Praise for the original *Inside Oscar*

"Gossipy fun and a browser's delight! Everyone may know bits and pieces, but no one has ever gathered this kind of material in such a convenient and diverting format."

—*The Philadelphia Inquirer*

"The fullest—and funniest—chronicle ever accorded the Golden Guy . . . A remarkable close-up of Oscar—warts and all."

—*New York Daily News*

"There are probably more solid laughs on any ten pages of this book than in the last ten years of Academy Awards telecasts."

—*St. Louis Post-Dispatch*

"It may be the only hilariously funny reference book in the world. At whatever point you open it, your total attention is engaged."

—*The New York Native*

"As addictive as a bag of Fritos."

—*The Village Voice*

INSIDE OSCAR 2

BY DAMIEN BONA

BALLANTINE BOOKS • NEW YORK

A Ballantine Book
Published by The Ballantine Publishing Group

Copyright © 2002 by Damien Bona

www.ballantinebooks.com

Library of Congress Cataloging-in-Publication Data is available upon request.

ISBN 0-345-44970-3

Manufactured in the United States of America

First Edition: February 2002

10 9 8 7 6 5 4 3 2 1

In memory
of
Mason Wiley

Acknowledgments

Happily, an acknowledgments page is not like an Oscar acceptance speech. One doesn't have to rush through it all in forty-five seconds or risk being drowned out by the orchestra. Which is a good thing, because so many people were instrumental in *Inside Oscar 2*.

As always, thanks for everything to my family: my mother, Alma, and late father, Arthur, my sister Amy, brother-in-law Neil Cohen, and, of course, three very excellent nieces, Emily, Elizabeth and Claudia Bona-Cohen, as well as Jo Peña, Agnes Racadio and Olive Peña.

Bill Condon and Joe Smith have each been particularly integral parts of *Inside Oscar* from the very beginning—and that's going back to the early months of the Reagan administration. Their support and generosity have been invaluable, and I'm extraordinarily lucky to have been blessed with their friendship.

The great Rosanna Arce-Arriaga has also been there from day one with her unsurpassed warmth, high spirits and ardent encouragement. And she and her husband, Marco Arriaga, both know from Rhoda Borgnine. Umm, Rosy, Jill is looking for you.

Every writer should be so fortunate to have as great an editor as Joe Blades; besides, without his energetic and steadfast support, there'd be no *Inside Oscar 2*. And my friend and trusty agent, Lynn Seligman, was tireless in making sure the book happened. Thank you, my wonderful pal Heather Smith—an author's dream publicist—and thanks also to the rest of the invaluable Ballantine team: associate editor Pat Peters, senior production editor Dave Barrett, and copy editors Heather M. Padgen and Nancy Inglis.

I'm also deeply indebted to Spencer Beckwith for the amazing, extensive help he rendered by reading early drafts of the manuscript and providing insights and laughs. Very special thanks also to Helen Wiley, Marian Payson, Margo Wiley and Gilbert Cole.

Heartfelt gratitude goes to the staff of the Billy Rose Theatre Collection of the Library for the Performing Arts, who collectively make up one of New York City's great unsung treasures: Bob Taylor, Karen Nickerson, Charles Squire, Roderick Bladel, Patricia Darby, Elisabeth Elkind, Christopher Firth, Christine Karatnytsky, Barbara Knowles, Mark Maniak, Annette Marotta, Jeremy Megraw, Brian O'Connell, Dan Patri, Louis Paul, Mary Ellen Rogan, Olive Wong, Henry Pierre, Donald Fowle, David Bartholomew and the late Ed Sager. Also, Eydee Wiggins, Elmer Sampaga, Farah Belizaire, Junelle Carter, Jehira Concepcion, Larry Forde, Nialah Holmes, Ronald Limage and Louise Martzinek. My thanks also to Kristine Krueger and Jeni Giancoli of the Academy of Motion Picture Arts and Sciences.

I tend to write late into the night, and Tiffany the Cat was great about staying up with me. She's also the perfect diversion whenever writer's block hits.

Ed Sikov—the best writer I know—has, as always, been a terrific inspiration. Zach Campbell's passion for film and his perspicacity did wonders for rekindling my enthusiasm about movies. Esteban Chalbaud and Ed Gonzalez provided valuable input on what I had wrought, and were great morale boosters. And all of the following people have helped me in a pleasing assortment of ways: Bob Montgomery, Mark Sullivan and Elizabeth Terhune, Susan Blair Ross, Gnarley O'Stain, Jack Morrissey, Bruce Finlayson, Jason Pomerance and Sam Destro, Tom Rhoads, Joel Cohen, Howard Karren and Ed Christie, George Robinson, Andy Dickos, M. Ira Hozinsky, Michael J. Giltz, Adam Orman, Jace Weaver, Jeff Zeitlin, Susie Day and Laura Whitehorn, Ron Fried and Lorraine Kreahling, Steve Garland, Lori Solinger, Rose Jannicola, Conrad and Tina Romanick, Irene and John Ofcharsky, Honey and Bob Hilzen, Lee Morrow, Judy Rhodes, Bob Hughes, Emily and Irv Fistorella, Margaret and John Galasso, Ann and Nick Vitale, George Callahan, Tom Phillips, Jane Croes, Julia Pearlstein, the San Francisco Giants, the gang at the Unofficial Academy Awards Discussion Board, Claude Daigle, Rhoda Penmark, Angie DeVito, Niambi Daniels, Tasha Guevera, Fr. Roger Fawcett, Eloise Eisenhardt, Lynn Kotula, Susan Davis, Doug Culhane, John Norwell, Ned Byrne, Dennis Russo, Vincenza Blank, Shelly Dague, Diana Shaw, Jim Nugent, Helen Kaplan, Kevin Dwyer, Sally Adams, David Beach, and M. Pache.

I must acknowledge all the people from newspapers, magazines, radio and television who have been fans of the original *Inside Oscar* and over the years have done so much to give it its long life. They are far too numerous to mention, but I hold them all in great affection.

And of course, most especially, the winner of my own personal Honorary Lifetime Achievement Award, Ralph Peña.

Contents

Introduction

Inside Oscar 2 picks up where *Inside Oscar* leaves off. Chronicling the Academy Awards for the years 1995 to 2000, it presents an in-depth look at what the late *New York Times* critic Vincent Canby called "this most particular of American phenomenon."

When *Inside Oscar* was first published in 1986, the Academy Awards were unmistakably America's—and probably the world's—preeminent annual popular culture event. Yet now, a decade-and-a-half later, the Oscars as they were then seem positively small-time.

Enormous changes have engulfed the Academy Awards in the years encompassed by *Inside Oscar 2*. Most pronounced has been the extravagant—some might say obscene—amount of money expended on advertising and publicity in the quest for Oscar glory. Although campaigning for the Academy Awards is a venerable tradition, marketing has escalated to unprecedented degrees in the last few years, as epitomized by the extraordinarily prodigal, intensely ego-stroking rivalry between Miramax and DreamWorks.

The vast amount of money spent, the proliferation of trade paper ads to absurd levels, the ingenious forms of subliminal suggestion and intense jockeying for persuasive personal appearances would have seemed like *Brave New World* material just a few years ago. Now they are a given. Another development since *Inside Oscar* was first published is that we've been inundated with magazines, television programs (entire networks, in fact), and Internet sites dedicated to, and obsessed with, "entertainment" and all its attendant froth. As a result, coverage of the Academy Awards has reached proportions bordering on the epic. The most obvious by-product of these new venues is the obsessive attention paid to Oscar night fashions. While the public has always been curious about what guests at the ceremony were wearing, it is only recently that the Oscar telecast has become truly the world's preeminent fashion show. The Awards are now as much a runway for the world's leading designers—and those newcomers hoping to join their ranks—as they are a celebration of Hollywood's outstanding achievements in motion pictures.

Inside Oscar 2 charts all these—and other—changes over the years. There is one constant, however: Hollywood itself is always in flux. With budgets spiraling and Hollywood's executive suites haunted by ever-greater paranoia regarding job security, mainstream American movies have continued—with the occasional aberrant good year—their steady decline in quality. This, of course, has made it a greater challenge for Academy voters to find, within their purview, worthwhile movies to honor, and the results of their attempts are often quite amusing. There is more than one year detailed in *Inside Oscar 2* that has been lambasted as "the worst year ever for movies." The book examines the output of each film year—and it's not always pretty.

As with the original *Inside Oscar*, I've tried to transport the reader to a specific time, to give a sense of what a particular Oscar year was like. Each chapter tells the saga of an entire twelve-month period, not simply Academy Awards season. Starting with an overview of the year's dominant movies and personalities, I've set out the cinematic events of each year—production backstories, critical reaction, release patterns, box-office results, controversies, advertising, personal (mis)behavior, and anything else that might have had an impact upon a movie's reception. Each chapter is designed to be somewhat of a suspense tale. Because the Academy Awards are, above all, a competition, each chapter is populated by all the potential players for that particular year. As relevant events are discussed, the winnowing of the possible contenders gets underway. The Big Night portion of each chapter details everything that happened on Oscar day—onstage, backstage, right outside the theater, and at parties. At the back of the book, you'll find a complete list of all the nominees for the years 1995–2000, as well as a listing of the more notable eligible movies and songs that *weren't* nominated.

While you're reading *Inside Oscar 2*, keep in mind what two-time Best Director winner Milos Forman once said: "The Academy Awards are a wonderful game, but if you take them seriously you're in trouble." Sometimes when I quote Forman I'm met with looks of incredulity because, after all, I have spent a good chunk of time writing on the subject. My point is that the Oscars should not in any way be considered the last word in what constitutes excellence in film. (The record shows that such icons as Cary Grant, James Dean, Montgomery Clift, Marilyn Monroe, and Richard Burton failed to win Oscars, that *Citizen Kane* was not named Best Picture and that *Singin' in the Rain*, *The Searchers*, *Breakfast at Tiffany's* and *2001: A Space Odyssey* weren't even *nominated*.) What the Academy Awards represent is simply the collective judgment at a particular point in time of several thousand people who work in, used to work in, or have some ties to, the film industry. Demographically, the average Oscar voter is politically liberal, well educated, and much better off financially than most Americans. Academy members are primarily craftspeople, and generally don't possess the critical faculties and scholarly approach of cinephiles and the best film reviewers,

nor are they as steeped in Hollywood history as your garden variety movie buff. They tend to be drawn to movies that are aesthetically conservative, but which contain humanistic or "uplifting" attitudes. Keep in mind that they are also people who decided that *Braveheart* and *Gladiator* were the supreme achievements of their respective years. In all fairness, though, sometimes Academy voters *do* get it right.

Inside Oscar 2 uses the Academy Awards as a mirror that reflects social, cultural, and political trends. But when all is said and done, the Oscars are simply a lot of fun. They are filled with intelligence, integrity, and inspiration. They also provide ample illustrations of silliness, cravenness, neediness, cheesiness, boorishness, (often-misguided) high-mindedness—in short, they are a microcosm of human nature.

1995

Suppose they gave Best Picture to a movie nobody cared about.

Hurling Toward Space

The year 1995 was shaping up like this: Only one movie released through the end of July managed to garner both generally favorable reviews and huge bucks at the box office. *Apollo 13* dealt with a relatively recent but little remembered piece of history: the 1970 moon launch during which an explosion crippled the spaceship, and NASA's subsequent efforts to return the three astronauts on board safely back to earth. Ron Howard needed only to take a look at a ten page outline of a book by the mission's commander, Jim Lovell, to know he wanted to do a film version. Christine James of *Box-Office* magazine noted the eclectic subject matter of Howard's movies, which most recently had included the slick newspaper comedy *The Paper* and the lambasted empire-building epic *Far and Away*. "About the only predictable aspect of Howard's film-making," she noted, "is the obligatory cameo casting of brother Clint Howard. In Howard's latest project, the new frontier is the space program (and Clint is a Mission Control worker)."

Jim Lovell instructed the director, "Listen, just tell our story as it happened, and you'll have a thrilling movie." Originally, the screenwriters worked on the script with Kevin Costner in mind because he bore a pronounced physical resemblance to Lovell and his production company was interested in the project. But Howard gave the part to Tom Hanks, whom he had directed in 1984's *Splash*, the actor's breakthrough film. Hanks was now the biggest star in America after his two consecutive Oscars and the phenomenal box-office success of *Forrest Gump*; Lovell said that when Hanks was announced for *Apollo 13*, his friends all teased him that he was going to be portrayed by Forrest Gump. And when doing publicity for the film, Hanks showed he still had some hyperbole left over from his two Oscar speeches, as he declared the story of *Apollo 13* to be a "saga as great as anything the Greeks put down on paper, or any story from Shakespeare or the Bible."

Director Howard, on the other hand, seemed most excited about the verisimilitude of his film, especially one piece of hardware. In interview after inter-

view, he gushed about the NASA KC-135, a jet that under certain flight circumstances causes weightlessness and which the Space Program used in training astronauts. Like a little kid, the director delighted in calling the contraption by its nickname, the Vomit Comet. Rather than attaching wires to the actors or relying on computer graphics to simulate weightlessness, Howard put his astronauts on the jet and filmed the real thing. One of them, Kevin Bacon, called this a "crazy idea," and acknowledged that Howard had to "convince me to go up in this stupid plane, that was a big job in itself."

While Hanks told CNN's Sherri Sylvester, "Well, now, none of us actually spewed," he and fellow astronaut Bacon did take boyish glee in the fact that although they managed not to throw up, celebrity photographer Annie Leibowitz, who had come onboard to shoot them for *Vanity Fair*, lost count as to how many times she vomited. Still, Bacon was man enough to admit that being on the jet "just scares the shit out of me." Lovell had great respect for the cast members because "the actors playing astronauts actually spent more time in the zero-gravity plane than any real astronaut ever did."

The previously best-known film based on actual events at NASA was Philip Kaufman's irreverent *The Right Stuff*, a 1983 Best Picture nominee and a box-office dud. The two movies had one common element: actor Ed Harris, who played John Glenn in the earlier film and was grounded here as the Mission Control flight director in Houston. Originally, Howard was reluctant to cast Harris because of his association with the earlier film, but Harris countered, "There are more than a couple of actors who've played cops or cowboys several times. So I don't see why there couldn't be more than one NASA employee in my career." Harris noted the difference between the two movies: *The Right Stuff* "was about the space program as a PR phenomenon, whereas *Apollo 13* is about men fulfilling a duty." Tom Hanks was reunited with Lieutenant Dan from *Forrest Gump*, Gary Sinise, who played the astronaut bumped from the moon mission after being exposed to measles, and Bill Paxton was also in orbit with Hanks and Bacon.

Despite his status as the number one box-office

draw in the business, Hanks insisted that in *Apollo 13* he was part of an ensemble piece and not the star of the film. "A movie like this would not exist as a star turn," he said. "You could do it as a star turn, but that would be unfair. It would be a disservice to the reality of it all." Nevertheless, Hanks did take top billing, instead of being placed alphabetically after Kevin Bacon.

Space Cadet

Hanks readily admitted that he was a science nerd growing up, his room decorated with models of rockets and spaceships; even now he could still spout off the names of all the astronauts and the purpose of each Apollo mission. He also stated that he'd always been "fascinated by spacesuits." *Entertainment Weekly* visited the set and reported that "Hanks has been going at the movie with the ardor of a boy reeling from his first crush." The actor recalled that when the real *Apollo 13* crisis was occurring, he was a 13-year-old who would rush home from school "waiting for [ABC-TV science reporter] Jules Bergman to explain what was going on in the spacecraft." On the other hand, Gary Sinise—one year Hanks's senior—said he scarcely had any recollection of the actual event because he was "too busy on Earth playing rock 'n' roll and looking for girls."

No Frills Thrills

Barbara Shulgasser of the *San Francisco Examiner* cheered, "Even though it focuses on what was then one of the space program's worst disasters, *Apollo 13* is a gripping movie about a time when America still worked. . . . With no frills and no commentary, Howard and company have made the kind of absorbing thriller we have in mind when we wistfully sigh, 'They don't make movies like they used to.' " And to the *Austin Chronicle*'s Mark Savlov, the film was "a riveting, nail-biting, two-buckets-of-popcorn return to form for Howard, filled with the almost unassailable heroics of the United States space program"; he added that *Apollo 13* "may be the only summer adventure blockbuster without bullets *or* warheads. At the risk of sounding like Michael Medved, that's a welcome change of pace."

Having a more temperate response was Kenneth Turan of the *Los Angeles Times*, who observed that "This film is wall-to-wall with straight-arrow, manly types like Lovell, inevitably played by Tom Hanks, who are such wholesome heroes that it's something of a shock to remember that all this took place in 1970, not the 1950s of *Father Knows Best*. Ron Howard, the master of Opie-Vision, is certainly well suited to the kind of sentimental, middle-of-the-road filmmaking of which *Apollo 13* is the epitome." And *Newsday*'s Jack Mathews noted, "Howard is not a flashy stylist, which is a tremendous plus on this movie."

Naysayers included Amy Taubin of the *Village Voice*, who complained, "Only twelve years separate Philip Kaufman's *The Right Stuff* from Ron Howard's straight 'n' narrow *Apollo 13*, but they seem to have come from different planets. . . . *Apollo 13* is so totally vacuumed of politics and history that a stray reference to 'President Nixon' is totally disorienting. If *Forrest Gump* was right-wing revisionist history, then *Apollo 13* represses history entirely." Lizzie Francke of *Sight and Sound* had a similar reaction: "One reason why the Apollo 13 mission was such a government priority was as a distraction from the Vietnam War. This political context is conspicuously disregarded here." She elaborated that "a more astute filmmaker might have teased out the ironies and contradictions of an event that, in retrospect, seems to signal the downbeat and fearful mood of the new decade. . . . Instead, Ron Howard tells a story of courage in which the crew and Mission Control pull together to work the problem through (much in the way that the firemen do in Howard's *Backdraft* or the family members in his *Parenthood*)."

Despite Tom Hanks's insistence that he was part of an acting ensemble on this film, his work managed to be singled out. For *Time*'s Richard Corliss, "Hanks provides the anchor. His Lovell—as strong, faithful and emotionally straightforward as Forrest Gump—carries the story like a precious oxygen backpack." Jim Lovell liked him, too, deeming Hanks "quite authentic" as Jim Lovell. Cowriter Al Reinert begged to differ, saying, "Actually, he's a bit more lovable than the real Lovell." Meanwhile, David Sterritt of the *Christian Science Monitor* liked the fact that Ed Harris "lends a hint of his patented weirdness as the Mission Control Chief."

Two observers with very specific agendas had differing responses to *Apollo 13*. *Satellite Orbit Magazine* thought it was really neat that the film went against the grain of the typical Hollywood space movie, in which "dilithium crystals are a whole lot cooler than jet propulsion engines, ooze-spewing aliens elicit a stronger response than malfunctioning solar panels and Klingons are more menacing than funding cuts to NASA."

And an Internet site called "Christian Spotlight on the Movies" had a unique take on *Apollo 13*: "Christians can marvel at the vastness of our Lord's creation as well as His manifold grace in loving rebellious sinners like us. His grace is especially evident as we watch virtually every central character incessantly blaspheme His name or utter other profanities whenever problems arise, yet God still grants them the vision and ingenuity to persevere."

Then there was director Oliver Stone, who lambasted the film as "an homage to bullshit patriotism. The fucking critics, they all loved it. I can't make movies anymore, I guess."

Heartland Heartbreak

The second most successful summer release in terms of melding more-than-respectable box-office returns and favorable reviews was *The Bridges of Madison County*. The receipts weren't surprising, but the critical hosannas were. For this was a movie based on a book that drove the literary intelligentsia crazy—a treacly novel awash in purple prose about a love affair in the American midsection, which went and became a publishing phenomenon. Besides remaining on the bestseller lists for three years and selling 6 million copies—and counting—the novel spawned a cottage industry of offshoot products, including an album of original songs by its author.

Anyone who found it improbable that Clint Eastwood would be directing the screen version hadn't been paying attention, for amid the action and violence in his movies were multifaceted treatments of male-female relationships. (His one out-and-out love

story as director—the May-December romance *Breezy* from 1973—was particularly deep-felt, although it made absolutely no money.) Meryl Streep was cast as a middle-aged Italian woman living in Iowa in the 1960s who, while her stolid husband is off at the state fair, has a Brief Encounter with Eastwood—a photographer hanging around in the area to take pictures of covered bridges.

A lot of folks who probably wouldn't have been caught anywhere near the book were filled with admiration for what Eastwood had fashioned out of his sow's-ear source material. In the *New York Observer*, Andrew Sarris declared that Eastwood "is a damned good director, and *The Bridges of Madison County* is a damned good movie." Geoff Andrew of *Time Out* opined: "Assembled with wit and sensitivity, this is one of the most satisfying weepies in years." On the other hand, Pauline Kael, retired but still silly, chatted with Peter Biskind for *Premiere* and said, "I don't understand the praise for *The Bridges of Madison County*. People were just surprised that it wasn't as bad as they feared. But it was dull, dull, dull."

Meryl Streep had the opportunity this time to accompany her mannerisms with an Italian accent. *Today*'s Gene Shalit raved, "Meryl Streep's performance is beyond extraordinary, it is incandescent, on the heavenly plane of her most exalted portrayals, creating an indelible personage." Somewhat less gaga was Gary Indiana of the *Village Voice*, who wrote "Streep gets off to a shaky start, unable to decide if she's Anna Magnani or some hotel chambermaid she once noticed in Venice, but she quickly becomes, as usual, completely believable." As an extra bonus, the movie revived interest in the late jazz singer Johnny Hartman, whose mellifluous voice somewhat implausibly kept emanating from a kitchen radio in the middle of Iowa.

Mel Gibson, Pornographer

Tom Hanks continued his remarkable run at the box office, with *Apollo 13* becoming his fifth mega-hit in a row, and Clint Eastwood—now a senior citizen—showed that he still had box-office clout. But another actor who had seemed to be just as dependably bankable was having a harder time of it.

Braveheart was Mel Gibson's second film as a director. His first was a not-terribly-well-received little movie called *The Man Without a Face*, about a lonely boy and a disfigured guy; in the novel upon which it was based, the fellow was gay, but Gibson would have none of that. In contrast, this second effort was a huge undertaking. Running three hours and filled with large-scale battle sequences, *Braveheart* was an epic recounting the story of William Wallace, a Scottish warrior circa 1300. To get the thing made, Gibson waived his salary and chipped in another $15 million of his own money. He, of course, starred as Wallace and, putting on a kilt, revealed a pair of stubby little legs.

Despite Gibson's track record, *Braveheart* could muster no better than a fourth-place finish at the box office on its opening weekend (behind two other new movies, *Casper* and *Die Hard with a Vengeance*, and a holdover, *Crimson Tide*). The notices were mixed. Gibson did score a rave from the *New York Times*'s Caryn James, although her review sounded more like a schoolgirl mash note than a piece of film criticism. James started off by cooing that Mel Gibson was "one of the prettiest guys in Hollywood," and concluded that *Braveheart* was "a great, ambitious gamble that pays off," declaring it to be "exhilarating." She was also tickled that "The war paint on [Gibson's] face is the same cornflower blue as his eyes and the sky."

But even many of the favorable reviews were strangely muted. Mike Clark of *USA Today* awarded the film his paper's highest rating, saying it was "uncommonly passionate." But then he added that it was also "lumpy and even redundant." *New York*'s David Denby cited *Braveheart* as "a lusty, crowd-pleasing movie, the kind of movie in which one man shows his affection for another by knocking him down."

The pans were far less ambiguous. Gibson said he'd seen a plaque honoring William Wallace near the spot in England where the Scotsman was executed which got him thinking: "To this day, they revere him. He never sought self-aggrandizement." Many critics wished that he possessed that same quality. Henry Sheehan of the *Orange County Register*, for instance, lamented that "as a director, Gibson is, like most actors who take a turn behind the camera, too fond of himself as a performer. Most scenes in which he appears

have been conceived as showcases for the benefit of his character's heroics or charms. . . . In the end, *Braveheart* doesn't amount to much more than theatrical chest-thumping by Gibson." Peter Stack of the *San Francisco Chronicle* complained that "The overstated depiction of the 'freedom'-crying hero in sequences reminiscent of the crucifixion scenes in *Spartacus* are so far-fetched they simply make Gibson look foolishly self-aggrandizing." Stack was also just one of a multitude of reviewers who decried what he called the "near-pornographic depictions of violence" in *Braveheart*: "The film repeatedly sabotages its best intentions by almost smirkingly forcing upon viewers a repugnant violence that after a while has a mechanical feel to it. It depicts with graphic realism enough eviscerations, decapitations, disembowelments, dismemberments, defenestrations and skewerings that the overall effect is numbing."

Too-Ra-Loo-Ra-Loo-Ral

Those in the know also castigated the film for its historical whoppers. Writing in London's *Daily Telegraph*, historian Allan Massie fumed about screenwriter Randall Wallace: "It would be a perversion of truth to call his way with history cavalier. He has no way with history." Experts in Scottish history were especially irked about the canoodling Gibson's William Wallace engages in with Isabella, the Princess of Wales, played by Sophie Marceau—the real princess didn't even leave France for the British Isles until several years after Wallace's death. In the *Irish Times*, Fintan O'Toole pointed out how simplistically the film had treated a complex historical situation, because, as opposed to the movie's version, "Wallace's undoubted courage and skill were deployed, not in a straight war between England and Scotland, but in a Scottish civil war that, in turn, created a power vacuum into which England, France and the Vatican rushed." The British consul-general in Los Angeles let everyone know that kilts weren't worn until the 1740s, some four hundred years after the movie takes place. That William Wallace and his men were seen mooning their English opponents was derided not merely for being anachronistic, but as emblematic of the juvenile tone of the whole enterprise. Academics also chortled over *Braveheart*'s clumsily obvious attempt to excuse its inaccuracies: At the beginning of the film a high-minded voiceover informed the audience that "History is written by those who hang heroes."

And despite all of *Braveheart*'s exhortations about nationalism and the glories of Scotland, Gibson actually shot the film in Ireland. He abandoned Wallace's homeland because the Irish government promised him tax concessions and the use of 3,000 soldiers from the Irish army as extras. Though that apparently wasn't enough, because digital computer effects were used to increase the number of "people" seen in the battle sequences.

Queen Edward

Braveheart created very little stir, except for news about Gibson's facing a tough old nemesis. Ever since a 1991 interview with a Spanish newspaper in which the preening actor asked rhetorically, "Who might think that with this demeanor I could be gay? Do I talk like them? Do I move like them?" Gibson had earned the enmity of gay activists. Now the Gay and Lesbian Alliance Against Defamation showed up at theaters where *Braveheart* was playing, angry at the way the film portrayed the gay prince, Edward II; GLAAD said Edward was "a throwback to the classic celluloid 'queer' played for laughs as a simpering weakling." On opening day, a parody of the film's poster was handed out, with the movie retitled *No Heart*, and a tag line asked, "How brave is Mel's gay bashing?" On the other side was a message that included these words: "Hate crimes are rising in America, and GLAAD would like you to understand a simple fact: Negative stereotyping breeds prejudice."

In addition to the portrayal of Prince Edward as a silly queen, offense was also taken at a scene in which Edward's father tosses his boyfriend out of a window; the sequence was played to generate laughter and cheers from audiences—which it inevitably did. When his beloved gets killed, Edward has a bit of a hissy fit but is certainly not grief-stricken—nothing like what Gibson's character felt when *his* inamorata was knocked off early in the film. This disparity in reactions really steamed James R. Keller, who wrote in the *Journal of Popular Film and Television* that Gibson chose to emphasize "Edward's seeming indifference when his lover is killed by the king, thus invoking the heterosexual presumption that no real affection could exist between gay men." GLAAD's Ellen Carton said that the stance of the film was that "all gay men are idiot effeminates, and when they're really annoying, it's okay to get rid of them." In gay circles, *Braveheart* was rechristened *Chicken Shit* and *Cowardly Asshole*.

Mel-t Down

Even before the film opened, Gibson had an inkling that the protests were on the horizon, and he was not happy. So he acted out. Frank Bruni of the Knight-Ridder News Service recounted his interview with Gibson: "By his own account, the shooting of the historical epic *Braveheart* was as grueling as moviemaking gets, a veritable endurance test of cold and rain and twenty-hour workdays, with Gibson wearing the triple hat of producer-director-star. By the accounts of others, he emerged from it with serious exhaustion and a seriously frayed composure. 'Mel Gibson,' opined the writer of a recent major magazine article, 'is on the verge of a nervous breakdown.' He seems to be having it right now." In his interview with Bruni, Gibson railed against those individuals who, because they urged civility and respect toward other peoples and cultures, were given the pejorative "politically correct" by conservatives. To the *Braveheart* director, they were "tantamount to Nazis. What, are they trying to tell us what to say and think? Fuck 'em."

And as for anybody upset at the swishy stereotype into which he had turned Edward II: "I don't even want to fucking talk about that. . . . When people sort of accuse me of that, I just want to whack them in the head, you know? What am I gonna say? What am I gonna do? It's my natural instinct. When I was younger, I did used to settle things like that. You can't do that in this country because you have to go to court."

The *San Francisco Chronicle*'s Ruthe Stein also interviewed Gibson. Her impression was that "the years . . . have not been kind to him. Deeply etched lines on his face make him appear older than his 39 years. He says that because of the sleep he's lost lately, 'I look like I'm carrying sacks under my eyes.' His heavy smoking has caught up with him, as has his reputation for drinking. . . . 'Sure I drank,' he says, sounding defensive. 'Didn't everybody? But I didn't drink on this set. I could not direct a film and sleep five hours a night and beat a bunch of 19-year-olds up a hill in the foot race scene if I were drinking.' " When the inevitable question of the film's homophobia arose ("I don't think an intelligent person would think that"), Stein reported that "Gibson's entourage, who have been listening quietly until now, perk up when they hear Gibson sounding riled. They appear about to come to his rescue, but Gibson signals them that everything is all right."

As to maybe saying he was sorry that he might have offended people, Gibson did an interview with *Playboy* and went into full macho mode, vowing, "I'll apologize when hell freezes over. They can fuck off." Besides, Mel made out as if he were really the victim here, implying that queer zealots were after his hide: "I've been chased by automobiles doing dangerous things on the freeway. It's made me totally paranoid."

And in an interview with *Newsday*'s John Anderson, Gibson was in full self-glorification mode. The director explained that in trying to finance *Braveheart*, "it was easier to get the backing with a bankable name. And of the really bankable names, I thought I might be the best one for this particular film."

One reason moviegoers were indifferent to *Braveheart* was that another adventure movie about a Scottish hero, *Rob Roy*, had opened in theatres just a month earlier. For people who didn't know much about Scottish history, Wallace was not nearly as appealing and readily identifiable a character as the eighteenth-century freedom fighter of the earlier film because, as *Time*'s Richard Schickel pointed out, "Sir Walter Scott never wrote a novel about William Wallace, and no one named a cocktail after him either." Plus, *Rob Roy*, which starred Liam Neeson and Jessica Lange, received much more favorable reviews than *Braveheart*. The *Boston Globe*'s Betsy Sherman said of *Rob Roy*, "In an age of big-screen cartoons, here is a genuine thinking person's epic," and *The New Yorker*'s Anthony Lane ad-

judged that *Rob Roy*, "with a salty, literate script . . . was much the better film, twenty times as intelligent and moody." And at different times, both Roger Ebert and Gene Siskel proclaimed that *Rob Roy* had the greatest sword fight—between Liam Neeson and Tim Roth—ever put on film. Hal Hinson of *The Washington Post* summed up Mel Gibson's dilemma when he said: "Actually, *Braveheart* might not have seemed quite so ordinary—or so monstrously long—just three months ago, before the release of *Rob Roy*; now it's merely the second-best film about Scotland around." Gibson had a ready response to all that, telling *Dramalogue*, "I read both scripts, and I was offered the other film. I get offered everything first."

Braveheart's mediocre business left Paramount executives perplexed: How could a Mel Gibson movie perform so tepidly at the box office? Thinking that perhaps *Braveheart* had simply been overwhelmed by the franchise pictures and higher-concept movies of the summer, the studio decided to put the $72 million vanity project back in theaters in September when its competition would consist of much lower-keyed movies. Again, the public was indifferent—a mere $6 million was added to the till, bringing the total up to $67 million, still below the movie's production costs and never mind the additional millions spent on prints and advertising. About the only solace Gibson could take—given his politics—was in *USA Today*'s announcement that the film was "the reported fave of three Republican presidential candidates"—including Pat Buchanan—who were seeking to oust Bill Clinton, a man Gibson referred to in his *Playboy* interview as "a low-level opportunist."

Animal Magnetism

The continued resistance of audiences to *Braveheart* proved once again that you can't force the public to see something it doesn't want to see. But an unheralded end-of-summer release—an Australian children's film, of all things, which cost about a third as much as *Braveheart* to make—showed that, conversely, there's no better tool for getting people into theaters than positive word of mouth. Produced by George Miller, the man who had directed Mel Gibson's first hit, *Mad*

Max, Babe was the story of a spunky orphaned pig who shares adventures with other animals on a story-book farm and wants nothing so much as to be a sheepdog. The warmth of the film had the critics melting, and they also seemed amazed that even though *Babe* was marketed as a kid's flick, it had genuine grown-up appeal. The movie even employed a bit of Brechtian distancing, as a chorus of mice sang the titles of the film's various episodes. *Newsday*'s Jack Mathews picked up on some unusual goings-on at theaters showing *Babe*: "For one thing, the children were so enchanted by the talking animals, they forgot to run up and down screaming. For another, the heartiest laughter was coming from the adults."

In *L.A. Weekly*, F. X. Feeney marveled, "If you had told me that I'd be raving to everyone I know about a talking pig movie, I would have called you insane, but I guess you just never know where you're going to be surprised by joy. Director Chris Noonan compresses an epic's worth of beauty and imagination into the ninety-one witty, exquisitely realized minutes that constitute *Babe*." Terrence Rafferty of *The New Yorker* noted, "This picture is the surprise hit of the late-summer season, and it deserves to be: it's a lovely, stubbornly idiosyncratic fable of aspiration and survival—a comedy of animal manners that is much funnier and much cannier than any recent movie about human relationships."

Curiously enough, *Babe* wasn't the first of its kind in 1995. Another talking pig movie, *Gordy*, had opened earlier in the year to no noticeable effect, and when *Babe* showed up, people were perhaps fearing more of the same. But *USA Today*'s Susan Wloszczyna said not to worry because "Unlike *Gordy*, an earlier disgrace to porcine pride, this witty piggy is closer to the lyrical grace of *Charlotte's Web*."

I Got You, Babe

Everybody who saw *Babe* wanted to know how in the world the film, with its dozens of loquacious animals, was put together. Producer Miller said, "The animal characters are so real that I felt we could best serve the story by using live animals; animation was never considered." This meant that he would only produce

Babe and not take on his usual role because, as he explained to the *Los Angeles Times*, "I'm very obsessive as a director. I would have got too caught up in which way the duck was looking." Instead, he hired his protégé Chris Noonan, who had made documentaries but had never directed a feature film. Noonan gave a discourse detailing his methodology. "Our story had animals that were true characters, so I wanted people to quickly abandon the idea that they were watching animals and just accept them as normal beings," he declared. "That meant treating them as actors and moving them so that the camera could operate around them as it normally does with humans." The director also sighed that, "It's easy to get a pig to walk across the room and sit. But to walk across, sit and look questioningly—that's a bit more difficult."

Trainer Karl Miller and his two assistants had to deal with five hundred different creatures during the production. Pigs were trained to work together in groups of six because, as Noonan explained, they "are all individual and have individual talents. There was always one pig in each group who really took to sitting. Others could pose for five seconds." Even with these teams of a half-dozen members, director Noonan acknowledged that "the number of takes needed for many shots was enormous." In addition, because pigs grow so rapidly, it was only when they were 16 to 18 weeks old that they had the right dimensions for the character of Babe. "Every three weeks, we'd start a new group so they'd be prepared when the preceding group outgrew its usefulness," the trainer explained. In all, a total of forty-eight Large White Yorkshire pigs enacted the title role, and the production also employed computer graphics and animatronic doubles to enhance the illusion that the creatures were talking.

Each type of animal was trained to react to a specific sound. Pigs responded to a clicker, ducks to a buzzer, sheep to a whistle and dogs to their master's voice, which meant that when members of different species had a scene together, the set was utterly cacophonous. Karl Miller had great admiration for American character actor James Cromwell, who played Babe's owner, Farmer Hoggett, because "His pockets were filled with food and many's the time, just before or after a shot, he was willing to have a pig's sloppy mouth eat out of his hand, knowing that that reward could make a big difference with the animal's performance." Cromwell acknowledged, "It is hard to get a pig that young to sit still . . . their only interest was in food." Despite the difficulties involved, producer Miller told the *New York Daily News*, "I don't like working with troublesome actors. I'd much rather work with a pig than Cher any day. And you can certainly quote me on that." He was still smarting over his run-ins with the actress nearly a decade after *The Witches of Eastwick*.

But what did it all mean? Different people had different interpretations. Dick King-Smith, the author of the book upon which the movie was based, said that because Babe was able to get sheep to do his bidding by asking politely, it was a tale about the value of courtesy. Producer Miller wanted the movie to be seen as a fable against prejudice, while director Noonan maintained it was an allegorical account of the importance of individualism in society. Mary Tyler Moore, a fan of the film, called *Babe* "one of the greatest life lesson movies that was ever made. It's a lesson in how to get along, how to integrate, how to share and respect each other. It's also funny, sweet and adorable."

Thousands of moviegoers claimed to have sworn off pork products after seeing *Babe*. People also worried about the fate of the four dozen pigs who essayed the title role, distressed that that they might be used for makin' bacon. A publicist on the film assuaged any fears. "It would have been kind of heartless just to dump them," said John Friedkin, "so we wanted guarantees from those who adopted them that they wouldn't be killed." In return, said another production spokesperson, the producers promised strict confidentiality, "so those that adopted the pigs wouldn't be bothered by fans."

Being an animal advocate did not necessarily mean you were going to love *Babe*. *Newsday*'s Linda Winer, who declared *Babe* to be "the best—okay also the first—vegetarian propaganda film," did admit that "a few purist animal lovers told me they hated the film because the animals talked, which they found demeaning to the creatures."

Dead Mail Department

Another non-American film opening in late summer also turned into a sleeper hit, although not quite as spontaneously as *Babe*—after all, *The Postman* (which also went by its Italian-language moniker, *Il Postino*) had the marketing savvy of Miramax behind it. The sole duty of the movie's title character is to deliver mail to Pablo Neruda after the Chilean poet is exiled to a small Italian island. As a friendship develops, the poet teaches the younger man about the ways of love so that, as publicity material for the film put it, he "discovers a sense of himself he's never had as his own inner soul blossoms." But in addition to its gentle, warm-hearted narrative, *The Postman* had something else going for it—a real-life human interest story that would be hooted at in a movie because it was so corny.

Comic actor Massimo Troisi was one of Italy's biggest movie stars, although, unlike his friendly rival Roberto Benigni, who had appeared in a few American films, he was unknown outside of the Continent. Hoping to change that, Troisi showed up at his friend Michael Radford's house with one of his favorite books, a Chilean novel about the relationship between Pablo Neruda and a teenager. Radford was a British director whose marriage had led him to put down stakes in Umbria, and Troisi set about to convince him that the book could be the basis for their working together for the first time. London's *Observer* described the filmmaker's state of mind: "With his marriage foundering . . . Radford was close to despair." And so, according to the *Observer*, "Radford, who had no desire whatever to make an Italian film, took on the project in sheer desperation."

The two men went to Los Angeles to put together funding and work on the script, changing the setting from Chile to Italy and making the youthful protagonist a man on the cusp of middle age. Troisi told Radford that before returning to Italy he was going to stop off in Houston for a medical checkup, and that they'd reconvene in Rome. It took longer than Radford expected for Troisi to show up, and when he did, the actor informed the director that he'd undergone minor surgery. And, recalled Radford, "he was not the same guy I'd left in Los Angeles."

One week into filming, Troisi collapsed. It was then that Radford learned that the cardiologist in Houston who had performed the operation had told the actor that he was in grievous need of a heart transplant. Radford urged his friend to take care of his medical concerns and put the movie aside, but Troisi refused, insisting, "I've got to finish the picture, no matter what." He did agree, though, that he would fly to London for the transplant as soon as filming was completed. Because of his frail health, the star wasn't able to come to the set until late in the afternoon, and then could work for a maximum of two hours a day. The personal and professional pressures were enormous on Radford. As he described the situation, "I had to look him in the face every day—a face of suffering and pain—and make him work. Not just do 'okay,' but to make a film to the standard we both wanted." On top of that, "I had to design a shooting style which could suit a man who could only walk a few steps and then needed to sit down." All the scenes showing his character in any physical activity—such as riding his bicycle—were done by his look-alike stand-in.

After the last shot was filmed, Troisi went to his dressing room. When he returned a little later, he embraced Radford and, in front of the cast and crew, said, "I'm sorry I couldn't give you everything. For the next five movies we do, I promise I'll give you more." Radford burst into tears. The next day, Troisi was at his sister's house and laid down to sleep. The 41-year-old actor never woke up. Michael Radford recalled that at Troisi's funeral, some mourners gasped when they saw his stand-in from the film, swearing it was the actor's ghost observing his own services.

Subtitles and Six-Packs

The film was a huge success in Italy, and when it was released in the States a year after Troisi's death, the Miramax publicity department made sure the critics and the public knew the unique circumstances of the production. Moreover, a title card dedicated the film "To Our Friend Massimo." Janet Maslin wrote in the *New York Times*, "As a rueful, warmly affecting film featuring a wonderful performance by Mr. Troisi, *The Postman* would be attention-getting even without the sadness that overshadows it." She went on to call the movie, "an eloquent but also wrenching tribute to Mr. Troisi's talents. The comic unease that he brought to this performance clearly has a component of real pain. But that hint of unease suits Mario's wide-eyed, wistful look and his slow, often dryly funny demeanor." In the *Los Angeles Times*, Kenneth Turan stated, "Made under unique and wrenching circumstances, it gained poignancy and a kind of purity from its troubles, and an already affecting film ended up suffused with emotion." John Petrakis of the *Chicago Tribune* cheered that the film "is many things, including a love poem to poetry, a paean to friendship and a homage to those with the audacity to wonder," while the *Philadelphia Inquirer*'s Desmond Ryan felt that "*The Postman*'s power, complexity and emotion belie its minimalist structure."

The Postman caught on with the art house crowd immediately. Because it featured a beloved Nobel Prize–winning poet, Miramax flacks were able to corral some distinguished people of letters to shill for the movie, providing blurbs to serve as the focus of a series of high-toned ads. Three Pulitzer Prize–winning novelists participated: John Updike ("A touching demonstration of art affecting life"), Oscar Hijuelos ("An emotional film that has much to say about life and art"), and William Styron ("A droll and tender movie of great heart and intelligence"), and also giving his stamp of approval was absurdist writer Kurt Vonnegut, Jr., who declared, "Cinema becomes poetry and poetry becomes cinema." But David Letterman, who hadn't seen *The Postman*, assumed from the film's title that it was about "a mailman who goes nuts with a gun and shoots people."

Michael Radford was a bit taken aback by his film's widespread appeal. "People seem to like it on different levels," the director observed. "The intellectuals like it because it's about poetry, and my sister's boyfriend, whose sole intake is *Die Hard 3* and a can of beer, absolutely loved it, even though he's never seen a subtitled movie before." On the subject of family matters, Radford's marriage, which was on shaky ground when he began the project, came to an end during production.

The film was such a niche hit that, just as a year earlier, *Four Weddings and a Funeral* had led to a resurgence in interest in W. H. Auden, *The Postman* brought about a Neruda revival. Miramax put out a small collection of his poems in a volume simply entitled *Love*. And the soundtrack album wasn't just your usual hodgepodge of musical interludes—it also included some of Neruda's poems read by movie stars and recording artists, including Julia Roberts, Sting, Wesley Snipes and Madonna. In *The New York Review of Books*, Michael Wood reported, "The readings range from dutiful to disastrous, with two exceptions: Glenn Close gets something of the feeling of 'Me gustas cuando callas'/'I like for you to be still'; and Ethan Hawke, without any showiness, catches all the magic of Neruda's fable about the Mermaid and the Drunks."

The Autumn of Our Discontent

If the success of *Babe* and *The Postman* were happy surprises, things were nevertheless terribly gloomy in the fall of 1995. October 13 (appropriately a Friday) saw three of the year's biggest critical and—more important for Hollywood—commercial disasters open on one day: *Jade,* a sleazy thriller written by Joe Eszterhas, and the second and last of the Howdy Doody-ish TV actor David Caruso's hapless attempts to become a movie star; *Strange Days,* an extremely expensive futuristic thriller from Kathryn Bigelow which was Ralph Fiennes's bid to cross over from highly acclaimed actor to top level box-office attraction; and most cockamamie of all, *The Scarlet Letter,* made by the once-upon-a-time-respected Roland Joffé and starring Demi Moore as a liberated Hester Prynne, with a happy ending entirely negating the point of the Hawthorne novel.

The following Tuesday, Bernard Weinraub reported in the *New York Times* that the three films would likely combine for a $150 million loss. He quoted one studio executive as saying, "It's scary," while another admitted, "I don't know what the lessons are here, except we're making a lot of movies that people don't want to see." In addition to this threesome, Weinraub also alluded to other such recent mega-flops as *Assassins,* which many were seeing as the

end of Sylvester Stallone's long-suffering career, and *Showgirls,* like *Jade,* based on a Joe Eszterhas script, and which went from being notorious, pre-release, for its NC-17 rating to being notorious as a new camp classic, a *Valley of the Dolls* for the 1990s.

Weinraub's article caught the attention of the *Times*'s powers-that-be, who ran an editorial titled "Hollywood Horrors." Said the Paper of Record: "Movie flops are like Tolstoy's unhappy families, each different in its own way. But a string of recent box-office calamities suggests a common thread, namely a growing public revolt against Hollywood's risk-free formulas and to 'bankable' movie stars who are asked to re-create earlier successes without improving on them." The editorial concluded that "Moviegoers do not wish the producers and performers ill. What they do not like is Hollywood's careless assumption that they are easy to manipulate and can be taken for granted." *Variety* noted that the terrible trio of *The Scarlet Letter, Jade* and *Showgirls* was joined by another fall release, *Fair Game*—an action movie starring no-can-act model Cindy Crawford—as the four worst reviewed films of the year.

Entertainment Weekly meanwhile was focusing specifically on the failure of *Showgirls* and *Jade.* An article entitled "Is T & A DOA?" answered its own question in the affirmative. The magazine quoted *Jade*'s producer Robert Evans lamenting that "I suppose somewhere between New York and Los Angeles there is such a thing as Bob Dole country," referring to the unpleasant Kansas senator who was the leading contender for the Republican presidential nomination and who was scoring some political hay by denouncing Hollywood movies, sight unseen.

Later in the year, the magazine's Anne Thompson described Hollywood's autumn as "staggeringly dismal," noting that there were only two major hits released during the season: *Se7en* and *Get Shorty,* crime films of vastly different temperaments. Directed by David Fincher, *Se7en* was dark and disturbing and attested to the enormous box-office clout of Brad Pitt, who played a detective tracking down one of the more ingeniously disturbed psychos the movies have offered up. Pitt had also been named *People*'s Sexiest Man Alive and was in a serious relationship with up-and-coming actress Gwyneth Paltrow, making them this year's version of America's Sweethearts. *Get Shorty,* a jaunty account of a loan shark in Hollywood, was based on an Elmore Leonard novel and proved that, in the wake of *Pulp Fiction,* John Travolta really was back big-time.

A Cheap Drunk

Amidst all the carnage of the fall releases, most of the critics were toasting an unheralded movie which couldn't have been more different from the big bloated bombs. Telling of the relationship between an alcoholic movie executive and the hooker he meets as he drinks his way to death, *Leaving Las Vegas* had a budget of under $5 million and was shot on Super 16mm. Executive producer Stuart Regen had happened across the semi-autobiographical novel at a secondhand bookstore and gave it to his friend, director Mike Figgis, who described the downbeat book as "like a breath of fresh air to me because it came along at not a very good time."

There were a couple of reasons why Figgis found the dark material particularly resonant. His parents were alcoholics and, he recalled, "On weekends they would drink themselves into stupors, be out of control, irresponsible." Like the novel's protagonist, Figgis himself was at a low point. His previous film, *Mr. Jones,* starring Richard Gere, had been a calamity, both commercially and personally. He had constantly gone head-to-head with the suits at TriStar, who according to Figgis, wanted the film to be a lighthearted tale of a manic-depressive. After a disastrous preview, the company took it away from the director. The film sat on the shelf for a year, and when it did see the light of day in 1993, nobody saw it.

Figgis later said of *Leaving Las Vegas,* "I knew going in that a film like this would have a low budget with a short shooting schedule, but I also knew that the material demanded and could attract a high-profile cast." He also knew that the major studios wouldn't be interested in such a downbeat little movie; he was thrown for a loop, though, when, looking for a company to bankroll the film, he got rejections from such supposedly edgier companies as Miramax, Sony Classics, New Line, Fine Line, Savoy and Gramercy. The money for the petite budget came finally from a French production company, Lumiere.

Made in the Shade

Nicolas Cage signed on as the dipso because "I'd been spending too many days in a sunny kind of moviemaking. I was ready to get out of the sun." He realized it wasn't going to be easy, though. "In order to play Ben, I knew I had to keep myself in the zone of meditating on death—and I figured I could do it, because it was a short suit," said Cage. "But believe me, I didn't like it because I'm a pro-life guy, and I had to go to a crummy little corner in my head to deliver my lines with any authenticity." For real verisimilitude, Cage also went on a two-week drinking binge. He checked into a hotel and did nothing but guzzle booze. Looking back, he said, "That's the beauty of staying in a hotel; you can drink and drink until you fall over, and no one need see you. I must admit, it was one of the most enjoyable pieces of research I've ever had to do for a part." Of course, the natural question is, under these circumstances, how did he remember any of his research, so that it could actually do him some good? Well, a buddy videotaped him while he was plastered, and the actor later surveyed the wreckage.

Cage also studied what he considered to be "the four great alcoholic performances": Jack Lemmon in *Days of Wine and Roses,* Albert Finney in *Under The Volcano,* Dudley Moore in *Arthur* (Oscar nominees all) and Ray Milland in *The Lost Weekend* (a Best Actor Oscar winner). And then he moved from celluloid inspiration to real life: Cage paid an alcoholic he knew— "a poet, an older man"—to hang around on the set so that he could observe him. The actor freely admitted that "many of his behaviorisms made it into the film. Sometimes he'd be curled up in a fetal position in my trailer, and I would just look at him while I was playing my bongo drums, getting ideas."

Cage's costar was Elisabeth Shue, whose previous on-screen encounter with alcohol was as leading lady in the Tom Cruise bartending saga, *Cocktail.* None of the movies she had previously appeared in, which included *The Karate Kid* and *Adventures in Babysitting,* had required the former Harvard student to exercise her acting chops much. But director Figgis, who had interviewed her seven years earlier for a film neither of them ended up making, had no doubts about her ability to play the prostitute, and hired her without an audition. The one worry he did have, knowing her from her goody-two-shoes roles, was that the film's seamy milieu and sordid situations might prove shocking. Not at all, said Shue. "As an actress, I think I've always had an exhibitionist side, so the nudity itself wasn't the issue. What scared me about doing nudity and violence in films was being portrayed solely as a victim or having it be one-dimensional. I wouldn't have felt comfortable with that, but because I knew I would be working with Mike, I knew that wasn't going to happen."

Everyone involved with the film sacrificed for their art. Nicolas Cage agreed to take $280,000 instead of his then-customary $4 million. Mike Figgis decided to forgo a trailer in order to be able to afford a focus puller, and everyone stayed in a low-rent motel where you didn't get fresh towels every day. And as if the working conditions and the material itself weren't downbeat enough, two weeks into preproduction, John O'Brien, the 33-year-old author of the novel, shot himself. His father said that the book was his suicide note. "Obviously, I was quite upset," acknowledged Figgis, "and considered not making the film. But eventually I decided that John wrote a great book, and the most I could do was to go ahead and make the film."

A Toast to Love

Most reviewers certainly seemed grateful that he did proceed, and that MGM/UA agreed to distribute the film. *Newsweek*'s David Ansen raved, "A love story like no other, *Leaving Las Vegas* is a bleak, mesmerizing rhapsody of self-destruction, defiantly uninterested in peddling Hollywood-style uplift. Figgis doesn't pretend, and I won't either, that this movie is for everybody.... But anyone who cares about ravishing filmmaking, superb acting and movies willing to delve into the mystery of unconditional love will leave this dark romance both shaken and invigorated." As was

his wont, *New York*'s David Denby came up with the most goofily pompous take on the film. He gushed that *Leaving Las Vegas* is "as lyrical and crazily emotional as any movie I can think of (this is also as close as the movies have ever come to the somber exaltation of Wagner's *Tristan und Isolde*)."

On the other hand, as if on cue, along came Michael Medved in the *New York Post* to bellyache, "Sitting through *Leaving Las Vegas* is such a powerfully unpleasant experience that some observers will automatically hail the picture as a triumph of courageous, cutting-edge cinema." Medved, in contrast, found it to be "painfully tedious and repetitive," and, although he enjoyed the cameo by singer Lou Rawls, decided that "it's still a good idea to leave *Las Vegas* to moviegoing masochists."

An unusual aspect of the film was that Cage's alcoholic had no desire to stop drinking and the prostitute was not out to reform him. The critics felt the two leads were certainly up to the demands of their roles. *The New Yorker*'s Terrence Rafferty enthused, "Amazingly, Cage sustains the improbable mixture of despair and insouciance throughout the picture, savoring its strange taste right down to the bottom of the glass. And he never violates the dignity of Ben's precarious, in-the-moment existence by imbuing it with either sad-sack pathos or anti-hero cool."

In *Film Comment*, David Thomson wrote an out-and-out love letter to Elisabeth Shue: "It's hard to recall another case of a familiar, albeit taken-for-granted actress so shattering expectations, or so exposing us to the horror of a system's waste. For Elisabeth Shue's Sera is one of the most moving and intelligent performances by an American actress in years. Her face is as changeable and compelling as the façade of Monet's Chartres Cathedral." Writing in *Premiere*, J. Hoberman declared that "Playing a whore as saintly as a Dostoyevsky heroine, Shue will never lack for a date after this movie."

Entertainment Weekly profiled the actress in an article entitled "A Different Kind of Girlfriend Role," and after calling hers an "astonishing performance," reported that "Shue downplays the idea that there was anything calculated about trading in her helplessly virginal *Karate Kid* knee socks for hooker heels." But the actress admitted that "I did feel a desperate need to play somebody more complex, and at a time when I was really unhappy and unsure of my career, the *Vegas* script just came in the mail." She was also feeling the pressure of having her younger brother Andrew suddenly emerge as a heartthrob on the television series *Melrose Place*: "Andrew's success obviously raised the question 'Well, *you*'ve been in the business for twelve years—what does that mean?'"

While Mike Figgis was reveling in the ecstatic reviews for his film, there was one bit of unpleasantness to deal with. As he admitted to a reporter, "Frankly, I'm broke."

Leaving New York

A month after *Leaving Las Vegas*, another, much more trumpeted movie set in Las Vegas arrived to kick off the Thanksgiving/Christmas season. *Casino* was Martin Scorsese's first film since *The Age of Innocence* and he was back in his familiar gangster terrain. This was perhaps the most anticipated movie of the year, and the one that his admirers hoped might finally be Scorsese's Oscar ticket. The director found Vegas particularly alluring because "If you won a lot of money or gained power there, it's different from doing it in Washington or Hollywood. It leads one to give in too much to indulgence and excess, and you bring about your own destruction, and the people around you. It's a dangerous place." *Casino* was an extremely violent tour of Las Vegas in the 1970s, when it was still controlled by the Mob and had not yet targeted family tourists. Scorsese was dismayed by what the place had become—"it's Disneyland"—and described the final days of the city's former self as "almost like the end of the Old West." His cowriter Nicholas Pileggi also grieved that whereas in earlier days, the casinos were filled with high rollers in tuxedos, "overweight people in spandex, often with little babies and children, that's who you see now."

The film was a fictionalized account of actual Vegas characters, with Robert De Niro playing a bookie who is given ownership of one of the biggest casinos on the Strip and Joe Pesci on hand as—what else?—an out-of-control lowlife. And in an unexpected piece of casting, Sharon Stone played De Niro's wife, a hustler whose life spins out of control due to those old demons, drugs and alcohol. Many people still considered Stone more eye candy than actress, a glamorous old-style movie star, not a thespian, and she was determined to change that perception. De Niro had pushed for former underage porno star Traci Lords, and a number of other actresses, including Nicole Kidman and Melanie Griffith, also tested for the role. But Stone had something extra going for her: She had called upon the spirit of the now-deceased woman on whom her character was based, and told her, "You've got to pick who you want to play you and who is the truth to you. I'm available—and thanks a lot."

The dead gal came through, and Stone agreed to work for $2 million rather than her $4 million asking price. Scorsese said it was Stone's reading that sold him, because "I sensed a relentlessness about playing the part, even in her body language. What we saw in the reading was a determination to lose herself, in a way, in the character. In certain scenes, remember, this woman is no longer in her right mind."

Stone, who had to yet to have a film that matched her success in 1992's *Basic Instinct*, claimed to be very surprised that she got the role: "Working with Marty was something that I didn't imagine would happen to me, because he doesn't often do pictures that require an artist of my type. But he watched everything I had ever done—all the schlock—and he saw what there was of value in all of that." Scorsese said he couldn't decide if Stone—whose pre-*Basic Instinct* films included such beauts as *Action Jackson* and *Police Academy 4: Citizens on Patrol*—had any talent from watching her movies, "since most of them are genre pictures. It was her presence and her look. She has a tough-edged look that seemed perfect for Vegas at the time."

No Girls Allowed

Reportedly, Scorsese generally referred to her on the set not as "Sharon" but as "the girl." And she fretted when she noticed that the director and his leading man seemed to have their own little club, hanging out together in private to work on De Niro's performance.

Stone's first reaction was to write in her diary, "Oh, shit. Oh, shit. Oh, shit. They're not going to let me in." Then she began hounding Scorsese when he was otherwise engaged on the set, pleading, "You've gotta help me here!" Finally, after several days, he responded with "Okay, what do you want from me?" What she wanted was for "you to push me 'til I drop dead." Among the ways cinephile Scorsese helped her was by giving her films to study, ranging from Carl Theodor Dreyer's *The Passion of Joan of Arc* to *What Ever Happened to Baby Jane?* and *Valley of the Dolls*.

The actress was quite pleased with the way her performance turned out, telling the *Los Angeles Times*, "I knew that I had abilities that I hadn't yet had an opportunity to demonstrate. But we went way beyond what I understood that I could do to things that I had never guessed I would be able to tackle." Stone, who described the intensity of her scenes with De Niro as "*Who's Afraid of Virginia Woolf?* meets *GoodFellas*," added, "I think people are gonna be pretty surprised when they see this."

Although Stone had garnered a reputation as being difficult on the sets of her movies, De Niro praised her to *Vanity Fair* because "we all had a lot of laughs during the fight scenes, like the one where I was dragging her on the floor. She was a good sport about it." The actress ended up completely black and blue, having refused all offers of a body double, even for a scene in which she was faced with the less-than-appetizing prospect of performing fellatio on Joe Pesci.

You Look Familiar

Despite the high anticipation for *Casino* there were several ominous signs shortly before the film's release. The movie had to be cut a number of times so it could avoid the dreaded NC-17 rating; some unpleasant business with an eyeball was especially troublesome to the ratings board. Scorsese was guest of honor, receiving the Cecil B. DeMille lifetime achievement award, at ShowEast, a convention of East Coast exhibitors and theater owners held in Las Vegas's rival, Atlantic City. He had received a standing ovation when he arrived, but then he showed an unfinished work print of *Casino*. *Entertainment Weekly* reported

that "finding someone who's still tickled 170 minutes later isn't easy," and quoted a representative from AMC Theatres at the post-screening cocktail party complaining, "He could have done this in an hour and forty." The trade magazine *Box-Office* mentioned the film's flirtations with NC-17, and observed, "the more apt rating—as disappointed exhibitors who attended the ShowEast screening would agree—would have been NS, for no see."

Moreover, even before anyone had viewed the film, there was an undercurrent of apprehension as to whether *Casino* wasn't simply going to be a case of Scorsese déjà vu. Screenwriter Pileggi, who had also worked with the director on *GoodFellas*, claimed the movie wasn't *really* about gangsters, it was about "dreams." Trying to instill a level of mythology to the enterprise, Pileggi said that the De Niro character's story "*is* the story of Las Vegas. And I always think that Las Vegas is to America what America is to the rest of the world—and that is the place you can go for a second chance." Producer Barbara De Fina insisted that *Casino* was "much more complex than *GoodFellas*, and much more sweeping." Scorsese himself would point out that the characters in *Casino* were on a higher socioeconomic level than those in *GoodFellas*. When the *New York Times*'s Bernard Weinraub asked Scorsese about the similarities in theme and tone between *Casino* and *GoodFellas*, the director "responded with some discomfort" before admitting, "I don't know what to say, I can't defend myself. I'm attracted to the same territory." Scorsese also tried to liken himself to two of his favorite directors: "John Ford made the cavalry trilogy—*Fort Apache*, *She Wore a Yellow Ribbon* and *Rio Grande*—basically the same picture. Hitchcock pretty much made the same picture."

Despite these attempts at spin-doctoring, a lot of critics nevertheless expressed disappointment that Scorsese had made, if not the same picture, then a film that was awfully reminiscent of *GoodFellas*. As the *Village Voice*'s J. Hoberman succinctly put it, "whole sequences . . . seem recovered from *GoodFellas* cutting room floor." "*Casino* is about as weak a film as can be imagined from the team of director Martin Scorsese and actors Robert De Niro and Joe Pesci," wrote Mick LaSalle of the *San Francisco Chronicle*. "Even the best

De Niro–Pesci scenes in *Casino* only call to mind better ones in their other Scorsese films, *GoodFellas* and *Raging Bull*. Watching them together here, in fact, is rather like watching Astaire and Rogers in their reunion picture *The Barkleys of Broadway*."

Andrew Sarris of the *New York Observer* brought up last month's little Vegas movie, but not in a way favorable to *Casino*: "*Leaving Las Vegas,* with its two sublime nobodies played by Elisabeth Shue and Nicolas Cage, gets more exuberance in a few cheaply shot sequences than Mr. Scorsese manages with all his voluptuous Steadicam camera movements."

Shortly after *Casino* opened, *Entertainment Weekly* ran a sidebar, leading off with "Describe *Casino* in two words? Wretched excess," and concluding, "By the end there's so much gold, greed, and gore, you won't believe you watched the whole thing." The piece then gave the lowdown on the film's numbers racket, ranging from "number of different instruments of destruction, including a cattle prod, a vise and a pen: 14" to "number of times F-word is used: 365." Despite all the high hopes, when all was said and done, 1991's *Cape Fear* still remained Scorsese's sole major box-office hit.

While reaction to *Casino* was disappointing for most of the people involved, Sharon Stone was at the apex of her professional life. *Variety*'s Todd McCarthy applauded, "Sharon Stone is simply a revelation. No part she's had to date has made remotely such heavy demands on her, and she lets loose with a corker of a performance." Peter Keough of the *Boston Phoenix* didn't like *Casino* ("begins with a bang and ends not so much with a whimper as with more than two hours of shrieking and gabbing"), but he loved its leading lady. He felt that Stone gave "a performance that galvanizes the movie despite its worst inclinations," and deemed her "the female equivalent of Nicolas Cage's doomed drunk in *Leaving Las Vegas*."

The actress received another treat besides the best reviews of her career—just before *Casino* opened, she was awarded a star on Hollywood Boulevard. She told Jay Leno on *The Tonight Show* that this honor "was always my dream . . . I really wanted to be part of film history." And Leno said to her, "I've noticed a calmness about you now. You always were somewhat feisty, like you had something to prove, and it seems to me

you've proved it in this particular role." Stone calmly concurred in his assessment.

To Bug or Not to Bug

Oh, well. If one high-profile director's eagerly anticipated movie didn't live up to expectations, there was another waiting in the wings. Amidst such typical Christmas releases as *Jumanji, Father of the Bride Part II*, and *Sabrina*, Oliver Stone unleashed a Grinch upon the world—the late, unlamented Richard M. Nixon.

Stone had followed up *JFK* with a Vietnam film, *Heaven and Earth,* which didn't cause much of a stir one way or the other, and the über-violent satire *Natural Born Killers*, which made professional moralists like William Bennett apoplectic. The director now decided to turn his attention to the man defeated by John F. Kennedy in 1960, only to rise—Lazarus-like if you were an admirer, zombie-esque if you hated him—to the presidency eight years later.

Despite his own leftish politics, Stone said that he was attracted to Richard M. Nixon because "he embodies everything that's right and wrong about America in general and American politicians in particular." Moreover, "Nixon is a giant of a tragic figure in the classical Greek or Shakespearean tradition. Humble origins, rising to the top, then crashing down in a heap of hubris." He also explained to the *Los Angeles Times* that in terms of his own career, *Nixon* was "the bookend of *JFK*, viewing the same era through a different prism."

To *Premiere*, Stone said, "Nixon is an easy target. He was an awkward man, and easy to ridicule. But he's got many sides." Besides, "to characterize a human being as a victim or a villain is to miss the point of Shakespeare's plays, in which villain and victim are combined in the same person." The director laughed when the *Los Angeles Daily News* asked whether he identified with his subject: "I see a lot of myself in him. I come in for a lot of criticism that other filmmakers don't get. Paranoia has definitely played a part in my life." Stone had never met Richard Nixon, but he told *Interview*, "I saw him once in Dallas when we were shooting *JFK*. We were shooting on a trailer—car shots—and he drove by in a limo waving to everybody on the crew like he was running for office. And no-body waved back at him. It was a strange moment."

After all the brouhaha about wild conjectures, nutty assertions and lunatic fringe conspiracy theories in *JFK*, Stone made sure to cover his ass this time: a completely annotated version of the script was published even before the movie's release, giving detailed sources for every scene, just like in a master's thesis. He commented to the *New York Daily News*: "The dramatic liberties we took were based on a feeling that this was possibly the way it was. We could be wrong. We could be right." And then, showing he was still smarting from the roasting he took from scholars on *JFK*, he added, "The last thing I want in the world is to take on the academic stuffy guys who think they own the history of this country." Stone also hired two of Nixon's real-life aides, John Dean and Alexander Butterfield, to keep him honest. Still, it seemed as if sometimes he just couldn't help himself, and so he threw in an indirect connection between Nixon and the Kennedy assassination.

More Human Than Hitler

Studio executives at Warner Brothers—which had released the director's three previous films—encouraged Stone to consider Warren Beatty, Jack Nicholson, Tom Hanks or even Robin Williams as his leading man. The director instead chose Anthony Hopkins, the Welsh-born actor who looked no more like the dead president than those bigger box-office names. Stone said that after seeing *The Remains of the Day* and *Shadowlands*, "the isolation of Tony is what struck me. The loneliness. I felt that was the quality that always marked Nixon." Moreover, he figured Hopkins could relate to the character because "he grew up poor like Nixon and wrestled with his own demons, so he's made that journey on his own."

Hopkins insisted, "I didn't want to do a Rich Little impersonation," so he was not made up to look like a Madame Tussaud version of Richard Nixon, although he was given the president's often-caricatured five o'clock shadow. He agreed with his director that, yes, he could identify with the guy: "I don't know why, but I know the pain—the inner essence—of this man. Nixon was a self-

destroyer with a strange damaged quality. He reminds me of *The Caine Mutiny*'s Captain Queeg."

The actor also told *Premiere* that he felt extremely protective of Richard Nixon because "He was a human being. I wouldn't say that about Hitler or Stalin, but Nixon—whatever he did—*he was a human being*." *Daily Variety*'s Army Archerd visited the set one day and reported, "I met Nixon several times and I can honestly say Hopkins has captured, sans caricature, Nixon's carriage, manner, total overall look and voice. And all with a minimum of makeup." The columnist also scooped, "Even Rich Little came over to admire Hopkins."

Tight Girdles

Stone surrounded Hopkins with many leading character actors to impersonate the Nixon Gang, including James Woods as Chief of Staff Bob Haldeman, J. T. Walsh as John Ehrlichman, Bob Hoskins as J. Edgar Hoover, E. G. Marshall as Attorney General John Mitchell, and Madeline Kahn as Mitchell's wacky wife, Martha (who may actually have been the sanest one in the whole bunch). For the key role of Nixon's enigmatic wife, Pat, Stone cast Joan Allen, who, although only in her thirties, had long been beloved by theater audiences. She had appeared in a handful of movies (including *Manhunter* and *Searching for Bobby Fischer*), none of which made her a household name despite memorable performances. Allen said of Pat Nixon to the *New York Times*'s Bernard Weinraub, "Do I like her? Very, very much. I would have liked to have sat down and had coffee with her, and I think she would have been a warm person, compassionate. People tagged her with the words 'plastic Pat,' but that's unfair and not true." The undergarments Allen wore were accurate to their period, meaning that many of her bras and girdles were pre-spandex; the constricting skivvies were a great aid to her in honing in on the constricted public persona of the First Lady.

Daddy's Girls

Warner Brothers decided not to continue its relationship with the director for this project; Stone characterized the studio's point of view of the project "as a bunch of unattractive older white men sitting around in suits, with a lot of dialogue and not enough action." So, instead, *Nixon* was released by Hollywood Pictures—part of the Disney conglomerate. The day before the film opened, Diane Disney Miller, Walt's daughter, wrote to the Nixon kids, Tricia and Julie, and wailed, "My father was a great admirer of your parents and our families enjoyed a special friendship for many years. I am ashamed that the Walt Disney Company—the company my father created—is associated with this disturbing distortion of history." She did her own bit of distortion in the letter by stating that Old Walt had "won more Academy Awards than anyone in the history of film," when this claim could be made only because he insisted on picking up the Oscars for films made by his underlings. And Diane hadn't, of course, seen the movie; her heartache emanated from what she was "reading and hearing." She concluded with a bit of Nixonian self-pity: "Our family, too, suffered from malicious attacks on our late father."

The feisty Nixon daughters hadn't needed any encouragement, though. The previous day, they and their husbands issued a statement—based on the published screenplay—calling the movie "reprehensible," a "character assassination" and an attempt to "defame and degrade President and Mrs. Nixon's memories in the mind of the American public." Stone said he could "understand the distress that any effort to examine the life of Richard Nixon might create for his family."

On the Couch with Dr. Stone

"Prepare for a surprise," advised a *Newsweek* cover story. "On the verge of 50, Oliver Stone has discovered complexity, ambiguity and even a measure of restraint." The magazine added that Stone's film "is no whitewash of Nixon. He's there with all his malevolence, his paranoia and his ruthlessness intact. His loyalists and family members won't like this portrait. But his bitterest enemies may not like it, either, for it forces the viewer to acknowledge the twisted humanity of the man." The article concluded admiringly that "the Stone who made *Nixon* is no demagogue. The propa-

gandist has been replaced by a bold portraitist." In a *Washington Post* profile of Stone and his movie, John Powers said, "Even as the movie spotlights the rotten truths of Nixon's checkered career—Watergate, the destruction of Cambodia, the cynical fanning of social hatreds—it offers an unexpectedly touching portrait of a man so exasperatingly human that you don't know whether to smack him or cry."

After the film's premiere—at Washington's Kennedy Center, no less—Bob Woodward, the one-time *Washington Post* reporter who had Nixon and Watergate to thank for his fame and fortune, commented, "I guess everybody gets the psychoanalyst they deserve, and Nixon got Oliver Stone." Woodward's old partner, Carl Bernstein, adjudged *Nixon* to be "very bad history," but he also found it "surprisingly empathetic," coming to the conclusion that it was "a psychodrama, not a docudrama." And while Bernstein agreed with Julie and Tricia that the film was erroneous, he did not share their belief that it was "malicious."

Janet Maslin opined that *Nixon* was "one of Mr. Stone's biggest gambles, a bold feat of revisionism that veers unpredictably between turgidness and inspiration. What it finally adds up to is a huge mixed bag of waxworks and daring, a film that is furiously ambitious even when it goes flat, and startling even when it settles for eerie, movie-of-the-week mimicry. Reckless, bullying and naggingly unreliable, this mercurial *Nixon* is also finally as gutsy and overpowering as it means to be." But *Time*'s Richard Corliss groused that "You might expect that Stone, our most vigorous and cinematically ambitious director, would be drawn to create a prismatic, Kane-like portrait of a potentate who was an enigma, not least to himself. But no. Stone is content to dramatize major episodes from the life. Some have voltage, but others are dry re-enactments inserted for the record. This gives much of the film an oddly pageantlike, perfunctory tone. It's a $43 million term paper."

Oliver Stone had said, "A lot of liberals really hate Nixon. But you have to be careful where hatred can take you." Some political columnists were not in as forgiving a mood as the director, and took exception to the film's strenuously balanced portrait. The *Boston Globe*'s Martin F. Nolan had had the honor of being placed on Richard Nixon's Enemies List—a document of unbridled paraphrenia featuring a crazy quilt of names ranging from Ted Kennedy to Dan Rather to "Miss Manners" to football's Joe Namath to Steve Mc-Queen, Tony Randall and Carol Channing. Nolan rolled his eyes at the film's hypothesis "that Nixon, certainly a victim of 'the system,' was probably too good—maybe too Gandhi-like—for America," and reminded his readers that Tricky Dick was the "ringleader of the most notable assault on the Constitution since Fort Sumter, all the while tossing his co-conspirators to the wolves as the troika sped across the ice." Then again, coming from the left-wing perspective of *The Nation*, Stuart Klawans argued, "Maybe the result isn't historically reliable; but we have books for that purpose and ought to use them. *Nixon* summons up the ghosts in our nation's haunted attic, and that's what a movie can do."

You Don't Know Dick

Nixon loyalists were disgruntled at seeing what they considered an unrecognizable Richard Nixon on screen. Presidential adviser John Ehrlichman, who somewhat incredibly emerged in the movie as the voice of conscience—cynics said it was because early on he had threatened to sue Stone—gave *Nixon* a mixed review. He acknowledged that it "wasn't nearly as bad as I thought it would be," but bristled at the film's notion that "nothing ever happened around Nixon except dark conspiracy and heavy drinking." Ehrlichman also reminded liberals that even though they may have loathed Nixon, he was, as frightening as it may be to contemplate, a hell of a lot better than what came later, because unlike Reagan's and Bush's, his administration was a proponent of such essentials as environmental protection and government support of the arts.

Other veterans of the Nixon administration who were still kicking around also weighed in. General Alexander Haig—Nixon's chief of staff—was on *Today*, saying that *Nixon* "made me schizophrenic. On the one hand, it was technically superb, the casting was outstanding and the acting was really quite brilliant. On the other hand, it abuses the truth in ways

that I find appalling and it's a real departure from historic fact." And while Oliver Stone had called *Nixon* "an attempt at a fuller understanding of Richard Nixon," Haig found it to be "a real hatchet job" noting that "he was not a lush. He wasn't a pill popper." Haig was played in the movie by Powers Boothe, and the general laughingly admitted that he did like how he was portrayed because "I was one of the good guys in the film in an otherwise dismal array of dismal personalities."

Special counsel Charles Colson—notorious for saying "I would walk over my grandmother if necessary to assure the president's reelection," and then later even less appealing when, after serving jail time, he became a proselytizing born-again Christian—also condemned the film: "I saw this man as a human being. He is not portrayed as a human being in this film. He is portrayed as some kind of monster. It's a dreadful film." Of course, Colson knew more about movies than other veterans of the Nixon White House: His autobiography, *Born Again,* had been turned into a 1978 movie, directed by Irving Rapper—who in better days had made *Now, Voyager*—and starring Dean Jones—who in better days had appeared in *The Million Dollar Duck.*

Jay Carr of the *Boston Globe* was bowled over by "a towering and complex performance by Anthony Hopkins that humanizes Nixon more than Nixon ever was able to humanize himself. . . . Even small gestures, like Hopkins's way of abruptly raising his hands to hide his face or jerkily defend it from the blows Nixon had to believe were ever poised to fall, are those of a first-magnitude stage artist comfortable playing Macbeth."

J. Hoberman of the *Village Voice*, however, groaned that "Hopkins's overheated, self-consciously self-conscious performance is an inorganic checklist of 'Nixonian' traits—he has less fun than even the real Nixon."

If response to Anthony Hopkins's interpretation was mixed, Joan Allen's portrayal of Pat received nothing but raves. Stephen Talty of *Time Out New York*, for example, called her "astonishing," opining that "repressed love and rage transform her face into a sharp-featured mask, but Allen uses it with great subtlety."

When Oliver Stone was in preproduction, he ran into Billy Wilder at a party and told him about his upcoming project. The incredulous octogenarian director responded, "Oliver, please. Nixon. Nixon. Nobody likes Nixon. Why would you do Nixon?" As it turned out, despite all the press, all the publicity, all the controversy, *Nixon* the movie ultimately was as unloved as Nixon the man. An unnamed source associated with the film sighed to the *Los Angeles Times* that "On paper, it looked like gold. *Schindler's List,* another three-hour film about an extremely dark subject, went through the roof. We've hit a brick wall trying to figure out what went wrong." For Paula Silver, a film marketing consultant, the answer was easy: "However well the subject is handled, Richard Nixon is no box-office draw." And Stone's spokesperson, Stephen Rivers, concurred, admitting that "we probably underestimated people's psychological aversion to Richard Nixon. Though the press finds him endlessly fascinating, the public's appetite is considerably less."

White House Washout

Nixon was the season's second disappointment set in the White House. Prior to its release, Rob Reiner's *The American President* had been touted as one of the year's main Oscar contenders, not because anyone was envisioning a major piece of filmmaking, but because the presumed liberal sentiments and middlebrow sensibility of the movie seemed perfectly suited to Academy voters. Michael Douglas was the widowed commander in chief, Annette Bening his sweet patootie, and the film represented the apotheosis of Hollywood's infatuation with Bill Clinton. But then it opened, and in terms of critical reaction, *The American President* ended up like a third-place finisher in the New Hampshire primary. The unenthusiastic response to the film meant that the Academy Awards would not—as *Entertainment Weekly*'s Gregg Kilday worded it—"boil down to a battle between Opie and Meathead."

Everything Old Is New Again

If 1970s mobsters and a 1970s president weren't cutting it at the box office, a figure from the much more distant past was doing quite well. Jane Austen seemed to be everywhere in 1995. A low-budget made-for-British-television adaptation of her novel, *Persuasion,* received some of the best reviews of the year when it was released in American theaters. Critics also found Amy Heckerling's *Clueless,* transporting *Emma* to present-day Beverly Hills, to be an unexpected charmer.

And at Christmas came the most highly anticipated of all, *Sense and Sensibility.* The project had its genesis back in 1990, when the then-little-known Emma Thompson was costarring with hubby Kenneth Branagh in his psychological thriller *Dead Again.* Chatting with that film's producer, Lindsay Doran, Thompson realized that they were both mad for Jane Austen and her early nineteenth-century comedies of manners. Thompson singled her out as "my top-favorite author. I started reading her when I was 10 or 11 and she just gets better and better." She added that, "I'll read those books and I'll get to a point where I'll have to put the book down because I'm laughing so much. People don't associate that with Jane Austen." And the way fate played out, not only was Lindsay Doran an Austen fan, but she also had long wanted to do a film version of *Sense and Sensibility*—if only she could find just the right screenwriter.

The actress's British television show, *Thompson,* was then being shown on public television in L.A. Some segments of that skit-based series—which Thompson wrote, as well as starred in—took place in earlier times, and Doran was a huge fan, especially of one episode in which a Victorian bride questions her mother about "the mouselike creature that had crawled out of her husband's trousers on their wedding night." "Emma's ability to write in period language seemed effortless," said Doran. "In short, it was exactly the kind of writing I'd been searching for. I knew that Emma had never written a screenplay before, but there was enough sense of storytelling even in those two- and three-minute sketches to indicate that writing a full-length screenplay wouldn't be too difficult a leap."

In between making such films as *Howards End* and *Remains of the Day* and becoming an Oscar-winning actress and international star, Thompson worked—in dribs and drabs—on the *Sense and Sensi-*

bility screenplay. As Doran explained, "Emma would make a film and write a draft, make a film and write a draft, over and over again. Sometimes she'd make a film and write three drafts." And meanwhile, as the actress became more and more of a hot commodity, Sidney Pollack's production company—for which Doran worked—was letting her know that sooner would be better than later. So she spent much of the latter part of 1993 working on the screenplay, while also dealing with the rumors that something was going on between Kenneth Branagh and Helena Bonham Carter, his costar on the film he was directing, *Mary Shelley's Frankenstein*. (Bonham Carter had also played Thompson's sister in *Howards End*.) Thompson insisted that Jane Austen is a "comedian, she's a satirist and an ironist of the first order, and her wit is biting and it cuts very deep." She took umbrage with the television versions of the author's works which were making their way to the States via *Masterpiece Theatre* and A & E: "They're just—well, I find them so offensive. They're so *cozy*—there's no sense at all that they're satire."

Signed to direct was Ang Lee, the Taiwanese-born filmmaker whose wry comedies centering on familial relationships, *The Wedding Banquet* and *Eat Drink Man Woman*, had been Oscar nominees for Best Foreign Film. Initially, there was some skepticism that an Asian director was being given an 1811 Jane Austen vehicle as his first Hollywood-backed project, but as Roger Ebert saw it, "surely a modern upper-middle-class Chinese person has more familiarity with Austen's varieties of family ties and marriage responsibilities than a modern Briton." In any case, Lee had been living in the United States—currently in the New York suburbs—since the late 1970s. Lindsay Doran acknowledged that Thompson's husband, Kenneth Branagh, "had shyly thrown his hat into the ring at one point early on," and that she had considered Rob Reiner because "he'd done *This Is Spinal Tap* with all that dry Brit humor."

Sense and Sensibility was the story of two sisters, one circumspect and proper, the other romantic and capricious, living in genteel poverty and facing various marriage prospects and the prospect of *not* being married. While working on the script, Thompson had en-

visioned Natasha and Joely Richardson as the Dashwood sisters. But Ang Lee told her that he had taken the assignment assuming that she would be playing Elinor—the "Sense" of the title. He cheerfully recalled that "It wound up a pretty easy twist-her-arm job—she jumped in right away." Admittedly, "I'm too old," said the 36-year-old Thompson—the book's Elinor Dashwood was 19—but on the other hand "we've bumped up the ages. We've had to age them for plausibility and, with makeup, I might look young enough." Cast as her sister, Marianne—"Sensibility"—was Kate Winslet, a 19-year-old with a cult following after her turn as a murderess in Peter Jackson's *Heavenly Creatures*.

At the end of 1994, Thompson met with Doran and Lee to go over the latest draft—number thirteen or fourteen by her account. It was decided that one more was necessary, and Thompson spent January alone at home with her word processor, "tears and a black dressing gown"—her marriage to Kenneth Branagh was through.

A Set of Friends

By coincidence, Winslet had just ended a relationship after four years, so the two on-screen sisters could commiserate with each other offscreen. Winslet told CNN that it was no problem acting opposite the film's screenwriter, and that if Winslet wasn't pleased with a bit of dialogue, Thompson's response would inevitably be a generous "Oh, God, that was a crap line. Why did I write that? I want to change that a bit." Thompson had written the part of one of the suitors specifically for her chum Hugh Grant; now a major star thanks to *Four Weddings and a Funeral*, he had a relatively small part. Thompson said, "I've done three movies with Hugh Grant and I'll be damned if I'll do another one without kissing him." She also maintained that, although *Sense and Sensibility* takes place nearly two centuries earlier, the situations in the film remained relevant. "Women still fall in love with the wrong guy," she said. "They still get jilted. They're still looking for people to marry." Alan Rickman, usually a cinematic villain, was cast against type as a shy and brooding suitor, and from reports on the set, actor

Greg Wise was helping Thompson to forget about Kenneth Branagh. Meanwhile two other old friends in the cast, Imelda Staunton and Hugh Laurie, jokingly stayed in character as they engaged in conversation for the benefit of E!: Imelda: "Did Emma write this?" Hugh: "No, she copied it out of a book." Imelda: "Straight out of a book?" Hugh: "She copied it out word for bloody word." Imelda (shaking her head): "There's not an original idea in this."

Thompson also kept a diary of the shooting experiences of *Sense and Sensibility*. In addition to jotting down occurrences during the production, the actress also included her take on other people in the production: "Ang presents a collection of intriguing contradictions. He does t'ai chi but his shoulders are constantly bowed, he meditates and smokes (not at the same time as far as I know), he hasn't an ounce of fat on him but eats everything going, especially buns." She also recorded that the first note she got from her director about her work was "don't look so old." Lee was used to having complete autonomy with his cast, and was taken aback when Thompson and Hugh Grant began asking questions and making suggestions about their interpretations of the characters. But above all, Thompson wrote with admiration, Lee's "sensibility very unsentimental, like Austen's. They're remarkably connected. She'd be astonished."

The down-to-earth Thompson also noted that "the horses have taken to letting off lengthy and noisome farts during the takes . . . it's the Devon oats. Privately I decide to lay off the porridge," and "Managed to pee on most of my underwear this morning (trailer loos are very cramped), so I'm in a very bad temper." After finishing his scenes, Hugh Grant went to Los Angeles, where he was arrested for dallying with a prostitute. Thompson's diary entry: "Hugh G. in a spot of bother up L.A., apparently. Something to do with a blow job. It's all right for some, I thought." Kate Winslet told *Entertainment Weekly* that *her* reaction to Grant's predicament was "I mean, it did make me laugh quite a lot, poor guy. But it's really not fair. Guys get up to that kind of thing. I hope he had a good time."

The Anglo-Asian Dream Team

Rita Kempley of *The Washington Post* had a wonderful time. "Based upon Jane Austen's satire of 18th-century dating games, this rapturous romance is not only laugh-out-loud funny but demonstrates how little humankind has evolved in matters of the heart," she enthused, and then put in a good word for the director: "Lee might be more familiar with green tea than Earl Grey, but it's hard to imagine anyone better suited to this material." *Time*'s Richard Schickel left *Sense and Sensibility* sounding almost giddy, writing of the movie's finale that this "kind of joyous catharsis is what the old movie masters of romantic comedy—Frank Capra, Leo McCarey—sometimes delivered. You don't expect to find it in adaptations of classic literature. You don't expect to find it in modern movies." And *L.A. Weekly*'s Ella Taylor declared Emma Thompson and Ang Lee to be a "dream team," saying that "Thompson plucks out the novelist's delicate wit, while Lee, a master of domestic dramedy, takes Austen gently over the top in a prankish farce with just enough heartburn to elicit the occasional sob."

National Review's John Simon marveled that "Miss Thompson has been remarkable in most of her many films, but—improbably—she keeps getting better. Just when you think she has reached her acme, she goes ahead and tops herself." And while Simon was adoring Thompson the actress, John Hartl of the *Seattle Times* was doing the same to Thompson the writer: The "script is a model of wit and compression, taking every opportunity to find humor in characters who are often overwhelmed by greed or caution or the need to express themselves openly in a society bound by decorum. Yet it never sidesteps the melancholy heart of a story in which love, money and social standing become hopelessly intertwined." Of Kate Winslet, *The New Republic*'s Stanley Kauffmann wrote: "At first she seems just one more English rose; but very rapidly she whirls into impulse and vulnerability and romantic intoxication with heart-aching verity. A captivating performance."

Kenneth Turan was one of the few party poopers, specifically taking Ang Lee to task. "Though he does a more-than-credible job of directing, he isn't sharp on the nuances of British behavior. . . . And with a precise writer who was as acutely conscious of intangibles of character as Austen, that lack is noticeable." Also voicing disapproval were the ladies and gentlemen of the Jane Austen Society, who let Columbia Pictures know that they did not take it lightly that Thompson's script hadn't shown absolute fidelity to the book, that it omitted a duel here, added a kiss there. Thompson laughed that she could imagine the "picket lines, with people in mobcaps chanting."

At year's end, *People* magazine selected Jane Austen as "One of the 25 Most Intriguing People of 1995." The British authoress found herself in the company of Hootie and the Blowfish, Louis Farrakhan, "Babe" and The Unabomber.

Prize Time

Everybody connected with *Sense and Sensibility* had to be feeling pretty good because, on the same day the film opened to outstanding reviews, it received the Best Picture and Best Director prizes from the National Board of Review in the year's first set of awards. On top of that, Emma Thompson was named Best Actress (both for *Sense and Sensibility* and *Carrington*, in which she played painter Dora Carrington). The following day, Thompson won an award from the New York Film Critics Circle; this one was for Best Screenplay and Ang Lee went two for two, garnering another Best Director prize. It was the third year in a row that the New York group showed no sense at all in deciding that the best directed *and* best written film was not the best film of the year. That honor went to *Leaving Las Vegas*. Jami Bernard of the *New York Daily News* began her account of the voting by reporting, "After a decidedly lackluster year at the movies and in the absence of any critical consensus, the New York Film Critics Circle unenthusiastically cast their ballots yesterday for *Leaving Las Vegas* as the best picture of 1995." She added, "Although several of the critics were solidly behind the Mike Figgis movie, the others were all over the map, offering practically one new nominee per critic."

Nicolas Cage took the Best Actor prize from the New York critics for *Leaving Las Vegas* as he had the previous day with the National Board. And Best Actress went to Jennifer Jason Leigh for *Georgia*, a Miramax film in which she played a troubled young woman who sings really badly. Analyzing the first two sets of awards, Thelma Adams of the *New York Post* wrote, "Pundits were predicting a strong showing for *Apollo 13* at summer's end, and there seemed a possibility of Tom Hanks getting a third Oscar nomination in three years for Best Actor. But that feeling appears to be fading fast."

These two New York–based groups agreed on the supporting awards. The National Board cited Kevin Spacey for the gimmicky crime thriller *The Usual Suspects*, in which he played a crook undergoing a lengthy interrogation—director Bryan Singer described it as "*Reservoir Dogs* meets *Rashomon*"—as well as for *Se7en*, in which he was the nutzoid killer. The New York Film Critics honored him for these two, but also cited his performances as a studio executive in the Hollywood satire, *Swimming with Sharks,* and as an army major in *Outbreak*, a medical thriller that tried to turn Dustin Hoffman into some sort of action hero.

The Supporting Actress winner both times was Mira Sorvino. She played a foul-mouthed and ditzy—but gold-hearted, natch—prostitute/porno actress in Woody Allen's *Mighty Aphrodite*; because this mean-spirited movie dealt with the subject of adoption, some observers saw it as a swipe at Allen's ex-companion Mia Farrow and her penchant for taking in stray children. Sorvino won the awards despite sharply dichotomized reviews. For example, *Newsday*'s John Anderson declared the actress to be "captivating, her Victoria Jackson impersonation quite ridiculous but endearing," while David Denby felt that the character "is lazily, insensitively written, and the untried Mira Sorvino gives a disconnected, defenseless performance, speaking in a high forced voice that is uncomfortable to listen to— she sounds like a man using his upper register in a puppet show." *Nixon*'s Joan Allen had received the same number of points as Sorvino in the New York Critics' voting, but because she wasn't on the requisite number of ballots, under the convoluted rules of the organization, this tie wasn't a tie.

Allen did make up for it on the West Coast, where

the Los Angeles Film Critics Association gave her its Supporting Actress award. The overall theme in L.A., however, was "Viva Las Vegas," as *Leaving Las Vegas* not only chalked up a third win for Nicolas Cage, but Elisabeth Shue, director Mike Figgis and the film itself all drew aces. (When Shue accepted her prize, she told the critics, "I haven't won an award since seventh grade, for most improved soccer player.") Emma Thompson continued on her roll, picking up another prize for Best Screenplay. The Supporting Actor winner on the Left Coast was Don Cheadle for *Devil in a Blue Dress*, a Denzel Washington vehicle based on one of Walter Mosley's popular Easy Rawlins crime novels and a box-office disappointment.

As usual, the National Society of Film Critics voted several weeks later than the other groups, after the dust had settled. The Society came up with the rather surprising choice of *Babe* as Best Picture of the year. And its Screenplay award went to a Jane Austen adaptation, though this time it wasn't *Sense and Sensibility* but Amy Heckerling's *Clueless*. Otherwise, the winners were all holdovers from the other groups: Nicolas Cage (making it a clean sweep of the four most significant critics' awards), Elisabeth Shue, Don Cheadle, Joan Allen and Mike Figgis.

With *Leaving Las Vegas* piling up the awards, more and more people got around to checking it out, including *Premiere*'s "Libby Gelman-Waxner." She reported, "I saw *Leaving Las Vegas* and afterward at least three people sitting near me turned to their friends and said, 'Okay, next time I pick the movie.'"

Penn in the Pen

In retrospect, the biggest mystery of this year's critics' awards was why one particular film had almost no impact on the voting. Gramercy Pictures did hold screenings of *Dead Man Walking* in time for the awards but perhaps, because it wouldn't be opening until after Christmas, a lot of critics figured they could catch up with it later, and concentrate on holiday shopping for now. *Dead Man Walking* had its genesis when Susan Sarandon was filming *The Client* down in Louisiana and met Sister Helen Prejean, a Catholic nun who had become a leading advocate against the

death penalty. She wrote a bestselling book detailing how she befriended two death row inmates and fought first for their lives and then for their souls. Sarandon gave the book to her companion Tim Robbins, and he found in it a project he wanted to direct as his follow-up to 1992's *Bob Roberts*.

Sarandon played Sister Helen, and the film followed the nun's experiences as a spiritual counselor, combining the two inmates into a single, swaggering murderer of a pair of teenagers. Sean Penn played the death row inmate and Sarandon felt that he was well cast because "You have to find someone who people will believe killed someone." Penn had a taste of prison life to draw upon, having spent thirty-two days in jail after punching out an irritating photographer; in the cell across from his was Richard Ramirez, the Night Stalker serial killer. (Tim Robbins referred to Penn's stint in the clink as "on-the-job training.") And even though Penn said he had retired from acting to devote himself to directing, Robbins recalled that "I sent him the script, and he said it really moved him, and he had to do it." *Dead Man Walking* was partially shot on location at the Louisiana State Prison at Angola, and Sarandon was deeply affected by the environment. "The day they executed one guy by lethal injection—he was from New York, actually—that stands out for me," she recalled. "It was very surreal, doing your work and going to lunch as a man waits to die."

What particularly impressed critics is that while Robbins and Sarandon were known for their left-of-center politics and were both adamantly against government-sponsored premeditated murder, the film was steadfastly well balanced. This was no ersatz *I Want to Live!* in which Susan Hayward was railroaded to her death. As Carrie Rickey articulated in the *Philadelphia Inquirer*, "Like Sister Helen, the movie's strength is in keeping an open mind—and heart. The film listens carefully to those who hold that killing murderers doesn't deter others from killing. Likewise, it listens to those who believe in eye-for-an-eye retribution. And, like Sister Helen, the movie cites testaments old and new, chapter and verse, about where the Bible stands on capital punishment: on both sides. As embodied by Susan Sarandon in the performance of her career, Sister Helen is our guide to what many have come to think of as the criminal injustice system."

Robbins himself said to the Associated Press, "If I were in a similar circumstance I'd probably have incredible rage. So I didn't want to make judgments on these people. I didn't want to make them the crazed parents calling for blood. I didn't think that would be honest." The director also told the *Los Angeles Daily News* that being among inmates while researching his role in *The Shawshank Redemption* removed any starry-eyed notions he might have had about criminals, but still, "I have a problem with the fact that it's a poor person's punishment. You'll never see a rich person killed."

For Sarandon, "it was always a movie about the power of love and redemption. Here's this woman with this incredible faith, and her job is to go in and be there for this guy, and to believe as Jesus did that no matter how horrible you are, you're still a child of God. She has to go from the company line of how this thing is supposed to work, to actually loving somebody who's despicable. And how do you do that?" The actress also admitted that this was a difficult role for her: "I prayed, I prayed often in the course of this movie, to be able to not comment on it, to have a certain purity in terms of my function in the story, to be able to put my ego aside and do all the things that she had to do."

Although Robbins and Sarandon were both lapsed Catholics, *Dead Man Walking* emerged as one of the most deeply religious films in eons. David Sterritt of the *Christian Science Monitor* found that "what makes *Dead Man Walking* one of the year's most encouraging screen events is precisely its insistence on carrying compassionate convictions to their logical extreme, challenging viewers to consider perspectives on crime and punishment—including the Christian mandate to love one's enemy—that aren't heard very often these days. All involved with the film should be very proud of it." Roger Ebert observed in the *Chicago Sun-Times* that Sarandon's Sister Helen "is one of the few truly spiritual characters I have seen in the movies. Movies about 'religion' are often only that—movies about secular organizations that deal in spirituality. It is so rare to find a movie character who truly does try

to live according to the teachings of Jesus (or anyone else, for that matter) that it's a little disorienting."

Debbie Reynolds on Death Row

Almost all of the interaction between the nun and the murderer occurred between a glass partition, which, Sarandon told CNN, made the film more difficult because of "the loneliness of not even being in the same frame as your costar." Despite this handicap, the performances in *Dead Man Walking* were as admired as the film itself. *USA Today*'s Mike Clark said, "Sean Penn humanizes a guilty-as-hell Louisiana death row con without trying to make us like the guy too much. This astonishing performance in an unexpectedly great movie would dominate year-end acting talk were it not for costar Susan Sarandon's comparably subtle work." Janet Maslin wrote, "Affecting a thick Cajun accent and a carefully groomed look suggesting equal degrees of Elvis and Mephistopheles, Penn gives an astonishing performance and delivers exactly what *Dead Man Walking* needs. Nothing about him suggests an innocent victim, but his surliness is so magnetic and mercurial that it holds the viewer's interest." Terrence Rafferty of *The New Yorker* analyzed that "Penn, having created in his initial scenes a lifelike portrait of a proud, fearless working-class loser, spends the rest of the picture painstakingly deconstructing it, stripping down layer after layer from it until he gets down to the roughest sketch of Poncelet's true self: a spare human outline that is, mysteriously, richer than the intricate designs that covered it."

"Using the simplest of acting techniques, which looks like no technique at all, Sarandon gives a stripped-down, gloriously effective performance as Sister Helen," panegyrized Edward Guthmann of the *San Francisco Chronicle*. "Acting rarely gets better than this. Sarandon, topping a decade of great performances, is luminous as the idealistic nun. She seems to have found this character at the perfect juncture in her career, and she brings to it all of her integrity and social commitment, her skill and maturity, and her gift for playing valiant, flawed women." And if that weren't enough, he concluded, "There's no division between Sarandon and her character in those final scenes. It's like watching Henry Fonda in *The Grapes of Wrath* or Gregory Peck in *To Kill a Mockingbird*—those rare occasions when actors not only are perfectly cast but also find parts that enrich and illuminate their humanity."

Stephen Talty of *Time Out New York* wrote that Sean Penn "delivers his scorching performance in spite of a big hairdo that Debbie Reynolds might have envied." Tim Robbins laughingly recalled that when he first got a load of Penn's pompadour, "I said, 'Wait a minute.' But then I looked at pictures of prisoners and Sean was absolutely right. You have a lot of time on your hands and not many avenues of self-expression. One thing you can do is spend a lot of time on your hair. Nails too, man; they have very nice nails." Sarandon was aware of appearances as well—she admitted "it's not easy to go without makeup and wear funny clothes and have a bad haircut."

Sister Helen was often on the set. Robbins quipped that "Helen's biggest fear was that I'd write some scene where she'd smuggle a cyanide capsule in her bra." The nun had told *Interview* that when Robbins first expressed interest in buying screen rights to her book, she didn't know who he was, so she and a friend rented *Bull Durham*. While watching the film, the friend turned to Sister Helen and said incredulously, "That pitcher with the garter belt is going to be the *director* of this film?" He had misconceptions as well, telling Charlie Rose, "I was raised a Catholic, so I have a whole other perception of nuns than, than the one that Sister Helen gave me. Mine was, you know, having to do with getting whacked on the knuckles." Robbins had also sent her the first draft of the script. "I had never read a screenplay," Sister Helen recalled. "I did not know what those POV things meant. But I am a nun. I did teach English, so I corrected his English."

Pathetic, Self-Loathing and over a Cliff

Back in October, Pat Broeske of *Entertainment Weekly* appeared on CNN and pronounced, "What a pathetic year it's been." For possible Best Picture nominees from among the movies that opened during the first ten months of the year, she cited *Apollo 13* and *The Bridges of Madison County*, "and you can practically stop there."

It was a theme that came up again and again in meditations on the films of 1995. In early November, *Variety* analyzed the year's likely Oscar contenders and the strategies being mapped out by the studios. "*Apollo 13* is considered the only certainty for a best picture nomination among releases to date." The article then quoted an Academy member as saying, "There are a handful of good pictures. But that's about it. I thought we hit rock bottom last year in terms of choices, but this year's films look even worse. It's becoming very hard to look upon the Oscars as a celebration of the best Hollywood can do." In *New York*, screenwriter-columnist William Goldman was the prophet of doom: "Hollywood is headed straight off a cliff," he warned. "The crash will occur in the next eighteen months, and very painful it will be—like sitting through *Four Rooms* twice." A source, identified only as "one of the most important people in the industry," told Goldman, "You are wrong when you say we're going over a cliff—we've already gone over. We're in free fall now." Another unnamed studio executive said of 1995, "Believe me, no one had a good year this year." Goldman's final warning was: "The quality of what Hollywood is turning out is so foul, people are beginning to turn away. . . . Broadway has been laughed at for years for not having enough quality stuff to nominate for the Tonys. Well, Oscar time is coming up. Welcome to the theater."

Entertainment Weekly heard the Hollywood buzz and, in early January, determined this year's Oscars were shaping up as "a dark-versus-light derby between the hottest contenders for Best Picture: *Sense and Sensibility*, the front-running filly, and *Leaving Las Vegas*, perhaps the broodiest Oscar dark horse to come down the straightaway since 1969's *Midnight Cowboy*." *Newsweek*'s David Ansen expressed the general sentiment that "as the Oscars approach, the movie industry finds itself in a quandary: it can't come up with five studio films to fill the bill. There are only two movies everyone concedes to be a lock, and only one of these is a homegrown, big-budget blockbuster." That would be *Apollo 13*. Ansen's other sure shot was *Sense and Sensibil-*

ity, and he commented, "It's an interesting face-off: the boys against the girls; high-tech American moxie vs. late-18th-century English reticence. Place your bets." He also quoted various studio executives, both named and off the record: "Hollywood is apathetic about its own product"; "The self-loathing is rampant"; "We're getting a lot of things wrong in this town."

Women on Top

There was also amazement that, for a change, it was among women that an abundance of deserving competitors could be found. In a mid-December edition of his "Talk of Hollywood" column, Bernard Weinraub of the *New York Times* wrote, "In recent years, Hollywood has endured the embarrassment of trying to find five nominees in the Best Actress category. For that matter, coming up with five Best Film candidates has often been a bit of a struggle, too. This year looks different. While the Best Film category once again appears thin despite 153 releases in wide release, there are more than enough contenders for Best Actress honors." Miramax marketing executive Cynthia Scwartz observed, "It's the only category where someone really deserving is going to get left out. It's the most exciting this year." Columnists Marilyn Beck and Stacy Jenel Smith had asked Sharon Stone who she felt her stiffest competition would be. "Anjelica Huston blew me away in *The Crossing Guard*," she responded. "Kate Winslet was remarkable in *Sense and Sensibility*; her commitment was so profound it came through her skin." These two women were potential *Supporting* nominees, however; Stone did mention one lead: "Elisabeth Shue made an enormous turn in her commitment to her work in *Leaving Las Vegas*. She was truly impressive."

Among actors, all those awards for Nicolas Cage made it highly unlikely he'd be left out of the final five, and *Apollo 13*'s Tom Hanks was seemingly on his way to becoming the Greer Garson of the 1990s—every year a nomination. *Entertainment Weekly* also put its money on the man Hanks had defeated last year: "John Travolta, consolidating his comeback, is sure to make a repeat performance. Even though *Get Shorty* is a lightweight amusement, his good sportsmanship as

he lost the Oscar to Hanks guarantees him another try at the prize." Beyond these three, the race was conceded to be wide open, with Sean Penn, Ian McKellen in *Richard III* and Anthony Hopkins (although *Nixon*'s poor showing had knocked his chances down a peg or two) among the names most frequently popping up in prognostications.

Harvey Weinstein Always Rings Twice

Surveying how wide open most of the races seemed to be, Miramax sensed an exciting opportunity for jumping in and seeing how adept it could be at manipulating voters' emotions. Although *The Postman* was well liked, it did not win any critics' awards (nor even show up as a runner-up in any categories), and few reviewers had the film on their Ten Best lists. Still, the studio did have certain intangibles on its side. Having already milked the human interest story of Massimo Troisi's dying for his art and the snob appeal of Great Authors rallying around the film to help turn *The Postman* into an art house hit, Miramax sent out videos of the film to 5,000 Academy members in November and dropped the soundtrack album in the mail. It also sponsored a poetry reading of Neruda's poetry in L.A.—Rod Steiger and Jennifer Tilly were among the participants. And then the ever-cagey studio hit upon a new tact to whip up interest among Academy voters.

Knowing that recent controversies over eligibility and selections by particular committees—such as the previous year's disqualification of Krzysztof Kieslowski's *Red* as a Foreign Film entry, and the whole *Hoop Dreams* fiasco—had made Academy members wary of the organization's seemingly arbitrary rules, Miramax devised an ad campaign to play to that sentiment. The company began plastering the trade papers with ads declaring what one would have assumed was bad news: "This year, Italy's official Academy Award nominee for Best Foreign Language Film is *not The Postman*." And as a P.S. there was a parenthetical: "(It was directed by an Englishman.)" The implication was clear: Italy was being spiteful and petty simply because

The Postman had the temerity to be directed by a Brit; surely if an Italian had directed it, *The Postman* would have been submitted as the country's entry. The next block of copy read: "In the tradition of past Best Picture nominees *Cries and Whispers* and *Z*, we respectfully submit *The Postman* for your consideration as The Best Picture of the Year."

Subsequent ads were less subtle. Before getting to the main point, they tried to convince the reader that "Every now and then a movie appears that captures the hearts of critics and audiences in a way few films can. This year, that film was *The Postman*. . . . American filmgoers have been seduced by the magic, the romance, the poetry and the performances of this extraordinary film." There were also some critics' quotations and other evidence of the respect in which the film was held, including, "In *People* magazine's Celebrity Poll, this is the one film cited more than any other as the best and most memorable movie of the year." (Among those voicing enthusiasm for *The Postman* in the magazine's survey were Fran Drescher of *The Nanny* TV show and model Christy Turlington, who declared, "*The Postman* is the kind of movie I like—a simple film without sex, violence or bad language.") Then, after all this build-up, the ads zeroed in on their main point. Whereas earlier Miramax had merely inferred nefariousness, it was now alleging a specific cause and effect: "Despite such unanimous acclaim," the movie was not eligible for Best Foreign Film "because of one technicality: it was directed by an Englishman." Actually, while it was true that *The Postman* was ineligible, it was not for the reason given, and the actual reason was hardly a technicality. There was no way that Italy could have had the movie compete in this year's Foreign Film competition—it had been released in its homeland in 1994, so it had no more business being in the '95 race than, say, Luchino Visconti's 1942 film *Obsessione*. Advertisements bemoaning the film's ineligibility were not confined to *Daily Variety* and *The Hollywood Reporter*, however; soon they were popping up in regular daily newspapers in big cities.

Good Money After Bad

At least Miramax seemed to have a reasonable chance of getting something back on its investment; as a marketing executive at another studio told *Entertainment Weekly*, "This is one of the weirdest races ever. If a talking pig has a chance, why not *The Postman*?" The year's most ludicrous waste of money—cash that could have gone to any number of worthy causes—was the push by Disney for *The Scarlet Letter* and, in particular, for Demi Moore's much-ridiculed impersonation of Hester Prynne. Academy members also received videos of the Roland Joffé foozle, which was very likely the first one they taped over. Although the hideously expensive Kevin Costner vehicle *Waterworld* was not quite the box-office or critical disaster that had been expected, Universal's two-page ads still had people shaking their heads; what was particularly notable, though, was that "Your Consideration" was requested for just about everyone connected with *Waterworld* except Kevin Costner. *Get Shorty*, *Nixon*, *Richard III*, *The Bridges of Madison County*, *Two Bits*, *Heat*, *Se7en*, *The Postman* and *Braveheart* (but not *Rob Roy*) were among the most heavily advertised features.

Pete Hammond, a senior producer of the *Extra* television series, commented that it's "becoming very quickly the Academy of Motion Picture Arts and Sciences on Videotape. And I know that's something the Academy frowns on, but what are you gonna do?" Paramount tried a psychological approach, attempting to make each voter feel special by sending videos in a container with the individual's name engraved on a plaque. In contrast to the seriousness of the film, screening videos for *Dead Man Walking* came in a coffin-shaped box. Disney got into a pickle with the Academy because its ads for the computer-generated children's film *Toy Story* showed miniature soldiers from the movie making off with an Oscar. It was payback time for Disney's having made legal threats over the Academy's use of Snow White in the 1988 Allan Carr farrago, and the organization sent the studio a letter advising that this was a clear copyright infringement. No hard feelings, because a couple of days later, the Academy announced that *Toy Story*'s director, John

Lasseter, was being awarded a Special Achievement Award Oscar for making the first all-computer-animated feature.

The Academy announced two Lifetime Achievement Honorary Awards. One was going to cartoonist Chuck Jones, who had joined Warner Brothers in 1938 and worked with all of the Merrie Melody and Looney Tunes stars. The Oscar officially was for "the creation of classic cartoons and cartoon characters whose animated lives have brought joy to our real ones for more than half a century."

The other was to Kirk Douglas, who along with Robert Mitchum and Richard Widmark, was one of the still-living major stars of the 1950s not to have received Oscar recognition. His award was marked for his "fifty years as a creative and moral force in the motion picture community." The thrice-nominated Douglas had recently suffered a stroke, and as far as Army Archerd was concerned, "No one is more deserving of an honorary Oscar than Kirk Douglas. He should also win the Jean Hersholt Humanitarian Award simultaneously for his (and wife Anne's) humanitarian contributions." Looking at the "fifty years" portion of his Oscar citation, Douglas told Archerd, "I always think of myself as a young guy trying to make a go of things. But I am delighted."

Spreading Gold Dust

While almost everyone else was decrying the current state of Hollywood, the voiceover announcer introduced the Golden Globes telecast by calling 1995 "the most exciting and successful year in entertainment history." This year the Hollywood Foreign Press spread its gold around. *Sense and Sensibility* was the night's big winner, which only meant that it won two awards, as opposed to everything else's single Globe. Besides Best Picture (Drama), the film won Best Screenplay for Emma Thompson. Ang Lee, however, lost Best Director to Mel Gibson for *Braveheart*. And *Babe* solidified its position as a serious Oscar contender by winning Best Picture (Musical or Comedy). Nicolas Cage proved to be a favorite not only with film critics but with the people who cover Hollywood for foreign newspapers and magazines, as he kept up his

streak with a Best Actor (Drama) victory. Mira Sorvino won the Supporting Actress award for *Mighty Aphrodite*.

The other acting winners, though, were new to this year's awards. Sharon Stone was named Best Actress (Drama), and the former sex symbol charmed the room when she said, "No one is more surprised than me . . . well, it's just, um, it's a, it's . . . okay, it's a miracle." Nicole Kidman won the Musical or Comedy award for playing a small-town wife whose quest to become a television personality leads to murder in Gus van Sant's black comedy, *To Die For*. The winner of Best Actor (Musical or Comedy) was John Travolta for *Get Shorty*, and he began his acceptance speech by acknowledging the startling career turnaround he had enjoyed in the last year and a half: "I don't know exactly what I've done to deserve the goodwill that I feel the public and the press and the industry has given to me recently, but I truly do appreciate it." But then he may have frittered away that goodwill when he proceeded to recite "a quote by a great man," who turned out to be not Gandhi, or Martin Luther King, Jr., or George McGovern or even Bill Clinton, but L. Ron Hubbard, the founder of the pseudo-religion Scientology, of which Travolta was a most earnest member. The great man's quote was fortune cookie stuff about how to be happy in life you need a goal and you gotta believe.

The Supporting Actor award went to Brad Pitt; the hottest young actor in the business played a mentally unbalanced animal activist in Terry Gilliam's futuristic thriller *12 Monkeys*. As half of the current "Golden Couple," he concluded his speech by thanking "the love o' my life, my angel," Gwyneth Paltrow. Pitt's victory did not sit well with Michael Welner, M.D., a psychiatrist on the faculty of the New York University School of Medicine. Dr. Welner wrote to the *New York Times* to protest that his "fatuous portrayal with its hyperkinetic hand gestures, campy grimaces and a cockeyed contact lens for accent, is as much an affront to audiences as Stepin Fetchit." While acknowledging that "the mentally ill can be fun, and funny as the rest of us," Dr. Welner said that to give this performance a Globe "is to illustrate a regrettable lack of sophistication behind the awards."

Whoopi-Do with 2

Gilbert Cates decided enough was enough, he wouldn't be producing the ceremony this year. Of course, he would have been better off if he had made that decision the previous year, before the David Letterman debacle, but that's another story. Academy President Arthur Hiller then asked the recipient of last year's Jean Hersholt Humanitarian Award, composer-arranger-producer Quincy Jones, to take over. Jones was no stranger to the Oscar show—besides having received the Hersholt, he was a coproducer of the 1985 Best Picture nominee, *The Color Purple,* and had been nominated six other times in the Song and Score categories.

What would Quincy Jones bring to the mix that Gilbert Cates hadn't? Jones's coproducer for the telecast, David Salzman, said, "When Quincy's involved, there are people who normally wouldn't want to do something but they say, 'Well, gee, you know Q's into this? Maybe I'll do that.'" Jones was asked his opinion of last year's notorious David Letterman–hosted show; his one-word response was "Barren." The producer turned to the host of the 1993 ceremony, Whoopi Goldberg, to reprise emcee duties. In the *New York Daily News,* gossipers Rush & Molloy reported that an "inside Oscar source" snitched that "certain members of the Academy's Board of Governors, as well as some of the creative talent involved in each year's telecast, were not happy that they were not consulted on the choice. 'We hadn't even gotten around to finalizing our short list when Quincy asked Whoopi,' the source said." But a spokesperson for Jones said that "when they asked Quincy if he wanted to produce the show, a part of that decision was that he wanted Whoopi to do it." Jones had a simple explanation for his choice of hosts: "I just wanted Whoopi. I know her capabilities and that she did a good job the first time she tried it." Looking back on her first hosting gig, Goldberg said her goal now was "to be faster. I want people to know whether they won sooner than they knew the last time." As for last year's host, David Letterman did tell Charlie Rose, "I still feel like one day I'll do it again." But on Valentine's Day, the "Top Ten List" on the *Late Show with David Letterman* was "Top Ten Signs You're Dating a Loser"; number two was "He keeps bitching about not being asked back to host the Academy Awards."

Whereas Gilbert Cates would attach an arbitrary and ultimately pointless theme to the show ("Year of the Woman," "Comedy and the Movies"), Jones was going to let the Awards serve as their own theme. This did cause a slight problem for the people in charge of the Governors Ball, where in recent years the decor had reflected the theme. The motif decided upon for the ball was "Artists and Their Works," spotlighting the somewhat florid sculptor Dale Chihuly.

But everyone had to be happy with the news that no Gil Cates meant that there would also be no Debbie Allen handling the choreography. Instead, because producer Jones was going younger and hip-hoppish, that chore would be shared by Jamie King, the 24-year-old host of MTV's *The Grind,* and Barry Lather, who had worked with both Michael and Janet Jackson, as well as skater Nancy Kerrigan. At the first day's audition, King told the hopeful terpsichoreians, "It doesn't really matter if you can do it or not. I just want to see the passion." He said that in contrast to the dance numbers on previous Oscar shows, his choreography would "be more exciting, more energy-filled. It won't just be straight dancing, there will be surprising elements to make it more spectacular. The dancers will be exhausted, but that's good." But he still praised his predecessor, saying of Debbie Allen, "She's one of my idols. I used to watch *Fame* when I was little."

A Change Is Gonna Come

New rules governed the nominations process for Documentary films this year. To cut the workload for the volunteers on the Documentary Committee, the Academy increased the viewing panel from fifty to two hundred people, divided into four groups, with each viewing different films; one group was in New York, the other three Los Angeles. Each individual panel saw approximately seventeen films, and the top four vote-getters in each group were then shown to the other gangs. At the same time, the panel's old stunt of shutting off movies they didn't like in the middle of the screening had become taboo. Moreover, to be considered, a documentary would now actually have had to play a week in a theater in L.A. or New York; a screening at a film festival would no longer do.

The Score category had been tinkered with many, many times since music was first acknowledged at the 1934 Awards, and this year the Best Original Score Oscar was split into two categories, one for Dramatic films, the other for Musicals and Comedies. It was understood that the unspoken reason for this bifurcation was that, beginning with *The Little Mermaid* in 1989, Academy members had voted for every new Disney cartoon as if by reflex. The Academy would never acknowledge it, but word on the street on Wilshire Boulevard was that Hans Zimmer's Oscar victory for his inconsequential contributions to *The Lion King* at the expense of David Newman's instant-classic score for *Little Women* had been the proverbial backbreaking straw.

The Nominations

Just moments before the announcement of the nominations, TV reporter Chantal reflected, "It's ten years that I've been standing here covering these nominations for *Good Morning America*, and if ever there was a morning where absolutely no one is sure what's gonna be on that board behind us, it's this morning." Jeff Margolis, who would be directing the Awards telecast, admitted that the playing field was so muddled that "I didn't even enter the office pool this year. I couldn't pick them out." On E!, Charles Fleming's analysis was that this was "a field of things that has no sure thing in it at all."

A few minutes later, after the nominations had been revealed, the consensus was that even though no one had quite known what to expect, there were still all sorts of surprises. Quincy Jones, who substituted for the flu-stricken Holly Hunter to join Academy President Arthur Hiller in making the announcements, said, "I'm happy to hear all the gasps this morning." Bob Werden, the Academy's former press chief, observed, "There are always a few gasps, but they were particularly loud this year." Making it all the more

odd, there was no consensus as to what the biggest surprise was.

Braveheart was the unexpected leader in nominations with 10, although it received no acting nods. Following were *Apollo 13* with 9, and then *Sense and Sensibility* and *Babe*, 7 apiece. But the shock was that neither *Apollo*'s Ron Howard nor *Sense*'s Ang Lee received nominations as Best Director. The fifth contender for Best Picture was *The Postman*, which, given the heavy spending for it, could not really be seen as a surprise by anyone who had been paying attention. The Italian movie—the fifth foreign language film to be nominated for Best Picture, and the first since *Cries and Whispers* in 1973—received five mentions, including Best Actor for its dead star, Massimo Troisi, who also had a nod for Adapted Screenplay; the film even picked up a nomination for Best Score, an indication that the soundtrack CDs Miramax sent out had done the trick. The *New York Post*'s Gersh Kuntzman quoted an Academy member who had received a *Postman* video: "They ran their campaign brilliantly. I had no intention of seeing the movie, but I popped it in. I loved it so much that I ended up voting for it." Or as Harvey Weinstein put it, "We created the excitement that got people to put the tape in the machine."

Massimo Troisi's sister, Rosaria, observed, "It's a very great satisfaction, but satisfaction doesn't signify joy." Michael Radford's take was "People say Hollywood's a hard, bitter place, but in fact, people go with their hearts." Harvey Weinstein, savoring a triumph by the Miramax publicity machine, gloated, "We're going to put the bookmakers out of business this year." Of course, Weinstein also had to be aware that his company's eleven nominations were exactly half the number Miramax had received the previous year. Tom Brokaw, prefacing a piece on Oscar campaigning for that evening's *NBC Nightly News*, said, "There may be someone somewhere who still believes in the tooth fairy and the idea that the Oscars are awarded on artistic merit alone."

The failure of *Leaving Las Vegas* to nab a Best Picture nomination raised eyebrows, although Mike Figgis received double nominations for directing and writing. And many people had thought that *Dead Man Walking*, which had been engendering a great deal of discussion, might be a finalist; Tim Robbins was anointed by the Directors branch, though. *Rolling Stone*'s Peter Travers was on CNN bemoaning the Academy's failure to honor these two films, complaining: "Anything edgy, anything with anything to say, the Academy said, 'No, I'll take a talking pig.' "

For any number of observers, the Best Actor race provided the most stunning result: the failure of John Travolta to be nominated for *Get Shorty*. As Chantal put it, "that blew us all away here." On CBS, *People* magazine's Mitchell Fink agreed, saying "everybody, including myself" had expected a Travolta nomination. Lewis Beale wrote in the *New York Daily News* that "next to the word 'screwed' in the dictionary, there's a picture of John Travolta." Over on *Today*, Bryant Gumble was likewise incredulous about Travolta and fumed, "I can't believe *Get Shorty* got blanked. It got shut out. Zero. Zippo. Nada." The *Today* crew was also surprised that *Babe* did so well, to which the show's Hollywood correspondent, Jim Brown, amusedly responded, "It just shows you how wrong you can be back in New York, doesn't it? This business about *Babe* has long been talked about out here, as ridiculous as that may seem."

Gene Siskel, appearing on *CBS This Morning*, felt the biggest surprises were "the very strong showing by *Braveheart*" and Ron Howard's non-nomination. Michael Medved of *Sneak Previews* was also taken aback by the "surging support for *Braveheart*," and his cohost Jeffrey Lyons agreed "because it didn't do *that* well . . . it didn't make that much money. They had to re-release it and they really had to promote it." Even Mel Gibson told the *Los Angeles Times*, "A few months ago, I would never have suspected it."

The headline of the *Philadelphia Inquirer* nominations article reflected the confusing state of affairs: "*Braveheart* and Muddled Minds." In the *New York Daily News*, Lewis Beale's lead-in for his article on the nominations was "Did Oscar go wacko this year? Well, yes." He added, "But that wasn't necessarily a bad thing. Given what a lot of observers felt was the overall mediocrity of film product in 1995, Academy Award voters were forced to think eclectically when filling out their nomination ballots."

Nicolas Cage in *Leaving Las Vegas*, Sean Penn in

Dead Man Walking and Anthony Hopkins in *Nixon* all made the cut, and Massimo Troisi's inclusion meant that he was the first posthumous acting nominee since Sir Ralph Richardson's Supporting nod for *Greystoke: The Legend of Tarzan, Lord of the Apes* in 1984. Also nominated was Richard Dreyfuss, whose performance in *Mr. Holland's Opus* was generally agreed to be his best since his young hotshot days in the 1970s. This sentimental saga in the *Goodbye, Mr. Chips* vein about a high school music teacher, with a deaf son no less, had opened in one L.A. theater in December for Oscar consideration and turned into a word-of-mouth sleeper hit—Dreyfuss's first in a while. Bob Strauss of the *Los Angeles Daily News* described it as "recommended for lovers of bathos and Richard Dreyfuss." Thus, in addition to Travolta, the also-rans included *Apollo 13*'s Tom Hanks and *Richard III*'s Ian McKellen.

The results in the Best Actress race weren't so much surprising as simply a reflection of the fact that there were too many acclaimed performances to wedge into the five slots, and several women who might easily have been nominated in a weaker year were left out. The nominees were Susan Sarandon in *Dead Man Walking* (her fifth nomination), Elisabeth Shue in *Leaving Las Vegas*, Sharon Stone in *Casino*, Meryl Streep nominated for the tenth time for *The Bridges of Madison County* and Emma Thompson, her fourth nomination, for *Sense and Sensibility*. Thompson was also up for Adapted Screenplay, thus becoming the first woman ever nominated for an acting and writing award in the same year. She and Massimo Troisi joined the A-list group of same-year acting/writing nominees: Charlie Chaplin, Orson Welles, Woody Allen, Warren Beatty. The omission in the Best Actress race that received the most press was *To Die For*'s Nicole Kidman, and for conspiracy theorists, there was the fact that she and Travolta, Golden Globe winners both, were Scientologists.

All ten Supporting contenders were first-time nominees: The men were James Cromwell in *Babe*, Ed Harris in *Apollo 13*, Brad Pitt in *12 Monkeys*, Tim Roth in *Rob Roy* and Kevin Spacey in *The Usual Suspects*. Those in the hunt for the Supporting Actress Award were Joan Allen in *Nixon*, Mira Sorvino in *Mighty Aphrodite*, Kathleen Quinlan in *Apollo 13*,

Mare Winningham in *Georgia* and Kate Winslet in *Sense and Sensibility*. Winningham's nomination was the biggest surprise among the ten supporting finalists, since she had been overshadowed by Jennifer Jason Leigh in their unloved film *Georgia*. But her making the cut did provide another human interest aspect to this year's Awards. She and Supporting Actor nominee Kevin Spacey had gone to Chatsworth High School together and were the Drama Club's stars; making the rounds on Oscar TV shows was a photo of them as Maria and Captain von Trapp in the school's production of *The Sound of Music*. *Babe*'s James Cromwell also brought an auld lang syne element to the Awards. His father, John Cromwell, had directed the1944 Best Picture nominee *Since You Went Away*, as well as guiding Charles Boyer and Gene Lockhart to acting nominations for *Algiers* in 1938, and doing the same for Eleanor Parker and Hope Emerson with 1950's *Caged*. Cromwell *père* was also the cohost with Bob Hope of the 1944 Academy Awards. James's wife, Julie, was the daughter of Lee J. Cobb, a Supporting Actor nominee in 1954 and 1958.

With what had been perceived to be the two front runners—*Apollo 13* and *Sense and Sensibility*—missing Best Director nominations, Best Picture now became anybody's race; of course, backers of those two films could try to convince themselves that *Driving Miss Daisy*'s victory in 1989 proved it was no longer necessary to have a Best Director contender to win. Jack Mathews wrote somewhat cryptically that Ang Lee's omission had "sinister implications" (presumably racism), but added that this "snub could actually help the movie in the final balloting." On *Entertainment Tonight*, Leonard Maltin noted that there were "no real front runners in any of the categories because it wasn't a great year, '95." Maltin was pleased, however, that the Academy did honor "the fella who's on my tie, Mickey Mouse. His latest short subject, *Runaway Brain,* was nominated—great recognition for one of the older stars at the Oscars."

It so happened that the directors of the two most nominated films were together when the news broke. Ron Howard was filming Mel Gibson's new vehicle *Ransom* in Queens. Interviewed by various news organizations over the course of the day, Howard said

things like "I would have liked to have gotten the personal invitation to the party" and "I'm really overjoyed by the support of the movie, including a Best Picture nomination, so I have to say all in all, it's a real good day." He also mentioned that Steven Spielberg wasn't nominated for Best Director even though *Jaws* was a Best Picture nominee in 1975. When *USA Today* brought up the "Opie Factor"—the question of whether people who had watched him from their living rooms as a little tyke thirty years ago had trouble taking him seriously as a 41-year-old man—Howard admitted that "It's crossed my mind. But there's not much I can do about it." Asked if director Howard would give him time off from the production to attend the Oscars, Mel Gibson jocularly replied, "Not now." Gibson noted that between them, Howard and his films received nineteen nominations, adding "It would have been nice if it were twenty." Howard could try to take solace in a gag gift Gibson had recently given him: a framed, large-size fake Oscar campaign ad, featuring the scene where the Scottish soldiers mooned their British counterparts, with the caption, "Best Moon Shot." Underneath "For Your Consideration" were further examples of Gibsonian wit, with entries including "Best Screenplay, Jean-Claude Derriere," "Best Actress, Sandra Buttocks," and "Best Supporting Actress, Katharine Hepbuns."

Apollo 13's other unexpected non-nominee, Tom Hanks, said maybe it was just as well, because after having won twice in a row, "I think they would have hurled rocks at my town car" if he had been nominated again. Kathleen Quinlan, whose Supporting Actress nomination for playing Tom Hanks's wife in *Apollo 13* was a minor surprise, deemed her director's omission "somewhat criminal." On the other hand, Emma Thompson said she was sure Ang Lee was "okay" about his snub "since Ang is one of the most philosophical people I know. With him it's 'Zen and the Art of Motion Picture Making.' " Thompson remarked that receiving two nominations "makes me feel very proud, bordering on the smug," and Sharon Stone declared that she took her nomination as Hollywood's way of saying "Hey, kid, we want you to grow!"

Tim Robbins, appearing on CNN's *ShowBiz Today*, commented that he and Susan Sarandon watched the announcement of the nominations with their six-year-old son, Jack Henry: "We told him he could go late to school so he could watch, 'cause he's very interested. Because last year when I didn't get nominated for *Shawshank* he threw something at the television and stormed out of the room."

And it was time for *Braveheart* to be unleashed yet again. Three days after the nominations, *USA Today* reported, "a lot of moviegoers still haven't seen *Braveheart*, a situation Paramount will try to rectify this weekend by re-releasing it into theatres." The third time for this film's release was not the charm; *Entertainment Weekly* reported that once again it "stalled at the box office." *Babe* was the nominee with friends in high places. Both Quincy Jones and Whoopi Goldberg told *TV Guide* that the Australian film was their favorite among the Best Picture nominees.

Dianne Houston, We've Got a Problem

It was looking like the smoothest pre-Oscar season in years—no wailing and gnashing of teeth over acclaimed documentaries that failed to be nominated; no bemoaning the fact that a reactionary movie with a revisionistic outlook on recent American history and filled with banal platitudes was going to defeat the film that critics considered the ne plus ultra in cutting-edge American cinema; a Best Picture race that everyone agreed was the most difficult to call since at least 1991, and a brand-new producer with a plethora of new backstage talent promising to revitalize the show—but then *People* magazine stirred things up. Two weeks before the Big Night, the magazine's cover blared HOLLYWOOD BLACKOUT, with the subhead, "The film industry says all the right things, but its continued exclusion of African-Americans is a national disgrace." And a sub-subhead added, "The 166 nominees at this month's Oscars include only one black and none of the stars at right"—on the cover were Angela Bassett, Denzel Washington, Laurence Fishburne and Whitney Houston.

The first page of the article contained a double-page overview photo of the audience at the previous year's Awards, with the caption "What's Wrong with This Picture?" To which was added, "At last year's Oscars ceremony, even the 'seat fillers'—ABC employees who slip into empty chairs during the telecast—were overwhelmingly white."

People said that it had conducted "an exhaustive four-month investigation" to reach the conclusion that "a shocking level of minority exclusion remains." In addition to the fact that only one African American had been nominated—Dianne Houston, director of the Live Action Short Film nominee, *Tuesday Morning Ride*—only 3.9 percent of Academy members were black, 2.3 percent of the Directors Guild and 2.6 percent of the Writers Guild. The article spoke of Hollywood as—despite predominantly progressive politics—an old boys' club. And "within that fraternity, studio executives, producers and superagents make handshake deals on the beach at Malibu or after backyard barbecues in Bel Air. And if blacks are shut out of the socializing, then they're also cut out of the wheeling and dealing that takes place." Eleven pages gave the dispiriting details on everything from salary inequities for African American stars, to the difficulties blacks have of getting into Hollywood unions, to the failure of Don Cheadle to be nominated as Best Supporting Actor for *Devil in a Blue Dress* despite his awards from the Los Angeles Film Critics and the National Society, to Fox's not sending out videos of the hit *Waiting to Exhale* to Academy members.

The article also had a sidebar profiling Quincy Jones: "Hollywood rarity: A brother with clout." The Oscar producer gave his opinion that, yes, "there's a lot of racism going on, and I'd be lying if I said there wasn't." But it wasn't simply racism involving African Americans, as he cited Ang Lee's failure to be nominated for Best Director: "To do such a good job with an English movie and not get recognized—I think it sucks." And while he acknowledged that things were better than when he first arrived in Hollywood in the mid-1960s—when the powers-that-be referred to him as "the *shvartzer*" (which he originally thought was Yiddish for arranger-composer)—Jones said, "The movies have always been twenty or thirty years behind the music business."

People roused the Reverend Jesse Jackson, who decided that the Academy Awards was the perfect event for his Rainbow Coalition to bring attention to racial inequalities in the film industry. "Actually the Rainbow formed a commission on fairness in media several years ago," Jackson said. "It was very difficult to get our position heard until *People* magazine said that the racism in Hollywood is a national disgrace."

The *People* article also provoked the expected reactions in its Letters to the Editor a few weeks later. Jeremy Gutwein of New Rochelle, New York, wrote in to share these sagacious words: "I am sure I will not see a *People* headline that reads 'NBA Whiteout.' Would it be fair to say that the basketball industry is a 'hotbed of black racism' and that whites are 'shut out' from the NBA? Why isn't that a national disgrace?" Travis Sabado of Los Angeles wanted everyone to know that "Cary Grant never received a single Oscar nomination [actually he received two]—and he was white." To Mary Coleman of Houston, the issue was much simpler. She wrote, "So what? I am sick and tired of hearing blacks whine."

Gifts for the Rich and Famous

The Academy was sick and tired of some of the methods studios were using to convince voters to support their films, and it was monitoring campaign practices more stringently than ever before. Over the course of a year and a half, the organization sent out three letters setting down and refining guidelines. Last year, Disney had to forfeit two tickets for the ceremony because of its *Lion King* coffee table book; this season, the same punishment was meted out to Miramax because the Academy decided the studio had engaged in unseemly practices by sending members a gift package consisting of a video of *The Postman*, the soundtrack-cum-poetry-readings CD, a photocopied booklet of some Pablo Neruda poems and the novel on which the movie was based. According to *Variety*, it was the book "that set off bells at the Academy," but Miramax countered that since the movie was nominated for Best Screenplay, it would be helpful for voters to have a look at the original source material. Meanwhile, a tote bag holding all of Disney's videocassettes passed muster. Academy Executive Director

Bruce Davis tried to clarify matters. "We don't mind the tapes in the sense that they are at least offering the thing that is to be judged," he said. "If you send a T-shirt or a leather-bound book of the script or something like that, then you've fallen over the line into something that's hard to find another word than 'bribe' for." Presumably, the Disney tote was okay because it was merely what the videos arrived in, even though once the tapes were removed it would have a useful life of its own; it was much the same way that the *Dead Man Walking* coffin carrying case could later be used to bury a hamster or other small household pet.

Since Massimo Troisi wouldn't be able to chat up Jay Leno or David Letterman, Miramax found another way to keep the actor in the public's consciousness. The studio arranged for a retrospective of his previous films at an L.A. theater and also announced it was founding a scholarship in Troisi's name.

Crap Shoot

"Never before that I can remember has Oscar been so open," stated Anita Busch, film editor of *Daily Variety*, who said that trying to predict the winners was "just a crap shoot. Nobody really knows this year." By the eve of the Oscars, while some of the races seemed to have narrowed down, Best Picture was still considered a toss-up, with *The Postman* the only one of the five nominees that didn't seem to have a realistic shot. The *Hollywood Reporter*'s Martin Grove declared that "the heat has built" for *Apollo 13* and most people were putting their money on that film—especially after Ron Howard received the Directors Guild Award. This prize was perceived as a self-conscious slap in the face of the Academy's Directors branch, in the tradition of the DGA Award to Steven Spielberg for *The Color Purple* a decade earlier. Tom Hanks would later aver that as far as he was concerned, Howard won the award on merit alone: "Ron's achievement on *Apollo 13* was the fact that he had a limited scope, and a story that everybody knows the ending of, and had to find out some ways in order to make it human and understandable and gripping. That he did it as well as he did is really . . . there's a reason he won the DGA Award that year 'cause it's *great* storytelling." Tellingly, among those Howard had defeated for the DGA citation was Ang Lee, meaning that outrage about snubs in the Director Oscar race had shifted to the All-American.

Babe was the wild card in the Best Picture race, because while it had passionate admirers, other people still maintained that a movie about a talking pig did not have the "stature" for a Best Picture Oscar. Martin Grove's take: "If it isn't *Apollo 13*, *Babe* would be my next guess." The host of TNT's program, *Inside the Academy Awards,* Robert Osborne, said, "Everywhere you go in Hollywood today, *Babe* is the movie they're all talking about," and so he thought it would be the one for which they'd be voting. Moving from his usual berth as theater critic, Ben Brantley of the *New York Times* switched to the cinema to talk up *Babe*'s chances, on the proposition that "Hollywood loves little movies that could (at least after they succeed), and particularly when they are about little heroes who could. It fosters the comforting illusion that movieland is a realm of equal opportunity in which individual initiative is rewarded."

Braveheart couldn't be counted out, simply because, unlike the two movies that had been expected to be clear front runners, its director was nominated. And Paramount had already pumped so much money into the film's life support that it wasn't about to stop now. *Apollo 13* had, however, also won the Producers Guild Award and the Screen Actors Guild Award for Best Ensemble, which is tantamount to SAG's Best Picture award. Robyn Carter of the *Day & Date* television show summed up the situation thusly: "Even though it is a wide-open year, there definitely is a consensus in Hollywood and there are a lot of people who believe very strongly that *Apollo 13* will nab Best Picture. . . . Hollywood loves Ron Howard, and a lot of people are upset that he did not get nominated."

Bob Strauss of the *Los Angeles Daily News* likened some of the Best Picture nominees to the clowns who were running for the Republican presidential nomination. He deemed *Apollo 13* to be a "Bob Dole–style front runner that came from deep inside the prevailing system but faltered in the early preliminary heats. However, after the voters took a look at some of those surprise upstarts, they appear to have closed ranks behind the original establishment candidate." Strauss felt that *Braveheart* resembled one of the Republican runners-up, and he called the movie "a literal realization of Pat Buchanan's 'peasants with pitchforks' rhetoric [that] upset the race when it earned the most nominations back in February. Like Buchanan, though, that's when it peaked; voters seem to have realized that, at its core, Mel Gibson's medieval military epic is just a really bitchin' *Conan* movie."

In *The New Yorker*, Roger Angell, taking a break from his usual baseball diamond beat, analyzed some of the year's contenders and happily concluded that "maybe it was the presence of the charming Australian-made porcinema *Babe* in the Best Picture category this year that first made me notice that intelligence—yes, yes!—might be what lifts and lights this year's lists. The prime footage in the multinominated Italian import, *Il Postino,* comes when its rustic letter carrier learns that he is capable of metaphor. The self-doubt and weariness of Susan Sarandon and the sneering, angrily crumbling defiance of Sean Penn transform *Dead Man Walking* into a succession of thoughtful and nearly unbearable difficulties—a story, instead of a tract about capital punishment. Emma Thompson wrote a light, unawed script from Jane Austen's *Sense and Sensibility*, and plays Elinor Dashwood in the movie: who else can she be but sense? The cool Ed Harris in Ron Howard's *Apollo 13* keeps his head while all at NASA are losing theirs. Brains everywhere."

Susan Sarandon received the Screen Actors Guild Award; at the podium, she said "This is so great, to get out of my seat for a change." She now had momentum on her side, and the fact that her nomination for *Dead Man Walking* was her fifth also provided her with the "Paid Her Dues" factor. The two actresses who were widely admired for revealing new depths to their acting skills—Elisabeth Shue and Sharon Stone—didn't seem quite so overdue. Stone was interviewed on *Dateline NBC* as part of a profile on how she had shed her sexpot image to be thought of as a Serious Actress. When host Stone Phillips mentioned that Vegas oddsmakers had her as the long shot in the race, she wasn't fazed because "for twenty years I've been the long shot." Everyone figured Emma Thompson would win Best Adapted screenplay, and Meryl Streep already had her two Awards. A Sarandon win for Best Actress was the closest thing to a highly likely result to be found in any of the races. Besides, when Sarandon appeared on the *Late Show with David Letterman*—where she said that the Screen Actors Guild award "is heavier than the Oscar, physically, and it has a penis, which the Oscar doesn't"—mind reader The Amazing Kreskin showed up to give her the good news that "If I were to read the thoughts of the entire film industry, 92 percent are convinced you're going to win."

If everyone had the same depth of feeling for her as London *Observer* reporter Nicci Gerrardi, Sarandon was a shoo-in. Gerrardi got positively rapturous over the actress, prefacing an interview article: "With her plush skin, her enormous and protuberant Bette Davis eyes, her curved body (cased in charcoal and black the day that we meet) that reminds you of Keats' 'Ode to Autumn,' her dark golden hair and light, clever Southern accent that descends like silk over the rise and fall of her sentences, Susan Sarandon is like a ripe fruit, a peach of an actress blooming with the years." Later in the article, the interviewer likened her to a "sleek, golden cat."

Nicolas Cage also won at the Screen Actors Guild, but *Dead Man Walking* was fresher in people's memories and there seemed to have been a slight shift in that all-important intangible, momentum. Audiences were responding more to Penn's redemption than to Cage's self-destruction, as the low-budget *Dead Man Walking* overtook the low-budget *Leaving Las Vegas* at the box office. WCBS-TV's Dennis Cunningham described the Best Actor race as "Brilliance vs. Brilliance," There was also talk of an upset by the comeback player of the year, Richard Dreyfuss. At the Nominees Lunch he had been asked to compare being nominated—and winning—in 1977—to being nominated this time around. "I'm much more aware of the day-to-day joy," Dreyfuss said. "I just kind of took it as business as usual, and I've grown up." Also at the luncheon, the nominees were shown a video on how *not* to accept an Oscar—it was Sally Field's "You like me!" speech.

Because *Nixon* had faded from public awareness, Anthony Hopkins had for a while now seemed like an also-ran. That didn't mean he wasn't still greatly admired as an actor. On ABC's morning talk show *Mike*

and Maty, Maty segued from a discussion of Nicolas Cage's performance: "Speaking of substance abuse, Anthony Hopkins has been very candid in saying that he was an alcoholic. Imagine what a talent we would have lost had he continued and not gotten some help, you know." In *Entertainment Weekly*, Gregg Kilday aptly said of *The Postman*'s Massimo Troisi, "Yes, he died, but Academy voters barely knew him. How sentimental can they really be expected to get?" Making the acting races even more intriguing was that the day before the Oscars, the Independent Spirit Awards went to *Leaving Las Vegas*'s Elisabeth Shue and *Dead Man Walking*'s Sean Penn. Accepting his Spirit statuette, Penn said "I guess this means you tolerate me. You really tolerate me!" *The New Yorker* reported that as late as the day before the show, the plan had been to show clips not just of the actors' current nominated performances, but also of their past work. "I mean, thanks a lot," said Elisabeth Shue. "I want to put that lot behind me."

The Supporting Actor competition was widely felt to be a toss-up between SAG winner Ed Harris and Kevin Spacey, but there was still the aura of the pig, and if sentiment did run high for *Babe*, then James Cromwell could well be clutching an Oscar. On the distaff side, the consensus was that this was a three-person race among Joan Allen, Mira Sorvino and Kate Winslet. Working against Allen was a perceived lack of affection for *Nixon* and working against Sorvino was the heavy-duty campaigning by Miramax, which was now turning off Hollywoodites. There was nothing working against Winslet, which is why there was a palpable late surge for her in the air.

An Antichoice President

At a press conference held by Quincy Jones and Academy President Arthur Hiller on the day before the Oscars, the emphasis of the reporters' questions was the Jesse Jackson boycott. Asked if they would be wearing a rainbow ribbon to show solidarity with Jackson's cause, Jones said, "If I get one I will," noting that Jackson's "concerns have a lot of merit." But Hiller sounded like a real politician, as he intoned, "I don't wear any ribbons because there are half a dozen different kinds of ribbons, and as president, I don't want to make choices." Jones and Hiller were much more interested in talking about this year's big innovation: the presentation of Best Costume Design, the first Award of the evening, would be preceded by a bevy of "supermodels" wearing the nominated frocks and walking on a runway, just like at an actual fashion show.

Jones had allowed that putting together the show was hard work, describing it as "like trying to hold water under your arm." Asked why he was putting himself through all of this anxiety, Jones told the Associated Press, "I love the film business. I love the people in it. The Academy hands you this kind of responsibility. . . . It's a killer job, but when they put it in your hands, they're trusting you with their baby."

Other celebrities weighed in on the Jackson controversy. Whoopi Goldberg was adamant that "I am not going to be wearing any pins or bows or anything, because if I did my entire dress would be covered." She also said of Jackson's tactics, "It is not the Oscar ceremony where the heat should go. I'm glad he's on board, that's all I can say. I'm pleased he's finally arrived." Jackson's fellow Chicagoan Oprah Winfrey, whom Quincy Jones had tapped to be the show's official red carpet greeter, was very peeved about the boycott threats. "This will be the most multiracial, multiethnic Oscar show anybody's ever seen," said the talk show host. Jackson did make one concession to Jones and Winfrey—he changed the site of his protest from the Dorothy Chandler Pavilion to the studios of KABC-TV, the local affiliate carrying the show.

The Big Night

Although he would be leading a protest outside the studios of KABC-TV and not at the ceremony itself, Jesse Jackson was at the Dorothy Chandler on Oscar morning. At 5:17 A.M., he was already speaking to *CBS This Morning*'s Mark McEwen, explaining that the picketing would take place at ABC affiliates in twenty-five cities because "We don't want the focus to get shifted to, 'Will Quincy will cross our picket line?' " Thrilled that the show's producer would be wearing a Rainbow ribbon in solidarity with the demonstrators, the Reverend Jackson said, "He is our ally." Jackson was also pleased that "a number of people are not coming tonight. They're simply not coming, because for many it would be like if Rosa Parks had to go to the back of the bus and then went to the annual Montgomery Bus Company party." When McEwen put forth the argument Oprah Winfrey had made—that with Jones producing and Whoopi Goldberg hosting, it was the wrong year to single out the Oscars—the civil rights leader countered that "Some say the timing's not right. Well, that's not logical because the timing for injustice is always wrong, the timing to fight for justice is always right." To another reporter, Jackson advised that the protests "would be much more vigorous, maybe even civil disobedience, if Quincy and Whoopi were not playing those roles." In the edition of *Variety* that hit the stands that day, editor Peter Bart wrote, "If 1995 proved not to be a good year for black Oscar nominees, it wasn't a good year for black movies, or for any movies. . . . But certainly the positioning of Quincy Jones and Whoopi, not to mention Sidney Poitier as a presenter, should give some clue that the Academy is hardly a bastion of racist sentiment."

Jackson stuck around throughout the day speaking to the press. He called attention to the fact that in addition to one solitary African American nominee, there were no Latin American, Asian American or Native American nominees, and pointed out that "We are 35 percent of the box office, yet 95 percent of the voters are white." But Jackson also agreed that the problems lie not simply with the Academy, but with the film industry itself, which he labeled "an institution of

Awards Ceremony

MARCH 25, 1996, 6:00 P.M.
THE DOROTHY CHANDLER PAVILION, LOS ANGELES

Your Host:
WHOOPI GOLDBERG
TELEVISED OVER ABC

Presenters

Costume Design	Pierce Brosnan, Naomi Campbell and Claudia Schiffer
Supporting Actor	Dianne Wiest
Makeup	Alicia Silverstone
Art Direction	Emma Thompson
Honorary Award to Chuck Jones	Robin Williams
Special Achievement Award to John Lasseter	Robin Williams
Short Films	Jackie Chan and Kareem Abdul-Jabar
Sound Effects Editing	Sandra Bullock
Sound	Steven Seagal
Supporting Actress	Martin Landau
Cinematography	Jim Carrey
Editing	Goldie Hawn and Kurt Russell
Scientific and Technical Awards	Richard Dreyfuss
Visual Effects	Will Smith
Documentary Awards	Nicolas Cage and Elisabeth Shue
Foreign Film	Mel Gibson
Honorary Award to Kirk Douglas	Steven Spielberg
Scoring Awards	Quincy Jones and Sharon Stone
Original Screenplay	Susan Sarandon
Adapted Screenplay	Anthony Hopkins
Original Song	Angela Bassett, Laurence Fishburne and Take 6
Director	Robert Zemeckis
Actress	Tom Hanks
Actor	Jessica Lange
Picture	Sidney Poitier

Performers of Nominated Songs

"Colors of the Wind"	Vanessa Williams
"Dead Man Walking"	Bruce Springsteen
"Have You Ever Really Loved a Woman"	Bryan Adams and Michael Kamen
"Moonlight"	Gloria Estefan
"You've Got a Friend"	Lyle Lovett and Randy Newman

race exclusion, of cultural distortion, of violence, of false depictions of people, unfair hiring practices, and lack of people of color in positions of authority." He also maintained that "one would think that this protest, challenging Hollywood to open up its eyes, expand its stage, open up opportunity, will ultimately be good for the industry." Quincy Jones told reporters, "*People* magazine is thirty-five years late. God bless 'em." Ultimately, about seventy-five people joined Jackson in demonstrating outside KABC-TV. Picket signs conveyed such messages as "End Hollywood Cultural Violence Against People of Color," "Same Slave Master. Different Plantation," and "Hollywood: This is 1996, not 1864. Wake Up!" What was described as a handful of folks were outside the network's New York studios.

The first person to get in line to enter the bleachers, Joey Marcus, 39, of East Los Angeles, had arrived on Wednesday morning—five days before the ceremony. He pretty much had the place to himself until the next day, when Sandi Stratton and her sister Babe Churchill arrived. The two women, who last year were taken down the red carpet by CNN's Gloria Hillard, were again featured in reports on CNN, as well as on *Day & Date*. This was Sandi and Babe's twenty-seventh time in a row watching the arrivals, and Sandi said, "A lot of people think we're crazy. But we think we're having fun." Babe, a Chino resident, told the *Baltimore Sun*, "I've always been a big movie buff. I've never grown up, that's the problem." Eliana Tomlin said she was at the Dorothy Chandler because "I just want to see somebody important." *ShowBiz Today*'s Bill Tush was in the bleachers, and conversed with Jenny Cowan, who came to L.A. from Brisbane, Australia, specifically to sit in the stands. Jenny said that being there in person made perfect sense because "We don't see 'em all like you guys do here all the time. We never get to see anybody."

Similarly, an unidentified woman told *Entertainment Tonight*, "When you're living in Europe you get all this talk about the stars and it's so hard to see them and when you're finally here, you should go and see it." Another woman told E!'s Art Mann that she found the best way to pass her day-and-a-half wait was to "read a romance novel, eat and gossip," and someone

else said that she'd manage fine because "I have lots of magazines and two Diet Pepsis." Then an unfortunate turn of events: A lady fell in the bleachers and broke her ankle. All the other people had to be removed so that a medical team could get to the hapless fan, meaning that folks like Sandi Stratton, who had camped out for days to get front-row bleachers, sadly were not guaranteed their choice locations when they were let back in.

Interviewing the arrivals on E! for the second year, Joan Rivers kicked things off by saying, "Tonight, stars like Meryl Streep and Anthony Hopkins and Emma Thompson will do so much air kissing tornado warnings have been posted all over Los Angeles." She also told viewers, "I'm thrilled, as we all are, to be here at the Dorothy Chandler Pavilion. No one, unfortunately, has seen Dorothy yet, but the bars are still opened, so she'll probably come staggering a little later." Gossip maven Cindy Adams tattled to her readers that Rivers was "schlepping a shopping bag."

The first celebrity arrivals were Roddy McDowall—a member of the Academy's Board of Directors—and his date, Kate Burton, who told Rivers that she had not attended the Oscars any of the seven times her father, Richard, had been nominated. And when McDowall said that he had never been nominated, Rivers said to the star of *Tuna Clipper* and *It!*, "Unbelievable, because you're one of the great ones."

Killing time as she waited for more celebrities, Rivers announced that Oliver Stone was making a new movie, *The Pat Buchanan Story,* and that she was lucky enough to be there for the filming of his fiftieth birthday party scene, where a Nazi jumped out of a cake. She added, "People say to me you shouldn't say that about Pat because his parents died in the Holocaust, which I found out, unfortunately, was true—they fell off a guard tower." Don Imus had told this same joke a few days earlier during his controversial gig at the annual Radio and Television Correspondents Association Dinner in Washington.

Then came the next celebrity, Christine Kavanaugh, who had provided the voice for *Babe*. Kavanaugh had a double rooting interest at the Awards, though—she was also in *Little Surprises*, a Live Action Short Film nominee directed by Jeff Goldblum. Kavanaugh had accessorized her pink satin Nolan Miller gown with a purse in the shape of a pig and told Rivers that she had to audition for her role in *Babe* and "I was competing against children." Model Tyra Banks, who would be participating in the ceremony's fashion show, said she'd be wearing a costume from *Sense and Sensibility*, in which "your body looks pretty, not sexy." Not nearly as many men wore banded collars as last year. One who did was Nathan Lane, the star of the current number one film in the country, *The Birdcage*. The Broadway actor parodied the role of new movie star to the hilt, saying to Rivers, "Joan, darling. I'm just a boy with a dream, and I made it to the Oscars. *And* I met you." Meanwhile the official Academy greeter, Army Archerd, got on Laurence Fishburne's bad side by referring to him by his former professional name. "If you call me Larry one more time, I'll break both your legs," the actor told the *Daily Variety* columnist.

Sam Rubin and Leanza Cornett, doing forecourt duties for Los Angeles's KTLA-TV and the WB network, came on the air an hour after Joan Rivers. One of their first interviews was with Daisy Fuentes, who was practically falling out of her low-cut green gown. When Cornett inquired what had brought the MTV personality to the Oscars, Fuentes responded, "What brings us to the Oscars? People. Stars. The Academy Awards. Movies. Fashion. Diamonds. Everything. It's exciting." Laurie Pike was standing by at the KTLA studios serving as a fashion analyst, and shortly after Rubin and Cornett had been making nice with Fuentes, she had this to say: "What was she thinking? She's not on MTV, she's at the Academy Awards. This is the ugliest dress so far tonight. The color is hideous, it's some neon green. It looks like she dropped cigarette butts down the front of her dress. And her hair has these horrible streaks. She needs to go home and change."

When Joan Rivers praised Tim Roth for his sublimely foppish performance in *Rob Roy*, he told her, "I was worried. I thought I was going to get fired, I really did. It was so over the top and crazy. When the studios got to dailies they would get me out of there." Leanza Cornett reminded him that at the Nominees Luncheon he had said that he wanted to be as drunk as possible before arriving at the ceremony. But now Roth said there was "too much adrenaline—you can't get drunk." Looking around, he said, "I couldn't imagine this. This is the most insane thing I've ever seen."

Roger Ebert was chatting up actors rather than critiquing them, as he again was on the red carpet for a preshow broadcast for a number of ABC affiliates. Kate Winslet—accompanied by her mother—and Tim Roth reached Ebert and his co-interviewer Lisa McRee at the same time, and each said they hoped and expected the other would win, but in their own races, Winslet predicted Mira Sorvino, Roth expected Kevin Spacey. Winslet also said that after she finished shooting Kenneth Branagh's *Hamlet*, "I'm going to do *Titanic*, which is a major, major thing, so it's very exciting." Roth told Ebert, "I love Basil Rathbone." Then Winona Ryder stopped by to say she was rooting for *The Postman*. *Women's Wear Daily* cheered that Ryder "must have the hippest stylist in town. She looked like something from this week's New York runway, with her beaded mocha-colored flapper dress from Badgley Mischka and marcelled hair." Making you wonder if they were looking at the same young woman, Orla Healy of the *New York Daily News* referred to "Ryder's matronly appearance," and felt that "frightening" was the word for "her slicked-down flapper gal 'do." *Entertainment Weekly* said simply, "Worst Hair: Winona Ryder."

The forecourt interviewers all treated Ron Howard almost like he was on his way to a coronation, as if an *Apollo 13* victory was a foregone conclusion. He remained characteristically modest when talking to Joan Rivers. "I think most people who are nominated here would all say the same thing, which is it's really impossible to pick the best of any movie or any kind of art form," he said. "But it's a great Hollywood tradition, and I love being a part of it." When Sam Rubin wondered, "I don't think this evening is melancholy for you, is it?" Howard said, "No, no, no. This is really, really exciting." And he said he was delighted to see a lot of the bleacher fans wearing *Apollo 13* T-shirts and holding placards in support of the movie. Leanza Cornett sent him off with good news about *Apollo 13*, that "You read all of the paperwork on it in the newspapers and that's everybody's pick." Howard did acknowledge to Lisa McRee that he was aware his film was the favorite among Las Vegas oddsmakers. Roger Ebert pontificated that "There's a theory going around that a director can't be nominated for Best Director unless he looks like he's filled with a lot of angst and suffering and pain, and you smile too much to be nominated." Howard replied, "I may just never get there then, who knows? Well, I enjoy it. I enjoy myself." According to Marilyn Beck and Stacy Jenel Smith, Howard hadn't planned on attending a ceremony where he wasn't a nominee, but his partner Brian Grazer convinced him that it would be "awkward" if he was a no-show.

Another TV commentator bumped into Rivers, causing the E! interviewer to complain, "People are so pushy here. No one should push except me." Cindy Adams made note of "everyone shouting for Alicia Silverstone as Karl Malden ambled by unnoticed." And Brad Pitt and Gwyneth Paltrow disappointed the bleacher fans when they wouldn't stop and chat.

Leanza Cornett told Emma Thompson that because of her double nomination, "You are making history at the Academy Awards." Thompson's response: "It's such a strain making history. Now I know how Mussolini felt." When the WB interviewer asked if, having now received five nominations in four years, she was getting used to the Oscars, Thompson answered, "You never get used to it. It would be like trying to get used to biological warfare. It's not possible. It's insane—let's face it." She told Joan Rivers that she kept the Oscar she won for *Howards End* "in the loo." When Rivers asked what she would do with a second Oscar, should she win tonight, the actress-screenwriter replied, "I might staple it to my head." As Thompson moved on, Rivers rhapsodized, "I think you're wonderful! I really do. You're the only person who ever says hello to me in real life."

Richard Dreyfuss told CNN's Bill Tush that the pair accompanying him were "just some people I met on the street a few minutes ago." Actually, they were his daughter, Emily, 12, and son, Ben, 9. Ben spoke to Tush about his dad: "He's always complicated." Emily told Sam Rubin and Leanza Cornett that "our teachers are a little different" than her father's character, Mr. Holland. Trying to bond with the boy, Rubin asked Ben the out-of-left-field question "Does this remind

you of going to school?" To which the youngster gave the only possible response: "Ummm. No!" The Best Actor nominee had a camera with him, and snapped a picture of Sam and Leanza and the two kids. Next they dealt with Joan Rivers, and when Rivers asked, "Who are you with?" Emily got in before Dad could speak: "He's with me. And him," pointing to Ben. Noticing his camera, Joan asked if the familial trio wanted to pose for a picture, but Dreyfuss declined, saying they had only six shots left, and had to save them for inside the Dorothy Chandler. But then they moved on to the Ebert-McRee team, and Dreyfuss took the interviewers' picture. Emily informed them, "We have to say Happy Birthday to a girl named Kiley in Idaho and we need to say hello to everyone in Idaho," and Ben looked into the camera and announced, "I'd just like to say hi to the people who asked us to say hi." Ben also carried a cell phone with him, and was giving a play-by-play to his mother, Dreyfuss's ex-wife, Jeramie.

"How can anybody look bad when there are all these free clothes available?" asked Meryl Streep, dressed in a black taffeta Donna Karan dress with an accompanying black taffeta wrap. But soon she was worrying that "Donna's gonna kill me. I put a hole in the dress. But it's her fault. It's too long." And Streep might have felt like killing Orla Healy, who said the night's "real shocker was Meryl Streep, looking downright dowdy in a bleak black Donna Karan ensemble." Catherine O'Hara laughed about her outfit: "I designed it and then Sue at Crown Cleaners made it for me." Asked to compare the Oscars and the Tonys, where she had won a Best Actress award for *Burn This*, Joan Allen said, "Well, there are a few more people here screaming and taking pictures, I have to say. It's a little more intense." And Mare Winningham spoke to her children, who were watching WB at home. "You make all of this a dream come true," she said. "This is your mom and her dream come true."

Back in the KTLA studio, Laurie Pike had a grand old time when she saw a picture of a woman making her way down the red carpet. "Here's a picture of what you see at the Academy Awards that other shows won't show you," she boasted gleefully. "We see tons of women in hideous outfits. We have no idea who this woman is, but look at this ugly cowprint thing. We've seen all kinds of women in, like, these tacky outfits with big shoulder pads. So this is a little dose of reality of what we reporters have to deal with."

Sharon Stone, whose date was her dad, described to *Day & Date* what it was like to be here as a nominee: "It's a big honor to know that I've made a space where there's room for my work to breathe, and I love that." Will Smith, dressed in a double-breasted Edwardian tux with ascot, joked about it all thusly: "It's a big social event. The only thing is the time that it takes to get dressed and, like, the bad thing is the time driving because you spend all your time getting your stuff straight, you get your gear straight and then you gotta bend it up, you know, yeah, you bend it all up." Girlfriend Jada Pinkett looked on admiringly.

"Coming up now is the happiest couple in California," announced Rivers, and it turned out to be Tom Cruise and Nicole Kidman, who was in a periwinkle Prada with a short bodice, piping and flowing skirt. Joan was really, really impressed by Kidman's opal choker, but the actress pulled away, leaving her husband to deal with Rivers. "Where did she get the necklace?" Tom Cruise paused, searching for an answer with a smile frozen on his face, and finally articulated, "Umm, I really don't know." And as Cruise edged away from her, Rivers asked, "How are the children? That's the most important thing." Rivers then expressed her amazement that reporters and other mere mortals had cleared a path for Tom and Nic so that the photographers could get some nice, unencumbered shots. Kidman told Ebert and McRee that she wasn't too disappointed about not being nominated because she had "just finished working on a great film," Jane Campion's *The Portrait of a Lady*. Cruise mentioned that he was working on a picture called *Jerry Maguire*, but McRee was more interested in his next release, which was predicted to be one of the summer's big blockbusters: "Do you expect to be up here next year with *Mission Impossible* for some awards?" As Cruise started to say something about never trying to predict, his wife playfully cut in with "No!"

Jackie Chan told the pair from ABC that he loved Gene Kelly "because his movements are kind of like my action," and also mentioned Buster Keaton,

Harold Lloyd and Charlie Chaplin as being among his heroes. Special Award winner Chuck Jones's response to Roger Ebert's congratulations was "You don't have to deserve something in order to enjoy it," and then Ebert informed Mel Gibson that "If *Braveheart* wins tonight, it would probably be the most violent picture that has ever won the number one Oscar."

When Susan Sarandon told Ebert, "You helped us quite a bit," his fawning reply was "You helped me a lot just by showing me that movie. It was a great film." Then two of Sarandon's competitors reached Ebert and McRee at the same time and put their arms around each other. Sharon Stone told Elisabeth Shue, "We're still standing." Ebert asked them why they thought so many performances as hookers had been nominated over the years. Shue said "You answer that one, Sharon." Sharon's answer was "I don't like to think of [her *Casino* character] Ginger as a hooker, since she had such a long life as also a drunk and a drug addict." Shue told Cindy Adams, "I've met some extremely beautiful hookers. Not necessarily tough. Sometimes vulnerable. I related to that. I had three brothers. It wasn't easy. Being a woman was my only power."

Both the WB and ABC broadcasts ended with Tom Hanks and his wife Rita Wilson. Asked by Leanza Cornett why an abundance of actors had recently turned to directing, Hanks answered, "It's megalomania of the highest order. We're out of our minds and we have to be stopped. We're ruining the industry—somebody may have to get a gun." And for Roger Ebert and Lisa McRee, the Hankses were joined by Oprah Winfrey. Hanks said, "I feel like I'm James Bond and these are my James Bond women." But Oprah Winfrey just wanted to talk about Hanks. "My regret is that we don't get an acceptance speech from Tom Hanks, who gives the best acceptance speeches in the world, because his speech about Rita last year was unbelievable," she cooed. Lisa McRee agreed, telling the actor, "Every woman in the country fell in love with you." Ebert made a suggestion: "He could be the pinch speaker. He could come in for someone who doesn't like to give speeches." But Oprah wasn't finished: "It just came out of his soul. You could tell that, you could tell that." McRee ignored Winfrey and added to Ebert's suggestion, "And just talk about *anybody's* wife." Hanks finally got a word in edgewise, asserting, "I'm ready to go at a moment's notice."

The telecast began with a POV shot of photographers taken from the vantage point of the red carpet, and then director Jeff Margolis cut to one of Oprah Winfrey's shoes and had his cameraman pan up her dress. Cindy Adams reported that "Oprah's diamond necklace was heavier than she." Winfrey had bragged to Adams, "Don't ask me if it's borrowed. The thing is mine. I even wore it last year!" Adams's take on things: "Gawd, how embarrassing. To be seen in the same damn eighty-five carats twice."

Speaking into the camera, Winfrey made the self-evident statement "I'm here at the Oscars." Then she announced, "It's my favorite night of the year. I've watched every single year, never missed since I was 10 years old." But instead of showing the talk show host chatting with the arrivals, the telecast switched to the standard opening shots—narrated by Les Marshak—such as Steven Seagal talking to Army Archerd, and Jeff Goldblum, who Marshak said was with "Oscar winner" Laura Dern. You would think that on the Academy's big night they would have had a fact checker, especially since this information is right there in the *World Almanac*, and one doesn't have to go into the bowels of the Academy's archives to find it. The opening segment cut back and forth between Marshak's announcing the likes of "smiling Ed Harris" and Oprah's mini-interviews. Among those with whom Winfrey was seen talking were Nathan Lane, who stated that because of the success of *The Birdcage*, "I'm drunk with power," and Dianne Wiest; Oprah sounded like she was hosting the Miss America pageant as she said to last year's Best Supporting Actress, "You're giving up the throne tonight."

This opening segment also revealed that the woman in the cow print outfit whom Laurie Pike had delighted in ridiculing was a member of the Randy Newman/Lyle Lovett party. When Oprah asked Emma Thompson if there was one of the Oscars she particularly wanted to win, the actress-writer insisted, "I want them both! I want them both!" The talk show host said to Nicole Kidman, "To die for, that's what

you look like tonight. To die for," and to Jackie Chan, "You look beautiful." Again sounding like she was at a beauty pageant, Winfrey asked Elisabeth Shue, "How has your life changed?" "It's changed dramatically in terms of opportunity and in changing my career," the *Leaving Las Vegas* star replied. "But my real life, my love for my husband and my family, and my dog, all the real things haven't changed." James Endrist, TV critic of the *Hartford Courant*, felt that "a starstruck Oprah Winfrey acted as if she'd never handled a microphone or asked a question in public before." The ABC cameras did not pick up what *Entertainment Weekly* described as "her omnipresent hairdresser."

The show moved to a sequence in which a picture of one movie star would morph into the face of another icon, to the accompaniment of Elmer Bernstein's elegiac theme from the early sixties documentary TV series, *Hollywood and the Stars*. It began with Gene Kelly turning into Clark Gable, who in turn became Jim Carrey. Some of the more interesting transformations were Toshiro Mifune into Eddie Murphy, Holly Hunter from *The Piano* into Bela Lugosi as Dracula, and Faye Dunaway into Jerry Lewis. *TV Guide* loved this opening, although the magazine did carp that "turning Hannibal Lecter into Dorothy from *The Wizard of Oz* may have gone a little too far." Mouthing "There's no place like home," Judy Garland herself transformed into an Oscar, and then the statuette dissolved into Whoopi Goldberg, who made her way onto the stage. Her black gown was a Donna Karan made of satin with a crushed velvet robe; her necklace came from Harry Winston and was valued at $7 million.

As the host basked in applause, the camera scoured the audience, alighting on power couples Brad Pitt and Gwyneth Paltrow and Mira Sorvino and Quentin Tarantino. Goldberg's throaty laughter could be heard over the clapping. She began her performance by asking, "So, did you miss me?" The audience's cheers answered affirmatively. Frank DiGiacomo of the *New York Observer* felt "The line was a veiled fuck-you to David Letterman, last year's host and, since then, the symbolic whipping boy for how the East Coast element screwed up the Oscars." Goldberg continued, "Welcome to the 68th Academy Awards, or as it's known in certain circles, *Cutthroat Island,*" a reference to one of 1995's biggest financial shipwrecks.

Whoopi then announced, "I want to say something to all the people who sent me ribbons to wear: You don't ask a black woman to buy an expensive dress and then cover it with ribbons," a statement that received applause. Then she went down the list of ribbons she supposedly had been sent, stating the cause each stood for. It started seriously, with "I've got a red ribbon for AIDS awareness," and then moved on to "I've got a milky white ribbon for mad cow disease" and, through a slip of the tongue, "I've got a rainbow ribbon for gay rights disease." Eventually Goldberg was on to "a seersucker ribbon to let Martin Landau finish his speech from last year" and "a blue ribbon that somebody swiped off Babe." After going through the ribbons, she mentioned Jesse Jackson and said, "I had something I wanted to say to Jesse right here, but he's not watching, so why bother?" The cheers and applause for this line were fairly thunderous, and Mel Gibson and Tom Hanks were among the audience members seen clapping. Tom Shales of the *Washington Post* noted that Goldberg "sounded surprisingly snide" with this comment. Then Goldberg got serious: "But there is somebody I want to give a ribbon to who I know is watching—Alec Baldwin. Bravo, baby!" There was another round of hearty applause for the actor, recently acquitted of assault charges after working over a member of the paparazzi who had gotten too close when Baldwin and wife Kim Basinger were bringing their newborn baby home.

Switching gears, Whoopi said, "I have to admit this show is a little different this year, you know. Quincy Jones is the producer, honey." She began clapping at this fact, and the crowd in the Dorothy Chandler followed suit. Then she elaborated that "the man has made some changes 'cause Oprah was on the sidewalk looking for Uma."

Now it was time for politics: "Oscar is sixty-eight. Younger than Bob Dole [applause]. I'm glad it looks like Bob's gonna get that nomination, honey, because it means he'll be too damn busy to go to the movies. Then we have Pat Buchanan, the original Boy 'n the Hood." This sentiment generated even more intense applause than her Jesse Jackson dig, although Mel

Gibson could be seen in the front row not clapping. Continuing with the far-right presidential candidate: "He had a profound influence on the movies this year. Pat's the man who inspired the titles *Dangerous Minds, Clueless* and *Dumb and Dumber.*" Backstage, Republican Kurt Russell was heard to say, "I wish somebody had the balls to make a joke about this idiot of a president we have."

Winding down, Whoopi mentioned *Showgirls*: "I haven't seen that many poles mistreated since World War II." The television audience saw Sharon Stone doubled over in laughter. There was the fact that "Elisabeth Shue played a hooker. Mira Sorvino played a hooker. Sharon Stone played a hooker. How many times did Charlie Sheen get to vote?" (Sheen had reportedly spent $50,000 as a customer of "Hollywood Madam" Heidi Fleiss.) And finally, "I thought *Dead Man Walking* was a documentary about Keith Richards." Gossipmonger Liz Smith called Goldberg "absolutely sizzling," while the *New York Times*'s William Grimes praised "a breathless, occasionally audacious monologue."

It was time for the Best Costume Design fashion show, presided over by Pierce Brosnan, who had successfully debuted as the new James Bond a few months earlier. He was joined by models Naomi Campbell and Claudia Schiffer. Schiffer announced, "We're doing it in a totally new way," and Brosnan elaborated, "Right. Sixteen of the world's top models are with us tonight to present the nominated costumes as you've never seen them before—trust me, as never before." Actually, there had been a number of times in which people onstage had worn the contending costumes, only they hadn't gone down a faux runway, with faux photographers and reporters alongside taking in the scene, and techno-pop music blaring. The other difference was that normally the models were nameless; this time, as Janet Maslin groaned in the *New York Times*, "An announcer intoned their names as if these mannequins were movie stars." Stephen Hunter of the *Baltimore Sun* thought that the fashion show "had no effect other than to suggest a concession; it was as if Hollywood was acknowledging it had lost its grip on glamour and beauty, and that those values have been entirely appropriated by the fashion industry."

Brosnan pushed his way among all the milling-about models, announcing that he was "coming through," and then revealed that the winner was James Acheson for *Restoration*, an elaborate period piece set in 1660s England, which had been heavily promoted by Miramax. Acheson, winning this Award for the third time, said, "Particularly I want to thank the wonderful team of people that cut and sew and print and dye the costumes that you see tonight. They're the real heroes of this." Backstage, the winner complained that he "wasn't thrilled" with the way the supermodels wore his outfits, and that he had no input on how the segment was handled. Onstage, Whoopi Goldberg wondered, "Why do supermodels have that look on their face all the time? They're getting ten grand an hour, *still* they look pissed off."

Dianne Wiest, wearing an angel pin representing a New York City AIDS organization, Friend in Need, announced that the Oscar for Best Supporting Actor was going to Kevin Spacey in *The Usual Suspects*. Spacey apparently hadn't heard of *Gandhi*'s Ben Kingsley regret about having worn a white tuxedo jacket on the night he won an Oscar, which he said made him look like a headwaiter. This year's Best Supporting Actor had chosen to be seen in the same thing, though at least it was an Armani and had satin lapels, so that if he were a headwaiter, it'd be at a pricey joint. Spacey began his speech by announcing that "Whoever Keyser Soze is, I can tell you he's going to get gloriously drunk tonight." Continuing, Spacey said, "And that's a question that I'm often asked, 'Who is Keyser Soze?' And I've always been very cryptic about my answer. But tonight I'm going to tell you who Keyser Soze is for me—the person who pulls the strings, the person who manipulates, who hovers over us, who gives us life and breath. For me Keyser Soze is Bryan Singer." After praising his *Usual Suspects* director, Spacey turned his attention to his date for the night, his mother: "Thank you so much, Mom, for driving me to those acting classes on Ventura Boulevard when I was 16. I told you they would pay off, and here's the pudding." With its references to Keyser Soze, Spacey's speech was utterly incomprehensible to the hundreds of millions of people watching around the world who hadn't seen *The Usual Suspects*.

Up next, to give the Makeup Award, was the star of *Clueless*, Alicia Silverstone. The 19-year-old actress, who had recently signed a $10 million two-picture production deal with Columbia, had undeniably put on some weight since appearing in her breakthrough film. The *New York Daily News* reported, "It was torture watching the nervous teen swathed in yards of material she clearly wore to hide her newly ample figure as she addressed the shocked Oscar crowd." The dress was an ice blue chiffon by Vera Wang, and *Women's Wear Daily* sniped that "her plump little arms need more than a matching sheer shawl to cover them." One person had kind words for the young actress, however. A bartender working at the Dorothy Chandler said that, as opposed to Brad Pitt, Ed Harris and Meryl Streep, all of whom stiffed him, "Alicia Silverstone tipped nice."

Silverstone announced that the winner of Best Makeup was *Braveheart*. Some observers wondered what was so noteworthy about dabbing blue paint on the faces of a bunch of actors—and why it took three individuals to do so. But very few people had seen the other two nominees in this category, *My Family, Mi Familia* and *Roommates*, so a *Braveheart* victory was pretty much assured, especially when, inexplicably, *Mr. Holland's Opus* wasn't nominated. Moreover, the Makeup prize is also for hairstyling, so *Braveheart*'s Oscar wasn't just for finger painting, it was also in recognition of the film's making the Battle of Stirling look, as *The New Yorker*'s Anthony Lane joked, like "stock footage of an Aerosmith concert." One of the winners was named Peter Frampton, and Whoopi Goldberg wasn't about to not make reference to a seventies icon. "That didn't look like Peter Frampton. I love your ways, too, baby."

Chris O'Donnell—Robin in *Batman Forever*—had put on a tuxedo merely to introduce Gloria Estefan. She had switched from the Armani she wore into the building to an Oscar de la Renta, and was singing the nominated song "Moonlight" from *Sabrina*, in lieu of Sting, who had sung it on the film's soundtrack.

Robin Williams, red ribbon on his lapel, declared, "I'm here tonight, ladies and gentlemen, because I have a problem. I am addicted to cartoons. I've been to Animators Anonymous. I've checked into the Betty

Boop wing of Betty Ford. I went to my therapist, knocked on the door, and said, 'What's up, doc?" and I realized it—I have a jones for Chuck Jones." Williams praised the legendary Warner Brothers animator—who worked with Bugs Bunny, Porky Pig, Daffy Duck, Sylvester and Tweetie, and all the rest—as a man who "has raised speech impediments to an art form." Williams also noted that "If you've seen the primaries, you've gotta believe that his characters are running for office," and likened the rich and robotic Steve Forbes to Marvin the Martian, the slow-talking Texas reactionary Phil Gramm to Elmer Fudd, and "Pat Buchanan is definitely Foghorn Leghorn. Now, if Chuck could only animate Bob Dole, we could have an interesting campaign." Even Mel Gibson clapped at this gibe, although Michael Medved called these attacks "particularly nasty," as if Republicans were dear hearts and gentle people. Finally, Williams told the audience, "Now you have to admit, there's a little bit of Chuck Jones lodged in the frontal lobe of everyone here tonight," and introduced a montage of clips by the Honorary Oscar winner by labeling him "the Orson Welles of animation."

Referring to the film clips, the 83-year-old Jones began his acceptance with "Well, what can I say in the face of such humiliating evidence? I stand guilty before the world of directing over three hundred cartoons in the last fifty or sixty years. Hopefully, this means you've forgiven me." He also quoted Robert Frost: "My object in life is to unite my avocation and my vocation, as my two eyes are one in sight." Jones concluded by giving his love to "the laughing denizens of Termite Terrace," a reference to his fellow cartoonists from the old days at Warners, including Bob Clampett, Friz Freleng and Frank Tashlin.

Robin Williams re-emerged to present another Special Oscar to another animator. "Now we take you to the world of computer animation," he said, "where director John Lasseter has proved that a boy with a hard drive can go a long way." Lasseter was the brains behind *Toy Story*, the first computer-animated feature film, and when Williams mentioned one of the characters from that film, the cowboy doll Woody, he stopped to wax nostalgic with a sly look on his face: "Boy, I had a Woody as a child, and what fun it was to

play with it in the morning." The laughter indicated that a good half of the audience could identify with him. The narrator of the behind-the-scenes clips of the making of *Toy Story* declared, "Artists and scientists spent four years designing every character, object and environment into the computer"—a far cry from Termite Terrace.

Williams announced that the Lasseter/*Toy Story* prize was "for one of the milestone achievements in the hundred-year history of film." Lasseter came out with dolls of Woody and another character from the film, Buzz Lightyear, and said they had hired their own limo to get to the show: "It was a real small one, and Malibu Ken was the driver." When the recipient left, he forgot the dolls and his Oscar on the podium, but this was just a set-up for an animated bit in which the pair gets freaked out by the golden statuette. "Freeze!" Buzz orders. "Woody, he's armed. Grab his sword before he kills us all!" Woody replies, "Buzz, if I take his sword, he'll be naked." Woody then begins to give an Oscar acceptance speech, which meant that Tom Hanks—the actor had provided the doll's voice—got to make another speech. Then the two dolls argued over who was the film's lead.

Randy Newman and Lyle Lovett dueted on Newman's nominated song from *Toy Story*, "You've Got a Friend." Jackie Chan—in a black jacket and white V-neck vest but no shirt—and Kareem Abdul-Jabbar came out together and, just for laughs, a clip of the 7-foot, 2-inch Abdul-Jabbar going up against Bruce Lee in *Game of Death* was shown. The award for Live Action Short went to *Lieberman in Love*, directed by 1984 Supporting Actress nominee Christine Lahti. Thus, Diane Houston, the evening's sole African American nominee, would be going home without an Oscar. The Animated Short winner was *A Close Shave*, a Wallace and Gromit film; receiving his third Oscar, the ever-goofy Nick Park thanked his parents "for allowing me to play with their 8mm Cine camera when I was 13. And I think they've regretted it ever since." Among the commercials in the break that followed was a Pizza Hut ad starring seven-time Best Actor nominee Peter O'Toole.

Taking the stage was the tap dancing/noisemaking group Stomp, who was here to demonstrate sound effects. These "downtown artists" were perhaps the clearest indication that Quincy Jones's Oscars were not a Gil Cates production. Whoopi Goldberg prefaced their appearance with "Bang it out, baby. Bang it out." As old film clips were shown, including Marilyn Monroe walking, Moe Howard and Larry Fine breaking rocks on Curly's head, James Cagney slapping Leo Gorcey, and a lot of doors opening and closing, the performers—through tapping, smashing the floor with poles, and, well, stomping—created the appropriate sounds to go with the images. When Stomp was through, director Jeff Margolis cut to Emma Thompson yelling "Bravo!" in the audience; off to the side an equally excited Sharon Stone could also be seen cheering.

Described by Goldberg as "the best bus driver since Ralph Kramden," *Speed* costar Sandra Bullock gave the Sound Effects Editing award to *Braveheart*. Steven Seagal, his black Nehru designed by Versace, came onstage to give the Sound Award. A couple of weeks earlier, the action star had been making noises that he really should be giving the more prestigious Foreign Film Award instead; when Quincy Jones heard this, he ordered, "Pretend he never existed! He was begging for a slot on the show, and then we give him one and he has to think about it?" Their differences smoothed out, Seagal announced that Best Sound was going to *Apollo 13*. Among the quartet of recipients was one fellow who seemed to be up for the wrong movie—he was wearing a kilt, unattractively set off by white knee socks.

It was time to settle the hotly contested Best Supporting Actress race. Martin Landau—who did not take advantage of his time onstage to finish his speech from the previous year—announced that the winner was Mira Sorvino in *Mighty Aphrodite*. Boyfriend Quentin Tarantino smooched her, and onstage, the winner—in a pearl gray beaded Armani accessorized by $1.6 million of Harry Winston jewelry—said, "When you give me this Award, you honor my father Paul Sorvino, who has taught me everything I know about acting." The ham actor was in the front row and gave an over-the-top performance, bringing his hands to his face and weeping. If he had known how negligible his daughter's subsequent career was going to be, he would really have had something to cry about.

When Jim Carrey materialized to present the Cinematography Award, he brought the *Toy Story* dolls with him. As he made Woody and Buzz walk on the podium, he started singing Fred Neil's "Everybody's Talking," and then had the two dolls imitate Jon Voight and Dustin Hoffman in *Midnight Cowboy*. Before opening the envelope, Carrey yelled, "Who will take home the lord of all knickknacks? The king of tchotchkes?" The answer was, for the second year in a row, John Toll, this time for *Braveheart*.

Whoopi Goldberg reappeared to say, "The last time our next presenters were on the Oscar show together was in 1989. So much has changed since then: the majority in Congress, the cost of living, many of the breasts in this room." There was some laughter, and as the tittering continued, Goldberg said, "I really wanted to say that." The presenters were Goldie Hawn and Kurt Russell, the Award was Editing and the winner was *Apollo 13*. The two victorious editors used their time onstage to praise Ron Howard and the camera cut to him beaming in the audience. Richard Dreyfuss relived the Scientific and Technical Awards banquet he had hosted three weeks earlier, noting that one of these awards was for "a device that pneumatically propels stunt people thirty feet through the air, safely."

After being at the ceremonies two years in a row as a nominee, Winona Ryder's purpose tonight was to introduce "a real hero of mine, and a real inspiration." That would be Bruce Springsteen, who was performing his nominated title song from what Ryder described as the "brilliant, brilliant, brilliant, *Dead Man Walking*." Dressed in black, Springsteen sang the spare, somber song—which he had described as "even a little further to the left" than his Oscar-winning "Streets of Philadelphia"—in simple straightforward fashion. He was accompanied by a quartet of musicians, whose parents must have been disappointed because the viewing audience never got to see their faces. And one couldn't help but wonder what Debbie Allen might have done for a dance accompaniment for the song.

Will Smith handled Visual Effects. In introducing clips from *Apollo 13*, he mentioned Ron Howard's beloved NASA KC-135, and said that the FX nominees for *Babe* "swore they'd never reveal their secrets." This tight-lipped quartet were the winners, and one of then held a stuffed animal pig above his head as he got out of the aisle. Whoopi Goldberg mulled over the seriousness of Bruce Springsteen's songs from *Dead Man Walking* and *Philadelphia.* Then she addressed the songwriter, "I just wanna say, Boss, I think you should lighten up a little. Maybe do a tune for *Ace Ventura.*"

She next introduced "the fun couple of the year," who were Elisabeth Shue and Nicolas Cage. They had the fun job of announcing the Documentary winners. The Documentary Short Subject category was tough on Oscar party pools, because there were *two* Holocaust films nominated this year. The winner was *One Survivor Remembers,* and director Kary Antholis brought an elderly woman wearing a jewel-encrusted Star of David, whom he introduced as Gerda Weissmann Klein, the subject of his film. After the director gave his thanks, the music swelled but the old lady remained at the podium, even as one of the onstage female escorts gently tried to pull her away. But she was determined to speak, and so she did:

> I have been in a place for six incredible years where "winning" meant a crust of bread and to live another day. Since the blessed day of my liberation, I have asked the question "Why am I here?" I am no better.
>
> In my mind's eye, I see those years and days [at this point the show's director Jeff Margolis began pulling in tight, resulting in one of the most extreme close-ups ever at the Oscars], and those who never lived to see the magic of a boring night at home. On their behalf, I wish to thank you for honoring their memory. And you cannot do it in any better way than when you return to your homes tonight, to realize that each of you who know the joy of freedom are winners.

This speech was a case in point about the self-defeating nature of time limits. If Klein hadn't stood up to the orchestra, the Oscars would have been deprived of one of the night's most emotional moments. Jim Carrey said that he was "pissed" that Klein almost got the hook, reasoning that "You go through the Holocaust, you should be able to say whatever you want."

The Documentary Feature was also Holocaust-themed *Anne Frank Remembered.* Winning director Jon Blair told the audience, "Anne Frank loved the movies. In October, 1942, she even wrote that she wanted to come to Hollywood." Among those he thanked was Steven Spielberg, "without whose eleventh-hour intervention, I would never have been able to make this film." Blair had also brought an older woman onstage with him, and he now introduced her as "the hero of the story of Anne Frank. The woman without which, quite literally, there would never have been a diary for us to celebrate for fifty years. Ladies and gentlemen, this is Miep Gies, who found the diary on the floor." (More important, she was also the woman who had hid the Frank family from the Gestapo.) She received cheers and a standing ovation and director Blair could be heard instructing her, "You don't need to speak." Gies, who rather resembled Pauline Kael, didn't talk, but bowed her head in appreciation. Meryl Streep could be seen in the audience shaking her head in admiration. Interestingly, Streep would star in—and be nominated for—1999's *Music of the Heart,* a film based on one of the documentaries that *Anne Frank Remembered* had defeated, *Fiddlefest.*

The shadow of a man carrying an umbrella and jauntily walking could be seen behind the large movie screen onstage, and then Savion Glover came out and tap-danced as the orchestra played "Singin' in the Rain." This led the way to film clips of Gene Kelly dancing, a tribute to the actor, who had died a month earlier at the age of 83. After some commercials, Glover—whose face had not been seen while he danced—was standing at the podium with Whoopi Goldberg. She introduced him to the audience, calling him a "sensational Broadway dancer." After he walked offstage, Goldberg observed, "Cute as a button, honey—but young. Very young for me."

Nathan Lane announced, "I just saw Ross Perot outside yelling and screaming. He wants to know why more nutty billionaires weren't nominated." He then introduced "a woman whose beauty surpasses even my own," Vanessa Williams, the singer of "Colors of the

Wind" from *Pocahontas*, who was wearing a Versace dress made of metal. Her performance was accompanied by what might be described as a Native American ballet, although two of the dancers were spinning around in the air on wires, as if this was a song from *Peter Pan*; others were fidgeting with floor-to-ceiling banners, which mostly had the effect of taking attention away from Williams. Afterwards, Goldberg grossed everyone out when she commented, "The question I really want answered, What color is *my* wind?" After some embarrassed-sounding laughter, she added, "C'mon, we've all wondered it from time to time," and then turned and looked down behind her.

Mel Gibson was the star Quincy Jones had preferred over Steven Seagal to serve as Foreign Film presenter, and he read off the TelePrompTer that the nominated "films remind us we're all part of one global village." He also got into pronouncing the Italian and Brazilian names accurately and with gusto. The winner was the entry from the Netherlands, Marleen Gorris's feminist, magic realism film, *Antonia's Line;* this marked the first time the Foreign Film Award went to a movie directed by a woman.

Goldberg next introduced "a very courageous man who gave me my first job in the movies," and Steven Spielberg blew his *Color Purple* star a kiss. "The dark has a life of its own," he began.

> Kirk Douglas said that in *The Bad and the Beautiful*, one of the best movies about movies ever made. We're celebrating and honoring Kirk Douglas tonight, because he's done nearly everything on film. He's directed, he's produced, and in the process he helped to hammer the blacklist to pieces. And of course, most memorably and most lastingly, he's acted.
>
> He's done that the way he's done everything—with grace and courage. Whether he's dealing with a character on screen, or with the all-too-real effects of a recent stroke, courage remains Kirk Douglas's personal and professional hallmark.
>
> Most stars of his stature are shaped out of mythic clay. Kirk Douglas never chose

> that. He doesn't have a single character that makes him *unique*; instead he has a singular honesty, a drive to be inimitable. That's what animates all his roles from Spartacus to Vincent van Gogh.
>
> There's a single thread drawing all his characters together, and it's called conscience. Every person he ever played had one, and because Kirk Douglas never made his characters simple—no good guys or bad guys. He shaded heroics with self-doubt and shaped his villainy with compassion.
>
> His characters weren't bigger than life, they were life reconverted, something we all could identify with, something that would touch us out there in the dark, something that gave the dark a life, and a light of its own.

Next came the film clips, which ended with Douglas saying in *Spartacus*: "As long as we live, we must stay true to ourselves."

Despite his stroke, the 79-year-old Lifetime Achievement honoree walked out very spryly to receive a standing ovation. The right side of his face was frozen, though, and Douglas spoke in a somewhat slurred manner that seemed all the more marked because his delivery had been so dynamic through the years. After acknowledging the standing ovation, Douglas said with a smile, "I see my four boys. They are proud of the old man. And I am proud, too. Proud to be a part of Hollywood for fifty years. But this is for my wife, Ann. I love you. [There was a shot of her sitting between two of the boys and sobbing. The most famous of the Douglas sons, Michael, was crying, too.] And tonight I love all of you, and I thank all of you for fifty wonderful years." He received another standing ovation, and despite his recent illness was still strong enough to raise the Oscar over his head as he walked offstage—no small feat. And the question remained: Why did Steven Spielberg present this award, rather than someone who had actually worked with Douglas?

After a commercial break, Whoopi Goldberg was standing next to a monitor and promised a surprise: an interview with "one of the hottest new stars of the year." It was Babe! But no sooner had the interview begun than the picture was lost and when it reappeared, the bad news was that *Babe* had been replaced by the passé Miss Piggy. For some years, now, the Oscars had been Muppet-free, but here she was doing the same old schtick from the late seventies. The puppet said things like "Did someone call for a babe?" and signed off with "You like *moi*. You really like *moi*." Whoopi apparently didn't because she said with a touch of comic exasperation, "I wanted this gig," to empathetic laughter. *Entertainment Weekly*'s Ken Tucker pleaded, "Can we please declare a moratorium on all appearances by the smug, tiresome Miss Piggy?"

Having established herself as Oscar night's most dependable old-style fashion plate, Sharon Stone stunned everyone by wearing a navy blue turtleneck from the Gap (made of a rayon-polyester combination), along with a black velvet jacket—but no bra—and skirt. To raise the glamour quotient, she did wear diamond cluster earrings from Van Cleef & Arpels. Her copresenter for the Scoring Awards, Quincy Jones, was wearing a morning suit, and was also the only participant to be sporting a Jesse Jackson Rainbow ribbon. Jones explained, "This year to increase the playing field, so to speak, the Academy has expanded the award for Best Film Score into two categories." After announcing the first award, Jones could be heard saying, "This sounds familiar," by which he was referring to the fact that one of the winners of the Oscar for Original Musical or Comedy Score was Alan Menken, this time collaborating with Stephen Schwartz, for *Pocahontas*. The television audience, meanwhile, could see nonwinning *Toy Story* nominee Randy Newman standing up to let the winners get by; he and Menken shook hands. Menken read a list of names, Schwartz said nothing, both wore red ribbons.

After the nominees for Original Dramatic Score were read, Stone said to Jones, "I don't have the thing"—she had given the envelope with their names in it to Menken and Schwartz as a souvenir, and had inadvertently also handed them the Dramatic Score envelope. While Jones walked offstage to see the men from PriceWaterhouse, the *Casino* nominee said to the audience, "I don't have the envelope, so I'd like us all to have a psychic moment. Let's just concentrate. It's coming to me." Jones came back and whispered into

Stone's ear. "Oh my God," she said. "It's *The Postman*." Winner Luis Enrique Bacalov, of course, dedicated the award to Massimo Troisi. *In Style* advised that the lesson to be learned from Stone's gaffe was, if you're on the Oscar show, "Don't be too spontaneous." And then Liam Neeson introduced the clips from *The Postman*, so the audience got to hear snippets of the winning score.

Just because Academy President Arthur Hiller hadn't made introductory remarks up front didn't mean viewers would be spared his oratory. After waving his arms as if he were conducting the orchestra, the Prez pointed into the camera and addressed the audience: "Just like you, I love movies." He then gave a platitudinous spiel about great movies becoming part of our lives and making our spirits soar, and how important it is to preserve our film heritage. Finally, "I believe that what makes film the transcendent medium of expression is the alchemy of collaboration," spouted the director of *W.C. Fields and Me* and *The Crazy World of Julius Vrooder*, not a man anybody ever accused of being an auteur. This all led up to the annual necrology film montage, with this year's list limited to Academy members who had died, meaning that Massimo Troisi, for one, wouldn't be included. Unlike previous years, there weren't different levels of applause serving as a popularity meter but, rather, the audience response was consistent throughout until one of the final entries, Louis Malle, who was greeted with cheers, a response that outdid even that given to the final participant, 100-year-old George Burns. Other Academy members who were remembered in the compilation included composer Miklos Rozsa, Dean Martin, Martin Balsam, Chuck Jones's old colleague Friz Freleng, Butterfly McQueen, Elisha Cook, Jr., Haing S. Ngor—the 1984 Supporting Actor winner had been shot in a robbery a few weeks earlier—producers Don Simpson and Ross Hunter, and Nancy Kelly, seen in her legendary role as *The Bad Seed*'s Christine Penmark, looking at Claude Daigle's medal.

Dressed in a Richard Tyler tux with the gimmick of having the buttons on the inside, Jimmy Smits was the next participant. He said, "Love songs. Love songs, they can lull, they can mess with your head and they can play with your heart. But if you wanna turn up the heat, you call on Bryan Adams." Adams was there, with his cowriter Michael Kamen on keyboards, to sing his nominated love song from *Don Juan DeMarco,* "Have You Really Loved a Woman." The Spanish-tinged song was accompanied by something resembling flamenco dancers, and *Entertainment Weekly* wondered of Adams, "Have you ever really washed your hair?" When Bryan Adams had finished asking "Have You Ever Really Loved a Woman?" Whoopi turned to the audience and said, "Now if I tell you the answer to that question, will you still be my friend?"

Wearing a pouffy copper-toned satin Dolce & Gabbana that matched her hair color, Susan Sarandon was the Original Screenplay presenter. Almost every postmortem on the ceremony wondered whether her spiked hair was dyed to match her dress or whether the dress was chosen because it resembled her hair color. Sarandon later revealed that the hair color came first, but right now she revealed that the winner was not the only nominee from a Best Picture contender, *Braveheart,* but rather Christopher McQuarie's script for *The Usual Suspects.* McQuarie concluded his speech, "And to my father, who offered me some words of wisdom. As the film was going into production, he said, 'Enjoy this time. This is the moment. The candy store is never so good as when you're looking in.' Well, Dad [his voice rising], I'm in the candy store. Put it there, kid [holding the Oscar aloft]. It's great!"

Before announcing the recipient of the Adapted Screenplay Award, Anthony Hopkins looked at the winner in the audience and smiled. That's because the name in the envelope was that of his two-time costar, Emma Thompson, for *Sense and Sensibility,* who was sitting with her mother, actress Phyllida Law. "Before I came, I went to visit Jane Austen's grave in Westminster Cathedral, to pay my respects and tell her about the grosses. I do hope she knows how big she is in Uruguay," said the winner. Among those Thompson thanked were executive producer Sydney Pollack "for asking all the right questions, like 'Why couldn't these women go out and get a job?'" She dedicated her Oscar to her non-nominated director, Ang Lee. Roger Ebert later said that Thompson "should get an Oscar for her speeches."

Announcer Les Marshak said simply, "Ladies and gentlemen, Christopher Reeve." The curtain rose to reveal the actor—who had appeared with Emma Thompson and Anthony Hopkins in *The Remains of the Day*—in his wheelchair. His appearance on the show had been kept a surprise (*Newsweek* called it "Oscar's biggest bombshell"), and a standing ovation immediately greeted the actor, who had been paralyzed the previous May in a riding accident. During the prolonged ovation, the television cameras showed Gwyneth Paltrow all teary, Kevin Spacey pumping his arm, Rita Wilson wiping away tears, and Marsha Williams crying—her husband, Robin, had been a classmate of Reeve's at Julliard. Steven Spielberg, who hadn't deigned to sit in the audience tonight, was also crying in the green room. Quincy Jones had planned to herald Reeve's appearance with the theme from *Superman,* but when the actor found out twenty minutes before he was to go on, he vetoed the choice and there was no musical fanfare to greet him.

Relieving the tension, Reeve said, "What you probably don't know is that I left New York last September and I just arrived here this morning." The audience laughed appreciatively and there was another round of applause. "And I'm glad I did," he continued. "because I wouldn't have missed this kind of welcome for the world. Thank you." This sentiment brought on a third round of applause. Then he got to the reason he had made the trek from the East Coast. "When I was a kid," he began, speaking haltingly as his lungs filled with oxygen from a machine attached to his chair, "my friends and I went to the movies just for fun. But then we saw Kubrick's *Dr. Strangelove*—it started us thinking about the madness of nuclear destruction. Stanley Kramer's *The Defiant Ones* taught us about race relations. And we began to realize that films could deal with social issues." This was the cue for a montage of "motion pictures that have courageously put social issues ahead of box office," which included *The Grapes of Wrath, In the Heat of the Night, Coming Home, In Cold Blood* (a scene of Robert Blake being hanged, a forerunner of Sean Penn in *Dead Man Walking*) and *Schindler's List,* with Liam Neeson saying, "I didn't do enough" and Ben Kingsley assuring him, "You did so much." Cut to Christopher Reeve saying,

"Hollywood needs to do more. Let's continue to take risks. Let's tackle the issues in many ways. In many ways, our film community can do it better than anyone else. There is no challenge, artistic or otherwise, that we can't meet. Thank you." And Reeve received another standing ovation.

The nominated costars of 1993's *What's Love Got to Do with It*, Angela Bassett and Laurence Fishburne— "together again and a lot more peacefully this time," joked Whoopi Goldberg—came out to present the Best Song Award. Unlike most presenters, however, they didn't get to announce the nominees. That task was handled by the vocal group Take 6, who sang the names of the nominated songs and songwriters a cappella. The winner was "Colors of the Wind" from *Pocahontas*, and once again home viewers got to see Randy Newman standing up to let Alan Menken and Stephen Schwartz get by. There was another shaking of hands, but this time Menken seemed almost embarrassed, as he looked at Newman and shook his head. On his second go-around onstage, Schwartz did speak: "I want to acknowledge my personal debt to the Native American poets and wisdom-keepers, who inspired my work on this project, most particularly in the case of this song, Chief Seattle."

Robert Zemeckis announced that the Best Director winner was Mel Gibson for *Braveheart*. In his lapel pocket, Gibson had some good luck beads given to him by his *Maverick* costar, Jodie Foster. Gibson nervously made some goofy faces and read from a list, calling those that worked with him on *Braveheart*, "one of the best casts and crews I've ever worked with," and, unusual for these occasions, not *the* best. He concluded with "Well, like most directors, I suppose what I really want to do is act," a line that Jay Leno had given to him after joking that Gibson was a terrible impromptu speaker.

At the Miramax party at Spago, Michelle Phillips was telling everybody that a psychic had informed her that Sharon Stone would win Best Actress. But when Tom Hanks opened the envelope, he revealed that the Oscar was going to Susan Sarandon in *Dead Man Walking*, which was ironic, since Hollywood's "Mr. Nice Guy" supported the death penalty. As Sarandon's name was announced, she closed her eyes and momen-

tarily put her hand to her forehead. All four nonwinners looked unusually happy, with Meryl Streep in particular appearing to be positively jubilant as she shook her head back and forth. But then again a whole lot of people in the Dorothy Chandler were delighted, because Sarandon was given a standing ovation, the first Best Actress winner to receive such a tribute since Jessica Tandy in 1989.

Among those Sarandon acknowledged were Sean Penn "for your intelligence and your courage and your humor. And your hairdo. It was a great dance." She referred to Tim Robbins as "my partner in crime and in all things of the heart" and told him, "Thank God for your stubbornness, Thank God for everything about you." Holding up the Oscar, she said, "This is yours as much as mine. Thank God we live together." After the laughter subsided, the winner concluded with, "May all of us find in our hearts and in our homes and in our world a way to nonviolently end violence and heal."

Tim Robbins was, of course, glowing at all this, but he was doing so in a shiny black tuxedo with a striped shirt. *The New Yorker*'s Anthony Lane said Robbins's "jacket was scaly, sharkish and distressingly similar to what he wore last year," and then inquired, "How can a guy of such evident sense, whose movies are a rebuff to bad glitz, opt on an annual basis for a garment that was apparently woven overnight from strands of crude oil?"

Belying his iconoclastic reputation, Sean Penn had said he would be at the ceremony. But his beloved, Robin Wright, was rushed to the hospital for emergency surgery shortly before the show began, so he remained with her, and his parents were in his seats. Penn's publicist said that the actor "had every intention of going; he was very proud to be nominated." The only other absence among the nominees was, out of necessity, Massimo Troisi. Jessica Lange announced that the winning streak had not ended; the Oscar was going to Nicolas Cage for *Leaving Las Vegas*. After kissing wife Patricia Arquette twice, he made his way to the stage. Elisabeth Shue stood up, and turning her head around, exhorted the rest of the crowd to do the same. Immediately behind her, Kevin Spacey got up, but only a handful of other people felt the need for a standing ovation. Cage thanked the Academy "for helping me to blur the line between art and commerce with this Award." His vision was certainly blurry because his next movie after *Leaving Las Vegas* was Michael Bay's expensive piece of junk, *The Rock.* Cage concluded by saying, "I know it's not hip to say it, but I just love acting." Interestingly, Cage's first film role was a small part in *Fast Times at Ridgemont High*, in which Sean Penn was top-billed, and this year's two top competitors also costarred in 1984's *Racing with the Moon.*

Whoopi Goldberg introduced the Best Picture presenter as "An actor who made Oscar history in 1963 by becoming the first black man to win the Best Actor Award, something that has yet to be repeated. He made a lot of other actors possible, including myself." Sidney Poitier then launched into an introduction of such high-minded incoherence that it rivaled Laurence Olivier's 1978 Honorary Award acceptance speech for poetic gibberish:

> Through pathways in the heart and across rivers of the mind, instinct guides us to a place somewhere in human consciousness that has no known address. There we look inside ourselves, confront our demons and do battle with a mystery called the creative process.
>
> Sometimes we win, sometimes not. Such battles, such journeys, are the stuff of which movies are made and dreams are spun.
>
> Among some of you here who have been there sit those of you who have brought us to this next moment. To all of you: the Academy's appreciation.

The winner was *Braveheart*, and much more memorable than anything the three winning producers, including Mel Gibson, said was the shock on Meryl Streep's face that such a thing could happen. As *Buzz* would later say, "Who can forget Meryl Streep's look of amused horror when Mel's Macho Mess won top honors?"

Whoopi Goldberg then reappeared one final time to say, "Well, we stomped our way through another Oscar show, and if you said three hours and thirty-five

minutes, you won the pool." And, recalling her sign-off from two years earlier, she concluded with: "Once again, a special good night for all you kids out there who are dreaming of being here someday: you have the power."

Aftermath

Susan Sarandon told reporters backstage that she didn't know what she said when she was accepting her Award, but that "I was either on the verge of getting completely hysterical or just kind of passing out. It's very surreal to see everyone standing up. . . . I was constantly fighting the impulse to just dissolve into kind of inarticulate sentimentality." Asked her opinion of the death penalty, she unsurprisingly responded, "I think killing for any reason is wrong. Morally, my bottom line is that." She also said she was sure the Oscar would go in the bathroom "where all our other awards are."

Nicolas Cage said that when he was onstage, he "kind of regressed into my Pinocchio stage, where I felt like I returned to a little boy." He also explained why he was wearing a Hugo Boss tuxedo. "I was voted the worst-dressed man in *People* magazine," he admitted. "And, in fact, companies like Dolce & Gabbana were gonna put me in clothes, but when they saw that, they didn't give the clothes to me. And Hugo Boss sent me five free suits, and I said well, these guys I gotta, I gotta just go down the line with these guys. I mean, that's great. So I wore the tux."

Kevin Spacey also addressed sartorial matters. He said that his white tux did not get on his body merely by happenstance, but that his choice in formalwear had a direct relation to his movies: "I just felt that I had had enough darkness this year and I would try to go a little lighter." But *In Style*'s Hal Rubenstein felt it was "a little too lawn party for Oscar night." Spacey said of winning an Oscar for *The Usual Suspects*: "It's a little embarrassing to be picked out of an ensemble because it was never conceived as anything other than that and it isn't anything other than that." He also talked about his high school pal, Mare Winningham. "When the show started, Mare was behind me," he recalled, "And I turned and said, 'Can you believe we're here? What are *we* doing here?' " When a reporter asked about a possible sequel to *The Usual Suspects*, the actor looked perplexed. "A sequel?" he asked. "No, this is not *Dallas* and I'm not Patrick Duffy."

Mira Sorvino, who said, "My heart is almost overflowing with love right now," was asked about the year's proliferation of prostitute roles. Hypothesizing, she said, "I do have a feeling that people like to see likable hookers. And my theory for this is that a hooker is about the most sexual character you can get, and we're a very uptight nation, but if you can make the audience like a hooker, then they can all forgive themselves for whatever their own sexuality may be." As for her father's waterworks shtick: "We cry a lot. I cry a lot. He cries a lot. We come by it naturally."

Emma Thompson was holding her shoes along with the Oscar when she met the press. Outside on the red carpet, she had complained about her high heels and said she was worried about falling and breaking her neck "because the sling backs aren't quite tight enough." Her reaction to being awarded an Oscar for writing was "I'm most astonished. And very, very honored. Very honored. I mean I can't even be ironic about it, I'm *that* honored." The Adapted Screenplay winner already knew what winning an Oscar meant, and she explained that "It's a huge pat on the back which says that you may be doing the right job. And God knows one doubts that sometimes in the still watches of the night. And so you get up at four o'clock in the morning, and get out the DuraGlit and go downstairs and polish it, and that makes you feel much better."

Kirk Douglas declared that of his eighty-two films, he liked twenty-two of them, most especially *Lust for Life*, *Spartacus* and *Lonely Are the Brave*. Christine Lahti told the press that she had become a director because "There aren't a lot of great parts for women over 35. They're all earnest moms waiting at home while the guys are having these great adventures. . . . I didn't want to play these two-dimensional roles." Although she hadn't spoken on stage, the Frank Family's protector, Miep Gies, did talk to reporters backstage. In broken English, she said, "To those people who say the diary is a lie—where are Anne and Margot? They leave the house with the Gestapo. . . . So tell me, where are those children?"

Mel Gibson said, "I'm just in it for the babes." And when asked if he would henceforth concentrate on acting or directing and producing, Gibson declared, "I've got a few balls in the air at the moment," and raised his eyebrows to make sure everyone got the double entendre.

"The long dark nights of Hollywood are over. The world's most colorful community has embraced color," cheered Karen Heller of the *Philadelphia Inquirer* about this year's fashion scene. "Eschewing the long-adored black, better for dinner parties than global media events, actresses went for a lighter shade of pale: white, cream, silver, shimmering pastels." She also felt that "Among the women, the predominant fashion statement was baring their biceps in sleeveless or strapless gowns that showed off their arms—to say nothing of all those borrowed chokers." Gianni Versace applauded that "It was a beautiful evening. Very elegant. Fashion is back in a great age." *People* was pleased that "Putting the kibosh on collarless tuxedo shirts, Tom Hanks, John Travolta and Steven Spielberg brought back the bow tie." But other fashion observers were dismayed that the banded collar was too often replaced by what *Entertainment Weekly* called "regular old neckties that make their tuxes look too casual." Brad Pitt was roundly criticized for his open-collar look; it seemed he was in a time warp from a mid-1970s Oscar ceremony.

A year later, *In Style* noted that Sharon Stone's "antifashion stance in a Gap mock turtleneck" was one of the biggest trendsetters ever among Oscar outfits. That night, though, the magazine's Hal Rubenstein was on E! and adjudged that "For such a designing woman, Sharon Stone miscalculated. Not that she looks bad, she actually looks very elegant. She looks like she's ready for a really important *lunch*." Stone revealed that the sweater had cost $22 and it wasn't even new for the Oscars—she had bought it last fall, and like her jacket and skirt, it had been hanging in her closet. Vera Wang, who had designed Stone's gown last year, and her old standby Valentino had provided dresses for her—reportedly she took three Valentinos home with her from Rome—but she said that since she was nominated for Best Actress, she said she wanted to be looked at this year as someone who was serious about her craft, and not simply a clotheshorse. She was aware of the impact her Oscar appearances had had in the past, though, and Gap executive Richard Crisman said, "She called yesterday to let us know we might get calls." Crisman also admitted, "She made that sweater look better than it has ever looked." But Karen Heller of the *Philadelphia Inquirer* gave thumbs down to the deglamourized Stone, maintaining, "It's never good for a diva to quit her day job and start thinking she's an *ac-tress*." And after calling Stone, "the single most beautiful woman there," fashion analyst Leon Hall tsk-tsked: "I just felt she sort of let everyone down. Yes, we now accept her as a serious actress. We know just what she wants to do. But c'mon, girl, give us some beads and some glamour, and drag a fox stole behind you! That's what you're all about."

Hollywood's other preeminent Stone was noticeably absent Oscar night. An Original Screenplay nominee for *Nixon*, Oliver Stone was instead in the southern Mexico city of San Cristobal de las Casas, meeting with left-wing Zapatista freedom fighters. Stone, who was accompanying a group called Pastors for Peace and members of Los Angeles's Humanitarian Law Project, told the press he wanted to examine the human rights conditions that had led to a violent uprising two years earlier. The director was greeted with a five-piece mariachi band and said he was in Mexico rather than the Dorothy Chandler "because I believe in their struggles."

Almost all of the reviewers were delighted that Gilbert Cates was gone. Michelle Greppi of the *New York Post* called it "the sassiest and slickest Oscars gala in memory." The *New York Daily News*'s David Bianculli asked, "Did Quincy Jones make a difference?" and answered his own question: "Yes, definitely. The musical production numbers were both listenable and watchable. In Oscar history, that would be a first." "It was the worst-case scenario for Oscar watchers itching to dish," complained a tongue-in-cheek *People*. "The most egregious crime at the 68th Academy Awards was—egad!—the relentless elegance and good taste that deprived viewers of genuine Grade A snicker fodder." *Entertainment Weekly* reported that the general reaction to the show was "something approaching ex-

ultation. Not only would producer Quincy Jones's ceremonies turn out to be a hip rethinking of the telecast's traditions, but they would be filled with enough human feeling to inspire some awe among the nominees, the live audience, and a billion viewers." Janet Maslin was happy that "with Whoopi Goldberg as its quick-witted host, the show soon established an energetic tone and a refreshing impatience with Oscar traditions; gone were the famously tomato-worthy dance numbers of years past. . . . the deadly dull spots were almost eradicated, as was Oscar's taste for sentimental sludge. This year's most touching moments were emotional without being maudlin," and she cited the appearances by Kirk Douglas and Christopher Reeve, and the Gene Kelly tribute.

The *Boston Herald*'s James Verniere said of Kirk Douglas's speech: "In a night full of reminders of why we love Hollywood and the movies, this reminder was the most memorable." Billy Crystal would later say his all-time favorite Oscar moment was "watching Kirk Douglas. I wept like a baby. He and I had been corresponding since *City Slickers*. He wrote to me, 'I was mad at you because you didn't consider me for the part of Curly. When I saw the movie, no one should've played this part but Jack Palance. I loved it. Yada yada yada. Kirk Douglas.' Jack went to the Oscars and the next day I get a hand-delivered letter: 'I would've thanked you. Jack didn't. Kirk Douglas.' So I wrote him a note after his appearance. 'Dear Kirk: It was one of the greatest things I've ever seen. I only hope that some day my kids will look at me with the love your boys look at you.' The next day, I get another hand-delivered note: 'Thank you so much. When I can talk, let's talk. Love, Kirk.' "

Andrew Sarris wrote: "Let's face it, guys and gals: Whoopi Goldberg and Quincy Jones achieved a miracle this year. Three hours and 35 minutes without a single stretch of silliness or bombast." Indeed, the host received mostly positive grades. *USA Today*'s Matt Roush raved that "Whoopi Goldberg came out swinging and sassy, and the audience loved her madly. She was the self-assured woman in charge, queen of the evening in the classiest of black velvet and diamonds and with comic material to match. She was going to have fun, and make sure everyone else did, too." *TV Guide* said: "Cheers to Whoopi. In her return engagement, she was fast on her feet, restraining her notoriously blue humor and dishing out some adroit political barbs." But Jay Carr of the *Boston Herald* damned her with faint praise: Comparing this appearance to her hosting job two years earlier, Carr wrote: "Her jokes last night were still lame, but she delivered them with much more comfort, warmth and confidence."

Goldberg swore that she did have people hitting her up to wear all those different ribbons, and it was not just the set-up for a joke. She explained that "whenever you do something like this, everybody wants to get their cause out there. And I thought, how can I do it, because I can't wear all those ribbons. Let me just deal with it this way. And so I think that [gag writer] Bruce Villanch and I found a really good way to acknowledge everything, and yet keep going."

Echoing most reviewers, Matt Roush said that "the show might have been a home run if not for an opening fashion disaster of a production number, with smug supermodels displaying the sort of self-absorbed attitude thankfully missing the rest of the night." As Gersh Kuntzman pointed out in the *New York Post*, "The problem was that the cameras were so intent on showing us the scowling supermodels that we never got to see the costumes themselves." Even *Women's Wear Daily*, which was much more familiar with the participants than most of us, said, "models, all of them described as 'super'—but most of them looking considerably less than that—showed how goofy fashion animals can be when they're torn from their natural habitat." Proving that absolutely nothing is ever unanimous, though, WCBS-TV's Dennis Cunningham raved about the "beautifully staged, knockout costuming nomination parade."

The show also received high marks from people in the industry. "There was a really great vibe there," reported Sandra Bullock. Liam Neeson said, "The show had real heart. It wasn't the phony emotion you sometimes see." Anthony Hopkins felt that of the seven Oscars he had attended, "this was the best because I think Whoopi made a huge difference, because she really drove it along, she's so funny." The *Los Angeles Times* quoted Scott Kroopf, production head at Interscope, who said, "I think anybody would tell you this year is

pretty entertaining compared to the last. It's not just the same old establishment show." Quincy Jones admitted, "This was the hardest thing I've ever done in my life." In case anybody doubted him, he further compared the experience to "running through hell with gasoline underwear on." He also vowed, "I'll never do it again. I'm 63 years old, not 30." He was going to sail down to Mexico and "just chill."

Newsday's Jack Mathews opined that "for once, the show was better than the Awards. It took the usual three-plus hours to get it done, and the ultimate victory for Mel Gibson's *Braveheart*—at 12:35 A.M. on the East Coast—seemed to lack what we might call . . . a reason." Michael Medved believed that "it makes sense that an industry that turns its big awards show into an endurance ordeal—a long day's journey into night, which this year ran to the unconscionable length of three hours and thirty-five minutes—would reserve its principal honors for the longest and most ponderous of the films in contention." Appearing on KABC-TV's post-Oscar show, Roger Ebert admitted being surprised by *Braveheart*'s victory, as he had expected *Apollo 13* or *Babe* to prevail. Ebert was on the same kick he had been with Mel Gibson before the show, noting: "This year, violence in Hollywood movies has been such an issue in the political campaigns, and if they had voted for *Babe* or *Apollo 13*, they could have been voting for a nonviolent, kind of positive values picture. Instead, they voted for the most violent film that has ever won an Academy Award, even more violent than *Silence of the Lambs*." Kenneth Turan wrote of the disappointment felt by "those who allowed themselves to hope that the Academy would truly open itself up to films that depart from the norm. It was probably too much to hope that *Babe* would win Best Picture, but wouldn't it have been swell, a vote for lightness and surprise in an otherwise ossified studio system, if it had happened? Instead, in the single biggest surprise in an otherwise completely by-the-book evening at the Dorothy Chandler Pavilion, the big winner was *Braveheart*, perhaps the most business as usual choice among the nominees."

Andrew Sarris felt that *Braveheart*, "for all its artistic deficiencies and devious sadism, is not the worst movie so honored"—and he came up with six others he deemed even less deserving, including *The Broadway Melody*, *The Great Ziegfeld*, *The Greatest Show on Earth* and *Ben-Hur*. Still, he wondered, "why did it defeat all the other contenders when it was the least well received when it opened?" and couldn't quite make sense of the result. In fact, no one had a satisfactory explanation for why *Braveheart* was named Best Picture. As Matthew Gilbert emphasized in *The Boston Globe*, "it was not one of the most talked-about or admired pictures of 1995. . . . it was absent from many Oscar nomination prediction lists in February. And jaws were seen dropping Monday night as Sidney Poitier announced it as the winner." Dave Kehr of the *New York Daily News* said that *Braveheart* was "a film that looks like an Oscar winner (with period detail and handsome cinematography) and even sounds like one (with the Academy's preferred Brit accents), but nowhere displays the spark of originality that defines a classic." Mike Littwin of the *Baltimore Sun* said simply, "If you're not surprised that *Braveheart* is, now and forever, the official very best flick of 1995, it can only mean one thing. You haven't seen the movie."

Nineteen-fifty-two Best Actress nominee Julie Harris was at an Oscar party in Boston benefiting the Massachusetts Film Office and said she was "heartbroken" at the results. "Did you see *Braveheart* and did it make you cry?" she asked. "*Braveheart* did not make me cry, but *The Postman* did. It'll stay with you the rest of your life, and that's why it should have won."

The *New York Daily News* front-page headline the next day was not about any of the winners. Instead, it simply read "Super Man" and was accompanied by a picture of Christopher Reeve on stage. Inside, the lead to the paper's Oscar story was: "Mel Gibson's Scottish war epic *Braveheart* won five Oscars, including Best Picture—but it was actor Christopher Reeve who was the soul of last night's Academy Awards."

Wolfgang Puck again handled catering duties at the Governors Ball, which *Premiere*'s Howard Karren described as "like a massive bar mitzvah." Puck had said, "I don't even know if the movies are that good as a matter of fact this year as the food is gonna be," and the menu consisted of pizza, Alaskan salmon—carved into the shape of an Oscar—with horseradish puree,

grilled free-range veal with ginger and orange glaze, and a chocolate and raspberry cake in the shape of a reel of film with a little gold Oscar on top. Live Action Short winner Christine Lahti said at the Ball. "I'm going to eat a lot of food. We've all been dieting like crazy to fit into our dresses. Every woman here is going to pig out tonight, and it's well deserved."

When she was heading into the Governors Ball, Susan Sarandon was asked by E!'s Steve Kmetko if she had had an opportunity to share "a private moment" with Tim Robbins. "Yeah," she answered, "and there'll be more to come." Kmetko asked Nicolas Cage what he hoped winning an Oscar would do for him. "What I hope it can do is next time I get a really out-there idea, maybe they'll listen, you know, like they'll say you're not nuts, let's see what happens and try it. I hope it'll give me more freedom and more of a chance to take chances." Kmetko also wondered if the Best Actor winner knew where he'd be putting his Oscar. He certainly did: "It's going on my old television set that I had when I was 6. That was the Zenith oval-shaped TV that was the first place where I think I decided I wanted to become an actor because I remember trying to go inside the TV set and be one of the people." On her way into the Ball, Emma Thompson said what she was most looking forward to was "taking my shoes off. That's all I need to do." Nicolas Cage's wife, Patricia Arquette, was also seen freeing her feet at the Ball. "My dogs are killing me," she admitted. "Why can't Manolo Blahnik team up with Birkenstock?"

Whoopi Goldberg did even better, exchanging her Donna Karan gown for jeans and a sweater for her party-hopping. Winona Ryder was overheard telling Kate Winslet, "Don't worry, there'll be a next time." Supporting Actor non-winner Ed Harris said, "I feel good, you know? Because I'm with my folks and my wife and I'm going back to see my little girl." He also instructed a sympathetic reporter, "Don't feel sorry for me." Asked how losing felt, Richard Dreyfuss said, "It's a big bummer for five minutes, but then you get over it." But *Apollo 13*'s Brian Grazer later spoke of his attitude that night. "I was depressed," he admitted. "As a producer, for me to say 'I don't give a shit that I didn't win' is, like, a fuckin' lie. Hey, look. I got in the race and I thought I was going to win." And read into it what you will, but Sharon Stone skipped all of the post-Oscar parties and instead headed straight home.

USA Today observed that Mira Sorvino was getting "her red lipstick smudged and her ear nibbled by filmmaker beau Quentin Tarantino." But the biggest draw at the Ball was not an Oscar winner, but Christopher Reeve. Tom Hanks said, "I think that when he came out we were totally surprised, we were totally shocked and totally awed by the power of the man." All of this year's winners and all of the show's participants had signed a commemorative poster for Christopher Reeve to take home and store in his memory box, but then some lowlife went and stole it. Liz Smith's reaction: "Ugh!!!"

It was Elton John's 49th birthday, and he had moved his party from the Four Seasons back to the more intimate Maple Drive, raising a quarter of a million dollars for his AIDS Foundation. On the menu were three appetizers: fried calamari, Scottish salmon with caviar, and tuna tartare; the main course was wild mushroom risotto with or without a grilled chicken breast, and a pear tart for dessert. John called this year's "the best show I've seen, without a doubt." He also pooh-poohed the thought that he might be disappointed that so few Oscar participants had worn AIDS ribbons: "I haven't worn a ribbon for ages—enough already." He did have one qualm, though: "I could do without all five songs being done in full. I'd do a little editing"—which would have been more meaningful if he had said it last year when the audience had to endure him performing "Can You Feel the Love Tonight." The *Washington Post* reported that John "looks positively glum." The paper said, "This is the living celebrity museum: Reporters are selectively allowed to walk through and gawk at—but not talk to—the stars who show up." Said stars included Steve Martin, Ian McKellen, Christine Baranski, Stevie Wonder, Herbie Hancock, Prince and Billy Corgan; dropping by after the show were Emma Thompson, Nicolas Cage and Patricia Arquette, Ed Harris and Amy Madigan, Jim Carrey, Steven Spielberg and Whoopi Goldberg. E!'s cameras also caught Allen Carr, the brains behind the 1988 Snow White Oscar bollix, sitting outside Maple Drive. But according to the *Los Angeles Times*, the place had pretty much cleared out by ten-thirty.

Whoopi Goldberg was both the host and guest of honor at a benefit for Covenant House at Planet Hollywood, where her Donna Karan dress was going to be mounted on the wall, although Harry Winston did take back his rocks. Investors in the tourist trap, including Arnold Schwarzenegger and Demi Moore, were there, as were Danny Glover, Charlie Sheen, Prince, Kenny G, Chris Farley and Chris Rock. "It's like a plumber's convention," said Rock of these Oscar night get-togethers. "We just happen to make movies and wear better clothes." Talking about the food that was served at this party, Kenny G simpered, "I liked the dessert best. The cigars you can eat. These chocolate cigars." Boxer Sugar Ray Leonard was also there, and Kenny G revealed that "We smoked a real cigar together once and we both got sick." This was at the height of the cigar fad of the mid-nineties, and Kathleen Sullivan, the E! correspondent at the party, said she understood about the proliferation of cigars at Planet Hollywood: "There are so many agents in this room. Which means not a lot of hair but a lot of smoke." Planet Hollywood was one of several parties Tom Arnold attended, and he said, "It's like your prom whenever you go to these things. Like you're not the coolest football guy and you can't get a date. You never really feel a part of these things."

Emma Thompson later went to the *Sense and Sensibility* revel at Drai's, where she sat in Greg Wise's lap. *The Washington Post* described this party as having "a very Jane Austen–like atmosphere of dark paintings and hushed tones." When Kate Winslet arrived, she confided that "The night is so unreal, almost like being in a movie." She did have one disappointment: "I wanted to meet John Travolta, but I didn't get the chance. I'm completely in love with him."

For the third time, *Vanity Fair* held a party at Morton's. There for the duration were Tim Allen, Billy Wilder, William Baldwin and Chynna Phillips, Steve Martin, Roy Lichtenstein, Raquel Welch, Julian Schnabel, Betsy Bloomingdale, a whole gaggle of cast members from *Melrose Place*, and three regulars from the old Swifty Lazar Spago parties, George Hamilton, Joan Collins and Jackie Collins. After the Governors

Ball thinned out, Morton's received fresh blood. On his way in, Tom Hanks described what Oscar night meant to him: "You dress up nice. I got the cutest girl in the hall on my arm. Sometimes I get to take home a brand-new waffle iron as a door prize, and other times we just get a souvenir program." Rita Wilson did her usual giggling at his every word. *Day & Date*'s Robyn Carter asked John Travolta what makes party-hopping so much fun. "For me," said the *Get Shorty* star, "it's just getting in with a niche of people that you like being with, getting a little tipsy, smoking a cigar and having some laughs." Carter also revealed that "John Travolta was really candid with me. He was talking about the fact that, you know, many people said he was snubbed, and he admitted to me that he felt he had been snubbed. He wasn't nominated, he was quite stunned by it. He said not only did he not get nominated, but people were predicting he was gonna win, so it was a double whammy. And he said that it took him a while to get over it."

Liz Smith was absolutely gaga reporting on this affair: "At one unbelievable point, right in the back of Morton's and all standing within ten feet of each other were Tom Cruise, Brad Pitt, John Travolta, Jessica Lange, Liam Neeson, Diana Ross, Chris O'Donnell, Kurt Russell and Goldie Hawn, Stephen Dorff, Ethan Hawke and Jacqueline Bissett. It was so intense that mere mortals caught in the starflow were convinced they had died and gone to heaven. Others couldn't take it and just headed to the bar." Smith also reported that Brad Pitt "was lip-locked with his steady, Gwyneth Paltrow. They kissed and nuzzled for some time. Strong women wept, let me tell you." Tom Cruise could be heard bragging that the show's "highlight is really my wife. She looked stunning." On the other hand, the *New York Daily News*'s Orla Healy wondered why Tom Cruise didn't "tell Nicole Kidman that her little Prada dress looked frumpy, not fabulous?" and fashion critic Patricia Jacobs complained that "Kidman's flimsy Prada gown made her look ready for bed, if it wasn't for the scratchy beading." Leon Hall said, "For someone who adopts all of her children, didn't she look awfully pregnant? It was just a limp, lifeless Prada *schmatta*."

Showing that tabloid newspapers possess some

sort of "genius," a couple of reporters for the *Star* rented a pig, stuck sunglasses on him and brought him to the *Vanity Fair* party in a limo. Because everyone assumed that this was "Babe," the pig—and the two newshounds—gained entrance into Morton's. Unfortunately, the crowd, the music and the noise caused the animal to panic and he had to make an early exit.

When Mel Gibson showed up at Morton's he was greeted by a bagpiper serenading him in the parking lot, courtesy of Jodie Foster. Mel gave the man fifty bucks. Gibson later put in an appearance at Paramount's party at Chasen's and then went to a private cigar club, where he put a stogie in his mouth. It was noted by several people on the scene that although she was at the Awards ceremony, Gibson's wife Robyn was not seen going into any parties with him.

A first-time party was adjudged a failure, but then again, it was all the way out in Santa Monica. *Buzz* magazine had hoped to start a new Oscar-night tradition, but by midnight there were only four women on the dance floor and a photographer who said the only celebrity he had seen all night was "someone from a soap opera."

Again considered the most A-list of all the A-list parties because of its intimacy was Dani Janssen's get-together at her Century City apartment. Jack Nicholson—whom Quincy Jones had originally asked to host the telecast's fashion show—was there, as was his old *Easy Rider* cohort, Dennis Hopper. Post-show arrivals included Nicholson's ex, Anjelica Huston, Susan Sarandon and Tim Robbins, Richard Dreyfuss, Robin Williams, John McEnroe and Patti Smyth, Tom Hanks and Rita Wilson and party-hopper Whoopi Goldberg. The Widow Janssen served homemade sweet-and-sour meatballs, marinated chicken, spinach soufflé and monkey bread. Sister Helen Prejean later said that, in addition to Susan Sarandon's victory, her favorite part of Oscar night was meeting Jack Nicholson: "He and I talked about the devil." Susan Sarandon was later asked what her kids thought of her golden statuette. "Frankly," she said, "I think they were more impressed with the chocolate Oscars they gave them at the hotel."

Where Swifty Lazar had once held court, Harvey Weinstein now reigned supreme. Spago was the home for the Miramax party, with Supporting Actress Mira Sorvino and boyfriend Quentin Tarantino playing the role of Homecoming King and Queen. And even though the way the Awards played out had made Sorvino the guest of honor, the decorative motif was the Italian countryside, in homage to *The Postman*. The *New York Post*'s "Page Six" claimed that Miramax had been so desperate to get good guests that studio "reps were calling all over Los Angeles, offering to send limousines to shuttle stars from other parties over to its bash at Spago." If so, the reps accomplished their mission as, all told, some seven hundred people made their way to the party, including Jay Leno, Jennifer Tilly, David Schwimmer, Winona Ryder, Tim Roth, Julianne Moore, Elisabeth Shue and brother Andrew, and Christian Slater. Chef-owner Wolfgang Puck—who helicoptered between here and the Governors Ball—commented, "Good to have a little young blood." Brad Pitt and Gwyneth Paltrow got to Spago in their limo, saw the huge crowd of gawkers and media people outside, and had their driver continue elsewhere. Although Miramax's four Oscars was the most yet for the studio, Harvey Weinstein was complaining at the party that "we didn't win the one we should have," meaning Best Picture for *The Postman*. And since this was a party hosted by New Yorkers, it was, as usual, the one that continued on while the whole wide world was fast asleep.

On the East Coast, Bob Dole had been invited to a Washington Oscar party at the home of socialites Peggy and Conrad Cafritz, but he was too busy campaigning to be there. Those who did hear Whoopi Goldberg's and Robin Williams's put-downs of Dole, included four-time Oscar nominee Jane Alexander, now doing battle with congressional Republicans as the head of the National Endowment for the Arts; as was befitting a Hollywood veteran, Alexander won the party pool. Others there included Sam Donaldson, Donna Shalala, Judy Woodruff, Ron Brown, Vernon Jordan, John F. Kennedy, Jr., and his girlfriend Carolyn Bessette, and Colin Powell, who was rooting for *Apollo 13*.

The *Los Angeles Times* wrote that while "Whoopi Goldberg got generally good reviews on her hosting duties . . . several observers and organizations inside and outside Hollywood found some of her jokes anything but a laughing matter." Elaborating, the paper said that "Leaders of several organizations, as well as some producers and directors, said they were angered and disappointed by Goldberg's remarks about the Reverend Jesse Jackson's protest and his fight to combat what he called institutional racism in Hollywood. They said her remarks belittled and dismissed a serious fight to gain diversity within the motion picture industry, and was an insult to African Americans and people of color." The paper quoted Guy Aoki, president of the Media Action Network for Asian Americans, as saying, "What Whoopi did was out of line. Some of the members [of the protest] are very frustrated with Whoopi. She went out of her way to be mean. She doesn't have to agree with what we're doing. But for her to go that far out is very sad and undermines the seriousness of what we're trying to do." Jesse Jackson said that although most observers felt that the protest fizzled, he thought that it was a good start. "We are at the center of debate," he said. "Once you raise consciousness, you change behavior. We are very serious about the struggle, and we will win."

Larry King was partying at Planet Hollywood when E!'s Kathleen Sullivan asked him about Jackson's assertions. The talk show host felt the answer was self-evident: "There's endemic racism" in showbiz and the media. As John Travolta was heading into the *Vanity Fair* party, KABC-TV's Marc Brown asked him his opinion of the boycott. Travolta responded that "I don't know enough of the details about that, but I dunno, I feel like I personally do a lot to help integration in films. Every one of my films has a nice integrated cast and I don't feel as burdened by that. I feel like I believe in that so wholeheartedly that, it's just a way of life for me."

After the Awards, Ceechi Gori—the Italian production company behind *The Postman*—placed an ad in the trade papers that at first glance looked like the many pre-Awards ads for the movie. But this one was a celebration of Miramax, and featured critics' quotations attesting, not to the excellence of the movie, but to the art of the Weinstein publicity machine. There was a rave from Janet Maslin that "*The Postman* would have remained a sweet beguiling and modest dark-horse candidate without the superstrategists at Miramax, who have brilliantly mastered the art of attracting Oscar's attention"; a cheer from Kenneth Turan: "If the folks at Miramax know anything, they know how to sell"; and a huzzah from Gene Siskel: "It was a masterful ad campaign, one of the greatest in history."

James Cromwell may have gone home empty-handed, but he did become one of the most sought-after character actors in Hollywood. It was quite a nice turnabout for a man who had been so disillusioned about his acting career that he had been on the verge of giving it up to become a probation officer. And he showed that his love of animals was not just a stance for *Babe*. When he heard that a 240-pound pig that mentally challenged students at a school in Florida had used in a 4-H project was going to be auctioned off to a butcher, Cromwell paid $1,700 for the swine and shelled out for the animal to stay at an animal sanctuary in Oklahoma, complete with swimming pool. He said that if the kids "knew what might have happened to their beloved pig, it would have broken their hearts. Now they will get to enjoy photographs of Dragon in his new home instead of fearing that he'd be someone's next ham sandwich."

Ten months after *Braveheart* won the Best Picture Oscar, Mel Gibson did something completely unex-pected: He joined in with producer Joel Silver on the set of his latest film, *Conspiracy Theory,* to meet with nine gay and lesbian filmmakers in a seminar organized by GLAAD. The participants felt it was important that Gibson, in the words of filmmaker Ted Sod, "see that there's a human face attached to those pejorative statements." Afterward, GLAAD's entertainment media director, Chastity Bono, tried to put on a positive front, writing in the organization's newsletter that the participants "felt we had made a connection with Gibson and were comforted by the notion that the next time he is in the position of representing a gay or lesbian image, he will remember our day together."

But as *The Advocate* put it, "the olive branch that most of the participants expected Gibson to extend didn't materialize." Gibson's camp didn't see a need for a peace offering anyway. His publicist said, "Mel Gibson does not have a problem with anyone who is gay. If members of the gay community have a problem with him, that's for them to work out." And the flack also advised that not too much should be read into Gibson's meeting: "Mel is passionate about film-making. He's spoken to Harvard about filmmaking, he's spoken to the University of Southern California about filmmaking. Why shouldn't he speak to a group of gay filmmakers?"

1996

It was every Hollywood executive's nightmare.

Cold-Blooded

In early March, while everyone was busy trying to figure out what in the world was going to happen at the 1995 Academy Awards, reviewers found the first movie of the new year that they collectively admired. The filmmaking entity known as the Coen Brothers—director-cowriter Joel and producer-cowriter Ethan—had followed their off-kilter *succès d'estime Barton Fink* with *The Hudsucker Proxy*, which found favor with no one; despite the marquee-friendly presence of Tim Robbins and Paul Newman, the $25 million film grossed a grand total of $3 million. There was nowhere to go but up.

The Brothers went Up North, specifically to the plains states of North Dakota and Minnesota—the seemingly quintessential New York siblings had actually grown up in the Minneapolis suburb of St. Louis Park. What they came up with was *Fargo*, the story of a kidnap plot gone very much awry, containing the usual Coen mixture of whimsy, violence and condescension. William H. Macy played a hapless, financially strapped car salesman—many reviewers noted the similarities between him and Willy Loman—who arranges for his wife to be abducted, with his formidable father-in-law set up to pay the ransom, and he and the kidnappers divvying up the spoils. Suffice it to say nothing works out as planned, and several people end up dead, one even going through a woodchipper. As Ethan Coen told CNN, "there's a sort of politeness and a little bit of a distance or reserve that's characteristic of a lot of people in the area that's oddly punctuated by these horrible, heinous crimes that you hear about more frequently than you think."

Forty-five minutes into the proceedings, a police investigator appears on the scene—a local sheriff played by Joel's wife, Frances "If She Were an Animal, She'd Be a Cat" McDormand. A plain-speaking, and very pregnant, prototypical midwesterner, the salient features of McDormand's Marge Gunderson are her deadpan attitude and her punctuating her speech with such regional colloquialisms as "You're darn tootin' " and "For Pete's sake." Thomas Doherty observed in *Cineaste*, "Marge

pretty much defies every Raymond Chandler cliché—no cynicism, no witticism, no eroticism."

Although Frances McDormand had been married to Joel Coen for a dozen years and had appeared in three of the brothers' movies, Marge Gunderson was the only role that her husband and brother-in-law had written specifically for her. She said laughingly that "it's the first time in twelve years of sleeping with the director that I got the job no questions asked." She also revealed to the *New York Times*, "I've always told them they write great women, but that there's always something missing from them, they just fall short." Marge, however, was different: "She has an inner life that is not immediately evident but which keeps revealing itself. As normal as she seems, there's something about her that people want to know more about because they don't fully understand her."

William H. Macy, a stage actor noted for his work with David Mamet and, onscreen, one of those character actors whose face everybody recognized without—until now—knowing his name, said, "I essentially begged these guys to cast me as Jerry. To me, *Fargo* is a perfect example of the dictionary definition of grotesque—it's at once beautiful and hideous at the same time." He joked that when he auditioned for the role, he told the Coens, "Guys, I don't mean to be pushy, but I'm not leaving until I get the role. If I have to kill your pets, I'll do it."

One of the essential components of *Fargo*—almost a supporting player—was the snow of the upper midwest, and the film opens with a blinding blizzard. No problem in Minnesota, right? Actually, the winter of 1995 was one of the mildest on record. "We were very unlucky," cinematographer Roger Deakins recalled. "We waited weeks and weeks for the blizzard we needed for that scene. And the one day we got really good snow, we were locked into shooting interiors." So the crew became meteorologists, tracking down where—anywhere—in the Minnesota/North Dakota area there might be even an inkling of snow and getting there immediately to shoot storm footage.

So here it was March, and Gene Siskel was already insisting, "There won't be a better film than this all year." Larry Worth of the *New York Post* observed that while the Coens' earlier films "have earned them countless fans, their major breakthrough has proved elusive. Not anymore. The Coens' talent for laugh-out-loud humor, unexpected violence, dead-on dialogue and arty camerawork has been honed to perfection. In short, *Fargo* is a work of art, painted with the Coens' penchant for details and mood."

Movieline's Stephen Farber loved how William H. Macy "deftly captures the unctuousness, the weaselly politeness of a pure unadulterated hypocrite," while Jack Mathews of *Newsday* felt that the leading lady "plays Marge Gunderson with such a perfect blend of professional wile and earnest folksiness that you have a smile on your face the entire time you're watching her." Mike Clark wrote in *USA Today* that "McDormand's uproariously sly-spry performance connects with Roger Deakins' bleakly beautiful photography to create one of the Coens' most consistently successful outings."

Dave Kehr of the *New York Daily News* was a dissenting voice: "From the camera angles to the set design, everything is calculated to make the viewer feel superior to the cloddish, geeky characters on display. Alas, this is something the Coens do with consummate skill." So was *Time*'s Richard Corliss, who found that "*Fargo* is all attitude and low aptitude. Its function is to italicize the Coens' giddy contempt toward people who talk and think Minnesotan. Which is, y'know, kind of a bad deal." (Laura McCarthy, of the Greater Minneapolis Convention and Visitors Association, however, said, "I thought it was hysterical.")

In a *New York Times* interview, Ethan acknowledged, "We'll do things that are less pat than critics or audiences are used to. A lot of people just accept that and appreciate the story in the spirit in which it's offered, but then there are those who want to either spit it out or chew it and turn it into something that they can accommodate more easily, which is weird." Joel allowed that "We're more reluctant to offer cues as to how the audience is supposed to react in different situations, which confuses certain people." That was all fine and good, but while Desson Howe of *The Washington Post* gave the film a generally favorable review, he also admitted, "I couldn't help wondering about Joel and Ethan Coen." Among his contemplations was: "All of their movies, from *Blood Simple* on,

seem so closed-in. Their stories are basically boxes within boxes: One revelation leads intriguingly to another. But the secret, the point, or the ultimate punch line becomes ever smaller. Do they just sit agonizing at their word processors as they concoct bizarre scenarios involving bloodshed, irony and the strangest bits of dialogue they can dream up? Do these guys ever step outside themselves? Do they have a worldview, a feel for humanity, a sense of the great beyond? Do they read the papers?"

Like Butta

Cannes was far away from Fargo, North Dakota, both in distance and sensibility, but the Coens and their movie were there in the south of France for the May film festival. Joel received the prize for Best Director, but the Cannes Film Festival's numero uno award, the Palme d'Or for Best Picture, was given to Mike Leigh's *Secrets & Lies*. In the film, a lower-class white woman meets the now-grown-up daughter she had as the result of a one-night stand and gave up for adoption. Oh, and the daughter is black. This sounded like the premise for a farce (and, indeed, was the essential set-up for the 1981 George Segal/Denzel Washington vehicle *Carbon Copy*), but Mike Leigh was too ornery a fellow for simple comedy. He'd always been fascinated by class distinctions in Britain, and the black woman is a successful optometrist, much better off than her birth mother.

Leigh made the film in his patented manner: To kick things off, he came up with the basic premise. Then for months he spent time with each of his main actors to develop a whole background and a personality for that actor's character, beginning at birth and taking things right up through to the present. At the same time, the actor was kept in the dark about the plot and the other characters, which the director was convinced made for greater realism and spontaneity. He told the *Boston Phoenix*, "It's about giving people their creative space. If, as an actor, you don't learn any more than your character knows, then it liberates you to absolutely create it. You only see events with your character as the center of the universe, like we all do in real life."

Generally, by the time a Leigh movie is being shot, everything has been well rehearsed. In *Secrets & Lies*, though, the actresses playing mother and daughter, Brenda Blethyn and Marianne Jean-Baptiste, met for the first time as the cameras rolled and their characters were similarly meeting each other. It was only then that Blethyn found out her character's daughter was black. "It must have been carried out with military precision, keeping *that* secret from me and the rest of the company," observed the actress. And Jean-Baptiste, who was making her film debut, laughingly recalled that an offshoot of Leigh's methods was: "For nine months people would ask me, 'What's the film about?' And I'd say, 'I don't know.' 'Have you got a big part in it?' 'Well, I don't know.' "

In addition to this mother-daughter relationship, *Secrets & Lies* featured other family members, including Blethyn's surly younger daughter and a bourgeois brother who is saddled with a snobbish wife, with tensions coming to a head at a birthday barbecue. As J. Hoberman of the *Village Voice* described it, "Two-plus hours of dense, interactional comedy culminates in the Mike Leigh equivalent of a musical production number: the ensemble freak-out."

Leigh would get good and mad when he'd hear a suggestion that as a filmmaker he was more interested in pressing a left-wing sensibility than giving the people a good show. "I am an entertainer," he insisted. "I see it as my job to make people laugh and to make people cry, to make people care. I am absolutely up there with Barbra Streisand and everybody else entertaining people."

A People Person

Four months after Cannes, *Secrets & Lies* appeared in America as the opening night attraction of the New York Film Festival, and then moved along on the art house circuit. The reviews were the best yet for a Mike Leigh movie, seemingly because the film was not nearly as sour as his previous work. Harper Barnes of the *St. Louis Post-Dispatch* commented, "The films of Mike Leigh are usually scathing attacks on contemporary hypocrisy. Leigh goes in for some of that in his new movie, but by his standards *Secrets & Lies* verges

on being mellow. It's almost, perish the thought, sweet. *Secrets & Lies* is also funny, touching and marvelously acted by a superb ensemble." Similarly, Edward Guthmann noted in the *San Francisco Chronicle* that "in the past, Leigh rode a thin line between satire and ridicule . . . and seemed more interested in displaying the folly of the working classes—mocking their gestures and accents, their lack of education, their tacky homes, their efforts at shabby gentility—than in granting them a shred of dignity. *Secrets & Lies* isn't the first indication of forgiveness on Leigh's part, but it's much kinder and wiser than anything he's done before."

In the *Los Angeles Times*, Kenneth Turan singled out the seven-and-a-half-minute, one-take scene where Blethyn and Jean-Baptiste meet and Blethyn suddenly recalls that, yes, she did have a brief fling with a black man: "In a breathtaking moment daringly presented in a rigorous two-shot unbroken by close-ups, that very memory comes back to Cynthia in a furious rush, flooding her face and bringing on uncontrollable weeping. If there are truer, more powerful moments to be found in modern film, they do not come to mind." And, again sounding like a PR person for the picture, Turan declared, "Like a well that goes deeper to get purer water, *Secrets & Lies* stretches the bounds of psychological truth on film, balancing humor and pain without ever tipping over."

A much more measured response came from Jonathan Rosenbaum of the *Chicago Reader*: "In the final analysis, what one thinks of *Secrets & Lies* depends on the films one compares it to. Set alongside most recent Hollywood pictures it looks like a masterpiece, but considered in relation to the best of Leigh—say, *Meantime* or *Grown-ups* or *High Hopes*—or the best of recent non-Hollywood films, it looks rather thin. The characters lack complexity, and though *Secrets & Lies* has the sort of actorly assurance one associates with a good night at the English theater, it's not the kind of show that sticks to one's ribs." Rosenbaum surmised that perhaps the problem was that "Leigh no longer has Margaret Thatcher to work up steam about."

Brenda Blethyn had won the Best Actress award at Cannes, staying in character with her acceptance speech: "Oh, this is livin', ain't it. Thank ye, sweet'art."

She found just as many admirers in America. Rita Kempley wrote in *The Washington Post* that "Blethyn and Jean-Baptiste are a joy to behold in tandem, but Blethyn's endearing portrait is transcendent." And *New York*'s David Denby simply said, "I can't remember the last time I fell so abruptly and violently in love with an actress."

Mike Leigh was enjoying his newly widespread acclaim. "When you've trudged, sort of barefoot, the broken-glass path as long as I have, it's very good news," said the 53-year-old director. "You kind of feel you're getting a bit back for what you put in, really." But how would he parlay these plaudits? "Do I have any desire to go to Hollywood?" he asked rhetorically. "None whatever, in any shape or form, in any circumstances. I cannot think of anything more disastrous. It would just be a complete fuck-up from A to Z. Everyone, especially me, would wish they'd never been born."

Looney Tunes

Another movie that caused a stir at a film festival was *Shine*. Well received when it was shown at Sundance in January, this Australian movie gained more attention because of some offscreen shenanigans surrounding it.

Not simply another feel-good, triumph-of-the-human-spirit-against-the-odds film, *Shine* also belonged to the dubious crazies-are-the-normal-ones school of moviemaking. It was the biography of pianist David Helfgott, a child prodigy who cracked up under the pressure of trying to make good in the cutthroat world of classical music. Mental institutions and Australian piano bars followed, before he sort of got his act together again. In the film, his father is the bogeyman, so it all played like a redux of *Fears Strikes Out*, Robert Mulligan's biography of Jimmy Piersall, except that that 1957 film was set on baseball fields rather than in concert halls. The patriarch in *Shine* had some serious family issues going on, with their roots in his memories of Nazi Germany. Between the uplift and the Holocaust connection, it was probably inevitable that Steven Spielberg would be heard to say, "This is a film I wish I'd made myself."

Director Scott Hicks—primarily a documentary director who did some of those interchangeable nature films you're always stumbling across on Discovery and the Learning Channel—said he first became interested in his fellow Australian back in 1985 when he saw a newspaper article that Helfgott would be playing in concert. Never mind that it was his wife's birthday, Hicks canceled celebrating her special day so he could see the pianist—which would seem to indicate, more than anything, that he was a jerk of a husband. "I was so captivated by his eccentric personality and virtuoso musicianship that I felt there must be the making of a story here," he reminisced. Hicks forced himself upon Helfgott and his wife—an astrologer—until finally, after a full year, they agreed to having a film made of his life.

When *Shine* received a standing ovation at Sundance, it became a sought-after commodity, with Miramax's Harvey Weinstein very much in the thick of things. The New York mogul was under the impression that he had nailed the rights, but then word got out that another independent company, Fine Line, had outmaneuvered Miramax and would be distributing *Shine*. The talk at Park City, Utah, was the scene when Weinstein ran into Scott Hicks at a local diner and began screaming at the director, "You fucked me! You fucked me!" The *Village Voice*'s J. Hoberman thought that Weinstein deserved the film, because "*Shine* is the generically perfect Miramax movie—emotionally effusive, English-language middlebrow glitz." For all the talk about *Shine* at Sundance, however, it didn't win any prizes there, the Grand Jury Prize going instead to Todd Solondz's paean to miserable adolescence, *Welcome to the Dollhouse*.

Rach On

Fine Line, meanwhile, was carefully programming *Shine* into a calculated sleeper. Even though the film wouldn't be hitting theaters until November, the studio began holding Oscar strategy meetings in August. And it had already sent out videos of the film during the summer, maneuvering to make people in the industry feel special, as they got to enjoy *Shine* at home months before the great unwashed had a chance to pay to see it; as intended, an aura was created about the film. Director Hicks and screenwriter Jan Sardi thought everybody should know something really cool about their movie: Since Rachmaninoff's Piano Concerto No. 3 is the centerpiece of Helfgott's musical world, they specifically structured the film itself like that musical form. According to them, *Shine* had the parallel exposition, development and recapitulation of a concerto. Or in the words of the guy who wrote the production notes for the movie, "Avoiding the straightforward, linear approach of conventional biography, *Shine* employed an impressionistic musical structure that intricately counterpoints past and present." What that meant was simply that the film portrayed Helfgott at three stages in his life—little boy, young adult and middle-aged—and jumped back and forth willy-nilly among the three.

This concerto structure presumably had something to do with Helfgott going, as described by Barbara Shulgasser of the *San Francisco Examiner*, "straight from fainting after triumphantly performing the notorious Rach 3 to the shock-treatment table . . . from a shy, shambling music student to a double-talking maniac who embraced and kissed everyone he met on first encounter," with no development in between. The sweetly nervous youth grew up to become an insufferable boor in the film, given to going around nude or wearing only a raincoat, and groping women—who are absolutely charmed by this unique form of pickup. Although doctors couldn't pinpoint the cause, Helfgott's most prominent characteristic as an adult was the breakneck speed with which he spoke, incessantly prattling repeated phrases.

Geoffrey Rush, who played the adult Helfgott, was an Australian stage actor with a handful of film credits. He hung out with the pianist in order to prepare for the role, and recalled, "I went round to the house, we had lunch, David would play, we'd have conversations across the room, and he'd have a lot of Beethoven going with his left hand. And he'd disappear and I'd be talking to his wife, Gillian, and then I'd see David running around naked in the background."

Jay Carr of the *Boston Globe* rather unimaginatively fixed on the dominant music in *Shine* to rave, "Like the piano concerto at its center—Rach's Third—

Shine is stormy, then shattering, then triumphant." For Gene Shalit of *The Today Show*, *Shine* was "Once seen, forever remembered. An exalting film to stir the soul." *Newsweek*'s David Ansen prefaced his review by mentioning the film's standing ovation at Sundance and said that *Shine* "has a lot of hype to live up to. A great film? Perhaps not. But a rousing, stylish and extremely well-acted one that, thanks to its vividly unconventional protagonist, pumps fresh blood into a conventional formula."

The *Los Angeles Daily News* decreed: "The performance by Rush, one of Australia's leading stage actors, is astonishing; besides mastering the playful, tumbling speech patterns, he performs the virtuoso piano movements as well, and despite the technical complexities of the part, emanates a kind of benevolent, uncritical affection for humanity that may have inspired the movie's title," and the *Hollywood Reporter* called Rush's "a truly poetic characterization." But Andrew Sarris confessed in the *New York Observer*, "I felt less moved than manipulated by this hyper-romantic musical biography. For one thing, Mr. Rush's undeniable histrionic virtuosity is expended on a note that is too much Johnny One-Note in its compulsive motormouth frenzy that makes Dustin Hoffman's gibbering idiot savant in *Rain Man* sound calm and collected." Helfgott's martinet father was played by Armin Mueller-Stahl, a veteran of both Rainer Werner Fassbinder and Barry Levinson, and Kenneth Turan adjudged that "At those moments when *Shine* threatens to get gooey, the integrity of Mueller-Stahl's chilling performance invariably stops it cold."

David Denby, not content with his usual guise as pedantic movie nerd, showed himself to be a pedantic classical music nerd, too. He went on *Charlie Rose* to cluck, "I'm gonna have the supreme bad taste here to do what no one else has done, which is to say that the guy isn't such a good pianist. I mean, I know these pieces. I can't possibly *play* them, but I know many different recordings of the pieces. To see this presented as the re-emergence of a great classical pianist is a little bit embarrassing if you know these pieces."

David Helfgott watched the movie and declared *Shine* to be "the best film I've seen since *Ben-Hur*."

The Miller's Tale

There was one film above all others that had Oscar written all over it, and it didn't need a showing at a film festival to gain its pedigree. Arthur Miller's 1953 play, *The Crucible,* an allegory of McCarthyism set against the Salem Witch Trials, had been a mainstay of high school drama clubs for decades. A French version was made in 1956 with Simone Signoret and Yves Montand. This time out, the stars were Daniel Day-Lewis, Winona Ryder, Joan Allen, Paul Scofield and Bruce Davison; at the helm was stage director Nicholas Hytner, who had made one previous movie, *The Madness of King George.* Eighty-one-year-old Arthur Miller himself was on the set, happily excising dialogue from his script so that it would play better on screen. The playwright told CNN's Cynthia Tornquist that even though he wrote *The Crucible* specifically in response to the atmosphere of the McCarthy era, he felt his work was relevant in 1996. "It's about panic, paranoia, about people believing in things that don't exist and going a little crazy because of that," Miller maintained. "And I'm afraid it doesn't go away."

The advance word on this one approached the extraordinary. In its Fall Preview issue, *Entertainment Weekly* described *The Crucible* as "a movie with such good buzz that even those at competing studios concede it could get nominations in every major category." In fact, there was already a creeping sense before the film opened that the Oscar race had pretty much already been decided, with the surest among the sure bets, of course, an Adapted Screenplay Oscar for Arthur Miller, who somewhere along the line had passed from mere playwright to Living Legend. *USA Today*'s forecast for *The Crucible*: "First, it will get rave reviews. Then it will carve out an audience—and a big piece of Oscar." Adding to the excitement, Daniel Day-Lewis married Arthur Miller's daughter shortly before the film opened. But then again, those who knew their Oscar history realized that a year earlier, Rob Reiner's *The American President* had also seemed to have things sewn up before it was released.

The reviews fell into place. *Playboy*'s Bruce Williamson exulted, "*The Crucible* achieves hurricane force. It's masterful, vibrant and compelling." And Owen Gleiberman of *Entertainment Weekly* went for the obvious with "*The Crucible* casts a more powerful spell than ever." But in one of the most extreme examples of how *not* to release a movie for maximum effect, 20th Century Fox opened *The Crucible* in just one theater, in New York, on Thanksgiving weekend. Meanwhile, the movie was featured on the cover of *Entertainment Weekly*, getting the magazine's millions of readers all hopped up on seeing a film to which almost none of them had access. That's how you deflate good buzz. By the time *The Crucible* opened wide a month later, nobody much cared anymore, having moved on to new interests.

Burned by Love

One of those new allurements was *The English Patient.* In lieu of a conventional narrative, Michael Ondaatje's 1992 book was filled with ruminations on the nature of love, war, loyalty and commitment. The metaphysical novel had turned into a fave rave of the literary set, but was deemed by most people as unfilmable.

Anthony Minghella, a not-too-well-known British writer-director, devoured the novel in one sitting and convinced himself that he should turn it into a movie. The next day he rang "the only producer I could think of crazy enough to countenance such a project," Saul Zaentz. Minghella advised Zaentz to get ahold of *The English Patient* immediately, because, after all, the producer of *One Flew Over the Cuckoo's Nest* and *Amadeus* had "made a brilliant career out of folly, and is one of the few moviemakers who loves to read." Zaentz, too, found the book irresistible, and told Minghella to proceed straightaway, even though he fully acknowledged the inherent difficulties in adapting this material, not to mention obtaining financial backing. Dismissing the fact that the director's previous films were all small scale, Zaentz noted that "people didn't know if Anthony could do a 'big' film. I told them, Vermeer painted very small paintings. Would you allow him to do a big painting?"

Minghella described his challenge as being "obliged to make transparent what was delicately oblique in the prose. It seemed to me that the process of adaptation required me to join the dots and make a figurative work from a pointillist and abstract one." Or, addressing the same subject on a different occasion: "With a novel that is so extraordinary and so complex, there is no room to do a conventional adaptation. For a book that is in itself so anti-narrative, so mosaic-like, so fractured in structure, you have to, as an adapter, invent a story that will lasso some of the more wonderful aspects."

Of course, no one wanted Michael Ondaatje to feel bad that his original work was going to end up completely different on screen. Zaentz prepared him by saying, "Don't worry, we'll fuck up your book." Then, as Ondaatje recollected with a smile, "Saul slipped me a copy of the short story that *Rear Window* was based on and I was horrified to discover that Grace Kelly's character did not even exist in it. If the film had followed the story it would have been about James Stewart and his manservant." Ondaatje got the point and prepared himself not to expect a faithful rendering of his novel. He would later say, "I didn't think it could be a film, quite honestly. How do you make a film with this kind of complicated story and swirling plots and stuff like that? It seemed too expensive, too vast, too full of no-nos."

The two-tiered film contained parallel stories: one about a man, burned beyond recognition during World War II, who is tended by a nurse in an abandoned Italian monastery; the other told, through flashbacks, of the doomed adulterous affair between this invalid—who turns out to be a Hungarian count—and an aristocratic adventuress.

Ralph Fiennes signed on as the title character, and to play his lover, a woman with a misleadingly cool demeanor, Zaentz and Minghella selected Kristin Scott Thomas, the British actress best known as the Other Woman in *Four Weddings and a Funeral*. Originally, Minghella hadn't been terribly interested in having Scott Thomas in his movie, and the actress recalled, "I wrote letters, I auditioned, I pleaded, I begged. I had to fight like mad." The reason she was so adamant was that "This mysterious woman in Cairo, she fascinated me. . . . It was so obvious to me, so painfully evident

that I had to be Katherine Clifton, that I am Katherine Clifton." Thomas got together with Minghella for lunch, which she labeled "a complete disaster," because she had sat down intending to tell him how, yes, she realized she was a nobody, but at the same time, she also knew she had the necessary talent for the role— and then forgot to mention the second part of the equation. The director agreed with her estimation of that meeting, saying that "she was so anxious it was palpable" and that she came across as "brittle, cool and insecure." Still, when Thomas wrote a letter pleading for an audition with Ralph Fiennes, Minghella acquiesced; seeing them together, he knew the two actors were perfect for each other. He said, "They're both these long-limbed, overbred, extremely high-strung people, rather like racehorses. You get the sense you can keep unwrapping them and there will be still another skin underneath." Kristin Scott Thomas joked to E!'s Steve Kmetko that "having a leading man prettier than I am is quite upsetting."

Juliette Binoche, who had appeared in Zaentz's 1988 production, *The Unbearable Lightness of Being*, and costarred with Ralph Fiennes in a little-seen 1992 version of *Wuthering Heights*, played the spirited nurse who takes care of the injured hero. She loved *her* role as much as Scott Thomas loved hers. Binoche said, "Hana was a character that was just so right for me. She can be very warm, very afraid, very serious. But also she has this happiness that I just loved."

No Moore Money

20th Century Fox had agreed to bankroll the project, but on the eve of production, the studio suddenly demanded that Thomas be dumped and replaced by a star, preferably Demi Moore or Uma Thurman. Once they had become convinced of Thomas's absolute rightness for the role, Minghella and Zaentz weren't about to cave in to studio executives. Nor would they get rid of Willem Dafoe, just because the potentates said that the role of an enigmatic thief would be better served by John Goodman, Richard Dreyfuss or Danny DeVito. And just like that, the financing was gone.

Members of the cast and crew agreed to remain on location in Italy without being paid while, for four weeks, Saul Zaentz scrambled frantically looking for funding. The project's savior turned out to be the Brothers Weinstein, who agreed to invest Miramax money in the project. But even with that contribution, Zaentz still had to add $5 million of his own cash, and just about everyone involved with the film deferred $10 million worth of salaries to get it made; after all, re-creating Northern Africa and Italy from the late 1930s and early 1940s wasn't going to be very convincing if it was done on the cheap. Zaentz later revealed that producer-director Sydney Pollock was instrumental in getting Miramax on board: "He read the script and liked it. He went out on a limb for us. Finally, Harvey listened to him."

Some of the book's fans were disheartened by the changes rendered by Minghella. Most troubling were eliminating the history of Willem Dafoe's Carravagio—so that this criminal now had only a tenuous relationship to the other characters—and the way that Kip, a Sikh bomb expert with whom the nurse falls in love, went from an integral and extremely complex character in the book to a happy-go-lucky minor figure onscreen. But Michael Ondaatje didn't mind, proclaiming himself delighted with the result; besides, the movie tie-in boosted sales of his book even more.

And the critics didn't much mind either, as many of them acted as if they were in a contest to see who could most effusively express appreciation for what Anthony Minghella had done. Richard Corliss of *Time* volunteered that "All year we've seen mirages of good films. Here is the real thing. To transport picture-goers to a unique place in the glare of the earth, in the darkness of the heart—this you realize with a gasp of joy, is what movies can do." *Newsweek*'s David Ansen proffered that Minghella has "given us an interpretation of the novel that succeeds stunningly on its own terms. He's seen that at the heart of Ondaatje's novel was a love story waiting to get out—and he's liberated that romance with wit, sophistication and passion." Peter Stack of the *San Francisco Chronicle* proposed, "*The English Patient* is the most stunning, tempestuous love story in a decade or two of moviemaking." But

going for broke was Susan Stark of the *Detroit News*, who came up with the startling declaration that "of some 6,000 films I've seen over my 28 years as a professional viewer, *The English Patient* is the best of all."

The cast got in on this critical acclaim as well. Janet Maslin wrote in the *New York Times* that Ralph Fiennes "makes himself the most dashing British actor to brood in such settings since the young Peter O'Toole." Maslin also praised Juliette Binoche for her "radiant simplicity"; Ella Taylor of *L.A. Weekly* called her "rosy and warm."

"In terms of screen time, Ralph Fiennes, Juliette Binoche and Willem Dafoe deserve to be billed over Ms. Thomas," noted Andrew Sarris in the *New York Observer*. "But with Ms. Thomas, there is something magical and mysterious in both the actress and the character, something that is lacking in the other players." It turned out that Kristin Scott Thomas was but the latest of Sarris's cinematic crushes, part of a litany that went back at least as far as bobby-soxer Diana Lynn. He claimed that "a growing number of cineastes have begun awaiting each new Thomas screen appearance with the eager anticipation of the Garbo worshippers during the first half of the century." Malcolm Johnson of the *Hartford Courant* must have been among them, for he believed that Thomas "matches the rakish Fiennes with a calculating sensuality and glamour that almost surpasses Dietrich."

As *The English Patient* developed into a financial success, Saul Zaentz said his biggest hope was that now everyone on the picture would finally get paid: "It's gratifying for the guys in the crew, who worked like dogs, through the difficulties in shooting and the deferred salary basis. It's that kind of vindication of their beliefs."

Arkansas Traveler

Miramax also had a smaller film in release for the holidays, and if *The English Patient* brought audiences to an exotic place and time, *Sling Blade*'s setting couldn't have been more mundane. Billy Bob Thornton was a 41-year-old Arkansas-born actor who had been kicking around Hollywood for a decade-and-a-half. During his stay, he had gravitated from movies like *Chopper Chicks in Zombie Town* to a featured role in the semi-successful TV series, *Hearts Afire,* which was produced by his fellow Arkansans, Bill Clinton cronies Harry Thomason and Linda Bloodworth-Thomason. He had also cowritten and appeared in the well-regarded but little-seen 1991 film, *One False Move.*

In 1993, Thornton had written and starred in a 25-minute movie entitled *Some Folks Call It a Sling Blade.* The film was based on a one-man show he had been performing since the mid-1980s in which he played a mildly retarded man who, on the eve of being released from a "nervous hospital," discusses the double murder that led to his being incarcerated. Now Thornton was pulling an Orson Welles by adding directing to his other duties on a feature film that reworked the interview sequence and then showed what happens when the murderer goes out in the world: He befriends a preadolescent boy, moves in with the kid and his mother, and watches out for the two of them against her no-account boyfriend. To make the film, Thornton was given a million dollars by the New York–based company Shooting Gallery; while acknowledging that it wasn't a great deal of money, Thornton praised the company for leaving him alone. He enlisted a number of friends—from both Hollywood and back home in Arkansas—as actors and crew members, and Miramax paid $10 million to pick up the finished product.

Considering that it was a Miramax film and that it played at the New York Film Festival, *Sling Blade*—longer film, shorter title—was released with relatively little fanfare and slipped into just a couple of theaters. Nevertheless, it emerged as one of the best reviewed films of the year; Andrew Sarris called it a "mesmerizing movie" and felt it was "a timely reminder of the surprising glories to be found every so often in the overhyped 'independent' cinema." *Sling Blade* found a true champion in Elizabeth Taylor, who saw the movie early on, fell in love with it and urged everyone she knew to check it out. She contacted gossip columnist Liz Smith, gushing, "I think about that movie every day, and it's been a month since I've seen it." Smith went to see *Sling Blade* for herself, loved it and began

talking it up in her column, as well as questioning why Miramax wasn't doing more to promote the film and highlight its auteur, and why in the world it wasn't giving it a wider release. During the Oscar nominating period, the film was only in two theaters, one in Los Angeles, the other in New York.

CNN's Paul Vercammon referred to Thornton's character, Karl Childers, as a "lovable murderer." Thornton revealed that he had created Karl—who wears his pants up high, leads with his jaw, has a guttural voice and is constantly clearing his throat—almost by accident while he was acting in a cable-TV movie over a decade earlier. "It was hot," he explained, "and I had a conductor's uniform on with a collar up to here. My part wasn't going well because the director [Daniel Mann] wanted me to overact. At lunch I was thinking how everyone else on the set was a real actor and I was a nobody. I started making faces at myself in the mirror and started talking in that voice. I looked so goofy, I just went, Eeeewegh. Then I came up with the monologue, with the voice. I thought it was a pretty good character." He elaborated to the *San Francisco Chronicle's* Ruthe Stein, "I based a lot of Karl's physicality on some of the old guys in a nursing home where I used to work." Thornton acknowledged that many reviewers saw echoes of *Forrest Gump* and Dustin Hoffman's *Rain Man*, but he thought the more appropriate antecedents were Frankenstein's monster and Boo Radley from *To Kill a Mockingbird*. In a bit of an homage to Boo, Karl Childers's father in *Sling Blade* was played by Robert Duvall, who had made his film debut as Radley.

In *The New Republic*, Stanley Kauffmann asked, "Who is Billy Bob Thornton? The question fascinates after seeing *Sling Blade*, the extraordinary first film that he wrote and directed and in which he plays the leading role. It's a question that I hope will engage many." Kauffmann then explained why he was so interested: "Actors love to play impaired people, mentally or physically or both. Simulating impairment is usually easy and easily wins praise. Very quickly in this film, Thornton convinces us that he is interested in Karl as a human being, not in showing how cleverly he can play a slow-speaking, slow-moving man. Thornton soon creates a conviction of someone resident in Karl.

Caught within that pigeon-toed, slightly round-shouldered, jut-jawed figure is a whole man trying to signal to us. Reconciled to his immured condition, all he wants from the world is the chance to make others aware of his capacity for feeling."

John Ritter, who knew Thornton from the *Hearts Afire* series and appeared as a gay nerd in *Sling Blade*, could answer Kaufmann's question. He said of his friend, "If Horton Foote and David Lynch ran at each other at 100 m.p.h. and collided head on, the result would be someone like Billy Bob." Little by little, word of mouth turned *Sling Blade* into the year's most conspicuous sleeper. And although most people were thrilled with Thornton's success as "the little filmmaker who could," one prominent celebrity was less than enamored of him. Thornton refused to fly, and because train connections to Chicago didn't work out with his schedule, he turned down a request to appear on *Oprah*. "Who does he think he is?" Madame Winfrey was heard to complain.

Tom Cruise Saved My Life

It was certainly more high profile a release than *Sling Blade*, though for a Tom Cruise vehicle, *Jerry Maguire* had remarkably little advance word. There were a few news tidbits a year earlier when the female lead went to an unknown actress, Renee Zellweger, but the buzz for *Jerry Maguire* just wasn't there. *Entertainment Weekly* reported that "production was eerily quiet." In fact, Nicole Kidman was expected to be much more in the spotlight this Christmas season, since Cruise's wife was starring in *The Portrait of a Lady*, Jane Campion's first movie since *The Piano*.

Earlier in the year, Cruise's action vehicle *Mission: Impossible* was a huge success, and on three separate occasions the actor made headlines for his offscreen feats. In March, he had tended to a woman injured in a hit-and-run accident in Los Angeles and paid for her emergency room bill, and then at *Mission Impossible*'s July London premiere, he saved a 7-year-old boy who was in the process of being crushed by out-of-control fans. Finally, while vacationing in Italy a month later, he rescued five members of a French family from a boat fire near the isle of Capri. As Barry Koltnow of

the *Orange County Register* characterized this state of affairs, "In a matter of a few weeks, he personally saved the lives of half the English-speaking world. . . . And his highly-paid publicist swears she didn't make any of this up." Despite these acts of heroism, Cruise insisted, "I don't feel like I'm a saint." The actor was also in the news for suing a German magazine for $60 million because it contained a "quote" from him saying that he had a "zero sperm count." Cruise dropped the suit after the rag admitted it had fabricated this and other statements.

Jerry Maguire told the story of a hotshot sports agent who finds redemption by rethinking his business practices and finding the love of a good, simple woman who has one of those gratingly "adorable" kids you come across only in the movies. Writer-director Cameron Crowe claimed the film had as its trajectory two classic films from the Eisenhower era. He envisioned Tom Cruise's character starting off as Tony Curtis's Sidney Falco, the unctuous press agent in *Sweet Smell of Success*, and becoming the reformed Jack Lemmon at the end of *The Apartment*. Cruise said he did the movie because "When I read the script I cried."

Variety's Todd McCarthy called *Jerry Maguire* "an exceptionally tasty contempo comedic romance . . . although it has conventional sit-commy elements and goes on a bit too long, the dialogue is so good and the performances so alive to the potential of the characters that the faults remain quite minor." *Entertainment Weekly*'s Steve Wulf found it to be "a big movie with a small movie's charms and quirks." Bernard Weinraub of the *New York Times* said that many reviewers admired the movie because "Unlike virtually any other studio film with a marquee star like Mr. Cruise, *Jerry Maguire* is almost impossible to characterize in one sentence." But *Newsday*'s Jack Mathews was one of the critics who thought that was actually a shortcoming of the film, and he opined, "Somewhere in *Jerry Maguire*'s overlong, overwritten and too often over-the-top romantic comedy there is a nice little movie struggling to get out, and it finally succeeds." Peter Keough of the *Boston Phoenix* said that the narrative of *Jerry Maguire* "is predictable, the ways of love and friendship and underdog struggles and cute kids in

Hollywood being what they are. But Crowe and company pull it off with a wink and a prayer—a sly self-parody and also a trace of genuine belief in what it's preaching. Not that the film doesn't have its share of gag-inducing moments. Jerry spends so much time bonding with Dorothy's weird and seemingly brain-damaged son Ray (Jonathan Lipnicki) that the movie seems about to turn into a juvenile version of *Rain Man*."

Amy Taubin of the *Village Voice*, though, didn't accept the film's romantic angle, saying she couldn't believe "Tom Cruise as a lover of anyone except himself." The *New York Post*'s Thelma Adams had no patience for the basic theme of the movie. "A sports agent in search of his soul? That merits 10 minutes, not 135," she insisted, and added, "When I want to watch a sports agent in action, not a pretty actor going through the motions, I'll take Robert Wuhl and *Arli$$* on HBO."

Gary Thompson of the *Philadelphia Daily News* declared that *Jerry Maguire* "defeats gender polarization in the most amazing way—guys walk out thinking it's a guy's movie, women walk out bawling about how sensitive it is." But others thought it was merely specious. One reason that Hollywood embraced *Jerry Maguire* is because it presented a moral dilemma Tinseltown could identify with: an agent's valiant self-abnegation in relentlessly trying to wangle the most money possible for just one guy, as opposed to doing the same for ten players. As CNN film critic Paul Tatara observed, "the whole movie comes off phony—even after Jerry has struggled for over two hours to become a better human being, his much-sought-after true happiness is triggered by the signing of a $10 million contract." *Newsweek* observed that "everyone in Hollywood thinks he's Jerry Maguire—the one suit with integrity."

Tommy and the Hand Jive

Larry King reckoned that this "might be Tom Cruise's best performance ever," while David Sheehan of KCBS-TV decided it was his "most passionate performance ever." Then again, Gary Arnold of the *Washington Times*, who deemed the movie "a strenuously

eccentric and misbegotten romantic comedy," groaned that "Mr. Cruise has never had a role that demanded busier use of his face and hands and arms. Indeed, Jerry at his most agitated is a veritable Rube Goldberg windmill of grimaces, hand jive and hyperbole."

One thing no one could argue about *Jerry Maguire* was that the movie did contribute to the vernacular. While doing on-site research for the film, Cameron Crowe had heard Phoenix Cardinal Tim MacDonald tell his agent, "Show me the money!" as he was about to sign with the San Francisco 49ers. Crowe gave the line to Cuba Gooding, Jr., who played Cruise's sole client, and the phrase entered the public consciousness almost immediately. *USA Today* declared that it "has become a mantra for the masses," and was "destined to become a 'Where's the beef?' for the '90s." *U.S. News & World Report, Entertainment Weekly, New York* and *Asiaweek* were just four of the publications using "Show Me the Money!" or variations thereof for headlines. One quickly got sick of hearing it.

The 300 Faces of Eva

Moviegoers had to wait until the last week of December for both the year's most eagerly awaited film and the film that would prove to be 1996's most controversial. And—you might have predicted it—Oliver Stone's name was on both of them.

Reserved seat tickets for *Evita*'s Christmas Day opening were available by mail beginning in September, calling to mind the old road-show musicals of the 1960s. If three months seemed like a long time to wait after ordering your tickets, that was nothing compared to how long it took for *Evita* to get on the screen. The main reason the film was so anticipated was because it was so damned long and boring.

A rock opera—there's a term you don't hear much anymore—by the team of Andrew Lloyd Webber and Tim Rice, *Evita* originally saw life as a concept album in 1975. The work intermingled fact and fantasy to convey the essence of Eva Peron, the First Lady of Argentina from 1946 to 1952, who became a legend by dying at the age of 33. Eva was born in poverty, became an actress and slept her way to the heights of power, combining a concern for the working class with a taste for high fashion and fascism. Part of the fantasy element was the use of Bolivian revolutionary Che Guevera as sort of a Greek chorus sardonically commenting on the proceedings. In 1978, the record had metamorphosed into a hit musical on the London stage, and a year later the show also became a smash on Broadway; many other companies of the musical crisscrossed the United States and set down all over the world. This was a hot property, and even if song-and-dance movies were no longer a cinematic staple, *Evita* was deemed a natural for the screen, especially with *Saturday Night Fever* and *Grease* showing that there was still an audience for at least certain film musicals.

It so happened that Robert Stigwood, the coproducer of those two John Travolta movies, had also produced *Evita* on the stage. (His track record wasn't impeccable, though—he also made 1978's *Sergeant Pepper's Lonely Hearts Club Band*.) Stigwood talked to director Alan Parker about the project, but Parker was working on *Fame* at the time and didn't wish to follow it up with another musical. A combination of hot newcomers and stolid veterans were touted to direct the film at various times, including Harold Prince—who had directed the show on the stage—Michael Cimino, Francis Ford Coppola, Herbert Ross, Richard Attenborough, Michael Apted, Franco Zeffirelli, Alan Pakula, John Frankenheimer and Hector Babenco. Some of these men were seriously considered, others were little more than rumors.

In 1981, Ken Russell—who had made *Tommy* for Stigwood—was hired. Russell conducted a number of screen tests and announced he had found his Eva Peron: Karla DeVito, a rock singer married to Robbie Benson. Stigwood told Russell to think again, because there was no way Karla DeVito was going to star as Evita. Russell then decided that Liza Minnelli in a blond wig would be perfect. Stigwood overruled him, and decreed that the original star of the London production, Elaine Paige, would be getting the part. Russell responded that Liza was his one and only, so the producer and director parted company.

Speculation about casting had been rampant from the beginning. By the time the movie finally came out,

Sid Smith of the *Chicago Tribune* could declare, "The search for Scarlett O'Hara pales by comparison." For a number of years, the entirely unsubstantiated scuttlebutt was that Barbra Streisand would star as *Evita* (and somewhere along the line the rumor was expanded so that she'd be enjoying a reunion with ex-hubby Elliot Gould playing Che). What wasn't mere rumor, however, was that even before the show had opened on Broadway, Streisand did offer Stigwood $2 million for the screen rights. Even though Stigwood had officially announced Elaine Paige for the role (with David Essex as Che), the next director attached to the project, Franco Zeffirelli, stated that Diane Keaton was *his* choice for the lead. Other would-be Evitas over the next several years included Olivia Newton-John (reportedly with John Travolta as Che and Elton John as Juan Peron), Bette Midler, Cyndi Lauper, Ann-Margret, Pia Zadora and Charo. Additional names for Che were Sylvester Stallone, Barry Gibb, Roland Gift, Patrick Swayze and Meat Loaf.

In the late 1980s, Madonna met with Robert Stigwood for the specific purpose of convincing him that she should be Eva Peron. She wasn't going to rely merely on her powers of persuasion; she went in for visual effects as well, wearing an old-fashioned evening gown and a late forties twist hairdo for their confab. Stigwood decided yet again that he had his Evita, and it was no longer Elaine Paige.

Shortly thereafter, Oliver Stone—then the hottest director in the business thanks to *Platoon*—came aboard. Things began to unravel when he and Madonna had dinner with Andrew Lloyd Webber and the singer—who had yet to solidify a position as a movie star—told the composer she wanted to rewrite the score so it would sound more Madonna-esque. She was also demanding script approval. Stone had heard enough and became convinced that he didn't want Madonna to star in his film.

Mercurial Streep

Stone envisioned the movie as a highly stylized Vincente Minnelli-esque musical, and he flew down to Argentina where he was assured by the Peronist president that the country would welcome the production. The director approached Meryl Streep—whose name had first surfaced in 1981—about the role, and she demonstrated her interest by rehearsing for two weeks and making a demo tape of herself singing with piano accompaniment. Stigwood deemed her vocalizing to be "just mind-boggling." Stone, Andrew Lloyd Webber and Tim Rice all concurred in that assessment, and the film was set to start in early 1989.

Streep decided to ask for a lot more money. The behind-the-camera principals agreed to take reduced salaries so she could get her pot of gold. High jinks ensued, though, as Streep's agent, Sam Cohn, sent Stigwood a two-line fax saying that, even though she had been working with choreographer Paula Abdul, Streep had decided against doing the film for "personal reasons"—it seems she was tired. Ten days later Streep had apparently caught up on her sleep and wanted in again. But Stone said enough was enough, and went off to work on his Jim Morrison biography, *The Doors.*

Next up was Glen Gordon Caron, who had made a name for himself with television's *Moonlighting* but whose one film, 1988's *Clean and Sober*—Michael Keaton in rehab—came and went. At this point, Stigwood's current production partner, Disney, pulled the plug because the budget had gotten too high for the studio's taste. By 1990, Oliver Stone was back in the picture, with Mariah Carey and Gloria Estefan among the newest names bandied about. Finally, it was decided that Michelle Pfeiffer would star as Eva, with Antonio Banderas—who was still known only as the star of Pedro Almodovar's art house comedies— playing Che, and Raul Julia or Julio Iglesias as Peron. Stone went back to Argentina and got the bad news that the formerly accommodating Peronists had decided that *Evita* was an affront to the memory of their beloved former First Lady and refused to grant permission to film there.

Once again Stone decided he had had enough of this *meshuga* project, and who should come back into the picture but Robert Stigwood's original choice. Alan Parker had made two musicals since *Fame (Pink Floyd: The Wall* and *The Commitments)* and was ready to have another go. His one stipulation was that he write his own script and not be saddled with Stone's,

saying it was a "matter of pride." He was faked out, though, when the Writers Guild decided that Stone would also be given credit. Interestingly, Stone had won an Oscar for writing the script for *Midnight Express*, the 1978 film which had marked Parker's first success as a director.

Hey There, Lonely Girl

By this point, Michelle Pfeiffer, having been attached at least tentatively to the film for a couple of years, concluded that she really didn't want to be saddled with a large-scale production that would take her away from her two small children. In February 1995, *Daily Variety* announced that the newest replacement names were Patricia Arquette, Robin Wright and, déjà vu, Madonna. Five days later, Robert Stigwood was quoted in the paper saying everyone could forget those first two and that as far as he was concerned the film wouldn't be made unless Madonna was in it. "Madonna's perfect for it," he insisted. "Just because she did a bad Letterman show, you don't not give her the role. That's Hollywood casting with who's hot at the moment." The Letterman reference was about a recent appearance in which she repeatedly said "fuck," and the host was not amused.

Meanwhile, Madonna hadn't been hanging back idly. As Kristin Scott Thomas had done with Anthony Minghella, so, too, the singer did with Alan Parker, writing in a letter that she just *had* to play the part, that no one else could possibly be as in synch with Eva—even though at this point Pfeiffer was still on the project. She would later declare, "I can honestly say that I did not write this letter of my own free will. It was as if some other force drove my hand across the page." To supplement her four-page epistle, Madonna went to psychics to have them use their influence on her behalf. The planets and stars aligned just right and Madonna was indeed going to be Eva Peron. Antonio Banderas was retained as Che, and Jonathan Pryce, best known to the general public for car commercials, was signed as Peron. Parker also managed to reunite Webber and Rice, who had been estranged for years, to write a new song for the movie, clearly with an eye on the Best Song Oscar. "It was the first time Andrew and Tim were in the same room for a while," said Parker. "But I was in the middle so it was easier."

Argentine President Carlos Menem had a partial change of heart, saying that Parker and company were free to film in Argentina, but not in the Peron home, where the character of Eva sings the show's best-known song, "Don't Cry for Me, Argentina." Menem also advised that the company should be prepared to face protests against the movie. The international press was filled with stories reporting that signs, posters and graffiti denouncing *Evita* and Madonna were everywhere throughout Buenos Aires. Eva Peron's former secretary announced, "We want Madonna dead or alive. If she does not leave, I will kill her. She is not going to offend any longer the name of our revered Evita." The reason the woman felt so strongly: "Evita is our mother, our flag, our motherland."

In the midst of the protests, Madonna chatted on the phone with Liz Smith, saying—with what the gossip columnist described as "just a trace of actressy melodrama"—"Is any movie worth dying for? I think not!" She also explained that the protests were confusing because they were coming from two polar viewpoints: "Some think of Eva Peron as a saint and are outraged at the idea of me playing her. Others think of her as a whore and are outraged we are even bothering to make a movie that will surely perpetuate her myth." And if it wasn't protesters giving Madonna a hard time, it was the paparazzi, ferocious in their single-minded determination to snap photos, or the fans camped outside her hotel, desperate for a glimpse. Sounding very Eva Peron herself, Madonna said she was pleased that the production would be employing thousands of local citizens because "judging from the number of people who stand outside my hotel all day long, not many people have jobs."

She also kept a diary, later published in *Vanity Fair*, in which she complained about being "stuck in an uncivilized country" and referred to her hotel room as "my prison cell." Revealing the soul of a poet, Madonna wrote in one daily entry: "As I descend further into this labyrinth called moviemaking I am stunned by the number of possibilities for feeling lonely and alienated." She even got invited to the

presidential estate and dutifully advised her diary, "I caught Menem looking at my bra strap, which was showing so slightly." Meeting the president paid off, though, for he eventually relented and granted her permission to sing "Don't Cry for Me, Argentina" on the Perons' balcony.

Madonna also constantly complained about the hardships she was enduring on the production itself—like being kept waiting for setups or swatting Argentine flies. "She was a pain in the ass," Alan Parker admitted, "but brilliantly prepared. Which is why you can't criticize her." The *New York Post*'s "Page Six" reported on the star's dedication, saying that she was eating lustily to make sure she retained Eva Peron's body type, and that even when she wasn't on the set, she kept wearing hazel contact lenses to match Eva's eye color, and remained in post–World War II hairstyles and couture. The *Post* added: "She's even supposed to have taken a vow of chastity for the length of the film shoot, although given Peron's own reputation, that seems to be going a bit far."

Madonna with Child

After filming was completed in Argentina, the production moved to Budapest for large-scale exterior shots because, not having been modernized like Buenos Aires, the Hungarian city looked more like the Argentine capital in the 1940s than the real thing.

Newsday was on the scene for the open audition call for extras in Budapest. Tunde Piret, who described herself as an aspiring actress, was enduring the long lines because she so wanted to be able to work with Madonna. "She is so brave to express herself. You don't see that a lot," was her estimation of the star. Another would-be extra, Maria Grob, concurred: "There's just something about Madonna that says I'm a true woman." Of course it wasn't just because of the leading lady that people were lining up for the casting call. Antonio Banderas "is the reason I'm here," gushed Lilla Simonyi. "He's so sexy. Not that I think I have a chance with him . . . but he told Melanie Griffith no sex until she loses ten kilos." Madonna would be putting on extra kilos, too. She was now a changed woman—she was pregnant. This meant rearranging her shooting schedule and adding inserts to her wardrobe to give her breathing space. The father was her personal trainer, Carlos Leon.

Director Parker came out with *The Making of Evita*, a coffee table book coinciding with the film's release, and revealed that, with eighty-five costume changes in the film, Madonna would be finding herself in the *Guinness Book of Records*, having easily bested Elizabeth Taylor's previous record of sixty in *Cleopatra*. the *Village Voice*'s Michael Musto was highly amused that in her preface for Parker's book, Madonna had written, " 'When I was asked to be in this movie . . .' Asked? Asked??? Excuuuuse me, but didn't the woman campaign for seven solid years, tracking down directors around the globe to demand the part and pushing everyone that stood in her way off a cliff with all the demureness of a dictator's wife?"

In its Fall Preview issue, *New York* advised, "Though the two-hour-plus musical doesn't open until December 25, brace yourself for October, when Madonna has her (well-timed) baby, re-emerges from her self-imposed exile on *The Rosie O'Donnell Show*, perhaps publishes a picture book called *Baby*, and genially grants many interviews in which she discusses her latest incarnation(s)." When she did appear on *Rosie O'Donnell* in December, Madonna said of her two-month-old daughter, "She's already making more sense than people in Hollywood."

Madonna was also on *Oprah*, where she fretted that having given birth, "Oh, God. Oh, God, it's going to be hard getting my waistline back." She also complained about eccentric basketball player Dennis Rodman's revealing details of their short-lived relationship in his bestselling book. "I don't have any respect for a man who kisses and tells." Which led the *Orange County Register*'s Anne Valldespino to comment, "Imagine, Madonna outraged at someone else's outfront sexuality." Madonna revealed to Oprah how she chose the name Lourdes for her daughter. The performer—whom Cardinal John J. O'Connor, the malicious head of the New York archdiocese, had tried to have excommunicated—said her baby was named after the town where Saint Bernadette (Jennifer Jones in the movie) saw the original Madonna. It's "the village of miracles," she explained.

An Elephant on Your Lap

Jack Garner of the Gannett News Service thought *Evita* was swell, and raved, "The film moves with relentless power, like a comet, exploding across the sky. The cameras and the editor's scissors must have been in constant movement; in that sense, *Evita* is the most spectacular musical video ever created. But to label *Evita* as an elaborate MTV spin-off is grossly unfair— this is a breathtaking and complex night at the movies. I wouldn't change a frame, a performance, or a note." Liz Smith told her readers, "Go and be challenged by *Evita*. Give yourself over to the all-singing concept. Forget any predisposition about Madonna. It's *not* your usual movie fare, but the rewards are great. It's stunning, impressive cinema."

But the way Megan Rosenfeld of *The Washington Post* saw it, "to say that *Evita*, the movie, is a stunning film is not to say that it is actually good. It stuns the way an avalanche would, or an elephant sitting on your lap. It is long, it is loud, it has enough extras to fill a small country, and it has more costumes than a New Orleans Mardi Gras. For 130 minutes it bludgeons you into submission; when it's over, you are numb." John Hartl of the *Seattle Post* referred to it as "this suffocatingly monotonous movie" and Peter Travers of *Rolling Stone* simply denigrated the film as "a $60 million Karaoke session."

The reviews were similarly divided on Madonna. Henry Sheehan of the *Orange County Register* declared that she "turns out to be a faultless Eva Peron, an iconographic screen presence who mirrors the scantily talented actress who became a political star." Richard Corliss concluded that "Madonna plays Evita with a poignant weariness, as if death has shrouded her from infancy. And dressed in sumptuous gowns or feeling life seep away, she has more than just a little bit of star quality." Among those laughing at Madonna's expense was Anthony Lane of *The New Yorker*, who felt that the title role "is ideal for Madonna, of course, because it seldom requires her to deliver her lines in normal human speech, which was never her forte." And Duane Byrge of the *Hollywood Reporter* gibed, "Madonna exudes a grim and relentless ambition but never ignites any real sparks. After a while, as we witness her methodical rise to power, the character becomes about as exciting and charismatic as Bob Dole."

As the critics were split, so too was the message from moviegoers ambiguous. The film was sold out through its initial exclusive New York and L.A. engagements, and when it went wider, *Evita* came in second to *The Relic*, a horror film which was in three times as many theaters. But the good news was fleeting. *Evita*'s ultimate $49 million domestic gross was $10 million short of its production costs alone. That the film would ultimately have limited appeal might have been gleaned from a *New York Post* piece that ran shortly before the film's opening. People on the street were asked if they knew who Eva Peron was. Most had no idea, but one woman from Brooklyn was sure of the answer: "That's Madonna's real name, right?"

Oh, You Nasty Man

When they were college roommates, Scott Alexander and Larry Karaszewski, who would go on to write the first two *Problem Child* pictures and *Ed Wood*, had decided that a biography of Larry Flynt would be a great idea for a movie. As the publisher of *Hustler*, Flynt went further with newsstand pornography than anyone ever had, bringing a new level of raunchiness and violence and an extremely infantile sense of humor to girlie magazines. The writers said they had become fans of Flynt when he campaigned for the presidency in 1984. A decade later, they were shocked when, after expecting the worst with their pitch meeting, "The studio people were laughing and jumping up and down," according to Karaszewski. "They said stuff like 'It's Capra with porn. Exactly what we want!' It turned out to be the best meeting we ever had." Oliver Stone came across the duo's three-page treatment for a Flynt biopic and was immediately intrigued. "I briefly considered directing it," Stone recalled, "but people told me to back off that kind of material. I was sort of being pressured not to do scumbags anymore." He figured that serving as producer was backing off far enough.

Stone thought that one particular director with a proven affinity for outsiders and rebels—"people whose behavior was not acceptable by normal standards"—would be the perfect fit for the material. But Milos Forman said that when he received the script and saw Larry Flynt's name, "the only association in my mind was pornography, sleaze and exploitation. So I put it down." Forman, who hadn't made a film since 1989's *Valmont*, finally got a call from his agent, who said, "You should read it as a courtesy to Oliver Stone." This was the first Forman knew about Stone's involvement with the project, so Forman read the script "out of courtesy" and loved it. Then, after Larry Flynt had a chance to read the script, Forman met with him and acknowledged that it contained "very, very embarrassing or unflattering things about you. You don't mind, I hope." To which, Flynt replied, "Of course, I do mind. I do mind very much. But they are true, so what can I do?"

Milos Forman's ultimate take on Larry Flynt was that "his taste is full of shit, but the man is not." The Czech-born director said, "I've lived long enough in totalitarian regimes, in a society where the censorship was rampant and the freedom of the press was practically abolished, that I know what kind of a devastating effect that has, how it chokes creativity in all fields." Forman elaborated that he had grown up first among Nazis and then Communists, and "I think it's significant that both these regimes started with crusades against those they classified as perverts: pornographers, homosexuals, Jews and blacks."

Bill Murray was everyone's first choice to play the pornographer, but Forman said Murray never returned phone calls. Others considered were Tom Arnold, Jim Carrey, even Tom Hanks, before Stone hit upon the idea of hiring Woody Harrelson. The two of them had already been in the trenches together with *Natural Born Killers*, but Harrelson wasn't immediately sold on the project. "I was initially attracted to working with Milos Forman, but I wasn't too jazzed up about the prospect of doing a movie about Larry Flynt . . . even though a good percentage of my early sexual experiences resulted from Larry's indirect help," admitted Harrelson. "I have to say I thought of him as a sleazebag. I didn't think there was anything worthwhile about him." But the actor did note that he and the magazine publisher had a certain kinship: "Both of us were poor white trash who somehow got a leg up in the world." And over time, Harrelson came to have a grudging admiration for the publisher. "With Larry," he stated, "you may not like the fact that he's a pornographer and you may not respect some of his outrageous antics, but you have to respect his honesty. He says what he thinks, even when it's crazy." Moreover, Harrelson pointed out to *U.S. News & World Report* that Bob Dole had called for boycotts of two of his last three movies (*Natural Born Killers* and *Money Train*) but, "Nobody is just all black or all white, and probably if I sat down with Bob Dole, I'd like the guy."

This was not, however, simply going to be a re-creation of the pornographer's colorful life, which included a stint as a bootlegger, drug addiction, getting shot by a white supremacist and becoming permanently paralyzed, showing up in a courtroom wearing an American flag as a diaper, being sentenced to twenty-five years in prison for obscenity, going to the U.S. Supreme Court in a landmark constitutional law case and becoming—briefly—a born-again Christian. Instead, his experiences would serve as a launching pad for an ode to the First Amendment. The movie's theme was Flynt's own declaration that "If the First Amendment will protect a scumbag like me, then it will protect all of you." Strangely, the case that brought Larry Flynt before the United States Supreme Court was not even obscenity-related. It was a suit brought by the Reverend Jerry Falwell for "emotional distress" because of a parody ad in *Hustler* which joshed that the fundamentalist preacher lost his virginity to his own mother in an outhouse.

Spreading Love

Courtney Love was cast as Althea, Flynt's bisexual fourth wife who eventually died of AIDS. Love, the leader of the rock band Hole and the widow of Nirvana's Kurt Cobain, had become a regular in the tabloids herself, thanks to Cobain's suicide, her former drug use and her unconventional child-rearing techniques. In addition to music videos, her acting experience consisted of cameo appearances in *Basquiat* and *Feeling Minnesota*. Forman admitted he had no idea who Love was when she showed up to audition for the role, "but I knew from the first moment I was in the presence of a really fascinating personality." The studio had reservations because of her notoriety and because she wasn't an actress per se, and *Variety* said, "If Love is chosen, some feel it might be difficult to insure the widow of Kurt Cobain, who is known to party hearty." Out of several dozen actresses auditioned, Forman narrowed things down to three choices: Love, Georgina Cates and Rachel Griffiths. He showed the three actresses' audition tapes to some friends, including Vaclav Havel, the novelist turned President of the Czech Republic. Forman said, "Havel and his wife were the only ones who were crazy about Courtney, so I was encouraged by that." And the director put up some of the money for Love's insurance in the picture.

Oliver Stone was pleased to report that during filming, Love was "a highly responsible, maybe eccentric, but responsible person. She would get it done." And CNN's Sherri Sylvester mused, "Courtney Love is a character too strange for fiction, which probably makes her ideal for the role of porn-peddler Larry Flynt's wife." The film was a learning experience for Love, who acknowledged to *USA Today* that "Freedom of speech stuff for Gen X people like myself is so boring. We forget how important it is. I'm just a spoiled West Coast little American rock star who screams and cusses and kicks stuff, and I have nobody trying to stop me. I've had tabloid articles about my life, but that's not anything close to what could happen if I'd been expressing myself as an artist in a totalitarian regime."

Besides Love, an oddball cast was sprinkled throughout the film. Flynt himself played a cantankerous anti-Flynt Cincinnati judge. ("It was a lot of fun," said Flynt. "I know how the old bastard acted in the courtroom.") Woody Harrelson's brother Brett made his film debut as Larry Flynt's brother Jimmy, and NYU Law School professor and former ACLU legal director Burt Neuborne was incongruously cast as Jerry Falwell's attorney. Also present as President Jimmy Carter's faith-healer sister was Donna Hanover, wife of the disagreeably despotic mayor of New York City, Rudolph Giuliani, and as an anti-Flynt prosecutor, former Clinton political operative James Carville. Carville had his own spin of the movie: "Think about it. Flynt's got a sixth-grade education. Becomes a millionaire. Gets mixed up with Falwell and Keating. Goes through the Supreme Court stuff. Almost gets assassinated. When you put it together, it's a *Forrest Gump* kind of thing."

"If Larry gets glamorized in the process, bummer," Courtney Love said sarcastically, and then, turning serious, said, "Larry has probably done some wicked things. But Larry has spent more money than he'll ever receive to fight for freedom of speech." Flynt claimed to cringe from the title of folk hero. "I have trouble with that hero label. To me, a hero is a result of the last act committed by a coward. If you lifted some of the boys' faces out of the mud in Vietnam and asked them if they wanted to do it over, I think their answer would probably be the same as mine. I wouldn't have given up my legs for anyone or anything, including the First Amendment. So I think that disqualifies me for the hero category." Besides, as he told the *New York Daily News*, "All I wanted to do was make money and have fun."

Risqué Business

In a nice bit of irony, the original ad for the film was censored by the Motion Picture Association of America. The MPAA felt that having Woody Harrelson crucified on a woman's pelvis and wearing an American flag as a loincloth was not in the best interests of the movie industry. An exasperated Milos Forman said, "I don't feel at all that the original artwork was obscene. I thought it was tasty and funny." The director explained that "what MPAA President Jack Valenti basically said to me is, 'I will have to protect more important freedoms for us through self-censorship so that we don't provoke very conservative forces.' I respect it, but I don't like it." The new ad showed a close-up of Woody Harrelson's face, with an American flag plastered over his mouth. Sid Ganis, who had been Columbia Pictures-TriStar's president of worldwide marketing when the advertising decisions were being made, put on his best face to say: "Though this campaign wasn't our first choice, it really does work. It talks to the movie. . . . We have to make sure not to create in the minds of the audience that this is a

sex film. It's better than the risqué one." The paradox wasn't lost upon Forman that when *The People vs. Larry Flynt* went into international release over the next few months, "Only the few countries where censorship is rampant will reject the original art."

The People vs. Larry Flynt was the closing night entry of the New York Film Festival. Frank Rich began a *New York Times* column about the movie by "calling Bob Dole, William Bennett, Joseph Lieberman, Al and Tipper Gore and foes of depraved pop culture everywhere: The next Hollywood exhibit awaiting your moral outrage is being unveiled." Rich then reflected: "After watching *The People vs. Larry Flynt*, which truly offers something to offend everyone, our cultural guardians may wish they had not wasted so much firepower on *Natural Born Killers*, *Striptease* and *Mighty Morphin Power Rangers*." Rich himself felt the movie "deserves a huge adult audience, because it is the most timely and patriotic movie of the year . . . an eloquent antidote to anyone who would jawbone the First Amendment to clean up the grotesque excesses of our culture." One of *Hustler*'s bestselling issues contained photos of Jacqueline Onassis in the nude. That didn't stop John F. Kennedy Jr.'s magazine *George* from running an admiring article in which author Barry Hannah sighed, "Flynt and I are the same age, and when you see him you feel, in the fight for freedom, a relative coward."

David Ansen noted that Flynt was "the least likely man to be the hero of a big-budget Christmas movie . . . . Yet here he is, wonderfully incarnated by Woody Harrelson, as the title character of *The People vs. Larry Flynt*, a brave, spectacularly entertaining— and unexpectedly stirring—account of Flynt's life that asks us to regard the publisher of *Hustler* magazine as an invaluable champion of our First Amendment freedoms." Bruce Williamson of *Playboy*, which seemed awfully tame and mainstream once *Hustler* arrived on the scene, called *The People vs. Larry Flynt* "an ultrapop masterpiece" and "the most scintillating and outrageous message movie of the decade." Rita Kempley of *The Washington Post* loved how Woody Harrelson "brings the zeal of an evangelist to his rollicking take on Flynt, who ironically becomes a pulpit pounder in promoting his own beliefs. More importantly, though,

Harrelson allows the character tenderness and love, pathos and loss, and dignity after shame." Rex Reed praised the film, even though maybe he didn't quite get it, since he felt it had "a detestable subject (in America you can get away with anything as long as you hide behind the First Amendment)." He also said, "Watching Ms. Love writhe around in a moaning ecstasy of heroin, you know it's the kind of stuff that wins awards, but I'm wondering, considering her own well-publicized addictions, if it's not a case of what Irving Berlin called, 'doin' what comes natcherly.' " But Janet Maslin felt, "When Althea goes to seed, she begins looking more and more like Courtney Love, but Ms. Love's performance is far too good to confuse one well-tended image with the other."

Where's My Scumbag?

Terrence Rafferty of *The New Yorker* had a bone to pick with *The People vs. Larry Flynt*. He complained that "the picture turns sentimental and smugly high-minded in its second half. . . . The filmmakers, having gone to great lengths to humanize these disreputable characters, make the mistake of trying to canonize them—Larry as a fearless point man for First Amendment freedoms, Althea as a sexually unconventional but fiercely devoted wife. Since the most attractive quality of both characters is the outrageous bluntness of their self-interest, the appearance of more conventional virtues is disappointing (and unconvincing)." Similarly, in the *Village Voice*, Laura Kipnis regretted that the movie "sanitized Flynt's career into one long noble crusade for the First Amendment, while erasing from the picture the very thing that made *Hustler* so reviled and persecuted—its scurrilous antiestablishment politics. Masterfully made, this movie nevertheless reeks of class condescension, taming Flynt's cantankerous, contrarian life into the most conventional story arc possible."

While Rafferty and Kipnis thought *The People vs. Larry Flynt* suffered aesthetically because of what they saw as its idealization of Flynt and his magazine, other voices angrily rose to declare that this candy coating had more serious ramifications. First up was *The New Republic*, in which Hanna Rosin expressed the view

that Hollywood had no business making a film about the publisher of *Hustler* in the first place. She was worked up because "in the movie, *Hustler* is almost accidentally in the nudie business," and then she made the judgment call that in reality the magazine contains a "relentless depiction of sex as beastly and of sexual creatures as beasts. Sex in *Playboy* is a barefoot romp in the park. Sex in *Hustler* is a freak show. The magazine's pictorials are violent, depressing and perverse." Rosin complained that Flynt "went to court to protect his bank account. In doing so, he accidentally protected the right of free speech. That's not particularly brave or heroic. The real protectors of American rights are rather boring. They're a few dour justices and the Constitution that guides them. But that wouldn't make much of a movie."

Gloria Steinem was next, and much more widely read, with a *New York Times* op-ed piece entitled "Hollywood Cleans Up *Hustler*." "Larry Flynt the Movie is even more cynical than Larry Flynt the Man," seethed the iconic feminist leader. "*The People vs. Larry Flynt* claims that the creator of *Hustler* magazine is a champion of the First Amendment, deserving our respect. That isn't true. . . . Let's be clear: A pornographer is not a hero, no more than a publisher of Ku Klux Klan books or a Nazi on the Internet, no matter what constitutional protection he secures. In fact, the Nazis who marched in Skokie, Ill., and the Klansman who advocated violence in Ohio achieved more substantive First Amendment victories than did Mr. Flynt. Yet no Hollywood movie would glamorize a Klansman or a Nazi as a champion of free speech, much less describe him in studio press releases as 'the era's last crusader,' which is how Columbia Pictures describes Mr. Flynt." In particular, Steinem, who had been subjected to attacks in *Hustler* and to being "depicted as the main character in a photo story that ended in my sexual mutilation," complained that the film omitted "the magazine's images of women being beaten, tortured and raped, women subject to degradations from bestiality to sexual slavery."

Milos Forman immediately fired back a letter to the *Times*, saying "I am puzzled and disappointed by Gloria Steinem's misrepresentations." He argued that Steinem "blurs or erases the clear distinctions between the goals, philosophy and themes of my movie and those of *Hustler* magazine." Forman surmised that Steinem had a personal vendetta against Flynt, and felt it was "regrettable that she uses my work as a weapon of retaliation." He concluded by stating that "the Supreme Court, not Larry Flynt, is the hero of my movie." Oliver Stone shrugged off Steinem's accusations by saying, "Larry is not into violence against women. He puts them in a meat grinder as a *joke*. Doesn't she have a sense of humor?" But at least one of the people involved in the film was a little uneasy. Courtney Love admitted, "I'm a feminist, so I would agree with Steinem on a lot of levels."

Forman had an ally in *Newsday*'s John Anderson, who scoffed at Steinem's "rusty-razored attack" for two reasons: "One: *Flynt* is a movie. A Hollywood movie. If one equates historical accuracy with cinematic quality, one can toss out everything from *Birth of a Nation* to *Braveheart*. Two: *Flynt* is a movie about ideas and a movie that without following certain conventions wouldn't have been produced at all. If you ask whether factual inaccuracies outweigh the importance of a crowd-pleasing film about the First Amendment, I have to say no."

New York Times columnist Bob Herbert echoed Steinem and argued that at the core of the magazine was "an extreme and unrelentingly violent hatred of women, a hatred every bit as fanatical as the Klan's hatred of blacks and the Nazis' hatred of Jews." Herbert said Milos Forman told him, "I could have splashed the screen with images from *Hustler* that would make people *scream* in disgust and throw eggs at the screen." Well, he should have done so, said the columnist, so the film "could then have chosen to make the case that even such extreme images—expressions of such fanatical hatred—deserve constitutional protection."

Coming from the right, *The American Spectator*'s James Bowman drew a similar conclusion to the liberal Herbert. After smirking that "Larry Flynt is the perfect hero for Hollywood: a man who manages to be utterly self-righteous about being utterly self-indulgent," Bowman complained that "All the way through the argument is basically this: that Larry Flynt is a scumbag (he proudly claims the title himself), but if free speech means anything it means the right of scumbags to speak too. It is an admirable point of view which the film then goes on to obscure by making the man only a theoretical scumbag. We never see him actually being one." *Time*'s Bruce Handy wrote: "Like journalists who pore over dirty magazines in order to debunk them, *The People vs. Larry Flynt* wants to have it both ways. A relevant point of comparison is with *A Clockwork Orange*, a far riskier and more complicated film that in arguing for the sanctity of free will dared to create a charismatic protagonist whose exercise of that free will was pointedly horrific. *Larry Flynt* has the nerve to argue for the sanctity of free speech but—for lack of a better word—censors its excesses." For Bill O'Reilly of Fox's *O'Reilly Report*, the problem was that a "loathsome vulgarian" like Flynt was embodied by the guy who played Woody on *Cheers* and "every night you see him on reruns and he's a pleasant, cute, bubbly guy." Therefore, Woody Harrelson "makes Larry Flynt more sympathetic than he is."

For Your Non-Consideration

Receiving pointed attacks from political columnists and personalities was not pleasant, but some goings-on in Hollywood had far more sinister consequences for *The People vs. Larry Flynt*. What should appear in *Daily Variety* under the traditional "For Your Consideration" heading but a full-page reprint of the Steinem article. The newspaper later said the ad was placed by a Washington organization called Public Citizen; the head of the organization admitted that Public Citizen had indeed arranged for the ad to run but did not pay for it. Her line was "We were approached by people from Hollywood who were afraid of retribution if they put their names on it." The National Organization for Woman denied chipping in for the ad; the president of its New York chapter said NOW wasn't interested in censoring the film, just making sure it wasn't honored with Academy Awards. Steinem played coy, saying that the money for reprinting it came from some women in the film industry who remained anonymous because "they were concerned about their ability to get jobs" and feared "retribution" from Milos Forman and Oliver Stone. As far as anyone could remember, this was the first ad taken out in the trade papers to encourage Academy members *not* to vote for a specific film. It recalled the atmosphere of the 1950s, when voting for Communists was strongly discouraged. The American Civil Liberties Union ran its own trade paper ad to counter Public Citizen's. This one praised Forman for being a "First Amendment advocate and an artist of unsurpassed creativity, ability and courage."

Columbia also took action. In full-page newspaper ads, the studio announced "Some people have attacked the film *The People vs. Larry Flynt*. They call it dishonest and guilty of whitewashing the ugly truth about Larry Flynt and *Hustler* magazine." The studio then requested "you to read the following excerpts from our country's most distinguished journalists and publications. YOU DECIDE." Rex Reed was one of the "distinguished journalists" quoted, as was the *Chicago Tribune*'s Mike Royko, who referred dismissively to "the ladies at NOW." Joanna Connor of the *Cleveland Plain Dealer* stated that "The real hero of the movie is America and the extraordinary (and often difficult) freedoms its citizens enjoy, but do not always fully appreciate. Thanks to Forman and a superb script, the movie prods you to appreciate and truly enjoy them—and it accomplishes that not by waving the flag, but by wrapping it around a pornographer's bottom."

Meanwhile, Sherlee Lantz, an old friend of the director, said, "Milos is in deep shock, depression and disillusionment."

I'm Larry, He's Jerry

Making it a little more difficult for the filmmakers to separate themselves from Larry Flynt the man, as opposed to Larry Flynt the symbol of First Amendment freedoms, was the fact that the publisher was making the publicity rounds himself, plugging his newly released autobiography. He had his own take on the controversy, telling *Entertainment Weekly*, "Gloria Steinem is an ancient, worn-out old relic whose only claim to fame is urging some ugly women to march."

Louis Menand, in *The New York Review of Books*—which, rather astonishingly, Flynt published at

one point—wrote: "Falwell and Flynt were each other's devils, but they were also each other's raison d'être." And the two adversaries had a reunion on *Larry King Live* on what the host declared to be a "rather historic night." The Reverend Falwell hadn't seen *The People vs. Larry Flynt*, as he said he'd been boycotting movies for forty-five years (with the exception of Clint Eastwood's 1985 Western *Pale Rider*, because Eastwood told him the title character was a Christ symbol). Falwell was all smiles and backslapping joviality, as he tried to make nice with the pornographer. The minister insisted that "I do love him and I do pray for him," and maintained that he never had any ill feelings against the publishing magnate. Flynt wouldn't get suckered in by such pleasantries, however, and he said, "I've always felt Jerry's a hypocrite, and I still feel that way. And I think some of the rhetoric that he spews out has caused more harm than any other ideas since the beginning of time."

Referring to Flynt's short-lived fling with a born-again lifestyle, Falwell said, "I'm a Christian. My interest is that the next time around, Larry, when he accepts Christ, he'll really mean it, and go on and get rid of that magazine and go for God." It wasn't likely, because Flynt said, "I have a message for those born-agains. If they just take a little lithium, they'd be fine."

Before the movie expanded to a wide release, Andy Seiler of *USA Today* reported, "Critics side with Forman, admiring the film's sweep, satire and politics, though it remains to be seen if mainstream Americans will buy into a movie about such an unsavory character." Eventually, despite all the press given to the film, the paper ran a headline: "Critics Love *Flynt* but the Heartland Turns Cold Shoulder." Just as last Christmas's most controversial release, *Nixon,* did little at the box office, now the paper was reporting that although it "hustled up a huge response from big-city moviegoers when it opened, *Flynt* has bombed everywhere else." *USA Today* also quoted Drew Devlin, from *Independent Marketing Edge*, a newsletter for independent theater owners, who said, "A lot of people don't realize that there's quite a statement in it about freedom of the press. But when they hear 'Larry Flynt, *Hustler* magazine,' they want nothing to do with it. They were fed up with Larry Flynt ten years ago and couldn't care less about him today." One commentator felt Flynt was a positive role model. *Entertainment Weekly*'s Ty Burr said, "Woody Harrelson playing a vibrant man who's in a wheelchair is something that disabled people would like to see."

Count Him Out?

The People vs. Larry Flynt wasn't the only potential Oscar nominee that was enduring scrutiny for fabrications and omissions. Count Laszlo de Almasy, the dreamily passionate character Ralph Fiennes portrayed in *The English Patient*—who Michael Ondaatje always acknowledged was based on a real person—was in actuality a great admirer of Hitler. Karen de Witt of the *New York Times* snitched that in the movie Almasy was "a romantic desert explorer spying for the Germans during World War II only so he can be reunited with his beloved, the wife of another man. The real Hungarian count, a homosexual, was an opportunist who spied for whomever suited him." Andrew Sarris heard the backlash against *The English Patient* because of the count's real-life escapades, and scoffed that this reaction was "about as cogent as an imagined complaint that Heathcliff in *Wuthering Heights* was a bad landlord to his tenants." Some viewers thought that even the movie's fictionalized version was no prize package. *The New Yorker*'s Hendrik Hertzberg observed that *The English Patient*'s "hero turns British military secrets over to the Nazis in exchange for an airplane with which to rescue his mistress. (This stands the moral world of, say, *Casablanca* on its head: it's as if the Ralph Fiennes character were saying, 'I guess the outcome of the war against Hitler doesn't amount to a hill of beans in this crazy world compared to the problems of two little people.')"

Sharing the Wealth

The critical consensus was that Hollywood had little to be proud of in 1996, but that American independents and filmmakers from other countries more than picked up the slack. The *Hollywood Reporter* surveyed the Ten Best Lists of twenty-six newspaper and magazine reviewers, and found them dominated by three movies that had played the Cannes Film Festival: *Secrets & Lies*, *Fargo* and *Breaking the Waves*. The latter was Lars von Trier's three-hour English-language, Dutch-French coproduction about a young Scottish bride who achieves spiritual redemption by becoming the village slut; Dave Kehr of the *New York Daily News* described the movie—which was filmed entirely with a handheld camera—as a fusion of Carl Theodor Dreyer and Frank Borzage.

None of these three was chosen as Best Picture in the year's first set of prizes, the National Board of Review awards. The Board instead picked *Shine*. Best Director was Joel Coen for *Fargo*, and his wife, Frances McDormand, was named Best Actress. The Best Supporting Actor award went to Edward Norton, generally considered 1996's major discovery; the 27-year-old was cited for all three of his performances: as a murder suspect in the mystery potboiler *Primal Fear*; a sweet young suitor in Woody Allen's musical *Everyone Says I Love You*; and Flynt's beleaguered lawyer in *The People vs. Larry Flynt*. The National Board had two big surprises. One was the choice of Tom Cruise as Best Actor for *Jerry Maguire*, the other awarding Best Supporting Actress to Kristin Scott Thomas *and* Juliette Binoche for *The English Patient*. There had already been considerable speculation about which of the actresses would be considered a lead, and which supporting for Oscar purposes, so the Board did nothing to clarify the situation. For that matter, Frances McDormand's screen time in *Fargo* was much less than that of most lead actresses. Binoche said that she and Thomas had seen *The English Patient* together four or five times, and every time they'd embrace and say to each other, "You were better."

The next group up, the New York Film Critics, didn't agree with the National Board in a single category. This body named *Fargo* Best Picture, although the film's star, Frances McDormand, came up empty. The New Yorkers' Best Actress choice was, instead, Emily Watson in *Breaking the Waves*, the 29-year-old British stage actress's film debut. *Breaking the Waves* also won Best Director for Lars von Trier. Best Actor was Geoffrey Rush in *Shine*, even though calling Rush a lead actor might be considered a bit of a stretch—as one of three actors playing David Helfgott, he was only on screen for about half an hour. Supporting Actor went to Harry Belafonte, who played a crime boss in *Kansas City*, Robert Altman's re-creation of the 1930s jazz milieu of his hometown. Courtney Love was named Best Supporting Actress for *The People vs. Larry Flynt*; as with Binoche and Thomas, no one was quite sure if Academy members would consider her a lead or a supporting player. Dave Kehr noted that *Fargo* "is a dicey, difficult film by Hollywood standards, though this will greatly improve its Oscar chances." He also observed that "the well-reviewed *The English Patient* proved surprisingly weak, winning no awards. *The English Patient*, though, will almost certainly be appreciated by the Academy, whose members have a well-established weakness for sweeping historical melodrama."

The big winner with the Los Angeles Film Critics Association was *Secret & Lies*, which received Best Picture, Best Actress for Brenda Blethyn and Best Director for Mike Leigh. Geoffrey Rush was named Best Actor, with Edward Norton the Angelenos' pick as Supporting Actor. Best Supporting Actress was Barbara Hershey as the manipulative Madame Merle in *The Portrait of a Lady*, Jane Campion's take on Henry James which turned out to be a little too out there for most people. *New York Post* gossip columnist Cindy Adams dubbed it "the downest, dullest, dourest, darkest movie in captivity," and Richard Corliss said, "You cannot underestimate the degree to which people hate *Portrait of a Lady* . . . people are scratching the screen"; things did not bode well for Nicole Kidman's Oscar chances.

Finally, members of the National Society of Film Critics found *Breaking the Waves* the 1996 release most to its liking. The film won awards as Best Picture, Best Director and Best Actress. Barbara Hershey was again named Best Supporting Actress, but the male acting winners hadn't previously shown up this awards season. Supporting Actor was split between one of Hershey's costars, Martin Donovan, who played a sweet-natured consumptive in *Portrait*, and Tony Shaloub as a volatile Italian chef in *Big Night*. Then there was Best Actor. The National Society went as far away from the flamboyant austerity of *Breaking the Waves* as imaginable. The winner was Eddie Murphy for *The Nutty*

Professor, a cornucopia of bathroom humor in which flatulence played a major role and Murphy played seven others, all of whom, despite extensive makeup, seemed like Eddie Murphy doing shtick.

Uninvited Guests

With the four main critics groups giving Best Picture honors to four different movies, it was no wonder that *USA Today*'s Andy Seiler said, "The Oscar crystal ball is mighty cloudy." But one thing seemed clear: what the Hollywood studios had come up with in 1996 wasn't going to cut it with Academy voters any more than it had with critics. In *Variety*'s last issue of the year, the front-page headline was "INDIES SPIKING OSCAR'S PUNCH: Studios fear losing party to crashers." The accompanying article stated: "Even the most optimistic executives admit that the majors have delivered perhaps the weakest lineup of Oscar prospects since the Awards began in 1927." The article also quoted an unnamed studio executive: "This doesn't look much like the Oscars; it looks like the Independent Spirit Awards. The majors are going to have to turn up the heat for their best movies, or Hollywood won't have any reason to attend this year's event."

Although it was new to the Oscar game, October Films was operating as if it were run by a Weinstein. The company's *Secrets & Lies* had the most ads touting it, and the company also went all out for *Breaking the Waves*. In fact, like the critics' Ten Best lists, trade paper ads were dominated by the independent companies, including Fine Line for *Shine*; New Line for *In Love and War*, a Richard Attenborough dud in which Chris O'Donnell was improbably cast as young Ernest Hemingway; Goldwyn's *I Shot Andy Warhol* (for Lili Taylor's performance); Castle Rock for *Lone Star*, John Sayles's drama about Texas cops, buried history and racism, Kenneth Branagh's four-hour version of *Hamlet* and Rob Reiner's White Man's Burden civil rights drama, *Ghosts of Mississippi*. And, of course, Miramax spent freely on ads, mostly for *The English Patient* but also giving attention to *Sling Blade*, *Marvin's Room*, *Emma*, *Trainspotting*, *Everyone Says I Love You*, *Citizen Ruth* and a handful of others.

At the New York Film Critics awards dinner, the

group's chair, Bob Campbell, joked that "Fine Line has finally figured out how to get a hit. Let's face it. If Miramax had released *Shine*, the whole country would be walking around naked under their raincoats." Gramercy Pictures came up with a unique promotional item for *Fargo*: a snow globe containing a miniature re-creation of the scene in which Frances McDormand throws up after finding a dead body next to an overturned car. The company had originally considered using the woodchipper sequence but decided "it was a little too much." But the goofiest promo came as part of the ads for the unsuccessful science fiction spoof *Mars Attacks!*, requesting that voters consider Lisa Marie as Best Supporting Actress. Playing a Martian, she didn't have a single line in the film—but she was the girlfriend of director Tim Burton.

Women's World

The year 1995 had been noteworthy for its surfeit of strong women's roles, but things this year were even more heartening. In fact Molly Haskell, author of the seminal book *From Reverence to Rape*, declared, "It's definitely been the best year for women in twenty years." The situation even led *Entertainment Weekly* to wonder, "How come nobody writes good parts for men anymore?" This portended a real scramble for Best Actress Oscar nominations. There were, first off, the women honored by the critics' groups—Brenda Blethyn, Frances McDormand and Emily Watson, all of whom had competed against each other at Cannes, where Blethyn had emerged victorious. Miramax decided that the flashback scenes were the emotional core of *The English Patient* so—screen time be damned—Kristin Scott Thomas would be pushed for Lead Actress, Juliette Binoche Supporting; the overall acclaim for the film bode well for both their chances at nominations.

The comeback story of the year belonged to Debbie Reynolds, who had the title role in *Mother*, the Albert Brooks comedy which won the Best Screenplay award from the New York Film Critics and the National Society. In her first starring role in twenty-five years, the one-time America's sweetheart played a no-nonsense, set-in-her-ways woman who has to contend with her grown-up son's moving back in with her; Andrew Sarris rhapsodized that "Debbie Reynolds gives the performance of the year, of a lifetime, in *Mother*." Debbie looked as if she was having a great old time being back in the spotlight. When she appeared on *Good Morning America*, she joked that "I lived so long I came back in style" and that she was "older than panty hose." She also climbed onto host Charles Gibson's lap because "Anything goes after 64!" Roger Ebert called Reynolds a shoo-in for a Best Actress nomination, while in *Entertainment Weekly*, Gregg Kilday predicted, "Debbie Reynolds should have no trouble being embraced for her performance as the slyly controlling mom in *Mother*. She not only got swell reviews but can count on support from two strong voting blocs: her own aging contemporaries, and pals of her hip daughter, Carrie Fisher."

Debbie Reynolds had hit records in the 1950s. Also vying for a Best Actress slot were two women who had had hit records in the 1990s. With the early box-office returns for *Evita* looking good, Madonna's name continued to be mentioned in connection with a nomination—provided the acting branch could be convinced that lip-synching *does* constitute acting. She didn't do her cause any good, though, when she was asked at a press conference for the London premiere of *Evita* if she expected to receive an Oscar nomination, and whether it would be a big deal for her. With the presumptuousness that came with being a star in the music world for over a decade, Madonna replied "Yes and yes." Since the New York Critics selected Courtney Love as Best *Supporting* Actress, that was the category in which Columbia had been planning to ask for your consideration. But Milos Forman insisted that she was a colead in the film, and so Oscar ads for *The People vs. Larry Flynt* followed suit. *U.S. News & World Report* asked Love how she felt about the prospect of competing against Madonna and Debbie Reynolds for the Oscar. "Oh, wow, that's so cool," she replied, caught herself, and said "I'm not competing with anyone. That's retarded."

Others in the mix included the two stars of *Marvin's Room*. This adaptation of Scott McPherson's play was a character study about death and families, starring Diane Keaton as a terminally ill woman and

Meryl Streep as her tough sister. *Variety*'s Emanuel Levy wrote: "Truly collaborating rather than competing (as could be expected), Keaton and Streep render brilliant performances. Part of the joy derives from watching how the two thesps, who have never worked together before, use different techniques that ultimately complement each other. Streep works at her role from the outside in, mastering the details of voice, movement, facial expression. Keaton, in contrast, is an instinctive actress who makes her lines sound more spontaneous." Streep was signed for the film first, and Harvey Weinstein had refused to consider Keaton even though every day for a month she sent him cartons of cigarettes and cases of Diet Coke as a way of stating her case. Streep knew of Keaton's interest and told Weinstein that no Diane equals no Meryl. When Keaton later heard about Streep's ultimatum, her reaction was: "I can't believe she did that. Isn't it incredible? But I don't know why. I mean why? I'm thrilled to hear it; it's such a great thing to say. I mean, God. From Meryl Streep!" When the Golden Globe nominations came out, Streep had made the cut, but Keaton had not.

In early January, *Variety* took a look at the bounty of possibilities in the Actress race in an article entitled "Year of the Woman (for real)." Among the other potential nominees mentioned were Laura Dern in *Citizen Ruth*, Gwyneth Paltrow in *Emma* (a performance that had received a good deal of attention in the summer, but seemed to have faded from memory in the winter), Winona Ryder in *The Crucible*, and Shirley MacLaine, reprising her Oscar-winning role from *Terms of Endearment* in *The Evening Star*, although the film was proving to be both a critical and a commercial disappointment.

Golden Rendezvous

Madonna received the validation she had been seeking—well, she at least received the Best Actress (Musical or Comedy) from the Hollywood Foreign Press. In doing so, she beat the likes of Frances McDormand and Debbie Reynolds. The Foreign Press also gave her vehicle a major boost in the Oscar race by declaring *Evita* the Best Musical or Comedy of 1996, over *Fargo* and *Jerry Maguire*. The *Cinemania* Web site advised, however, that "As for Madonna and *Evita*, the Academy is less likely to be as enthralled as the Hollywood Foreign Press. Madonna, like last year's winner Sharon Stone, has long courted the HFPA, but she is not so well thought of in the movie industry itself." Backstage, Madonna declared that Frances McDormand should have won.

Brenda Blethyn received the Best Actress (Drama) Globe and Tom Cruise won for Best Actor (Musical or Comedy). His Drama counterpart was *Shine*'s Geoffrey Rush, and the previously unknown-in-America actor was accorded a standing ovation. Rush allowed as to how he was "very proud to be part of a film that has taken such a vulnerable, peculiar, unfamiliar and very human character from the margins of our experiences and placed him so deservedly at the heart of the narrative." He concluded by thanking "my newfound friends at CAA." Rush announced in the press room that this was the first time in his life he had ever worn a tuxedo.

Also receiving a standing ovation was Supporting Actress winner, Lauren Bacall, who played Barbra Streisand's tart-tongued mother in the romantic comedy, *The Mirror Has Two Faces*. Bacall's performance was about the only thing critics had liked in Streisand's latest directorial effort. Jack Mathews said it was "otherwise wretched"; Todd McCarthy called the film "all but impossible to watch with a straight face" and found that "the narcissism on display is astonishing to behold." And about Bacall, *Newsweek* insisted, "you've got to love a character who's mean to Barbra Streisand." Backstage at the Globes, Bacall said, "Well, it just goes to show if you live long enough and keep working, anything can happen." The Supporting Actor winner was Edward Norton for *Primal Fear*.

Showing that they weren't bothered by the *People vs. Larry Flynt* hubbub—which was kicking into high gear around the time Globes were being voted upon—the members of the Foreign Press named Milos Forman Best Director and Scott Alexander and Larry Karaszewski the Screenplay winners. Forman joked, "I am inviting all the members of the Hollywood Foreign

Press to see the outtakes." But then, at the end of the evening, the group's choice for Best Picture was not *The People vs. Larry Flynt*, but *The English Patient*.

Even though the film had lost out on the big prize, it still had to be adjudged a good night for *The People vs. Larry Flynt*. Joining in the celebration was Larry Flynt, himself, although he was seated not with Milos Forman, Woody Harrelson and Courtney Love at the main Sony/Columbia table, but was in the back with writers Scott Alexander and Larry Karaszewski. Flynt's presence admittedly didn't have quite the same inspirational feel that was in the air the last time someone associated with an Oliver Stone production attended the Golden Globes in a wheelchair: Ron Kovic, the subject of 1989's *Born on the Fourth of July*. Jack Mathews fretted that Flynt's "presence there seemed to contradict the filmmakers' denials that the film glorifies him." Flynt was asked by reporters about protests against the film. "It disappoints me that they are taking away from something that is entertaining and engrossing and allows the audience to make up their mind," he said, before adding reflectively, "I've been harassing feminists for a quarter of a century. I guess I should have expected this."

In the *New York Observer*, Andrew Sarris groused that the New York Film Critics' choices for Best Actor and Actress, Geoffrey Rush and Emily Watson, hadn't bothered to show up at the critics' party to pick up their awards, but "then, lo and behold, a few weeks later, both Mr. Rush and Ms. Watson are sitting in the dining room where the Golden Globes are being held. If I know my colleagues, that's the last time Mr. Rush and Ms. Watson are going to get anything from us." He added, "Ms. Watson lost at the Globes (tee-hee)."

He's Back!

Despite having produced the best reviewed Oscar show in years, Quincy Jones was true to his word and would not be returning to guide the 1996 ceremony. Instead of forging onward, the Academy reverted to Gilbert Cates. Once upon a time, Cates had said he would not do the show more than thrice, but this would be his seventh time as producer.

Whoopi Goldberg had made clear that she wanted no part of the show this year: "I did it. I'm done. Two years from now I might do it again. But I don't need to do it every year." Whoopi then said that, "There isn't anybody else who can do it in my opinion but Rosie." Goldberg happened to be appearing on *The Rosie O'Donnell Show* when she made this pronouncement, and she urged viewers to write to the Academy to second her opinion. Cates instead went back to Billy Crystal; even though Crystal was roundly panned for his last appearance in 1992, Cates proclaimed, he "plays the unexpected events of the live telecast like a Stradivarius." In early December, *USA Today*'s Susan Wloszczyna surveyed the potential Best Picture nominees and declared, "As for the prime choices so far, funny man Billy Crystal may regret his decision to return as Oscar host when he sees the material he's working with. These are films more likely to inspire funeral orations than comic monologues."

"Once Barry Scheck turned it down, I had a feeling they'd come to me," said Crystal in a piece of topical humor. He told the *Los Angeles Times* that he most likely would have done the show last year with Quincy Jones, but that nobody asked him. Never mind that Jones had had his sights set on Whoopi Goldberg from the get-go, Crystal asserted, "I think they assumed I wouldn't do it." He also admitted that being on the show would give him a grand podium for reminding the world that his new picture *Father's Day* would be coming out in May and it's "a really funny movie." Crystal promised he would do his best to get through the entire evening without saying, "Show me the money!" *New York* laid three to one odds that the host would do " 'You look maaaavelous' spoken in a Minnesota accent," and six to one that he would make a joke about cloning the Coen Brothers. But the odds that Crystal would say "anything either controversial or funny" were fifty to one.

After the infinitely cooler Tom Scott handled musical chores for Quincy Jones last year, Cates hauled out Bill Conti to be musical director for the twelfth time. But in what may have been the biggest surprise of this year's Oscars, Cates was not recycling Debbie Allen as choreographer. Instead, he chose Otis Sallid, who had created dances for a number of Spike Lee films. It was explained that this was not a sea change in Gilbert Cates's thinking, but simply that Allen was unavailable. Sallid philosophized about his approach to Oscar dance numbers: "We don't want to overkill it, like it's usually done. It's always been so big and like a circus, not to put anybody down. Everybody tells me they hated it."

And of course, since this was a Gilbert Cates production, it had to have a meaningless theme attached to it, and this year's was a pip: "The Togetherness of Moviegoing."

Give the Kidd a Hand

Over the decades, the Academy had come up with some jaw-droppers among its choices for Honorary Oscar, but this year it may have outdone itself. A Lifetime Achievement Award was going to Broadway choreographer Michael Kidd. Kidd was by no means an integral part of motion pictures, having choreographed a mere ten movies—most famously the macho dance numbers of 1954's *Seven Brides for Seven Brothers*—and appearing in a handful of others. He also directed one film, a 1958 Danny Kaye vehicle nobody remembers called *Merry Andrew*. Academy President Arthur Hiller intoned, "Michael Kidd's choreography has given us some of motion picture's greatest moments. It is only fitting that the Academy recognize the joy he has brought to so many moviegoers throughout the years." Curiously, two men with whom he had worked, Stanley Donen and Blake Edwards, were major filmmakers who never received a Best Director nomination from the Academy and would therefore have been much more deserving recipients. Kidd himself admitted, "When the telephone call came through I was startled 'cause the last big musical I had done was *Hello, Dolly!*, which was about twenty-eight years ago. It came out of the clear blue sky and it took me some time to adjust to it."

The Irving G. Thalberg Memorial Award recipient was also a strange choice. Since he was the producer of *The English Patient*, Saul Zaentz clearly was going to be a factor at the Oscars this year. By announcing him the Thalberg winner, the Academy

Board of Governors seemed to be signaling their support to his film in the Best Picture race. Zaentz's output as a producer consisted of a mere eight movies; as was the case with Michael Kidd's ten films, this was a pretty skimpy body of work for special recognition. Furthermore, Zaentz had already won Oscars for producing Best Picture winners *One Flew Over the Cuckoo's Nest* and *Amadeus*, so it wasn't as if he'd been shortchanged by the Academy; his other six contributions to cinema included the cartoon *Lord of the Rings*, *The Mosquito Coast*, and *At Play in the Fields of the Lord*. Zaentz reflected on some of the people who had won the Thalberg in the past—including David O. Selznick, Darryl F. Zanuck and Cecil B. DeMille. "These are the guys who made the industry," Zaentz said. "They didn't just produce films like we do now. They had a lot of intelligence and guts. Some of them weren't very nice people." He added, "But some of us today aren't very nice people."

On the eve of the nominations, John Hartl of the *Seattle Times* observed, "This is shaping up as one of the least predictable races since . . . well, since last year, when *Braveheart* and *Babe* turned out to be amazingly popular on nominations day, and the early favorites, *Sense and Sensibility* and *Apollo 13*, lost their momentum." The locks for Best Picture nominations were assumed to be *The English Patient*, *Shine* and *Jerry Maguire*, all of which had proven to be extremely popular within the industry, and which, to varying degrees, had performed well at the box office. *Fargo* also appeared to have consolidated a good deal of support. Other independent films with a leg up included the L.A. Critics favorite, *Secrets & Lies*, and *Lone Star*, indie stalwart John Sayles's most popular movie yet; Meryl Streep told CNN, "Well, *Lone Star*, I really liked." Roger Ebert cited *Secrets & Lies* as a dark horse, and averred that "For a Leigh film to figure in the Academy Awards is an unmistakable sign of changing times." There were two major studio films besides *Jerry Maguire* still in the hunt, although both had factors working against them: for *Evita* it was, as Mark Caro of the *Chicago Tribune* put it, that "the movie seems to have impressed more people than it has excited"; for *The People vs. Larry Flynt*, Gloria Steinem. And *Daily Variety*'s Army Archerd had a word of advice for all prognosticators: "There will always be one nomination where you say, 'How did that get in?' "

The Nominations

Newspaper headline writers had to scramble to come up with variations on a theme: as expected, the 1996 Oscar nominations were dominated by independent features. Indeed, some of the same headlines seen in 1992 were popping up again, such as "Independents Day for Oscars" in the *Los Angeles Times* and "Independents' Day at the Oscars" for Roger Ebert's *Chicago Sun-Times* piece. Even *Entertainment Weekly*, which had several days during which to come up with a clever heading, fell back on "Independents Day."

The trade papers managed to avoid the independent theme in their page 1 headlines. *Hollywood Reporter*'s line was "Oscar Spin: A Lot of 'English,' " while *Daily Variety* had "Oscar's 'English' Accent"—references to *The English Patient*'s leading the competition with twelve nominations. Saul Zaentz talked to Barry Koltnow of the *Orange County Register* on nominations morning, and the reporter gathered that revenge was on the producer's mind. "It truly is sweet," admitted Zaentz and said, referring to having been blindsided by 20th Century Fox on the eve of production, "I'm not new at this business and I have been in plenty of situations where a studio passed on a project. They usually say something like, 'It's not for us,' and there are no hard feelings. But they really treated us shabbily." Zaentz added, "You never plan on Oscar nominations because it's hard enough to make a movie without worrying about that." Then, harping on a favorite theme, he said, "We had a different definition of success. For us, the film will be considered a success when we get paid. Then we'll know that a lot of people have seen it."

Competing against *The English Patient* for the top prize were *Shine*, which garnered seven nominations, *Fargo*, also with seven, and two films with five nominations, *Secrets & Lies* and *Jerry Maguire*. Andrew Sarris called this year's "the most offbeat field of entries in the history of the once big-studio-bossed Academy of Motion Picture Arts and Sciences," and a hyperbolic Peter Travers went on CNN's *ShowBiz Today* to say,

"I'd never believe that four out of five of the nominees are independent movies. It's a revolution." (*Daily Variety* pointed out that it was not entirely accurate to label most of this year's big Oscar contenders as independent studios. Miramax was a subsidiary of Disney, Fine Line belonged to Time-Warner, and Gramercy was part of Holland's gigantic PolyGram; only October Films was an indie in the true sense.)

Jay Carr of the *Boston Globe* analyzed, "In an amazing reversal of last year's denial-filled cleanup by the retrograde *Braveheart*, the message was clear: The Academy has caught up with the rest of the world in acknowledging that most of the quality and vigor is to be found in personal filmmaking, not in the huge special-effects-dominated entertainment machines favored by studios, which seem more intent on replacing the aerospace industry than regenerating Hollywood's golden age." The *Hollywood Reporter*'s Kirk Honeycutt observed that "seldom if ever has box-office performance had so little to do with the Academy voters' choices," and Bob Thomas of the Associated Press noted that "the production and marketing cost of one Best Picture nominee, *Jerry Maguire,* is more than double the costs of making and marketing the other four combined." In *Los Angeles* magazine, William Goldman said this year's slate of nominees was the Academy's way of telling the studios "Stop making shit."

Premiere's Anne Thompson did want to remind everyone that, of course, the Hollywood studios had not intentionally set out to make no films that would appeal to Academy voters. "The releases that were intended to be in competition lost steam or were not embraced by critics or were flops," she said, citing *The Crucible* as an example. Paramount's Sherry Lansing played hometown cheerleader, asserting, "I think the nominated films are wonderful. But I think there were many wonderful movies that were overlooked, many from the major studios. I'm just sorry it's not possible to have more nominees." Stu Zakim, a vice president at Universal—which scored a total of four nominations—sounded almost happy when he said, "It's true we didn't get the nominations this year, but we did get the box-office revenues."

The People vs. Larry Flynt ended up with only two

nods; one was for Milos Forman, who knocked Cameron Crowe out of the Best Director race. The rest of the nominees were the helmers of the four other Best Picture contenders: Anthony Minghella, Scott Hicks, Joel Coen and Mike Leigh; when Coen's picture went up on the board during the announcements, his name was spelled "Cohen." *Larry Flynt*'s other nomination was Woody Harrelson for Best Actor; he was up against Tom Cruise in *Jerry Maguire*, Ralph Fiennes in *The English Patient*, Geoffrey Rush in *Shine* and Billy Bob Thornton in *Sling Blade*. Even though *USA Today*'s Susan Wloszczyna imagined that "a collective cry of 'Who?' was heard nationwide" when Thornton's name was announced, it was his nomination that seemed most to delight observers, along with the fact that Thornton was also nominated for Adapted Screenplay. *Good Morning America*'s Chantal Westerman effused, "I *love* that Billy Bob Thornton was nominated." And in the *GMA* studios, Charles Gibson's reaction to Thornton's double nomination was "Terrific! Terrific!" Even two of Thornton's competitors were fans. Woody Harrelson said, "I just love the movie and Billy Bob. . . . I love that that kind of work is getting recognized." (Thornton had appeared with Harrelson in the 1993 film *Indecent Proposal*.) And when he heard that the *Sling Blade* star was in the running, Geoffrey Rush exclaimed, "Billy Bob Thornton—oh, fantastic!"

If everyone was happy for Thornton, the greatest sympathy pains were over an omission in the Best Actress race. *Good Morning America*'s Westerman said "My first reaction, I was so surprised that Debbie Reynolds was not nominated for *Mother*. I thought she did such a wonderful job, and it had been so long since we'd seen her." Also in the spotlight for missing the cut were Madonna and Courtney Love. Those who safely made it in were all from independent movies: Brenda Blethyn in *Secrets & Lies*, Diane Keaton—but not Meryl Streep—in *Marvin's Room*, Frances McDormand in *Fargo*, Kristin Scott Thomas in *The English Patient* and Emily Watson in *Breaking the Waves*.

Lauren Bacall received a nomination—her first in a career that began with 1944's *To Have and Have Not*. On the other extreme, *Secrets & Lies*'s Marianne Jean-Baptiste was nominated for her film debut. The other Supporting Actress nominees were Joan Allen in *The Crucible*, Juliette Binoche in *The English Patient* and *The Portrait of a Lady*'s Barbara Hershey, who having made her debut in 1968, would have qualified as the sentimental favorite in this category if it hadn't been for Lauren Bacall. The Supporting Actor nominees were Cuba Gooding, Jr., in *Jerry Maguire*, William H. Macy in *Fargo*, Armin Mueller-Stahl in *Shine*, Edward Norton for *his* film debut, *Primal Fear*, and James Woods as the killer of Medgar Evers in *Ghosts of Mississippi*.

Liz Smith sighed that most of the nominees were "not exactly the sort that bring high ratings or glamour to the annual Oscar telecast. Can't see too many people tuning in to check out what Emily Watson is wearing!" If Smith seemed disappointed about the new names crowding the nominations list, she had nothing on Cindy Adams, who wrote, "Excuse me, but I'm a movie fan. I buy popcorn, eat the junky hot dogs, do the neighborhood theaters rather than screenings. I mean, I am a wall-to-wall, triple-A card-carrying fan. I love movies. Even lousy ones . . . I therefore have the right—just like a know-it-all cabbie—to bitch about the Academy Awards. What is it with those twinkies out there who make the nominations? Who are all these nominees with the three names? Billy Bob Who? Armin Mueller Which? Marianne Jean What? Kristin Scott huh?"

The oddest nomination—arguably the oddest in Oscar history—was Kenneth Branagh's for Best Adapted Screenplay for *Hamlet*: he had filmed the complete text of Shakespeare's play. The Academy defended the nomination, spokesperson Andrew Levy arguing that any movie based on a play is by definition an adaptation, "whether the dialogue changes or not." The reasoning was that an adaptation encompasses changing stage directions and "everything that separates a screenplay from a stage play." In an unusual breaking with tradition, there were no Best Song nominations from the year's Disney animated films, *The Hunchback of Notre Dame* or *James and the Giant Peach* (both *were* nominated for Original Musical or Comedy Score), but the studio did have two nominees in the category anyway, with "You Must Love Me" from *Evita* and "That Thing You Do," the sixties pastiche title song from Tom Hanks's directorial film debut. Also noteworthy was the Live Action Short nominee *Dear Diary*. This marked the first time that an unsold television pilot—a vehicle for *Cheers*'s Bebe Neuwirth—had been nominated for an Academy Award; it was also the first ever nomination for DreamWorks, the company begun by Steven Spielberg, Jeffrey Katzenberg and David Geffen in 1994, which had yet to release a feature film.

Daily Variety's Michael Fleming revealed that Roderick Jaynes, nominated for Best Film Editing for *Fargo*, was actually a pseudonym for Joel and Ethan Coen. This meant that each of the Coens had received three nominations this year. The reporter's source said, "They invented the moniker years ago because they didn't want to clog up the credits by repeating their names." When asked how the Academy would handle the situation, Academy Executive Director Bruce Davis impishly suggested that "if the name Jaynes is in the envelope, the first person to reach the stage wins the Award."

USA Today's Susan Wloszczyna noted the irony that "Miramax, that perennial champion of art house underdogs like *The Crying Game*, is suddenly out in front with its David Lean–style epic *The English Patient*." "We're loving it," said Harvey Weinstein. And well aware that Miramax led with a total of twenty nominations, he told Army Archerd, "We're not pouring glasses of champagne, it's magnums!" The Miramax chairman said that he surmised that about half the Academy's membership had seen *Sling Blade* on videocassette and that Thornton's Best Actor nomination was "the greatest surprise we've ever had." But in anticipation of possible Oscar recognition, Miramax had expanded *Sling Blade*'s release, from four theaters to sixteen. Another New York–based company, October Films, received six nominations (five for *Secrets & Lies* plus Emily Watson). Bingham Ray, one of the heads of October, said, "There was hope and there was faith. But I don't think we really *expected* all these nominations. When it happened it was amazing." Mike Leigh had an explanation for the strong showing of *Secrets & Lies*: "I think Hollywood is maturing, partly because a lot of Academy members are dying and the younger ones are more sophisticated and have taste."

Daily Variety asked Milos Forman if he were surprised that *The People vs. Larry Flynt* hadn't been nominated for Best Picture. "I was surprised that Woody and I *were* nominated in light of the negative campaign," he replied. Forman told the *New York Times* that he was still angry at what he characterized as the "unprecedented campaign against the film to sway the votes of the Academy," adding "I expected controversy, but not controversy based on a false premise." Forman also reminded Army Archerd that he still considers *Hustler* "tasteless, vulgar and brutal." Janet Maslin thought that even apart from the feminist backlash, the film "self-destructed." Appearing on *Charlie Rose*, the *New York Times* critic lamented, "They let Larry Flynt out in public, that's what happened. It's very simple, it really is. The fact that they did not distance themselves from him either creatively or personally really hurt the film." But Milos Forman countered such arguments by asking, "It's his life, so what does one do? I would feel very embarrassed to tell Flynt, 'We have to shove you under the carpet because you're hurting the film, you shouldn't be visible.' "

Diane Keaton was in her bathtub reading a script when she got a phone call telling her of her nomination. Her reaction was "I think that all the actresses nominated were astonishing. With the exception of me, of course." Brenda Blethyn was doing the *Today* show when she heard her nomination; in the green room she was given a standing ovation by her fellow guests, members of the O. J. Simpson civil trial jury. Blethyn told Bernard Weinraub of the *New York Times*, "This only happens to famous people. Who ever heard of me?" Having done publicity in New York, Billy Bob Thornton was on a train heading back to Los Angeles when he received a call from L.A. radio personalities Mark and Brian giving him the news. "I was half asleep and stunned," said Thornton. "I mean, these other actors are seasoned pros. It's like those test questions in school: 'There's an apple, an orange and a goat. Pick the one that doesn't fit.' "

Barbara Hershey acknowledged that she had slept only fitfully during the night. "But this is much better than coffee for getting up in the morning. If Starbucks could package this, they'd make a fortune. I really woke up, I'll say that much." For Juliette Binoche,

"Living in France, Hollywood is far away, and so I was very surprised. It's like being accepted by another family." James Woods said of the racist assassin he played in *Ghosts of Mississippi*, "I don't think I've ever understood or grasped the core of this character, and I wouldn't want to." Shortly after the announcements, Tom Cruise and Cuba Gooding, Jr.—both of whom were in London—were on the phone congratulating each other. "We screamed at each other for ten minutes," explained Gooding. "It was nothing intelligent, just 'Arrrggghhh. Ahhhhh. Yeahhhhhhhh!' I yelled. He yelled. Then he went hoarse." Gooding admitted he had been anticipating good news and "If I had not gotten that nomination, you know what I'd have done? I'd have cried like a girl." One of his competitors, William H. Macy, said, "The phone started ringing and I opened my eyes and I realized it was still dark outside. So I thought there's a death in the family or I got nominated, one or the other."

Looking at a list of acting nominees that your average moviegoer had never heard of, Gilbert Cates said to members of his staff, "We've got our work cut out for us, getting folks in Middle America to watch this. Thank God Tom Cruise was nominated."

Dan and Debbie, Sitting in a Tree

Madonna told the *London Sun*, "I'm disappointed, but I've got my priorities straight." Despite this even-tempered reaction, the *New York Post* characterized the *Evita* star as "stunned." A few weeks later Courtney Love told the *New York Daily News*, "Oh, I don't care. It wasn't my turn yet. I'm from the rock world and we don't get recognized the first time out." While Love was saying this to a reporter at a party, Heather Matarazzo—Dawn Wiener in *Welcome to the Dollhouse*—came over to tell Love she had been robbed of a nomination. "You're my idol. You rule," said the 14-year-old actress. Debbie Reynolds told Army Archerd, "I didn't expect it, but it was sweet of those who even thought of it."

Reynolds may have taken her non-nomination in stride, but one prominent American was incensed. Dan Rather wrote an op-ed article for the *Los Angeles Times*, headlined "No Debbie? Get *Real*, Academy."

The news anchor called her performance in *Mother* "sassy and sexy and smart . . . a detailed, deft portrait of a real woman who just happens to be over 60." He contemplated, "Maybe she's been able to do this sort of thing all along, but who knew? Nobody made a picture with her in the last quarter-century. That's a stunning injustice to her and to all of us." Finally, Rather concluded: "Reynolds has given us a glimpse of the possibilities that are in acting, in moviemaking, in *life*—for anybody who takes a chance, no matter what his or her age. For this, she deserves a medal, not merely an Oscar." And so, in lieu of an Oscar nomination, Rather gave her a "Danny Award."

A Less Lustrous Shine

The proverbial iron was hot, so somebody had the bright idea of unleashing David Helfgott. On March 4—three weeks before the Oscars—the *Shine* pianist began his first North American concert tour. All of his shows across the country sold out—some, according to press reports, doing so in just three hours.

Scott Hicks was there for the first concert, held at Boston's Symphony Hall, and he and Mrs. Helfgott substituted when the pianist decided against attending his scheduled press conference; Helfgott remained in his hotel room doing pushups. The *New York Times* reported that "Mrs. Helfgott and Mr. Hicks sought to dispel criticism that the '*Shine* Tour,' as the promoters have dubbed it, is exploitative, putting a circus-sideshow freak on display, as some music critics have suggested, and endangering Mr. Helfgott's frail health." The *Times* also spoke to Melissa Brown, an investment executive, who said she was coming to the show "because he is mentally ill, which is what makes it more amazing." The scene inside Symphony Hall was not unlike the high days of Beatlemania, as audience members ran to the stage to try to touch the pianist.

To say the critics were unimpressed with Helfgott's performance in Boston would be a huge understatement. The *Boston Globe*'s Richard Dyer felt that "last night's sad spectacle made clear that Helfgott is far from well, even with the help of medication." He also likened the event to the days when aristocrats would "buy their way into Bedlam to amuse themselves watching the antics of the forlorn and the disturbed." Tim Page of the *Washington Post* found the concert to be "a painful and disturbing experience," and concluded, "We have reached the point where a disturbed man who can barely play the piano is suddenly the hottest person in classical music, duly hailed for bringing in a 'new audience'; it's a little like the Peter Sellers film *Being There* come to life."

USA Today's David Patrick Stearns reported that "few found it to be a relaxing evening. Aside from the muttering and neighing noises he makes while playing, he's unpredictable. When the audience began to applaud during a particularly long rhetorical pause in Chopin's Ballades No. 4, he stood up and bowed before sitting down to finish." Stearns added that "At best, he sounds like a well-coached child prodigy. At worst, he's so casual he misrepresents the music." Still, the *USA Today* critic declared, "I'd much rather hear him mumbling over Chopin than endure the corny poems Van Cliburn often recites during his concerts." Stearns admitted that "One hopes that Helfgott is making lots of money at this: His celebrity shelf life is bound to be short." The assessment of Helfgott's manager regarding the Boston concert was "Overall, it was pretty good."

The *New York Times* even wrote an editorial about the tour, opining that "Mr. Helfgott, at times, seems to be the captive of an entrepreneurial enterprise being manipulated for maximum profit by his managers and the makers of *Shine*. He seems reduced to serving as part of a merchandising campaign, a spin-off marketed with *Shine* the way plastic velociraptors were sold alongside *Jurassic Park*." *Newsweek*'s "Conventional Wisdom" gave him a down arrow: Formerly "An inspiration to us all." Now: "He stinks." Scott Hicks's response was to make like Oliver Stone attacking *his* critics; the director denigrated the music reviewers as "self-appointed guardians of the elite. Maybe there are barricades that need to be stormed." Helfgott's reaction to the pans was "One mustn't be so serioooso. It's all a game. Must be grateful." Among the things the pianist had to be thankful for: his recording of the Rach 3 was the number one selling classical CD in the country, with the *Shine* soundtrack number two.

If the lousy reviews weren't enough, Helfgott's oldest sister, Margaret, was conducting a personal campaign against the film. She wrote letters to various newspapers in Australia to say that *Shine* was filled with lies and that the character of the demon dad was a complete figment of the filmmakers' imagination. She called the portrayal of her father a travesty and said, "It breaks my heart that the man behind David's genius, his father, Peter, should have been needlessly misrepresented for dramatic effect." She argued that their father had never beat her brother, and maintained that he lovingly took care of the youth when he had his breakdown. Moreover, the elder Helfgott moved to Australia from Poland prior to the Nazis' invasion of his homeland, meaning the film's Holocaust trappings were bogus.

The question arose as to whether the negativity directed toward the "*Shine* Tour" would hurt the film's Oscar chances. A second, parallel negative was the fact that, because it was now clear that David Helfgott was still mentally ill, the film was exposed as having prettified the truth—the same sin *The People vs. Larry Flynt* had been accused of committing. Scott Hicks must have been feeling a bit like Milos Forman, as he said, "I would hope people are sophisticated enough to see the distinction between David's tour and the film as an entity." He also averred, "Perhaps it's a benefit. It's kept the film in the public eye. We haven't had the means or the giant publicity of *The English Patient*. It's also sparked all sorts of debate about the nature of high culture and entertainment. Some of the criticism of David Helfgott has lost sight of the fact that the public is entitled to choose whom they want to see."

Getting to Know You

At the Nominees Luncheon, Billy Bob Thornton wore a John Deere cap, along with black jeans and a black T-shirt, but said that on Oscar night he'd be in a Hugo Boss tux with western accents. Asked if he would be accessorizing his formalwear with the tractor company chapeau, he said that the Academy wouldn't let him. "I asked 'em. They said, 'Show a little class.'" Thornton also said that on the awards circuit he'd gotten to be friends with Geoffrey Rush: "He's such a good guy. We're both married, with two kids about the same age, so mostly we talk about our kids."

Mike Leigh said, "There's a tremendous allegiance and friendship between all the independent Oscar nominees." Sharing the microphone with Leigh, Brenda Blethyn announced, "I'm an Oscar virgin." "That's the only kind of virgin she is," joked Leigh. "It's such a huge thrill. I feel like a child of six," said Kristin Scott Thomas, despite being jet-lagged from having flown in on the Concorde from Paris. Frances McDormand admitted she never watched the Academy Awards when she was a kid: "Didn't grow up in a household watching 'em. So I don't have any fantasies about that. My fantasy as a child was playing Lady Macbeth. I thought I was going to be doing classical theater. So there you go." McDormand was asked how the nomination had changed her life. "I've been taking more showers and worrying more about clothes and matching shoes than ever before in my life," she replied, and said also that she had no hopes for winning. When asked to do her *Fargo* accent, McDormand declined, saying, "I did her; she's gone." Cuba Gooding, Jr., was luckier, as no one asked him to do his trademark line. Gooding said being nominated was "sort of cool," and that "Steven Spielberg invited me over his house and told me how much he liked the movie. Wow!"

James Woods said he was nine the first time he watched the Oscars on TV. He recounted how, "They had Best Supporting Actor and I asked my mom, 'What's Best Supporting Actor?' And she said, 'Well, it's kind of like these are the guys who really aren't like big stars, they just work all their lives and once in a while they give them awards just to make them feel good.'"

You Must Love Madonna, But Barbra . . .

Despite the Acting Branch's treatment of her, Madonna had let the Academy know almost immediately that she would still be honored to attend the Awards and sing "You Must Love Me," the Best Song nominee from *Evita*. By contrast, several weeks before the Awards, the "Hot Copy" column in the *New York Daily News* reported that not only would Barbra Streisand not be performing *The Mirror Has Two Faces*'s "I Finally Found Someone," she wasn't even planning on attending the Oscars, despite having been nominated for Best Song. "Babs is confiding to friends (who've been confiding to us) that she got unfairly snubbed for Best Director and Best Actress for her work in *Mirror*. Other sources say Streisand's disdain for the Academy Awards actually goes back to the time she developed a grudge over not being nominated for Best Director for *The Prince of Tides*. Barbra, let go," suggested columnists A. J. Benza and Michael Lewittes.

When Billy Crystal said he had "tremendous respect" for the "really classy" Madonna for agreeing to appear on the show, most people took it to be as much of a slap at Barbra Streisand as it was a compliment for Madonna. The *New York Post* reported that "Streisand's people defended the diva director's snub of Oscar. 'Can you blame her?' said a source close to Streisand. 'She's pissed off because the Academy is just one big boys' club. They didn't nominate her for *Yentl*, they didn't nominate her for *The Prince of Tides*, and they didn't nominate her for *Mirror*. She takes it personally.'" The song she had cowritten would be sung by Natalie Cole, and *USA Today*'s Jeannie Williams reported, "Barbra Streisand and James Brolin will be cozy at her home."

Laying Odds

The overall consensus had *The English Patient* as the most likely Best Picture winner—Edward Guthmann of the *San Francisco Chronicle* said, "Take a long whiff of *The English Patient* and tell me if you don't smell Oscar bait. It's got history and epic sweep, a literate script, magnificent photography and high-pedigree actors in safari-chic clothes." Because of its inspirational qualities, *Shine* had been seen as the film with the best chance to snatch the top Oscar away from *The English Patient*; Kenneth Turan wrote that a number of people found *The English Patient* "cold and distant. These folks have made *Shine* and its retelling of pianist David Helfgott's emotional roller-coaster career the likeliest choice to upend *The English Patient* if any up-ending is to be done." But this analysis was done be-fore Helfgott had begun tinkling the ivories across America and had done no good for the cause.

This year, the Screen Actors Guild did something totally unexpected by deciding that the year's out-standing ensemble was in *The Birdcage*, Mike Nichols's remake of the French gay farce *La Cage aux Folles*, star-ring Robin Williams and Nathan Lane. The only Oscar nomination the film received was for Art Direc-tion. In the other categories, things ran more accord-ing to form as the SAG winners were Geoffrey Rush, Frances McDormand, Cuba Gooding Jr., and Lauren Bacall.

Giving his pronouncement on the Actor race his best sardonic spin, David Letterman insisted, "They'll pick Pretty Boy Tom Cruise." Dave Kehr's position was, however, "In a year of no clear favorites, the Academy is likely to go for what seems familiar, and Geoffrey Rush delivers a performance—as a physically or mentally challenged person who triumphs—that has won countless times in the past." Shortly before Oscar night, Roger Ebert wrote, "Until a few weeks ago, I thought the front-runner was Geoffrey Rush. . . . But now there is a current in the air. A drift. A feeling I get as people tell me they've caught up with *Sling Blade*. And I actually believe Billy Bob Thornton may pull off the upset of the season and win this category. He de-serves to." Wouldn't it be pretty to think so, felt Rene Rodriguez of *The Miami Herald*, who urged, "Keep your fingers crossed for underdog Thornton"; but Rodriguez was resigned that even though "Thornton's performance was the best of the bunch . . . Rush will still walk away with the Oscar, because *Shine* was bright and tony where *Sling Blade* was edgy and dark."

Post-nominations ads for *Sling Blade* showed Billy Bob Thornton as he really looked rather than in character as Karl, and announced, "From the Heart of America Comes a New Voice in Movies—Writer, Director and Actor Billy Bob Thornton." It was Miramax's not-too-subtle way of reminding people—particularly Academy voters—that Billy Bob Thorn-ton in real life was a far cry from Karl Childers. When *ShowBiz Today* cohost Jim Moret commented on how

he didn't at all resemble his character, the actor re-sponded, "It's a darn good thing I look different, I think. Otherwise I probably wouldn't be married and have two kids right now." Also helping Thornton's chances was that he was playing the Oscar publicity game like a pro, dutifully making all the possible ap-pointed rounds. But because he was so self-effacing, he came off as charming rather than Sally Kirkland-desperate, and his low-keyed nice-guy persona fit in perfectly with his Cinderella story. There was one thing about Thornton, though, that was pure Hollywood—his current wife was number four.

In the Best Actress race, the Associated Press's Bob Thomas noted that Brenda Blethyn "appears to be the favorite." Any number of other people said the same thing about Frances McDormand. Nobody said it about the other three nominees, although it was con-ceded that Kristin Scott Thomas did have an outside shot as part of an *English Patient* sweep.

Best Supporting Actor was tight. Many prognosti-cators felt that Cuba Gooding, Jr.'s ebullience as he made the post-nomination publicity stops had regis-tered favorably with voters. Jay Leno commiserated with Gooding about how annoying it must be to have people coming up to him in public and insisting that he do "Show me the money!" The actor looked into the camera and told America, "We're over it. Just let it go." Still, a persuasive case could also have been made for Edward Norton, and, especially if their films did better overall with voters than expected, for William H. Macy and Armin Mueller-Stahl, as well. Only James Woods seemed predestined to be at the Shrine Auditorium merely as an observer.

My Lousy Career

There was one race that every single Oscar ob-server knew was a lock. In fact, Lauren Bacall's victory as Best Supporting Actress was one of the surest things in Oscar history. Although by her own admission, "I've had a lousy career in many ways. Very sparse, very up and down, in and out," she was a true cinematic icon (even if that status had been achieved through just three or four of her three dozen movies—*To Have and Have Not, The Big Sleep* and *Key Largo*, and maybe *Designing Woman*). In addition, her first husband, Humphrey Bogart, was also all over the place recently, undergoing one of his periodic revivals during which the world rediscovers just how unbelievably cool he was. Their son, Stephen, had authored a book about his father and was also was appearing on Turner Classic Movies as part of a week-long showing of Bogart movies; two other new biographies of the actor had recently hit stores, as well. An earlier, alternative version of *The Big Sleep* had been discovered in the Warner Brothers vaults and was being released theatrically. All the omens portended a Bacall victory. As Michael Medved put it, there was "not a chance" of an upset by any of her fellow nominees. Fellow nominee Juliette Binoche told *TV Guide* that she wasn't preparing a speech because "Lauren Bacall is going to win for sure, so I can go there and feel safe."

Big Boys Bonding Against Dirty Armpits

Brian Grazer, Ron Howard's producing partner, told the *Los Angeles Times*, "I think the studios all feel kind of badly on the day of the Oscars because they're not going or they're watching it at some party. But that's fleeting. Two weeks later they're back to making high-concept movies with big movie stars." Nevertheless, so many people in Hollywood were so dispirited by the look of things that, with gallows humor, this year's Awards were referred to as "the Prozac Oscars." Bernard Weinraub reported that "The countdown to the Academy Awards which pits a lone studio film, *Jerry Maguire,* against four independent movies has struck a discordant note in Hollywood. It's Us vs. Them." He said that the vast majority of studio executives seemed to be casting their ballots for the TriStar release because, as a Disney member of the tribe explained, "I feel there's a little patriotism involved here." This was all fine and good, but the numbers said that all this jingoism was probably irrelevant—of the 5,227 people in the Academy, management types constituted only 394.

Gossip columnist Cindy Adams still hadn't gotten

used to this year's slate. Appearing on *Geraldo*, she declaimed that "there is no glamour. I mean, it's dirty armpits and it's spitty kisses and it's everything that's grungy and creepy and ratty and lousy." But another guest on the show, *Premiere* deputy editor Howard Karren, stood up for the Academy, saying, "I think that it's time that the Academy got better taste, and now that they do, everybody's blaming them for not having glamour. It seems a bit unfair." To which an incensed Rex Reed shot back, "These nominations are not about good taste. There's an entire political movement afoot in the Academy to disgrace the industry for the comedies and action pictures it's been turning out."

Adams was also angry at the nominees for not being established movie stars. "Who *are* these people?" she asked. "They're hyphenated nobodies. . . . The security guards at the Oscars don't even know who to protect this year because they don't recognize anybody." Geraldo Rivera chimed in with "Some years you love them all. This year you wonder who the hell they are." He admitted, "Can't say I've ever heard of *Breaking the Waves*," and after showing a clip with Emily Watson and Dorte Rømer as a nurse, he said, "We didn't know who was Emily Watson in the clip, but it was the patient, not the nurse."

With critics praising the Academy for its "daring" choices, and some columnists bemoaning the lack of glamour and glitz among the nominees this year, perhaps the most clear-eyed assessment of things came from John Hartl of the *Seattle Times*. "In terms of quality and innovative filmmaking, there's . . . little that's new among this year's major nominees. *Shine* is simply an Australian variation on the Hollywood artist biography, complete with debatable facts and an overreaching of its hero's musical abilities. *Fargo* could be described as a police drama with a female Columbo. *The English Patient* is an elliptical variation on a David Lean epic. *Secrets & Lies* is a far more accessible film than most of Mike Leigh's movies, including his previous one, *Naked,* which won every best actor prize in the world for David Thewlis—but not even a nomination from the Academy."

The Bonehead-Haters Club

Instead of serving their usual function as providing a hipper, parallel universe to the Oscars, the Independent Spirit Awards this year seemed to be almost a dry run. Appropriately, this was the first year the Awards were broadcast live on the Independent Film Channel. October Films' Bingham Ray noted the proliferation of stretch limousines pulling up to the event in Santa Monica and commented, "The cost of renting three of those limos could be half the budget of some independent films."

Serving as keynote speaker, Mike Leigh bored everyone to distraction by going on for half an hour—but then again, his movies are often criticized for being longer than they need be. Leigh said that independent filmmaking meant being free from "the interference of boneheads." By this he meant studio executives. *Fargo* was the big winner at the Spirits, with Best Picture, Best Actress, Best Actor, Best Screenplay and Cinematography awards. *Sling Blade* won Best First Feature and *Secrets & Lies* was named Best Foreign Film. At the Awards ceremony, Joel Coen admitted he was at a loss to explain why *Fargo* had found such favor among Academy voters when it was not "any more remarkable" than any of his other films. He also said of the Oscars, "I think this year was a fluke. It wouldn't surprise me if next year there are five great movies from the studios nominated."

Brenda Blethyn expressed amazement over what she called "everyone's obsession about what we're wearing" to the Oscars. Kristin Scott Thomas was also confused by the fashion issue. "This dress thing is terrifying," she said. "It's totally out of proportion. What is it about? It's ridiculous. But that's all that people talk about. I feel like I'm going to be like one of those people wearing sandwich boards, everyone staring." Frances McDormand was pretty much in agreement: "Let's face it: There are a few more important things in the world than fashion, but that's what's so crazy about this whole process. It ends up being the thing that's on your mind the whole time. Did I get the right shoes? Does black go with blue? It's completely insane."

Out Like Flynt

A movie about his life had impressed Academy voters enough to have garnered two nominations, but Larry Flynt was not going to be at the Oscars. It wasn't by choice, though: the studio wouldn't hand over tickets. "These actions by Columbia Pictures just reaffirm this city's reputation that when they need something from you, they suck up to you big-time, and when they get what they want, they drop you like a bad habit," said a disgusted Flynt. "I think they would really like to blame me for the movie's bad performance at the box office, but it really was their incompetence at marketing the film." A spokesperson for Columbia took the tack that "Like every other distributor, we have been given a limited number of tickets" for executives and stars of nominated pictures. And the studio did have to think of the people associated with its other nominated releases, *Jerry Maguire* and *The Mirror Has Two Faces*. Roger Ebert wasn't buying that excuse, noting, "If somebody makes a movie about you when you're alive, it seems appropriate for you to attend the Academy Awards." For instance, Muhammad Ali and George Foreman, the subjects of the Documentary nominee, *When We Were Kings,* would be in attendance. Flynt wasn't on the guest list for the studio's post-Oscar party either, although the studio said he wouldn't be turned away from the door if he did show up. The First Amendment hero declared, "I'll get over not going to the Oscars. It's a shame that a film about someone with integrity was made by a studio without any." At a press conference the day before the ceremony, Gilbert Cates said of Flynt, "I won't miss him."

As luck would have it, David Helfgott had a Los Angeles concert scheduled for the day after the Oscars. This naturally fueled speculation as to whether, unlike Larry Flynt, he would be in attendance at the Awards and, even more tantalizingly, might he be coaxed to play the piano on the show. Gil Cates adamantly denied such a scenario, and Neal Travis of the *New York Post* reported that the Academy had ruled against having him perform. Travis quoted "a source close to the Oscar production team" as revealing, "They had toyed with the idea of having Helfgott on stage playing the Rachmaninoff concerto. But then they learned that the man is quite goofy, still. It would have been a terrible embarrassment—and would have exposed *Shine* as a movie that isn't based on the facts." *Newsday*'s Linda Winer felt this was very good news because "we have been spared the spectacle of an upsetting or even disruptive international spectacle."

Among those who definitely would be at the Shrine, *Fargo*'s William H. Macy was looking forward to the event because in the past he'd be at Oscar-watching parties, and "everybody'd bet on the documentaries even though none of us had seen any of them and just saying these deliciously catty, cutting things about the way they were dressed up there and how full of crap they were. I just love that people will be doing that watching me." James Woods was feeling buoyant about taking his mother to the show. He relayed how he had decided he wanted to be an actor while he was attending M.I.T. and that his mother had said that if he was truly following his heart, she would support his decision. He promised her then and there that when he was nominated for an Oscar, she'd be there with him. In 1986, he was nominated for *Salvador*, but the film was released by a very small studio, Hemdale, which was able to give him only two tickets. Woods was engaged at the time, and his mom insisted that he take his fiancée. "So of course I don't win, the marriage is a disaster and, of course, I don't get nominated for another ten years." Some time in the intervening years, his mother had had a serious heart attack. When she was coming out of the anesthesia, she told him, "I guess I'll never get to go to the Oscars, will I?" Immediately, the actor became determined that she *would* attend an Oscar ceremony, and this year he finally had the opportunity to keep his promise. Before the ceremony, though, he did clarify his situation to the press: "She's coming, but I will have a date. I may be only a supporting actor, but I'm not *that* pathetic!"

Billy Bob Thornton laughed that his wife, Pietra, "used to be kind of threatened by the movie business, until Valentino called." Just prior to the Oscars, he told *USA Today*'s Jeannie Williams that he was "fairly stressed out" by all the attendant froth of the last six weeks, but

admitted that "there are worse things that happen to people" than being an Academy Award nominee.

West of the Mississippi, East of the Oscars

The town of Fargo was planning to go all out to celebrate its eponymous Best Picture nominee, even if not all the citizens were crazy about the film. Mayor Bruce Furness scoffed, "The idea of having hit men in Fargo is not real." The fete would be at the city's Fargo Theater, and the theater's director of development and party organizer, Margie Bailly, kidded that, "Dress will be strictly North Dakota formal. That's fur hats, overalls, huge parkas and everything else everybody else thinks we all wear." CNN's Sheri Sylvester traveled to Fargo to give viewers a sense of what the city was really like. Among the sites she was shown was the Fargo Walk of Fame, where celebrities who came to town put their hand- and footprints in cement, just like at Graumann's Chinese. Viewers could see only John Updike's slab, because all the others were covered by ice. The Walk's founder, Mike Stevens, told the story of how Metallica lead singer James Hetfield made an obscene gesture in the cement, so his imprint had to be altered by adding another finger and turning it into a peace sign.

Hangin' with Mr. W.

The night before the Awards, Miramax held a party at the Beverly Wilshire celebrating all twenty of its nominees, who were presented with chocolate Oscars. They had to perform, though, to get their special statuettes. Anthony Minghella, for instance, was pressed into service imitating Billy Bob Thornton, and many people noted how similar the two men looked, definite "Separated at Birth" material. Thornton said he was thrilled that Lauren Bacall had sent him a note congratulating him on his success. He described her as "just one of those people you don't even think exists until you meet her. She's just that lady that says, 'Put your lips together and blow.' "

The *New York Daily News* "Hot Copy" column observed that "Thornton got pretty chummy with Laura Dern. The two were holding hands during the cocktail reception. Must be old friends—that's all." Thornton was becoming more and more of a familiar face— by Oscar weekend, *Sling Blade* was up to a thousand theaters. And whereas on nominations day the film had grossed a mere $500,000, the total was now $12 million.

Michael Ondaatje was at the party, and he told the *New York Daily News*'s Rush & Molloy that he found the Oscar competition "terrifying," that it was "like a blood sport." *The English Patient* author also said, "I hate public competition. It reminds me of *They Shoot Horses, Don't They?*"

Diva Drama

Word got out that Natalie Cole was under the weather and would not be able to sing Barbra Streisand's "I Finally Found Someone." People around town were buzzing that maybe Streisand would come to the Academy's rescue and perform the tune after all. This "will she or won't she?" provided as much of a cliffhanger element to the show as any of the races themselves.

The Big Night

On Oscar morning, one of Larry Flynt's kids, Tanya, whom he had described as a "lying little wacko," held a press conference along with media hog attorney Gloria Allred, to denounce *The People vs. Larry Flynt* and vent some personal demons against her dad. When hardly anyone showed up to hear what they had to say, they decided they should probably hightail it to the Shrine for some attention. By contrast, another daughter, Theresa, took out a full-page ad in the trade papers that day saluting her father. Aping the ads for the movie, this one had shown the American flag covering Flynt's mouth. Theresa railed against Gloria Steinem, likening her to Joe McCarthy, and admitted to being "appalled" by what she saw as the success of Steinem and her allies in depriving *The People vs. Larry Flynt* of more than a pair of Oscar nominations. Speaking also for her sister Lisa and her brother, Larry Jr., Theresa wrote, "Our dad has loved us unconditionally and always treated us with respect. For these and so many other reasons, we are proud of Larry Flynt: the man, the businessman-pornographer and, above all, the father. . . . He has inspired us, fired our ambitions, and taught us to live our lives honestly, courageously and without fear of public opinion. He is our hero."

Another Oscar day trade ad came from People for the Ethical Treatment of Animals, praising those Oscar nominees—including Woody Harrelson, Lauren Bacall, Diane Keaton, Billy Bob Thornton, Edward Norton, Barbara Hershey and Ralph Fiennes—"who have chosen tonight's attire from designers who shun fur." According to the ad, these designers included Armani, Calvin Klein, Todd Oldham, Ralph Lauren and Donna Karan.

A year after being at the center of the Academy Awards, the Reverend Jesse Jackson contented himself with a conference call press meeting. In Jackson's estimation, "There has been at best moderate improvement." There was a 100 percent increase in the total number of African American nominees this year: two instead of one. Latinos were nominated as producers of two of the Live Action Short Films, and two Asian-Americans were in the running, one as a coproducer of

Jerry Maguire, the other as a Documentary Short producer. Jackson said, "There is an opportunity deficit, not a talent deficit. We said it a year ago and we say it today: Hollywood must do a better job in reflecting the cultural diversity of society. Until then, every Oscar night is a celebration in excluding people of color from fair shares, equal opportunity and access, a slap in the face to the American dream of a 'one big tent' society." Jackson concluded that this fight was "a long-term struggle, not a short one, and we will definitely continue."

Larry Flynt hired an advertising airplane to fly above the Shrine, pulling a banner that read, "Columbia Studios Suck—L. Flynt." That wasn't the only flying banner, though. Another plane carried the message "Disney Uses Sweatshops—30 Cents an Hour in Haiti." Employees of *Hustler* were outside of the red carpet area with signs saying "People for Larry Flynt," and anti-Disney protesters were down on earth, too. Another group, called Bastard Nation, voiced its support for *Secrets & Lies* and called for the opening of adoption files of adult adoptees. A representative from a Fargo, North Dakota, newspaper was handing out T-shirts reading "Fargo Woodchipper Mfg. Inc."

One woman in the bleachers was dressed up as Marlon Brando's 1972 proxy, but she got the name wrong, calling herself, *Sascha* Littlefeather. In stereotyped Native American dialect, she told E!'s Greg Agnew, "If somebody doesn't want to pick up their award, I take home." Having camped out for four days outside the gates, Sandi Stratton and Babe Churchill were at ground zero for year number 28. Frank Marquez was here for the eighteenth time, his fourteenth time at being first in line. He deserved his premier spot because he had gotten to the Shrine ten days before the Awards. This despite the fact that "I'm not starstruck anymore. It was great to see Peter Sellers and Doris Day, but the new guard, they don't have the respect for what the Academy represents. I can't understand how they think they're above it." Forty-eight hours before the show, when the gates were opened, a woman wearing homemade Ralph Fiennes earrings and identifying herself only as Tina could be seen losing it on TV as she barked, "I've been out here for fucking five days, and people getting here this morning get in line in front of me, and I am not patient or in a good mood." Things were much better on Oscar morning, when she said, "I feel like a million bucks." She also told E!'s viewing audience, "I want to see Ralph Fiennes. He's got the best buns, and I've just got to see them." India Wood of Harrisburg, Pennsylvania, informed CNN's Bill Tush, "We flew in on Friday. US Air." Hairdresser Larry Buckland of San Diego was talking to Paul Hodgins of the *Orange County Register* about the quality of this year's nominees: " 'People just love a good story, not all that superficial fluff. Oooooh, bad hair, *baaaad* hair,' Buckland exclaimed as a passing actress momentarily diverted his attention. He quickly raised his camera and captured the transgression."

Los Angeles Daily News reporter Glenn Gaslin was covering the bleachers, and he wrote, "Those who work as hard at fandom as the bleacher creatures deserve their own awards: Best Costume Design: Clad in a shiny gold jumpsuit, topped in a swim cap and painted gold, Hyundo Seung, 19, was lucky Tom Cruise didn't pick him up and take him home."

Gaslin also talked to "a 23-year-old wanna-be actor from Germany wearing a white wig, a gauche lapel-crazy disco shirt and bowling shoes." "It's not fair. I'm protesting," said Alex Ramirez. "A woman, she can wear a dress and she can be sexy. A man has to wear a tuxedo and he cannot be sexy. I want to be sexy." Some girls from Norway were nearby, and one of them delivered the bad news: "He doesn't turn me on."

In addition to interviewing arrivals for E!, Joan Rivers was also being simulcast on the radio. Waiting for celebrities to show up, she told some jokes, such as "Later on, Paula Jones will be here trying to get another look at a Governor's Ball." Meanwhile, handling forecourt duties for L.A.'s Channel 5—KTLA-TV—and the WB network, Sam Rubin and Leanza Cornett pointed out that the red carpet was divided down the middle by a red rope. Rubin explained that the Academy's scheme was "those that they don't feel the press or that you at home maybe are necessarily interested in seeing, though they are deserving Academy members, some are nominees, are sent on the far side of the line." The crowds were proceeding very quickly in that lane, and Rubin mentioned that food was being served inside the Shrine and the bar was opened "in the hopes that they will move through."

Fashion critic Laurie Pike was standing by at KTLA studios again this year, and she said that "With the onslaught of all the independent film nominations and nominees, I'm hoping we'll see maybe a little bit more originality in the dress this year." The station also had a camera set up in Randy Newman's limo as he and his wife wended their way to the Awards. The musician was nominated for Best Original Musical or Comedy Score for *James and the Giant Peach*, and Rubin asked him what was special about this year's Awards. "I think I'll lose again more gracefully," said the nine-time nominee. "I've been working on my standing up for Alan Menken to go by, and I've really worked on a beautiful, sort of a reverse curtsy kind of thing."

At 3:45, Joan Allen was the first star to arrive. Joan Rivers's initial interviewee, Claire Danes, who had recently been seen as Juliet to Leonardo DiCaprio's Romeo, said she was here "with my very sweet Daddy." When Scott Hicks was talking to Rivers, his preadolescent son could be seen in the background getting Danes's autograph. Sam Rubin referred to Hicks's having skipped his wife's birthday party to see David Helfgott play the piano. The director's wife confirmed the story, but looking around at the forecourt carryings-on, said "What a birthday party I've got eleven years later!" "I've been forgiven," declared Hicks.

Helen Hunt was with boyfriend Hank Azaria, and as they headed off, Rivers told the actress, "Get an engagement ring!" She also joked that the Academy passed a rule that "Emily Watson must wear a name tag and carry a passport because nobody knows who the hell she is." A few minutes later, the oblivious Watson stopped by, and Rivers gushed, "You were wonderful!" And as Watson and her husband strode off, Joan sent them away with "I wish you such luck. You were wonderful!" A little later, when Susan Sarandon called *Breaking the Waves* "one of my favorite films this year," Rivers said, "Hated it!" Inside the Shrine, Watson told KABC's George Pennacchio that the studio had hoped she'd plant herself down in Los Angeles after being nominated so that the community would get to know

her better, but her husband had just returned home from a theater tour in Wales, so she wasn't about to go anywhere.

Barbara De Witt of the *Los Angeles Daily News* noted, "Anne Jeffreys—you remember her from *Topper*—looked very glam in a bright green gown by Nolan Miller with a white fox stole, which several guests carried over a shoulder, signaling the demise of the no-fur phase." Sam Rubin asked Meg Tilly if there were any friends she was particularly hoping to run into tonight. The 1985 Supporting Actress nominee answered, "Just happy to be here. It's fun, you know. I have nothing intelligent to say. I'm sorry." The WB hosts talked about the rumor that Barbra Streisand was going to show up after all. Leanza Cornett admitted, "I can't even take it. I just have to say I'm about to weep." By contrast, when Rubin asked Courtney Love, "Who have you seen that's excited you tonight?" she deadpanned, "I'm so jaded nothing excites me." Love, who was linked romantically to Edward Norton, also announced: "I'm engaged to Kevin Spacey."

"How do you do it?" Rivers queried Randy Newman. "How do I lose every year?" he specified. Rivers saw Mrs. Billy Bob Thornton and effused, "What a great-looking wife! ... She was the wife *before* you were a major star. Then she really likes you." Thornton's mother, a fortune-teller, was also with him; her date for the evening was country singer and *Sling Blade* heavy Dwight Yoakam. Mother Thornton wanted to make sure that people didn't assume she and Yoakam were an item, telling *USA Today*, "We don't want to see in the *Enquirer* that Dwight brought an old lady." When the Rubin-Cornett team commented on the huge ovation Thornton received from the bleacher fans, he said he believed they thought he was Anthony Minghella. Thornton was wearing a floppy string tie to go with his Hugo Boss and he said he wanted to look like Gary Cooper in *High Noon*. Laurie Pike proclaimed that "Billy Bob Thornton looked finger-lickin' good in his Kentucky colonel outfit." James Woods was walking behind the Thornton entourage, and he kidded, "Billy Bob, you're the slowest damned nominee there ever was, I swear to God. We've got a traffic jam all the way back to 35th Street." Woods had arranged to borrow $2 million worth of

Harry Winston diamonds and sapphires for his mother to wear; "now that's a nice son," said a spokesperson for Winston. Woods brought not only Mom and a date, as promised, but also his brother. The actor told Rivers that his sibling "blew up my tugboats with firecrackers when I was a kid," and remarked to *Entertainment Tonight*'s Julie Moran: "I smoked three cigars before breakfast out of nervousness, and I don't even smoke."

Red Buttons, the 1958 Best Supporting Actor for *Sayonara*, went unnoticed by the fans, and he shouted to Army Archerd, "I'm changing my name to Billy Bob Buttons." Anthony Minghella told the press that he was carrying a horseshoe, the very same one that Sidney Pollack had with him when he won for *Out of Africa*. Geoffrey Rush's amulet of choice was a plastic Daffy Duck. Debbie Reynolds said, "I want everyone to win. We should have a hundred Oscars!" She also went up to the bleachers and proudly declared to the fans, "I'm Princess Leia's mother, kids."

Taking time out for a wisecrack, Joan Rivers mentioned that cinematographer Dante Spinotti had left *The Mirror Has Two Faces* during production because of "creative differences" with Barbra Streisand, "which is a fancy word to mean 'that bitch is out of control.'" Then a quartet dropped by to chat—Ed McMahon and his wife and Sally Kirkland and her date, whom she introduced as Nick Corri, her costar from *In The Heat of Passion*, which turns out to be a 1992 movie. Sally was all excited because she was working on some directing project for Showtime, and when Rivers tried to ease them along, Corri insisted on letting her know, "I'm doing a film now called *Soft Toilet Seats*." As they left, Joan could be heard saying, "I believe it."

Kristin Scott Thomas allowed that "I've never actually fantasized about the Oscars because I never dared fantasize about the Oscars," and Juliette Binoche said she chose Sophie Sitbon to design her gown because "She's an independent costume designer and I'm doing an independent film, so I thought it was a good idea to choose somebody who's not well known." Brenda Blethyn stepped on the train of Binoche's dress. Valli Herman of the *Dallas Morning News* marveled that "Compared to the look of her pitiful *Secrets & Lies* character, Brenda Blethyn was virtually unrec-

ognizable as a stunning woman." Blethyn was in a lime Armani with matching stole, and she wore a $1.5 million, 122-carat diamond necklace with a 13-carat pendant courtesy of Harry Winston, while costar Marianne Jean-Baptiste wore Isaac Mizrahi "because he kindly lent me something very, very early on, before anyone had even seen the film, so I was loyal."

Meanwhile, Army Archerd was having Cuba Gooding, Jr., work up the crowd by doing his "money" line. When the *Jerry Maguire* actor got to Rubin and Cornett, he insisted, "If every movie I do after this bombs, I'll still love America." And he enthused to *Access Hollywood*'s Larry Mendte, "I couldn't prepare myself for this if I went to Vietnam and back and went to the moon and won the lottery three years in a row." While talking to Roger Ebert and Willow Bay on KABC-TV, Gooding hugged Lynn Redgrave, who played Mrs. David Helfgott on screen, and told her that *Shine* is "the most wonderful movie other than *Jerry Maguire*." Much of the time George Plimpton, present as part of the *When We Were Kings* entourage, could be seen milling about, gawking.

When Milos Forman arrived on Army Archerd's dais, some sixty-five people in the bleachers calling themselves the Pure Love Alliance, jumped up, brandished posters with such sentiments as "Porn Is Pollution" and "No Perversion of the First Amendment," and began chanting against Larry Flynt, the man and the movie. They were loud enough to drown out Forman's responses to Archerd's questions, and as Forman left, the beloved *Daily Variety* columnist yelled at them, "Sit down and shut up!" They couldn't sit for long, because security forces soon removed them from the premises. Joan Rivers asked Milos Forman, "They wouldn't invite Larry Flynt. Why were they that *stupid*?" "I think it's silly because I think politics should be taken out of this kind of event," said Forman to Joan. "I think it's sad." To Leanza Cornett, the director said he had anticipated some controversy over his movie, "but I didn't expect it from the extreme *left*. I expected it from the extreme *right*." As for Columbia's refusing Flynt an entry ticket, Forman said, "Knowing Larry, I think he'll be here."

As it turned out, Céline Dion, who was already going to be on the show to reprise her version of the nominated "Because You Loved Me," offered to sing the Barbra Streisand song as well. Gilbert Cates said that when Natalie Cole had to bow out, he considered not having the song performed at all, "but that has ramifications," so he accepted Dion's offer. Sam Rubin broke the news to Dion that word on the street had Barbra Streisand showing up at the Awards after all. The chanteuse looked shell-shocked. "How does that make you feel?" he asked. "Well, if she's there, she sings the song, no problem."

Lauren Bacall said to Joan Rivers, "I'm thrilled, I think. But I'm nervous. I'm waiting to hear another name called." Rivers assured her that "all the odds are for you." Bacall countered that "there are always surprises, always surprises at these events, and I think there could be one tonight." Meanwhile, in the eastern and central time zones, Bacall was being seen on Barbara Walters's pre-Oscar show, where Walters promised to reveal "the undisclosed interior life of a woman who has been a star for half a century." On the program, Bacall and Walters went shopping at Zabar's together, and the Supporting Actress favorite revealed that "there were years I couldn't get a job at all. I was doing all the game shows." She also said she thought that Humphrey Bogart would "be very happy that at last I am at least being given credit for being an actress because, you know, I never really have been. I've always been thought of as a personality." Unusual for a guest on a Walters program, Bacall laughed but did not cry.

Kevin Spacey, who wore a white jacket last year, was now entirely in black, courtesy of Armani. Rivers assessed it as "a simpler outfit than last year." Spacey told her, "Well, I know you didn't like what I wore last year." "No," agreed Joan. "I'm not crazy about this year, either." The actor apparently didn't hear this crack, because he said, "You thought I looked like I should be selling ice cream, so do you feel better this year? I tried hard in your honor." Spacey's date laughed when Rivers responded, "This year you look like you should be collecting Dr. Kevorkian's people. I'll dress you next year."

Sam Rubin grilled Kenneth Branagh about his *Hamlet* Adapted Screenplay nomination: "Typing? Good Xeroxing?" Branagh laughed good-naturedly, and said "I think maybe it's a four-hundred-year-old

nomination for William Shakespeare." Next came a man Rubin described as a "noted Shakespearean actor," heavyset comic Chris Farley. Farley predicted, "I'll probably be thrown out. I just took pictures of Tom Cruise and they were, like, going, 'All right, beat it, pal.' " And then the KTLA cameras caught Larry Flynt, who had come down to the Shrine, although the question remained as to whether he'd be able to gain entrance into the building. The protestors had been ejected by the time Flynt had arrived, so he was spared from seeing their "Free Dumb of Speech" placards. Though, being Larry Flynt, he would probably have relished the attention. He had arrived in a white stretch limo with a reclining nude woman painted on the side.

"I never say" was the answer Joan Rivers got when she asked Roddy McDowall the name of his designer; for the second year in a row he was with Kate Burton. *Philadelphia Inquirer* fashion critic Susan Sterner's catty take on Jane Fonda was that the at-least-temporarily-retired actress "was every bit the mogul's moll in a golden yellow, sequined Versace that accentuated her new breasts but did nothing for her not-yet-done eyes." While Fonda was telling Rivers that she'd been coming to the Oscars since the fifties and that her gown was not new, her very rich husband, Ted Turner, reached down to Joan's container of Altoids and took one without asking. "Please, help yourself," said Rivers with a whiff of contempt.

Ralph Fiennes told Sam Rubin and Leanza Cornett that he and his beloved, Francesca Annis, had been watching them on their limousine's television set and "You're doing very well. I don't know how you keep all the balls in the air all the time. It's very impressive." But Roger Ebert had the Best Actor nominee completely perplexed when he went on about how people in England tend to mispronounce his first name. Another KABC reporter, Harold Greene, declared, "When you're that good looking and you have that much talent you can be 'Ralph' or 'Rafe' or whatever you darn well please."

Quentin Tarantino told Rubin and Cornett that he and Mira Sorvino were not watching television in the car, but "I was drinking in the limo, man. I knocked off a little bottle of Yaeger and did a dent in a bottle of Christoff." While Tarantino was thusly articulating, Tom Cruise and Nicole Kidman could be seen walking by. They didn't stop to talk to Joan Rivers either. Sam Rubin told the WB audience that they were going to try to grab Cruise and Kidman, and when Tarantino heard that, he went back to the microphone and said, "You were talking to me while Tom Cruise was walking by. So sorry, Channel 5. I know how it is, like 'Get this fuck out of the way.'" Realizing what he had said on live TV, he covered his mouth, and added, "Oops, sorry." Rubin and Cornett were a combination of shocked, embarrassed and amused. "Whoops," said Leanza. "It's the Yaeger talking." And Rubin said dryly, "Quentin Tarantino, who may not be back on our program next year, but we welcome him and appreciate his efforts this year."

Roger Ebert said admiringly to William H. Macy, "You almost imploded in some of those scenes" in *Fargo.* "I feel like I'm going to implode here," replied the Supporting Actor nominee. Barbara Hershey likened the scene outside the Shrine to a Marx Brothers movie. Vivica Fox was with Dennis Rodman, who was in the most intentionally outrageous outfit of the night, a self-designed long blue brocade coat, black pants, rust-colored shirt and, most pronouncedly, a tall hat that called to mind The Cat in the Hat. Joan Rivers asked if there was a romance going on, but what she got from Fox was "I'm here with the Mad Hatter. And I am the goddess at the end of the rainbow. My dress is my goddess and we designed his look for the evening as the Mad Hatter." Rivers asked the basketball star—who once showed up in public in a wedding gown—how he chooses his costumes. "I just wake up in a weird way and things just happen, you know. They just happen." Even though Fox had costarred in *Independence Day*, the year's highest-grossing film, Roger Ebert asked her, "What's your name?" He had seen her even more recently than in *Independence Day* because she thanked him for giving thumbs-up to *Booty Call.*

Winona Ryder was hemmed in by Dennis Rodman's large-scale bodyguard and couldn't move, the crush leading her to say, "It's really not even fun at this point, is it?" Sam Rubin observed to Ryder that the years when she was nominated, "You looked beautiful but a little shaken up." The actress began her discourse: "I'm completely relaxed because I'm not nominated and I don't have that pressure and it's a really exciting year because there's so many—You're not even listening to me!" A mortified Rubin sputtered, "She caught me ! She caught me!" Cornett attempted to salvage things by telling Ryder, "You know what. I'm listening. I'm listening." Rubin made the excuse that he was trying to get the attention of "your friend Jodie Foster" so she could join them. Ryder gave him a look that said "whatever" and headed off. Jim Carrey was with wife Lauren Holly and joked, "We're just happy to be nominated. We're not expecting to win anything." Laurie Pike observed that "her boobs look a little lopsided. She needs to work on them when she gets inside."

Renee Taylor told Joan Rivers, "Nice to see you. And this is the boy from *The Nanny*, Benjamin." Taylor's date was Benjamin Salisbury, who was appearing with the actress on the Fran Drescher sitcom. And then who should appear but another actor from TV, and his girlfriend: James Brolin and Barbra Streisand, having changed their minds about attending. What had transpired was that, the night before, when Streisand heard of Natalie Cole's indisposition, she told the Academy she could be pressed into service if need be. Cates decided there wouldn't be enough hang time for her to rehearse and decided to stick with Céline Dion. As the show's director, Louis J. Horvitz, explained the situation, "Barbra called us after saying no several times, but the ship had sailed." Despite all this inside intrigue, the question Rivers had for Streisand was "They wouldn't let you sleep over at the White House because you're not married?" "That's ridiculous," replied the *Mirror Has Two Faces* auteur. "People make up these strange stories that have nothing to do with the truth." Before they took off, Rivers said to the couple, "I hope it's forever."

Streisand was cordial enough to Rivers, but she greeted Sam Rubin by calling him "my friend." This was, she explained, because "You've always been very nice to me." Then she summarized what her last eighteen hours had been like. "We almost didn't make it because he was making a promo for his new series, *Pensacola,* in La Jolla," she said proudly. "So he flew up. I just met him at the airport. I had to drive in today and almost sang the song, too, because we found out late last night that Natalie Cole was sick, and so I thought that would be kind of interesting. I have nothing to wear or anything like that, but he was willing to drag me in at twelve o'clock last night." Brolin was also speaking part of the time, saying that there hadn't been enough rehearsal time for her to practice the song and that "it would have put the brakes on Céline." Streisand said of Céline Dion, "She's wonderful." Barbra added, "I'm like most people. I like to stay home with a pizza and watch it on TV." Her boyfriend interjected, "The best seats are from your bed, you know that." Streisand finished by explaining, "But I wanted to honor Betty Bacall and the picture I made, and I thought, I'd better come." The Academy had given her Natalie Cole's tickets. As proof that theirs was a last-minute decision, Streisand pointed out that she was wearing an old Donna Karan she had pulled from her closet, and her beau wasn't wearing a tuxedo, but a black suit with black t-shirt. Streisand got even more specific for *Access Hollywood*, saying that Brolin was going to "take me to the record store so I could get a copy of the song to relearn the lyric. We were going to Tower Records at ten o'clock last night. And then they said they already committed it to rehearsal with Céline. She'll do a great job."

Sam Rubin ended the WB broadcast by saying, "Leanza's life is made—you saw Barbra Streisand." And as the E! pre-show wound down, Joan Rivers commented, "Barbra Streisand. Boy, love has changed her. She recognized me." Her daughter and cohost, Melissa, said, "I know. I was speechless. I'm sitting here staring at a monitor going 'Omigod, I can't believe she's actually speaking to you.' "

The Oscar telecast itself did not employ a celebrity interviewer, like last year's Oprah Winfrey. Instead, home viewers saw the usual montage of star arrivals. Announcer Randy Thomas referred to the *Fargo* Supporting Actor nominee as "Bill Macy," Beatrice Arthur's husband on *Maude*. Lauren Bacall was called "first-time nominee, all-time star," and Mira Sorvino was seen kissing Quentin Tarantino on the cheek and then wiping off her lipstick. The announcer also informed us that "second only in interest to the Oscars themselves are what the ladies are wearing." In

the corner of their screens, the home audience could see that this program was rated TV-PG.

Academy President Arthur Hiller kicked things off by saying, "Thank you for dropping by on your way to the party," punctuated by a nervous laugh. The ceremony's theme of "Togetherness at the Movies" hadn't been well publicized, but the president's address touched upon the motif. Starting with, "There are over 6,000 of us in the Academy, who share at least one wonderful and fulfilling thing with over a billion of you out there—we love movies." Then he made like he was an existentialist: "In what sometimes feels like an era of isolation we find ourselves too often alone with our technology, sitting alone to read our computer screens, or listening to radio and watching television alone. Fortunately, we still have our houses of worship, ball games and movies to remind us that we are related by humanity, not machinery." Tom Maurstad of the *Dallas Morning* News sneered, "Really, what chance does a show have that opens with Academy president Arthur Hiller?" and Tom Shales sighed in the *Washington Post* that the "show started out badly with a pompous speech by gnomic Arthur Hiller."

After Hiller promised, "You keep going to the movies and we'll keep making them," a screen descended with scenes from *Star Wars*, which had been having a fabulously successful reissue. Yoda was saying, "You must go," and the person he was addressing turned around. It was Billy Crystal, who said, "Go? Go back to host the Oscars again? You mean in Hollywood?" There then followed scenes of Crystal interjecting himself into clips of the Best Picture nominees and addressing the issue of whether he should emcee the show. For instance, when Brenda Blethyn picked up the phone in *Secrets & Lies*, it wasn't Marianne Jean-Baptiste on the other end, but Crystal, who addressed her as "Mom," and wanted her advice on taking the gig. The premise of this segment showed Crystal's ego at its most unbridled, as if whether or not he hosted the show was of earth-shattering consequence. The comic highlight of the bit came from an unlikely source. In a scene from *The English Patient*, Crystal was walking in the desert—and plugging his upcoming *Father's Day*—when a small plane began descending near him. Piloting it was David Letterman, who shouted, "Hey, Billy! How're ya doing? Here's what you oughtta do. Introduce Uma to Oprah and then Oprah to Uma and then Uma to Oprah [at this point the 1994 host was looking wild-eyed] and then introduce Oprah to Uma. And then do it again. [The plane was perilously close to the ground now.] Uma! Oprah! Oprah! Uma! Keep doing it, Billy!!!" And then he crashed, and Crystal ran through the screen into the Shrine Auditorium, where he received a standing ovation as the band played, "It Had to Be You." Andrew Sarris assessed that, "By making these supposedly obscure movies the proper subject for the wildest parodies, he legitimized them for the billions of people watching the Oscars around the world."

"All right, good night, everybody," he began. "Welcome to Hollywood. The world of *Secrets & Lies*." Among his other opening quips: "It's great to be back here at the show, or as it's known this year, Sundance by the Sea"; "It's the year of the independent film. Great performances. New faces among the nominees. I mean *really* new faces. Who *are* you people?" Alluding to the 200-mile-per-hour winds in *Twister*, he joked, "That's almost enough wind to blow Gloria Steinem into a screening of *Larry Flynt*." The camera cut to a smiling Larry Flynt himself—the magazine publisher had scored a place inside the Shrine after all. (Woody Harrelson gave Flynt his agent's tickets, and the agent sat with another client, Ralph Fiennes. One story had Jack Nicholson giving Flynt *his* tickets, but Nicholson had merely called Columbia to complain about its shabby treatment of the man.) Noticing him, Crystal commented, "Apparently there was a little bit of a breeze today, because Larry's here with us. Nice to see you, Larry." The audience applauded, and there were even some cheers. "Glad you're here." Then, "Tonight, nobody knows who's going to go home with the Oscar. The only one guaranteed of waking up with a statue is Tipper Gore."

The montage sequence wasn't in lieu of Crystal's Best Picture medley, and soon he was singing "It's a wonderful night for Oscar . . ." Among the components this year were *Secrets & Lies* sung to the "Theme

from *The Brady Bunch*": "And so one day then, this mother met this daughter/And she knew that it was much more than a tan./So she had to make the big confession/You should know that Dennis Rodman's your old man." With cockney accent and to the music of "Wouldn't It Be Loverly," Crystal sang, "He's in pain and he's out of luck/He's as crispy as Peking duck./He cheats, he spies, what a schmuck/No, he's Ralph, *The English Patient*." And the Notre Dame fight song was used to highlight *Jerry Maguire*, ending with, "And even if you don't score this goal/You still go home with Nicole," as television viewers saw Tom Cruise laughing.

Introducing the presenter of the Best Supporting Actor Award, Crystal said, "I certainly hope her dad has stopped crying by now." "The beautiful and talented" Mira Sorvino announced that the Oscar was going to Cuba Gooding, Jr., in *Jerry Maguire*. The actor kissed his wife, and when he got onstage, Gooding did a little hotdogging, just like a wide receiver in the end zone. At the microphone, the victor said, "I know I have a little bit of time, so I'm gonna rush and say everybody, and you can cut away, I won't be mad at you." After saluting his wife—who, he revealed, was his high school sweetheart—and his children and parents, he went on to "God. I love you. Hallelujah. Thank Father God for putting me through what you put me through. But I'm [momentarily switching into a little boy voice] happy. I just want to . . ." And then the music started to play. "Oh, here we go," he commented, and then with the speed of David Helfgott continued, "Okay, the studio, I love you! And Cameron Crowe! And Tom Cruise, I love you, brother! I love you, man!" He listed a group of names that need not concern us, and then got to his leading lady, "Regina King! I love you! We did a great job when we made the movie!" The orchestra rose in crescendo but still he managed to shout over the music. "Everybody involved with the movie! I love you! Oh, my goodness! [holding the Oscar aloft] Here we are! I love you! I love you! I love you all! I love you! I love you! [dancing around on the stage] Everybody involved!" The music swelled and much of the crowd got on its feet . . . Army Archerd would call this "the most exuberant acceptance speech—and performance—ever seen." Bob Thomas loved that Gooding "refused to be intimidated by the police-state insistence on half-minute acceptance speeches."

After the commercial break, Billy Crystal announced, "If there's anyone who has not been thanked by Cuba, if you give me your names, he's waiting backstage." The host then introduced, "The star of *Speed* and *Speed 2*, the only person in this room who's actually ever ridden on an L.A. city bus." Sandra Bullock revealed that the winner of Best Art Direction was *The English Patient*. Steve Martin came out and said, "I couldn't tell. Did Cuba thank me?" Martin was there to introduce the clip from *Jerry Maguire*, and he orated, "*Jerry Maguire* is a moving and funny American film which accomplished an impossible task. It makes you feel sorry for an agent. And tonight, rather than show a clip of the film, we're going to show the entire film."

Next, Juliette Binoche was onstage to announce that the Costume Design winner was the woman who had designed her army fatigues for *The English Patient*. Ann Roth nearly fell forward from the weight when Binoche handed her the statuette. Her speech was a reworking of the "film is the universal language" bromide: "I'd like to use my thirty seconds to say that my crew was from Italy, Tunisia and the United States. But we're all costumers and costumers know one language and work beyond maps and boundaries."

"Ladies and gentlemen, before I introduce Madonna, I want to say one thing," began Crystal. "Even though she was not nominated—and there was a lot of speculation that she was going to be—she accepted the invitation, actually she called the show to say that she wanted to sing and come here tonight. And I thought that was showing a great deal of class." The audience applauded and cheered, and director Louis J. Horvitz mischievously cut to Barbra Streisand in the audience, who was chatting with James Brolin. "So here she is," continued the emcee, "to sing the song, 'Don't Cry for Me Because I'll Get Back at You If It Takes the Rest of My Life.'" In actuality, the singer was of course warbling "You Must Love Me." Appropriately, she was wearing an outfit from Eva Peron's favorite house of couture, Christian Dior, a low-cut

black lace and chiffon gown with a long train. Choreographer Otis Sallid said, "When you've got Madonna, you don't want to surround her with Argentine tango dancers. You just put her in the spotlight and go for it." So it was simply Madonna in the center of the stage and a piano player off to her right, and when she finished, the auditorium was again filled with cheers.

Crystal mentioned that he had set up an Oscar Web site, called www.whyistheshowsolong.com, and solicited jokes from the wired public. He then gave what he deemed to be the three best. From a contributor named R. Lang: "Why is the show so long? Because there are just so many little people." The gag elicited mild laughter. "It's cute," said the host, before reminding everyone, "These are Web site jokes, folks." J. Phillips had provided, "What was Bill Clinton's favorite movie last year? *101 Donations*." The joke had a better reaction than some of Crystal's own, as solid laughter followed. Crystal allowed that "it's not bad." And finally, D. Snow wanted the host to say, "You know, I expect to win an Oscar next year. I'm making a move called *Price Is Very Sexy, and Waterhouse Is a Genius*." Not bad, acknowledged Crystal. "And speaking of PriceWaterhouse, there is a gentleman from the firm who is retiring after twenty-one years of servicing Oscar—*that* sounds terrible," as the audience chuckled. He brought out accountant Frank Johnson, a familiar face to Oscar aficionados.

In introducing the next two presenters, Crystal enthused, "From MTV to their own hit movie, these animated characters are what happens when Sylvester the Cat and Tweetie Bird make it with Leopold and Loeb. Here are the bad boys of MTV." Beavis and Butt-head were actually wearing tuxedos, and Butt-head kicked things off by articulating, "Good sound effects editing can make the difference between a boring chick movie with some English dude and a really cool movie with lots of explosions and stuff." Beavis jumped in with "Yeah, yeah like *Under Siege 2*." Butt-head continued, "For example, when I smack Beavis, sound effects create the illusion of pain." He then whacked his pal, who went flying to the floor and said, "Ow, that really did hurt." Beavis opened the envelope, announcing, "And the Oscar goes to . . .check it out, Bruce Stambler for *The Ghost and the Darkness*," a big game hunter movie. Backstage, Stambler laughed about receiving the Award from Beavis and Butt-head: "My son is a big fan of theirs, and sometimes he makes me watch an hour of it, and I want to commit suicide."

The *New York Daily News*'s Laurice Parkin wrote of the Makeup presenter, "It appears rocker Courtney Love has shed her 'grunge diva' persona once and for all, wearing a fabulous white satin number by Versace complete with a semi-plunging neckline and perfectly coiffed 'do with nary a black root in sight." Love gave the Makeup Award to *The Nutty Professor*, but in announcing the Award mentioned only David Leroy Anderson, and not his cowinner, Rick Baker. Baker was unfazed, and paid tribute to Eddie Murphy, who "made seven rubber characters come to life, sat in the makeup chair for over seventy days, and he never complained once. He's the most talented and cooperative actor I've ever worked with." Backstage, *Premiere*'s Steve Pond heard Love apologizing to the winners. "I fucked up," she admitted. "I'm so fucking sorry, you guys." Then she added, "Well, it was just human error. It wasn't like adultery or something."

Winona Ryder was in her customary flapper look—this one a beaded black tulle Chanel, which *People* said made her look like Wednesday Addams; Tom Shales of the *Washington Post* snickered that "The very strange Winona Ryder seemed stranger than ever in a dress that looked as if an angry mob had tried tearing it from her pale little body on her way into the theater." Ryder had the duty of picking up the "Togetherness at the Movies" theme and running with it. "Last year over a billion of us bought tickets to see a movie," she claimed. "All over the world we sat together in the dark for a few hours and shared the experience of film." This was the segue for a particularly pointless montage of film clips about going to the movies with a cover version of the Drifters' "Saturday Night at the Movies" providing the soundtrack. We saw people like Mia Farrow and Daffy Duck entering theaters, Simon Fenton at the concession stand in Joe Dante's cult film, *Matinee,* Roger Rabbit and a slew of Gremlins sitting in the auditorium, and shots of audiences watching scenes from *Casablanca* and *A Streetcar Named Desire. Daily Variety* said this "montage featur-

ing movie houses and oddly packaged film clips appeared to be a tribute to popcorn." The mélange would have an afterlife: for years, moviegoers at Sony theaters would be subjected to it in between the Moviefone ads and the trailers.

Before Kevin Spacey could get around to announcing Best Supporting Actress, Crystal made him do his Christopher Walken imitation. Spacey paid homage to the nominees, saying "These are my fellow alumnae of high school drama clubs who have already won our admiration and respect. . . . They have done for film what the Cheshire Cat did for Alice—they have left an indelible impression." Spacey then proceeded to announce Lauren Bacall's name. Except it wasn't what was in the envelope. The winner was Juliette Binoche in *The English Patient.* The winner looked absolutely stunned, as did three of her fellow nominees. Joan Allen's eyes widened, and Barbara Hershey and Marianne Jean-Baptiste were both open-mouthed at the news. Lauren Bacall was expressionless at first, but then she smiled broadly and applauded. Cindy Adams reported that it was such a stunning upset that "In memoriam, even journalists in the press room stopped eating for a second. And nobody ever saw a reporter pass up free food."

Walking to the stage, Binoche was shaking her head in disbelief, and at one point put her hand up to her head. There was a cut to Lauren Bacall, who was clapping, but her son Stephen was poker-faced. Onstage, the winner stated the obvious: "I'm so surprised." She added, "It's true. I didn't prepare anything. I thought Lauren was going to get it, and I think she deserves it." The audience applauded. "Where are you?" Turning to her own project, Binoche said, "I think we all tried our best on this film, and Anthony was there to help us—I'm so amazed. This is a dream. It must be a French dream, I think. Bye." With Binoche winning, John Hartl of the *Seattle Times* noted it "looked like this elliptical World War II epic was going to collect everything in sight." A clean sweep, twelve victories, would mean a new Oscar record.

Next, the title song from "That Thing You Do!" was lip-synched by actors pretending to be the film's The Wonders. This was choreographer Otis Sallid's only number, and the band was hidden by a giant radio much of the time, as the dancers exuberantly performed an approximation of the greatest dances of the sixties.

Holly Hunter introduced a clip from *Fargo* by calling the film the "story of chilling mayhem and bad planning," and David Spade and Chris Farley showed up onstage to announce the Short Film winners. Farley, who was all sweat and heavy breathing, looked out in the audience and said, "I see a lot of confused people out there!" Going into his agitated routine, he began yelling, "What are we doing? We don't belong here!" Spade's response was "Maybe there was some sort of mix-up, and right now Jeremy Irons is performing at the Improv." The Live Action Short was Dream-Works' busted TV pilot, *Dear Diary,* and as the two victorious producers walked down the aisle a middle-aged guy with no class could be seen in his seat talking on a cell phone—an Oscar first. Onstage, one of the winners said, "I'd like to thank the Academy for recognizing that TV networks do produce innovative work—they just don't show it to you." He also thanked "the three wise men of DreamWorks and their Apostles," indicating that he wasn't overly familiar with the particulars of the Bible.

Farley, who would die nine months later from a cocaine overdose, loudly pretended to get a paper cut from the Animated Short Subject envelope. Ellen Gray of the *Philadelphia Daily News* wrote, "Who knew these two would make Beavis and Butt-head look so . . . erudite?" Tyron Montgomery, one of the producers of the winner, *Quest,* asked, "Oh, gee, what do you say in a moment like this?" which of course he was supposed to have figured out before he got to the podium. What he came up with was "I actually just wanna say one thing. I'm very, very happy that Billy Crystal is doing this night. He was always my very favorite show host of the Oscars and I'm very honored and very happy that he's doing this," which was both too much information and too much self-involvement, as if he believed that Crystal had returned just to be there for him. His cowinner, Thomas Stellmach, apologized for being "very nervous" and then visibly shook as he stammered while reading from a piece of paper in a heavy Teutonic accent. Later in the show, Crystal said,

"I'd like to thank Thomas and Tyron for thanking me. Cuba didn't."

When the orchestra began playing "The Sound of Music," it could only mean that Julie Andrews was here. Her task was to present the Honorary Oscar to Michael Kidd, whom she described as "a dear friend and my favorite curmudgeon." Film clips followed, and the Academy did, in a backdoor way, get Barbra Streisand to sing on the show—the closing moments of the compilation were accompanied by her version of the title song from *Hello, Dolly!,* which Kidd had choreographed. The recipient said, "My wife, Sheila, who was my assistant on many of these pictures and naturally bore the brunt of my grouchiness, said to me, 'Michael, the Academy is honoring you. For once, stop being Mr. Bah-Humbug and try to enjoy it, at least for your family and friends' sake.' Well, she's not only beautiful, she's right. . . . Once the reality of all this sinks in, I promise to enjoy it." The audience responded with laughter, and Kidd added, "I even had my glasses tinted slightly rose-colored." Turning serious, the choreographer proclaimed, "So many of today's films suggest the terrors that await us. Perhaps this award signifies an awareness that we have been missing something, namely the vitality and the joy of living that movie musicals can express in song and dance." For this sentiment, Kidd received a nice hand.

During the next commercial break, there was an ad for something brand new on the market, the DVD player; Panasonic pronounced it "the next thing." Appropriately, Helen Hunt was up next with a report on the Scientific and Technical Awards banquet, which she had emceed. "As the host, I made sure that each and every one of you received an invitation. What happened?" she asked the Shrine audience. "If you had been there with us . . . you could have seen how James Kajiya and Timothy Kay grow hair on creatures in movies, or as they put it, render fur with three-dimensional texture. I'm not kidding."

Crystal had to explain what was going on with "I Finally Found Someone": "Natalie Cole was to have been here tonight to sing the song and she has been taken ill with the flu. So, graciously stepping in with one day's notice" was Céline Dion. The singer had on what Susan Sterner of the *Philadelphia Inquirer* called "what may well be the ugliest expensive necklace of all time, a giant pavé-diamond necklace with a star and meteor shower"; like her dress, it was by Chanel. Dion had the sheet music in front of her, and added a few Streisand-esque vocal mannerisms to her rendition. The crowd gave her a great hand, for her "graciousness" if nothing else. But Barbra Streisand didn't catch the number—she was in the bathroom.

Tommy Lee Jones and Will Smith, the stars of an unheralded upcoming summer film, *Men in Black,* were together to present the Documentary Awards and greeted each other: "Hello, Mr. Smith." "Good evening, Mr. Jones." The Short winner was *Breathing Lessons,* about a paralyzed writer who has spent forty-one years in an iron lung. Winning director Jessica Yu said, "You know you've entered new territory when you realize your outfit cost more than your film," which *Newsweek* called the "best line of the night" and which immediately went into the annals as one of the all-time great Oscar speeches. The Feature winner, as expected, was *When We Were Kings,* about the 1974 Muhammad Ali/George Foreman "Rumble in the Jungle" fight in Zaire; because of legal and financial entanglements, the film had taken over two decades to complete. Ali, who was suffering from Parkinson's disease, could be seen in the audience, more rubbing his hands than clapping. As the winning producer and director were leaving their seats, Barbra Streisand could be seen coming down the aisle, returning from the ladies' room. Onstage, director Leon Gast thanked "George Foreman for being who he was back then and who he is now . . . and The Man. The man who realized a long while ago [applause was mounting] that he could make a difference [a standing ovation]. And as President Bill Clinton said, it's about time that we as Americans start paying him back for everything he's done, Muhammad Ali." The orchestra rose in volume as Foreman and a slow-moving Ali came to the stage to the sound of wild cheering from the audience.

Jim Carrey asked, "And how was *your* weekend? Mine was good," a cunning reference to the fact that his new movie *Liar, Liar* had just opened to huge numbers. Turning his back to the audience, Carrey pretended his rear end was talking. He then announced that the Visual Effects Oscar was going to *In-dependence Day,* the only one of the three nominees that didn't rely entirely upon computer graphic imagery. One member of the winning quartet who didn't get to speak held up a card with his list of people to thank, and the show's director Louis J. Horvitz accommodatingly moved in for a close-up. Chris O'Donnell awarded Best Sound to *The English Patient.* This made it official that *The English Patient* was in full sweep mode, since its sound was decreed more impressive than that of a musical (*Evita*) and three very loud summer movies (*Independence Day, The Rock,* and *Twister*). One of the winners thanked the Academy "for honoring a film that could be as exciting and engaging in its quiet moments as in its loud ones. Thanks for listening."

Nicole Kidman, putting on her distance glasses for the TelePrompTer, read the nonsense the writers had given her to say about Film Editing: "In many ways, it's like the dance, moving back and forth in a particular pace, always pushing deftly and percussively to its climax." Then she brought out "the phenomenal" Michael Flatley and his Lord of the Dance troupe. What transpired next was, in a nutshell, the difference between Gilbert Cates and Quincy Jones. Whereas last year, Jones had brought a hip and innovative troupe, Stomp, to the Awards, Cates—pitifully trying for something he thought was in the same vein—mustered only pure kitsch, starting with the buffoonery of the pompous Michael Flatley (whom Conan O'Brien referred to as "Swishy McJackass"), and continuing through the silly pseudo Irish jigs his dancers performed. Whereas Stomp's appearance actually made sense on the Awards—creating noises to go along with film clips to illustrate what Sound Effects Editing is—the only thing members of Lord of the Dance accomplished was blocking the movie screens where a tired Chuck Workman montage was running. The segment ended up coming across as a salute to the Rockettes, rather than Film Editing, and took its place with the Rob Lowe/Snow White on the all-time Oscar camp short list. *Daily Variety* observed that the "production number appeared to have little to do with genuine editing, aside from those who edit while dancing Irish jigs chorus-line style." The next morning, *Today's* Jim Brown gibed, "There's a lesson to be learned from last night's show if you're an entertainer: Be in Los Angeles at Oscar time and you may appear on the show. Michael Flatley and his Lord of the Dance troupe made it into a segment about editing. One had nothing to do with the other, but the troupe was in town." The audience did give the dancers a rousing response, however.

Then Nicole Kidman returned, and announced that *The English Patient* had won another one. Editor Walter Murch, who had just received a statuette for Sound, thanked his wife, whom he called "the patient English."

"I'm not going to lie to you," began Debbie Reynolds, "I was a little disappointed by not being nominated myself, but what I did was I took to my bed for two weeks and then I discovered this wonderful support group, called the Non-Nominees Anonymous, or Non-Anons. Well, maybe not so anonymous. Courtney Love, Madonna, Barbra Streisand . . ." When Reynolds first began speaking, the camera caught a bored-looking Barbra Streisand turning to talk to James Brolin, but now that she heard her name she seemed transfixed by what Reynolds was saying. ". . . and these wonderfully generous, gifted, *uncomplicated* women . . ." The audience laughed, but TV viewers saw Barbra Streisand now looking embarrassed. ". . . took me in and nominated me as their friend. So it is to them that I would like to express my gratitude for helping me out of my deep funk into this shallow one. Now to the TelePrompTer." And with comically exaggerated elocution, she began reading: "The precious gift of laughter film comedy provides . . ." as the audience applauded her comic aplomb. Then Reynolds stopped and asked, "Who wrote this drivel?" prompting the guilty party, her daughter Carrie Fisher, to come onstage. Fisher told her not to bother reading it because "the show could be shorter anyway." "Well, you couldn't," shot back Debbie. Carrie had agreed to write for the show, even though she admitted to feeling "some bitterness" that her mom wasn't nominated, "especially after I saw some of the other nominated performances." Reynolds announced that the Best Original Musical or Comedy Score winner was Rachel Portman for *Emma*—she was

the first woman to win an Oscar for writing a musical score.

Announcer Randy Thomas said, "Please welcome a memorable performer on previous Oscar shows," and Gregory Hines gave the Dramatic Score Oscar to Gabriel Yared for *The English Patient*, the film's sixth Award. Glenn Close introduced the *Shine* excerpt, and then returned with a surprise: "Ladies and gentlemen, David Helfgott." The pianist entered the stage talking to himself, and the *Shine* contingent in the audience unsuccessfully tried to get a standing ovation going. The pianist was also jabbering as he played "The Flight of the Bumblebee," but because he wasn't miked, the audience couldn't hear what he was finding so interesting. Everyone sighed in relief when he finished without going off his trolley and doing something outrageous, such as running down and groping Nicole Kidman in the front row. Reportedly, Helfgott's handlers and Gilbert Cates had initially been against his appearance, fearing it might put too much pressure on the pianist. It was Mrs. Helfgott who pushed to have him on the show, supposedly as a way to show the world that those cruel music reviewers along his tour had it all wrong. The *Hollywood Reporter* called it a "reasonable rendition" of the piece, but *USA Today*'s Matt Roush said that his appearance ironically had the effect of "vindicating the nation's music critics with his sloppy technique." David Daniel of the *Wall Street Journal* winced that "By normal concert-hall standards, it was pitifully bad, full of missed notes and arthritic runs. Bumblebees had a right to picket the Shrine Auditorium."

Tim Robbins gave *The English Patient* its seventh Award out of seven tries. Cinematographer John Seale referred to Saul Zaentz as "one of the world's gentlemen," and thanked one of his second unit d.p.s who "shot all the beautiful camels." Walking off, presenter Robbins could be seen making eye contact with someone in the audience, shrugging and pointing to the envelope he was carrying—presumably it was *Fargo*'s losing nominee, Roger Deakins, who had photographed Robbins's *Dead Man Walking*.

Billy Crystal's take on things so far was: "Apart from wheat and auto parts, America's biggest export is now the Oscar." Kenny Loggins sang the nominated song "For the First Time" from *One Fine Day*, and then Randy Thomas declaimed, "The Academy is proud to welcome a two-time Oscar winner. The distinguished actor-producer who brings honor to the family name, Mr. Michael Douglas." Honor was in the air, for Thalberg Award presenter Douglas called Saul Zaentz—with whom he had produced *One Flew Over the Cuckoo's Nest*—"an honorable gentleman who exemplifies the Motion Picture Academy's support of independent filmmaking." Zaentz talked about passion in movies, quoted screenwriter Samuel Hoffenstein's saying "The Holy Grail is not in the finding, it is in the journey," and ended by saying, "My cup is full."

The Foreign Film presenters were introduced by Crystal as "She's from *The English Patient* and he's from the Johnson administration": Kristin Scott Thomas and Jack Valenti. The MPAA head intoned, "To millions of people around the world, Kristin, we're speaking a foreign language right now. And, I might add, you speak it eloquently." "Thank you," the actress replied, and because somebody had to, she said, "But the universal tongue is the language of movies." *Entertainment Weekly* chided, "Kristin, at least act like you like him." The winner was *Kolya*, which was essentially a Czech reworking of *The Champ*. The kid who appeared in the movie was among the four people who mounted the stage, and Jack Valenti petted him on the cheek. Director Jan Sverak spoke directly to his statuette, saying, "Dear Oscar, I was not able to sleep last night. All night long I was wondering where you are going to end up tonight. You are going to Prague— you don't know where it is. It's in Europe. And this is your new family." He introduced his father, who wrote and starred in the film; the producer; and the little boy, Andrej Chalimon, whom he simply called "Kolya." Sverak concluded with "We promise you that our next film will not shame you, and maybe one day we will make a brother for you."

Céline Dion returned to sing the song with which she was more familiar, *Up Close and Personal*'s "Because You Loved Me," a number one single for six weeks the previous spring. Having now heard them performed, one realized that the nominees from *The*

Mirror Has Two Faces, *One Fine Day* and *Up Close and Personal* were more or less the same song, drippy generic ballads all; Roger Ebert denigrated the trio as sounding "like they were written for a Vegas lounge act."

Angela Bassett began the year's necrology segment by saying, "To quote a wise man, 'They are not where they used to be, but they are now wherever we are.' " The ones who were there in the Shrine Auditorium ranged from 25-year-old Tupac Shakur to cinematographer John Alton, 94. Included were such superstars from the 1930s and 1940s as Claudette Colbert, Greer Garson and Dorothy Lamour, the irrepressible character actors Sheldon Leonard and Jack Weston, directors Krzysztof Kieslowski and Fred Zinnemann, as well as title designer Saul Bass, *James Bond* producer Albert Broccoli, and Joanne Dru, Marcello Mastroianni and Lew Ayres.

The three stars of *The First Wives Club*, Goldie Hawn, Diane Keaton and Bette Midler, entered *ensemble* to present Best Song. Midler stated that all five nominees had been "rendered tonight in full-throated ferociously committed performances." She also corrected Hawn's pronunciation of "Streisand," insisting the accent was on the second syllable. Goldie still begged to differ because, "God, I've known her for twenty-five years." Bette told Keaton, "I voted for you, darling," and Hawn piped up that she had, too, and she and Keaton hugged. "But you do already have one," Midler pointed out, "so it won't be the end of the world if you don't get one." Regarding the business at hand, the winner was "You Must Love Me" from *Evita*. "Well, thank heavens that there wasn't a song in *The English Patient* is all I can say," commented composer Andrew Lloyd Webber, and he heard a lot of laughter for having said so. Lyricist Tim Rice called *Evita* "a jolly good film." About the presenters, Crystal kidded, "There they go, the Yentas of Eastwick."

The host then reminded everyone that he had appeared as a gravedigger in Kenneth Branagh's film version of *Hamlet* and said, "It was wonderful getting laughs with something that was four hundred years old. I actually felt like Anna Nicole Smith." Kenneth Branagh popped up to introduce another time-waster:

film clips of Shakespeare on the screen. This included not just adaptations of the plays, but the use of his words in films like *L.A. Story.* Popeye and Olive Oyl were also on hand as Romeo and Juliet, and the montage ended with Roy Rogers and John Wayne in Raoul Walsh's *Dark Command.*

Critiquing the evening's fashions, designer Vera Wang called Writing presenter Jodie Foster "the poster girl for Armani," and deemed her outfit "a very, very interesting long coat in fish-scale sequins worn over pale gray trousers that created a very artistic unusual combination." Foster prefaced the Writing Awards by saying, somewhat sheepishly, "In a word, the writer's God. That's why so many studio executives in this town are agnostics." With *The English Patient* having so far won all seven of the awards for which it'd been nominated, and with Anthony Minghella's screenplay being the single most praised component of the film, one had every reason to expect the film to win the Adapted Screenplay Award. But instead, in a testament to his personal popularity, *Sling Blade*'s Billy Bob Thornton was the winner. "Well, Lord have mercy," he declared. Among those he thanked was his early promoter, "Miss Elizabeth Taylor," and he concluded by saying, "This is a terrific honor, you know. This is the big one. What can you say?" In addition to Anthony Minghella, Thornton had defeated *The Crucible*'s Arthur Miller, whose days as the front runner seemed very long ago.

The Coen Brothers won the Original Screenplay award for *Fargo.* Joel said, "I would particularly like to thank Frances, without whom the part wouldn't have been written, the movie wouldn't have been made, and we wouldn't be standing here." Five years later, Adapted winner Thornton would be starring in a film for the Original winners, the Coens' *The Man Who Wasn't There.*

Best Actress presenter Nicolas Cage opened the envelope and shouted out the name of Frances Mc-Dormand, with whom he had appeared in 1987's *Raising Arizona.* In the audience, Lauren Bacall could be seen rising to her feet for her fellow Upper West Sider, and the entire audience followed suit. *Today*'s Jim Brown noted that the winner "did a little strutting as she approached the podium." "It is impossible to maintain one's composure in this situation," McDormand began. "What am I doing here?" She spoke of her fellow nominees and said, "We five women were fortunate to have the choice, not just the opportunity but the choice, to play such rich, complex female characters. And I congratulate producers like Working Title and PolyGram for allowing directors to make autonomous casting decisions, based on qualifications and not just market value [huzzahs from the crowd]. And I encourage writers and directors to keep these really interesting female roles coming, and while you're at it, you can throw in a few for the men as well." Finally, she thanked her brother-in-law, Ethan "who helped make an actor of me," her husband, Joel "who made a woman of me," and her son, "our moon and sun, Mr. Pedro McDormand Coen, who's made a real mother of me."

Susan Sarandon quit reading the introduction for the Best Actor Award, suggesting "Why don't we just cut to the chase and let's give this lucky guy an extra eleven seconds." The lucky guy was Geoffrey Rush in *Shine,* and the winner kissed his wife, and then his screen wife, Lynn Redgrave, who was sitting behind him. Like Frances McDormand, he received a standing ovation. (Army Archerd speculated that this ceremony "must have set a record for standing ovations"—there were eight.) Rush said, "The Academy has honored me by choosing to seat me as David Helfgott at a table with Larry Flynt and Count Laszlo de Almasy and Karl Childers and Jerry Maguire. I can't quite imagine where the conversation might lead that night, but it has really enriched me as an actor to be seated at that table." The actor then addressed David Helfgott to say, "You truly are an inspiration, and to those people who say it's a circus, then with your celebration of life, you've shown me that the circus is a place of daring and risk-taking and working without a safety net, and giving us your personal poetry."

Mel Gibson, who had been Geoffrey Rush's roommate in 1979 when they were doing *Waiting for Godot* together in Australia, was onstage to give what he had received last year, the Best Director Oscar. After having lost three Awards in a row, *The English Patient* was back in the winner's circle. Anthony Minghella thanked "my wife who taught me the meaning of the word 'uxoriousness,' " and he blessed Bob and Harvey Weinstein.

Billy Crystal heralded "a great actor" and Al Pacino ran out with a grin on his face. "We have come to the part of the show now that you've all been waiting for," he said. "It's the halfway mark." The audience laughed at the remark, not so much because it was particularly funny, but because it was Al Pacino cracking a joke. "Thought I'd try that," he explained. The winner, of course, was *The English Patient*, and Saul Zaentz was back onstage to declare, "I said my cup was full before. Now it runneth over." He also said, "I'd like to thank actors. I love actors. Producers are supposed to not be in love with actors. And I love writers and directors, too." While Zaentz was recounting how everyone stayed faithful to the project even when the financing was taken away, the telecast cut to Ralph Fiennes, who was holding up two handwritten signs with hearts drawn on them. One read, "Hello, Ivanov Babes," a reference to cast members of the London production in which he was currently starring; the other, "Hello, Becky," who was his personal assistant. Zaentz stated that "Harvey and Bob Weinstein came through and financed the picture—we had final cut, though." He then mentioned, apropos of nothing really, a line that he liked, namely that "Shakespeare was defined as an early plagiarizer of Freud." Anthony Minghella came out from the wings to remind the producer to thank Michael Ondaatje. Zaentz did so, and he concluded with "Thank you to the boys on the corner of Myrtle and Monroe and the gang up in Berkeley."

All that was left was for Billy Crystal to say, "Well, it's been a great night. Stay tuned for *Good Morning America*."

Aftermath

The *Los Angeles Times* reported that, not surprisingly, "Juliette Binoche's upset win over Lauren Bacall was the talk of the industry." Backstage, Binoche said, "I want to say something about Lauren Bacall, because I admire her. We were sure, all of us, we were sure she was going to get this. I hope she has an honored *[sic]* Oscar next year, because she really deserves it." Asked,

"Is winning kind of bittersweet because Lauren lost?" Binoche replied, "No. I don't know why I got this, you know. It's not my fault." Binoche appeared on *Good Morning America* at five A.M., having gotten two hours of sleep, and said she had seen Bacall after the show: "She came over and she hugged me and I hugged her and she said to me, 'Between actresses we shouldn't have competition because it's not about that. We're storytellers and we're trying to give the best we can.' " Binoche also recounted that Bacall "said she was happy that I mentioned her, and she was touched, I think."

Cuba Gooding Jr., exclaimed to reporters backstage, "That music came in quick! Did you all notice that? I mean, they got four hours for the show!" Gilbert Cates later said, however, "I wanna make one thing really clear. We did not play Cuba Gooding Jr., off. We thought he was done and we started the music." When Gooding stopped for interviews on his way into various parties, he was still as exuberant as he had been onstage. "I was two seconds away from backflipping, so I think that was one of the most restrained moments in my entire life," he laughed. "I was backstage still saying my acceptance speech. I didn't realize I wasn't up there anymore." *Access Hollywood* had a camera at the home of Gooding's brother, Omar, and the winner was shown a tape of the jubilation and celebration that had broken out when he won. Cuba's reaction was, "Don't break anything—the lease is in my name!"

Marge Gunderson struck a chord with audiences because "she's just nice," said Frances McDormand. "She's nice, but she's good at her job." The actress also said that the Minnesota dialect was "something exotic for Americans, because not many people have traveled there." When a reporter inquired how Joel Coen "made a woman" of her, McDormand said, "No, I'm not going there."

Geoffrey Rush defended David Helfgott's piano playing. "Music critics hear things through very sophisticated ears, but somehow David is offering a kind of musical experience that is different than what they want to hear," said the Best Actor winner. "I mean if they want to hear technical virtuosity, then maybe David's not the person to give that sort of concert, because he's pouring out his life at that keyboard." He also said he had been "pretty certain" that Billy Bob Thornton was going to win.

Anthony Minghella pooh-poohed the suggestion that he might be disappointed he hadn't won Adapted Screenplay. "When you've won nine Academy Awards for a movie, I think it's very grumpy to say anything. I love Billy Bob Thornton. It's a great movie." Minghella did acknowledge that "it is ironic that the screenplay was the biggest challenge in this film, but I think we have been so blessed this evening that I'm very happy to take one of these guys home with me." And he said, laughing, that "One thing that's really awful. The screenplay for *English Patient* took me two years. Billy Bob wrote his in two weeks." Minghella later revealed that when he phoned his father at home on the Isle of Wight after the ceremony, "I said, 'Dad, how are you doing?' He said, 'Why didn't you win Best Screenplay?'"

Somebody wanted to know if Billy Bob Thornton's psychic mother had predicted his Screenplay victory. "I told her I didn't want to know." He said he would be putting the Oscar "where my two- and three-year olds can't get to it because, boy, will they get to it. My Spirit Award is already ruined." Thornton stole away from the Miramax party to appear on *Today* at 4:16 in the morning. Matt Lauer asked the Adapted Screenplay winner what it was like to go from "somewhat obscurity" to being an Oscar winner. "It's a little bit like a Frank Capra movie," said Thornton. "It's quite a fairy tale because I lived pretty much as an anonymous character actor for sixteen years now." Adding even more of a fairy-tale quality to his life, a few days later Thornton and his wife were Elizabeth Taylor's guests at her Bel Air home.

Harvey Weinstein also chatted with Matt Lauer, and said, "This is probably, business-wise, the most exciting night of my life." He laughed about *Sling Blade*'s success, saying that he told Billy Bob Thornton, "I never even heard of half the towns where his movie's a hit." As for an Oscar follow-up, the Miramax head mentioned Michael Winterbottom's *Welcome to Sarajevo* with Woody Harrelson, and "we'll see if we can come to the prom next year." He also noted that "Quentin's gearing up for his next one, too." Kenneth Turan wrote, "Who but Miramax could have focused

the Academy's attention on a deserving urchin like *Sling Blade* and gotten the Best Adapted Screenplay Oscar for Billy Bob Thornton? Like the polished lobbyists they are, the Miramax team has perfected the technique of putting just enough pressure on Academy voters to get results but not so much as to appear unseemly."

Saul Zaentz was later asked if he had received congratulatory calls from any executives at 20th Century Fox. "Are you kidding?" he replied. "They were sick. If they could have had a cement truck run me over, they would have." Executives at Fox had always denied the veracity of Zaentz's account of their pulling out of *The English Patient*, saying it had nothing at all to do with the issue of Demi Moore and star power but that, as paraphrased by the *Los Angeles Times*, "the project unraveled instead because of Zaentz's struggle to secure financing."

David Frankel, winner of the Live Action Short, said it was a "strange feeling" to have won DreamWorks' first Oscar. But "I know there are a lot more Oscars coming from the man at the top there. And I think next year, with *Amistad*, you'll see Steven Spielberg right here." Courtney Love said she initially had a case of butterflies before going on, but "then I realized I've rocked theaters way bigger than this." She also said she cried when Frances McDormand won. Before the show, Mike Leigh had said, "I've had quite a few fantasies, but none of them involved the Oscar," which was just as well, since *Secrets & Lies* ended up the only Best Picture nominee not to receive a single Award. October Films would also lose its status as a true independent, with Universal buying a 51 percent share in the company in the summer of 1997. Two years later, it would cease as a separate entity altogether when Barry Diller combined it with Gramercy Pictures to form USA Films.

Wolfgang Puck was in charge of the menu at the Governors Ball for the third time. Hors d'oeuvres consisted of roasted new potatoes and caviar, Chinois vegetable spring rolls with apricot mustard sauce, smoked sturgeon on crisp potato galettes, and pizza with smoked salmon and dill cream. Appetizers included marinated lobster salad, artichokes with white truffle vinaigrette, chopped chino ranch vegetable salad, asparagus with orange mustard, tuna tataki with wasabi cream, Parmesan bread sticks wrapped with prosciutto and smoked salmon on Oscar matzoh. Main course was roasted salmon with horseradish mashed potatoes and tomato basil fondue and Chinois rack of lamb with mint cilantro vinaigrette and stir-fried vegetables. For dessert, it was "Oscar's Decadent Delights." The tent was decorated by artist Hiro Yamagata, with images from his Earthly Paradise collection projected on the ceiling, while his renditions of flowers and butterflies adorned the walls. Frances McDormand was heard saying, "I'm starved, I've gotta eat," when she came in after fulfilling her Best Actress obligations with reporters. Jack Sheldon's orchestra provided the music at the Ball, which lasted about two hours, at which point people moved on to the other soirees.

There was an official East Coast Academy Party this year held at New York's "21" and hosted by Official Academy Historian Robert Osborne. Dining on shrimp, smoked salmon, grilled tournedos of beef, and apricot yogurt with chocolate Oscar were Jane Powell and Dickie Moore, Kim Hunter, Ruth Warrick, Arlene Dahl and Arnold Stang.

Bill Higgins of the *Los Angeles Times* had written, "There are less parties this year because there aren't any studios celebrating the Oscars this year except Sony. So the pressure to get into the parties is even crazier than usual." The Sony/Columbia party was held at Eclipse, and Cuba Gooding Jr., was, of course, the belle of the ball. Woody Harrelson was there, as well, wearing a classically tailored Armani tuxedo—which was made entirely of hemp. Asked by E!'s Gina Cook what he thought of Geoffrey Rush's victory, the *Larry Flynt* star said, "Personally, I would have voted for Billy Bob," then with an artful little dig, added, "But I thought Geoffrey Rush definitely delivered thirty-five minutes of a solid and great performance." Despite his airplane banner, Larry Flynt came to the Sony party, though he did say he was "depressed" that Harrelson and Milos Forman went home Oscar-less; Dennis Rodman and California Governor Pete Wilson were also among the revelers at Eclipse. Frank DiGiacomo of the *New York Observer* called this party "mirthless," declaring that "its only oxygen a gracious but bummed-looking

Cameron Crowe, a grim-looking Lauren Bacall and a chowing down Cuba Gooding Jr." At this party, Bacall did let it be known that " 'How did it feel to lose?' is *not* my favorite question."

To get from the *Jerry Maguire* bash to the *Vanity Fair* party, Tom Cruise and Nicole Kidman had only to walk across Melrose. E! Online's Ted Casablanca had reported, "*Vanity Fair,* which always reserves Morton's for its Oscar fete, is *furious* that Sony is having its *Jerry Maguire* bash right across the street at Eclipse, which is, ironically, right where Morton's *used* to be. I swear, these partiers are worse than gals caught in the same dress." The *Observer's* DiGiacomo claimed that at Eclipse "the noise of the band couldn't quite drown out the roaring out on the sidewalk that occurred each time *another celebrity* walked into Morton's." When Bette Midler arrived at the *Vanity Fair* bash, she nodded in the direction of Eclipse and jested, "I might go across the street just to see what the hoi polloi are doing." *Daily Variety* took note that "the annual fete at Morton's seemed to be the most controlled invite in town, and the magazine turned away a number of partygoers who hoped to segue there from the Sony soiree." Despite *Vanity Fair's* exclusionary tendencies, the *Hollywood Reporter* complained that "the party trappings were on the ordinary side, with waiters offering unremarkable hors d'oeuvres amid a quietly throbbing techno beat." Cuba Gooding was there saying, "I blew a gasket" onstage. "I am so gone right now. All conversation is flying over me." Cindy Adams saw Tony Curtis at Morton's, "with his blonde woman in tights so tight that her navel must be an 'inny' or I'd have seen it. And Mira Sorvino with Quentin Tarantino, who stuck closer to her than that lady's tights." Curtis was also heard to declare that the triumph of independent films at this year's Oscars was "like the Berlin Wall coming down. The studios are out of business." He was also still smarting that he and his *The Defiant Ones* costar Sidney Poitier had lost the 1958 Best Actor race to David Niven in *Separate Tables.* "Did you see that performance? It's a lot of shit," Curtis insisted, continuing that "We saw a bit of that elite British concept of movie making tonight with *The English Patient.* They don't act, they posture."

Steve Martin accidentally knocked Diane

Keaton's glass out of her hand; when the sound of breaking glass had everyone looking their way, Martin pretended he was a wedding rabbi and yelled, "Mazel tov!" The president's brother, Roger Clinton, was at the same table as Mick Jagger, and when Ellen DeGeneres saw Dennis Rodman's outfit she told him, "I almost wore that." DeGeneres also saw actress Anne Heche at this party, and it marked the beginning of their highly publicized relationship. Painter David Hockney called the show "longer than *Tristan und Isolde*." Winona Ryder and Gene Siskel were seen having an intense conversation, with Siskel at one point declaiming, "Remarks like that are threats to my show!" And as Mel Gibson entered the party, he told E!'s Jules Asner, "If somebody threw up on me, I might throw up back on them."

At Elton John's benefit party—held at Maple Drive and cosponsored this year by *In Style* magazine—the *Fargo* contingent made an appearance, although Frances McDormand said she couldn't stay out too late because son Pedro had an eleven A.M. play date. Sting, Lionel Ritchie, Fran Drescher and Sean Young were here, as was 6-year-old Jonathan Lipnicki, the kid from *Jerry Maguire*, and his 9-year-old sister, Alexis. When Muhammad Ali arrived other partygoers began chanting, "Ali! Ali! Ali!" and "We love you!" On the menu were grilled prawns, crab cakes, calamari, roast lamb and stuffed artichokes. A quarter of a million dollars was raised for the Elton John AIDS Foundation, but even though John was turning 50 at midnight, the party ended on the early side. *Daily Variety* quoted "one Maple Driver who later was spotted at the *Vanity Fair* fete: 'It got dull pretty fast.' "

The Beverly Hills Hotel was the scene of the Night of 100 Stars Gala, a benefit for the Film & Performing Artists Foundation, which helps out entertainment industry-ites having a rough go of it financially. Partygoers enjoyed chicken, pasta, asparagus and fudge mousse. Attendees included Milton Berle, Kato Kaelin, Rod Steiger, Richard Benjamin, Flip Wilson, Shirley Jones and Marty Ingels, Barbara Eden and Tom Arnold. A debut charity soiree this year was the Oscar Night Gala for the Environment, raising money for three green and animal-friendly organiza-

tions: the Earth Communications Office, the American Equine Rescue Organization and People for Children & Animals. The party was held at Wolfgang Puck's new pan-Asian place, Oba Chine, and it was only right that *Babe*'s James Cromwell was here, as were Bruce Davison, Swoosie Kurtz, David Carradine and Tippi Hedren.

USA Today's Jeannie Williams reported, "Hollywood hostess-with-clout Dani Janssen's party showed the impact of independent wins. Usually her Century City penthouse has several Oscars arriving with winners. None this year, though the traditional power group inhaled her smothered chicken." That group included Clint Eastwood and Jack Nicholson, as well as some visitors from New York—Susan Sarandon, Tim Robbins and Lauren Bacall.

At one point, fire marshals refused to let anyone into the Mondrian Hotel because there were so many people at the Miramax party; *Daily Variety* put the number at "more than 1,000," the *New York Observer* said "1,200 all told." Hotelier Ian Schrager had eighty-five valets handling cars at the bash. In addition to nominees from Miramax releases, the guests at the hotel's Skybar included Al Pacino, Jay Leno, Bill Maher, Mick Jagger, Tori Spelling, Keith Richards and Michael Eisner. "It doesn't get better than this," declared Harvey Weinstein of Miramax's eleven Oscars. The possible downside was "I just hope the press won't expect us to do this every year." A helicopter hovered overhead, using the latest digital technology to congratulate the company on its success tonight, but Weinstein denied he had anything to do with it. Heading into Mondrian, Kristin Scott Thomas said one result of *The English Patient*'s sweep was that "I've got aching cheeks from smiling so much." Jay Leno quipped, "All over the world there are a lot of English patients lying in hospitals, and I think this movie will be an inspiration to them." Holding his Oscar and Thalberg, the portly Saul Zaentz joked, "These are my new dumbbells. I'm starting to work out with weights!" The *New York Observer* was at this party and noted that "independent filmmakers, who have always been in the Miramax stable, were there that night, some of them in their usual turtleneck-and-blazer shtick. But they looked woefully out of place at the Mondrian on Oscar night. Harvey and Bob Weinstein had finally stopped being guests at the table; they were getting initiated as members of the Hollywood establishment." *Entertainment Weekly* reported that a security guard standing near where Harvey was positioned told a comrade, "We have to watch this area. That fat guy is the head of this whole thing, and everybody wants to hang around him."

Because of local liquor laws, the hotel's bars closed down at two A.M. and drink-filled glasses were taken away from party-goers in mid-gulp, even though such guests as Leonardo DiCaprio, Claire Danes, Winona Ryder and Glenn Close were just arriving. Brenda Blethyn was heard inquiring, "Where can you get a drink in this town?" With the bar closed, the party moved up from the ground floor to a suite on the twelfth floor of the hotel. Andrej Chalimon, the 7-year-old who had the title role in Miramax's *Kolya*, was photographed fast asleep at the party long before that, and at 11:45 was carried out. Quentin Tarantino was the last to leave—at 5:30.

And the shindig in Fargo, North Dakota, was by all accounts a smashing success. Organizer Margie Bailly noted, "We need a party right about now. We're smack in the middle of the snow and flood seasons." In fact, it was snowing on Oscar night, and the 3 new inches brought the winter's total to 109.6 inches. Making like one of the giant-sized Oscars outside the Shrine Auditorium was Olie, a mannequin from a local department store dressed in long johns and a hat. Kristin Rudrüd, the Fargo native who played William H. Macy's kidnapped wife in the movie, was the guest of honor—arriving not in a limo, but a blue pickup truck—and nearly nine hundred people attended. Most were dressed in overalls, flannels, hooded parkas and duck boots. Marv Bossart, a reporter for local station WDAY-TV arrived in a tuxedo, went home and changed into more comfortable Fargo-wear. There was a wood-chipper demonstration and a live polka band, and refreshments consisted of local favorites, such as lime Jell-O, pickled herring on Ritz crackers and rommegrot, which one out-of-town reporter described as "a fatty white pudding." T-shirts were on

sale with such sayings as "Fargo: It's flat but it's cold," "Fargo: The movie is deep, but the snow is deeper," and "We don't talk like that movie—OK, then?" Noting that this had been Fargo 's worst winter ever, NBC's Jim Avilla reported that each win by *Fargo* "was cheered as though the sun had somehow broken out in mid-January." Taking stock of the evening's results in Hollywood, a local radio personality suggested that the sequel to *Fargo* be called *The Norwegian-American Patient*. And Kristin Rudrüd said, "I'm much happier coming to this. This is huge. The Oscars are just the Oscars."

People was impressed that, fashion-wise, the Oscar ceremony, "despite its dearth of glitzy nominees, still pulled off a high-style—and virtually guffaw-free—display of good taste." Appearing on *The Today Show*, *Premiere* senior editor Holly Millea, though, said this year's trend was to be "very revealing on top." She observed that "these women forget that when they step into a cold auditorium we're not necessarily looking at their dresses anymore," and, as a case in point, the television monitor showed Sigourney Weaver, with her right nipple very prominent through her dress. Millea's conclusion: "A lot of these women should have had bras on, frankly."

Millea called Jodie Foster the best-looking of the night, saying she was "totally classic." Maureen Jenkins of the *Chicago Sun-Times* wrote that Frances McDormand "transformed from *Fargo* frump to Hollywood star. Her sleek midnight-blue gown with criss-crossing back straps was an Oscar 'Do.' " Acting as fashion critic for *Good Morning America*, 1994 Supporting Actress nominee Jennifer Tilly analyzed, "It seemed like the European actresses seemed to go for the Gothic influence. It's almost like they forgot it's not really winter here in Los Angeles. Maybe over in England and France it's winter."

One of the actresses of whom Tilly was speaking, Kristin Scott Thomas, generated the most votes for this year's best dressed. She wore a low-cut black taffeta Christian Lacroix ball gown with shawl collar, sheer sleeves and a tulle bustle, accessorized with a jeweled broach at the waist. Vera Wang gasped, "She was positively staggering, with the beautiful makeup, the refined hair and the incredible earrings that she wore." The *Orange County Register* felt that "Thomas evoked classic Hollywood glamour." And Joan Rivers's compatriot Leon Hall said simply, "You don't get much better than that."

W's Merrill Ginsburg deemed it a toss-up between Thomas and Juliette Binoche for sartorial honors, and Barbara De Witt of the *Los Angeles Daily News* said, "If there was an Oscar for Best Entrance on the Red Carpet, the women of *The English Patient* took that award, too. Juliette Binoche and Kristin Scott Thomas would have tied in terms of fashion." Backstage, Binoche said she had been working with designer Sophie Sitbon "for seven years, and I had other offers coming here. And I said, 'No, no. I'm going back to my friend.'" The outfit, a rust-colored velvet dress and jacket with a stand-up portrait collar, was the most divisive of the evening. Sitbon designed the dress, but Binoche chose the color. *People* called Binoche "the picture of retro elegance" and Susan Sterner of the *Philadelphia Inquirer* said "the collar was a tad too much, but she still managed to look like something out of a Sargent painting." Laurice A. Parkin of the *New York Daily News* was one of several fashion critics who decided "it looked more appropriate for the evil queen from *Snow White*" while Cruella de Ville's name also came up in criticisms. Mimi Avins of the *Los Angeles Times* also evoked the *Snow White* villainness, but added that "the color was spectacular." The *Miami Herald* printed a picture of the actress backstage holding her Oscar, with the caption: "Best performance in a Count Chocula outfit."

Nicole Kidman also heard both pans and panegyrics. KTLA's Laurie Pike said "Nicole Kidman is officially forgiven for that hideous nightgown last year. She looks flawless. . . . She looks fantastic. In chartreuse. It takes guts to wear chartreuse to the Academy Awards." Joan Rivers, though, said Kidman was "in the ugliest green you've ever seen." Mimi Avins had it both ways with Kidman: "Her chartreuse satin embroidered gown with tassel trim by John Galliano for Christian Dior couture was sure to rile those with limited tolerance for that difficult color, but her sleek figure-eight chignon was above reproach."

On *E!'s Academy Awards Fashion Review*, Joan Rivers said, "Dennis Rodman should kick himself in the groin. He looked like the doorman at a gay bed-and-breakfast." And Billy Bob Thornton "looks like Karl in *Sling Blade* dressed him." Hearing that it was Hugo Boss who did the outfit, Rivers said, "It's Hugo Boss on drugs."

The telecast received a mixed response, although enthusiasm for the opening comic film montage was near unanimous. *Daily Variety* wrote: "Billy Crystal showed them how it's done with an Oscarcast hosting gig that had more pure verve and spunk than any of the previous three telecasts that lacked his glib presence." Otherwise, the paper found the show to be "at turns absurd and funny, warm and awkward, classy and strained." The *Orange County Register*'s Kinney Littlefield enjoyed how "like a smart parent, witty Crystal knows just how to chide, ride or take pride in his egocentric Hollywood children."

Tom Maurstad of the *Dallas Morning News* called it "a really long and strikingly mediocre television show" and Tom Shales sighed in the *Washington Post* that the show was "hideously overlong." Shales also said that "Throughout the night, Crystal was bouncy and engaging—not as wickedly funny as Johnny Carson or Bob Hope was in the very gold days, but generally a pleasure to have around." Brian Lowry of the *Los Angeles Times* said that the "few memorable moments belonged almost entirely to the recipients . . . in a telecast that proved less compelling—indeed, during stretches, more downright dull—than recent predecessors." He also felt that Billy Crystal's jokes "felt a bit forced and stale." Frazier Moore of the Associated Press remembered that Billy Crystal had "killed the audience in 1991, yet died a year later when nothing he said got a laugh . . . Monday night Crystal was back, an actor whose career has faded in the interim and could use a pick-me-up. A socko performance could've worked wonders for him, as well as for the show. It didn't happen."

Emotional highlights were deemed to be the appearance of Muhammad Ali onstage—even if director Louis Horvitz cut to commercial just as Ali got there—and, especially, Cuba Gooding Jr.'s speech. "How could you not love a moment like that?" wondered *Entertainment Tonight*'s Leonard Maltin. "He started thanking people and apparently couldn't stop," joked David Letterman. "This morning he called me and thanked me for not hosting." Letterman's Top Ten list the night after the Awards was "Top Ten Things Overheard at the Oscars." While number seven was "I'm sorry. Those seats are reserved for the two people who actually saw *Secrets & Lies*" and number four was "I hope Richard Gere wins 'Weirdest Celebrity Rumor,' " number one was "Who's the geek in the crashing airplane?"

Entertainment Weekly said David Letterman was "mordantly funny" in his bit part in the opening film and *TV Guide*'s Jeff Jarvis declared, "The class act of the night had to be David Letterman, coming on doing 'Oprah-Uma, Oprah-Uma' and making fun of himself." Jarvis also appreciated Debbie Reynolds's bit saying, "That's entertainment. The Oscars are supposed to be good old-fashioned entertainment, and Debbie Reynolds is a good old-time entertainer and she knew that. And it was a relief." Billy Crystal's own critique of the program: "I feel it was the best first half-hour of any Oscar show I've ever seen." Despite his plug for it in front of a supposed billion people, however, Crystal's film *Father's Day* tanked at the box office.

On the internet, an AOL member named PUZZLR wrote, "ok I was like watchn tv n I saw this show. it seemed pretty cewl so i watched, like big mistake. it was sooo borrin n long n it was a jyp two like I thout they wood show a hole movie but they only shwd bits n pecces . . . but 4 some reason like thay had a lot of big starrs I didn cee lio decaprio but I no he was hot wereever he was tom bruise in his heels toms wife wering I-glasses like im so smart but if yous so smart why r you still with tom . . . melvin spacee talkn like he had a labottomee . . . n evreebodi that got up thank peoples I nevr herd of why didn thay thank me 4 watchn this crap the bess part was bevis n buthead but they like was not on looong enuf n they nevr said this sucks so win this show comes on next week join me in boycotton it."

That singular species known as Barbra Streisand fanatics was also busy on the internet, and they were not happy about what they had witnessed. Guy McGuire, online in the middle of the show, said "You know, I used to love the Oscars . . . until 1983, that is, when Barbra didn't receive a single nomination for *Yentl: The Masterwork*. And then 1987, when Barbra was overlooked for her staggering performance in *Nuts*. And then 1991 when Barbra received no personal mention for *The Prince of Tides*, despite its seven nominations . . . Lauren Bacall—a true Hollywood legend, never before nominated—is supposed to be a LOCK for Best Supporting Actress. A SURE THING. And what happens? No Oscar for Bacall. After 53 years in the business, they tell her once more she's not good enough . . . As soon as Madonna's four-note wonder or Céline Dion's shriek-fest wins the Best Song award, off I go. This is it for me. Screw the Academy."

Five minutes later, Guy was back to add, "Seems to me no one complimented Barbra for her 'class' when she sang in 1976 despite having been denied an actress nomination [for *A Star Is Born*]. No one complimented her for her 'class' when she showed up for the 1991 ceremony . . . haven't been this angry since Nolte lost the Actor Award five years ago." A fella calling himself RoadRPH shrieked, "I cannot believe this. That queen Billy Crystal takes a dig at Barbra when he introduces Madonna . . . I saw a little of *A Star Is Born* because it looked as if James wanted to jump up and protest when Billy Boy made his little comment."

GoldenCat wrote, "Céline may not be a Barbra, she may have an unfortunate chin, but the lady is a pro and is deserving of much honor for her professionalism. Merci, Céline—I'll never bad-rap you again . . . I was *so* happy to see Barbra there, and to see her be gracious to that filthy Rivers creature." AllieCat70 typed, "Can I too express my opinion on how extremely pissed off I am at the cut to Barbra after that one guy (I refuse to type his name) mentions Madonna's 'class'???? What a f******g cheap shot!! I am still furious and its been over for like 3 hours now!! . . . I want to hit something or someone!!! . . . I haven't seen *The English Patient* so I can't say whether or not it deserved to win as much as it did, but I'm glad it did because Barbra and Jim were sitting right behind that group so we got to see them a lot!! . . . Everyone remember to take their high blood pressure medication tonight! I'm sure we'll all need it."

Later in the week, Liz Smith said that, from what she'd been hearing, Lauren Bacall had been the victim of anti–Barbra Streisand sentiment: "Bacall would most certainly have hailed Barbra to the skies," she observed, and "Hollywood insiders insist this *is* why Bacall—expected to win in a walk—lost to Juliette Binoche. The Academy voters won't give Streisand a break."

Bacall told Cindy Adams, "I never expected anything. I've been honored for my stagework, but I've been dismissed in films. Mentally, I understand what's happened. I'm not stupid. There was just too much focus. It's always a mistake to think it's a shoo-in. They've had more than one surprise at the Awards." Andrew Sarris's heart went out to Bacall, "one moment a screen legend and the next a pathetic 72-year-old woman victimized by a combination of advance expectations and Oscar's periodic reminder that Hollywood is somewhat less sentimental than Caligula on a particularly cruel day." Bacall had been at a number of post-Oscar parties and didn't look "pathetic" or dejected at all. *Entertainment Tonight* showed her dancing at the Governors Ball with Kevin Spacey, the very man who had opened the envelope with Juliette Binoche's name in it.

Two weeks after the Awards, Marilyn Beck and Stacy Jenel Smith reported, "Lauren Bacall wants to make something perfectly clear. She is not—repeat, not—devastated that she didn't win an Oscar for *The Mirror Has Two Faces*. She never expected to nab the Award and felt just fine when Juliette Binoche was announced as Best Supporting Actress. Bacall is making her feelings clear at this time because of the many press reports that she was crushed at the Oscar loss and hasn't gotten over it. Simply 'tain't true, says she." And later in the year Bacall had the distinction of being a Kennedy Center Lifetime Achievement honoree; the only downside was that the impassioned liberal had to share the spotlight that night with right-wing gun nut Charlton Heston. One thing was made absolutely clear by the 1996 Academy Awards—never again would there be a "sure bet."

Gillian Helfgott appeared on *Good Morning America* to talk about Oscar night and said, "It was so exciting. David was thrilled to bits about it . . . he couldn't get the grin off his face." She also revealed that "He couldn't stop cuddling Glenn Close, and I don't blame him." A year later, David Helfgott's sister

Margaret went beyond her letters-to-the-editor campaign against *Shine* and wrote a book, *Out of Tune*. In it she again denounced the movie by chapter and verse and attempted to set the record straight about her family and, in particular, her father. Subtitled "David Helfgott and the Myth of *Shine*," the book inveighed against Scott Hicks and everyone else connected with *Shine*—which, among other things, Margaret condemned as anti-Semitic; her greatest venom was saved for Gillian, who was portrayed as a manipulative and exploitative harpy. After the book was published, Hicks maintained that it was Margaret who had a distorted view; he said, regarding the film, "In fact, some people who knew David Helfgott's father have commented to me that it is, if anything, a rather kind portrait."

The day after the Oscars, Cindy Adams still hadn't forgiven this year's Oscar players for being new faces. The headline of her morning-after column was "Fame's Apt to Be Fleeting for This Bunch." She began: "The Oscars. Borrowed jewels, borrowed schmattas and, this year, borrowed limelight that for some may get repossessed fast."

It would be hard to think of a faster turnabout from Academy Award bliss to personal turmoil. On Oscar night, Pietra Thornton was clinging onto husband Billy Bob like Velcro. Heading into the ceremony, she had told reporters, "I am so proud. You have no idea." Two and a half weeks later, she sued Billy Bob for divorce, citing irreconcilable differences and alleging that he beat her, something he adamantly denied. *Newsweek* reported: "In a restraining order she's obtained against him, Pietra slings accusations of physical and emotional abuse that include murder threats and knocking her down when she was pregnant. She says Billy Bob is a manic-depressive who's violent when he doesn't take his lithium." In response, the actor said, "I'm sorry that Pietra's advisers have convinced her to take this malicious and untruthful course of action." They divorced a few months later, and she would have her own starring role when she got naked for *Playboy*.

Another turnabout was in the love-fest between *The English Patient*'s gang and Miramax. On nominations day, Saul Zaentz had said, "For us, the film will be

considered a success when we get paid." Three years after the producer praised the Weinsteins from the stage
of the Shrine, the *Hollywood Reporter* wrote, "the filmmakers and the cast (who deferred fees to get the picture made) are still waiting for distributor Miramax
Films to pay them," and quoted an unnamed source
that "right after the Academy Awards, Harvey gave a $5
million advance, but no one's gotten a nickel since."
The post-Oscar $5 million was spread among the cast
and crew and no more money had been forthcoming—
even though the $31 million film had grossed $232
million—so Saul Zaentz hired a law firm to conduct an
audit. The *Reporter* quoted someone "with a direct
interest," bemoaning, "There is this ongoing audit
that never ends. They are very slow in producing
documents. Meanwhile, we keep getting statements
from [Miramax] showing us that the movie is in the
red. It just doesn't make any sense." More time passed,
and in the beginning of 2001, the *Reporter* again
checked in on the situation and found that "The waiting for payment continues for the filmmakers and cast
of *The English Patient* . . . including the company's current *Chocolat* star, Juliette Binoche." And the audit
went on.

1997

So much for small independent films.

The Ghost of Tom Joad

The summer of 1997 saw the usual suspects. Although the season lacked the overwhelming one-two punch of last year's *Independence Day* and *Twister*, there were *Men in Black*, *The Lost World: Jurassic Park* and *Air Force One* to keep happiness alive in studio corridors. But Jonathan Rosenbaum of the *Chicago Reader* spoke for serious film people everywhere when he admitted to being "rattled . . . by the mindless rapidity of such empty junk heaps as *Speed 2: Cruise Control* and *Batman & Robin*." In the midst of all this noise, there was a much quieter movie critics found more to their liking.

Directed by Victor Nunez, *Ulee's Gold* was the story of a flinty widowed beekeeper, estranged from his ne'er-do-well adult son, who in a time of crisis opens himself up to reconcile with both family obligations and the ability to love. Todd McCarthy of *Variety* rejoiced, "A gem of rare emotional depth and integrity, *Ulee's Gold* is the cinematic equivalent of a wonderful old backwater town, a community bypassed by the interstate of the mainstream American film industry that possesses virtues and knowledge that travelers in the fast lane never stop to appreciate." Dave Kehr wrote in the *New York Daily News* that "it may be trite to say it, but in a summer dominated by digital dinosaurs and flying psycho-killers, the real gold is here, in the irreplaceable human stuff." He felt that the film "unites the clear, classical style of a John Ford Western with the prickly humanism of Jean Renoir."

But the real story about *Ulee's Gold* was its leading man. In the *New York Times*, Janet Maslin cited "Peter Fonda's quietly astonishing performance. It would be accurate but barely adequate to call this the finest work of Fonda's career. Lionized nearly 30 years ago as the epitome of hip complacency, then dormant for a long while, he emerges here as a figure of unexpected stature." She added, "Almost wordlessly, in a way that also suggests Clint Eastwood or even the John Wayne of *The Searchers*, he conveys stubborn bitterness along with the inner strength of a man described by another of the film's characters as 'an old-fashioned, ties-that-bind kind of guy.' " Kenneth Turan of the *Los Angeles Times* was equally impressed: "Fonda, wearing metal-rimmed glasses that echo his father's . . . brings a deliberateness and a weight to Ulee's stillness that say more than pages of dialogue could. His performance holds the film together, and it's one that all generations of Fondas can be proud of." In *Newsweek*, Karen Schoemer exulted that "Fonda achieves a subtle miracle: he brings to life a man who's virtually *out* of life, etching him in passions so deeply buried they barely flicker across his face. Not since 1969's *Easy Rider* has he connected so emphatically with a role."

Although Fonda had been making movies on a regular basis in recent years, *Ulee's Gold* brought him more attention than he had been accorded in decades. He acknowledged that a lot of Hollywood decision makers just assumed he was busying himself with illegal substances on his Montana ranch. "Well, no, I wasn't," he said. "I took drugs, but I wasn't a druggie. I made an average of 1.3 films a year. Some were, you know, bad. But I did my job well. My father took everything he was offered. I'm sure he wasn't thrilled with being in *The Swarm*, but there he was."

Many reviews noted how Fonda's performance conjured memories of his father's work, and director Nunez went so far as to say, "There were moments when I was directing Peter that I'd look into the camera and see the ghost of Henry Fonda." The actor said of his father, "He could get up on stage or screen and have a conversation, but at home it was hard for him. He was very, very shy. And I saw that in Ulee's character. I realized that this man was a lot like how my father was for all of his life until the end. He was quiet, he didn't say much, he'd become more and more uneasy the more we would all demand he talk to us. Poor guy. But ultimately everything was fine. I had—what's the buzzword, closure? I had great closure with my dad. One of the last things he said on the planet—he looked at me and said, 'I want you to know, son, that I love you very much.' " Peter did make the distinction that "I wasn't playing my dad, but I was playing that type of character."

During production in Florida, a woman saw Fonda and came back with her copy of a *Tammy and the Doctor* video for him to sign. Observed Victor Nunez, "You realize he's not just the art film or the specialized filmgoer's actor. He's like a country singer who had a couple of top-ten hits a few years ago and he's still loved."

Macho Dancers

Audiences needing an antidote to the summer's behemoths embraced another small film which, like *Ulee's Gold*, had first made a splash at Sundance and found its way into theaters during the warm-weather months. A British comedy set in the 1980s during Margaret Thatcher's reign, *The Full Monty* told of a group of northern England steelworkers who, their jobs having been eliminated, hit upon a scheme to bring in some dough. They're going to go one better than Chippendale dancers by baring it all for the local women of Sheffield, which means they have to deal with their inhibitions, learn—pretty much from scratch—how to dance, and face the fact that they are not your usual pin-up types.

The *Full Monty* incorporated two distinctive components. As John Anderson of *Newsday* characterized them, "One is the baggy-pants, no pants slapstick of relatively unattractive men strutting their stuff; the other is about their willingness to humiliate themselves to an excruciating extent because they need to feed their families, pay their rent and rebut the official government position that they're obsolete." Andrew Sarris reflected in the *New York Observer* that "Their blue-collar travails remind us as few American films do of the horrors attendant on downsizing for the sacred causes of industrial efficiency and the free market."

Director Peter Cattaneo, who was graduating from music videos and short films to make his feature debut, said that even though his background was far different from that of the men in his movie, he was highly empathetic to their plight. In fact, the first film he made at the Royal College of Art dealt with striking miners, although in retrospect he said that effort was "a load of artsy bullshit." But while in school, "We used to do collections and join the miners on the picket lines. Margaret Thatcher was an evil woman."

Cattaneo said that when casting actors for the film, "I did ask some of them to take their shirts off and do a twirl, to make sure they were un-muscled or puny enough. Mostly I asked them if they could dance. If they said yes, then they didn't get a part." He appreciated having Susie Figgis as his casting director because "It was good to have a woman involved, just to be sure that they weren't in any way attractive." He was looking for "a very motley crew. I wanted a short, fat guy, someone older, etc. The poster for *The Usual Suspects* kept popping into my head."

Critics appreciated *The Full Monty* on both its humorous and more serious levels. "This exuberant charmer still manages to be roaringly funny and subtly heartbreaking," said Peter Travers of *Rolling Stone*. The *Washington Post*'s Rita Kempley called the film "a warm, ribaldly funny, stubbornly upbeat story . . . with witty, appropriately rough-hewn repartee and genuine poignancy." And she tapped into the aspect of the film to which audiences would especially respond: "Size, as the women of Sheffield can attest, is not the true measure of a man, nor, for that matter, are youth, beauty and bulging muscles. There's nothing new in that, but sometimes the non-Chippendales of the world need to be reminded that courage, kindness, honesty and being able to laugh at yourself count for more than washboard abs and a full head of hair."

I'll Show You Mine . . .

The movie's climax had the sextet on stage and baring it all. The director recalled having to film take after take because "one of the guys would always get kind of caught up in his Velcro leather thong, and their bums got very sore as well. It was funny for about three takes, and then it became a bit of a problem." Leading man Robert Carlyle remembered that "the camera went behind us and we did the whole strip scene through, ending with a ten-second freeze. The women went wild. And we just stood there. It was terrifying, absolutely terrifying." Natasha Walter of London's *Observer* felt gypped. She complained that the film "presses forward the idea that now that women are getting hold of more economic power, men have to get used to giving pleasure as well as getting it. The final shot is the apotheosis of that theme, when six men stand naked facing a screaming crowd of Sheffield lasses. It's all right for those lasses; but the women in the cinema can't see what they're so excited about. We get a set of bottoms in long shot; where, we might ask, is the full monty?" But Michael Medved of the *New York Post* had seen plenty, and said that even without full-frontal nudity, "the audience feels well-informed about the individual equipment of the individual characters."

"As soon as we saw the dailies, we knew we had something special," said a marketing executive at Fox Searchlight. The company then held an unusually large number of pre-release screenings for the film, designed to generate positive pre-opening word of mouth. In fact, another Searchlight executive admitted, "Theater owners started complaining and getting nervous that we were giving away too many tickets and cannibalizing our whole audience." The strategy worked, though, for when the film opened in a few cities, house records were broken. That same word of mouth, as if by wizardry, spread out to smaller burgs, and when *The Full Monty* hit those towns, audiences were waiting eagerly. The little $3 million British film turned into a major hit across the country. Fox Searchlight's head, Lindsay Law, thought he understood the key to *The Full Monty*'s success. "It was a summer in which we were presented with movies that had no resemblance to our world or our lives," he posited. "In this movie, the audience actually understands and loves these guys. You can't say that about too many other movies."

Newsday's Jack Mathews told of a friend who saw the movie in a Connecticut theater and "said the audience was so wired at the end it began an impromptu party, dancing in the aisles to the music over the end credits." That was nothing compared to what happened in Santa Monica. *Variety* reported that "after the film played, an audience member got so excited he took off all his clothes and ran naked down Wilshire Boulevard."

Men Behaving Badly

While Fox Searchlight was praised for its marketing savvy with *The Full Monty*, Warner Brothers didn't seem to know quite how to sell its film, *L.A. Confidential*. Actually the studio hadn't known what to do with the project in the first place. Three very different—and morally ambiguous—cops were the starting point of James Ellroy's unwieldy novel, a labyrinthine story inundated with all forms of corruption and evil. The book was so relentlessly brutal and profane that it teetered on the daft; its rather out-of-control narrative even featured a Walt Disney–like character doing unspeakable things to children. Warners had optioned the novel in 1989, and though at one point the book was penciled in to become a miniseries, *L.A. Confidential* stagnated as a project. Ellroy said he was used to getting option checks for his novels, without ever seeing the books metamorphose into movies.

Enter Curtis Hanson, a director in Hollywood's good graces because of the financial success of his two most recent films, the psycho baby-sitter opus *The Hand That Rocks the Cradle* and Meryl Streep's Big Adventure, *The River Wild*. Once he read the book, Hanson said, "I couldn't get Ellroy's characters out of my mind. It was the characters more than the specifics of the plot that kept my interest. It also touched upon a theme that I've always enjoyed playing with: exploring the difference between how things appear and how they are." Ellroy might have disagreed about that analysis, for in his estimation the general theme of all his books was "bad white men doing bad things in the name of authority."

Hanson was a cinephile who, when he was in his twenties, had founded *Cinema*, a highly regarded film journal. He salivated thinking how *L.A. Confidential* would offer him the opportunity to put his own mark on a genre he loved: moody 1950s crime melodramas set in Southern California, as epitomized by Robert Aldrich's *Kiss Me Deadly* and Nicholas Ray's *In a Lonely Place*. It wasn't just movies of the period he felt kinship for; the L.A. native was also fascinated by the city itself at that point in time because it was "when Los Angeles started to become what it is today. That's when the first freeways were built, when cops on the take were replaced by a military-style police force popularized in *Dragnet*, when the tabloid industry started. I wanted to create the world of *L.A. Confidential*, then put it in the background and shoot it like a contemporary movie."

Because he was a hotter commodity than he'd ever

been, Hanson made his move. He said, "It was like I was at a poker table and had won all these chips, and this was the moment where I pushed them all into the pot and said, 'Whether anybody wants to do it or not, this is the movie that I want to make.' " At the same time, he realized that because *L.A. Confidential* would be "related to film noir, which is a genre that's less than commercially viable," it was not likely to be embraced by a big studio. So Hanson took his project to Regency and, in a most unorthodox way, convinced company head Arnon Milchin to back the movie: he simply had the producer look at photographs from the fifties. Milchin recalled, "He came in and started to show me a lot of pictures of kind of the mood he wanted for the film. Basically, what he was saying through his ten- or fifteen-minute presentation was 'Arnon, this is not just another period movie in the fifties,' which for us would normally mean we would go run for the hills, 'but I'm talking *Young Guns* and James Dean. I'm talking a totally different language. I'm talking today.' " Milchin agreed to finance the film even though there was no script, which Hanson would cowrite with Brian Helgeland. And the beauty part was that Regency had a deal with Warner Brothers, so the film was guaranteed distribution.

Hanson defied expectations by casting two fairly obscure Australian actors as prototypical Southern California policemen: the up-and-coming Russell Crowe to embody—on the surface at least—brutality and volatility, and Guy Pearce, last seen as a drag queen in *The Adventures of Priscilla, Queen of the Desert,* to play a mixture of self-righteousness, priggishness and ambition. Hanson cast these two men from Down Under because "I wanted actors about whom the audience has no preconceived notion. I wanted the audience to accept these two characters at face value and not make assumptions about them based on roles the actors had played before." The third lead, a charmingly amoral detective, was played by Kevin Spacey; Hanson had tried to cast Spacey in *The Hand That Rocks the Cradle,* but in 1992 the future Oscar winner simply wasn't a big enough name for Disney executives. One of the actors Spacey had defeated for the Academy Award, James Cromwell, was cast as his superior officer. Danny DeVito was a sleazy

tabloid publisher, and Kim Basinger played a prostitute whose greatest selling point is that she supposedly looks like Veronica Lake, even though Lake's heyday was a decade before when the film takes place.

For the two Australians the hard part of the movie wasn't fine-tuning an American accent or becoming comfortable inhabiting characters from nearly half a century earlier. Pearce found the sheer act of being in Los Angeles itself very tough. "Everyone has come to L.A. because they think that this is the land that they can live out their dreams in," he said. "There's all this smog, there's all this traffic, there's all this anger. I developed some sort of chest infection when I got there. There are so many people who carry guns. There's always animosity. There's this image of Hollywood and movie stardom that you grow up hearing about. Then when you turn up at LAX , all you can see is smog and attitude, a desperate sort of attitude."

Crowe had his own particular cross. Even though the actor argued the point, author James Ellroy told him his character didn't drink beer but was a Scotch man. And so, the Method actor recalled, "I didn't drink a beer for five months, and as an Australian, that's a helluva damn hard thing to do. I kept saying, 'You're killing me, Ellroy!' " As for developing a taste for Scotch, "I had to bloody learn, didn't I? Now I can tell what's blended and what's single malt. But I haven't actually had any since the moment we finished shooting this movie, because it's disgusting."

Studio Behaving Badly

The deal that Regency had with Warner Brothers was a mixed blessing. While it meant *L.A. Confidential* would have the backing of a major studio, Hanson soon had an inkling that the company was kind of clueless regarding his movie. For instance, when he and Arnon Milchin decided that having the film in competition at the Cannes Film Festival would be a great way of building advance word four months before the official release date, people at Warners didn't see the point—and so the director and the producer sent a print directly to the festival themselves without informing the studio. Milchin shared his memories of Cannes with the *Hollywood Reporter*'s Martin Grove:

"We got, with the exception of one paper, probably the greatest reviews—from *Newsweek* to the *L.A. Times* and the *New York Times*. They just flipped over the movie. So we know in advance that this movie's going to get wall-to-wall raves. What we decided was to take the gamble early enough so that if we're wrong, we still have time to do something, and if we're right, we'd get a real jump-start here. You can't explain the mood of the movie, how much depth it has. You have to see it." The film didn't win anything at Cannes (the Palme d'Or going to Abbas Kiarostami's *A Taste of Cherry*), but Jack Mathews wrote that "it has aroused American filmgoers here in the same way *Pulp Fiction* did in 1994." It would also receive additional positive feedback at the Toronto and San Sebastian festivals. And in September, it faced the general public.

"Curtis Hanson's resplendently wicked *L.A. Confidential* is a tough, gorgeous, vastly entertaining throwback to the Hollywood that did things right. As such, it enthusiastically breaks most rules of studio filmmaking today," rejoiced Janet Maslin in the *New York Times*. "Brilliantly adapted from James Ellroy's near-unfilmable cult novel, it casts anything-but-A-list stars (yet) in a story with three leading men, no two of whom can be construed as buddies. It embroils them in a cliché-free, vigorously surprising tale that qualifies as true mystery rather than arbitrary thriller and that revels in its endless complications. Take a popcorn break and you'll be sorry." Duane Dudek of the *Milwaukee Journal Sentinel* enthused, "Based on James Ellroy's bear of a book, it has been made into a bulldog of a film by the director Curtis Hanson. The film doesn't have the book's muscle but it has the serrated tenaciousness of a carnivore. Like its central characters, both cops—a clever college boy and a streetwise bone breaker—the film is both complex and confrontational. It is rich with plot, explodes with violent action and integrates these elements with style rather than force. Hanson is like a gondolier steering this unstable vessel along an open sewer, toward clarity, with surprising velocity and a strong sense of purpose."

Most neo-noir films are sloughed off as *Chinatown* wanna-bes but *L.A. Confidential* was the rare movie that critics compared favorably to the Roman Polanski classic. ("The first L.A. movie in more than twenty years to come within hailing distance of the historical, cultural, and mythic resonance of *Chinatown*," hailed *Mr. Showbiz*'s Richard T. Jameson.) The entire cast received kudos, with full-fledged stardom predicted for its Australian leading men. Kim Basinger's career of late had been more notable for off-screen legal woes than onscreen accomplishments, and she told Jay Leno, "I'm so happy to be in a good movie for a change." Edward Guthmann of the *San Francisco Chronicle* praised her for bringing "a tragic weariness to her icy-blond role." The one aspect of *L.A. Confidential* deemed most impressive, though, was that a cohesive narrative had been extracted from James Ellroy's book. Mike Clark of *USA Today* declared, "It appears as if screenwriters Brian Helgeland and Curtis Hanson have pulled off a miracle in keeping multiple stories straight. Have they ever. Ellroy's novel has four extra layers of plot and three times as many characters. Like Daniel Taradash adapting James Jones's *From Here to Eternity*, the writers have trimmed unwieldy muscle, not just fat, and gotten away with it."

But David Walsh of the *World Socialist Web Site* had a bone to pick with *L.A. Confidential*. "Indeed the film does not paint a pretty picture of the city, the film industry, tabloid journalism and so forth," he wrote. "But none of this unpleasantness is going to astonish anyone. There is hardly a hint in Hanson's film of a *genuine protest* against corruption, racism, stupidity or greed. The film, in fact, lives parasitically off these elements, as their enthusiastic chronicler. One might even say that the film contributes, in its relatively vulgar fashion, to the generally debased quality of contemporary life. How does that help anyone?"

By year's end, *L.A. Confidential* had grossed a less-than-smashing $38 million and Curtis Hanson took Warner Brothers to task for its ad campaign and advertising. He griped that the marketing people "took a glance at the movie, saw it was about cops and concluded that *L.A. Confidential* was a movie for males and should be sold accordingly. They never listened to the audience. In our test screenings we found out that women liked the picture as much as men." Hanson also believed that the ad campaign turned people off: "We had a trailer and TV spots featuring cops and guns. The key art and poster showed cops approaching a man standing over a dead body. We're still trying to overcome the negative impression of this movie as dark and forbidding. Thank goodness for the critics, who almost uniformly have described the movie as rich, rewarding entertainment." Warner's head of distribution, Barry Reardon, seemed to imply that it was Hanson's own fault. "Here is a terrific movie, but unfortunately it has no big movie stars," said Reardon, and he maintained that Hanson had made a film whose main appeal was to an older constituency, which is "sometimes a difficult crowd to get out." But Hanson wasn't the only faultfinder. *Entertainment Weekly* quoted a marketing executive from another studio: "You have to ask [if] they understood the potential of this movie," and the magazine said that he "questioned the film's murky promotional campaign, obscure poster art, and particularly, its release in the no-man's-land of September." Agrees another rival exec: "I don't think they knew what they had." Chris Pula, Warner's head of marketing, told the magazine in response: "They can kiss my ass. It's easy to piss on someone else's campaign. We've got a brilliant movie—but anyone who thinks it's an easy sell is an idiot."

Shake Your Groove Thing

A pair of the fall's most discussed releases were alike in two ways: They were set in the 1970s and they focused on sex. But their milieus, characters and sensibilities were vastly different.

Having triumphed with *Sense and Sensibility*, Taiwanese director Ang Lee was back in the twentieth century with *The Ice Storm*. Based on Rick Moody's novel, *The Ice Storm* takes place in the wealthy bedroom community of New Canaan, Connecticut, during Thanksgiving weekend 1973. The film used the trappings of the period—from Watergate to spouse-swapping "key parties"—to enhance its character studies of two generations of dispirited individuals. For research, Lee watched *Bob & Carol & Ted & Alice* and he presented his cast with self-help books from the Nixon era, such as *I'm O.K., You're O.K.* Once again, the director was dealing in familial relationships, but the empty and despairing WASPs on view here—embodied by Kevin Kline, Joan Allen and Sigourney

Weaver and their offspring Tobey Maguire, Elijah Wood and Christina Ricci—were a far cry from the exuberantly human people in his other works. Still, Lee said, "My Oriental upbringing made me bring sympathy to them."

In *Newsweek*, David Ansen wrote, "This may be Lee's most haunting movie: delicately balanced between comedy and tragedy, it holds you rapt without having to raise its voice." Joe Baltake of the *Sacramento Bee* felt that "while *The Ice Storm* has been meticulously researched and executed, its chief strength is that it's a film of lovely, disturbing intangibles. This is a film that's interested in the pain of the period, not the good times. We get 'plot' and a cast of renowned actors, sure, but everything here is in service to the symbolism of the film's haunting title—to the metaphorical rain storm that immobilizes its characters, forcing them to stop and think. *The Ice Storm* is composed of deep, hushed nuances of a time, a place and its people, all of which Lee has somehow captured with his camera."

The *New York Times* sent a reporter to see what the good people of New Canaan had to say about the film. Most people agreed with the town's first selectman, Richard Bond, who deemed the film "terrible." He contended, "There's nothing redeeming about it or any of the characters . . . it was a very dark, depressing film. Everyone was so unattractive, even Sigourney Weaver." The reporter could only find one person leaving the New Canaan Playhouse who would admit to liking the film—but he was from Darien.

The *Times* noted that in Manhattan the film was enjoying terrific word of mouth. As it turned out, though, the rest of the country was more in line with New Canaan. Director Lee had said, "This movie is about uncomfortableness. Whatever you do is somehow wrong." That's not how you entice 'em into theaters. A film that received major coverage in the national press, *The Ice Storm* made a pittance, grossing less than half its $18 million cost.

Wild and Crazy Guys

Like *The Ice Storm*, the season's other sex-in-the-seventies film played at the New York Film Festival.

But while the Ang Lee film took place among well-heeled New England malcontents who detest their family situations, *Boogie Nights* focused on damaged individuals who looked to the porno movie industry of the San Fernando Valley to find surrogate familial relationships; the movie's production notes referred to the pornographic film community as "a misunderstood underworld." Twenty-seven-year-old director Paul Thomas Anderson, whose one previous film, *Hard Eight,* had proved inconsequential earlier in the year, had grown up in the Valley, and he recollected how "the Van Nuys industrial section had large warehouses, with people walking in and out of them who were not there to pour concrete." His only actual contact with the adult film business, though, was his "watching a ton of porno movies." Anderson's take on the genre was "I can see something in pornography that can be either incredibly funny, either in a campy way or an honest and dark way. But then it can become sad and depressing. I love it and support it as much as it disgusts me and saddens me."

The movie was loosely based on the life and career of John Holmes, a.k.a. Johnny Wadd, whose claim to fame was his Brobdingnagian endowment. Anderson had wanted Leonardo DiCaprio to star in his film, but the actor was busy making *Titanic.* DiCaprio suggested the director consider his costar from *The Basketball Diaries,* Mark Wahlberg, who despite having made a handful of movies was still best known for his days as rapper Marky Mark and for his stint as a Calvin Klein underwear model. Anderson took DiCaprio's advice, and if Wahlberg was lacking Johnny Wadd's certain *je ne sais quoi,* well, there was always prosthetics. Gossip columnist Cindy Adams gibed, "Let us all thank Allah for Marky Mark not having this particular prop in his Calvin Klein underwear days. The size of the jockey shorts on the billboard would have eclipsed Times Square."

Boogie Nights covered the years from 1977 through 1984, and Anderson was clearly looking back on his childhood years with a rose-colored tint, for he said it was "a wonderful period of music and fashion." This was a movie in which what passes as a tragic event is the changeover from adult films being shot on film to videotape. As Roger Ebert stated it, "There is hope,

at the outset, that a porno movie could be 'artistic,' and less hope at the end." Michael DeLuca, the president of New Line, was a mite extravagant when he said, "*Boogie Nights* takes on the adult entertainment industry the way *GoodFellas* explored organized crime or *The Player* exposed the cutthroat nature of studio politics." But damned if some people didn't buy into this statement, which was dutifully reprinted in the press kit they were handed when going into screenings, and the names "Scorsese" and "Altman" kept popping up in reviews of the film.

After calling the movie "a sprawling and incredibly entertaining epic," Andrew Johnston of *Time Out New York* gushed, "*Boogie*'s structure and presentation owe a lot to *GoodFellas,* but in a California context, the Scorsese vocabulary seems remarkably fresh." Mike Clark of *USA Today* thought, "With its ceaseless music, large canvas, shrewd casting and flawless ensemble acting and the dexterity of its whiplashing mood switches, the movie recalls Robert Altman's *Nashville* more than any subsequent movie has—though the one scene that Anderson all-out lifts is transparently out of Martin Scorsese's *Raging Bull.*" *Time*'s Richard Corliss said, "*Boogie Nights* has panoramic ambitions: a tapestry-style narrative, labyrinthine tracking shots, explosions of random, firecracker violence. *Nashville* meets *GoodFellas* meets *Pulp Fiction* . . . it packs a wad of compelling entertainment." He added, though, that "Holmes, who died of AIDS in 1988, had a life far more bizarre and instructive." *Entertainment Weekly*'s Owen Gleiberman called *Boogie Nights* "a movie that may well leave Quentin Tarantino and Martin Scorsese drop-jawed with envy." ("That sad combination of dropsy and lockjaw?" wondered Godfrey Cheshire of the *New York Press,* one of the few critics to see that there wasn't too much *there* there in *Boogie Nights;* Cheshire also pointed out that "Scorsese and Tarantino, whatever one thinks of them, have styles that most people could recognize on a 12-inch screen at 20 paces with the sound turned off. P. T. Anderson's style is pleasant and able, but it could belong to Michael Winner. Or do I mean Michael Ritchie?")

The favorable reviews were nice, but Anderson said that what he really wanted was "a seal of approval from people in the industry, whose opinions I respected, like

Veronica Hart, who's in the film and was a wonderful actress, the Meryl Streep of porn. She loved the script which made me feel good." But two other stars of dirty movies from the seventies thought Anderson's version of their former world was flaccid. Actress Candida Royalle said that Anderson had it all wrong when he showed the adult film industry filled with "people who have sad lives, who don't have many options in life." Bobby Astyr, a veteran of literally hundreds of blue films who was now on the board of directors of a housing project in New York's East Village, scoffed, "I think everything was overblown. It was a caricature." And Robert Hofler, who was an editor at *Penthouse* in the 1970s and ghostwrote *The Happy Hooker's Sex Fantasies*, complained in *The Advocate* that "Anderson has a view of the era and the hard-core porn business that could make sense only to someone who wasn't there to live it." Hofler pointed out that while Anderson blamed the demise of a "golden age" of porno movies on the advent of video and the general avariciousness of the Reagan years, the industry's glory days were in reality already over by the time *Boogie Nights* begins. In the early seventies there was an attempt to bring creativity to the genre and a certain naive respectability—"porno chic," as Truman Capote called it—followed, but it all fell by the wayside when X superstar Harry Reems was brought to trial by a yahoo Tennessee prosecutor for obscenity and was actually found guilty. Hofler concluded, "Anderson doesn't let the complexities of history get in the way of telling a good story."

Two members of the large cast were particularly singled out for praise. Julianne Moore portrayed a veteran porno actress named—the movie's single most inspired element—Amber Waves, and Kenneth Turan called her "that most adventurous of actresses" who brought "a sad and inescapable poignancy" to the character; *Rolling Stone*'s Peter Travers wrote, "Moore pierces the heart." Burt Reynolds played a filmmaker who functions in the picture as a Father Figure. *The New Republic*'s Stanley Kauffmann said he "seems to have invested his whole career in preparation for Jack Horner. Ease used as ethic, a seriousness that is meant to be transparent, all the qualities that marked his unctuously inveigling performances lead directly to Jack, a man of a dependability that is limited only by self-

interest, with an embrace that is part smother." Michael Wilmington of the *Chicago Tribune* cheered that the actor "has just the right aging charisma and frayed warmth for Jack Horner. . . . Reynolds finally gets to use the irony and self-reflexive humor that were trademarks in his '70s–'80s heyday. This seems as much a possible career-reviving movie for him as *Pulp Fiction* was for John Travolta." And in *Premiere*, Todd McCarthy wrote that his performance "reminded everyone why he became a star in the first place."

Reynolds, the country's biggest star during the period in which *Boogie Nights* takes place, had most assuredly been having a less than spectacular time of it lately, making television movies—on *basic* cable—straight-to-video items like *Frankenstein and Me* and *The Maddening*, and just-plain-bad theatrical releases, such as *Cop and ½* (although he was in the acclaimed, if little seen, *Citizen Ruth*), enduring bad publicity for an unseemly divorce with Loni Anderson, declaring bankruptcy. The story went that after Reynolds saw *Boogie Nights*, he was so appalled that he fired his agent. The actor said that was just another of the rumors that had dogged him, that his only reservation about being associated with the film was that, as Burt Reynolds, he brought certain baggage that might deflect from the people's perception of the film.

Grooving on his reviews—and the mainstream attention that had eluded him for a long time now—the 61-year-old Reynolds told Liz Smith that a year earlier he had called friends at William Morris, ICM and CAA, and nada. "Nobody wanted me. I couldn't get arrested. Now my phone rings. Nice." He also cited those pals who remained steadfast during his down period, including Van Johnson, Clint Eastwood, Elizabeth Taylor, Angie Dickinson and Elizabeth Ashley, and said, "All I hope is that I can accept this new phase graciously, and not make wisecracks that sound sour and inevitably backfire." One of Reynolds's latest jokes, in reference to his director, was "I got socks older than him."

A Perfect Blendship

Actors Ben Affleck and Matt Damon were Gen-X contemporaries of Paul Thomas Anderson. They were in that nether region between obscurity and familiarity, known to die-hard movie fans if not the general public. Damon received some attention with a small part as a heroin-addicted soldier in 1996's *Courage Under Fire,* and then was given the lead in Francis Coppola's version of a John Grisham book, *The Rainmaker,* a November 1997 release. Affleck's most notable work was the "I fell in love with a lesbian" movie *Chasing Amy,* where he came across as the poor man's Ethan Hawke. But if Harvey Weinstein was putting Miramax's resources behind a movie that these two childhood friends had written, then something had to be up.

In quintessential Miramax fashion, studio flacks made sure the press knew the back story of *Good Will Hunting.* (That the publicity people did their job was evidenced by the opening line of Janet Maslin's review: "Everybody loves a Cinderella story and *Good Will Hunting* has two of them: one on screen and one behind the scenes.") Damon and Affleck had been best pals since childhood in Cambridge, Massachusetts. Typical good-looking but struggling actors, living in Eagle Rock, they were, in Damon's words, "frustrated, because all we got to look at were the scripts everyone on the short list passes on, then it's you and everyone else brawling for these meager table scraps." Then in 1994, a brainstorm—if they weren't getting top-notch scripts sent their way, why not pull a Mickey-and-Judy, nineties version, and write their own screenplay, as if no other struggling actor had ever thought of that. Making things easier for the guys was that they didn't have to start from scratch—they dug up a short story Matt had been working on in a creative writing class when he was attending Harvard in 1992. They reworked it as a screenplay, which in its earliest form was a conspiracy thriller ("Basically, we tried to make each other laugh," Damon said of the writing process), and gave it to Damon's agent, who turned it over to a script agent, and within a few days, a bidding war was on, with Castle Rock emerging victorious. But ultimately the film went into turnaround and director Kevin Smith, a friend of the budding writers, intervened by prevailing upon Harvey Weinstein to read the script, which is how the project ended up at Miramax.

Good Will Hunting was about a young mathematical genius who conceals his gift under his South Boston blue-collar swagger and works as a janitor at MIT. He's also an orphan and a rowdy troublemaker, and the dramatic centerpiece of the film is his relationship with a somewhat prickly psychiatrist who's no emotional prize package himself. Gus Van Sant, who first made his name as the director of subversive independent films about young people on the fringes—up to now his most mainstream movie had been *To Die For*—got ahold of the script, and said "It was probably the best-written screenplay I had ever read. We called it a color-by-numbers script: if you just filled in the scenes as they were written, it would come to life." His wishing to helm *Good Will Hunting,* though, didn't make it a done deal. "There were people like Harvey Weinstein who weren't sure," recollected Van Sant. "I tried to sell myself by saying that *Ordinary People* was my favorite film, which it is. Ben and Matt, however, had faith. Maybe it was harder for the executives to make a leap, because Hollywood people put you in a category. Ben and Matt never had those preconceptions." In fact, the two writers were adamant about Van Sant. "As an actor," Affleck said, "you see these great performances he gets. He has his own sensibility. We said, 'You're the indie guru. It's yours.'"

Not that Damon and Affleck were in much of a position to do anything. They had undersold the script in return for the guarantee that they'd get to star in the movie, but once Miramax had bought it, the studio didn't seem particularly eager to push a Matt Damon/Ben Affleck vehicle into production. But, said Van Sant "all of a sudden Francis Coppola cast Matt in *The Rainmaker* and then Miramax said 'we're going.' A lot of the film is owed to Francis for casting Matt." Van Sant suggested Robin Williams to play the nurturing shrink. The thought of it made the writers laugh because while they loved the idea, as Affleck said, "We never thought we'd get him. We thought we'd end up with, you know, maybe William Shatner." The two writer-stars familiarized Williams with the Boston bar scene, which is a key element of the film; Williams, a recovering alcoholic, joked, "It was like taking Gandhi to a deli." When a TV reporter came to the set to observe, Affleck and Damon said working together was a piece of cake because they were lovers.

The Eros of Algebra

"The situation is clearly contrived and not a little fantastic," admitted Andrew Sarris. "Yet the film works as a character-driven narrative because Mr. Van Sant and his co-screenwriters are not afraid to unlock the psychological mysteries of their five major characters with clear and concise dialogue. Unlike many contemporary 'independent' films, which pride themselves on keeping the audience guessing at motivations even beyond the final fade-out, *Good Will Hunting* tells you not only *what* happens, but also why. . . . Talk, talk, talk; there is nothing like it when it is cogent and coherent, and when the actors can deliver it with flair and feeling." Roger Ebert thought that "the outcome of the movie is fairly predictable; so is the whole story, really. It's the individual moments, not the payoff, that make it so effective." Shawn Levy of *The Oregonian* surmised that *Good Will Hunting* was "the only movie in memory in which prowess in abstract mathematics has seemed sexy."

In the *San Francisco Chronicle*, Peter Stack advised that "The film is a departure for director Gus Van Sant—this one has warmth as well as edge. That may disappoint hard-core Van Sant fans, but it shows the director applying a sure hand to a more mainstream story without forsaking the offbeat." Jonathan Rosenbaum of the *Chicago Reader* concluded "this is good, solid work that never achieves either the art or poignance of Van Sant's earlier and more personal projects *(Mala Noche, Drugstore Cowboy, My Own Private Idaho)*, though it's clearly superior to something like *Dead Poets Society*." Peter Keough of the *Boston Phoenix* noted that Van Sant "presents a grittily detailed Southie somehow devoid of racism, homophobia, or genuine desperation. Uncharacteristically for Van Sant, this film wants to believe that even in the heights and the depths of human experience, some redemptive decency can be found. It may be a spurious happy hunting ground Van Sant is offering, but with the help of Damon and Affleck, he makes good."

"The real magic," thought Bruce Kirkland of the *Toronto Sun*, "is Damon's deeply moving performance as the title character. Overplayed, and Will Hunting would be a Hollywood cliché. Underplayed, and he would lack the charisma that pulls us into his world. The 27-year-old Damon has an unusual talent—the ability to simultaneously play good and bad and blend both into a coherent whole that makes sense. Contemporaries such as Brad Pitt can't seem to hold or even find that precarious balance. . . . Damon's dazzling smile and sparkling eyes give him movie star appeal but his innate sense of darkness makes him as dangerously real as people we know in life." That was nothing compared to what Joe Morgenstern had to say in the *Wall Street Journal*: "He has a coiled strength that has not been seen since the young Marlon Brando, and an unaffected vulnerability all its own; it's the year's best performance to date, and don't hold your breath waiting for anyone to top it." "You may have to go back to Jack Nicholson's Bobby Dupea, the pianist-cum-oil-rigger in *Five Easy Pieces*, for a similarly blessed marriage of star to role, and Damon's performance is no less magnetic," raved *Newsday*'s Jack Mathews. "He has a commanding presence on screen, mixing boyish good looks with a voice fermented in oak, and he has the ability to seem simultaneously dangerous and sympathetic."

David Sheehan of KCBS-TV declared that "Robin Williams delivers a portrayal filled with strength and wisdom." But Stephen Talty of *Time Out New York* thought the character's "speeches are often recycled, prefabricated and dull, and Williams doesn't help by delivering them with faux humility." "As for its notions about therapy," scoffed Stephen Holden in the *New York Times*, "one good cry, no matter how wrenching, doesn't cure anything; it's just a beginning." And *Entertainment Weekly*'s smart-ass "Jim Mullen's Hot Sheet" said of the film, "Robin Williams teaches a boy genius how to cope. If the kid is so smart, why didn't he figure it out himself?"

Magazine profiles painted Damon and Affleck as genuinely nice and unaffected young men who were fairly stunned by their newfound success (as the title character of the film, Damon did receive much more attention than his buddy, and, besides, Affleck was playing a schlemiel). Damon was even on the cover of *Time*, heralded as "Hollywood's Newest Golden Boy." Their personae quickly became established: Damon was the sincere one, Affleck the sweet-natured jokester. When they were guests on *Oprah*, the host asked Affleck to describe what kind of friend Damon was. He said, "Matt's the first guy I'd call if I woke up in a hotel room with a dead hooker." Adding to the fairy-tale quality of the real-life scenario was that Damon and Minnie Driver, his rich-girl romantic interest in the film, fell in love while making the movie. Driver told a reporter for the *New York Daily News*, "I'm loath to even speak about it because I don't want to curse it. I adore him. He's one of the best people I know." Driver's joy was short-lived, though. Appearing on *Oprah* a month after *Good Will Hunting* premiered, Damon said, "I was with Minnie for a while, but we're not really romantically involved anymore. We're just good friends and I love her dearly." A miffed Driver claimed that this public announcement was the first she had heard that they were no longer an item, and she wasn't shy about telling that to the press.

Christmas Baubles

Two household-name directors were represented by Christmas releases. For Steven Spielberg, the set-up was a replay of 1993: Have a popcorn movie in the summer and follow it up with a socially conscious historical film at Christmastime. The first half of the equation worked fine. *The Lost World: Jurassic Park*, like its predecessor, was a cacophonous mess that brought in boxcar numbers at the box office. For Christmas, Spielberg presented what was intended to be DreamWorks's first major Oscar contender, *Amistad*, his re-creation of a slave ship revolt in 1839 and the consequences of the uprising. The film starred the actor who, a year earlier, had been deemed the Next Big Thing and had yet to deliver, Matthew McConaughey, and featured Morgan Freeman, Nigel Hawthorne, Anthony Hopkins as ex-President John Quincy Adams, and Anna Paquin as the Queen of Spain. A few months before *Amistad*'s release, author Barbara Chase-Riboud sued DreamWorks, claiming the film appropriated parts of a novel she had written about the incident. She thought that $10 million might make things right and also asked for an injunction to prevent the film's release. That request was de-

nied, meaning *Amistad* could open as planned, but it now did so saddled with bad publicity.

Once it was released, *Amistad* became saddled with indifferent reviews. "Spielberg's historical epic doesn't stir the imagination. It informs. It interests. It probably will do something to raise consciousness. But it's not the great work that this subject demanded," sighed Robert Denerstein of the Scripps-Howard News Service. In the *San Francisco Chronicle*, Edward Guthmann said, "As much as he wants to do the right thing in his serious films, Steven Spielberg inevitably falls back on old tricks, technical dazzle and twinkly sentiment," and he called *Amistad* "a film that veers between stoic political correctness and mushy pop-Hollywood platitudes." Cindy Fuchs of the *Philadelphia Citypaper* complained, "While the Africans are tremendously sympathetic, the film maintains a distance from them, granting emotional access instead to the well-intentioned white guys." Along with the bland critical reception, the public was apathetic—in contrast to *Schindler's List*, no one was talking about *Amistad*.

It had been three years since *Pulp Fiction*. Although there had been plenty of movies made by Quentin Tarantino wanna-bes, the original was primarily spending his time not behind the camera but in front of it. Tarantino did direct one segment of the four-part 1995 film, *Four Rooms*, one of the worst reviewed movies of the decade, and an episode of *ER*, but mostly he was following his dream of becoming an actor. Finally, it was time to pleasure his acolytes, not to mention Harvey Weinstein, who had been hankering for a new Tarantino to put into release.

As Josef von Sternberg once devoted himself to the glorification of Marlene Dietrich, with *Jackie Brown*, Tarantino set out to do the same for the Queen of 1970s Blaxploitation movies, Pam Grier. Based on the novel *Rum Punch*—in the book, the lead character is a white woman named Jackie Burke; in 1974, Grier had made a movie called *Foxy Brown*—*Jackie Brown* told of an airline stewardess involved with smuggling, gunrunning and selling drugs, and the nub of the film was double and triple crosses between the law and her own lawless crowd. In *Pulp Fiction*, the director had cast an actor he had liked in the seventies, John

Travolta, even though his current career had been on the skids. Similarly, in *Jackie Brown* he employed Robert Forster, whom he knew from the seventies Depression-era cop show *Banyon* and whose recent output had included *Maniac Cop 3: Badge of Silence* and *American Yakuza*. Forster said of his role as a world-weary bail bondsman, "That's a sweetheart of a part, isn't it? It's like something your dad or your brother gives you for Christmas." Tarantino also wanted it understood *Jackie Brown* would not be *Pulp Fiction* 2. "I felt I'd gone about as far as I could with my signature shooting style, so this one is at a lower volume than *Pulp*. It's not an epic, it's not an opera. It's a character study. I knew I didn't want to go bigger than *Pulp*, so I went *underneath* it."

Time's Richard Corliss reported, "Now everyone can stop wondering what Quentin Tarantino will do next. The answer, in *Jackie Brown*: more of the same, and less. The film is an elaborate, fitfully funny Tarantoon about chatty folks with big guns." Corliss concluded, "As for Tarantino, he is playing peekaboo with his sizable talent. *Jackie Brown* marks time, lots of it, between *Pulp Fiction* and his next great project. The wait goes on." Janet Maslin, who was one of *Pulp Fiction*'s more prodigal cheerleaders, wrote disappointedly, "for all its enthusiasm, this film isn't sharp enough to afford all the time it wastes on small talk, long drives, trips to the mall and favorite songs played on car radios." After saying that *Jackie Brown* "plays like a conventional, well-crafted crime comedy," John Hartl of *The Seattle Times* concluded, "Perhaps the most attractive single aspect of *Jackie Brown* is the casting of Pam Grier as a compromised flight attendant and Robert Forster as Max Cherry, the dependable bail bondsman who turns out to be the only man she trusts. Both actors have gone through long lean periods since their heydays in the late 1960s/early 1970s, and it's a treat to see them dominate a movie that also happens to feature Samuel L. Jackson, Robert De Niro, Bridget Fonda (who's never been better) and Michael Keaton." Hartl also wondered, "Did this picture really need to be longer than *Amistad*?"

But in London, *Time Out*'s Geoff Andrew called *Jackie Brown* "Tarantino's finest, most mature movie to date," praised the "terrific acting (Grier and Forster make you wonder where they've been all these years)," and found that "perhaps most surprising and welcome is that this is a subtle, poignant account of middle-aged people trying to come to terms with failing faculties, fading looks, diminishing options and a need to make their lives count somehow."

Fruits and Nuts

The first movie TV producer James L. Brooks directed had Jack Nicholson in it. It was *Terms of Endearment*. His second movie featured Jack Nicholson in a cameo role. It was *Broadcast News*. Movie number three did not employ the services of Jack Nicholson. It was *I'll Do Anything*. Brooks was back to using Jack Nicholson.

In *As Good As It Gets*, a character study of three needy New Yorkers, Brooks, as usual, combined studiously eccentric characters with would-be laughter and tears. As described by the *New York Daily News*'s Dave Kehr, Nicholson was "a romance novelist who, with rather too obvious irony, hates humanity in general and women in particular." Nicholson's splenetic Melvin also suffers from obsessive-compulsive disorder. Even though she was ten years younger than the character's original age, Helen Hunt was cast after *Broadcast News*'s Holly Hunter balked at a paycheck that was about one-fifth the size of Nicholson's; Hunt, beloved across America for her TV series *Mad About You*, played a wisecracking, lonely single-mother waitress, whose son is badly asthmatic. And Greg Kinnear was a dolorous gay artist. Despite his immense success and fame, he conveniently doesn't have health insurance, so after he's badly beaten up, he loses his money to medical expenses, and because they're shallow homosexuals, almost all his friends abandon him. Maybe you didn't see it coming, but Nicholson's misogynistic and homophobic cretin is redeemed by the friendship of this wan woman and whiny gay man. Laurie Stone of the *Village Voice* sighed, "Not even the thick-waisted hets green-lighting Hollywood could buy this fable, though they must believe there's a demographic out there that will."

An example of how grounded in reality *As Good As It Gets* was: In the opening scene Nicholson's character, who has a pathological fear of germs, is seen picking up his neighbor's dog, Verdell, as he's urinating, and putting the animal into a germ-ridden garbage chute. It was also a movie taking place in New York that seemed as if it was made by people who had never stepped foot in the city or even met a New Yorker. Stephen Holden of the *New York Times* rolled his eyes that "Only Hollywood could imagine Brooklyn as a predominantly white suburban adjunct of Manhattan."

Then there was the issue of the 60-year-old star being coupled with a 34-year-old romantic interest. (Helen Hunt was 6 when Nicholson hit it big with *Easy Rider*.) "The obligatory love interest for the middle-aged leading man is a cliché of the movies that I don't like as a member of the audience and am always a little offended by," Nicholson said. "But Helen disarmed that at the first meeting, and I stopped thinking about it."

It was not a tension-free set. Brooks said of working with Nicholson, "I swear to you, this is the truth, that some of the times where he had an idea for doing something a certain way, which I thought somewhat secretly was the worst idea I ever heard, just chilled my blood and I thought it would bring the movie to ruin, and I know I had ideas that chilled his blood; some of those are in the movie. I promise you." On the other hand, Helen Hunt trilled that Nicholson "treated me like a queen" and that they "immediately connected. It wasn't even what we said; it was just some frequency we both could tune into that was very, very compatible." Brooks chuckled about how "Helen had to smile in the last scene. So she said to Jack, 'If you can say anything nice about me just as the cameras are rolling, that would help me.' So when the cameras were rolling, he said, 'Tits.' "

Critical judgment was very much mixed. An admiring Gene Siskel wrote, "*As Good As It Gets* promotes the idea that if we really engage the eyes of the people we meet in daily life and recognize them as special creatures because of their human status, we have a chance to truly enjoy life. That sentimental strain of the story is then matched with the wickedly funny bile of Nicholson's character, one of his best performances in years." Jay Carr of *The Boston Globe* said, "This new

James L. Brooks film plays like sitcom on a huge budget—so huge and, at two hours-plus, so lengthy that it sometimes seems bloated. Yet it reminds us that things like coherence and seamlessness can become unimportant when the screen is filled with entertaining characters."

Back in the city where the film takes place, Daphne Merkin of *The New Yorker* said that the movie "wants us to accept its sitcom rendering of life as bonafide reality. Other viewers may cotton to the film as much as they did to *Terms of Endearment* and *Broadcast News*, but Brooks's gleaming manipulativeness and trendy pieties made me grumpy." Xan Brooks of *Sight and Sound* had no patience for the way Nicholson's character "moves from racist, sexist villain to curmudgeonly philanthropist in an eye blink, his protracted conversion apparently triggered by nothing more than a liquid look from a little dog."

Newsday's Jack Mathews declared of Nicholson, "He's in rare form. One moment he's doing screeds on homosexuals or immigrants; the next, he's arching that most famous of all archable brows, trying to comprehend what in the world he's done wrong. It's one of those performances that make you aware how much fun the actor is having, and you're pleased to go along with him." But Stanley Kauffmann of *The New Republic* felt that Nicholson "is quite visibly uncomfortable in his role. It needed an actor who could easily be viciously stuffy, like William Hurt. Nicholson struggles for the core of the man but never gets it; so in most scenes, he resorts to working his face, with grimaces and sneering smiles and lip-pursings in place of acting."

To *USA Today*'s Mike Clark, "truth is, Brooks is great with actors, period. Hunt delivers one of the year's most appealing performances as a Brooklyn single mother whose feet are both figuratively and literally on the ground, given her dubious lot in life." *New York*'s David Denby said, "Helen Hunt, holding the screen at times in silence, has never seemed more powerfully sane." Uh-uh, felt Michael Sragow, who wrote in *New Times Los Angeles*, "In her struggle for a meat-and-potatoes manner, she resorts to a furrowed-brow sincerity that would have made her the winner on the old *Queen for a Day*."

Thelma Adams of the *New York Post* put forth that "Kinnear steals the movie. He matches emotional range with perfect timing and a wicked Nicholson imitation." Brooks said he had wanted a gay actor to play this role because "I just wanted it to have integrity. I didn't want it to be glib." And claimed that when he cast Greg Kinnear, he thought that was exactly what he was doing. Brooks realized the actor was straight only when, during filming, the actor told him he was getting married. Brooks's reaction: "It was a bummer for me. I guess I didn't look as enthusiastic as I should have when a guy tells me he's in love." Brooks's pronouncement about using a gay actor sounds as bogus as the movie itself and more than a little self-serving, when you realize he said this to a journalist from the gay magazine *The Advocate* and even more so when you find out that Ralph Fiennes, Geoffrey Rush, Woody Harrelson and Sean Penn had all been considered for the role.

The director said he wasn't sure what the moral of the movie was while he was working on it, but once he saw it, he knew. There were two: "That which makes us safe, imprisons us. And that life is tough." As was the case with last year's *Jerry Maguire*, which Brooks exec-produced, audiences didn't stop to think about the how superficial this all was, the movie just made them feel good. *As Good As It Gets* was a big hit.

The Return of Erich von Stroheim

Despite all the studios' putting forth their Christmas best, no one could deny that one end-of-the-year release towered above others in terms of publicity and anticipation. In 1987, James Cameron, the special-effects-obsessed director of such movies as *The Terminator* and *True Lies*, had seen a National Geographic documentary about the discovery of the *Titanic* on the ocean floor. He wrote down notes: "Do story with bookends of present-day scene . . . intercut with memory of a survivor." When his intended adaptation of the *Spider-Man* comic books wasn't coming to fruition, he went back to those notes, thinking about how yet another movie about the 1912 sinking of the *Titanic* would allow him a lot of nifty effects. And there could be a really neat moral to the story, too. See,

Cameron figured the early part of the twentieth century "was a time of very, very rapid technological progress: the invention of the airplane, the mass production of the automobile, the invention of cinema. And you know, hey, it was a very, very interesting decade just before the *Titanic* sank. And I think of the sinking as the kind of wake-up call, the alarm clock going off, saying, 'Guess what, guys: It's going to be a rough century.' " Not only that, the totally cool thing was "We're going through the same kind of boom time. Maybe we have to get whacked again before we remember it. But hopefully, if we remember *Titanic* a little bit, we won't, y'know?"

Before convincing 20th Century Fox to make the film, Cameron first got it to ante up for a dozen deep-sea dives on which he surveyed the remains of the *Titanic*. The experience jizzed him up so much that he tirelessly went to work on swaying Fox executives until they gave in. The studio agreed to a $100 million budget but then suffered a panic attack with the realization that James Cameron movies always tended to go way over budget. So Fox went into a partnership with Paramount, which would put up $65 million—but no more, no matter how high Cameron ran up his budget—in exchange for domestic rights; Fox would cover all other production costs and retain international rights.

Sure enough, the expenses quickly mounted, and the ongoing production of *Titanic* led many to snicker that the project was as doomed as the original vessel. *Daily Variety* even had a special column called "*Titanic* Watch," charting the production's setbacks and spiraling expenditures along the way. Estimates put the film's final cost in the $200 million range, while rumors had it as high as $285 million. The ever-expanding budget was particularly problematic, because as *Variety*'s editor-in-chief Peter Bart noted apprehensively, "Leonardo DiCaprio is the biggest name in the movie"; that being the case, Bart added "one can only assume that the 250 special effects are the true stars." Similarly, *Entertainment Weekly* observed, "Despite the prestige of a cast that includes three Oscar nominees, the film doesn't have a single international box office star."

In addition to the huge scale of the production,

the costs had resulted from a new studio facility—containing the world's largest water tank—that Cameron had convinced Fox to build on a Mexican beach, and from the 90 percent scale replica of the ship which served as the film's set. Construction costs turned out to be higher than expected and the complicated logistics involved in re-creating the sinking caused shooting to be extraordinarily time-consuming, especially with the director demanding take after take. When Fox chairman Bill Mechanic presented Cameron with a list of scenes to be cut from the script to bring down expenses, the melodramatic director said, "If you want to cut my film, you'll have to fire me. And to fire me, you'll have to kill me." He did eventually agree to a few of the demands. But a couple of months later, the studio again grew alarmed at the seemingly out-of-control expenditures, so Cameron gave up both his producing-directing salary (in the $8 million range) and his share of any profits. It wasn't as if he was a pauper, though: he did hold on to the $1 million-plus salary he was paid for his screenplay. Cameron stated, "Contractually, it is now impossible for me to make any money beyond my writing fee. But I'm satisfied that I did things honorably."

There were also reports of a cast and crew miserable over being at the mercy of a maniacal director, a throwback to Eric von Stroheim and Otto Preminger, but without the same level of talent. Bob Strauss described the situation on E! Online: "His increasingly agitated behavior prompted characterizations of a captain going down with his ship." "I hear some people call me General Patton, bossing the set like a military operation," Cameron said. "But I don't have to strut around and try and prove I'm the clever guy. The only thing that counts is making a great film. Everything else is bullshit." Members of the crew wore T-shirts bearing one of the director's mantras, "You either shoot it my way or you do another fucking movie." Cinematographer Caleb Deschanel left the production after a few weeks, appalled by the director's temperament.

Early on, even before Cameron and company got to Mexico, there was dissension on the production. The film's present-day scenes were being shot in Nova Scotia, and during a midnight clam bake, everyone became sick. It turned out this was not a simple case of food poisoning: Somebody had put PCP into the lobster chowder. A doctor who treated some of those affected gave his diagnosis: "These people were stoned." Actor Bill Paxton recalled that "People started line-dancing, slapping themselves in the head, and some people had crap coming out of their nose." It was fun to imagine that the sabotage was done by a disgruntled crew member fed up with Cameron's martinet ways and the acquiescence of everyone else to his childish petulance, but the culprit was never apprehended. Cameron himself put forth, "My theory is it was a bullshit, internecine thing between two people who had nothing to do with the production, and we just got caught in the crossfire."

In "Memo: to James Cameron," Variety's Peter Bart cited "the horror stories from the Titanic set—nightmarish hours for the crew, extras having to stay in the water for 18-hour stretches, your temper tantrums over mistakes and malfunctions." Reporter Claudia Puig told of the on-set problems in a Los Angeles Times article entitled "Epic-Size Troubles on Titanic," detailing how "Titanic crew members say the massive, grueling water-borne production was made even more trying by the perfectionistic demands of its famously bombastic director. 'Yeah, the horror stories are true,' said first assistant director Sebastian Silva. Many cast and crew members say they admire Cameron for his single-minded focus. But his abrasive manner, frequent angry outbursts and intolerance of imperfection are what they usually bring up first."

So many negative reports were coming from the shoot that Cameron took time out from his busy schedule to write a "Counterpunch" article in the Times responding to Puig's piece. The director declared, "Just as it does not serve a mountain climber, in the retelling of the tale, to suggest that the mountain conquered was a gentle grade, it does not serve those who have been tested by fire on one of my films to describe the experience as routine. It is therefore easy for a journalist with what appears to be a negative agenda to assemble quotes from my cast and crew, taken out of context, and paint a picture of a cruel and heartless production that cares only about commerce and not people. Nothing could be further from the case." He said, "Most of my team are people who have worked with me before, some of them for more than 10 years. . . . Nobody forces these people to work on my films. They are not slaves or indentured servants. They love the intensity and the challenge. And because they are the best, they get paid as the best. And when the hours get long, they are paid overtime, as is fair. They love this, too." Cameron also wondered, "When did this country cease to celebrate the work ethic, and the principle of striving for excellence? It seems to have become a dirty concept these days to work too hard, to care too much, to give your all." Puig had written of "a number of filming-related accidents. (A Fox spokesman acknowledged 'eight or nine,' but some reports cited more.)" To which the director countered, "On the issue of safety, my safety record on my films has been far above the industry norm. My safety methodology is rigorous and, as a result, time-consuming." Cameron concluded, "Am I driven? Yes. Absolutely. Out of control? Never. Unsafe? Not on my watch."

He also told an interviewer that people were being naive if they thought someone at the helm of a megaproject like *Titanic* could be Mr. Nice Guy at all times: "I have to turn my hat around and become the cantankerous artist and say, 'Because I think this is how it's supposed to be, goddammit.'" Making Cameron's Type A personality much worse than normal was the fact that he had become enamored of a toffee-and-milk-chocolate confection called a Crunchie. The resultant sugar high made him James Cameron to the nth degree. Even he realized this was not a good thing and he hired an assistant whose duty was to prevent him from enjoying more than one Crunchie per day.

Shortly after she had completed her work, Kate Winslet, the film's 21-year-old female heroine, opened up to the *Los Angeles Times* about her experience, which she called "an ordeal." It was not an interview that would make a pleasant addition for James Cameron's memory book, as she let it be known that "during the course of production she nearly drowned, contracted influenza and suffered extreme chill from being immersed in cold water." Winslet said that the result of the physicality Cameron put her through was "I looked like a battered wife," and observed, "He has

a temper like you wouldn't believe. . . . As it was, the actors got off lightly. I think Jim knew he couldn't shout at us the way he did to his crew because our performances would be no good." Winslet said that "there were times I was genuinely frightened of him," but then again, "A couple of times I felt he was someone I could take a country walk with, and enjoy it." She also discussed the costs of the film. "I normally don't even think about things like budgets, but everyone on set was talking about it," she said. "It makes you think, doesn't it? How many houses could you build for that money? How many people could you feed?" She concluded, "For the first time in my life on a film set I was thinking, 'I wish I wasn't here.' Some days I'd wake up and think, 'Please, God, let me die.'"

Delay of Departure

While all this was going on, a musical about the ship's demise—also called *Titanic*—became a surprise hit on Broadway, winning the Tony as the year's Best Musical. Originally, a Fourth of July weekend opening had been planned for *Titanic*, the movie, but in April, Cameron delivered the bad news: With filming having been completed in late March, the extensive postproduction work would prevent him from meeting the scheduled premiere date. Cameron did take time out in the summer to marry his long-time girlfriend, Linda Hamilton, who had starred in his *Terminator* movies, but he and his fourth wife put off their honeymoon so that he could return to editing. Fox decided that July 28 would give Cameron plenty of time and yet still be early enough to cash in on those big summertime bucks. This turned out to be a problem for Paramount. *Air Force One,* Wolfgang Petersen's dopey action movie about a take-charge chief executive, was also opening that day, and star Harrison Ford let it be known that if the studio ever wanted him to make another Tom Clancy movie, it'd seriously think twice about making his film go up against *Titanic.* So much for July 28. Paramount thought Thanksgiving would be ideal, but Fox balked because it already had two what-it-hoped-would-be-major-releases scheduled then, the cartoon *Anastasia* and *Alien Resurrection.* So

Titanic would not see the light of day until just before Christmas—in the States, that is. Fox was unveiling it at the Tokyo Film Festival in November.

The two Hollywood trade papers dispatched their first-string critics to Tokyo to pass judgment, and executives at Fox and Paramount could smile when they read the dispatches. From *Variety*'s Todd McCarthy: "A spectacular demonstration of what modern technology can contribute to dramatic storytelling, James Cameron's romantic epic, which represents the biggest roll of the dice in film history, will send viewers in search of synonyms for the title to describe the film's size and scope." The *Hollywood Reporter*'s Duane Byrge said the film "is no soulless junket into techno-glop wizardry but rather a complex and radiant tale that essays both mankind's destructive arrogance and its noble endurance." Byrge added, "Undeniably, one could nit-pick—critic-types may snicker [despite what he did for a living, Byrge apparently did not consider himself a critic-type] at some '60s-era lines and easy-pop '90s-vantage hindsights—but that's like dismissing a Mercedes on the grounds that its glove compartment is drab."

Me Write Good

Unlike *A Night to Remember*, the 1958 British film against which all other *Titanic* movies had been measured, Cameron's *Titanic* did not rely on real people and actual situations. Instead, it hearkened back to Jean Negulesco's 1953 *Titanic*, in that they both plopped fictional characters on board to be the film's centerpiece. In the earlier movie it was an unhappily married couple played by Clifton Webb and Barbara Stanwyck; here it was Leonardo DiCaprio and Kate Winslet enacting the old one about the poor boy and the rich girl whose love transcends class lines. "We're holding just short of Marxist dogma," bragged Cameron.

What Cameron made was essentially a 12-year-old boy's idea of a romantic epic. The "left-wing" element of which he was so proud had Winslet playing Rose—frisky despite her stuffy background—who is liberated by the love of DiCaprio's Jack; at one point,

this well-bred young woman of the Taft-era even flips her middle finger at an adversary. Cameron must have read up on his Hemingway Cliffs Notes because Jack is a free spirit who gets his bohemian credentials from hanging out in Paris cafés. He also draws crummy magazine-illustration-style drawings—actually done by Cameron himself—which send Rose into paroxysms of ecstasy. Jack, who freely roams the decks of the ship despite his third-class ticket, changes his raison d'être from doodling to saving Rose from a forced marriage to Billy Zane's Cal Hockley, a sadistic Brahmin so unremittingly and one-dimensionally nasty his name might as well have been Snidely Whiplash. The dialogue included such gems as "So, this is the ship they say is unsinkable" and "Picasso—he won't amount to a thing." And in Cameron's telling, the reason the *Titanic* went down was because voyeuristic sailors on the bridge were too busy ogling Jack and Rose as they smooched to notice that iceberg.

It could be argued that the most astonishing thing about *Titanic* was not its special effects or its re-creation of the sinking, but the number and intensity of rave reviews it received. Janet Maslin went particularly off her nut for the movie. "Cameron's magnificent *Titanic* is the first spectacle in decades that honestly invites comparison to *Gone With the Wind*," she enthused. "What a rarity that makes it in today's world of meaningless gimmicks and short attention spans: a huge, thrilling three-and-a-quarter-hour experience that unerringly lures viewers into the beauty and heartbreak of its lost world. Astonishing technological advances are at work here, but only in the service of one spectacular illusion: that the ship is afloat again, and that the audience is intimately involved in its voyage." A week later, when she compiled her Ten Best list, *Titanic* was number one, and she praised the film for "bold storytelling."

In the *New York Post*, Michael Medved preached that "James Cameron delivers awesome spectacle, rich and captivating characters, a great love story, rousing adventure, and a seemingly endless succession of images so grandly cinematic, so poetic and so breathtaking, that they unequivocally earn the adjective 'unforgettable.' " *Entertainment Weekly*'s Owen Gleiberman called *Titanic* "a resplendently old-fashioned cornball love story that, in its collision with the reality of technological disaster, takes on the resonance of genuine tragedy"—this was good enough for Gleiberman to name *Titanic* the third best film of the year.

Plenty of reviewers would have none of that and saw the film as just so much nonsense. Barbara Shulgasser of the *San Francisco Examiner* winced: "Cameron gives writing-directing, and the tradition of making multi-hour movies, a bad name. The guy might be gifted at spending money on computer graphics and *Poseidon Adventure*–like special effects, but he sure as hell hasn't the slightest clue how to write a scene. . . . As moviegoers, we are programmed to look forward to love scenes. The Pavlovian response is so strong that even in the face of one awful, clunky scene after another between Rose and Jack (in one courtship interlude, Jack demonstrates to the untutored Rose how to spit from the back of her throat) we still cling to the hope that the next encounter will engage us. Forget it." She also laughed that "at one point, Cameron has his first-class passengers discussing the clever Dr. Freud and the piquant—for 1912— observation that men are obsessed with size. I'm not sure if Cameron recognizes his own pathetic weakness in this regard."

Salon's Stephanie Zacharek groaned that "Jack gets stuck with lines like 'When you've got nothing, you've got nothing to lose' and 'You could just call me a tumbleweed blowin' in the wind.' (The script credit goes to Cameron; shouldn't they have added 'Inspired by the words and music of Bob Dylan'?)." Referring to the present-day sequences in which high-tech fortune hunters are looking for the *Titanic*'s remains, the *Village Voice*'s J. Hoberman said: "To call the framing story 'tacky' does an injustice to its torpor." As for the rest of the movie, he called it "a tiresome cliché parade," and said, "Not only is the dialogue as floridly stilted as the least literate silent-movie intertitles, but the correlation between the characters' personal lives and impending doom is absolute." Hoberman's conclusion: "Two thousand passengers and not one recognizable human being!"

"Just as the hubris of headstrong shipbuilders who insisted that the *Titanic* was unsinkable led to an un-

paralleled maritime disaster, so Cameron's overweening pride has come unnecessarily close to capsizing this project," wrote Kenneth Turan. "What really brings on the tears is Cameron's insistence that writing this kind of movie is within his abilities. Not only isn't it, it isn't even close. Cameron has regularly come up with his own scripts in the past, but in a better world someone would have had the nerve to tell him or he would have realized himself that creating a moving and creditable love story is a different order of business from coming up with wisecracks for Arnold Schwarzenegger. Instead, what audiences end up with word-wise is a hackneyed, completely derivative copy of old Hollywood romances, a movie that reeks of phoniness and lacks even minimal originality. Worse than that, many of the characters, especially the feckless tycoon Cal Hockley and Kathy Bates' impersonation of the Unsinkable Molly Brown, are clichés of such purity they ought to be exhibited in film schools as examples of how not to write for the screen."

Bad Is Good

An odd thing about the response to *Titanic* was that several critics spelled out the groan-inducing elements of *Titanic* and then, in the manner of a willful child, chose to ignore them. Dave Kehr of the *New York Daily News* gave the film his paper's highest rating, saying, "*Titanic* is not merely good. It is a magnificent object, a feat of engineering and an overwhelming visual, aural and emotional experience that alone justifies all the worrisome tendencies of recent American movies." This despite the fact that he found the movie to be "a simplified tale of class conflict that, filmed as a Biograph one-reeler, could have played to the nickelodeon audiences of 1912." Michael Wilmington of the *Chicago Tribune* made the mature pronouncement, "You could say that Cameron's film . . . is overblown, a travesty of the truth. And, of course, you'd be right. But so what?" The *Chicago Reader*'s Jonathan Rosenbaum declared *Titanic* to be a "Must-See." This was even though "Cameron insists on having everyone speak '90s dialogue; he clearly doesn't know how to make his characters speak 1912 dialogue without alienating the audience. And he makes the ludicrous decision to give the 1912 Rose a recently acquired collection of paintings ranging from Picasso's *Les demoiselles d'Avignon* and one of Monet's water lily canvases to familiar pieces by Degas and Cézanne, all of which presumably sank to the bottom of the ocean." And even though "Cameron is no Cecil B. De Mille—as spectacle the sinking of the *Titanic* lacks the power of the toppled temple in *Samson and Delilah* or the train wreck in *The Greatest Show on Earth*—and he's at best a fledgling pupil of Kubrick and Spielberg when it comes to evoking vast spiritual reaches." And even though "As a screenwriter Cameron clearly has plenty to learn." And even though "Morally and conceptually, this movie could almost have been made in 1912." That's some "Must-See."

Critics also split on the performances. *Slate*'s David Edelstein, as always slavishly imitating Pauline Kael's writing style, seemed to be in heat over Kate Winslet and was fairly keen on Leonardo DiCaprio as well: "Her porcelain skin can flush with feeling, so that she seems translucent, and she's more graceful for the trace of clunkiness that attends her movements—her tremulousness is unforced. In *Titanic*, under a mane of red hair, she has a period plushness, and she helps to anchor the slender, boyish DiCaprio—who is spring-heeled and suave, light without ever being lightweight. Even the bangs that fall into his eyes seem not the work of a hairdresser, but the extension of his cheerfully mussed personality. It's hard to imagine another pair of ingénues who could hold us in our seats for two hours while we wait for that iceberg to show up, justify the movie's budget, and put an end to all that terrible dialogue." On the subject of Winslet, Bob Strauss of the *Los Angeles Daily News* argued, "spunk has its charms, but I preferred when she actually bothered to act in *Heavenly Creatures* and *Sense and Sensibility*." Gene Siskel said of Leonardo DiCaprio, "I thought that the best special effect in the picture was just how pure and innocent and how compelling this young actor can be." Au contraire, said Mick LaSalle of the *San Francisco Chronicle*, who lamented "There's something almost pitiful about *Titanic*," and cringed because "The first-class passengers, even the Americans, talk as if they're auditioning for a Restoration comedy, while Leonardo DiCaprio, as a young man in third class,

sounds like DiCaprio in any other picture. DiCaprio fares better than Winslet—at least he's not playing a stick-in-the-mud. . . . But the two look odd together. She's 21 and looks 30. He's 22 and looks 14." Rex Reed told the women of *The View* that the sex scene between the slight DiCaprio and the full-bodied Winslet in *Titanic* "was like a Chihuahua trying to mount a Golden Retriever."

It was unanimous—even among *Titanic*'s admirers—that Billy Zane was terrible ("the worst performance ever in a great movie," said Peter Travers on CNN), although it was also agreed that nobody could have done anything with such a ludicrously written role. And everyone found the presence of Gloria Stuart, the 1930s ingenue who had appeared in James Whale's *The Invisible Man* and John Ford's *The Prisoner of Shark Island*, to be a lovely surprise; now 86, the actress played Kate Winslet's character as a very old woman. The *Hollywood Reporter*'s Duane Byrge wrote that her "luminous portrayal of the 101-year-old Rose is an inspirational joy" and Stanley Kauffmann called her "completely winning." Cameron had originally planned on casting Fay Wray, but the 89-year-old *King Kong* star wouldn't submit to reading for the director.

The consensus in Hollywood was that *Titanic* would be fighting it out with the latest James Bond movie, *Tomorrow Never Dies,* for the top spot on their mutual opening weekend. *Titanic* came out on top, $28.638 million to $25.143. It would be a long time before the film relinquished this position.

Scram, Pipsqueaks

Even before *Titanic* and the other Christmas releases showed up, *Variety* reporter Dan Cox divined that "the Academy is going to rebel against the independents this year." He described studio executives as "furious" over the way the Academy had disrespected the major studios last year, that "They told everyone, 'We're the ones financing this industry and you can't even nominate us?'" Terry Lawson of the *Detroit Free Press* wrote: " Call it the Revenge of the System, but most people in Hollywood now consider it a foregone conclusion that when the Oscar nominations are announced next month, the Reign of the Independents will be interrupted, if not repudiated.

Even a leading light of the world of independent films, October Films' copresident Bingham Ray, conceded, "The media hype generated from the 1996 independent films has played a huge part in the heightened expectations for 1997. The perception was that the independents had come of age, but the market is roller coaster in nature, and this year there are fewer impact independent films." October, which among the players at the 1996 Oscars had alone been a true indie and not a subsidiary of an entertainment conglomerate, no longer enjoyed that status. In July, Universal had bought 51 percent of the company. A pre-nominations edition of CNN's *ShowBiz Today* showed footage of *Secrets & Lies* director Mike Leigh from a year ago, stating that the major Hollywood studios were run by "boneheads." Cohost Sherri Sylvester said, "This year, score one for the boneheads."

L.A., L.A., L.A. Go! Go! Go!

By the time *Titanic* opened, James Cameron already knew he wouldn't be attending any critics' awards ceremonies. The National Board of Review, the New York Film Critics' Circle and the Los Angeles Film Critics Association already had all turned their balloting into a celebration of Curtis Hanson and *L.A. Confidential*. The film won Best Picture and Best Director from all three groups, and Best Screenplay in New York and L.A., the National Board inexplicably not having a screenplay award. Three different actors were honored: Jack Nicholson in *As Good As It Gets* by the National Board; Peter Fonda in *Ulee's Gold* by the New Yorkers; and on the West Coast, Robert Duvall as a Pentecostal minister in *The Apostle*, the character study he himself wrote, directed and spent fourteen years getting financed.

Both the National Board and the L.A. organization honored Helena Bonham Carter for *Wings of the Dove*, a Henry James adaptation in which she played a penniless woman ruthlessly trying to get ahold of a dying friend's fortune. *Interview*'s Graham Fuller opined

that Bonham Carter had "taken all that Merchant Ivory experience and now turned it into something pretty dark here." Bonham Carter acknowledged that people sometimes made fun of her penchant for appearing in period pieces and "I thought that in doing yet another costume period drama, I'd be completely ribbed for it, certainly in my country, and that people would just be so bored it'd just engender one big yawn because it would be such a predictable role for me to do. But then having said that, when you look beyond the costume, it's actually quite a dramatically different kind of part for me, and much more ambiguous morally. It's probably my first grown-up part." In New York, Julie Christie was the winner for *Afterglow*, a typically quirky Alan Rudolph film about two adulterous couples; Janet Maslin said "maybe there's a more ruefully beautiful screen actress than Julie Christie. But that's hard to imagine while watching her radiant performance."

The Supporting Actress awards went to three different women. The National Board of Review's winner was Anne Heche in *Wag the Dog* and *Donnie Brasco*; Heche had gained much greater fame this past year for her role as Ellen DeGeneres's girlfriend in real life rather than for her film performances. The New Yorkers' prize went to Joan Cusack for her comic work in *In and Out*, in which she played deeply closeted Kevin Kline's put-upon fiancée; the L.A. group's to Julianne Moore in *Boogie Nights*. Although the National Board anointed Greg Kinnear Best Supporting Actor for *As Good As It Gets*, the other two groups kept Burt Reynolds's comeback moving along nicely, and he now had a pair of awards to go with his excellent reviews.

After the new year, the National Society voted and it was more of the same. *L.A. Confidential* was again named Best Picture, and Curtis Hanson had his fourth Best Director award; the film also received the Society's screenplay prize. The acting winners had all been previously cited by other groups: Julie Christie, Robert Duvall, Julianne Moore and Burt Reynolds. *Titanic* had not won a single thing from the four most prominent critics' societies.

Director Alan Rudolph observed that at the New York Film Critics ceremony, the assembled reviewers "were coming up to Julie like she was Elvis or something." Burt Reynolds said that the New York Film Critics Award was especially meaningful for him because "I felt like an artist. I felt like a real actor." Nevertheless, accepting his award at the Rainbow Room, he was still ready with the quips: "I've been doing this for forty-four years. My chances of being here tonight were like having a Richard Simmons, Jr., in the world." When Marilyn Beck asked him, "Why do you think you've had to work so hard to get recognition from the critics?" he replied, "I think in their eyes I was the same personality they saw on *The Tonight Show*—a bit irreverent and cocky and all. And you know, when you do those shows, it isn't your personality. I was being Peck's bad boy with Johnny. I was far too accessible and far too open about a lot of things. I should have watched and learned from Mr. Redford, Mr. Eastwood and Mr. Newman: If you don't say anything at all, you're given credit for a higher IQ."

Leo Is My Stud

Not only had *Titanic* beat out *Tomorrow Never Dies* its opening weekend, week after week after week it was the number one movie in America, with huge box-office totals, even after Christmas vacations were over and the kids were back in school. After all that turmoil during production, it became clear by early January, as it indefatigably held on to the top spot, that *Titanic* was no mere hit movie, it was a phenomenon. During production, the head of one studio told *Variety*, "The lesson of *Titanic* is that Jim Cameron won't work within the accepted structure of a conventional budget." Now that the film was an indubitable success, Cameron said that the lesson to be learned should be that "the media doesn't get to hang a movie with a rush to judgment."

A good portion of *Titanic*'s lucre was coming from preadolescent and teenage girls who swooned over the film's love story and kept returning to the movie to get another hit. (Score one for James Cameron: if he had added any complexity to the romance, it wouldn't have had the same resonance for youths with disposable income.) Coproducer Jon Lan-

dau opined, "People are getting something out of this on an emotional level. It's like when you were younger and you used to listen to the same record over and over again." In *Newsday*, Linda DeLibero wrote, "Cameron is being hailed as a genius, and he certainly is—a marketing genius. It was inevitable that after 20-odd years of the Lucas and Spielberg juggernaut (boys 'n' their toys flicks) someone would figure out that if you put a girl, a romance and a little history at the center of the action, you'd increase your audience—and your revenues—by more than half."

The *New York Observer* wrote, "Not since the rise to stardom of Frank Sinatra or the arrival of the Beatles have New York City teenagers found themselves so willing to surrender themselves en masse to a pop cultural sensation. Once again the parents don't quite know what to make of their children's new passion." The *Observer* quoted 17-year-old Spence School student Jamie Beilin who had seen the film seven times in its first two months of release. "The first time I went and saw it was on a Monday and I came home and my parents weren't home and I was just crying so much and I couldn't stop crying and my parents came home and they were like, 'What's wrong? This isn't right—you've seen lots of movies.'" On her second go-around, "I was so embarrassed. I was hysterical. Guys like it because it's like sinking for 45 minutes. That's what they like—they don't get the love part, they like the sinking part." Fifteen-year-old Manuel Candal, a sophomore at Xavieria High School in Bay Ridge, Brooklyn, would likely have disagreed with her estimation. Seeing it for the eighth time, he told the *Observer*, "The first time was like the *bomb*. I cried like every other scene." Referring to his girlfriend, Manuel said, "She usually cries after me. Whenever I start she follows. We're like the same person—we're inseparable." Manuel also said, "I read a biography of Leonardo DiCaprio. Don't think I'm gay or anything. I just think he's cool. I wanna *be* him. I'm not attracted to him. I just think he's hot and I would like to be him."

Indeed, it was cute, nonthreatening Leonardo DiCaprio whom most of *Titanic*'s repeat customers obsessed upon. (*Entertainment Weekly*'s Jess Cagle joked,

"Leonardo DiCaprio can't be called 'sexy' until he goes through puberty.") DiCaprio had already achieved pinup status by dint of last year's *William Shakespeare's Romeo + Juliet*, although he was merely one of a number of teen idols vying for pre-eminence, along with Jonathan Taylor Thomas, Devon Sawa and Brad Renfro, and he hadn't been able to make girls flock to *Marvin's Room*. But a month after *Titanic* premiered, he was on the cover of *People* being called "Hollywood's Hottest New Star." His fans—contemptuously dubbed "Leotards" by nonbelievers—were like a plague on the internet, filling cyberspace with single-minded veneration to his eternal glory. There were innumerable posts along the lines of Maceykay's "Leo Is My Stud," in which she declared, "I am convinced he is the hottest creature on earth!!!" And Coolbn7345's "My only wish is to meet him, then I can die a happy person." There were also over three hundred fan Web sites dedicated to DiCaprio, and in the first three months after *Titanic* opened they had some 8 million hits.

A reporter for WABC-TV in New York, Michelle Charlesworth, was posed outside the Sony Lincoln Square theater to get some comments about the actor. Along with the giddily enthusiastic teenage girls, she did find an infidel, an elderly man with a white beard who said Leo didn't do anything for him because he's "too sweet and innocent." And a doe-eyed preadolescent boy told Charlesworth, "I think he's overrated." When the reporter said, "Truth be told, you've got it going on over him," the little boy nodded in agreement.

The odd thing was DiCaprio claimed he wasn't interested in superstardom but aimed to be a character actor, an assertion which was given credence by his earlier career choices, ranging from the retarded younger brother in *What's Eating Gilbert Grape?* to Rimbaud in *Total Eclipse*. *Entertainment Weekly* said, "It's possible DiCaprio may be about to break Hollywood's heart. Primarily an indie-film actor, the baby-faced performer reportedly doesn't want to be a mainstream movie star." *Newsday's* Jack Mathews hoped Leo stayed to this course, because "if he isn't careful, he could end up being compared more with Fabian than Dean and Clift." Ironically, James Cameron had had reservations about hiring him in the first

place. The director said, "He didn't strike me as necessarily having the qualities I wanted for my Jack." And the actor wasn't sure he wanted to do the movie anyway. Cameron recollected how DiCaprio "had decided the character wasn't quirky enough. He wanted, I don't know, warts or a hump or a cocaine addiction, I told him that wasn't the character and that Jack was like Jimmy Stewart, pure of heart. Then the lightbulb went on for Leo and he realized that would be a really hard thing to make great." The director did have some problems with his leading man during the shoot. DiCaprio, he said, "was like a cat. He always made this big drama about getting wet." And in regards to *Titanic*, DiCaprio said, "After the whole experience, I know it's *really* not my cup of tea—all respect to Jim and the actors who do that type of thing."

As further evidence of *Titanic's* unique hold on the populace was the *New York Times Book Review* paperback bestsellers list, where at one point, eight of the fifteen entries were *Titanic*-related, ranging from James Cameron's *Titanic*—all about how he made the film, minus the Sturm und Drang; a reprint of Walter Lord's classic account of the sinking, *A Night to Remember;* and three biographies of Leonardo DiCaprio, one of which was called *Modern-Day Romeo*. "My Heart Will Go On," the treacly theme song sung by Céline Dion, was number one for weeks on end—until it was displaced by Will Smith's "Gettin' Jiggy Wit It." James Horner's banal score—sort of Chieftains-lite with some Enya thrown in—became the top-selling instrumental soundtrack album of all time.

Ruined by Television

Taking effect for this year's Academy Awards was a bylaw stating that a documentary could not have been shown on television prior to its theatrical run if it was to qualify for Oscar consideration. Academy executive director Bruce Davis noted that the 1995 Documentary feature winner, *Anne Frank Remembered*, had actually won an Emmy before it received the Oscar. Arthur Hiller, who was Academy president when the rule was put into effect, said, "We need to find ways to pare our field down from the current seventy to the twenty-odd films each year with a legitimate theatrical existence and to persuade the others to seek their rewards over at the Television Academy."

This regulation brought documentaries under the same guidelines as feature films. But two distributors were awakened rudely that the Academy was taking a strict constructionalist approach with its "no television" law, one with a documentary, the other with a popular Japanese feature. It didn't matter that a movie had been shown in America only within the confines of theaters, if a foreign film had been shown on TV in its country of origin, that was enough for the rule to be invoked, even if the movie premiered in a theater in its homeland. Disqualified was a documentary, *Marcello Mastroianni: I Remember, Yes I Remember*. Fine Line, the film's American distributor, tried to find the logic of the movie—originally a theatrical release—being rendered ineligible for Oscar consideration simply because it had been shown on French television as part of a salute to the actor, but there was none to be found. Harvey Weinstein also had a movie affected: *Shall We Dance?*, one of the year's top-grossing foreign pictures in the United States, and the National Board of Review's choice for Best Foreign Film, was incontrovertibly a bona-fide movie; having been released theatrically in Japan early in 1996, it swept the Japanese Academy Awards. But in March 1997, its theatrical run completed, the film then appeared on Japanese television. Four months later it was released in the United States, being seen in America only in theaters. Weinstein contended that the no-TV-first decree made sense only as it was applicable to American films. He argued—in vain—that the completely irrational rule was "simply hurtful to foreign films and foreign filmmakers."

Academy executive director Bruce Davis said the rule was "absolute." Academy President Robert Rehme was more sympathetic, counting himself an admirer of *Shall We Dance?* and acknowledging, "It's a problem area." Ellen Little, the president of First Look, which released the Mastroianni film, said that in other countries movies are presold to television companies with specified air dates. "What is a producer supposed to say in the contract with the TV company? You can't broadcast until it qualifies for Oscar consideration?"

Golden Oldies

Receiving eight Golden Globe nominations, *Titanic* set a new Hollywood Foreign Press Association record. But the highlights of this year's Globes presentations occurred on the television side of things, as Ving Rhames, winner of Best Actor in a Special or Mini-Series for his portrayal of boxing promoter Don King, insisted that one of the losing nominees, Jack Lemmon, come onstage and take the award. The Best Actress in a Drama Series, Christine Lahti, also livened things up by being in the bathroom when her name was called.

In the movie realm, the overall theme was less a coronation of *Titanic* than a celebration of old friends, starting with Burt Reynolds, who won the Supporting Actor Globe. "If you hang on to things long enough, they get back in style—like me," he said in accepting the award. "It's been real quiet for about three years. Seen a lot of television." The *Boogie Nights* actor also declared that he was "excited just to rubberneck here with you people whom I haven't seen in a long time," and concluded by saying, "Just remember that the old Stradivarius plays better than the new ones." When Best Actor (Drama) winner Peter Fonda got to the stage, he exclaimed, "God, it's great to be back!"

It wasn't all comebacks, though. *L.A. Confidential*'s Kim Basinger defeated Gloria Stuart, the two stars of *As Good As It Gets*, Jack Nicholson and Helen Hunt (beating *Jackie Brown*'s Pam Grier), took home Globes, and their film was named Best Musical or Comedy. Aping his character in the film, Nicholson—who received a standing ovation—accepted his trophy with his hand in a plastic bag. Being boisterously vulgar, Nicholson said, "For those of you who were wondering, it was number two—for Miss Lahti," and then said, "I want to thank my fellow nominees," and then turned around and bent over, essentially mooning the audience with his pants on. He said, "I warned Jim [Brooks], this'll give me another decade of not having to behave myself, and here I am."

Matt Damon lost in the acting race to Peter Fonda, but he and Ben Affleck did triumph in the Screenplay category. Onstage, Damon addressed his father back in Massachusetts: "Dad, I got a better seat than Jack Nicholson!" Best Actress in a Drama went to Judi Dench, the British actress who played Queen Victoria in Miramax's *Mrs. Brown*; she was onstage in the West End, so wasn't around to meet and greet Hollywood.

Titanic did win four of the eight awards for which it was nominated. Two were for music, the others for Best Director and Best Picture; this marked the first time that the film had beaten out *L.A. Confidential*. When he accepted his Best Director Globe, James Cameron said, "Directors are supposed to be in control all the time. I can barely control my bladder right now." And then he praised Fox and Paramount for putting up the money for *Titanic* and insisted that "I just think that we should all give a big round of applause for the people who had the *huevos* to make this nutsy movie." When he was back to pick up the Best Picture Globe, Cameron said, "So does this prove once and for all that size *does* matter?" His conclusion was "The thing that I think this film does prove in our cynical and jaded time is that true love is still the greatest power of all." Shortly after the Globes, a man called the *Los Angeles Times* and got ahold of an editor, telling him he hoped that "now that *Titanic* is the best film of the year, you'll take that guy who didn't like it outside and shoot him"—meaning Kenneth Turan.

Gunning for Eve Harrington

With the dust settling, the Oscar race was becoming clearer. Any film that swept the critics' awards could not be ignored, so *L.A. Confidential* was a definite Best Picture nominee. And a movie that touched the popular imagination as strongly as *Titanic* was also guaranteed of being an Oscar contender; Kenneth Turan reckoned that for all of *Titanic's* success, James Cameron was not necessarily a shoo-in for a Director nomination because "his lack of what might be called a winning personality could cost him votes." And although not in as ostentatious a manner as *Titanic*, *Good Will Hunting* had also struck a chord with moviegoers. That, combined with the Miramax publicity apparatus, signaled Oscar recognition; in predicting a Best Picture nomination, Su Avasthi of the

New York Post said *Good Will Hunting* "is making grown men weep at theaters—need we say more?" And between its strong Golden Globe showing and healthy box office, *As Good As It Gets* also looked like a finalist; for those who believed in omens, Jack Nicholson and Helen Hunt were featured on the cover of the issue of *Entertainment Weekly* containing its nominations predictions article, which this year was called "As Good As Gold."

With these four movies appearing to be definite nominees, several films would be fighting it out for the fifth spot. Movies that prior to, or just after, their premieres, had seemed like good bets were hurt by middling box-office response and an overall lack of enthusiasm, films such as *Amistad*, *The Ice Storm*, *Wings of the Dove*, Jim Sheridan's latest Daniel Day-Lewis vehicle, *The Boxer*, Martin Scorsese's Dalai Lama epic, *Kundun*, and *Boogie Nights*, which wasn't faring much better at the wickets than last year's "respectable" sex pic, *The People vs. Larry Flynt*. Atom Egoyan's mournful Canadian drama, *The Sweet Hereafter*, earned some of the best reviews of the year, but—although it had come close a number of times—the small film did not win a single critics' award; that kind of recognition would have helped it immeasurably in its attempt to catch the attention of Academy voters. Then there was also *The Full Monty*, which could rightly be called "beloved" by audiences. The head of Fox Searchlight, Lindsay Law, contemplated the film's Oscar chances: "I think in some people's minds they can think of it as a guilty pleasure , 'cause they had such a good time. And then they have to equate, yes, but is it of the quality for a gold statuette?"

The Academy deprived the studio publicity departments of some of their window of creativity, setting down a hard and fast rule that the only allowable campaign perks for Academy members were videos of the movies themselves—they could no longer be presented in a nice tote bag. Academy President Bob Rehme put it this way: "You can send a video of the movie but can't send it in a musical pop-up box."

After two years of it being otherwise, the Best Actress race was looking like old times, meaning there was a dearth of critically acclaimed women's performances. *Entertainment Weekly* couldn't even come up with an actress to include as its "Lovable Long Shot" in this category, and had to include the dubious likes of Jodie Foster in *Contact* and Julia Roberts in *My Best Friend's Wedding*, just to fill up a one-page discussion of the contest. By contrast, the magazine listed thirteen men who had a legitimate claim on Best Actor consideration, and that was *without* including any of the three stars of *L.A. Confidential*. The studios, which as always were throwing away money on Oscar ads for people who hadn't even a remote chance for recognition (Lee Evans as Best Actor for *Mouse Hunt*, Bruce Willis in *The Jackal*), couldn't find even weird choices to push for Best Actress.

The most intriguing question regarding the nominations was whether *Titanic* would best *All About Eve*'s 47-year-old record of fourteen nominations. It was now evident that the film was going to topple another record. Having become, in two and a half months, the fourth highest grossing movie ever and still number one at the box office week after week, *Titanic* was well on its way to becoming the biggest moneymaker of all time.

The Nominations

"*Titanic*'s Ship Comes In" was *Daily Variety*'s headline. The film, however, had to settle for a tie with *All About Eve* and its fourteen nominations. That *Titanic* did not set a new record James Cameron had only himself to blame—the much maligned script that he insisted on writing solo was passed over by the Writers Branch. (Kenneth Turan said that "denying a nomination to James Cameron and his cobbled-together *Titanic* script" was "the sane thing" to do.) Purists also pointed out that one of *Titanic*'s nods came in a category that didn't exist in 1950: Sound Effects Editing (not that *Eve* would have been nominated in that field), and also that *Eve* didn't have an insufferable song to be nominated like *Titanic*'s "My Heart Will Go On." John Anderson of *Newsday* believed that the tie between these two movies was "both ironic and apt . . . because their disparities define what made two eras of Hollywood tick." His reasoning: "*Eve* was built around one of the smartest, most caustic screenplays ever (by Joseph Mankiewicz, the film's

director). Director James Cameron's *Titanic* screenplay, at its best, suffers from dry rot." Ironically, the 1953 version of *Titanic* received but a single nomination: for its screenplay (it won). Even without being an Original Screenplay finalist, though, Cameron was nominated in three categories: as Director, coproducer and coeditor. Although it had been over thirty years since a film won Best Picture without a Screenplay nomination, Cameron could assuage himself that the film that accomplished the feat was another crowd-pleaser, 1965's *The Sound of Music*.

Going up against *Titanic* for Best Picture were *L.A. Confidential* and *Good Will Hunting*, each with nine nominations, *As Good As It Gets* with seven, and *The Full Monty*, which received four. Just as had happened with his *Broadcast News* ten years earlier, James Brooks was the one man who made a Best Picture nominee and did not receive a concurrent Best Director nod; his spot instead going to Atom Egoyan for *The Sweet Hereafter*. Like James Cameron's movie, Egoyan's involved a tragedy in a body of water—a school bus crashing into a lake—but his film cost $5 million; Egoyan's inclusion was one of the few surprises among this year's set of nominations. Edward Guthmann of the *San Francisco Chronicle* felt that "there appears to be a quality backlash in the directing and writing categories, with Canadian filmmaker Atom Egoyan winning two nominations. *The Full Monty*'s Peter Cattaneo was the only Director nominee with previous Oscar experience: his 1990 film *Dear Rosie* had been nominated for Live Action Short in 1990.

Leonardo DiCaprio was not among the finalists, although another actor of his generation was, *Good Will Hunting*'s Matt Damon. Damon hadn't even been born when his conominees had made their film debuts. Jack Nicholson was in the running for his performance in the Brooks film; this was his eleventh nomination, a new record among male actors, as he left Laurence Olivier's ten nominations in his wake. On *Live with Regis and Kathie Lee*, Claudia Cohen averred that Nicholson managed a nomination "despite what some people thought was a somewhat unattractive acceptance speech at the Golden Globes." In a nicely symbiotic contest, Nicholson's competition included the man who had given him his big main-stream break twenty-eight years earlier in *Easy Rider*, his friend, *Ulee's Gold*'s Peter Fonda; although Fonda had shared a screenplay nomination for *Easy Rider*, this was his first for acting. Receiving his fifth nomination was Robert Duvall for *The Apostle*, while Dustin Hoffman, nabbed nomination number seven for imitating producer Robert Evans in *Wag the Dog*; Hoffman's inclusion for this smug little satire was the most surprising in this category. *Daily Variety* analyzed the race: "The characters are flawed and neurotic, but none is nearly as extreme as those in last year's race (a deeply troubled pianist, a wheelchair-bound pornographer, a yokel with mental retardation and a severely burned nobleman." Immediately after the five Best Actor nominees were announced, somebody amidst the press corps at the Academy's Samuel Goldwyn theater began screaming in protest that radio's Howard Stern hadn't been nominated for his film, *Private Parts;* on television, however, it sounded as if he was shouting "Gloria Stuart!"

The Actress race was jokingly referred to as Four Brits and a Yank, as Helen Hunt in *As Good As It Gets* was the sole American in contention. Her competitors were Helena Bonham Carter in *The Wings of the Dove*, Julie Christie in *Afterglow*, Judi Dench in *Mrs. Brown* and Kate Winslet in *Titanic*. Claudia Puig of *USA Today* wrote that "Americans' legendary inferiority complex when it comes to matters of culture often can propel people to hand over awards to the seemingly more cultured and refined British." Helena Bonham Carter told Puig, "There's the patina, the accent. Perhaps because we come from that theater tradition, people credit us with a certain amount of respect above American actors. There's a veneer of respectability about being British." The actress slyly added, "I don't mind. I'll play it for all it's worth."

For the first time ever, two people were nominated in one year for playing the same character, as Gloria Stuart was a Supporting Actress finalist for portraying the aged version of Kate Winslet's Rose. (Marlon Brando and Robert De Niro had both been nominated for playing Vito Corleone, but two years apart, and over the years several actors had been nominated for impersonating Henry VIII.) Stuart,

at 87, also displaced Jessica Tandy as the oldest acting nominee ever. Her competition consisted of three women who had won other awards: Kim Basinger in *L.A. Confidential*, Joan Cusack in *In and Out* and Julianne Moore in *Boogie Nights* and one newcomer to the award scene this year, Minnie Driver, who was carried along on the popularity of *Good Will Hunting*.

Burt Reynolds received his first Oscar nomination for *Boogie Nights*. Two other Supporting Actor nominees were first-timers: Robert Forster in *Jackie Brown* and Greg Kinnear in *As Good As It Gets*. The other two, *Amistad*'s Anthony Hopkins and *Good Will Hunting*'s Robin Williams were each nominated for the fourth time, although their previous nominations all came in the lead category.

The *Orange County Register*'s Henry Sheehan led off his analysis with "Lack of surprises is the hallmark of this year's Academy Award nominations." The only omission that could be deemed even close to jarring was the failure of Rupert Everett to receive a Supporting Actor nomination for *My Best Friend's Wedding*. As Julia Roberts's gay pal, he gave one of the year's best liked—and most discussed—performances; cynics speculated that the openly gay actor was adjudged to be simply "playing himself," while a straight actor, Greg Kinnear, received a nomination for going queer. Tom Selleck had been given a slight outside chance for a nomination as a proudly gay reporter—who kisses Kevin Kline—in *In and Out*. Sheehan observed, "Playing a gay-but-not-too-gay character is always a good bet, as Greg Kinnear's nomination shows. Can you be too gay, though?" He said that because of the omissions of Everett and Selleck, "you might think so. But accusations of homophobia against the Academy just don't fly as well as its reputation for poor judgment. Kinnear's character was cheaply sentimental; Everett's and Selleck's weren't. So Kinnear got the nod." And Raymond Murray, author of *Images In the Dark: An Encyclopedia of Gay and Lesbian Film and Video*, took note that the gay character who was portrayed as a victim got the nod, not the men who were "comfortable in their own skin."

Woody Allen's surprise Original Screenplay nomination for *Deconstructing Harry*—the rancid film was not particularly well liked—meant he now had one more writing nomination than Billy Wilder. John Hartl of the *Seattle Times* griped about "an unnecessary 13th nomination for that strained collection of recycled gags, *Deconstructing Harry*. Kevin Smith's *Chasing Amy* and Neil LaBute's *In the Company of Men* (neither of them nominated for anything) both took a much fresher look at the battle of the sexes." That *The Ice Storm* was completely shut out did raise eyebrows. Although the movie had not been a hit, Joan Allen was considered a strong possibility for Best Actress, as was Sigourney Weaver for Supporting Actress, Ang Lee for Best Director and James Schamus for Adapted Screenplay.

Nominations day on E! usually finds various golly-gee personalities brought in to cheerlead for the brilliance of the Academy and its nominees. But one of this year's in-studio guests, Kristine McKenzie of the *Los Angeles Times*, was hilarious as she made no attempt to hide her contempt for the morning's results. While E! anchor Gina St. John was besides herself over the finalists in the Best Actor race—"an amazing lineup there"—McKenzie said, "None of these performances really meant anything to me," and rued that Sam Rockwell was not nominated for *Box of Moonlight*, a film which grossed all of $780,000. And she had only disdain for Supporting nominee Robin Williams because "Judd Hirsch gave that performance in *Ordinary People* several years ago, so I hope he doesn't win."

One of the year's most acclaimed foreign films, *Ma Vie en Rose*—the sweet-tempered account of a 7-year-old cross-dresser—had been submitted by its country of origin. But even though the Belgian film had won at the Golden Globes, it inexplicably did not make the Academy's short list. And the critics' favorite among documentaries, *Fast, Cheap and Out of Control*, was a non-nominee, meaning that Errol Morris, arguably the premier documentarian of the last two decades, was still looking for his first Academy Award nomination. Kenneth Turan said that the ritualistic snubbing of Morris "bespeaks a traditionalism so rigid it wouldn't be a surprise to hear that Whistler's mother was a voting member." The best known of the Documentary nominees was *Four Little Girls*, Spike Lee's

widely praised look at the 1963 Birmingham church bombing. "We're happy we got the nomination," said Lee. "I automatically thought about the parents who were the key to making this film. I did not make this film to get a nomination. To be honest, since *Do the Right Thing*, I haven't thought much about nominations. I think if you do good work it stays much longer than an award." He also said, "Well, the Academy—they have their own way of thinking, especially in the Documentary branch. *Hoop Dreams* they left out, and that was a great film—so, I mean, I didn't expect this at all." Coretta Scott King took out a full-page ad in *Variety* congratulating Lee on his nomination and thanking him "for making it impossible for us to forget the four little girls."

While the major studios were back in control, the independent companies weren't quite as scorned as some had predicted. Miramax, of course, once again stood tall, with seventeen nominations, led by *Good Will Hunting*'s nine, and *Wings of the Dove*'s four. Noting *Good Will Hunting*'s strong showing, Chantal of *Good Morning America* declared, "I'll bet you the guys over at Miramax are really cheering because once again it shows Miramax's uncanny ability to choose Oscar material." Harvey Weinstein told CNN, "If Jim Cameron is saying size matters, then we at Miramax are saying less is more." Mark Ordesky, the president of Fine Line, which received recognition for *The Sweet Hereafter* and *Deconstructing Harry*, observed, "People were implying that this would be the year of the studios. It actually turned out to be a very balanced year. It's incredibly heartening to see that." October Films had the most precipitous drop among the independent companies, going from six nominations last year to only Robert Duvall's Best Actor nod now.

Bill Mechanic, the Fox chairman, who had battled James Cameron over *Titanic*'s expenditures, maintained, "It wasn't a vote for budget. It was a vote for picture. And that crazy passion that drove us to make a picture of this size." As far as independent films, "Last year was a Cinderella year," said Uberto Pasolini, producer of *The Full Monty*. "Now, *The Full Monty* is the Cinderella movie." He acknowledged, "I'm not sure we have much chance on the night, when you look at the opposition. But I'm not complaining." One reason for his lack of complaint was that from his vantage point, *The Full Monty* has "become an event, not just another successful movie. Even the title is back in the vernacular. The film will stay in people's minds longer than most." And Fox Searchlight head, Lindsay Law, said, "We're holding the torch for the independent community." But, he added, "I think it's healthy that the awards encompass a whole range." In terms of the ratio of gross to cost, *The Full Monty* was a much more successful picture than *Titanic*.

"Every Academy Awards ceremony has at least one solid triumph-over-adversity story to stir the tears," wrote Jan Stuart in the *Los Angeles Times*, "but this year the number of comeback kids could push the stock index on Kleenex to a new high. For Best Actor nominee Peter Fonda, Best Actress contender Julie Christie and Best Supporting Actor candidate Burt Reynolds, the recognition spells a new lease on careers stalled by one too many indifferent movies. In the case of supporting performance nods for Robert Forster and Gloria Stuart, the nominations mark the end of a Rip Van Winkle sleep that has gone on for so long that their names have little or no meaning to more than half of the moviegoing public."

Peter Fonda wouldn't hear anything about a comeback. "You just haven't gone to the art houses," he told a reporter who used the term. Fonda also said his twice-Oscared sister, Jane, called immediately after the nominations were announced. "Every time she tried to talk, she burst into tears," he said, so she e-mailed him instead. She started off by writing, "Yes, I am crying." Peter said his one disappointment was that he had hoped his daughter would be nominated as well. Edward Guthmann of the *San Francisco Chronicle* concurred, calling Bridget Fonda "a versatile actress who consistently delivers original, quirky performances that more often than not get lost or ignored. She was tremendous as the pot-smoking beach bunny in *Jackie Brown*—once again showing a new slant to her ability." Robert Duvall said, "I was so punchy going coast to coast doing publicity I forgot today was the day." His estimation of his work was "I tend to get better as I get older." Duvall was continuing his publicity blitz, appearing on *Live with Regis and Kathie Lee* immediately after hearing his Oscar

news, and he got to see Regis Philbin's imitation of his performance. Matt Damon issued a statement saying he was "staggered just to have two nominations, one with my best friend and another in the company that I am in. I can't even comprehend this. I feel like I've won, just being nominated."

Julie Christie was getting out of a cab, having just returned from a poetry reading in Holland, and ran into a friend on the street who told her about her nomination. Although she had won the New York and National Society Awards, Christie's nomination was a bit of a surprise, only because *Afterglow* hadn't found an audience and its somewhat flaky essence was off-putting to many who did see it; moreover, she was neither a Golden Globe or Screen Actors Guild nominee, two bellwethers which of late had had a better prophecy rate than the slightly more esoteric critics' groups. *Premiere* asked Christie, "How do you think Hollywood perceives you today?" "I don't think it *does* perceive me. Maybe as an old lady," replied the 57-year-old actress. "What I find strange is a kind of respect. Where did I earn that respect?"

The 63-year-old Judi Dench was the least known—in the United States—of the five nominees, but her face had become more recognized now that she was playing Pierce Brosnan's boss M in the two latest James Bond movies. Having her name mentioned as a possible nominee over the last several months also helped make her more familiar in the States. "I love the fact that Americans know me now, that they say to me, 'Have you done anything else besides the Bond films and *Mrs. Brown*?'" This is absolutely fine with me," laughed the woman who had been acting since the 1950s. Dame Judi said of her nomination, "I hope it means somebody will give us more money for our film industry. I think there is a renaissance in British films, but we need cash. It's wonderful that films at last are being made here, like *The Full Monty*."

Comparing this year's nomination with the one she received two years ago as Supporting Actress for *Sense and Sensibility*, Kate Winslet said, "It felt very unreal last time, and it sort of feels the same this time." Her older alter ego, Gloria Stuart, said, "It's a real trip!" *ShowBiz Today*'s Sherri Sylvester visited Stuart at her Brentwood home, and asked her how it felt to be the oldest acting nominee in history. "I don't think about my being 88 this year," she said, and added that, except that "there are very few of us left, my old friends left, I don't feel old, I don't think old."

"Everybody always said, 'film noir, film noir,' but that never had any meaning to me," said Kim Basinger. "But the old movies of the forties and fifties were always my favorites because I watched them with my father." Her director, Curtis Hanson, said that when he heard that Basinger had been nominated, "My heart leaped. I am so proud of Kim and her work in this picture. What's so stunning about her performance is the spareness of it, the lack of apparent technique." *Access Hollywood* imagined that the nomination must have been bittersweet for Minnie Driver, because of the breakup with Matt Damon. "That's just the way it goes," she philosophized. "I'm on a particular path, and Matt is on a particular path, and I wish him well." An Associated Press reporter used the same word, and this time Driver said, "It's certainly bittersweet, but it's more sweet than bitter from where I'm standing, because I have learned an enormous amount and all I can ever ask of life is that I have learned."

Burt Reynolds was on *Today*, from the Banff, Canada, location of his new film, *Mystery, Alaska*. He said, "I'm just so truly—and this is hard for anybody to believe, I'm sure—humbled by this," he said. On the subject of whether he was back to stay, Reynolds revealed that "Mr. Eastwood called me last night and said, 'I know you, and if you just keep your mouth shut, you'll do really well.' " After the interview, *Today*'s Matt Lauer commented that Reynolds was "almost at a loss for words, which may never have been said in the past." Reynolds told Ruthe Stein of the *San Francisco Chronicle*, "You appreciate everything more when you have a second chance. It has taken me forty years or so to learn to act, and I was afraid I wouldn't have a chance to show it." And whenever the word *comeback* was brought up, Reynolds would insist, "I didn't go anywhere. *They* did."

"I didn't expect it" was the immediate response of another of the "comeback kids," Robert Forster. "I didn't get Golden Globe or the Screen Actors Guild nominations, so I figured, 'Who am I to worry about the Academy Awards?' " And he said, "God, I hope it

means steady work." Greg Kinnear laughed that "Jack won't be up until probably noon, so I'll call him at that point and we'll share the excitement, I'm sure."

Director Atom Egoyan got the news of his nomination almost by accident: "My son wanted to watch cartoons. I was flipping around when I was nominated. It was incredible news." Curtis Hanson seemed already resigned to *L.A. Confidential*'s Oscar fate: "*Titanic* is titanic. Like the ship, its namesake, it's huge. What can you do about that? Nothing." The *Hollywood Reporter*'s Martin Grove commiserated with Hanson, saying that in another year *L.A. Confidential* might well have been the front runner. Hanson was getting something he had wanted, though—a new ad campaign. Warner distribution head Barry Reardon said, "Hopefully I can reinvent the movie and expand it." The new ads attempted to convey an old-style romantic feel, with nominated femme fatale Kim Basinger front and center.

Although casual observers expressed surprised at *Amistad*'s relatively poor showing (four nominations), serious Oscar watchers had known that it was destined to be an also-ran. Offsetting, at least somewhat, the disappointment for Steven Spielberg, Barbara Chase-Riboud dropped her plagiarism suit against him and DreamWorks the previous day. *USA Today* reported, "Chase-Riboud settled for a reported $1 million. Sources at DreamWorks say that although Chase-Riboud did not win what she claimed to want most— a mention in the film's credits—she did manage to affect the performance of the film, which has grossed about $40 million."

Janet Maslin was on *Charlie Rose* after the nominations were announced, and her fellow panelists, Richard Corliss, David Denby and Graham Fuller, as well as Charlie Rose himself, all made fun of her passion for *Titanic*. When Rose emphasized, "*Titanic,* for you, was a spectacular movie." "I stand by that, even in this crowd," Maslin insisted.

The Leotards were out in force on the net, bewailing the injustice and stupidity of a world in which Leonardo DiCaprio is denied an Oscar nomination. Lizardbick declared that DiCaprio "is the best actor alive! He rox!" and his non-nomination "pisses me off beyond belief! He is better than any of the other actors nominated! Whoever decided not to nominate him are stupid fools, who don't know anything. I bet your just jealous!" Sorry3078 declared, "Who ever decided not to nominate him should pay!!!!!!" And Chinson899 wondered "Where do they find these stupid people who decide who's a nominee?" and knew that "The only way those other people were nominated was because they bribed the judges!" Some DiCaprio admirers sprung into action. The Academy received a few hundred e-mails and phone calls demanding a recount. An Academy spokesperson reported, "The calls did not just come from teenagers. One older woman called and said the whole state of Florida was upset." *Titanic* songbird Céline Dion got in the Leo action, too: "To me, he's James Dean. He's wonderful—I can't believe he's not nominated!"

Gloria Stuart was at a loss at why DiCaprio was not an Oscar finalist. "I don't understand it. I think their performances together were beautiful. But you see, it's so iffy. That's why I was so happy this morning. It's so iffy." Philip Wuntch of the *Dallas Morning News* felt, however, that "the Academy's decisions can be justified. Mr. DiCaprio's impact is due to a buoyant personality; he remains chipper even when icicles are forming on his eyebrows. But Ms. Winslet's Rose makes the film's real emotional transition, and the actress navigates the dramatic waters with eloquence and elegance."

Gloria-ous

Gloria Stuart told the *New York Times*'s Bernard Weinraub that she had been sent a number of scripts since *Titanic* opened. "I was offered a script where I play a space woman," she said, "I don't see myself as a space woman." The actress was greeted with a standing ovation when she was a guest on *The Tonight Show with Jay Leno*. When Leno said, "you had a huge career," she corrected him: "a huge *unsuccessful* career." To give the audience an idea of what the actress was like in the 1930s, a clip was shown, only it was of Alice Faye singing and not Stuart, who thought it was hilarious and said, "I couldn't sing a note." She said that when her agent retired seven years earlier, she didn't bother to get another, and explained how she got the

role in *Titanic*: "James Cameron was looking for an actress of the 1930s that was still upright, you know, could talk, remember lines, things like that. But he didn't want anyone like Katie Hepburn because it would be too recognizable, and he wanted someone that was still more or less professional, and I happened to be it." She admitted that Cameron had one reservation about her: "He wasn't sure I could look 101—but he hadn't seen me in the morning." Leno asked who she'd be taking to the Oscars, and she said "Well, all my beaus are dead. I outlived them all." And in closing, Leno informed the audience that "This woman was instrumental in the anti-Nazi movement in the 1930s here in Hollywood, too. So God bless you for all your good work."

The next night, Stuart was on *The Late, Late Show with Tom Snyder*, and he mentioned the film clip snafu on *Leno*. Stuart laughed that her daughter had been watching and when she saw Alice Faye said, "I didn't know Mother was so plump." She told Snyder that she quit movies in 1939 because she was waiting for Oscar-caliber roles to come her way but she was "marooned in the B unit at 20th." Of all the actors she worked with, George Sanders was the best kisser, and "he married Zsa Zsa Gabor, you know—that takes some doing." She also recounted how, because she was going to be playing Kate Winslet as an old lady, she wanted to meet the younger actress before filming began, so Winslet dropped by for a visit. "I put my arms around her at my house, at the front door," recalled Stuart, "and said, 'I have a beautiful tea for you,' and she said, 'Oh, I'd rather have a drink.' So I said, 'Well, I have champagne in the fridge. It's the way I live.' So we killed a bottle of champagne in an hour. She told me her life story, I told her mine. We had a wonderful time." Winslet similarly had fond memories of her first meeting with Stuart, telling *Good Morning America*'s Joel Siegel that the octogenarian actress was full of anecdotes of Old Hollywood, and was "telling me tremendous stories about naughty things she got up to and she had so much life, and so much exuberance."

Both Jay Leno and Tom Snyder evinced genuine respect and affection for Gloria Stuart. Not so Gene Siskel, who apparently never saw a sentimental Oscar choice he didn't dislike. Siskel complained on the *Late Show with David Letterman* about the possibility of Gloria Stuart winning. "Think about it, Dave. She played someone—what a stretch!—15 years older than she is." "Well we don't need to get catty," reprimanded the host. When Letterman mentioned another perceived sentimental favorite, Burt Reynolds, Roger Ebert said, "I don't know that they really want to see Burt come back." On her *Late Show* appearance, Helena Bonham Carter said that since being nominated, "everyone keeps on congratulating me, which is very nice, so I'm in 'auto thank you mode'—people say 'Good morning,' I say thank you."

Peter Fonda also made an appearance on the *Late Show* and brought with him a piece of wood he was having people touch for good luck. Letterman did so upfront, but later in the interview, as the host gesticulated while speaking, a laughing Fonda would hold out the block so that Letterman would again touch it. "What is wrong with you? Stop that!" demanded a jokingly-flummoxed Letterman. Fonda then tossed the wood behind him through the "window" on the set where Letterman frequently threw pencils and cards containing bad jokes. Now that he was without his block, the actor knocked on Letterman's desk. Fonda also said, "I remember beating the pavement in New York when I was 20, a wannabe actor on stage, getting as many readings as I could. And whenever we heard, a small group of us, that Bob Duvall was in town, we'd go over to where he was and just sit like acolytes at his feet because we thought he was the coolest. And now I'm included with this group, one of my heroes, it's terrific." A little later when Fonda was on *Late Night with Conan O'Brien*, he asked if the host's desk was made of real wood. When O'Brien told him no, Fonda knocked sidekick Andy Richter's head instead.

The *New York Daily News* team of Rush & Molloy had talked with Robert Duvall and they mentioned a rave review by David Denby, in which the *New York* reviewer emphasized his admiration for Duvall's performance in *The Apostle* by noting that he had not "always been a fan" of the actor whose performances he often found "dry and overbearing." "So David Denby is throwing me a bone?" snorted Duvall, who didn't bother reading him. "Well, fuck his bone. I

don't think he ever taught an acting or directing class. Who should I listen to: Marlon Brando, who wrote about me in his book? Or David Denby?" When Denby spoke to Rush & Molloy, he tried to puff himself up with, "He said the same thing about Pauline Kael." But then Rush & Molloy faked him out by telling him that, coincidentally, the actor had denigrated him as "a Pauline Kael clone."

A Grace Note

Perhaps the process started during the presentation of last year's Honorary Award to Michael Kidd. During the clip from *Seven Brides for Seven Brothers*, surely it must have occurred to somebody that while the Academy was giving an Award to that film's choreographer, a man who had worked on ten movies, its director had never been recognized by the Academy. And Stanley Donen had directed or codirected twenty-eight pictures, ranging from *Singin' in the Rain* and *Funny Face* to *Charade* and *Two for the Road*. Plus there were nine others he had choreographed. This year, in one of its most refreshingly sensible moves, the Board of Governors voted him an Honorary Oscar, "in appreciation of a body of work marked by grace, elegance, wit and visual innovation." Academy president Bob Rehme said, "Stanley Donen has directed some of the most memorable films ever made. His films are genuine landmarks of technique, of choreographic grace and color design and story structure." Donen's reaction, as rendered to CNN's Cynthia Tournquist, was "It's very nice to have them give one to me."

Y'all Come Back, Hear?

This was the seventieth anniversary of the Academy Awards, so it was thought that a nice gesture for the momentous occasion would be to invite all the living acting Oscar winners back to the show. And it was promised they would be treated with respect and affection, not like at the fiftieth Awards, where the returnees were quickly shuttled across the stage in an Allan Carr opening number.

Army Archerd kept tabs on the RSVPs for this segment, but five days before the Awards, he reported,

"Barbra Streisand doesn't want to again be an on-again, off-again award show participant—this time for next Monday's Oscars. You recall last year's in-again, out-again appearance to sing her nominated song, 'I Finally Found Someone' (which was eventually done by Céline Dion). Then followed the Grammys, when she was to duet with Dion but Barbra became ill and Dion did a solo. Now, Barbra was invited to attend the seventieth Oscars as a previous winner. But today she is notifying Gil Cates that she cannot attend this year's Oscars. She has a bulging spinal disc, she's in and out of traction and undergoing therapy. And rather than say yes on one day when she's feeling okay and then having to cancel the next day when she's in pain—she's declining today. Further, she's suffering remnants of bronchitis, adds Marty Erlichman. Barbra was also to have joined fiancé Jim Brolin and his 10-year-old daughter on the latter's spring school break skiing vacation, but there's also no snow biz for Barbra."

Billy Crystal would be returning as well. He initially told Gilbert Cates no, but—according to Crystal—Cates, Academy officials, personal friends and fans kept pestering him until his resistance gave way. This would be his sixth stint as a host, putting him in second place only to Bob Hope's seventeen. He told *USA Today,* "I so liked *not* doing the show after doing the show so well the years that we did it. And I needed a break. And it went really well last year. People liked it. So I didn't want to do it this year. But they wore me down." He did promise that he wouldn't be taking off his clothes on stage in a *The Full Monty* tribute. Writer Bruce Villanch was happy with the nominees. "Last year it wasn't easy coming up with Brenda Blethyn jokes," he laughed. "This time we've got Burt Reynolds, Dustin Hoffman, Robin Williams and Jack Nicholson nominated, and they're all sitting ducks. Jack loves jokes made at his expense. In fact, nothing makes him happier."

Debbie Allen was busy portraying Harriet Tubman in a local play, so she wouldn't be available to bless the show with her choreography. Certainly at one point she had been hoping to attend the ceremony as a nominated producer for *Amistad,* but of course that didn't pan out. This year's choreographer would be Daniel Ezralow, who had worked on videos with U2 and David Bowie. He had also created a "multimedia event," *Mandela,* which would be playing at the UCLA Center for the Performing Arts, the school where Gilbert Cates was chair of the Film, Television and Theater Department. A few days before the show, Cates told CNN, "We have a little dance number that's quite exciting this year."

Chat and Chew

The Nominees Luncheon had a record turnout of 120 people. Addressing the assembled press, Gloria Stuart said, "I think everyone needs approval. And you know, the older you get, the less attractive you get, so you worry more about approval." Helena Bonham Carter said, "It's sort of like a roller-coaster. Everyone is so excited for you and of course you *are* excited, but you can't be excited for six weeks perpetually—that's something I've learnt." Curtis Hanson, who shortly after the nominations had seemed almost to be conceding a *Titanic* sweep, was now chin up, saying that it was no done deal: "It was a foregone conclusion that the ship was going to get to New York." James Cameron said, "The Oscars are a bonus round for me. It's not a career make or break. If we win, we get drunk. If we lose, we get drunk. But with fourteen nominations, we're definitely going to walk out with some trophies."

CNN's Jim Moret described Greg Kinnear as "someone who is envied by anyone who's ever been in television, because he's made the leap from television to the big screen so successfully." Kinnear himself was amused that Dustin Hoffman was walking around the luncheon wearing a name tag. As the nominees posed for a group picture, Peter Fonda said, "I love the idea of being in a class photo. I'm in a really good class." Fonda gave his fellow nominees silver pocketknives as a sign of affection. Matt Damon later said his father saw the photo of the five Best Actor nominees posing together and told him that "it looked like one of those pictures where they have a cardboard cut-out and somebody puts their head on there, because it's like these four legends and me." Indicating Damon, Robert Duvall said to another nominee, "Hey, Dustin, if you think you're a ladies' man, you should see this guy!" *USA Today* scooped that during the photo shoot,

Damon "didn't make eye contact with *Good Will Hunting* cast mate and ex-girlfriend Minnie Driver, who stood one row down with fellow supporting actress nominees Kim Basinger and Joan Cusack." As always, the nominees were told what to strive for if they got to accept an Oscar. Julianne Moore said her reaction was "Oh my God, to be brief and be funny on top of it?"

The night before the Nominees Luncheon, the SAG Award for Best Male Actor had gone to Jack Nicholson. In accepting, Nicholson reminisced about how "I worked for ten years, I never got one dollar more than Screen Actors Guild minimum. Not one." He also expressed his "love" for his *As Good As It Gets* collaborators, and admitted he never thought he'd be saying that word in a movie. The Awards presentation featured a special tribute to Gloria Stuart, who had been one of the founding members of SAG, and then she tied for the Best Supporting Female Actor with *L.A. Confidential*'s Kim Basinger. In accepting, Stuart said, "After the birth of my beautiful daughter, this is the next best thing that's ever happened to me." Helen Hunt won Best Female Actor for *As Good As It Gets*, after her work in *Mad About You* lost in the television category to *Seinfeld*'s Julia Louis-Dreyfuss. *Good Will Hunting*'s Robin Williams defeated Burt Reynolds for Supporting Male Actor, and in accepting, said the award looked like it was swiped off the hood of a Bentley. There was a major surprise in the Ensemble Acting award. The prize went to *The Full Monty*, even though its cast members had still not become household names. James Cameron said of *Monty*'s victory, "All the energy in that film comes from the group dynamic. *Titanic* doesn't fit that. There's logic to it."

Telling Tales out of School

Because Matt Damon and Ben Affleck seemed so *nice*, theirs was a rare instance of a success that nobody seemed to begrudge. But then forces appeared seeking to bring down the pair. *Variety* reported that "a curious set of potentially damaging rumors—none of them, evidently, with any foundation—are doing the rounds" about the *Good Will Hunting* script. Among the gossip was "that Damon and Affleck had bought

the story from someone else; another that the script had been written by veteran William Goldman and a third—reported everywhere from *Entertainment Weekly* to *Daily Variety*—that Damon had initially written the story at Harvard as a one-act play. The latter was conceivably the most devastating, jeopardizing the Best Original Screenplay nom if it could be proven that the story had been performed or published beforehand." Publicist Tony Angellotti noted, "This has been going on for months. The calls are coming in anonymously. Who's got the most to gain?" Angellotti said that Damon had purchased the *title* but not the story from a pal of his; that the basic story had been written for a writing class at Harvard but had not gone beyond that; and that William Goldman had spent a day going over the script with Damon and Affleck when the project was still at Castle Rock. Academy officials pointed out that the Writers Branch Executive Committee had checked into the screenplay's gestation and found no indication that it did not belong in the Original category. William Goldman said, "I spent a day working with them on it, and thank God I didn't damage their talent."

The Days Dwindle Down

Janet Weeks of *USA Today* felt that a tight Best Actor race had become less so as the Awards approached. "Each candidate had ample reasons to win: Duvall, beloved by fellow thespians, wrote, directed and financed *The Apostle* himself; Fonda is a member of a famous acting family and somewhat of a comeback kid; and Nicholson—well, Hollywood loves Jack. Then came Nicholson's rowdy Golden Globes appearance, during which he mock-mooned the audience, wore a plastic glove and told an off-color joke. Some predicted his bawdy behavior would sink his Oscar chances. Since the Globes, however, Nicholson has been Mr. Nice Guy. He gave a dewy-eyed speech to Screen Actors Guild members when they honored him, saying how much he loved writer/director James L. Brooks and castmates Helen Hunt and Greg Kinnear. He also was well mannered at the Oscar nominees lunch. And now he's the front runner." William Goldman also felt Nicholson would win, despite "his swell behavior at the Golden Globes." Goldman didn't think a Nicholson victory was warranted, however, writing in *Premiere*: "Easy part, Bill Murray would have been terrific, or Robin Williams or Gene Hackman, or if you want to go young, Jim Carrey would have been sensational." Barry Koltnow of the *Orange County Register* was hoping that Peter Fonda would win, but was expecting a Nicholson victory because "If you want to have Jack smiling at the cameras from the front row each year, you gotta give him a prize once in a while."

John Hartl of the *Seattle Times* wasn't so sure about a Nicholson victory: "Jack Nicholson's popularity could win him a third Oscar for his highly enjoyable performance in *As Good as It Gets*, but does anyone believe the radical transformation his character went through?" Gene Siskel thought Peter Fonda deserved to win since, of the five nominees, "he had the least flashy part and did the most with it" and, tweaking Roger Ebert's choice, added that Fonda "doesn't rant broadly like Robert Duvall." *Entertainment Weekly* felt that because "he dished up a showy role for himself," Duvall would win. Fonda joshed that "I told Jack, I'd vote for him if he votes for me. Of course, I was lying."

Janet Weeks also believed Nicholson's costar had an advantage over her British competitors, because "this year, the Academy seems to be circling its wagons and celebrating films made in town." Glenn Whipp of the *Los Angeles Daily News* observed, "Everyone likes Helen Hunt. Biological terrorists who toil underground take a break from developing new strains of anthrax to watch Helen in *Mad About You*." *Entertainment Weekly* also predicted a Hunt victory over Judi Dench, although the magazine acknowledged that Hunt's "come-and-go Brooklyn accent is a minor but noticeable flaw" that could work against her. Bernard Weinraub of the *New York Times* reported that, "Like many political candidates, Ms. Hunt is juggling several jobs, including her television series, *Mad About You*, yet managing to speak to as many journalists as possible, often from her car phone." Henry Sheehan of the *Orange County Register* saw in Helena Bonham Carter a possible long shot coming up from behind: "The once decorative English actress has steadily worked at

her craft, turning in an impressive performance as a conflicted lover in *Wings of the Dove*." And Dave Kehr of the *New York Daily News* felt that with "her charisma undiminished, her beauty intact and her insight and discretion even greater," Julie Christie would be a deserving winner. During the voting season, the L.A. County Museum of Art presented a career retrospective of Christie's films, reminding the town of why she was a star and why the industry should be happy that she was back.

The *New York Post*'s Rod Dreher called Supporting Actress "the night's toughest call. Basinger was an early favorite, but she's going to have to hang tough to resist a surge of sentiment. It's going to be Stuart in a squeaker." Lisa Scwarzbaum of *Entertainment Weekly* agreed about the result but not on the closeness of the race, saying that Stuart "has the ship to herself." Jami Bernard of the *New York Daily News*, like most observers, saw the Supporting Actor race as between Robin Williams and Burt Reynolds; unlike most, though, she gave the edge to Reynolds, saying "even Burt doesn't seem to realize how good he was," and that Williams didn't "block out the memory of Judd Hirsch in *Ordinary People*." Henry Sheehan thought Williams would win, but hoped for a Burt Reynolds upset, saying "Reynolds gets the respect a hardworking veteran with a lot of ups and downs deserves, but it seems not many Oscar voters have seen *Boogie Nights*. I'd give it to: Reynolds. It's a joke among supporting players that they, rather than the leads, held a picture together, but in the case of *Boogie Nights* and Reynolds, that's exactly true." Bob Strauss reasoned that Williams would win because, "In *Boogie Nights*, Burt plays a guy who can't distinguish vulgarity from art. In *Good Will Hunting*, Robin tells a self-proclaimed genius that nothing's his fault. Which role do you think Hollywood types find more reassuring?" Robert Forster said, "I was a long shot to begin with and I snuck in—so I got my prize. I'm gonna be the most relaxed guy in the joint on Academy Award night. I will let the other guys worry about who takes home the statue. I've got my prize—thank you very much."

It would be hard to find people who'd bet against *Titanic* winning Best Picture. So, just as prior to the nominations when the question was how the film would do in relation to *All About Eve*, now the discussion became more about whether the film would break *Ben-Hur*'s thirty-eight-year-old record of eleven Oscar wins, or would have to settle for a tie or even a place or show position—or, improbable as it seemed, something less than that. Desmond Ryan of the *Philadelphia Inquirer* wrote, "Among industry executives and seasoned Oscar watchers, the consensus is that the charioteers of *Ben-Hur* are in a real horse race for the first time in four decades. There have been long-shot contenders over the years—most recently, 1996's *The English Patient*, which went into the ceremony with twelve nominations and took home nine awards—but nothing has posed such a, well, titanic threat to *Ben-Hur*'s towering achievement." His findings were that "Expert speculation on whether *Titanic* will break *Ben-Hur*'s record ranges between 'no way' and 'difficult, but quite possible,' with some fence-straddlers forecasting a tie." Bob Strauss of the *Los Angeles Daily News* said the record "will end up resting on the dear, frail shoulders of Gloria Stuart. Figure Kate Winslet won't win in the Best Actress category and *Men in Black* gets the makeup award. Cameron has Best Director nailed, of course; the film should take all the other tech and craft races; and the most annoying song automatically wins every year, so [the writers of "My Heart Will Go On"] should start writing an acceptance speech. That's 11 statuettes; the highly competitive and traditionally unpredictable Supporting Actress race will tell the tale."

When James Cameron won the Directors Guild Award, he joked at the podium "*Titanic* was a labor of love or, some might say, a crime of passion," showing a wit that was noticeably lacking in his script. Jack Shea, the president of the Directors Guild, opined "I didn't think it had any kind of chance at the record until after our dinner. Now, I think it might tie *Ben-Hur*. You could tell from the reaction in the audience that *Titanic* is something different and special in people's minds. It's a tidal wave. I think its prospects are very good." Judah Ben-Hur, a.k.a. Charlton Heston, said that if *Titanic* did supplant his film, "Obviously, I would be disappointed."

But Saul Zaentz, producer of last year's big win-

ner, didn't think *Titanic* was even guaranteed to win Best Picture, let alone set a new record. "I don't give it to *Titanic* automatically," he said. "It doesn't have a good script. It's like saying *Twister* has a good script. They're always saying, "Hold on, I'm coming." *The English Patient*'s producer concluded, "I think *L.A. Confidential* has a chance." And since this year his film wasn't the front runner, Harvey Weinstein was back to his standard position of spouting that an upset was in the offing. "It's a battle," Mr. Miramax insisted. "*Titanic* has great special effects, but in *Good Will Hunting*, the special effects are the words." Miramax's favorite actress, Gwyneth Paltrow, told *TV Guide* "I hope anything other than *Titanic* wins Best Picture."

Ten days before the Oscars, the new Leonardo DiCaprio movie, the latest version of the old warhorse *The Man in the Iron Mask*, opened. But Jack Mathews believed the dual roles in the swashbuckler "was not the Leo the fans wanted to see. In one role, he's an effete womanizing man-brat who takes ladies by force and doesn't even give them a hug afterwards. And the twin is a prison gray innocent whose only romantic moment is an affectionate glance exchanged with a giggly dairy maid. There's neither a Rose nor a Juliet to be seen, to be identified with, to be envied. The opening night audiences apparently left the theaters urging everyone to get back in the *Titanic* line. Business for *The Man in the Iron Mask* dropped so dramatically on Saturday and Sunday that it came up $8 million short of its predicted gross." Still, it was the first movie since *Tomorrow Never Dies* back in December that had given *Titanic* a run for the number one position. It finished just $307,000 short.

Rage Against the Machine

On Oscar weekend, *Titanic* set a new record. It was number one at the box office for the fourteenth week, breaking the previous mark held by both *Tootsie* and *Beverly Hills Cop*. That very Saturday, Kenneth Turan took stock of *Titanic*'s popularity and, in an essay entitled "*You* Try To Stop It," wrote more in sadness than anger. In response to assertions that his pan of the film has been proven wrong by its sensational box-office numbers, Turan put forth the proposition that "Film critics, general opinion notwithstanding, are not intended to be applause meters. Just as restaurant critics don't send couples seeking that special anniversary meal straight to McDonald's on the 'everybody goes there, it must be the best' theory, the overall mandate of critics must be to point out the existence and importance of other criteria for judgment besides popularity." The *Times* critic understood the appeal of the movie, writing, "Deadened by exposure to nonstop trash and willing to confuse the on-screen chemistry of Leonardo DiCaprio and Kate Winslet with writing ability, audiences have been sadly eager to embrace a film that, putting the best face on it, is a witless counterfeit of Hollywood's Golden Age, a compendium of clichés that add up to a reasonable facsimile of a film. 'It's close enough' is how one Oscar-winning screenwriter accounted for the film's success. 'If you give today's audiences just an idea of what the film is about, they'll go for it.' "

Turan believed that as a portent for Hollywood's future, *Titanic*'s success was worrisome for two disparate but related reasons. One was that "though Cameron is not someone to be trusted anywhere near a word processor, he is a master of the physical side of filmmaking and one of the few people who can make effective use of $200 million. What will happen when Cameron wanna-bes with considerable studio clout start turning out grotesquely bloated, *Postman*-type disasters on a regular basis is not a pleasant scenario to contemplate." Conversely, "what Cameron does naturally—write lowest common denominator screenplays that condescend to their audience—other writers have to be forced into. The more a movie costs, the bigger its audience tent has to be, the more it has to appeal to every person on the planet if it's to have a hope of breaking even. So these movies ruthlessly bludgeon writers into dumbing down their scripts, removing any trace of intelligence that might put off even a single potential viewer." As Turan saw it, the ultimate result of the *Titanic* phenomenon would be "the wholesale jettisoning of the notion of anything resembling a literate script as a necessary part of the filmmaking process, a change in the very nature of film that is not going to be any less fatal for being largely unrecognized. Never in the past has a film with a script as lacking as *Titanic*'s" been so universally (well, almost universally) acclaimed as the acme of the medium."

Wherefore Art Thou, Leo?

What Barbra Streisand was to last year's Oscars, Leonardo DiCaprio was to the 1997 version. Although he wasn't nominated, the Academy—and ABC—was certainly hoping that the centerpiece of *Titanic* would participate in the Awards. At the gala premiere for *The Man in the Iron Mask* at New York's Ziegfeld Theatre three weeks prior to the Oscars, he told columnists Rush & Molloy, "I really don't know if I'm going to go." His mother was with him, and piped up, "Why should he go? He wasn't nominated." Marilyn Beck and Stacy Jenel Smith reported that in Hollywood, DiCaprio's "getting roasted as a bad sport," and now, a few days before the Awards, he "may be having a change of heart about joining his *Titanic* comrades." A day later, though, the *New York Post*'s "Page Six" declared that he "will *definitely* be a no-show at the Academy Awards on Monday. But the *Titanic* hunk insists he isn't staying away out of spite." His publicity representative said he wasn't going because "he feels it would take away from everyone else's moment. This is really a moment for James, for Kate, for Gloria." DiCaprio had told his director, "I'm not going. It just ain't me, bro'." Cameron was not happy with his leading man because "I felt that it was kind of a snub, not of the film per se, but of all the other people who did care and sweated blood for the movie. So I kept calling and saying, 'You gotta go for the team and for yourself, because the consequences of your not going is that you're going to look like a spoiled punk.' "

Cameron almost sounded like he wished he could be a no-show. He said to Bernard Weinraub that he was "petrified" at the thought of addressing those supposed one billion people watching the Academy Awards. "Directors choose that role because they want to be behind the camera, not in front of it. That's for actors. It's horrifying to me. You reach a point at one of these ceremonies where you hope someone else wins so you don't get up and embarrass yourself."

The Big Night

At the 1994 Oscars, CNN's Gloria Hillard thrilled bleacher perennials Sandi Stratton and Babe Churchill by taking them for a walk down the red carpet outside the Shrine Auditorium. This year, Hillard did even better by them. She took the sisters on a limo ride to Beverly Hills, where they went to Fred Hayman's boutique and had front-row seats as models showed off the Academy fashion consultant's latest goods. Sizing up one model, Sandi commented, "I don't think she has underwear on." "None of them probably do," responded Babe. They also had their hair done and got to model million-dollar jewelry, all of which led Sandi to marvel, "We felt like *Pretty Woman* the whole day." Except, said Babe, "We just don't have Richard Gere." Hillard reported that as the limo headed down Rodeo Drive at the end of the adventure, "all Babe could think about was what she would tell the girls at work," and Babe's voice could be heard declaring, "At the shop, they're just going to go bazonkers."

On Oscar day, Sandi and Babe were back in the bleachers and had been given a remnant of the red carpet to take home as a souvenir. Steve Hennigan and Tim Baker came from Boston to put oversized papier-mâché *Titanics* on their heads, and mentioned to CNN's Bill Tush that they knew Sandi and Babe. Tush later told the two sisters, "You guys are legends to everybody." Hennigan and Baker talked to the *Hollywood Reporter*'s Josh Chetwynd, telling him the reason behind their two-foot-long headwear was that "*Titanic* is the greatest movie ever made. We wanted to do all we could to help it break all the Academy records." Any number of adolescent girls carried placards extolling Leonardo DiCaprio and wore "Leo or Bust" T-shirts, hoping that their idol had changed his mind and would be making an appearance. On this hot sunny day, a marimba band entertained the bleacher creatures and Revlon gave baseball caps and T-shirts to everyone, but for nourishment, complained Chad Wilkerson of Lakewood, "All we got was a biscuit and a single bottle of water, and we didn't get the water until we started chanting, 'Water, water.' " E!'s Suzanne Sena chatted with a 6-year-old named Amanda who was dying to see the star of the just-released *Primary*

Awards Ceremony

MARCH 23, 1998, 6:00 P.M.
THE SHRINE AUDITORIUM, LOS ANGELES

Your Host:
BILLY CRYSTAL
TELEVISED OVER ABC

Presenters

Supporting Actress . . . . Cuba Gooding, Jr.
Costume Design . . . . Elisabeth Shue
Supporting Actor . . . . Mira Sorvino
Sound . . . . Cameron Diaz
Sound Effects Editing . . . . Mike Myers
Visual Effects . . . . Helen Hunt
Short Films . . . . Ben Affleck and Matt Damon
Actress . . . . Geoffrey Rush
Original Dramatic Score . . . . Antonio Banderas
Original Musical or Comedy Score . . . . Jennifer Lopez
Makeup . . . . Drew Barrymore
Film Editing . . . . Samuel L. Jackson
Scientific and Technical Awards . . . . Ashley Judd
Honorary Award to Stanley Donen . . . . Martin Scorsese
Song . . . . Madonna
Documentary Short Subject . . . . Djimon Hounsou
Documentary Features . . . . Robert De Niro
Art Direction . . . . Meg Ryan
Actor . . . . Frances McDormand
Foreign Film . . . . Sharon Stone
Writing Awards . . . . Jack Lemmon and Walter Matthau
Cinematography . . . . Denzel Washington
Director . . . . Warren Beatty
Picture . . . . Sean Connery

Performers of Nominated Songs

"Go the Distance" . . . . Michael Bolton
"How Do I Live" . . . . Trisha Yearwood
"Journey to the Past" . . . . Aaliyah
"Miss Misery" . . . . Elliott Smith
"My Heart Will Go On" . . . . Céline Dion

Colors; her homemade T-shirt read, "John Travolta, I love you so much that I want to kiss you 101 times. Love, Amanda."

Leanza Cornett, interviewing arrivals with Sam Rubin for Los Angeles's WB affiliate, KTLA-TV Channel 5, noted "I've been doing this for five years now, and never ever ever have I seen such an immense security patrol." (*Entertainment Weekly* printed a picture of Jack Nicholson being subjected to a body search by a gendarme on his way into the Shrine.) On E!, Joan Rivers said that the red carpet "has been Scotch-guarded just in case June Allyson stops by and makes a mistake." Her daughter Melissa was perched on scaffolding high above the Shrine forecourt, and Rivers told her, "Don't look down my dress. It will just bring back painful memories of my inability to breast-feed you." Rivers's first celebrity interview was with Steve Guttenberg, who she said was "looking very thin." He thanked her for the compliment, and added, "I'm working out—I'm on the program." "I've lost fifty pounds," said Shelley Winters, one of the seventy prior Oscar winners who were returning tonight. She also told Rivers that "thirty or thirty-five of the seventy were members of the Actors Studio, and I saw a lot of old friends" at rehearsals. In a red low-cut Fred Hayman and wearing beaucoup diamonds, Sally Kirkland cooed to Rivers, "I get to play Marilyn Monroe over 50!" She was referring to some straight-to-video thing she was filming. *Buzz* fashion writer Laurie Pike was again on hand for KTLA, and she ragged on Kirkland: "Every year she doesn't disappoint. She always looks like a huge drag queen."

Vanessa Redgrave was with Franco Nero and her mother. She told the Sam Rubin/Leanza Cornett team, "There are plenty of crazy things happening in the world. But one of the best and most inspiring things are the filmmakers who gather here at the Academy Awards." Her pale wool and silk tuxedo coat dress was created by Catherine Walker, who had been Princess Diana's favorite designer. Rivers, a Reagan Republican, would later say of Redgrave, "I hate her politics, but I have to admit I like her dress." Last year Red Buttons claimed he was changing his name to Billy Bob Buttons; this year he got a laugh out of the fans by saying, "Hi, I'm Leonardo DiButtons!" Asked

about Leonardo, Billy Zane said "I think he's going to be airlifted in a little bit later if I'm not mistaken." Zane's head was completely shaven, and to Rivers, "He looks like Tyra Banks's left breast with a face painted on it." Shirley Temple Black boasted that she'd had her Oscar longer than any of the other returning winners; when Army Archerd heard that she would be turning 70 next month, he had the bleacher fans serenade her with "Happy Birthday." Cindy Adams saw Archerd talking to Jack Palance, "whose wife got introduced as his daughter. She was thrilled. He was not."

Access Hollywood's Giselle Fernandez gave Robin Williams a hand fan with her show's logo on it to try to beat the heat. "Oh, chile, it's like a Baptist reunion," he said, launching into an imitation of Robert Duvall in *The Apostle*. Williams told Rivers that his knee-length tuxedo with no buttons and a white stand-up collar was "from the Armani Amish collection. Comes with a carriage." The Best Supporting Actor nominee was there with his wife and his mom, and Rivers asked Mother Williams what her son was like as a child. Her reply: "Funny, but serious, too. A fantastic student, great athlete, what more can I say? What were *you* like as a child?" "Funny, serious, a great athlete. What more can I say?" responded Rivers. During this exchange, Marty Ingels was showing the *Good Will Hunting* nominee a picture of wife Shirley Jones with Burt Lancaster as the two Academy Award winners looked on Oscar night 1960. When Williams got to Sam Rubin and Leanza Cornett, he began reading their note card for Helena Bonham Carter: " 'She has worked with Kenneth Branagh'—more than *worked*!" And when it was suggested that Williams could someday host the show, he said, "The censors would go nuts," he said. "It would be like Gandhi in a delicatessen."

Joan Rivers informed her viewers that Judi Dench was "much younger looking, much softer looking than what she looks like as Queen Victoria." Rivers wondered aloud, "Is it F. Murray Abraham behind her?" "Ben Kingsley," informed an off-camera voice. Dame Judi's husband, Michael Williams, was opening in a play in the West End that night, and the Best Actress nominee said she had just phoned her husband and the premiere "went wonderfully. So I don't mind now what happens." Dame Judi had also been treading the boards in London, but she and the producers of her play, *Amy's View,* reached an agreement whereby she was allowed to go to the Oscars in exchange for doing the play for another week. The actress was treated to an Altoid and a bottle of water by the KTLA duo. Ben Kingsley, as he had been the night he won his Oscar, was decked out in a white tux. On the *E! Academy Awards Fashion Review* a few days later, Joan Rivers said, "Obviously he thought the Oscars were being held in Panama. Give me a tutti-frutti to go."

Designer Deborah Milner had based Helena Bonham Carter's gown, which had a corset-like top, on a fragile old Dior that the actress had discovered in her mother's attic; *Newsday* called this a "luscious lilac confection," and *Vogue*'s Katherine Betts gave her "the ethereal Uma Thurman award." Bonham Carter said, "I've never attached that much importance to what I wear. Now it's monumental."

Rivers told ex–*Talk Soup* host Greg Kinnear, "E! is so proud of you," and then she asked Djimon Hounsou, the star of *Amistad,* "Do you have your speech ready?" "No, I am not nominated," he said. Hounsou said to Leanza Cornett and Sam Rubin, "It's an honor to be doing the walk of my heroes," and that the most exciting aspect of being on the red carpet was seeing Robert Duvall. In response to Joan Rivers's inquiry, Supporting Actress nominee Joan Cusack said that her baby was now nine months old. Armed with that knowledge, Rivers inquired, "So did you need undergarments—have to wear anything to support yourself?" "Yeah, a little. A little," was the answer. Before she let Cusack leave, Rivers wanted to know "How long were you in labor?"

Peter Fonda's wife, Becky, referred to the Harry Winston necklace she was wearing as "wretched excess—wonderful!" She also said that if her husband won an Oscar to go along with his Golden Globe, "We'll have a little wedding for them." Best Director nominee, *The Full Monty*'s Peter Cattaneo was in front of Joan Rivers the same time as Walter Matthau and said he was born just around the time that Matthau won his Oscar. Ernest Borgnine said he and wife Tovah had a night of partying ahead of them and that he expected to "go home with a headache." Asked by the KTLA team whom he really hoped to run into

tonight, the star of *Marty* responded, "Karl Malden, that's all I want to see." *L.A. Confidential*'s cowriter, Brian Helgeland, joked to Cornett and Rubin that here on Oscar night, his movie was "the iceberg waiting for the *Titanic.*" Curtis Hanson was very excited because "I was just introduced to Fay Wray, which to me sums up the Seventieth Anniversary Academy Awards. You know, as a kid, *King Kong* was one of the movies that made me fall in love with movies in the first place, and to see the past and the present and the future here all at the same time is pretty amazing."

Leanza Cornett called James Cameron and his wife, Linda Hamilton, "the prom king and queen." The *Titanic* director responded, "I never even went to the prom when I was in high school." Sam Rubin asked Hamilton, "After the huge success, is he easy to live with, is it easier or more difficult now?" "He was always a jerk, so there's no way to really measure," replied Mrs. Cameron.

Gloria Stuart said this was all "a great adventure." Her pale blue Escada was highly praised, and the designer colored the gown to match exactly the tint of her eyes. The Supporting nominee also wore a $20 million Harry Winston diamond sapphire necklace—bodyguards from the jeweler never let her out of their sight. Rubin asked last year's Best Actress, Frances McDormand, "You've been here before, does it make it all easier?" "No, the shoes never get easier." Laurie Pike was delighted by McDormand's outfit, a long pomegranate-colored Vera Wang and a gold-embroidered black coat: "She's the only one there working hippie chick drag and I love it." Pike also loved "Anne Jeffreys, or whatever her name is"—the forties RKO star who had moved on to daytime dramas. "Look at that stunning, stunning dress, with like a queenly scepter stuck in there and the weird thing on the shoulder. This is my favorite dress so far tonight." Richard Dreyfuss was true to his Brooklyn roots when he described the forecourt activity as "very loud, and screaming and yelling and crazy. It's like going to Coney Island, except you're the ride." Asked by Sam Rubin how this the Oscars had changed, Dreyfuss said, "It's gotten bigger. There is nothing but Oscar for like a week in America. Everything shuts down. Like Monica Lewinsky doesn't exist this week."

Sporting a "Pre-Raphaelite" hairstyle, Minnie Driver wore what *Time* said was a " 'take that, Matt Damon' Halston." *Newsday*'s Barbara Schuler described her outfit as "stunning simplicity—a red Halston gown designed by Randolph Duke, accessorized with a ruby and emerald bracelet and a fox wrap dyed to match the dress." The actress told *People* that she chose an unadorned gown because "*You* have to sparkle, not your gown." She informed Joan Rivers that "pretty much every major designer" had contacted her and "Banana Republic, I think, would have liked me to wear some chinos with some rhinestones." When Driver went up to Army Archerd's podium, her shoulder strap came off, but she quickly righted it, and laughed over the fact that the fans in the bleachers had seen more of her than she and Randolph Duke had intended.

Susan Sarandon and her pal from *Thelma and Louise*, Geena Davis, were together for the WB interviewers. Sarandon had recently been on the *Today* show saying she wasn't sure if she'd attend because "I didn't know whether I could deal with the hassle of finding another dress." She did find a low-cut Dolce & Gabbana with a bouquet on the back; the *New York Daily News* scolded that "the actress scooped up last night's booby prize for indecent exposure." Tim Robbins was in Houston shooting *Arlington Road*, so Sarandon's date was their 8-year-old son, Jack Henry. His tuxedo was by Ralph Lauren and he had a diamond stud in his ear. Jack Henry informed Sam Rubin, "It's my favorite earring, so I wore it here."

Joan Rivers told Julie Christie, "I hope you're gonna make some more movies now." "Probably not," said the *Afterglow* star. "That's not my plan." Asked how he felt about his sweetheart, Helen Hunt, being considered a likely winner tonight, Hank Azaria told Cornett and Rubin, "All of us actors are self-absorbed. I want to see how this affects me." "What was your day like?" Pat O'Brien of *Access Hollywood* asked Hunt. "Oh, I woke up, threw on some lipstick, Hank made this dress and then we left." Drew Barrymore had glitter on her arms and real daisies in her hair—which Laurie Pike deemed "a very nice touch"—and Cornett marveled that "They're in perfect shape." "Thank you," said Drew. "I'm very happy. I feel a part

of the earth and yet I feel a part of the glamour with the glitter, so I'm kind of balancing both." Mira Sorvino, here for the third year in a row, felt the red carpet hoopla was "a little crazier this year than it's ever been." That was the general consensus, and Sam Rubin often used the term "celebrity gridlock" to describe the non-movement of people trying to work their way into the Shrine. Joan Rivers mentioned how patient the stars were and how everyone seemed eager to chat with interviewers this year, crediting the reunion of past Oscar winners for creating an especially festive party atmosphere and putting everyone in a great mood.

KTLA had a video remote from Robert Forster's limo as he made his way to the Shrine. He had the chance to speak with his costar Samuel L. Jackson, who dropped by to talk to Cornett and Rubin; in the car, Forster also showed viewers one of his good luck charms—a small tool that his elephant trainer father had used in his work. When he got to the Shrine, Forster described the goings-on as "an amazing human event." He also said that, thanks to *Jackie Brown* and the Oscar nomination, his was "a legitimate career now." And he revealed that his father had died before the film was released, but that he had come to the set and was utterly delighted at what certainly seemed to be an upswing in his son's fortunes.

Rivers asked Ben Affleck and Matt Damon, "Are your lives totally changed?" "No," said Matt, "this pretty much happens every day." Ben jumped in with "This is what my backyard looks like, as a matter of fact. And I can't get Madonna out of there." Joan then wondered, "Who was nasty to you in high school that you're glad is watching tonight?" After beginning earnestly with "Everybody liked us in high school," Affleck switched to his jokester persona and said, "We were such losers that no one even wanted to pick on us because we were so pathetic." To *Access Hollywood*'s Giselle Fernandez, Affleck said, "Matt's just become insufferable. There's no talking to the guy." Ben told *Entertainment Tonight*'s Julie Moran that he had spent the day looking for his cummerbund, which some friends had thought would be funny to steal; he never did find it. *Entertainment Tonight*'s cameras caught Damon introducing his mom to Charlton Heston, who was next to him on line. Affleck's girlfriend Gwyneth Paltrow remained behind in England on the set of the film they and Judi Dench were making, *Shakespeare in Love,* so, like Damon, he brought his mom as his date. Damon's new girlfriend, Winona Ryder, would be watching from the *Vanity Fair* party at Morton's.

"Oh my," said Joan. "Coming in now is Rosa Parks. Legendary." The civil rights pioneer, who was a guest of Spike Lee's, admitted that she was "overwhelmed" by the Oscar hoopla. When Rivers saw newlywed Sharon Stone—wearing Vera Wang—she instructed her husband, San Francisco newspaper editor Phil Bronstein, "You take care of her! She's the best, the best." Mike Myers told the world that Dennis Quaid, who was behind him, "just pinched my ass." Dustin Hoffmann told KABC-TV's Roger Ebert, "I went to a proctologist last week and got a thumbs-up." "Oh, that is an inside joke," replied Ebert. And continuing to show himself a man of erudite wit, Hoffman told Joan Rivers, "I haven't been this excited since I had a premature ejaculation on my fifty-ninth birthday."

The telecast began with three minutes' worth of shots of the arrivals and first-time announcer Norman Rose declaring, "The stars are out tonight in all their glory to celebrate Oscar's seventieth anniversary. And the movie fans have been gathering since early this morning to catch a glimpse of them. And here are the stars they came to see: two Hollywood legends, Luise Rainer and Roddy McDowall." It was true—everyone waiting on line to get to the bleachers kept saying, "Damn, I hope we get to see Luise Rainer and Roddy McDowall." Others Rose announced were "the beautiful newlywed" Sharon Stone and "Who else but Cher?"—she was, of course, wearing Bob Mackie for her "tribute to *Titanic*," complete with a headpiece that was variously described as "Statue of Liberty-esque," a "cookie jar," a "space-age headdress," a "giant ice cream waffle cone" and "The Acropolis." Liz Smith called Cher's outfit "the hoot of the night."

The ceremony itself kicked off with Academy President Bob Rehme, who—like Grover Cleveland—was in a nonsequential second term as president. A much more eloquent speaker than Arthur Hiller,

Rehme said, "The world's most enthusiastic movie fans are those people who make movies . . . This is Oscar's seventieth birthday and we baked a cake big enough for the millions who share our enthusiasm." After briefly thanking everyone who helped out on the show, Rehme concluded, "Because I'm as anxious to get to the party as you, that's my speech. Now let's celebrate our great year in the movies."

The *Titanic* showed up on a giant movie screen on stage, with Leonardo DiCaprio teaching Kate Winslet how to spit real good. Of course, his saliva hit Billy Crystal in the face. Writing for *Salon,* Camille Paglia said, "Here comes tonight's host, Billy Crystal, who year after year is given an insane amount of Oscar time to do his tedious shtick." As on last year's show, the host had interjected himself in scenes of the nominated movies in a ritual of self-glorification, and he announced, "I didn't want to do the show this year, but the Academy talked me into it." In the world of this parody, the Academy had the cops of *L.A. Confidential* shove his head in a toilet and hang him out the window by his feet. Having thus been convinced to host, Crystal then had to decide what to do on the program—which led to his taking over Hugo Speer's role of the exceptionally well-endowed dancer in *The Full Monty.* When the other cast members looked at him in shock after he pulls down his pants, Crystal said, "Too Jewish?" He then showed up as Kim Basinger in *L.A. Confidential,* looking much like Milton Berle in drag. He mused, "Maybe I do some stuff that makes fun of myself: 'Hey, I had a great year. Between *Fathers' Day* and *Titanic,* we got fourteen nominations.'" Crystal did a Jack Nicholson imitation and showed up as Sammy Davis, Jr., amid the cheerful third-class passengers on the *Titanic.* In Davis's unctuous manner, Crystal said, "You steerage cats are exciting, and I mean that. What a hot crowd on a chilly night! Here come de ice. Here come de ice." Back as himself, Crystal also was seen posing nude for Leonardo DiCaprio. In an appearance akin to David Letterman's last year, Kevin Costner showed up in the film to make fun of his ludicrous mega-bomb, *The Postman.* Costner fell to his death from the *Titanic,* but not before telling Crystal, "I'll be fine, but you, you got another three hours." Crystal responded, "Yeah, but there's no Lord of the Dance this year—it's just gonna fly by." Finally, Crystal was at the prow of the *Titanic* addressing the audience: "So that's what happened. They beat me up, spit on me, pushed my head into a toilet. But in this town, it only means one thing: They like me! They really like me!"

The host arrived onstage on a fake *Titanic*, and said, "We are just like that great ship. We are huge, we are expensive and everybody wants us to go a lot faster. So we will try to do that tonight." And then, in defiance of that goal, he began the Best Picture medley. *Titanic* was saluted to the melody of the "Theme from *Gilligan's Island*." "Just sit right back and you'll hear a tale/A tale of a giant ship/That started many years ago/With an overbudget script. The boss was a loud director man/Who made accountants sick [there was a cut to James Cameron not looking too amused]/Two studios teamed up to pay/For a three-hour flick, a three-hour flick. It's made a billion dollars now/I hope it springs some leaks/Some other films deserve a break/Like *My Giant* in three weeks, *My Giant* in three weeks."

As Good As It Gets was given the Gershwins' "Let's Call the Whole Thing Off": "Jack is compulsive and Jack is obsessive/Helen's impulsive and Greg is depressive/Compulsive. Obsessive. Impulsive. Depressive. This is *As Good As It Gets*." Going down into the audience, Crystal addressed Jack Nicholson, singing: "Sit back and relax. Forget about *Mars Attacks*." He then sat on Nicholson's lap and handed Helen Hunt a camera so she could take a picture. Back onstage, the host mentioned the Best Actor nominees and joked, "Matt Damon must feel like he's playing on the Seniors' Tour." And then, to the tune of Cole Porter's *Night and Day*, sang "Matt and Ben/You are the ones. Your script was tight, and damnit/So are your buns." In the audience Affleck looked embarrassed. It was back to the Gershwins as *L.A. Confidential* got "Fascinatin' Rhythm": "*L.A. Confidential*. You put on quite a show/*L.A. Confidential*. But it's confusing. Is the plot sequential? How will I ever know?/ Are there any good guys?/My mind I'm losing."

Finally, "Hello, Dolly!" was the music for *The Full Monty*. "It's *The Full Monty*. It's *The Full Monty*/Yes, my pants are on the floor where they be-

long. But there's a draft, *Monty*. It's a half-*Monty* [Crystal looked down at his crotch]. It's not showing/it's not growing/ It's not going strong." Ed Bark of *The Dallas Morning News* groaned that Crystal, "bestowed another of his increasingly laborious musical tributes to the five Best Picture nominees." And *Entertainment Weekly* declared, "Deadest Horse: Crystal's seventh song-parody intro. Enough!"

Before announcing the winner of Best Supporting Actress, Cuba Gooding, Jr., gave "one quick word of advice to the lady that graces this stage this evening. While giving your acceptance speech, take your time. Don't listen to the music. Do your thing!" The audience clapped in approval of the sentiment. The winner was Kim Basinger in *L.A. Confidential*. Minnie Driver, wide-mouthed with surprise, said "Wow!" when she heard the news. Louis Gossett, Jr., stood up in tribute to Basinger, as did Jack Nicholson, who kissed her on her way to the stage. "Oh my God!" the visibly shaking winner said, and television viewers saw her husband, Alec Baldwin, whooping. "We only get thirty seconds to give a thousand thank-yous," said Basinger, who then paraphrased Maureen Stapleton's acceptance speech: "I just want to thank everybody I ever met in my entire life." After thanking a few of those people by name, she said, "If anyone has a dream out there, just know that I'm living proof that they do come true," and ended by proclaiming, "Daddy, this is for you." Gloria Stuart's loss was an early blow to *Titanic*'s quest to set a new record.

After the commercial break, Billy Crystal referenced Bill Clinton's escapade: "You know, so much has changed in the last year. A year ago, the White House was complaining that there was too much sex in *Hollywood*." The response consisted of whistling and applause. Continuing, Crystal said, "A billion people are watching this tonight, except for Linda Tripp, who's taping it." This reference to the hideous woman who recorded conversations with her supposed friend, Monica Lewinsky, received loud laughs and Crystal added, "Is it just me, or does she look like Michael Caine in *Dressed to Kill*"? Caine was seen in the audience having a good laugh.

Bill Conti's orchestra played "All The Things You Are" as Elisabeth Shue arrived onstage to present Best

Costume Design. That the merely serviceable clothes in *Titanic* beat the extravagantly opulent designs of *Kundun* and the character-defining costumes of *The Wings of the Dove* indicated that *Titanic* was going to be doing very well tonight, despite Gloria Stuart's loss. Winner Deborah L. Scott said, "Thank you, Jim Cameron, for the first-class passage," the first of the night's nautical references in acceptance speeches. Billy Crystal gibed, "And the best thing is, those costumes are drip-dry."

Introducing Dustin Hoffman, Crystal said, "In over thirty years in the business, he has starred as a street hustler, an idiot savant, a pirate and a movie producer—so, basically the same guy." Here to present a montage of previous Best Picture winners, Hoffman again showed class by noting, "All sixty-nine of them. I wonder if that number is as significant internationally as it is here at home." The clip from *Cavalcade* featured a shot of a life preserver from the *Titanic*; *The Sound of Music* was the first clip to receive applause, but the biggest cheers went to *One Flew Over the Cuckoo's Nest*.

Announcer Norman Rose introduced "the bright young star of *Scream 1* and *2*, Neve Campbell." She was on the show to introduce the performances of the two Best Song nominees from cartoons; the writers had given her a list of Oscar-winning songwriters to read, but the fact-checkers proved a disgrace to their profession because Cole Porter's name was included. Campbell said that *Anastasia*'s "Journey to the Past" would be sung by "the brilliant young artist" Aaliyah, while "Go the Distance" from *Hercules* was going to be performed by "the exciting" Michael Bolton. Both renditions were no-frills and straightforward—inasmuch as any performance by the tumid Bolton could be called straightforward. Among tonight's dresses, Aaliyah's was unique—it was off the rack. After the two numbers had been completed, home viewers saw an expressionless Céline Dion in the audience clapping politely.

Arnold Schwarzenegger showed himself to be quite a card when he noted that he had made three films with "my friend" James Cameron, *The Terminator*, *Terminator 2* and *True Lies*. "That was, of course, during his early low-budget art house period." Before

getting to the *Titanic* clip, Schwarzenegger pointed out that "Some say its box office will grow so large it may actually show profits that no accountant can hide—and that's painful for the studio executives, may I remind you." After the scenes from *Titanic* were shown, Crystal said, "That clip cost $15 million," and "The only thing I saw retain water quicker than that was my Aunt Sheila after eating shellfish."

The host then said that last year's Supporting Actress winner, Juliette Binoche, couldn't be here to present the Supporting Actor Award because she had broken her foot while performing onstage in London, "but here to fill in for her is Céline Dion. No, I'm just kidding." There was a shot of Dion in her seat looking shocked, and then laughing with relief when she realized it was just a joke. The actual substitute was "a great actress," 1995 winner Mira Sorvino. The *Boogie Nights* clip for Burt Reynolds had him saying, "This is the film I want to be remembered for." The winner, though, was Robin Williams in *Good Will Hunting*. As the victor made his way to the stage, he hugged Matt Damon and Ben Affleck, and TV director Louis J. Horvitz cut to Billy Crystal clapping for his *Fathers' Day* costar. Williams began with "Oh, man. This might be the one time I'm speechless." He said, "Thank you, Ben and Matt. I still want to see some ID. Thank you, Gus Van Sant, for being so subtle you're almost subliminal." He praised the people of South Boston, where some of *Good Will Hunting* was filmed, saying, "You're a can of corn," and his wife, "Marsha, for being the woman who lights my soul on fire every morning. God bless you. [She was crying.]" And he concluded by thanking his deceased father, "the man who when I said I wanted to be an actor, he said 'Wonderful, just have a backup profession, like welding.'" Earlier, Billy Crystal had said his fear was "if Robin wins on Monday, the show will end on Tuesday," but the usually manic recipient spoke for only just over a minute. Crystal came over to hug him, and then Williams went off in a Groucho Marx stoop; the camera followed him into the wings where he could be seen bussing the next presenter, Cameron Diaz. Crystal's take on Williams's victory: "Boy, Comic Relief is going to be rough this year for me"—he was now the only one of the trio of comedians who organized and hosted the semi-regular telethons for the homeless to be without an Oscar, Whoopi Goldberg having won in 1990.

The *San Francisco Examiner*'s Cynthia Robbins was aghast that Cameron Diaz, "who was so pert and classy last year in powder blue Prada, looked like a rag picker in the accordion-pleated bell-sleeved top and sarong number John Galliano overdesigned." Diaz awarded Best Sound to *Titanic*, and one winner addressed James Cameron, "whose passion for filmmaking makes all of us do our best work." He added, "with the great success of *Titanic*, I hope that you attain the self-confidence you'll need to succeed in this business." And one more joke: "I'd like to thank Jon Landau for the promise of points."

Mike Myers interrupted the presentation of Sound Effects Editing to complain, "the Academy has overlooked and besmirched—oh, yes, I said besmirched—the contributions that animals have made to motion pictures, and I'm gonna do something about it right now." So, despite Crystal's pledge up top that this was going to be a shorter show, footage of animals in the movies began running. Besides being pointless, the montage made no sense thematically because, although some real animals were shown—Asta, Benji, Francis the Talking Mule—there were also cartoon characters and computer generated creatures, such as the cow from *Twister*. The soundtrack segued from Kool and the Gang's "Jungle Boogie" to the Beatles' version of "Act Naturally," with Ringo on lead vocals. The last animal seen in the clip was a grizzly bear, and then Norman Rose announced, "Ladies and gentlemen, the star of eleven motion pictures, including *The Clan of the Cave Bear*, *Legends of the Fall* and, most recently, *The Edge*: Bart the Bear." The bear, Gilbert Cates's big surprise attraction this year, was onstage his paws holding a large envelope, which he dropped; his trainer jammed it into his mouth, took it back and gave it to Mike Myers, who trotted back to the podium. "I just soiled myself," he said. The Sound Effects Editing winner was *Titanic*, and the night's theme was emerging: the difficulty of working with James Cameron. Tom Bellfort read a list of names and then spoke to the director: "Jim, although the seas were a little rough at times, I really thank you for this

voyage and for building a ship that will last forever." Cowinner Christopher Boyes said, "I'm more overwhelmed now than I was the first time I met Jim Cameron. I want to thank you for demanding nothing less than my excellence."

After the next set of commercials, Billy Crystal pointed into the audience and said "There's Charlton Heston. Hi, Mr. Heston," and waved to the actor, who was returning to his seat. Crystal then announced, "We had a little problem backstage. You know the old joke—there's a bear in the woods? In the green room." Crystal reminded everyone that Helen Hunt had played his agent in *Mr. Saturday Night*, and the Best Actress nominee introduced another montage, this one illustrating old-timey special effects up through the 1930s, and ending with a guy getting hit by a train. The winner of the Visual Effects Oscar was *Titanic*.

Crystal said, "Many years ago, the world was stunned by the appearance of the strongest, scariest presence in Hollywoood. But Joan Crawford would turn . . . I'm sorry, no." It was really King Kong of whom he was speaking, and there followed clips of Faye Wray and the giant ape, after which Crystal was standing in an aisle in the audience. "Ladies and gentlemen, the beauty who charmed the beast," he announced. "The legendary Faye Wray." Even though the host was standing next to her, she was openmouthed by the introduction, and stood up to be kissed twice by him. Wray was not miked, but you could hear her say, "It's wonderful . . . What do I do now?" Crystal replied, "You can just wave to everybody," which she did, and he said, "I'm Ralph Edwards—and *This Is Your Life*." She said, "Goody, I'm so glad my life is with you," and then helped him introduce Short Films presenters Ben Affleck and Matt Damon. Curiously, Wray was seating directly in front of James Cameron, who didn't give her the part in *Titanic* when she wouldn't read for him.

Affleck and Damon announced that the Live Action Short Film winner was *Visas and Virtues*, about a Japanese diplomat based in Lithuania who helped save Jews during the Nazi era. Among those that cowinner Chris Donahue thanked were "my Jesuit Brothers in East L.A.," while Chris Tashima—whose parents had been thrown into an American internment camp during the war—persuasively said, "I hope we can begin to embrace every race. Diversity is the ingenue. She's the true American star, and she's ready for her close-up." The Animated Short went to *Geri's Game*, a Pixar production; while the winner was reading his laundry list of names, Louis Horvitz cut to Joe Pesci and Marisa Tomei laughing hysterically about something.

Even though the show was only at one hour and sixteen minutes, Geoffrey Rush was onstage to present Best Actress. The winner was the hometown girl, Helen Hunt in *As Good As It Gets*. Hank Azaria kissed her hand, as did Jack Nicholson. Hunt said, "The first time I saw *Mrs. Brown*—I saw it three times—the first time I saw it I leaned over to my beloved and said, 'She's going to win an Academy Award.' And in my mind tonight she has, and so has Julie Christie and so has Helena Bonham Carter and so has Kate Winslett, and for that matter so has [*Mrs. Brown* leading man] Billy Connelly, and so has Ben Affleck, and so has Joan Allen, and I'm honored to work in a year where there were so many magnificent performances." Hunt insisted that "I'm here for one reason and that's Jim Brooks." She told Jack Nicholson, "I worship you, you know it," and said to Greg Kinnear, "I hope you hold in your heart how beautiful your performance in this movie was." Finally she thanked Hank Azaria, "the very best man I know."

Antonio Banderas was the presenter of the Original Dramatic Score Award, and Bill Conti and the boys—onstage and in white tie and tails—played snippets of the nominees. The winner was *Titanic*, and the fey James Horner wanted everyone to know that "I've been so close quite a few times, but never actually won. I've got to get my wits about me," which entailed thanking his wife and family. Backstage, a reporter said that the score was awfully reminiscent of Irish musician Enya's work. Horner countered, "Almost anything that's Irish and has a woman's voice in it is going to sound like Enya." The night's one dance sequence preceded the presentation of Best Original Musical or Comedy Score and consisted of interpretations of the nominees. Most of the dances were balletic, of the Agnes de Mille school, although the *Men in Black* number had hip-hop touches, and a woman in the

Anastasia portion was flying around on a very visible wire; the dances were all much more graceful and spare than what was usually seen on this program. Army Archerd wrote that the number, "in its simplicity of production, was praised for its artistry." Then "the exciting and talented" Jennifer Lopez presented the Oscar to Anne Dudley for *The Full Monty*, which was somewhat surprising, since the music most remembered from the film was such disco hits as Hot Chocolate's "You Sexy Thing" and Sister Sledge's "We Are Family." Although Dudley had scored other movies, she was best known as a member of the British techno group Art of Noise.

Billy Crystal brought out Drew Barrymore by saying, "She's been acting for eighteen years and she's only twenty-two. The other four years I guess she was directing." Barrymore—the flowers in her hair holding up fine—announced that last year's winners, Rick Baker and David Leroy Anderson, were again taking home Oscars, this time for *Men in Black*. Next, Alec Baldwin introduced the *L.A. Confidential* clip by saying, "The film's intricate tale of deceit is both gripping and enticing. I think the girl in the movie's kind of cute, too." This line elicited more laughter than Crystal's next bit of business, the favorite movies of famous people: Hillary Clinton, *Conspiracy Theory*; Kenneth Starr, *I Know What You Did Last Summer*; Michael Jackson, *Face/Off*; Robert Downey, Jr., *In and Out*; and Bart the Bear, *My Dinner Was Andre*.

When Samuel L. Jackson came out to present Best Editing, director Louis J. Horvitz cut to Lou Gossett and then to Spike Lee. *Titanic* was the winner, and James Cameron was one of its three editors. He took the opportunity to speak to his kid: "For my daughter, Josephine, who's five years old, watching at home. Honey, this is the thing I described to you. It's called an Oscar and it's really cool to get."

Ashley Judd strode onstage in a Richard Tyler dress with the left side slit so high that thousands of 14-year-old boys who had taped the show would undoubtedly be playing her entrance in slow motion and employing the freeze-framing button. *Entertainment Weekly* dubbed the dress "shockingly revealing"; *People*, "truly shocking." Judd had been the host of the Scientific and Technical Awards banquet and showed

videotape of the event, including Gordon Sawyer
Award winner, Don Iwerks "the first man to bring a
napkin from his table to wipe my fingerprints off his
Oscar."

Billy Crystal said, "Please welcome one of the
world's greatest directors." Martin Scorsese began by
saying "I'm gonna tell you a story with a happy ending,"
a statement which provoked laughter, presumably because of its source. He continued,

Once upon a time, a lonely boy in South
Carolina was sparked by the wonder of
movies, where he was captivated by everything from cowboys to comedians to movie
monsters. And then he saw his first musical,
Flying Down to Rio, which introduced him to
two magical people named Fred Astaire and
Ginger Rogers.

They took the boy into a fantasy world
of such delight that he changed his mind
about going into his family's dress business
and started taking dancing lessons. He was
nine years old, and he kept on dancing and
when he graduated high school, the shy and
awkward 16-year-old danced his way up
north and into the chorus of a Broadway hit,
Pal Joey.

And it was there he met the star of that
show, who was to become his mentor, friend
and, in time, his collaborator on a series of
films that would revolutionize dancing in the
movies. The star was Gene Kelly, the boy was
Stanley Donen, who followed Gene to
Hollywood as his assistant first, and then as
his codirector. And the first film he directed
by himself starred his boyhood role model,
Fred Astaire.

Stanley Donen had made the big time,
and for the next thirty years he directed and
often produced a string of classic films.

Scorsese added color commentary to the presentation of clips from Donen's films, such as "At the ridiculous age of twenty, he got Gene Kelly to dance
onscreen with Jerry the Mouse" and "His stories are al-

ways refreshingly adult, sometimes heartbreaking,
sometimes wickedly funny, always profoundly stylish."
The montage included *On the Town, It's Always Fair
Weather, Funny Face, Indiscreet, Two for the Road, Charade* and, of course, *Singin' in the Rain,* and Scorsese
concluded, "Stanley Donen's entire career is distinguished by elegance, wit, visual innovation and extraordinary grace." Then he said, "And here's that
happy ending I promised you: an Academy Award for
Life Achievement to Stanley Donen."

The orchestra played "Singin' in the Rain," and
Donen began by addressing the presenter: "Marty, it's
backwards. I should be giving this to you, believe me."
Donen then began the most wonderful acceptance
speech in the entire history of the Academy Awards.
"And I wanna thank the Board of Governors for this
cute little fella which, to me, looks titanic. Tonight
words seem inadequate. In musicals, that's when we do
a song, so . . ." And Donen began singing, "Heaven,
I'm in heaven . . ." Irving Berlin's "Cheek to Cheek"—
a 1935 Best Song nominee from *Top Hat*—and doing
a tap dance. When he sang the words "cheek to
cheek," he held his Oscar to his cheek. The cheers
from the audience were deafening, With the orchestra
continuing to play, Donen switched from singing back
to speaking:

I'm gonna let you in on the secret of being a
good director. For the script you get Larry
Gelbart or Peter Stone or Huyck and Katz or
Fredric Raphael, like that. If it's a musical, for
the songs you get George and Ira Gershwin,
or Leonard Bernstein and Comden and
Green, or Alan Lerner and Fritz Loewe, like
that.

And then you cast Cary Grant or Audrey Hepburn, Fred Astaire, Gene Kelly,
Sophia Loren, Richard Burton, Rex Harrison, Gregory Peck, Elizabeth Taylor, Burt
Reynolds, Gene Hackman or Frank Sinatra,
like that.

And when filming starts, you show up,
and you stay the hell out of the way [a huge
roar of laughter]. But you've gotta show up,
you've gotta show up. Otherwise, you can't

take the credit and get one of these fellas. Thank you very much.

Entertainment Weekly said that Donen's time on-stage "pointed up the resounding gracelessness of most of his fellow honorees." Gene Siskel said it was "a classic Oscar moment," while Tim Johnson of the *San Francisco Examiner* said simply, "Stanley Donen, you're the bomb." And *Entertainment Tonight's* Leonard Maltin gave "a special salute" to Donen, stating "I'd like to ask today's hot young directors, How many of you can sing and tap-dance?" Backstage, the Lifetime Achievement recipient said, "It was difficult to come up with what I wanted to do. I didn't want to do something boring and list people. I figured I'd sing and dance, since I've done a little bit of that before."

Matt *Dillon* introduced the *Good Will Hunting* clip, after which Billy Crystal said, "Matt *Damon* looks so young results in his category are tabulated by Fisher Price Waterhouse." He then brought out "the hottest working mom in show business," who was Madonna. Army Archerd reported that "Glamorous Madonna and Elisabeth Shue, backstage in the Green Room, were talking about babies—Madonna's daughter, Elisabeth's son!" Onstage, Madonna was presenting the final three song performances, and said, "Just as the songs represent a contrast in styles, so do the films from which they come and the artists who will perform them." Trisha Yearwood sang "How Do I Live" from *Con Air*, another cookie-cutter ballad from Diane Warren. Elliott Smith, who also wrote the song, sang "Miss Misery" from *Good Will Hunting*; strumming his guitar, he seemed like he might have been playing at Folk City thirty years earlier, and his simple, unadorned style recalled Keith Carradine's performance of *his* song, "I'm Easy," at the 1975 Oscars. *Entertainment Weekly's* TV critic, Ken Tucker, however, thought "Smith looked like Beck on quaaludes." Whereas Yearwood and Smith were alone onstage, dry ice smoke and Bill Conti's orchestra joined Céline Dion for *Titanic's* "My Heart Will Go On." Only once did Dion do her signature mannerism—hitting her chest, as if trying to jump-start herself. She was wearing a 170-carat diamond and sapphire replica of the Star of the Sea necklace from *Titanic* valued at

$2.5 million while she sang, so a misplaced pounding could have done some costly damage. *Daily Variety's* Ray Richmond denigrated the song as "seemingly destined to become the 'Feelings' of the 1990s." When she read what was in the envelope, Madonna editorialized, "What a surprise." It was "My Heart Will Go On." Composer James Horner said, "Jim Cameron, thank you for being in a good mood that day when I brought you the song."

Djimon Hounsou gave the Documentary Short Subject Oscar to *A Story of Healing* about a hospital, and Robert De Niro handled the Feature category. He said that "making a documentary feature is the cinematic equivalent of jumping out of a plane." What was surprising in this category—normally a hotbed of liberal humanism—was that two right-wing documentaries were nominated, one scolding the federal government for ending the stand-off instigated by scary anti-government crackpots in Waco, Texas, the other about Ayn Rand, the wacky proponent of the Selfishness-as-a-Way-of-Life philosophy, who did at least write the screenplay for a great movie, William Dieterle's deliriously romantic *Love Letters*. The winner was not Spike Lee's *Four Little Girls*, but a movie about the Holocaust, *The Long Way Home*. Producer Rabbi Marvin Hier, wearing a yarmulke, had also won in this category in 1981 for a movie about the Holocaust. He dedicated his Award to "the survivors of the Holocaust who walked away from the ashes, rebuilt their lives and helped create the state of Israel." Billy Crystal said, "What a night when your rabbi wins an Oscar. First my best friend, now my rabbi. Who's next?" He pointed to somebody in the audience and said, "You? Come on up. Get one."

Whoopi Goldberg quoted from the Book of Ecclesiastics (and Pete Seeger): "For every thing there is a season, and a time for every matter under heaven. A time to be born and a time to die." This was the lead-up for the necrology segment, and Goldberg said, "As we celebrate the achievements of our fellow artists and craftspeople tonight, we also acknowledge the passing of those whose lives were dedicated to bringing the artistry of the movies into *our* lives." Lloyd Bridges was the first person acknowledged, and others included Brian Keith, Richard Jaeckel, William Hickey, Stubby

Kaye, Red Skelton, Toshiro Mifune, Chris Farley, Burgess Meredith, J. T. Walsh, cinematographer Stanley Cortez, blacklisted writer Paul Jarrico, studio executive Dawn Steele, director Sam Fuller, Jacques Cousteau (who received a huge amount of applause) and finally, to the cheers of the audience, Robert Mitchum and James Stewart, who had died a day apart the previous summer. It was a reminder that the Academy hadn't bothered to give an Honorary Oscar to Mitchum, the greatest actor never to receive an Academy Award.

Billy Crystal said, "I was Harry. She was Sally. And now we meet again. The scene we did together in a deli brought new meaning to the term 'happy meal' . . . a great actress, Miss Meg Ryan." She announced that the Art Direction Oscar was going to the pair who copied the plans of the *Titanic*. Art Director Peter Lamont said, "The day I left *Titanic*, James said to me, 'It's been a hell of a trip.' Believe me, it was."

Robin Williams imitated Robert Duvall in *The Apostle* ("Sometimes there's a boom shadow. The devil puts that there. You don't want that!") and Dustin Hoffman in *Rain Man*, his spot-on impersonation of the latter showing how easy that gimmicky, Oscar-winning performance was. Tonight's Best Supporting Actor winner then introduced yet another montage, this one of "Seventy years of people receiving the golden dude. Seventy years of Oscar's greatest moments. Check it out." Scenes from Oscar ceremonies ensued: people accepting, people presenting, Robert Opel streaking. It ended with James Stewart saying, when he received his Honorary Oscar in 1984, "You've given me a wonderful life. God bless you."

"Okay, guys," said Frances McDormand. "Sit up straight and act presentable." She then announced that the Best Actor winner was Jack Nicholson in *As Good As It Gets*. Robert Duvall was stone-faced at the news, but Peter Fonda looked absolutely delighted. Nicholson did a little dance onstage and said, "Thank you very much, the members of the Academy for this Award, and the other nominees, some of them are very good friends of mine. And I'm honored to be on any list with you Bobby, Dusty, and you and your father, Mr. Damon [laughter]. My old bike pal Fonda." Nicholson admitted, "I dunno, I had a sinking feeling

all night, right up to now." He said that there were "so many producers on this picture, I can't remember them all." He continued, "I'd like to thank everybody here tonight for looking so good. I'd like to dedicate this to Miles Davis, Robert Mitchum, Shorty Smith, Joe Vetrano, Ray Kramer, Rupert Crosse, J. T. Walsh and Luana Anders. They're not here anymore, but they're in my heart." The last thing Nicholson did was hold out the Oscar and say, "Fonda." The Acting Awards had all been presented—none of the year's comeback stories would be taking home an Oscar.

The Foreign Film presenter was Sharon Stone; the *New York Daily News* felt that Stone "dressed in a tailored, menswear-style white shirt worn totally unbuttoned, and a dusty pink sarong skirt by N.Y.C. designer Vera Wang was a scene stealer." She announced that the winner was *Character* from the Netherlands. Pumping his arm onstage, director Mike van Diem said to Stone, "Okay, Sharon, it's just another, you know, another crazy Dutch director, you know 'em [a reference to her *Basic Instinct* director, Paul Verhoeven]. The film is *Character*. It opens next Friday, I'm not going to advertise it. This oughta tell you that it probably has, you know, like damn stunning subtitles."

Jack Lemmon and Walter Matthau handled Screenplay duties. The Adapted winner was, as expected, *L.A. Confidential,* the film's second Oscar. As the cowinners walked to the stage, announcer Norman Rose mentioned that Brian Helgeland had written *The Postman*, the movie Kevin Costner had made fun of in Billy Crystal's opening segment. Onstage, Helgeland, who had spent the early part of the day finishing his income taxes, said, "My sons relentlessly play with action figures at home, and I'm constantly left out. And that's all gonna change tonight, because I'm bringing this guy home." Curtis Hanson said, "To be handed this by the two actors whom I will always associate with Billy Wilder makes it all the sweeter." Hanson called James Ellroy's novel "our inspiration and our challenge."

Lemmon was really happy that *Good Will Hunting* won Best Original Screenplay because he exclaimed "Yeah!" and "Yahoo!" after making the announcement. The victorious boys were embraced by their moms. But the most interesting aspect was that Minnie Driver was standing for her ex, though she was blank-faced when the camera cut to her after the winners thanked her. At the microphone, Ben Affleck started with "I just said to Matt, 'Losing would suck, and winning would be really scary.' " At a fever pitch, he excitedly started naming names, including "My mother and Matt's mother, the most beautiful women here [both moms were Cambridge lefties]," and his buddy excitedly gave him more names to add. Matt jumped in with "My dad, right over there. Jack said hi to you!" Ben added, "And Cuba Gooding for showing how to give our acceptance speech!" Ben: "I know we're forgetting somebody!" Matt: "Whoever we forgot, we love you!"

The Acting and Writing Awards may have been taken care of, but there was still Cinematography, and it was up to Denzel Washington to announce that *Titanic* had won Oscar number nine. Russell Carpenter said, "We're running so late, this is becoming sort of a Depends moment for me." Nobody laughed. He continued, "A year ago today, exactly, principal photography completed. And what a year it's been, it's gone from being a ship of fools to a ship of dreams." *Daily Variety* reported that "Backstage, the press corps was so exhausted with the *Titanic* sweep that when cinematographer Russell Carpenter, carrying his first Oscar, faced two hundred reporters, not a single one had a question for him. 'You got off easy,' the backstage handler said."

Susan Sarandon, dragging a train, came onstage. "They were all, and will be for all time, Oscar winners," she said. Hearing voices emanating, the 1995 Best Actress winner laughed. "And I think they're still getting in their places. The loudest actors and actresses over the years. Ladies and gentlemen, Oscar's Family Album." Partitions opened and there was a spontaneous standing ovation as four rows of people who had won lead, supporting, Honorary or the now-defunct Juvenile Oscars were revealed. The members of the Album were introduced in alphabetical order and the camera lingered on each; on the bottom of the television screen were a scene from his or her winning movie and a shot of the person accepting the Oscar or, if he or she wasn't present on Oscar night, another Academy

Award appearance. It took just under twelve minutes to go from Anne Bancroft to Teresa Wright. The eldest member of the group was Claire Trevor, 89, the youngest 15-year-old Anna Paquin, who tonight was wearing her first strapless dress, a lavender Pamela Dennis. The earliest recipient was 1934's Shirley Temple, though the earliest winner of a competitive Oscar was the Best Actress of 1936 and '37, Luise Rainer. Jack Nicholson held up tonight's Oscar to the camera, and three of tonight's non-winners, Julie Christie, Robert Duvall and Dustin Hoffman, were also on board. Once all the previous winners had been saluted, "the newest additions to Oscar's Family Album" came onstage: Kim Basinger, Helen Hunt and Robin Williams.

After a clip from *As Good As It Gets* was shown, Billy Crystal said of Jack Nicholson's character in the film, "That is a tough role. Playing that, really. Playing a bigoted, anti-woman, anti-gay, anti-minority millionaire. Not only won an Oscar, but he's the front runner for the Republican nomination." There was an appreciative response and a cut to Republican millionaire Arnold Schwarzenegger, who had a smile on his face.

What Crystal had to say about Best Director presenter Warren Beatty was, "He comes from a family that features eight generations of actors, seven of them his sister Shirley." Beatty announced the inevitable and James Cameron kissed Kate Winslet and Gloria Stuart as he made his way to the stage. What he said once he was there was "I don't know about you. But I'm having a really great time." He announced, "I had a killer cast. They really threw down for me." He also thanked "my lovely wife Linda [applause]" and "my original producers, my parents, who are here tonight, Phillip and Shirley Cameron." Spiraling along on his descent into Oscar infamy, Cameron told his parents, "Mom, Dad, there's no way that I can express to you what I'm feeling right now, my heart is full to bursting except to say, I'm King of the World! Whooop!" Ed Bark of *The Dallas Morning News* mused, "Perhaps you were jolted from a sound sleep when *Titanic* director James Cameron shouted." Among one's reactions to Cameron's self-aggrandizement was the realization that he wasn't king of anything, he was merely an Oscar winner for Best Director, which meant he was the same as Delbert

Mann. *Entertainment Weekly* called Cameron the "Least Winning Winner," and *New York Times* columnist Frank Rich felt, "Sally Field should cheer him for at last topping her 1984 'You like me!' in the annals of embarrassing Oscar effusions."

All that remained was for *Titanic* to be named officially as Best Picture, and it fell upon Sean Connery to do so. Coproducer Jon Landau began by saying, "So this morning I woke up and I couldn't wait for the day to be over. Now I don't want it to stop. So I can't act and I can't compose and I can't do special effects, so I guess that's why I'm producing." Landau then read—at breakneck speed—a list of more than four dozen names. He finished off by showing himself to be delusional: "We would not be here without an incredible screenwriter who wrote a great script, James Cameron," a statement one would think even the most sycophantic schmo would not want to be on record as having made.

Because of the rapidity with which Landau had read his list, Cameron said, "I think Jon saw *Shine* too many times." Then, as if he was purposely seeking to debase himself further, "In the midst of all this euphoria, it's kind of hard for us to remember that this euphoria and the success is for a film that's based on a real event that happened, where real people died, that shocked the world in 1912. So I'd just like everybody to go with me just for a second on something here. I'd like to do a few seconds of silence in remembrance of the 1,500 men, women and children who died when the great ship died. The message of *Titanic*, of course, is that if the great ship can sink, the unthinkable can happen, the future's unknowable. The only thing that we truly own is today. Life is precious, so during these few seconds, I'd like you to also listen to the beating of your own heart, which is the most precious thing in the whole world. Join me please in a few seconds of silence for *Titanic*." Fifteen seconds of dead air followed. Then the King of the World said, "Thank you very much, that's about as much as I'm sure Gil Cates can stand," a statement that was greeted with applause. "All right. You've really made this a night to remember in every way. Now let's go party till dawn!" The final tally for *Titanic* was eleven Oscars. It had tied *Ben-Hur*.

Billy Crystal reappeared to say, "It's been a great night. We're all tired. Matt Damon just hit on Shirley Temple. Good night, everybody. See you next year."

Aftermath

Meeting the press backstage, Jack Nicholson said, "Usually I just come out 'cause I like movie stars and having a good time and all that, but I was real nervous tonight." The father of two little kids also said, "If you have young children you always wish they can get to see you do something big, so I know they were sitting home having a ball. They don't know the difference between this and bowling, but they know Dad won, and that was great for me." As to his future career, Nicholson expected "peaks and valleys. I'll put a real tanker out next."

When she was asked the inevitable "Is this is as good as it gets?" Helen Hunt shook her head and said, "I hope not. I hope I have a long career ahead of me." Earlier in the day, NBC had announced that she and her *Mad About You* costar Paul Reiser would return to do another year of their TV series, with each of them pulling in a million bucks a pop. Television was on the minds of the reporters, with Hunt pleased to acknowledge that "The blacklist that existed before between TV and movies is gone. People have realized that work is work." She was sure, for example, that today, unlike in 1980, no one would give a second though to Robert Redford's casting Mary Tyler Moore in *Ordinary People*. Hunt was also asked to compare the Oscar with the two Emmys she had won for *Mad About You*. "It's thinner, and without wings." She wasn't the only winner tonight with television connections. Robin Williams had, of course, first become a star on the *Mork and Mindy* series, and Kim Basinger appeared on two very short-lived shows in the late seventies, *Dog and Cat* and *From Here to Eternity*. For that matter, Jack Nicholson never hid from the fact that some of his earliest acting gigs back in the fifties were on the tawdry syndicated series, *Divorce Court*.

Although he was uncharacteristically serious onstage, back with the press it was business as usual for Robin Williams. He said that winning was "extraordinary. It's like I'm sailing. It's much cheaper than

Prozac." On the issue of why comic actors tend to be overlooked at the Oscars, Williams conjectured, "Maybe it's because we're unusual people. We scare you." When someone wondered if his comedic background was detrimental to playing dramatic parts, Williams said, "I was trained as an actor. It's not like they have to medicate me." And asked if *Good Will Hunting* was the nomination for which he would have awarded himself the Oscar, Williams replied, "Oh yes . . . the other ones were just foreplay."

Kim Basinger said that she hadn't lined up another movie because "I've been very spoiled by *L.A. Confidential*. It's taking me a whole year to decide what to do." She also said that she had dedicated her Oscar to her father because he "was my very first acting teacher. I used to spend many nights on the floor with my father watching old forties and thirties and fifties movies with him and he would question me about Humphrey Bogart and Walter Huston and John Huston. So by the time I left at age seventeen, I had a pretty good background in film." Basinger also told the press that as far as she was concerned she was not an Academy Award "comeback kid": "I left to have a baby." Two years later, she described her Oscar night experience to *Vanity Fair*: "I was all ready to stand up for Gloria—and then Cuba Gooding turned to me and said my name, and everything went silent. Everything was in slow motion. My whole brain switched off. Alec was mouthing, 'Get up! Get up!' But I had no thought process. I know God helped me out of that chair." Once onstage, "the Oscar was wet and it was slipping out of my hand; and I remember looking down all of a sudden and I saw the actual thing in my hand and I thought, 'Uh—did I steal this from the bathroom?' I'm still in shock to this day."

Her director was asked if he was disappointed that *L.A. Confidential* had taken only two Awards. Curtis Hanson quoted what Frank Capra had said regarding *Mr. Smith Goes to Washington*: "Don't make your best picture the year *Gone With the Wind* comes out."

"I feel gratified that I went into this dark place— the bottom of the sea—and I experienced something and I was able to share that experience," pontificated James Cameron, who was holding his three Oscars. But in addition to gratified, did he feel vindicated? "I

feel happy. Vindicated has a negative connotation. There's nothing negative here."

Cameron may have been the big winner, but Mark McEwen of *CBS This Morning* called the Original Screenplay victors "the darlings of the night," and *People*'s editor Janice Min said, "it was really Matt Damon and Ben Affleck's night. They were just having the time of their lives." Would they be doing other projects together? "Not only do we plan on it, but we are contracted to do it," said Damon. "Have you ever worked with Harvey Weinstein? You never do only one." To which Affleck added, "You sign up for one and end up doing nine at five dollars apiece." Referring to his Oscar statuette, Affleck also said that his mother was "considering this her grandson and she's holding it for ransom until she gets her real one."

As they were going to the Governors Ball, E!'s Steve Kmetko asked the guys how it felt to be the subject of a Billy Crystal song. For Matt, it was "literally, the most incredible thing," while Ben said, "That was my all at one." And when Kmetko kidded them about their "buns" being mentioned in the song, Ben declared, "You know what, he doesn't have very tight buns . . . mine are rock hard." He also said, "For me, what was really cool was just having our families here and having them to share it with. So it wasn't just me that met Charlton Heston, my mom got to meet him, too." Damon chimed in, "Yeah, my mom was over in the corner talking to Frances McDormand. She was like, 'I'll see you later.' " Inside the Ball, Alec Baldwin tried to offer some brotherly advice to the wunderkinds: "Stay off the booze, stay off the drugs, and we're all pulling for you." A startled Damon replied, "Tonight? The *booze*?"

The *Los Angeles Times* reported, "The stars usually stop off at the official post-Oscar gathering, the Academy's Governors Ball, for just a few dutiful moments before rushing on elsewhere. Not this year." And a delighted Chairman of the Ball, Sid Granis, rhapsodized, "They're staying!" One aspect of the Ball everybody oohed and aahed over was the blue and green mosaic dining tables, fashioned from tiles imported from Italy, which eliminated the need for tablecloths. Although he admitted the Oscars were heavy, James Cameron said, "Yes, I can hold them all at once." But Linda Hamilton held on to one of his trio anyway because, said Cameron, "I can't do that and be sociable." Gloria Stuart was one of the centers of attention at the Governors Ball, and she joked "us two broads"—Kate Winslet and she—were about the only two aspects of *Titanic* that went away Oscar-less. Stuart was delighted at being a player for the first time in eons: "Tonight I'm part of the action. I'm basking in the evening." However, before she had even left the Shrine, the Harry Winston bodyguards whisked her necklace away from her, so she couldn't show it off at the post-ceremony parties. On her way into the Ball, Kate Winslet said her party plans were to "have lots of fun and get very drunk." Shortly after, she was fretting: "It's all a bit desperate. You're desperate to have a drink. You're desperate to eat something. You desperately want to dance and no one is really dancing yet."

Minnie Driver and Helena Bonham Carter were desperate for a smoke, so they lit up despite the ordinance against doing so. Asked what she thought the evening's most exciting moment was, Bonham Carter said, "I'm still waiting." But 1986 Best Actress Marlee Matlin knew what *her* highlight was: "I was overwhelmed when Shirley Temple told me there in the Oscar Family Album that she was a big fan of mine. I was like, 'Hello?' " Kim Basinger told *Entertainment Tonight*'s Julie Moran that winning the Award was "like pretending to be an astronaut and finally making it to the moon," and she laughed to CBS's Mark McEwen, "The only Oscar I've ever known is on *Sesame Street*, and I have to be up for that in the morning." Jennifer Jones was overheard telling Cher—who had slipped into something more comfortable—that she's a big fan.

The *Los Angeles Times* said the *Vanity Fair* party guests were, "short of having the Chinese Politburo and the British Royal Family, about as eclectic a mix of Who's Who as can be stuffed in one room." Among those who watched the ceremony at Morton's were Oliver Stone, Matt Drudge, David Hockney, Jean Claude Van Damme, k. d. lang and Angie Dickinson, who told Cindy Adams, "I especially thought this was the very best Academy Awards show ever." On her way in, Jackie Collins made sure reporters knew she was wearing "my own diamonds, of course." Madonna went to the Oscars with her brother, but came to Morton's alone; inside, she shared a table with Joni Mitchell and Cher. *Entertainment Weekly* observed that Ben Affleck, Gwyneth Paltrow's current guy, kept away from her former beau, Brad Pitt, who arrived solo; Warren Beatty was also stag. Geena Davis walked in, saw her ex-husband Renny Harlin and left. Brendan Fraser said, "I'm totally going to meet movie stars. I'm getting whiplash." Ellen DeGeneres and Anne Heche were both positively glowing as they told reporters outside Morton's that this was their one-year anniversary and that it was, in fact, at this very party they had met. They also showed off the anniversary gifts they had given each other: Anne had earrings, Ellen a necklace. Musician Melissa Etheridge said she and her girlfriend Julie Cypher would be celebrating with Ellen and Anne, and while DeGeneres was on camera with a TV reporter, Etheridge sneaked up behind her and made devil's horns with her fingers. Despite her status as an Oscar winner, Kim Basinger was kept waiting outside by fire marshals until the party thinned out.

Wolfgang Puck had approached Elton John about holding his AIDS fund-raiser at Spago, so the party moved from Maple Drive to Swifty Lazar's old haunt; John said that Maple Drive was just too small for the crowds and that fire marshals were always problematic. Fran Drescher, Teri Hatcher, Lionel Richie and Joely Fisher were at Spago for the duration, while Sharon Stone, Michael Douglas, Jay Leno, Jeremy Irons, Pam Grier and Atom Egoyan dropped by post-show. As usual, this party emptied out fairly early.

Columbia TriStar rented out Chasen's—the legendary restaurant had become more or less an upscale catering hall—for its celebration of *As Good As It Gets*. This was essentially a party for management rather than talent, although the *Los Angeles Times* did report sighting "a few genuine stars, including Sean Connery, Paul Sorvino and Larry King, whose mad night of party hopping would *not* include *Vanity Fair*'s event. 'They did an article on me that was preposterous,' said the still-miffed TV personality." Jack Nicholson and Helen Hunt were at the party, although most other guests might not have known it, since they were in a separate VIP area. Nicholson also left early, going out through the back door, heading off to Dani Janssen's get-together which this year was a tribute to him. Also in that special section at Chasen's was Jill the Dog, who had played Verdell in *As Good As It Gets*; she wore a costume jewelry necklace worth $250 and ate lamb and crème brûlée.

The party coproduced by Paramount and Fox in honor of their joint enterprise, *Titanic*, wasn't held in a restaurant at all, but a tent set up in a parking lot on Canon Drive in Beverly Hills. E!'s Jeanne Wolf asked James Cameron if his feelings were hurt that Leonardo hadn't shown: "No. I spoke to Leo. I can tell you this is no Hollywood gesture. Leo is genuinely shy." Because she had been having such a good time at Morton's, Kate Winslet didn't arrive here until almost two A.M., by which time the *Titanic* bar had closed for the night. James Cameron did not "party till dawn," as he had exhorted others to do. He returned to his hotel at three A.M.

And as usual, Miramax's fete was the place for night owls. The party at the Polo Lounge of the Beverly Hills Hotel was just beginning to pick up steam around midnight—the shank of the night for Los Angeles. On his way in, Robin Williams pointed to his Oscar's rear end and said to a reporter, "Look at that—no crack." But when E!'s Patrick Stinson remarked to Williams that he seemed subdued, the Oscar winner responded, "It's a shock," and that hearing his name called was "a jolt. It's like someone grabbing you in a very interesting place." *Entertainment Weekly* wrote that if you were at the Miramax party you were likely to get "a giant bear hug from Ben Affleck, who was squeezing everyone like they were rolls of Charmin." A *Los Angeles Times* reporter asked Peter Fonda how he was handling Oscar night after losing. "It feels great," said the *Ulee's Gold* actor. "I love my friend Jack. It's not like we both played Hamlet and he beat my pants off. I've been nominated by my peers. They don't unnominate you." Miramax partygoers did take note of Minnie Driver studiously avoiding Matt Damon; Rush & Molloy of the *New York Daily News* reported that "The end of the night saw nominee Minnie Driver crying in her mother's arms. Bad enough that Kim Basinger walked off with the Best Supporting Actress Award, worse still was that Driver bumped into ex-boyfriend Matt Damon, sharing his Oscar triumph

with Winona Ryder. (One consolation for Driver: Ryder and Damon went home separately.)"

Four months later, the *New York Post*'s "Page Six" had a story headlined "Oprah Tale Driver-s Damon Nuts." It detailed that the Matt Damon was "sick and tired of hearing once again how he cavalierly dumped Minnie Driver on national TV. Now that Minnie, his costar in *Good Will Hunting*, has told the story for the umpteenth time—and appeared on the covers of *Cosmopolitan* and *Elle*—he realizes there is no end in sight. But friends are trying to control the damage. They say the story of his swinish behavior simply isn't true, and that Minnie is flat-out lying." One friend of Matt's insisted that Driver "knew about the breakup for at least a week, probably ten days before *Oprah*" and that Driver's sister concurred in this version of the breakup. The *Post* snickered that "the *Oprah* angle makes it a better story, one that Minnie apparently intends to keep telling for the rest of her life." The article also talked about the Academy Awards, indicating "Minnie has also said how much it hurt her on Oscar night that Matt and fellow Oscar winner Ben Affleck shunned her and never spoke to her. But sources say Matt avoided her specifically at Minnie's own request. 'She and Matt have the same agent, Patrick Whitesell at CAA,' said our insider. 'She called him up before the Academy Awards and he said, "Matt will do whatever you want to make it easier." And she said it would be better if they didn't meet face to face in public. Matt's not talking to her was a direct request.' "

Early, the morning after, Robert Duvall appeared on *Oprah*. The host told him, "I thought you held your face pretty well last night when the camera was on you, Mr. Duvall. Were you really disappointed?" He answered in the affirmative, and insisted, "It's very competitive. Artists are very competitive. People tend to minimize that, but it's not true. So you always like to win." Not only that, but *The Apostle* "didn't write itself and it didn't direct itself, so I would have liked to, even last night, to have been accepted in a more broad way." Searching to find something he might be upbeat about, Winfrey mentioned that people in her audience had found the Family Album very touching, and asked, "Was that as moving for you all there?" "It wasn't moving, but it was nice."

Peter Fonda appeared on the same program, and was the upbeat counterpart to Robert Duvall's Sore Loser. He said the whole experience had been "terrific." He said he expected Nicholson to win and while "I would have liked to have won ... everything's cool."

Not only did Leonardo DiCaprio stay away from the Shrine Auditorium on Oscar night, he didn't even watch the Academy Awards. The *New York Daily News* scooped that at the same time the Oscars were beginning, the actor was in Manhattan's NoHo, waiting on line to get into the Tomoe Sushi restaurant. "Wearing a light blue knit cap, baggy jeans and layers over a thermal shirt, the 23-year-old screen star got antsy and began to playfully kick-box with his male friends on the sidewalk while waiting for his table at the popular sushi joint," according to witnesses. The paper also said that "DiCaprio was recognized by an employee of nearby Liam's, who invited him to the restaurant's Oscar bash. But the star politely passed on the offer. 'No, man, thanks,' the actor said, shrinking a bit. 'Not gonna go.' " According to *Extra*, he and his buddies also had a snowball fight.

Marilyn Beck said, "So after all these weeks of will he? Won't he? Leonardo DiCaprio did not show up for the Academy Awards, but you know that didn't bother me as much as the fact that so many former Oscar winners were no-shows." Among those she mentioned were Tom Hanks, Jodie Foster, Paul Newman and Joanne Woodward, Liza Minnelli and Sally Field. "It's called giving back a little to the industry that's given you so much," she instructed. Liz Smith agreed, and also mentioned Loretta Young, Joan Fontaine and Olivia de Havilland. She pointed out, "If the famously jittery Jennifer Jones could overcome her shy misgivings, others should have been there."

Smith later reported that she had chatted with de Havilland, who was nursing her seriously ill ex-husband, Pierre Galante, at her Paris home and couldn't abandon him for the Oscars. *Entertainment Weekly* sent out investigative reporters to find out where the 63 other no-shows among the 134 living Oscar winners had been. The subsequent article said, "Clearly, no one expected such stars as Frank Sinatra and Katharine Hepburn, with their well-publicized

health problems, to show up. And was anyone holding his breath for Marlon Brando or George C. Scott?" The magazine reported that 1956 Best Supporting Actress, *Written on the Wind*'s Dorothy Malone, never received an invitation. Gilbert Cates hazarded that "Maybe it went to the wrong address. I would have loved to have Dorothy there." Malone's spokesperson said she was "a little pissed." The same thing happened to Tatum O'Neal. Although the magazine couldn't track down the whereabouts of Mickey Rooney or Linda Hunt, among others, the most frequently given excuse was that the person was working on a film and couldn't get away, even though some of them weren't away on location but were right there in L.A. So why Nicolas Cage couldn't bring himself to show up— particularly when the movie he was making was *8mm*—was a mystery. Tom Hanks was in New York working on *You've Got Mail*, but his costar, Meg Ryan, was an Oscar night presenter. Among some other excuses given by spokespersons: Jason Robards: "We didn't even know he was invited." Gene Hackman: in the South Pacific. He and his wife "committed to an expedition before he received the invitation." Patty Duke: "She lives in another state and doesn't usually come to L.A." Paul Newman and Joanne Woodward: "Probably at their home in Connecticut. They are very private." Meryl Streep: "If it wasn't for her kids' spring break, she would have been there." Glenda Jackson: "She is a full-time politician and she can't just get on a plane and fly out to Hollywood." Maureen Stapleton: "The actress who doesn't fly or take trains was at home in Massachusetts, 'she would have had to have been chauffeur-driven 3,000 miles, which is quite prohibitive.' " As for Miyoshi Umeki: The magazine called her "MIA. She's dodged the press for years."

Mimi Avins, fashion editor of the *Los Angeles Times*, wrote, "Thanks to a refreshing emphasis on personal style, the Academy Awards were an entertaining evening of fashion, not the overdressed high school prom they've sometimes resembled. On the one night a year when glamour traditionally rules, most of the women of Hollywood showed up dressed as Tasteful Ladies, while maintaining their individuality." Julie Szabo of the *New York Post* was also pleased, declaring that "young and old, famous and nearly forgotten, all entered the Shrine Auditorium looking impeccable, And for a change, most everyone did themselves justice."

Cindy Adams decreed that "Gownwise, the knockout was the very busy green *schmatta* Kate Winslet wore." Julia Szabo agreed: "Inspiring full-figured gals everywhere, Winslet proved that, if there was an award for Best Dressed Actress, it would go to her (or is that her stylist?). Her bottle-green Givenchy, with its strategic draping, made her look almost as statuesque as Oscar himself." *Glamour*'s Charla Krupp said Winslet "wins my 'best body' award because she showed women out there that you don't have to be rail thin." In *Salon*, Camille Paglia found Winslet to be "truly titanic in her magnificent green dress, which makes her look like the Grand Duchess Anastasia at a medieval tournament. She should get the Oscar for best bust. Anyone with those floaters doesn't need a lifeboat." But Mimi Avins was more mixed about Winslet: "As overwrought as her deep green Givenchy gown was, she carried it off in high drama." Winslet said that she would have nothing to do with trying to lose weight for Oscar night. "I wouldn't starve myself," she insisted. "I'm a girl. I need feeding. I had a scone this morning, some fruit and loads of coffee."

An entirely different body type than Winslet, Helen Hunt also received glowing reviews for her satin ice-blue strapless satin gown designed by Tom Ford for Gucci. Martha Stewart said, "If I were thin enough, I would have worn Helen Hunt's dress. I thought that was beautiful." Ilene Rosenzweig, senior editor of *Allure*, felt that Hunt "looked incredibly elegant and very thin. I think you want to give this girl a big steak and a plate of mashed potatoes."

Cynthia Robins of the *San Francisco Examiner* declared, "Probably the classiest gown of the evening was Minnie Driver's cranberry Randolph Duke for Halston. Driver likely incurred the wrath of PETA people with her dyed-to-match double fox stole, but it was the perfect Hollywood moment: the divine melding of class with crass." Randolph Duke was on *Entertainment Tonight* to say, "One of my favorites had to be Minnie Driver. I did do the dress, so I'm a little partial, but she did wow the crowd." The *San Francisco Chronicle*'s Trish Donnally thought Kim Basinger

"looked lovely in a pale green satin gown with a cowl neck, cowl back, bustle and long train, her hair in soft waves," while *Entertainment Tonight*'s Jann Carl said Basinger "evoked Grace Kelly in her Escada gown."

Cindy Adams observed, "Halle Berry, with four gowns to choose from, did a yellow Vera Wang. It showed so much that you can't understand why her marriage broke up." Camille Paglia cooed, "Sharon Stone is fabulous! As usual, she is uniquely dressed and makes everyone else look like lemmings. She's doing a Jean Seberg this year—the gorgeous garçon haircut, the white beachwear blouse with raffishly turned-up collar, wittily set off by a mauve satin sheath skirt. La Stone always has it." Stone revealed that the shirt she was wearing belonged to her husband, so looking at a picture of her and her husband on *E!*'s *Academy Awards Fashion Review*, Joan Rivers joked, "Under his tuxedo, he's wearing her bra."

While many observers professed to be shocked, shocked! by Ashley Judd's ultra-revealing gown, Cynthia Robins thought the actress, "groomed to look like a cross between Ava Gardner and Hedy Lamarr, took the prize for the most skin, in a fly-away, slit-up-or-down-to-there (take your pick) white number in which she was so secure and sassy, she wins the Babe-a-licious Award." (Judd's mother, Winona, joked to the press that *her* gown came from the "third aisle in Walmart.") Madonna was slammed for combining a puffy Gaultier skirt with a black vest by Olivier Theyskens, adding body glitter on her chest, arms and face. Trish Donnally said, "Madonna didn't know whether to go tender or tough. Her muscular arms bared by her sleeveless black gown gave her the look of a bricklayer, and the maiden blond curls cascading down around her face made her look like a character out of a medieval fairy tale." *People* sneered that she "resembled a biker chick from the Black Forest."

While Leon Hall selected Madonna as the night's worst dressed, the four other participants on *E!*'s *Academy Awards Fashion Review* picked Cher. Joan Rivers mentioned Cher's ex-husband, who had recently been killed in a skiing accident: "Sonny saw her in that dress and that's why he aimed for the tree." Cher did have a defender in Liz Smith, who wondered "What was *so* wrong about Cher's sexy, beaded Bob

Mackie number or her amusing headpiece? . . . It was all very Cher, very showbiz, very Oscar night. From the violent criticism, you'd have thought Cher had brought the plague into Hollywood!"

People noted that "After years of seeing their counterparts go collarless, tieless and monochromatic . . . almost unanimously, the males wore the traditional soup-and-fish." The man who received the most attention—almost entirely negative—was Gus Van Sant in a multicolored striped Gaultier jacket and black T-shirt. "So Elton John," harrumphed designer John Gibson to the *San Francisco Examiner*. Four of the five participants on the Joan Rivers show deemed Van Sant the man who looked the worst. "He was up for Best Director in Stupid Clothes," cracked Rivers, while Leon Hall ruminated, "You know, sometimes Jean-Paul Gaultier can help you to make some of the worst mistakes in the world, and this was a mistake." Stylist Phillip Bloch disagreed with the others and said the worst dressed man was Sally Kirkland.

The *New York Daily News* felt that "veteran actress Julie Christie upstaged a string of starlets in a statuesque silver beaded Badgley Mischka scoop-necked, cap-sleeve gown." Christie's was one of the best reviewed gowns of the night, but the actress herself panned it after the Oscars. She learned from the People for the Ethical Treatment of Animals that her designers had created a line inspired by *Doctor Zhivago* which employed fur. "I should have made a more thorough investigation before I chose my Oscar dress," Christie told the two designers in a fax. "I had already ruled out Valentino, Dolce & Gabbana and Max Mara because, looking at their clothes, I had been absolutely shocked to note that, suddenly, real fur was used in their collections." As for Badgley Mischka, Christie sighed, "It just never occurred to me that two young American designers would have thrown in the towel so easily."

Reviews for the show were all over the place. John Carman of the *San Francisco Chronicle* raved, "It was the best Oscar show in two decades. Maybe even in twenty-five years, which transports us all the way back to *The Sting* and David Niven arching his eyebrow at a streaker. You knew last night's telecast was going to be good when that harbinger of all things screwy, Cher,

sauntered into the Shrine Auditorium in a get-up that looked as if Busby Berkeley had upchucked on her head." Carman also praised the emcee: "A year ago, Billy Crystal returned to host his fifth Oscar telecast after a three-year layoff, and he seemed tense and just plain rusty. But last night, Crystal was back in razor form." "Kinda lame, what a shame, Billy," began Kinney Littlefield of the *Orange County Register*. "Yet it turned out it hardly mattered. Despite Crystal's flat delivery—the fault of a dull script he fought all the way—this year's telecast was warmly rewarding, although about forty-five minutes overlong. And its success had little to do with television production values. This year Oscar gave us fans what we love best— big personalities in moments of oh-so-personal public triumph."

Entertainment Weekly's Ken Tucker simply deemed the show "excruciating," and said it "came down to a debate as to what was the worst moment." Tucker found that "As television, this Oscar broadcast . . . was just about as bad as it gets; I've watched Country Music Association Awards ceremonies honoring Minnie Pearl that had more vigor." The *Hollywood Reporter* complained "It was a generally dull night with the usual flat, sterile scripts. How many years must we be told that music helps the movie moods or that script and cinematography are important for making films? Even host Billy Crystal seemed unusually timid and couldn't pump up the much-needed volume." The paper made note of the abundance of film clips, "some of which were pertinent (the Donen montage) and some of which were hard to explain (a group of animal stars in films)." Ray Richmond of *Daily Variety* called this "a yawner of an Oscarcast," although he advised, "Don't blame Billy. He did what he could as host, even if many of his off-the-cuff one-liners sank faster than the great ship herself. . . . Crystal still turned in his usual cleverly written piece of pointed foolishness."

On *Entertainment Tonight*, Leonard Maltin enthused that "for any lifelong movie lover, the emotional highpoint had to be the Oscar Family Album. . . . Most of all, I loved seeing Shirley Temple, ageless Shirley Temple, still a star for young and old, and living proof of the impact that movies have on each and every one of us." *Daily Variety*'s Richmond said that the Family Album "was plenty swell but was dropped in with little regard for pace or continuity, a problem that paced the Oscarcast all night." Young, angst-ridden singer Fiona Apple—attending with *Boogie Nights* director Paul Thomas Anderson—told *Entertainment Weekly*, "I liked seeing Gregory Peck onstage—that's my boy!" One of the few people to express displeasure with the Family Album was Henry Sheehan of the *Orange County Register*: "Filling a couple of bleachers full of actors who had won various acting Oscars was a dubious idea to begin with, and in its execution, it made a large group of distinguished performers look like seniors stranded on a bus trip."

On the other hand, Sheehan loved Stanley Donen, saying his acceptance "was pure magic. . . . He cradled his statuette and started crooning, apparently spontaneously, 'Cheek to Cheek.' When the orchestra came in on time and in key, it was clear that it was a rehearsed bit, but it didn't matter; the moment was flying on its own wings, and the music was just right. Then, when the septuagenarian broke into a soft shoe, man, that was Hollywood: a lifetime of experience, practice and talent. It's not supposed to be spontaneous, after all—it's just supposed to look that way." Robert Dominguez of the *New York Daily News* said a "song-and-dance number by a Hollywood legend lent a moment of class to an Academy Awards ceremony otherwise punctuated by toilet humor and sex jokes," adding that Donen "nearly stole the show from host Billy Crystal."

The telecast, at three hours and forty-six minutes, was the longest ever; it would only hold the record for a year, though. The good news for the Academy and for ABC was that, undoubtedly propelled by the popularity of *Titanic*, this was the highest-rated Oscar telecast ever. The bad news for Billy Crystal was that his new movie, *My Giant,* which opened two and a half weeks after the Oscars, was yet another bomb. Thelma Adams of the *New York Post* opened her review with, "As funny as Billy Crystal was hosting the Oscars, there was a melancholy to his delivery. When the funnyman's *Fathers' Day* costar Robin Williams received the Best Supporting Actor nod, the emotion crested. Why? Crystal knew something that the audience didn't. He was following the desperately unfunny

Day, not with *Good Will Hunting*, but with the abysmal *My Giant*."

That *Titanic* would win was so much of a foregone conclusion that no one much complained about its sweep. Rod Dreher of the *New York Post* squawked about the lead actor winners, saying that Jack Nicholson's performance was "lovable but lazy" and that "Helen Hunt was fine . . . but losers Judi Dench and Helena Bonham Carter really showed how good acting could get. But they were in smaller films that were perceived as less accessible to the public—the kind of movies that were said last year to have finally arrived." Philip Wuntch of *The Dallas Morning News* observed, "One of the year's most haunting performances was Peter Fonda's *Ulee's Gold* beekeeper. But he lost to long-ago *Easy Rider* costar Jack Nicholson for *As Good As It Gets*. Mr. Nicholson's crusty character in the comedy was an apogee of all Nicholson performances. Yet when future film buffs look back at the remarkable Nicholson career, they'll rank such un-Oscared turns as *Chinatown*, *The Last Detail* and *Five Easy Pieces* higher than *As Good As It Gets*." Bob Strauss of the *Los Angeles Daily News* said, "You gotta love the irony. Produced by Miramax, the company behind last year's big indie winner *The English Patient*, *Hunting* was this year's only multiple Oscar-winning independent—and it was more conventional than many of this year's major studio contenders."

Spike Lee was asked if he was disappointed that he hadn't finally won an Oscar for his *Four Little Girls* documentary. Lee cited the entry that had defeated him, *The Long Way Home*: "When the film is about the Holocaust and one of the producers is a rabbi and it comes from the Simon Wiesenthal Center, there are not many sure things in life, but that was a sure thing when you consider the makeup of the voting body of the Academy of Motion Picture Arts and Sciences. I'd have rather been the New York Knicks in the fourth quarter, down ten points, a minute left in the United Center, than have the odds we faced of winning an Oscar against the Holocaust film." *Entertainment Weekly*'s Chris Nashawaty asked Lee, "Did you like *Titanic*?" "It was all right," said Lee. "But I don't understand why he is upset it didn't get nominated for Best Screenplay. I think Mr. Cameron is a great technical director, but he can't write, and he definitely can't write dialogue."

As *Titanic* had dominated the box office all these many months, so too did James Cameron's behavior dominate post-Oscar discussion. Bernard Weinraub wrote in the *New York Times* that Cameron's comments "startled many producers and executives in Hollywood, who are accustomed to Oscar speeches with a degree of humility." Su Avasthi of the *New York Post* gave a special award for "Most Out-of-Control Acceptance Speech" to the director's "arrogant celebration of his victory." Jack Mathews wrote, "Cameron lacked what one might call humility throughout the Oscar show, as his crew of technicians . . . paused at his aisle seat for a paternal hug on the way to the stage, and when he got up there himself, he was both pompous and ministerial." Mathews also called Cameron's silent prayer, "an awkwardly inappropriate way to end a more than three-and-a-half-hour celebration of one motion picture." Tim Goodman, the *San Francisco Examiner*'s TV critic, asked, "After James Cameron won, then gave his acceptance speech, didn't you want to take it away from him?"

The *Los Angeles Daily News* wrote, "James Cameron's film *Titanic* may have won 11 Oscars Monday, but the filmmaker had not won a popularity contest, according to Dr. Arnold G. Abrams, a body language expert. Abrams said that other than James Horner, who won an Oscar for Best Original Dramatic Score, the winners from *Titanic* appeared as if they were thanking Cameron because they had to." Dr. Abrams's findings were that "It was ritualistic, You did not see a lot of warmth coming to Cameron." The *Daily News* also reported, "As a contrast, Abrams said that Helen Hunt, the winner in the Best Actress category, indicated a genuine affection for screenwriter James L. Brooks."

As Oscar night revelries were winding down, Cameron said he was going to try to catch up on his sleep. But five days after the Oscars, it was revealed that he had spent his post-Oscar period on a new writing project. Kenneth Turan's pre-Awards treatise on the detrimental effects *Titanic* may have on future movies had gotten under the triple Oscar winner's craw, and so Cameron wrote a long letter to the *Los Angeles Times*, which was printed as an article in the Calendar section. He began, "I have shrugged off Kenneth Turan's incessant rain of personal barbs over the last few months, since he clearly is not man enough to admit when he is wrong, and it has been amusing to watch him dig himself into a deeper hole each time he tries to justify his misanthropic personality with regard to *Titanic*. But it's time to speak up when Turan uses his bully pulpit not only to attack my film, but the entire film industry and its audiences." Cameron looked down upon "Poor Kenny. He sees himself as the lone voice crying in the wilderness, righteous but not heeded by the blind and dumb 'great unwashed' around him. It must be a great burden to be cursed with such clear vision when your misguided flock bray past you, like lemmings, unmindful." Cameron instructed Turan that he apparently had lost sight of what a film critic is supposed to do "if he ever knew": "When people spend their hard-earned money on a movie at the end of a long work week, all they ask is that their local critic steer them toward the good ones and help them avoid the turkeys. . . . What you don't get to do is grind on and on, month after month, after the audience has rendered its verdict in the most resounding of terms, telling everybody why the filmgoers are wrong and you are right." Cameron ended with "Forget about Clinton—how do we impeach Kenneth Turan?"

Cameron probably figured that the directors of the world would genuflect before him in grateful agreement. But his tantrum gained nationwide attention, and hard as it was to imagine, he was now adjudged to be even more of an ass than he had seemed on Oscar night. In the *New York Times*'s Week in Review section, Hubert B. Herring meditated, "Now, one might think that a king, especially of the whole world, would rise, magnanimously and majestically, above such a fray, glancing down, perhaps, with benign amusement. Alas no. Mr. Cameron [is] unable to rest until the *Titanic* verdict is unanimous." Frank Rich also weighed in for the paper, and employed the director's own petard: Cameron, he noted, "was particularly enamored of his own 'earnest and straightforward' script. 'Audiences around the world are celebrating their own humanity by going into a dark room and crying together,' he wrote with deadly seriousness of moviegoers' responses to *Titanic*, hilariously unaware that sentences like this would lend credence to Mr. Turan's criticism that Mr. Cameron is 'not someone to be trusted anywhere near a word processor.' " Rich also quoted "an industry observer" on Cameron's two Oscar acceptances: "In the first speech he was going for king—in the second he decided to go for God." Rich concluded, "While hurling thunderbolts from his throne, he seems to have forgotten the moral of his own movie, in which the powerful, arrogant and celebrated are portrayed as the bad guys who sink everyone else."

Jack Mathews of *Newsday* found Cameron's piece to be "astonishingly angry." Mathews pointed out that Turan had attacked the film in print on four different occasions but asked rhetorically, "What harm could one dissenting critic do? It wasn't as if Turan was getting away with anything. His paper's letters section was boiling with angry rebuttals from readers, and it was clear his criticism was having no impact whatsoever on *Titanic*'s business. But Cameron couldn't have taken much solace from that. The fact is, the leading voice of the paper of record in Southern California is heard by everyone in Cameron's kingdom, and it had to be taking some of the fun out of the party." Mathews said he had talked on the phone to Turan—whom he'd known for two decades—and told him, "Don't go outside without your flak jacket." Turan's response: "I'm not sure you're kidding." "This isn't unusual" for Cameron," noted Anne Hurley, the executive film editor of the *Los Angeles Times*, who felt "It seems to have really hit a nerve with him that one critic is not getting aboard the train." *The New York Post* quoted an

"insider" from the film industry, "The piece he sent to the *Times*, along with that speech and a number of other things lately, have reminded everyone of the magnitude of his ego." The *Post*'s film critic, Rod Dreher, addressed the director: "Earth to Jim: *Dude, you won!* How about a bit of kingly noblesse oblige?" Dreher also figured that "Cameron's carping in this case looks extremely petty, and surely must churn the stomachs of industry types who will have to contend with the Great Helmsman's ego in the years to come. . . . Mad King James, determined to smite his enemies, is setting himself up for a nasty fall—which he will have earned as much as he's earned the success he now enjoys." As for Turan's reaction to Cameron's attack, he told *Newsweek*, "If this is the way he tolerates dissent, I have increased empathy for people who have to work for him."

Sometimes Hollywood studios are forced to acknowledge that fair is fair, so 20th Century Fox worked out a deal where, despite having given up his salary and points in *Titanic*, Cameron would still be paid close to a reported $100 million dollars for making the highest-grossing movie of all time. That was the sweet part of Cameron's post-Oscar life. Not so pleasant was that just weeks after his Oscar night triumph, the king's queen, Linda Hamilton, made him move out of their castle—he had resumed his relationship with Suzy Amis, which had first begun when she was appearing in *Titanic*'s present-day sequences. This truly was the cruelest month for, after fifteen weeks, *Titanic* fell from its number one spot at the box office over the first weekend of April, vanquished by *Lost in Space*.

1998

Battles were raging everywhere.

Candid Camera

For months, upscale magazines carried a three-page ad for a movie opening in late spring. The centerpiece of the campaign was a number of quotes from David Thomson of *Esquire*, with the first page simply saying, "The movie of the decade and it stars Jim Carrey!" Turn the page, and Thomson went on to say, "One of the most spectacularly original American movies in years . . . here, out of nowhere, comes a picture that knows there is no subject as weirdly compelling as our strange relationship with television." Most people might take exception to this last assertion, but the main thing was that Paramount had created an extremely high level of awareness for its offbeat movie.

Directed by Peter Weir, *The Truman Show* was a satire of media manipulation and the supposed obsession of the public with television, making its points through the tale of a genial Everyman who discovers that his entire life has been broadcast to the world at large. The previous "serious" Jim Carrey movie was the critical and box-office disappointment, *The Cable Guy*, so to have a shot at another relatively straight role, the comic actor had to sacrifice by working for $12 million rather than the $20 million he could have gotten for a broad farce. With memories of *The Cable Guy* fresh, it was only natural that people were apprehensive about this new vehicle, and E! reported that when theater exhibitors were shown preview clips at the ShoWest convention in Las Vegas, they had a "cool reaction." Hence the need for a pre-release advertising blitz.

Some reviewers concurred with David Thomson's appraisal. Kenneth Turan of the *Los Angeles Times*, for instance, called *The Truman Show* "the nerviest feature to come out of Hollywood in recent memory," deeming it "adventurous, provocative, even daring." Others weren't nearly as impressed. Peter Rainer of *New York* found *The Truman Show* "a clever but empty movie," which "was about as 'subversive' as *Forrest Gump*, another soothing film about an innocent stumbling through his existence. This is a profound movie for people who don't like to think." Ella Taylor of *L.A.*

Weekly said, "As a 1984 for the millenium, the movie lapses into glib and lazy social critique, with an ending that is 98 percent sentimental Hollywood glop and 2 percent cynicism about our capacity for empathy." And *Entertainment Tonight*'s Leonard Maltin was one of a number of people who pointed out that "*The Twilight Zone* used to do this sort of thing—better—in half-hour segments."

As for the Serious Guy, Roger Ebert opined, "Carrey is a surprisingly good choice to play Truman. We catch glimpses of his manic comic persona, just to make us comfortable with his presence in the character, but this is a well-planned performance." Marjorie Baumgarten of the *Austin Chronicle*, however, said, "For all the talk of Carrey's toned-down dramatic performance here, it is, though serviceable, still awfully broad and hammy . . . His behavior is that of an insanely cheerful overgrown kid—too exaggerated to be believable as the world's most famous "real" person and too limited to convey the psychological turmoil he experiences as he begins to suspect that the whole world revolves around him." *The New Yorker*'s Anthony Lane wrote, "Carrey has been lauded for tamping down his instinctive mania in favor of a more lightly tortured soul. To me, the spectacle is admirable but painful; he looks like a drunk who is not only making do with Pellegrino but pretending that he likes the stuff." He added, "What is unclear is why on earth half the planet would want to watch a man like Truman."

As the omnipotent figure orchestrating the broadcasting of the title character's life, Ed Harris had replaced Dennis Hopper, who bolted after a single day of filming. the *Sacramento Bee*'s Joe Baltake wrote, "Harris, who worked with James Cameron on *The Abyss*, seems to have modeled this megalomaniac after Cameron." Stephen Farber of *Movieline* was thinking along the same lines: "Harris captures the single-minded passion of every megalomaniacal director, and the film offers the savage last word of egotistical auteurs who see themselves as 'king of the world.' "

This time the sober-sided Jim Carrey did very well with audiences: *The Truman Show* grossed $125 million.

Playing Army

A month after the serious Jim Carrey arrived at theaters, the serious Steven Spielberg also made an appearance. Those two current-day avatars of a cozy, pre-Vietnam-era, middle-American sensibility, Steven Spielberg and Tom Hanks, had long wanted to work with each other. Bringing them together was *Saving Private Ryan*. The film centered on a World War II company sent to retrieve a soldier whose three brothers have been killed, so as to save Mother Ryan any more grief; the title character hasn't been captured by the Germans or anything, he's just a normal grunt doing his job on the battlefield. It's a rather preposterous premise, made more so by the fact that the order is given by Army Chief of Staff George Marshall, as if he didn't have anything on his mind other than some lady who lives on a Norman Rockwell farm in Iowa; and, shucks, General Marshall was inspired by a letter Abraham Lincoln wrote. (When he saw this scene, Vincent Canby—in a one-shot return to writing about movies after having moved over to the *New York Times* theater beat—laughed, "On the first or second day after the General helped to start the biggest, riskiest military operation in the history of the Western world, his Washington office is as serene as that of the dean of a small New England college on a midsummer afternoon.")

During his involvement with *Apollo 13*, Tom Hanks's mantra was "All I Ever Wanted Was To Be An Astronaut." Now it turned out that, "This is my boyhood dream, to be playing a soldier in a World War II movie. I would do this for free." He wasn't exactly doing it gratis, but both Hanks and Spielberg took hefty points in the project—which was being coproduced by Spielberg's DreamWorks and Paramount—in lieu of salaries. Spielberg, too, had enjoyed army fantasies when he was a child. His father, who had been a radio operator on a B-25 bomber in the Pacific, "intoxicated me with bedtime stories about the war," and one of the director's first homemade movies was *Fighter Squad*, in which he accessorized his pals in the military paraphernalia his father had around the house as keepsakes.

But this was no longer child's play. At the gala premiere screening of *Saving Private Ryan*, attended by D-Day veterans and those families who had lost loved ones at Normandy, Spielberg got up and made a speech, stating that "If Hitler's armies were able to stop the invasion and then drive the British, Canadian, and American forces back into the sea, he would have been free to move major forces from his western to his eastern front, enough maybe to win a victory—and almost certainly enough to impose a stalemate. The war would have gone on; the Holocaust would have gone on. It really is too terrible to imagine." Saluting the former soldiers in the audience, the director declared, "It is to honor these men and their buddies—the men who put an end to the Holocaust and saved Western Civilization—that I made this movie."

Although *Saving Private Ryan* wasn't intended to be escapist entertainment, the decision was made to release it at the height of the escapism season because come the end of the year there would be too many other heavy films around. Terry Press, the head of marketing at DreamWorks explained, "It's hard on the press and the Academy members who are expected to absorb and process these deep dish dramas at a rate of about one per day"—in other words, in July *Saving Private Ryan* would have the field to itself. The title role in *Saving Private Ryan* was enacted by Matt Damon; Robin Williams had brought him along to meet Spielberg when they were making *Good Will Hunting* in Massachusetts and the director was working on *Amistad* in Rhode Island. Damon filmed *Ryan* before *Good Will Hunting* was released and DreamWorks was hoping he'd pull in those moviegoers who might otherwise avoid a war film.

Violence is Golden

A great deal of fuss was made over the D-Day landing sequence that came early in *Saving Private Ryan*. Using a grab bag of different film stocks, exposures, and camera speeds, as well as frenetic editing, hand-held cameras, and the *ne plus ultra* in sound recording, Spielberg, cinematographer Janusz Kaminski, and the technical crews came up with twenty minutes of bravura filmmaking that filled the theater with the sound of bullets flying and the screen with blood and guts. Spielberg himself embarked on a press junket for the first time since 1981 and he emphasized that because of the graphic nature of the picture, "anybody under the age of fourteen should not see this movie. But I also believe that if you can drive a car and fight in a war, you should see it."

Once the D-Day portion was over, *Saving Private Ryan* pretty much became business as usual, with Hanks commanding a unit made up of a cross-section of ethnic and socioeconomic types. There was the Italian, the Jew, the guy from Brooklyn who cracks wise, the veteran, the sensitive soul, the hillbilly, and so on—it was right out of a Warner Brothers feature from 1943 and you half-expected Dane Clark, Sam Levene, George Tobias, Alan Hale and Robert Hutton to show up. Spielberg would have you believe that in no way was the main portion of the film a let-down for viewers, though: "I felt in a sense that the Omaha Beach landing was not unlike basic training for an audience, that once they got through that—if, in fact, they allowed themselves to get through it—they would be on the alert just as our kids are aware as they walk through the hedgerow of France looking for Private Ryan that any moment something like that could happen to them again"—making German snipers sound like just another version of *Jurassic Park*'s dinosaurs lurking in the jungle or Bruce the Shark preparing for business in *Jaws*. At the end of the picture, there was another big set piece highlighted by a brainy soldier being made out to be a weak sister, a slap in the face to all the intellectuals who fought gallantly in this and other wars. And never mind that Spielberg swore, "He was me in the movie. That's how I would have been in war."

Much of the response to *Saving Private Ryan*—particularly in regard to the opening sequence—was so unrestrained that one could be forgiven for thinking that many of these people had never seen a war movie before, or at least certainly not a war movie by Robert Aldrich, Anthony Mann, or Samuel Fuller. *Good Morning America*'s Joel Siege chirped that "Every once in a while, a film transcends the art form. *Saving Private Ryan* does that." Stephen Hunter of the *Washington Post* effervesced, "There are movies and then there are movies. And then there is Steven Spielberg's *Saving Private Ryan*. Searing, heartbreaking, so intense it

turns your body into a single tube of clenched muscle, this is simply the greatest war movie ever made, and one of the great American movies. In one stroke, it makes everything that came before—with the exception of two or three obscure European variants on the same theme—seem dated and unwatchable. And it redefines the way we look at war." *The New Yorker*'s David Denby, anxious as ever to show that he had taken the required Humanities class as an undergraduate at Columbia—and had retaken it recently—went on about the Omaha Beach scenes and gurgled that Spielberg's accomplishment was such that only "Homer and Tolstoy have attained a comparable cruel magnificence." Janet Maslin was equally keyed up in the *New York Times*: "This film simply looks at war as if war had not been looked at before." As for those battle scenes, Maslin advised, "Imagine Hieronymus Bosch with a Steadicam."

Owen Gleiberman of *Entertainment Weekly* even managed to decide that the D-Day landing sequence was somehow "revolutionary." In reality, other than recognizing Tom Hanks from *Sleepless in Seattle* and other movies, the soldiers in this opening assault are not characters we know, just so many movie extras, and therefore the sequence was at heart just a Spielberg thrill-ride for people with strong stomachs—it was ultimately escapist entertainment.

The director claimed he was doing publicity for the film primarily because "I just want people to know that this movie is extremely close to reality. It doesn't glorify or titillate, as violence in summer movies usually does. This movie in effect may re-sensitize people who thought they were desensitized to violence." Gleiberman would describe the D-Day scene thusly: "For nearly half an hour, Spielberg uses his unparalleled kinetic genius to create an excruciatingly sustained cataclysm of carnage, nausea, and death. Everywhere, there are men with their limbs blown off, their insides hanging out, and the lapping tides run dark with blood." *Newsday*'s John Anderson observed that Spielberg made the violence in this episode "so overwhelming and inescapable that the only way to survive it . . . is to be a lead actor in his movie."

Ironically, because Spielberg was so reliant on technical cinematic wizardry—and throwing blood on the camera lens—the effect was to draw the viewer away from the carnage, not into it, since one could not help but be aware of the effects the director and his cinematographer were employing. As Vincent Canby wrote, "This is the way Omaha Beach must have looked and sounded. So it goes for five minutes, ten minutes, fifteen minutes and on. But then you, too, begin to suffer your own kind of shell shock. You are, after all, watching a movie. You can see the red exit sign at the side of the screen. You smell the aroma of the simulated butter on the popcorn being wolfed down by the person next to you. You become conscious of the editing, of the technology of the aural effects, of the fact that the gruesome images aren't much different in degree from those featured in commonplace, R-rated slasher films made for teenagers. There are just more of them, packed more closely, and, unlike those in slasher movies, you're supposed to believe them." Still, Owen Gleiberman's conclusion was "*Saving Private Ryan* says that only by confronting the pitiless horror of World War II can we truly know its heroism. For the first time, a movie has shown us both." Whatever.

Some critics besides Canby did manage to keep their wits about them. Tom Carson of *Esquire* averred, "Honestly, I can't see much that Hitler would have changed in *Saving Private Ryan* except the color of the uniforms," and he called the film "one of the most mindlessly adulatory war movies of all time—one that treats combat as horrific, but only on the way to making it sublime." Carson did accept that Spielberg was no hypocrite, though, "mainly because hypocrisy requires some forethought; for all his gifts, Spielberg is less reflective than almost any director of his caliber." Jonathan Rosenbaum of the *Chicago Reader* panned *Saving Private Ryan* in the same column that he raved about Joe Dante's *Small Soldiers* ("a trenchant satire masquerading as a summer kids' movie that's rude enough to suggest that the emotions and fancies underlying the make-believe war games boys like to play are not so different from the sentiments and fabrications underlying real wars, including our escapades in places such as Vietnam and the Persian Gulf."). Rosenbaum wrote, "I never could shake the impression that all I was watching was every other war film Spielberg

had ever seen. The same chestnuts implicitly critiqued in the opening mayhem soon reappear, and it becomes clear that the major lesson Spielberg has to teach us about war is what he's learned from a lifetime of moviegoing. And what he's learned turns out to be something for everyone rather than a single vision: war is hell, war is absurd, war is necessary, war is unnecessary, war is uplifting, war is depressing, war is a lesson in morality, war is a lesson in immorality, and so on." Rosenbaum also sighed that the film contained "nothing that suggests an independent vision, unless you count seeing more limbs blown off than usual (the visceral opening sequence) or someone getting graphically shot underwater."

There were philosophical themes underpinning *Saving Private Ryan*, most particularly the question of the relative value of individual lives, as personified in the main plot device of eight men being forced to risk their hides in order to try to save one person. But neither Spielberg nor screenwriter Robert Rodat—nor the many rewriters on the movie—seemed interested in or—more likely—capable of delving into this issue with any depth and clarity. David Sterritt of the *Christian Science Monitor* concluded that, "What holds *Saving Private Ryan* short of excellence, despite the vigor of its acting and the impact of Spielberg's technical skills, is its failure to explore these moral dilemmas with all the depth and dignity they deserve." And Louis Menand of the *New York Review of Books* felt that in the context of the film, the soldiers are not so much on a mission to rescue Ryan as they are fighting for his mom, and, therefore, the entire concept of "Motherhood." Menand felt that things would have been a lot more interesting if Private Ryan was "a character of less than admirable proportions." Instead, Matt Damon's Ryan is "so fresh-faced and noble he refuses the offer of safe conduct home; moved as he is by the news of his brothers, he'd rather stay and face death side by side with his comrades. It's that kind of movie." David Hinckley of the *New York Daily News* chuckled, "You've got to admire Steven Spielberg. He discovers war is hell and, suddenly, that's news."

Honor Thy Father and Mother

USA Today's Mike Clark liked the star of *Saving Private Ryan*: "A complete ensemble effort, the film still gains much of its power from Hanks, who looks appropriately drained, disoriented and on the verge of nervous collapse." But Stanley Kauffmann of *The New Republic*, finding that "once the Private Ryan mission starts, the picture becomes a good war movie, not much more," wrote "add to the disappointments the performance of Tom Hanks, usually an engaging deputy for us all, as the captain. His dialogue is a bit starchy—because he was a schoolteacher in civilian life, I guess!—but, unlike the men around him, he never seems to have quite burrowed into the earth of battle."

Hanks wasn't merely fulfilling his little boy dream of starring in a war movie, he was on a mission. "I can't fight in World War II," he said, "but maybe I can do my part to help people understand." And just as he had done his darndest to make America proud of its heroic astronauts, he was soon huckstering for World War II soldiers, serving as spokesperson for a campaign to get them a kitschy monument down on the mall in Washington. Hanks had produced an extended series on HBO dealing with the U.S. space program and, with Spielberg, he would eventually go on to do the same for the Second World War. Spielberg said *Saving Private Ryan* was also designed to be a learning experience, intended to make Americans rethink the way that "the deep pride we once felt in our flag" had been overtaken by "cynicism about our colors." Indeed, *Saving Private Ryan* set into motion the process of sentimentalizing the men and women who participated in World War II and, in fact, the entire generation that grew up in the Depression—the very people that now-middle-aged baby boomers had rebelled against in the '60s. Which just shows you the cyclical nature of historical perceptions.

This canonization turned into something of a phenomenon. Tom Brokaw's exaltation of the people now in their seventies and eighties, *The Greatest Generation*, was a number one best-seller by year's end and among those on *People*'s list of the "25 Most Intriguing People of 1998" was The World War II Soldier. *New York Times* op-ed columnist Maureen Dowd wrote of the anguish of having been born too late: "Suddenly, baby boomers realize that, despite a buzzing economy and a passel of luxury goods, we are going to die without experiencing the nobility that illuminated the lives of our parents and grandparents. They lived through wars and depressions, life and death, good stomping evil. Our unifying event was *Seinfeld*." Writing in *The New Yorker*, John Gregory Dunne scoffed that "The post-*Ryan* patriotism of the middle class is a virtual patriotism, meaning you do not have to do anything about it except express it and wish you had been at the conflict in question. It comes not from the actuality of a war but from a movie about a war. To find patriotism at the cineplex reduces it to a style, a look." Dunne, who was born in 1932, also posited that, "The fact that one was born in the years immediately before or after 1948 does not mean that he or she is automatically morally inferior. Ordering up a world war or a global economic crisis seems a heavy price to pay just to test a generation's mettle."

Although it was still the height of summer, Oscar talk had already begun and it all centered on *Saving Private Ryan*, which was being called a shoo-in for Best Picture, especially after the film turned into a box-office bonanza. Of course, there was always the possibility that this July release would be eclipsed by movies released in the fall and at Christmas, movies that would be fresher in the minds of Academy voters. Spielberg would have you believe it really didn't matter to him, as he insisted, "I don't make movies to win awards. I mean, I've never made a movie to win an award in my lifetime." At the same time, though, he did show himself to be a student of Oscar history, telling a reporter, "I really believe movies can come out any time. *Silence of the Lambs* came out in February and won Best Picture. If a movie can stand the test of time, it certainly can stand the test of a couple of months."

Unloved

One of the films expected to be a likely contender against *Saving Private Ryan* was the pet project of a woman Steven Spielberg had cast in her first movie. Oprah Winfrey coproduced and was starring in the adaptation of Toni Morrison's Pulitzer Prize–winning novel *Beloved*—which she had wanted to turn into a movie since reading it in 1987. Directed by Jonathan Demme, *Beloved* told the story of an escaped slave haunted by the ghost of her murdered child. The benevolent Winfrey informed *TV Guide* that the movie was "an offering, a gift, so people can see the humanity of our history, see the humanity of ourselves," and she told CNN, "This wasn't just work, this was necessary, this was *necessary*. This was part of the reason I was born." Winfrey insisted that giving the lead role to herself "really isn't about my ego at all. I just wanted to see it get done with earnestness and truth." And as a show of her seriousness of purpose, "I literally just removed myself from all communication with the world. I did not turn on the television, with the exception of Princess Diana's death."

The film contained brutal portrayals of slave life and the supernatural scenes, too, were unusually graphic; some people referred to *Beloved* as "a cross between *Roots* and *The Exorcist*." Winfrey told her loyal television audience, "I won't shut up about it, I will not . . . I hope you all go see it this weekend. I feel like I'm giving birth to my baby after ten years of labor." She also treated her viewers to footage of her attending four premiere screenings of the film in four cities (opening night in New York was described as "one of the most magical nights"; while premiere number four in Los Angeles "was a storybook ending to making the movie of my dreams"). On the second of two successive *Oprah* programs dedicated to *Beloved*, Winfrey announced, "I believe that it will touch America's heart . . . You have never seen a movie like this before." And after clips were shown, she wiped away the tears. Winfrey did acknowledge that the movie was not necessarily what her television audience would have expected from her, and that, in fact, they might have a hard time seeing her appearing in *any* movie: "With me there's a familiarity that movie stars don't get. When Liz Taylor's in a restaurant, people stare and whisper. When they see me, they pull up a chair and tell me Liz Taylor's over there."

"Majestic, confounding and rich with secrets, *Beloved* runs bravely against the grain of market-driven Hollywood entertainment. Here's a film, nearly three hours long, that doesn't sanitize its tale of African American loss and survival—the way Steven Spielberg's *The Color Purple* did—but delves deeply, heartbreakingly into an American tragedy," raved Edward Guthmann of the *San Francisco Chronicle*. "The movie is tough and frightening and devastatingly sad—how's that for a commercial recipe?—but also gorgeous and haunting, a drama to chew on for days afterward." Kenneth Turan wrote in the *Los Angeles Times*, "*Beloved* is ungainly and hard to follow at times, like the proverbial giant not quite sure how to best use its strength. But that power exists, present and undeniable, and once this film gets its bearings, the unsentimental fierceness of its vision brushes obstacles and quibbles from its path."

Three weeks after the film opened, Bernard Weinraub asked in the *New York Times*, "What happened to *Beloved*?" He noted that the $80-million film had been "one of the most lavishly advertised films of the fall and received generally respectful reviews. Its star and producer is one of the most popular figures in America, Oprah Winfrey, who aggressively promoted the movie on her talk show and in numerous newspaper, magazine and television interviews. So did Jonathan Demme, the Academy Award winning director and one of the most respected filmmakers in Hollywood. And yet the film has grossed only about $21.2 million since it opened, less even than many of those who predicted tough box-office sledding had foreseen." "All there is is pain," Joe Roth, the chair of Disney told Weinraub. "You try to do something good, artistic, adult. It's like barking in the wind . . . I feel badly for Jonathan and Oprah." The *Hollywood Reporter*'s Martin Grove observed, "The problem seems to be that when a movie is three hours long, and word of mouth says that it's depressing and brutal, most people would rather do something else." If, as Winfrey claimed, *Beloved* was a gift to the American people, it was akin to giving a pair of socks as a birthday present to an eight-year-old boy.

By early December—just weeks after the movie's release—*Journey to Beloved*, the elegant coffee table book containing Winfrey's journal from when she was making the picture, had been dumped into the 50 percent off bin at Borders and Barnes & Noble.

Camp Humor

While one of the most famous people in America struck out at the box office, a little known figure from Italy was hitting the big time—Winfrey probably should have made *Beloved* with Miramax rather than Disney. Roberto Benigni was a major comic star in his native Italy, but he was a vague figure in the United States, known, if at all, for supporting roles in a couple of Jim Jarmusch pictures, *Down By Law* and *Night on Earth*. He also starred in *Son of the Pink Panther*, where his mugging made the audience long not just for Peter Sellers but even for Ted Wass in *Curse of the Pink Panther*.

In *Life Is Beautiful* (*La Vita è bella* in Italy), which he wrote, directed, and starred in, Benigni aimed to have fun with the Holocaust. He played Guido, an Italian Jew in the Mussolini era who, in the first part of the film, woos and captures the beautiful Dora, played by his wife; that she is irresistibly attracted to his goofball ways is just the first of the film's many implausibilities. (Despite his numskull behavior, audiences were asked to accept Guido as an intellectual whose dream is to open a bookstore.) Time goes by, they have a good time and they have a son, but then the Nazis come to town and they are whisked away to a concentration camp—the wife's not Jewish but she insists on going, too, another indication of a none-too-credible narrative. In this one particular camp, the Nazis seem not to follow the usual protocol of separating parents and children, so Guido gets to stay with his son and tries to make things nice for the kid by pretending it's all just one big game.

The film was immensely popular in Italy—despite considerable controversy about its lack of respect for Holocaust victims—and Miramax picked up the American rights. Most die-hard American film fans had the same initial reaction when they heard that a Holocaust comedy was on its way: Why don't they just release *The Day the Clown Cried*, the 1972 Jerry Lewis movie about a clown who leads children in a concentration camp to the gas chamber? (The *New York Post's*

Rod Dreher said of *The Day the Clown Cried*: "The legendary film is said to be in such hideous taste that Lewis himself has locked up the only print in a vault and won't show it to anybody," not even Benigni, who had requested a screening.)

Benigni knew the right things to say. When asked at a press conference if he was Jewish, the Catholic comic responded, "I don't have that honor," which was exactly how Charlie Chaplin had replied to the same question while he was promoting *The Great Dictator*. "The Holocaust belongs to everybody," Benigni asserted, upon hearing the suggestion that it'd be better to reserve this kind of material for Jewish filmmakers. "It's a story about humanity. Whenever I read one of Primo Levi's books, or other books about the Holocaust, I am not the same as the day before. It changed my life. It belongs to me." *Life Is Beautiful* had been shown in Israel before its American engagement, and the hyperactive Benigni—who seemed to think he was being delightful by playing up Italian stereotypes when he spoke English—wanted to make sure that everyone in the States knew that "In Israel, mamma mia, they gave me a lot of prizes. The mayor of Israel and the president, they planted for me some trees in Israel. *This* is my Oscar."

The film was shown at Cannes, where Benigni gave a preview of the schtick America was in store for once he got to the United States to plug the film: When *Life Is Beautiful* received the runner-up prize at the festival, he ran to the stage and laid prone on the floor before an embarrassed jury president, Martin Scorsese, and then began extravagantly kissing his feet. Having put his mouth all over Scorsese's shoes, Benigni proceeded to kiss the other jury members on the face.

The Return of Colonel Klink

In Italy, *Life Is Beautiful* swept the Donatello Awards. In America, reaction ran the gamut. Mike Clark of *USA Today* said, "Art house sentimentalists will likely go for *Beautiful* in a big way, but even those who aggressively resist manipulation can find a lot to admire. To see someone even attempt a bittersweet treatment of this subject is surprising, but to largely pull it off is a major feat." (Despite his praise for the movie, Clark said, "One has to take it on faith that Braschi's Dora character would instantly find Benigni's calamity-prone Guido so thoroughly cute—and that Guido's fellow camp inmates would put up with his boisterously elaborate schemes to convince the boy that their enforced camp tenure is really just a game.") Jami Bernard of the *New York Daily News* said, "If you can get past whether the subject can ever be mined for laughs or used as a backdrop to illustrate a lesser theme, Roberto Benigni's *Life Is Beautiful* is a rare blend of comedy and tenderness whose point is not the horrors of war but the lengths a parent will go to protect his child's innocence."

Given that he was a clown of a movie reviewer, one might have expected *Slate*'s David Edelstein to love *Life Is Beautiful*. Instead, the ever-eloquent Edelstein wrote, "Benigni's movie made me want to throw up," and deemed the film "a monstrous ego trip—a clown's megalomania"; he was disgusted by "the power of Benigni to celebrate, Jerry Lewis-like, his own beautiful martyrdom. Imagine Harpo Marx giving the hot foot to a pompous official, who takes out a machine gun and blows him away: That's how cheap Benigni's hash of farce and tragedy is. It's a gas, all right." *The New Republic*'s Stanley Kauffmann carped that, "Any repugnance we might feel is supposed to be swept away by the wash of paternal love, Guido's intent to protect his son from the facts. This protection is so blatantly impossible that the paternal love begins to seem theatrically phony. Even a small child (if he had been able to survive with his father) would have seen fairly soon that the object of the camp was not to have fun, a fact that renders Benigni's idea much less a moving instance of love than an actor's shallow conceit." *National Review*'s John Simon wrote, "Hard to tell who is the bigger idiot: the smart, precocious kid who falls for this running lie, or the audience that falls for this movie."

Kauffmann surmised that Benigni "couldn't devise enough material to set the whole film in the camp, so he fills the first half of the picture with his slapstick" and Andrew Sarris wrote in the *New York Observer* that "there are no real laughs in the first half of the movie but instead just a series of forced slapstick con-

trivances." *Salon*'s Charles Taylor, who was disturbed by "the sheer callous inappropriateness of comedy existing within the physical reality of the camps," was another of the critics who didn't find the film's early sections any great shakes either, largely because of the shortcomings of the star: "He's an adequate physical comic, though he lacks a coherent persona, seeming too canny for the scrapes Guido keeps walking into. Benigni also lacks the effortless precision of the great physical clowns, and the manic spark beneath their surface calm. The funniest gags in Keaton or Chaplin or Mack Sennett two-reelers feel at first unexpected, and then inevitable. Benigni lays out the gags so we see them coming. When he accepts eggs as payment for helping out on a farm, it's only a matter of time before they end up on somebody's head. But obviousness doesn't equal offensiveness, and for an hour or so, *Life Is Beautiful* is nothing more than uninspired bits and worked-up whimsy." John Simon asked, "Comics do not have to be good-looking, but must they be as unappealing as the inverted-eggplant-headed, chinless wonder Benigni, with his passive-aggressive charmlessness and fish-eyed simpletonism?

Miramax knew that its subject matter made *Life Is Beautiful* a dicey proposition, and that the film had to be handled very carefully. The studio tried to deflect criticism preemptively by sticking an essay by Andrew Stille, an expert on Italian Jews in the Mussolini era, in the press kit. Stille assured everyone that the gang at Miramax and Benigni himself were cognizant that "the concentration camp that Benigni describes in no way approximates the horror of the actual camps." But that's okay because "the film is not striving for straightforward realism." Stille's little treatise wasn't very persuasive because scores of detractors found the pristine condition of this camp to be particularly noisome. *The Nation*'s Stuart Klawans said it "looks like the courtyard of a little factory," while Ella Taylor of *L.A. Weekly* complained, "The director gives us not just a pop Holocaust but a prettified, palatable Holocaust, guaranteed to convince any naive observer that Auschwitz was a slightly unsavory boot camp whose minor discomforts could be hurdled with a little ingenuity and a sunny outlook." Richard Schickel of *Time* groaned, "The place is clean, and though the work is hard and the rations are short, no one seems to sicken or die. There are references to mass extermination, but that brutal reality is never vividly presented. Indeed, the prisoners don't seem to see much of their jailers, who, when they do turn up, act as if they've drifted into this film from a *Hogan's Heroes* rerun—barking incomprehensible orders to cover their comic ineptitude." On the other hand, Michael Wilmington of the *Chicago Tribune*, in the midst of cooing that this thing was "a deeply moving blend of cold terror and rapturous hilarity," somehow managed to think that it took place "in a notably grim concentration camp." Well, maybe the bulb on the projector where he saw it was dim.

Benigni himself had a ready answer anytime *Life Is Beautiful* was criticized for sugarcoating the terror of the Holocaust. The movie wasn't supposed to be true-to-life, it's just a "fable," you see—which would mean that Nazi guards had no more basis in reality than a fairy tale witch. Miramax hadn't gotten to where it was by not knowing that you sell this material by emphasizing the "humanistic" feel-good elements. It also made sure that prominently displayed on early Oscar ads for the film was a testimony from the *Jerusalem Report* that "*Life Is Beautiful* is a dazzling exposition of the way in which love, tenderness and humor can sustain the human spirit." And the studio had its radar out, looking for any possible rumblings that could upset the pretty picture it had so studiously tried to present. When the author of *Inside Oscar 2* was quoted in *USA Today* as saying that there could well be controversy over "the issue of whether or not it trivializes the Holocaust," he received a phone message from someone working on Miramax's Oscar campaigns saying, "I'd love to share with you some of the responses we have gotten from the Jewish community, which are just extraordinary, from survivors, etc."

Prosciutto

Benigni stormed the United States on a long-term publicity campaign, demonstratively proclaiming how much he loved people and how much goodness he had in his heart and how the mass exterminations in the concentration camps pained him so. His appearances on talk shows were marked by a contrived zaniness intended to endear him to America. Nothing the man did seemed spontaneous, from his dancing onto the stage and leaping into the arms of both Jay Leno *and* Conan O'Brien, sprinting into the audience to nuzzle with women, staring at and pawing the female guest sitting next to him (on Leno's *Tonight Show*, Sarah Ferguson, the former Duchess of York, looked to be genuinely appalled and maybe even a bit frightened by him), or pretending he didn't speak English well, so that he would make gibberish come out of his mouth. He told Jay Leno he found him "handsome and sexy . . . a cross between Gene Kelly and Sharon Stone." On *Live with Regis and Kathie Lee*, he kneeled before Kathie Lee Gifford and kissed her hand, and then tried to smooch Regis Philbin, who would have none of it. As part of his calculated antics on television, he'd inevitably jump out of his seat and run around, amusing the audience in the same way that, say, a misbehaving trained chimpanzee would. Tellingly, when he was profiled on *60 Minutes*, he spoke nearly flawless English and was low-keyed and serious. Realizing that many people found Benigni's being a horse's ass funny and endearing, the minority who were hold-outs could only paraphrase what author Martin Amis once said about Ronald Reagan: "Roberto Benigni. Everyone you know hates him. Everyone you don't know loves him."

"Whether or not the tears it jerks are artistically earned, they come as surely as the rising of the sun," said Andrew Sarris. This was the ace that Benigni and Miramax were holding on to, for the true antecedent for *Life Is Beautiful* was not a Holocaust picture like *Schindler's List* or *The Shop on Main Street*, but *Cinema Paradiso*. The 1989 Italian film that had brought Miramax one of its first Oscars was every bit as maudlin as *Life Is Beautiful* and now, once again, many people, sobbing as the lights came on in the theater, mistook bathos for profundity. And they recommended *Life Is Beautiful* to equally gullible friends, who recommended it to more equally gullible friends, and before you knew it, *Life Is Beautiful*—aided by a deep-pocketed Miramax advertising campaign—was a huge art house hit. John Simon shared that "Two middle-aged women who recognized me and queried me about it on the bus simply could not get it through their heads that I was calling the film not excellent but execrable." Essayist Ron Rosenbaum pondered in the *New York Observer*, why do "so many Jews—starting with the Weinstein brothers at Miramax—celebrate this hideously condescending trivialization of their tragedy. A film so self-congratulatory, so self-reverential about its star's puny posturing, it ought to be called not *Life Is Beautiful* but *I Am Beautiful*."

In ballyhooing his movie, Benigni said, "I believe that laughter saves us, it forces us to consider the other side of things, the surreal and funny side. Being able to imagine prevents us from being reduced to ashes." Which was not the most judicious choice of words, since millions of people literally were reduced to ashes in the Holocaust. And if they had followed Benigni's advice and laughed on their way into the gas chambers it would not have changed a thing.

Rio-Realism

Roberto Benigni's Holocaust farce wasn't the only foreign film garnering attention in the fall. Sony Classics was counting on its Brazilian film, *Central Station*, to find a cross-over audience. The tale of an embittered retired schoolteacher who helps a young boy try to find his father may have sounded, at first blush, like the standard saccharine stuff that was currently plaguing art house theaters. But *Central Station* was much tougher than most films of this genre. As F. X. Feeney wrote in the *L.A. Weekly*, "A cranky loner and a helpless, headstrong child make a journey that changes both their lives. If that isn't the oldest story in movies, it's close. *Central Station* appears to be yet another, but [the characters] are freshly observed, and their adventure is beautifully devoid of manipulating inflection . . . a gradual alchemy transpires between the two that is all the more deeply moving for defying predictable sentiments." *Time Out New York* said, "In Hollywood's hands, this would amount to a heaping helping of schmaltz, but director Walter Salles, a former documentarian, brings an unexpected degree of honesty and wisdom to the tale." And *Time*'s Richard Schickel felt, "Theirs is an odyssey of simple problems, simple emotional discoveries, a relationship full of knots that

Salles permits to unwind in an unforced, unsentimental fashion. His imagery, like his storytelling, is clear, often unaffectedly lovely, and quietly, powerfully haunting."

In contrast to Roberto Benigni's middling reviews as an actor, the star of *Central Station*, Fernanda Montenegro was universally praised. Rex Reed raved, "the great, expressive, baggy-eyed Fernanda Montenegro combines the volcanic energy of Anna Magnani with the terrific innocence of Giulietta Masina" and called her "galvanizing." Troy Patterson wrote in *Entertainment Weekly*, "Montenegro acts the part superbly by playing it with her eyes," and Tom Meek of the *Boston Phoenix*, said, "Montenegro, gracefully dignified as the reluctant matriarch, gives one of the year's best performances."

Central Station did well, but it couldn't touch the Italian film's grosses. *Central Station* director Walter Salles specifically said of his film, "This is not a fable."

Worshipping the Gods

When *Gods and Monsters* played at Sundance, it was shown out of competition. This situation prompted *Entertainment Weekly*'s Lisa Schwarzbaum to contemplate in her wrap-up of the festival, "Why wasn't *Gods and Monsters* up for an award? If it had been, writer-director Bill Condon's satisfying, inventive cinemaphile fantasy about the last years of *Frankenstein* director James Whale and a young gardener he fancies, would have been a shoo-in for honors. It's got *Death in Venice* depth and great performances by Ian McKellen and Brendan Fraser."

Even with that endorsement and an enthusiastic audience response, *Gods and Monsters* had a difficult time finding a distributor—while Miramax, for instance, in one of its stupidest blunders, was shelling out $6 million for the romantic comedy, *Next Stop Wonderland*, as well as another $3 million for the Australian film, *The Castle*, and $2.5 million for *Jerry and Tom* (which was never released) after their Sundance screenings. Finally, *Gods and Monsters* was picked up by a fledgling company, Lions Gate, and, after playing at a number of additional film festivals, including Seattle, Deauville, and New York, it was released in the fall.

Shot in twenty-four days on a $3-million budget, the film used a character study of two disparate individuals, an ailing, openly gay former movie director and his young straight yard man, as a starting point for an examination of the nature of friendship, love, and longing, and a look at sexual identity during Hollywood's Golden Age. It received rapturous reviews. "*Gods and Monsters* is a nearly perfect movie," hailed Bob Stephens of the *San Francisco Examiner*. "When film historians write the cinematic history of this decade, it will surely be included. Bill Condon, who demonstrated his talent with quirky, imaginative screenplays for two cult films of the '80s, *Strange Behavior* and *Strange Invaders*, has written one of the most complex and powerful literary scripts in recent times. And his direction, which relies on an imaginative use of the medium in editing and pictorial composition instead of special effects, is outstanding." Bob Strauss of the *Los Angeles Daily News* said, "Mary Shelley couldn't have imagined the movies when she wrote *Frankenstein, or The Modern Prometheus* in 1818. Had she known a film like *Gods and Monsters* could be made, she might not have been so pessimistic about man's presumptuous determination to create something that could live forever."

Now that *Gods and Monsters* was in theaters, Lisa Schwarzbaum could go on about it at length, and she enthused, "Bill Condon has made a deeply touching, elegant, and inventive biographical fantasy. *Gods and Monsters* is an extraordinarily graceful film about desire, aging, and the creative harnessing of personal pain into art (low and high), which is, of course, what a good chunk of moviemaking is always about." *USA Today*'s Susan Wloszczyna said, "Chances are, the more you love classic cinema, the more you will find *Gods* is your cup of tea. As Whale, who feigns indifference about his accomplishments, finally admits, 'Making movies is the most wonderful thing in the world.' Watching movies this well-done isn't bad, either." And, in *The Advocate*, Jan Stuart cheered, "*Gods and Monsters* is a triumph on all levels, a movie for people who love movies and for people who love people who love movies."

Gods and Monsters contained a brief epilogue, featuring Brendan Fraser's gardener character and taking place several years after the rest of the film. Dave Kehr of the *New York Daily News* said it was "the most beautiful ending of any American film in years, a coda of reconciliation and remembrance set in a gentle L.A. rain," while *The New Yorker*'s Anthony Lane called the closing shot "one of the loveliest I have ever seen."

Praise for the cast of *Gods and Monsters* was equally enthusiastic. Kenneth Turan marveled, "There are so many colors to McKellen's performance, so many diverse emotions fleetingly play on his face, that resisting his art is out of the question. Better work by an actor will not be seen this year." Rene Rodriguez of the *Miami Herald* echoed that sentiment: "In *Gods and Monsters*, Ian McKellen gives the performance of the year. It's not just McKellen's lascivious, tremendously enjoyable flamboyance that makes his work such a standout (Whale flaunted his homosexuality at a time when few dared to do so, which McKellen illustrates in little touches, such as the manner in which he smokes his cigars). It's McKellen's ability to capture the poignance of a man confronting his own mortality with a mixture of nostalgia, dignity and desperation that makes the performance so profoundly moving."

In addition to McKellen, Brendan Fraser and a heavily made-up Lynn Redgrave, who played Whale's devoted Hungarian maid, were also cited for their performances. Robert W. Butler of the *Kansas City Star* insisted, "We should feel fortunate any time a movie delivers a great performance. *Gods and Monsters* has three of them," and maintained that the "most amazing turn comes from Fraser (that's right, George of the Jungle) who nicely holds his own against the overwhelming McKellen. It's Fraser's performance that gives the film heart." Chris Vognar of the *Dallas Morning News* also lauded Fraser: "Going toe-to-toe with an all-time great, the young actor shows what he can do with a meaty role that doesn't require swinging from vines . . . He doesn't just hold his own in the one-on-one scenes; he sells the part and brings out all of Clayton's emotional wrinkles. After several years of passable performances in thin roles, Mr. Fraser has become an actor."

Rolling Stone's Peter Travers, who called the film "elegantly witty and haunting," said "Lynn Redgrave is fantastic in a role that combines high comedy with aching tenderness." *The Daily Show*'s resident gay cut-up, Frank DeCaro rhapsodized, "Georgy Girl plays a Nazi fag hag in a French maid's uniform! What's not to love?" Continuing a resurgence that began with *Shine*, Redgrave noted that in recent years she "couldn't get arrested in Hollywood." Of her work in *Gods and Monsters*, she laughed, "I'm delighted to say that a lot of people don't recognize me in this, at least not until the closing credits. They don't expect it, and that is actually the best compliment I could have." The film was a professional reunion for Redgrave and McKellen: the two old friends had first worked together on the stage in the early 1960s.

Sir Ian was the most prominent openly gay actor so it almost seemed preordained that he should be playing the openly gay director. But he admitted that, prior to reading the script, he was completely unfamiliar with James Whale who, in addition to the first two *Frankenstein* movies, also directed the 1936 version of *Show Boat*. As he researched the character, McKellen was amazed at the similarities he had with the filmmaker: "I discovered that the Lyric Theatre Hammersmith is where Whale first acted in London. It's where I first acted. The Savoy Theatre in London is where he had his first production; it's where I directed for the first time. In London he lived at 410 Kings Road, I lived at 306A. And when he moved to Hollywood he lived just up the road." The *San Francisco Chronicle* wanted to know if his costar was "uncomfortable with any of the material, the sexual undercurrents?" McKellen replied that Brendan Fraser "had no embarrassment about anything in the story. He's resolutely straight but resolutely gay-friendly, as so many young people are nowadays. We got on very, very well and worked together on the script and would go to the director and discuss it with him. It was an entirely satisfactory relationship, and now we're good friends."

Considering that *Gods and Monsters* gave the fifty-nine-year-old Ian McKellen by far the best reviews of his film career, it was ironic that he originally had doubts about doing the movie. "My agent kept harassing his agent until he finally read it," said Bill Condon. "Ian was interested, but his concern was that he had already agreed to do *Apt Pupil*, in which he plays a seventy-seven-year-old ex-Nazi, and in this movie, he

would be at death's door. He's really throwing himself into the idea of becoming a presence in film, and he didn't want people perceiving him as this ancient codger. So I told him that we would also be shooting flashback scenes of Whale in the 1930s shooting *Bride of Frankenstein*, and we showed him these pictures of Whale, who was this very handsome, dashing man and this impeccable dresser. Ian looked at those and said 'Oh, he's very dishy.'"

Condon got a laugh when he heard *Gods and Monsters* described as "a gay *Sunset Boulevard*" because that "seemed redundant to me." Liz Smith wrote that, "*Gods and Monsters* has turned into quite a little moneymaker. But here's a bit of inside dish. Originally, Fraser had agreed to complete exposure in the scene in which he poses nude. But the week the scene was scheduled to shoot, Fraser's family comedy for Disney, *George of the Jungle*, opened to surprisingly big box office, and Brendan's 'people' persuaded *Gods and Monsters* director Bill Condon to suggest rather than show all of the star's gifts. Image still counts in Hollywood-land." The movie was based on Christopher Bram's novel, *Father of Frankenstein*, and the title was changed largely because of Brendan Fraser; the original name sounded too cheap and exploitative said the star of *Airheads* and *Encino Man*.

I Knew Her Before She Was a Virgin

Queen Elizabeth the First has been a staple of the movies, going back at least as far as Sarah Bernhardt's portrayal in 1912. Her latest screen incarnation came with the advance word that it was going to be a new kind of historical biography. Gone would be the stilted dialogue and reverential treatment; instead, *Elizabeth* was promised to be a full-throttled melodrama, with passions akin to a 1980s' prime-time soap opera transported to the sixteenth century. Star Cate Blanchett referred to the film as "*Dallas* in tights."

Elizabeth takes place in the periods immediately before and after the Queen took the throne at age twenty-five in the midst of a maelstrom of intrigue between Catholic and Protestant factions in England.

Coproducer Tim Bevan said, "We wanted to stamp a contemporary feel onto our story, and with the early part of her reign being filled with such uncertainty, we decided to structure it like a conspiracy thriller." Another of the film's producers, Alison Owen added, "We were a lot more influenced by films like *The Godfather* than by previous historical dramas. Although it is a film that is very true in spirit to the Tudor times, historical veracity has not been our main point of contact. We have not changed facts but manipulated time periods." And even though the monarch went down in history as "the Virgin Queen," adding to the movie's contemporary feel was a passionate affair with Robert Dudley, the Earl of Leicester. By the end of the film, she reverts to her virgin status for the good of Protestantism.

The British producers imported a director from India, Shekhar Kapur, whose film *Bandit Queen*, a violent feminist action movie, had caused a sensation in his native country; Tim Bevan acknowledged that Kapur, who had never directed an English-language film, didn't know the first thing about Queen Elizabeth, but he considered that a positive attribute because Kapur wouldn't be hemmed in by any history book preconceptions. Kapur declared that his challenge on *Elizabeth* "was to break the rules. I think the cinema has too many rules. I thought the sheer madness of doing this was so exciting, to make a very human story which, although historical, has the essence of something quite contemporary." The director's pet name for the film was *Thoroughly Modern Lizzie*.

Kapur may not have known anything about Queen Elizabeth, but somewhere along the line he discovered that "It's been a tradition in England, and perhaps all over the world: The prime role every actress wants to play is Elizabeth. Why? Because she was the fantastically greatest and most powerful woman who ever lived." The intent of his film was to show the Queen before her "image was created," a woman "able to look vulnerable, in love, inept. So I needed an actress who could look extremely strong and extremely vulnerable in the same movie." After Emily Watson turned down the role, he cast Australian actress Cate Blanchett, having seen clips of her in the Gillian Armstrong film, *Oscar and Lucinda*: "I saw a face that, at

times, looked like it belonged to a spirit and not a person. That was great for a character who some would say becomes a shell, an image. And Cate also had a face that looked like it could belong to 400 years ago." In *Oscar and Lucinda*, she played opposite Ralph Fiennes. This time out, her leading man was Ralph's brother, Joseph, while the man who beat Ralph for Best Actor in 1996, Geoffrey Rush, was present as a court adviser.

Well, it certainly *was* a different sort of historical drama. "If you're interested in cinematic folly at its most outrageous, you should definitely check out *Elizabeth*," advised Joe Baltake of the *Sacramento Bee*. "Ostensibly about the tumultuous forty-four-year reign of England's Elizabeth I, Shekhar Kapur's film is really a loony feminist/historical remake of Francis Ford Coppola's *The Godfather* and *The Godfather Part 2*, with young Queen Bess standing in for young Michael Corleone." Mike Clark of *USA Today* lamented that "humor—once a vitalizing component of virtually every Hollywood costumer—is nowhere to be found. It's as disdained as Elizabeth is by Queen Mary of Tudor, her pro-Catholic half-sister whose death paves the way for international turmoil." It was difficult to recall a film with so many arbitrary baroque camera angles and off-kilter cuts—you'd probably have to go back to the 1960s when aping the French New Wave was all the rage for filmmakers no matter what genre they were working in. Jack Mathews of *Newsday* said that director Kapur "will have his Hollywood career. He's a bit of a pack rat, ordering camera moves that would please Brian De Palma and staging a purge of conspirators as an almost direct homage to Francis Ford Coppola. But the film looks fabulous, and in the costume dramas he prefers, that's often enough."

Some people did like the film, though. Roger Ebert adjudged *Elizabeth* to be "A brilliant historical reconstruction and a beautiful film," and would put it on his Ten Best list. Walter Addiego of the *San Francisco Examiner* said, "Often riveting and occasionally ridiculous, *Elizabeth* offers a fresh, highly entertaining view of the storied Virgin Queen . . . The offbeat choice of director suggests that the producers wanted an outsider's perspective on this most celebrated of British monarchs. They got it. This isn't the kind of stodgy costume drama that often gets shipped across the pond. It's thoroughly modern in spirit, not shy of violence, and almost gleefully steeped in realpolitik." Eleanor Ringel of the *Atlanta Journal-Constitution* wrote, "Shekhar Kapur isn't worried about the cliches of historical drama: the portentous, history-in-the-making dialogue, the elaborate royal entertainments, the whispered court intrigues. Rather he embraces them, thus investing them with a renewed vitality. True, there are a few lingering clinkers, but for the most part, the movie's opulent production design (look for some Oscar nominations), accomplished cast and raucous, event-filled narrative win out. . . . The bottom line is simple: *Elizabeth* is a really good story. The story of a girl becoming a woman, of a woman becoming a queen."

Cate Blanchett had to compete with Kapur's extravagant camera movements and most reviewers felt she held her own. Peter Travers found that the actress "has a passionate fire and wit that command attention . . . Blanchett makes Elizabeth's transformation from mouse to marriage-hating monarch such a hypnotic spectacle that you're happy when she stops diddling." Janet Maslin chortled, "The captivating Cate Blanchett rules England in *Elizabeth* as if the monarch's principal responsibilities were being bejeweled, choosing consorts and saying 'Leave us!' with a wave of the hand. This is indeed historical drama for anyone whose idea of history is back issues of *Vogue*." But Maslin did feel that Blanchett "brings spirit, beauty and substance to what might otherwise have been turned into a vacuous role."

Good Will Loving

Queen Elizabeth made an appearance in another late-year release, and coming along with her from *Elizabeth* were Joseph Fiennes and Geoffrey Rush. In late November, *Entertainment Weekly* reported that because among its five Christmas releases there was "no obvious front-runner into which to pour its advertising and energy, Miramax will have to follow the leads of reviewers and position its films with care so as not to have them cancel each other out." Once he got the lay of the land from press screenings, though, Harvey

Weinstein knew that, along with *Life Is Beautiful*, it was *Shakespeare in Love*—and not Woody Allen's *Celebrity*, the kitchen-sink fantasia *Little Voice*, the Maya Angelou adaptation *Down by the Delta* or the Altman wanna-be ensemble piece *Playing By Heart*—that would be the company's Oscar bait. Prior to the screenings, there had been next-to-no pre-release buzz for *Shakespeare in Love*, which only finished post-production a few days before it was shown to critics.

Shakespeare in Love had its genesis when screenwriter Marc Norman's college-age son told him that what he'd like to see someday was a movie about William Shakespeare when he was just starting out as a playwright. Norman mulled it over, and eventually came up with the inherently humorous concept of the Bard having writer's block while he was working on *Romeo and Juliet*. Producer-director Edward Zwick lived nearby and when Norman told him the concept while exchanging neighborly pleasantries, Zwick was so delighted by it he helped the scripter pitch the project at Universal. Norman wrote the screenplay and playwright Tom Stoppard—the author of *Rosencrantz and Guildenstern Are Dead* was an old hand at comic revisionist treatments of Shakespeare—did a touch-up, amplifying the ambience and the literary references, and the project was set to go in 1990 with Daniel Day-Lewis and Julia Roberts in the lead roles. Things fell apart, however, as the two stars moved on to other pictures; Kenneth Branagh and Winona Ryder were the next pair of stars considered but things never materialized and *Shakespeare in Love* went into movie limbo.

Zwick slipped the script to Harvey Weinstein, and Miramax took on the production even though it meant paying not only for the screenplay but covering all the expenses Universal had already laid out—it was the most money Miramax had ever put up to obtain a project. Signed to star were Joseph Fiennes in the title role and Gwyneth Paltrow, who was pretty much becoming the Miramax house actress. Another Miramax regular, Ben Affleck, had a secondary role and Geoffrey Rush played a debt-ridden producer. John Madden, who had made *Mrs. Brown* for Miramax, was the director, and his Queen Victoria from that picture would be Queen Elizabeth here. Judi

Dench was playing the monarch from the other end of the spectrum than Cate Blanchett in *Elizabeth* and she announced, "As the film is set towards the end of Elizabeth's life, she is not in great physical condition, so for example she has the most awful teeth which I'd like to make clear to everyone watching the film, are not my own!"

The plot centered on a broke Shakespeare in desperate need of a muse and finding one in a young woman who is posing as man in order to follow her heart and perform on the stage. The film was peppered with references to the Elizabethan theater scene as well as containing proudly anachronistic humor. Because she had to play many of her scenes as a man, Gwyneth Paltrow revealed, "I learned how to talk much lower and how to walk. The costume department made me this heavy, triangular-shaped bean bag which I stuffed in my tights, and it's great to have that weight, that shift of gravity. It's the only form of Method acting I've ever done, but it really helped." On the *Tonight Show*, Jay Leno commented to Paltrow, "You play a girl playing a guy, which seems like a stretch." The actress shrugged, "Well, depends on where you're looking from." Leno then gave her a deliberate once-over and concluded, "I can't imagine any place where I would look, 'cause there's no place I can see where you can pass for a guy. Maybe a tooth."

Philip Wuntch of the *Dallas Morning News* called *Shakespeare in Love* "a feel-great movie. It stirs a terrific awareness of both the exhilaration and pain of artistry and creativity. And you can also be assured that it makes you feel terrific about love, romance and sex. The exquisite movie has a quality that few contemporary comedies can claim—genuine verbal wit. Almost every line of dialogue provokes a smile, a chuckle or a guffaw." Kenneth Turan found the movie to be "a ray of light in a holiday film season that was starting to look as gloomy as the scowl on Ebenezer Scrooge's face. A happy conceit smoothly executed, this is one of those entertaining confections that's so pleasing to the eye and ear you'd have to be a genuine Scrooge to struggle against it." *Time*'s Richard Corliss beamed, "The true, rare glamour of the piece is its revival of two precious movie tropes: the flourishing of words for their majesty and fun, and—in the love play between

Fiennes and his enchantress—the kindling of a playfully adult eroticism."

Rod Dreher of the *New York Post* was sweet on the leading lady, bewitched by "the breathtaking performance of Gwyneth Paltrow. She's ravishing, she's vulnerable, she's irresistible—and she's never been better. Her way with Shakespearean dialogue suggests a future on the stage, should she so choose (and after this movie, Paltrow will have her pick of anything). Glowing with the incandescence of a true movie star, the magnificent Gwyneth illuminates this entire, many-splendored production." Janet Maslin was equally captivated: "Gwyneth Paltrow, in her first great, fully realized starring performance, makes a heroine so breathtaking that she seems utterly plausible as the playwright's guiding light. In a film steamy enough to start a sonnet craze, her Viola de Lesseps really does seem to warrant the most timeless love poems, and to speak Shakespeare's own elegant language with astonishing ease. *Shakespeare in Love* itself seems as smitten with her as the poet is, and as alight with the same love of language and beauty." But Duane Dudek of the *Milwaukee Journal-Sentinel* felt that, "Dressed as a man, she resembles an anorexic Leonardo DiCaprio."

Ruthe Stein of the *San Francisco Chronicle* wrote of the leading man, "The cast is near perfect. Fiennes is every bit as talented as his older brother, Ralph, but appears to be having more fun onscreen. He brings humanity to Will, showing how he wasn't that different from any other struggling writer." Liz Smith threw caution aside and declared, "The love scenes between Paltrow and the astonishingly magnetic Joseph Fiennes have to be the most genuinely magnetic and passionate ever put onscreen." Judi Dench had just three scenes and was on screen for about eight minutes but that was enough to make an impression. *Variety*'s Lael Loewenstein wrote, "The unassailable Dench plays Elizabeth with gusto: She provides a brilliantly wry counterpoint to her last monarch, Victoria."

Amy Taubin of the *Village Voice* didn't much like *Shakespeare in Love*, and she said, "you can bet that Stoppard is responsible for the clever Elizabethan in-jokes that let anyone who took one of those Shakespeare-and-his-world courses feel really smart." *Salon*'s Laura Miller felt that director Madden "clearly wants the movie to feel like one of Shakespeare's sunny, mature comedies—a bit of melodrama, a few clowns, some disguises, a touch of philosophy, some bawdy jokes, all wrapped around a romance—a grab bag of whimsies transformed by the Bard's uncanny alchemy into something sublime. Of course, not even Stoppard is Shakespeare, and the end result resembles one of Neil Simon's middlebrow romps more than it does *As You Like It*."

The Christian Film and Television Commission compiled a list of the year's most "immoral, anti-Christian movies." Topping the roster was *Shakespeare in Love*. Its offense? "*Shakespeare in Love* has a banal plot that distorts history. It demeans Shakespeare's genius by neglecting the nobler passions that permeated Shakespeare's work." In other words, the Christian Commission was certain that the real William Shakespeare had been inspired by a higher authority than his mojo.

Hello, Stranger

If young William Shakespeare was suffering from writer's block in *Shakespeare in Love*, he had nothing on director Terrence Malick. After making two of the seminal films of the 1970s, *Badlands* and *Days of Heaven*, the Rhodes Scholar and former MIT philosophy professor became a legendary figure by dropping out of sight professionally. Adding to his mystique was that he kept mum on what he'd been doing for twenty years, although it was known that he'd been living in Paris and then Austin—where he became an ardent bird-watcher. At one point he had a production deal with Paramount but never finished the script, and made a living by working on screenplays from time to time. That he was back with a new movie was one of the most anticipated cinematic events of 1998. Making it even more tantalizing, given the laudation for *Saving Private Ryan*, was that Malick's *The Thin Red Line* was also a World War II movie, and Malick's partisans were betting their man would show Spielberg how it should really be done.

This project had its gestation in the late 1980s when Bobby Geisler and John Roberdeau, a theatrical producing team who had made only one film, Robert

Altman's *Streamers* in 1983, dedicated themselves to getting Malick back behind the camera. When they approached the filmmaker, he said that he wasn't in the mood to direct a movie but he could be talked into writing an adaptation of *The Thin Red Line*; the novel was by James Jones—best known for *From Here to Eternity*—and told of an infantry unit during the battle of Guadalcanal. When Malick completed his first draft, Geisler and Roberdeau painstakingly went over the script with him, lavishly making suggestions. After this rather arduous process had been completed, the producers used all their powers of persuasion to get Malick commit to directing the film. He was skittish about the idea, but ultimately did come around, at least tentatively.

Geisler and Roberdeau realized that to keep Malick on board, they'd need to cater to his whims—including his rabid procrastination—and respect his continued insistence on extreme privacy. They also put up the scratch to enable him to write a theatrical adaptation of the Kenji Mizoguchi film, *Sansho the Bailiff*. Geisler said of Malick, "He was the center and circumference of our lives," and told *Vanity Fair*, "It wasn't an easy day's work, but it was a great day's work. Terry was the Holy Grail. He was thought to be unfindable, unapproachable, unconvincible. Others had failed; we would be successful. We realized how much that might mean to our careers." But the long-gestating workshop production of *Sansho* at the Brooklyn Academy of Music, directed by Polish filmmaker Andrzej Wajda, was a disaster and when it was over, the producers were broke, forced to sell their furniture in an attempt to stave off creditors. This state of affairs convinced them they had coddled the filmmaker long enough—they wanted something to show for their efforts. In early 1995, the duo approached producer Mike Medavoy, who had been Malick's agent in the 1970s; he agreed that his new company, Phoenix Pictures, would loan the pair money to keep the project afloat.

It didn't take long for friction to develop between industry insider Medavoy and the New York-based Geisler and Roberdeau; the pair refused to share producing credit with Malick's old friend George Stevens, Jr., whom he had brought in on the project. Meanwhile, Sony—with whom Medavoy had a co-financing deal—dropped out of the project, because studio head John Calley thought the $52-million budget was unrealistic. Fox 2000 agreed to come in, but only on the condition that Malick go against his inclination and hire some stars for the film; the studio didn't care if they had supporting roles, it just needed to know that some marquee-friendly names would be in the film.

That was no problem because when word got out that Malick was looking to get back into the game, a large percentage of the acting community expressed interest in being part of the project. Mike Medavoy told Marilyn Back and Stacy Jenel Smith, "Almost every actor I know in town has asked to be a part of it. Major stars have called Terry and asked him to write in a part for them." Roberdeau said that an agent called pitching an actress for the film. After being told there were no women in the film, "only a photograph of a woman in one scene," the agent cheerfully said, "She'll play that! She'll be the photograph." According to the *New York Post*'s "Page Six," Sean Penn was so keen on a new Terrence Malick movie that he encouraged other prominent actors not only to get with the program, but to be willing to work "for little more than scale." *Movieline* confirmed that the cast "signed on for surprisingly little money. Malick's mystique was a lot of the draw for those who were drafted but not all. The script has, many feel, a lyric beauty unusual in a war story, and the remarkable quality of giving each of the many characters his own moment." Among the people Fox was happy to see involved were such iconoclastic figures as Penn, Nick Nolte, Woody Harrelson and John Cusack, as well as John Travolta—who had been Malick's first choice for the Richard Gere role in *Days of Heaven*—and George Clooney. Newcomers cast by Malick included Jim Caviezel and Adrien Brody, who was given the film's lead role. On the flip side, Harrison Ford, Edward Norton, Tom Cruise, and Leonardo DiCaprio declined the opportunity to come and be part of the experience.

The production finally had a start date, but this was not the happy, momentous occasion Bobby Geisler and John Roberdeau had anticipated all these years: Malick decreed he didn't want them anywhere near the film's Australia location. The director felt so strongly about this that, even as he was consulting them for casting advice, he had a clause inserted in his contract ensuring that they would be prohibited from being on the set. Geisler recollected, "We just wanted the pleasure of seeing him say 'Action!' for the first time in twenty years, feeling we had earned that, and he would not be there were it not for John and me." But "Basically he said I should be grateful to him for directing the material." Roberdeau said he was at a loss, telling *Entertainment Weekly*, "I wish I could say there was one fight, but there wasn't." It got worse, as the pair was threatened with having their screen credit removed; Mike Medavoy maintained they had violated an agreement not to speak to the press when they revealed secrets to *Vanity Fair*. That very same offending *Vanity Fair* article quoted an unnamed source, "The two guys are trying to get their careers started on Terry. They wore out their welcome." A second unnamed source: "They're people Terry got involved with and wishes he hadn't." In short, the back story of *The Thin Red Line* would always have a bit of *Rashomon* to it.

The Thin Red Line had been filmed before and turned into a conventional war movie in 1964. Nobody would call Malick's version "conventional," which had been clear to the actors who were participating in the movie. During production, John Cusack said, "I don't know if this will make sense the way a normal film does. Terry's wildly intuitive and impressionistic. He wrote a script based on the novel, and he's making a film based on the script, but he's not shooting the script. He's shooting the essence of the script."

When he arrived in Australia, Gary Oldman was told not to bother, his part had been written out. During post-production, Malick hired Billy Bob Thornton to record the film's narration, decided he didn't like the result and replaced Thornton's one voice with those of eight of the actors in the film. Malick had ten months to edit his one-million feet of film; his first cut was six hours and he was still working as its December premiere date—and voting for critics' awards—approached. The movie was screened for the press even though it was not yet in its final cut, and Medavoy admitted, "Terry was livid because he felt, how could we show a film that was not finished?" Between the early December screenings and the December 23 premiere, Malick, with Sean Penn at his side as an advisor, cut another five minutes. At that point it probably didn't matter to Adrian Brody. In the script, the young actor's character had been pre-eminent, and Fox publicity was playing him up as the star of the film. He brought his family to a screening and was probably asking, "Where's the rest of me?" as he saw that his lead role had been reduced to two lines ("incomprehensible ones at that," said *Variety*'s Todd McCarthy) and five minutes of screen time. Still, he did better than Lukas Haas, Mickey Rourke, and Bill Pullman who were completely cut out of the film. At the film's premiere, Jim Caviezel, an unknown actor who was given a good deal of screen time, said of Malick, "I love him like a father. And that says a lot 'cause I love my father. He put his reputation on the line for me." He also brought *The Thin Red Line* in on budget, sticking to the $52 million he had been allocated.

Malick had not spoken to the press since 1974 when *Badlands* was released, and his contract contained a clause stating that he did not have to start now. Others took up the slack, though. Mike Medavoy said of the director, "He has a sense of irony and humanity that is very special. This is a unique voice and vision. Then he disappears after making these two films. This only adds to the fascination of the man. In this world, you make two movies like that and most people would go on to make more because they are looking always at making more money. Terry didn't do that. This perplexes a lot of people." Executive producer George Stevens Jr. pointed out, "It's possible to live an interesting life without making movies."

Nature Boy

"Some films deal in plot truth; this one expresses emotional truth, the heart's search for saving wisdom, in some of the most luscious imagery since Malick's last film, the 1978 *Days of Heaven*," declared *Time*'s Richard Corliss. J. Hoberman wrote in the *Village Voice*: "The year's most enigmatic studio release, written and directed by one of the most puzzling figures in Hollywood, *The Thin Red Line* projects a sense of wounded diffidence. Terrence Malick's hugely ambitious, austerely hallucinated adaptation of James Jones's 1962 novel—a 500-page account of combat in

Guadalcanal—is a metaphysical platoon movie in which battlefield confusion is melded with an Emersonian meditation on the nature of nature." Hoberman concluded, "As mystical as it is gritty, as despairing as it is detached, Malick's study of men in battle materializes in our midst almost exactly a century after Stephen Crane's *The Red Badge of Courage*—an exercise in nineteenth-century transcendentalism, weirdly serene in the face of horror." The *Christian Science Monitor*'s David Sterritt felt that, "Although the story seems disjointed at times, no other war movie has tried so valiantly to convey not only the suffering of combat but the awful fissures it leaves between humanity's ideal oneness with itself and the world we live in."

The Thin Red Line had no stronger advocate than Godfrey Cheshire of the *New York Press*. He wrote, "Once a year, if I'm very lucky, a movie comes along that changes my life by doing that magical thing: sweeping me away on its torrent of images, ideas and feelings so decisively and thoroughly that I remain lost in its spell for days afterward, rapt and wonder-struck." Cheshire said *The Thin Red Line* "is one of those inebriating films that draws its power from radically rediscovering the way we view the world through cinema." As much as he adored the film, Cheshire seemed resigned that it was not for most moviegoers: "The film recurrently dips into the memories and off-hand musings of its many characters. It pauses to look at a branch, a leaf, a splash of light, a spray of clouds. This is something far beyond the superficial 'realism' of most war movies, because it gives us something a film's plot can't touch: the momentary sensation of life lived in very close proximity to death." Finally, Cheshire said, "Its burble of voices and perspectives invoke *The Waste Land* and *Ulysses* and their countless descendants. It is Mahler versus Spielberg's Sousa, Rimbaud and Whitman (*Leaves of Grass*: great title for a Malick film) versus Disney rhymesters, the impressionists versus the worthy but limited lineage of N.C. Wyeth."

Obviously, there would be plenty of reviewers who didn't appreciate what Malick was doing. Stuart Klawans of *The Nation* denigrated *The Thin Red Line* as "the first New Age World War II movie" and "meta-

physical guff." *Entertainment Weekly*'s Owen Gleiberman snorted, "This is a war film made by a very
somber flower child." In his weekly column, *Variety*
editor-in-chief Peter Bart *kvetched*, "Plotlines start and
vaporize. Characters blend into one another. Voiceover
perorations march off in opposite directions. Visual
images are constantly at odds with physical action."
Roger Ebert seemed not to understand the movie, so
he covered his flank by being condescending. "The
movie's schizophrenia keeps it from greatness (this film
has no firm idea of what it is about), but doesn't make
it bad. It is, in fact, sort of fascinating."

The Thin Red Line featured ruminative voiceovers
expressing the inner feelings of various characters. *The
Miami Herald*'s Rene Rodriguez did not like them:
"With lines like 'This great evil—where does it come
from?' and 'Oh my soul, let me be with you now!' the
men in Company C come off like a troop of bad poets
in need of a remedial creative writing class." Gary
Thompson of the *Philadelphia Daily News* said, "*The
Thin Red Line* is, very obliquely, the story of the
American attempt to wrest Guadalcanal Island and its
strategic airstrip from the Japanese during World
War II. The circumstances and strategy of that horrific
battle are virtually ignored by Malick, to the great disappointment of anyone who expects something on the
order of *Guadalcanal Diary*, the fine 1943 actioner
starring William Bendix and Lloyd Nolan. *The Thin
Red Line* is more, uh, contemplative. If you thought
the middle part of *Saving Private Ryan* was slow, you'd
better hit the coffee shop for a double espresso before
The Thin Red Line."

Just as once the world was divided into Willie
Mays people and Mickey Mantle people, now there
were *Private Ryan* folks and those who preferred *The
Thin Red Line*. Coming out for Spielberg was
Lawrence Toppman of the *Charlotte Observer*, who argued that "Spielberg's narrative is linear, direct, neatly
forecasting actions and then delivering the expected
payoffs. Malick wanders through the jungles of
Guadalcanal like a soldier, pausing to peer at exotic
bats, marvel at water trickling down giant leaves, suck
up snatches of conversation from the other guys in the
platoon. Spielberg's a storyteller, Malick a painter and
poet. But the poet has so little to say!" In his review,

Toppmann also spoke of his experience seeing *The
Thin Red Line*: "Much of the atmosphere comes from
the sinister waves of grass and frightening descent of
fog. Folks at the sneak preview didn't give two hoots
about those things. (Or, to be more literal, they gave
many hoots at the end.) They were like diners who
wanted apple pie and were served spun sugar, fine and
novel but not remotely filling. Like them, I was hungry for another movie two hours later." Barry Koltnow
of the *Orange County Register* contended, "*Saving Private Ryan* was not only a box-office success, it changed
how war movies will be made for the next twenty years
and triggered a catharsis nationwide among World
War II veterans. *The Thin Red Line* might also spark
veterans' memories, but it is more likely to make a lot
of people scratch their heads, wondering what the
heck Malick was trying to say." *Politically Incorrect* host
Bill Maher thought *Saving Private Ryan* was the best
film of the year. In contrast, "I walked out on *The
Thin Red Line*. People in the theater were laughing at
it and I don't blame them . . . The movie is stupid."
The *Washington Post*'s Stephen Hunter sneered, "It's
pointless to compare or contrast *The Thin Red Line*
with Steven Spielberg's *Saving Private Ryan*, because
their intentions are so vastly different. With *Ryan*, a
kind of generational tribute, Spielberg's ambition was
to commemorate the men who won the war. Malick's
seems to be to photograph as many parrots as possible.
Polly want a movie?"

On Malick's side were Jonathan Rosenbaum: "In
contrast to *Saving Private Ryan* it's the work of a
grown-up with something to say about the meaning
and consequences of war." Dave Kehr of the *New York
Daily News* said "*The Thin Red Line* is not a film that
will reveal all of its secrets in one viewing; like *Days of
Heaven*, it's a dense and allusive work, with references
as disparate as the German silent cinema and Buddhist
philosophy"; he submitted that, "It is too dark and
cluttered and mysterious ever to achieve the popular
acceptance of Spielberg's movie, but as an artistic creation, it is a far more original, far more challenging
piece of work . . . Where Spielberg's film is a straight-
line narration with a clearly defined hero, rock-solid
values and a sentimental underpinning, Malick still
lives in the experimental atmosphere of the 1970s, a

time when American movies were dedicated to sub-
verting those conventional certainties."

Peter Keough of the *Boston Phoenix* averred that
Malick's "film won't garner anywhere near the business
or praise or awards of Steven Spielberg's excellent *Saving Private Ryan*, but while *Ryan* is indeed the more
fully realized work, *The Thin Red Line* offers us a
chance at a cinematic renaissance, of startling possibility. Put it this way: I will one day encourage my son,
while he is still a boy, to watch *Saving Private Ryan* for
its lesson in fulfilling those missions that destiny hands
us. But I will encourage him, when he is a man, to
watch *The Thin Red Line* for its misshapen but magnificent vision of a soulful quest—in the thick of
misery and fear—for the meaning of our lives."

The Thin Red Line did extremely well in its initial
big city engagements, but then sputtered when it
opened wide. While *Saving Private Ryan* would ultimately be the top grossing 1998 release, *The Thin Red
Line* was simply too cerebral for mass acceptance.

Spielberg Faces Resistance

There was a general assumption that given the
widespread deification of *Saving Private Ryan*, coupled with the undeniable societal impact it had had,
all other films would lie down before it in supplica-
tion at the critics awards. But Spielberg's movie was
shot down right at the beginning. In what the *Hollywood Reporter* called a "stunning upset," the National
Board of Review named *Gods and Monsters* the Best
Picture of the Year. The film's leading man, Sir Ian
McKellen was the Board's choice for Best Actor, although *Elizabeth*'s Shekhar Kapur won Best Director.
Fernanda Montenegro received the Best Actress award
for *Central Station*, which itself defeated *Life Is Beautiful* for Best Foreign Film. The supporting winners
were Ed Harris in both *The Truman Show* and—even
though he had little to do in this Susan Sarandon/Ju-
lia Roberts tear-jerker—*Stepmom*, and Christina Ricci
for three independent movies, *Buffalo '66,* John Waters's *Pecker* and Don Roos's *The Opposite of Sex*, in
which her wonderfully incorrigible Bad Girl was
clearly the lead character. For the first time, the Board
voted on a Screenplay Award, giving it to Scott Smith

for adapting his novel *A Simple Plan*, about good people who go bad when they find a fortune in a downed
airplane.

The Los Angeles Film Critics convened next and
they were loyal to the hometown hero. *Saving Private
Ryan* and Steven Spielberg both won. Ian McKellen
and Fernanda Montenegro repeated their National
Board victories, although Montenegro had to share
hers with Ally Sheedy; the ex-Brat Packer played a dis-
solute, reclusive, heroin-addicted, lesbian photographer in *High Art*. The voting for Supporting Actor
ended in a tie, as well, with awards going to Billy Bob
Thornton, a dim-witted rube—though still several
rungs above *Sling Blade*'s Karl Childers—in *A Simple
Plan*, and Bill Murray, a comically sleazy lawyer in the
sex-and-crime melodrama *Wild Things* and a bemused
millionaire in Wes Anderson's magical comedy of eccentric manners, *Rushmore*. The Supporting Actress
winner was Joan Allen for playing a June Cleaver–type
who becomes liberated in *Pleasantville*, Gary Ross's
tolerance allegory taking place in the world of a 1950s'
sitcom. The Screenplay award went to *Bullworth*, the
Warren Beatty political satire, and the L.A. group's
choice for Best Foreign Film was Thomas Vinterberg's
The Celebration, a Dogma 95 (i.e., only natural lighting, hand-held camera, real sound, etc.) production
from Denmark, about a family reunion during which
all sorts of "ugly truths" are revealed, just like in a
Broadway play from the 1950s.

The New York Critics' Awards worked out like a
replay of 1993, when Steven Spielberg's *Schindler's List*
won Best Picture, but the award for Best Director
went to Jane Campion for the more imaginative and
poetic, *The Piano*. This time, Steven Spielberg's *Saving
Private Ryan* won Best Picture but the award for Best
Director went to Terrence Malick for the more imaginative and poetic, *The Thin Red Line*. Best Picture had
been voted upon first, and when it came time for Best
Director, those whose first choice was Todd Solondz
for *Happiness* or Paul Schrader for *Affliction*, joined the
Terrence Malick contingent to prevent a Spielberg victory. The *New York Post*'s Thelma Adams divulged that
"Spielberg apparently was so confident of a win that
his people called Critics' Circle chairman Godfrey
Cheshire in August, asking when the awards dinner

would be held so that the DreamWorks SKG mogul could reserve the date on his calendar."

Best Actor here was Nick Nolte for playing a self-destructive small-town sheriff in *Affliction*, Paul Schrader's adaptation of a Russell Banks novel; the film had been kicking around for a year-and-a-half when it was finally picked up for an end-of-the-year release by Lions Gate, the same company that distributed *Gods and Monsters*. Bill Murray received his second Supporting Actor award, though this one was for *Rushmore* only and not *Wild Things*. Lisa Kudrow was named Best Supporting Actress for her hilarious, vinegarish performance in *The Opposite of Sex*. Best Screenplay went to Marc Norman and Tom Stoppard for *Shakespeare in Love* and, as in Los Angeles, the Foreign Film prize went to *The Celebration*. The New York Critics' most intriguing result, though, came in Best Actress, with Cameron Diaz in *There's Something About Mary*, the rude and very popular comedy in which the comic highpoint involved her putting semen in her hair.

What had transpired was that *Central Station*'s Fernanda Montenegro had a commanding lead on the second and third rounds of voting. In those heats, however, one must appear on over half of the critics ballots to win and Montenegro didn't make it. On round four, a simple majority suffices, and that's where everyone who wanted a babe at the awards ceremony rather than a sixty-nine-year-old Brazilian who spoke broken English came together for Diaz. Andrew Sarris confessed, " I originally intended to vote for Vanessa Redgrave for her portrayal of Mrs. Dalloway, but I sensed that Ms. Redgrave didn't have a chance with a vehicle that opened so early in the year. So why should I make a futile gesture when I could make a fun statement instead? To my delight, Ms. Diaz surged from behind to victory." The people who voted for Diaz figured they were being audacious and a little naughty, and *People*'s Leah Rozen called Diaz's fourth round surge a "groinswell." One does wonder if any of Diaz's proponents really did find her to be a convincing doctor, which is what she played in *There's Something About Mary*. *Entertainment Weekly* looked at this result, and stated, "You know the planets are misaligned when the New York Film Critics' Circle announces

that in its collective opinion, 1998's master thespian was Cameron Diaz."

The National Society of Film Critics has a reputation for often making offbeat selections as a corrective to earlier awards, but this time the group's statement was completely unanticipated. To head off Steven Spielberg's war movie, the anti-*Private Ryan* contingent closed ranks around Steven Soderbergh's *Out of Sight*, resulting in Best Picture and Director Awards for the caper film, a summertime box-office disappointment. Best Actor was Nick Nolte in *Affliction*, Best Actress, Ally Sheedy in *High Art*, Supporting Actor, Bill Murray in *Rushmore*; the one winner here who hadn't been crowned by another group was Judi Dench for *Shakespeare of Love*. The National Society named Abbas Kiarostami's *A Taste of Cherry* Best Foreign Film, meaning that *Life is Beautiful* had completely struck out at the various critics' awards; the Iranian *Taste of Cherry* was so much more complex and daring than Roberto Benigni's movie that the two seemed to be existing in separate universes. And when all was said and done, Steven Spielberg had won but a single Best Director prize.

Waiting for the Fat Lady to Sing

In the first week of January, *Variety* published a front-page story which began, "Last July, an Academy of Motion Picture Arts and Sciences member blurted out what seemed like the obvious: 'Should we just FedEx the Oscars over to Spielberg's house now and save everybody the trouble of voting?' The summer sentiment had DreamWorks's *Saving Private Ryan* as not just the favorite, but the out-and-out winner for best pic. Many also predicted Steven Spielberg was a shoo-in for Best Director, and Tom Hanks and his palsied hand were ready to clutch the Best Actor statuette. Six months later, the industry is re-evaluating." The article, entitled "Will Dark Horses Win Gold?", went on to announce, "Suddenly the other studios have caught Oscar frenzy," and quoted an "industry honcho" as saying, "The feeling is, 'We have a chance here, let's go for it. Advertising is beginning to get feverish.' " Also quoted was publicity ace Tony Angellotti who was working on the *Shakespeare in Love* campaign; he said that when the film was shown to Academy members, "There hasn't been one screening that was less than through-the-roof. People have an affection and passion for the film. *Chariots of Fire* also had a passion, and I think that's why it won."

This same front page of *Variety* contained—along with an ad for *Shakespeare in Love*—another article, written by editor-in-chief Peter Bart. Under the headline "Hot Race Stokes Harvey's Hunger," Bart wrote, "Two roly-poly fellas, Santa and Harvey can always be counted on to strut their stuff at this time of year." But "Harvey Weinstein, we were told, has been too fixated on launching his high-profile magazine with Tina Brown, too busy being a friend of Bill and Hillary and too preoccupied with the New York social whirl to perform his customary end-of-the-year pyrotechnics. That's what people kept whispering in my ear . . . Well they were wrong. It's 'Harvey Time' yet again. Two Miramax films, *Shakespeare in Love* and *Life Is Beautiful* have emerged as serious Oscar dark horses."

Saving Private Ryan regained its momentum when the Hollywood Foreign Press named it Best Picture (Drama) and gave Steven Spielberg a Golden Globe as Best Director. Spielberg received a standing ovation and said, "I want to thank all the veterans that are out there who saved civilization and stopped the Holocaust in 1945." *The Thin Red Line* wasn't even nominated for the Globe, a situation that Fox ascribed to the Foreign Press having been shown an unfinished cut, even though it was that version that the New York Film Critics had viewed before naming Terrence Malick Best Director. *Shakespeare in Love* ended up with one more Globe than *Private Ryan*, as the Miramax movie won for Best Musical or Comedy, Best Screenplay, and Best Actress, Gwyneth Paltrow. Paltrow became weepy on stage when she thanked her mother, Blythe Danner, and "my dad, who's had a tough year, and to my grandpa, Buster, who's had an even tougher year. Hang in there, Grandpa." She later revealed that her grandfather was suffering from stomach cancer.

Paltrow's Drama counterpart was Cate Blanchett in *Elizabeth*. The big shock of the night, however, was that the highly favored Ian McKellen lost Best Actor (Drama) to Jim Carrey in *The Truman Show*. In his acceptance speech Carrey pontificated, "It's gonna be so hard to talk out of my ass after this . . . But I'll manage." Word later came out that a former president of the Hollywood Foreign Press Association was a huge Carrey fan and he pressured his colleagues to vote for the Truman Show star, which, out of deference for their ex-leader, they did. The most memorable speech of the night came from Best Actor in a Musical or Comedy, Michael Caine. He won for playing a sleazy talent agent in *Little Voice*, one of the year-end Miramax releases that had been shunted aside by *Shakespeare in Love*. After musing, "My career must be slipping, this is the first time I've ever been available to pick up an award," Caine thanked Harvey Weinstein "for the picture, and for the other one I've just done and for the next one I'm hoping to do because without him, I don't work a lot." Finally he said, "I always behaved out of fear because I never believed that I was ever going to be a success in this business. So I used to take every script that came in. And so I made a lot of crap. And a lot of money. So now I have enough money to be artistic and wait."

The Supporting winners were Ed Harris in *The Truman Show* and Lynn Redgrave in *Gods and Monsters*. Redgrave noted that thirty-two years earlier she had received a Globe for *Georgy Girl* and she thanked, "My husband and partner of thirty-two years, who's been there from Globe to Globe." *Life Is Beautiful* was not eligible for Golden Globes—the Foreign Press had a different cutoff date for international films than the Academy—and *Central Station* won Best Foreign Film. Roberto Benigni was in the house, though, as the presenter of the Best Musical or Comedy Award; he received a standing ovation, which indicated just how much Hollywood had fallen for his act.

Final Protocol

As the announcement of Oscar nominations approached, three films were seen as definite nominees: *Saving Private Ryan*, *Shakespeare in Love*, which was finding as much favor among audiences as it had with critics, and *Life Is Beautiful*—the Miramax publicity experts and the inexplicable personal appeal of Roberto Benigni had drowned out dissenting voices about the film. Based on nominations for various guild awards, box-office and general buzz, it was evident the remaining two nominees would be coming from a field of five films. Most likely seemed to be *The Truman Show* and *Gods and Monsters*. Others still in the chase included *The Thin Red Line*, which had genuinely impassioned supporters, although greater numbers of people in the industry seemed perplexed or bored by it, the box office was less than stellar and word of mouth was even worse. Gramercy was pushing hard for *Elizabeth* even though the movie hadn't lived up to its pre-release hype. There was also *Waking Ned Devine*, a wee Irish comedy that Fox was trying to position as this year's *The Full Monty*, regardless that audience response didn't remotely approach that for the earlier film; indicating that it was a possible contender, however, was a strong print campaign in the trade papers and the fact that it did receive a nomination as Best Picture from the Producers Guild (along with *Gods and Monsters*, *Life Is Beautiful*, *Saving Private Ryan* and *Shakespeare in Love*.)

The Nominations

"Oscar is wearing combat fatigues. And a codpiece," was the lead for *Daily Variety*'s report on the Oscar nominations, as the Best Picture nominees consisted of three films taking place during World War II, and two set in Elizabethan times. Bob Strauss of the *Los Angeles Daily News* ruminated, "It sure seemed like some of last year's good movies weren't about World War II or sixteenth-century England. But in their infinite wisdom, the voting members of the Academy of Motion Picture Arts and Sciences have said not so." The *Hollywood Reporter* headline, meanwhile, was "Wherefore art thou, Oscar?" reflecting that the most nominated movie was *Shakespeare in Love*, with thirteen nods. As anticipated, *Saving Private Ryan* and *Life Is Beautiful* were also in the running, with the two "open spots" going to *The Thin Red Line* and *Elizabeth*. *Private Ryan* was second in total nominations with eleven, and Barry Koltnow of the *Orange County Register* felt it was "remarkable that a light, entertaining comedy called *Shakespeare in Love* got two more nominations than the deadly serious *Private Ryan*." The *Hollywood Reporter*'s Martin Grove said he had ex-

pected *Shakespeare* to do very well with Oscar voters because, "This is a movie that makes Academy members feel good about themselves for getting all the references." *Life Is Beautiful* became the most nominated foreign film ever, with seven citations (a record that would stand a mere two years). Roberto Benigni received three nominations, for writing, directing, and starring in the film, which was also nominated for Best Foreign Film, the first such same-year double nomination since *Z* in 1969. Harvey Weinstein threatened, "I'm now going to make the Germans re-release it"— Germany was one country where *Life Is Beautiful* was not a success.

The Thin Red Line had seven nominations, including two for Terrence Malick for Director and Adapted Screenplay. *Elizabeth* snared its Best Picture nomination even though it received neither a Director or Screenplay nomination, an indication that the film's backers were from the technical categories, fans of its period opulence; it was a finalist in seven categories. A few days after the nominations, Bernard Weinraub asked around about why *The Truman Show* hadn't been nominated and reported that the executives and producers he talked to all "said that while some newspaper and magazine critics lavishly praised the movie, people in Hollywood didn't quite get what all the hoopla was about. 'It was a critics' phenomenon, and the town never liked the movie,' one top producer said."

Henry Sheehan of the *Orange County Register* spoke for most Oscar observers when he declared, "The biggest surprise this year has to be Ed Norton's Best Actor nomination for *American History X*. It's not that the performer, among the most talented of his generation, did an unworthy job. But the movie was an overhyped sermonette that lacked any sort of credibility, didn't find a public, and was a huge post-production headache. It is good news for young Norton, however; it means the Academy likes him—it really does." A treatise about the skinhead movement, *American History X*'s greatest attention had come from a feud between the producers and first-time director Tony Kaye, who squawked that they ruined the film when they took it from him and recut it. Some commentators expressed surprise that *The Truman Show*'s

Jim Carrey did not make the final cut, but his similar failure to receive a nomination from the Screen Actors Guild indicated that other actors did not equate his toning himself down with giving an exceptional performance. As Bob Strauss said, "The actors recognized Carrey's work for what it was: a promising transitional performance, but not the real goods just yet." More surprising was the failure of Joseph Fiennes to be nominated for *Shakespeare in Love*, given the overall affection for the movie, his Screen Actors Guild nomination and his emergence as a heartthrob. *Shakespeare* director John Madden's take was, "I can't tell you how dismayed I am. You can't celebrate this film without celebrating his performance." Competing against Norton were four expected nominees: Roberto Benigni in *Life Is Beautiful*; Tom Hanks, his fourth nomination, for *Saving Private Ryan*: Ian McKellen in *Gods and Monsters*; and Nick Nolte, nomination number two for *Affliction*.

The Best Actress contenders were the five women most Oscar watchers had predicted: Cate Blanchett in *Elizabeth*; Gwyneth Paltrow in *Shakespeare in Love*; Fernanda Montenegro in *Central Station*; Meryl Streep with her eleventh nomination as a mother dying of cancer in the box-office flop, *One True Thing;* and Emily Watson receiving her second nomination for only her third film, *Hilary and Jackie,* in which she played Jacqueline du Pre, the emotionally unstable cellist who succumbed to multiple sclerosis.

Appearing on CNN immediately after the announcements, *Entertainment Weekly's* Lisa Schwarzbaum said, "The idea that Bill Murray would not get a nomination for *Rushmore* breaks my heart. We all wanted this to happen. He so deserved it. We thought this would be his moment. And it went by him . . . I was saddened by it." In the estimation of the *Philadelphia Inquirer's* Desmond Ryan, Murray was "rudely rebuffed." What may have hurt Murray's chances was that, in a terrible strategy decision, Disney opened *Rushmore* for only a week in December and then removed it from theaters. Therefore, no one was talking about the film, which was the kind of small movie dependent upon word-of-mouth; Wes Anderson's original screenplay may also have been a victim of this blunder. Nominated in Murray's stead were James

Coburn as Nick Nolte's abusive father in *Affliction*; Robert Duvall, his sixth nomination, as the attorney for the bad guys in the fact-based social drama, *A Civil Action*; Ed Harris in *The Truman Show*; Geoffrey Rush as a comic-relief impresario in *Shakespeare in Love*; and Billy Bob Thornton in *A Simple Plan*; these last three actors were each receiving their second nomination. Two of the contenders were minor surprises: Coburn because he hadn't figured in any earlier awards, and Rush because his hammy performance was not as highly praised as those of two of the film's other supporting actors, Tom Wilkinson and Ben Affleck.

On the distaff side, the Supporting nominees were Kathy Bates as a political operator in Mike Nichols's Clinton *cinema à clef, Primary Colors*; Brenda Blethyn, an overbearing mother in *Little Voice*; Judi Dench in *Shakespeare in Love*; Rachel Griffiths as Emily Watson's sister in *Hilary and Jackie*; and Lynn Redgrave in *Gods and Monsters*. It was the little-known Griffiths's first nomination; for the four other women, this was the second time around, the first ranging from 1966 for Lynn Redgrave to last year for Judi Dench. Blethyn's nomination was the most unexpected among this group because her over-the-top acting was far from universally praised; Glenn Whipp of the *Los Angeles Daily News* said "her garish performance was the acting equivalent of an explosion at a paint factory." Kathy Bates was only slightly less unexpected. Both Joan Allen in *Pleasantville* and Lisa Kudrow in *The Opposite of Sex* had heard much greater acclaim than these two nominees.

Four of the Best Picture nominees had corresponding Director nominations, with *The Truman Show's* Peter Weir replacing *Elizabeth's* Shekhar Kapur. "I had to stop and consider why I didn't feel disappointed about not being nominated," Kapur said. "And certainly some of the reasons are rationalizations like the fact that it took the Academy a long time to recognize Mr. Spielberg." Stuart Klawans of *The Nation* complained about two of the nominees in this category: Klawans called *Life Is Beautiful* "a film of conspicuously inept direction," and referred to *Shakespeare in Love's* nominated director as "John (Point and Shoot) Madden."

Miramax was out in front with twenty-three

nominations—one more than its previous record in 1994. This year also marked something new for Harvey Weinstein. He had a producer's credit on *Shakespeare in Love*, so the East Coast mogul received a personal nomination for the first time ever. Weinstein gushed, "This is for every kid who ever dreamed of being in the movies; I am that kid." Seeing that his film was one shy of the record fourteen nominations held by *All About Eve* and *Titanic*, Weinstein laughed, "I kept telling John [Madden] to put a rap song in the middle so we could qualify for that, too."

Rolling Stone's Peter Travers said, "Everybody already sees [Spielberg] up there receiving that award. But we gotta look at this, too—that *Shakespeare in Love* actually got more nominations so maybe there's a contest. Hey, I'm hoping." Henry Sheehan noted that *Shakespeare in Love* had two more nominations and "all that makes for interesting long-term analysis, but it doesn't detract too much from *Saving Private Ryan*'s overall chances. Steven Spielberg's D-Day saga, which has not only garnered critical praise and popular acclaim but ridden the wave of generational tributes, nabbed eleven nominations, including two for which it is a prohibitive favorite: Best Picture and Best Director." And *USA Today*'s Susan Wloszczyna pointed out that *Private Ryan* had been at a disadvantage in the numbers game: "With no major female characters, it was shut out of at least two categories."

When he heard it suggested that *Saving Private Ryan* was a sure bet, Harvey Weinstein said to *USA Today*, "All five are fantastic. And this from me who didn't like *Titanic*. But shoo-in? No way. You start talking to voters as we do, and you'll find this is a race and a half, not like last year." Ads for *Shakespeare in Love* began proclaiming, "The Year's Biggest Crowd Pleaser Is Now Nominated For More Oscars Than Any Other Motion Picture!"

Spielberg was in Berlin where he was presenting a Holocaust documentary for which he had served as executive producer, the Shoah Foundation's *The Final Days*. His reaction to *Private Ryan*'s eleven nominations was, "I think this is a tribute to the veterans. It's important that, before the century is out, ample recognition is paid to the veterans who saved the world." Having received the news that *The Final Days* was nominated for Best Documentary Feature, he said, "How appropriate it is to get the news about the two films while I'm in Berlin." Spielberg also admitted, "Last year was a piece of cake with *Amistad*. It was so mired in controversy that I didn't think we had a chance. But I thought we did have a chance this year, and I was very anxious. In fact, I think I set a new record for anxiety this year."

Needless to say, Terrence Malick did not speak to reporters about *The Thin Red Line*'s strong showing, but Grant Hill, the line producer who shared credit for the film with the banished team of Bobby Geisler and John Roberdeau, told *USA Today*, "I talked to a very excited Terry. He said, 'It's not a bad way to come out of retirement.' He's very pleased the picture got the attention."

Ian McKellen was at the Yorkshire Playhouse in Leeds, England, where he was about to open in *The Tempest*. He said, "I was told to sit quietly in an office and wait for the phone to ring, which it didn't do. And I thought, 'Ah, well.' " Then, he logged on to the official Oscar Web site to see who had been nominated, and saw his name. "I was stunned. Then the phone began ringing." As for the three nominations for *Gods and Monsters*—in addition to McKellen and Redgrave, Bill Condon's adapted screenplay was nominated—McKellen reflected, "It's not bad for a small, $3 million movie made for love and not money." Between *Gods and Monsters* and *Affliction*, Lions Gate had five nominations. Company head Mark Urman said, "It's a major day. The company is only a year old. To Miramax, this is a paltry sum. To us, my God."

Roberto Benigni said that when he got the news, "I jumped in the air because I was transported with joy!" *Access Hollywood*'s Pat O'Brien asked him how he would act if he actually did win an Oscar. "When this happens, don't worry," said Benigni. "I'll find a way to demonstrate my love and gratitude." Nick Nolte said he was particularly pleased because *Affliction* "was a small picture, $6-million-budget picture, to gather this much attention. One doesn't anticipate that. You make those kinds of films for the sake of making them . . . it's just the love of filmmaking. It makes it very special in that sense." He was also delighted that his other 1998 release was nominated for Best Picture, and he called *The Thin Red Line*, "One long epic poem. It's not conventional filmmaking at all. People who love it really love it. People who want to see something in a more traditional storytelling way are a little confused by it. But it's a beautiful film." Nolte's seventy-year-old nominated costar, James Coburn, agreed with him about *Affliction*, "We didn't make any money doing it. It was the project, the work. That's what it's all about." He also disclosed that he patterned his fierce performance on director Sam Peckinpah. One of Coburn's competitors, Billy Bob Thornton, said that his girlfriend, Laura Dern, heard about his nomination first and tried to get their dog to convey the news to him, but that it didn't work so she had to tell him in English. Geoffrey Rush disagreed with his director about Joseph Fiennes, saying, "Joe is the lucky one. He got to sleep with Gwyneth Paltrow and Cate Blanchett. I only got an Oscar nomination."

"It is exciting because this was a little British film with a small budget that we shot in the middle of winter where we had daylight for only a few minutes for eight weeks," said *Hilary and Jackie*'s Emily Watson. "We were very passionate about it, but you don't know what is going to happen without a huge studio oiling the way." The *New York Daily News*'s Denis Hamill wondered, "Is there deep sadness in Watson's own background from which she draws such powerful and convincing performances? 'Actually no,' she says. 'Sorry to disappoint you, but I had a strangely untroubled and happy upbringing, I'm afraid. A very happy childhood, and I'm a very regular girl, really. I like home life, movies, theatre, friends. I'm not crazy or climbing the walls. Well, only occasionally." Watson's nominated costar Rachel Griffiths joked that, because of all her screaming, "I think the neighbors must think I'm being systematically raped every time the phone rings." The Australian actress also said, "My mother's already discussing whether she should wear Issey Miyake or some local designer.'"

Lynn Redgrave reflected back on when she had been in the running with *Georgy Girl*: "When I was nominated the first time, it was all very exciting and I was the new flavor of month. I didn't know that intensity doesn't last. That year, I won the New York Film Critics and a Golden Globe and was nominated for an

Oscar—I thought, boy, you do a big role in a film and that's what happens to you. I will be fifty-six by the time of the Academy Awards. If I can have that renaissance, anybody can."

Randy Newman received three nominations this year, for contributions to three different movies: Best Song for "That'll Do," from the box-office bomb of a sequel, *Babe: Pig in the City*; Best Original Musical or Comedy Score for *A Bug's Life*; and Best Original Dramatic Score for *Pleasantville*. This brought his total number of nominations to twelve; *Showbiz Today*'s Sherri Sylvester referred to him as the Susan Lucci of the Oscars. Oprah Winfrey's dream wasn't completely ignored: *Beloved* received a nomination for Best Costume Design.

A Sunday Kind of Love

For people who treasure tradition, it was the worst possible news. The Academy Awards were being moved from their usual Monday night setting to Sunday. Although the ceremony had not *always* been held on Monday, that day had become identified with the Oscars, as integral a part of the Awards as the presence of PriceWaterhouse, as well as adding to an overall holiday atmosphere for the ceremony. The Academy had fixed upon Mondays because it's traditionally the slowest night of the week for movie attendance, meaning theater owners took a smaller hit if people stayed home to watch the Awards. But Sunday was the evening with the highest levels of television viewing, and both the Academy and ABC hoped the move would increase ratings—apparently they weren't satisfied with the supposed one billion people who watched the show worldwide. ABC Entertainment Chairman Stu Bloomberg would have you believe that in terms of important events, "On a scale of one to ten, this is an eleven!"

Another factor cited was the traffic problems that occurred when a phalanx of limousines made their way to the Academy Awards at the very same time regular folks were driving home from work. But many in Hollywood were distraught that scheduling the show on Sunday meant that there'd no longer be a three-day Oscar weekend. Beverly Hills hostess Nikki Haskell wailed to Liz Smith, " 'They've taken away a day from us and destroyed the schedule. I think it's an awful shame that you can throw out a tradition just to get better television ratings. After all, the Oscars are supposed to be about movies, not TV." Another industry-ite complained to *New York Post* columnist Neal Travis, "The old way was best, with the fun starting Friday and building through to Monday night. Now Monday's going to be just another working day out here."

The Oscar ceremony once again would be in the hands of Gilbert Cates. Billy Crystal was adamant about not hosting this year, telling E! "I need to take a break. It's good to step away a little bit." He added, "I am just getting a little upset that people get mad at me when I'm not doing it." Crystal also kidded to *Us* that "I don't want to spend two months worrying about writing *Saving Private Ryan* jokes." His replacement wasn't a new face, however, as Whoopi Goldberg would be back for her third go-around. Writer Bruce Villanch said Goldberg was wondering, "How did I get a year where there's nothing to make fun of?" Debbie Allen hadn't weaved her particular brand of magic for a while, so after four years of non-cringe inducing dance numbers, Cates brought her back. Allen had apparently been watching the show in the interim, though, because she declared, "Smaller is better. I didn't want to return with an entire army like I've had in the past." Instead, she would be employing only five dancers. The producer was mum about a theme for the show, although the *New York Daily News* did report "Insiders say the show will use the show to look back at movies as the art form of the twenieth century."

In addition, the starting time of the ceremony was being moved up from 6 o'clock to 5:30, in the hopes that more East Coast viewers would still be awake when the show came to its conclusion. Seeing how popular the various preceremony programs had become, the Academy would, for the first time, be presenting its own show from 5 o'clock to 5:30. Academy President Bob Rehme promised that it would "take advantage of unprecedented access to areas not available to non-Academy preshows, such as lobbies, backstage areas and the auditorium itself." Hosting the program would be Geena Davis, whose career had been stalling of late. In fact, her current ambition had been not to

be in a blockbuster movie, but to make the United States Olympics archery team. At a news conference announcing her participation in the program, Davis got in a little dig at Joan Rivers when she stated, "The one thing I can virtually guarantee that it will not include, however, is anybody yelling, 'Who made your dress?' " Rivers later got back at her by reflecting, "She may turn out to be fabulous—there may be more to her than dimples and boobs."

A Rat's Tale

The Board of Governors announced that Honorary Awards would be going to two veteran filmmakers. Norman Jewison was to receive the Irving G. Thalberg Memorial Award. Because Jewison was primarily thought of as a director (most of the films he produced he also directed), it would be one of those times—as was the year Steven Spielberg received the Thalberg—that the Award's specific purpose of honoring the work of producers was distorted. But this was hardly the stuff of controversy.

The Lifetime Achievement Award, though . . . . Pressed by Board member and former Academy President Karl Malden, the Board of Governors decided—unanimously—that it would be a good idea to give an Honorary Oscar to Elia Kazan, even though the eighty-nine-year-old director already had two golden statuettes at home in New York. Malden would tell the *Los Angeles Times*, "When I got up to talk, I suspected there would be a big fight, but no one debated it at all." In announcing the vote, President Rehme declared, "Elia Kazan is one of the most extraordinary directors of this century. Both on the stage and on film, he made pronounced and lasting changes in the nature of our dramatic forms."

Although he was generally acclaimed for such films as *A Streetcar Named Desire*, *On The Waterfront*, and *East of Eden*, many people despised Kazan because of his behavior during the McCarthy era. To avoid being blacklisted, the director, who had been a member of the Communist party for a year-and-half in the '30s, cozied up to the House Un-American Activities Committee, giving the names of people—theater colleagues from the 1930s and 1940s—he said were members of the Communist Party. (Membership in the Communist Party was not illegal.)

While other people in the film industry had fed names to Congress to save their careers, Kazan was reviled for several reasons. One was that, unlike most of the others who squealed, he never apologized, expressed regret, or even admitted that his actions were less than admirable; instead, for decades, he arrogantly continued to argue that snitching had been the honorable thing. Also, he didn't simply testify against old comrades and leave it at that. A day after ratting to HUAC, Kazan—as if to rub it in people's faces—placed self-serving ads in the *New York Times* and *Daily Variety* in which he declared What A Good Boy Am I and said that all good liberals like himself should follow his lead and do what they could to destroy Communism and Communists. In addition, Kazan didn't *need* to testify in order to protect his livelihood. At the time, he was the preeminent director of the New York stage, and was balancing his Hollywood and Broadway careers. Even if he had been blackballed in movies, he would have continued to have fruitful—and highly profitable—work in the theater. As Victor Navasky wrote of Kazan in his history of the blacklist, *Naming Names*, "From 1946 on he had *de facto* first-refusal rights on any Broadway-bound play. And since the blacklist never dominated the New York theatre as it did Hollywood, the conventional wisdom was that he wouldn't have, in the vernacular of the day, to sing for his supper." Rumors circulated that Kazan had signed a Faustian deal with 20th Century Fox, receiving a huge sum of money in return for making nice with HUAC. Finally, many people believed because Kazan was such a big deal in the movies at the time, that if he had stood up to HUAC, the Committee might have been discredited and the studios might have backed away from the blacklist. For all these reasons, in previous years, both the American Film Institute and the Los Angeles Film Critics Association voted down motions to honor Kazan.

When he heard about his Honorary Oscar, Kazan told the *New York Times*, "I feel very happy about this. I'm flattered to death. I'm pleased with it. What more can I say?" Interestingly, at first little was said about Kazan's Award, and two-and-a-half weeks after it had

been announced, Bernard Weinraub reported in the *New York Times* that "what seems most surprising about the overall response to the Academy's announcement is how muted it has been. The emotions and fury that stamped the blacklist days and lingered for decades finally seem to have faded."

Weinraub spoke a little too soon. Kazan's testimony had been in 1952, but forty-seven years could not dilute the sense of outrage that a person who, in the words of Oscar–nominated blacklisted screenwriter, Walter Bernstein, "went over to the side of people who were bigots and racists and gave them his name and his eminence, which was considerable and helped the forces of oppression," would be honored for Lifetime Achievement. Shortly after Weinraub's piece, the *Hollywood Reporter* brought word that, "A group called the Committee Against Silence said it will stage a demonstration on Oscar night to protest the Academy of Motion Picture Arts and Sciences' presentation of an Honorary Award to famed director Elia Kazan." The Committee issued a statement, saying:

> The bad old days of HUAC and McCarthyism were the time when fear ruled the land—fear of dissent. Without dissent, without the freedom to express unpopular ideas or to make unpopular associations, there is no democracy and no chance to move government to the popular will.
>
> Elia Kazan cooperated with HUAC, validating their reign of terror, blacklisting thousands of men and women, not just in Hollywood, but throughout the country, destroying all progressive organizations and crippling the trade union movement.
>
> As a result, our country has suffered a fearful regression. Internally, we have become a nation ridden with crime, poverty and homelessness and an atrocious increasing gap between wealth and poverty; externally, we have moved from "The Land of the Free" to become the international bully, envied, perhaps, but feared and hated. Let's not reward HUAC, McCarthy and Elia Kazan for helping to bring about this dreadful transforma-

tion. We must protest everything that Citizen Kazan has stood for.

To that end, "There will be a protest demonstration among all the lovely gowns and black ties at the Academy Awards ceremony." In addition to those who had been blacklisted, the protesters would include a variety of progressive organizations, such as Los Angeles Greens, Orange County Greens, and the California Association of Professional Scientists.

Blacklisted writer Bernard Gordon, the cochair of the Committee Against Silence, said he wasn't looking for people to boycott the Oscars; instead he put forth the suggestion that those in the audience show their disapproval by not standing or clapping when Kazan received his Award. "I got the idea of not applauding when I watched President Clinton's State of the Union and the Republicans sat on their hands. I think the same thing of [repulsive congressman] Bob Barr and Elia Kazan. One is not a good director and one is a good director. But they're the same." Gordon said, "This is not an attempt to keep people from going in. We want to convey our basic position that it is shameful to honor a man who knuckled under to the House Un-American Activities Committee, a man who had such prestige and financial invulnerability that there was no need to do this in order to protect his own career." Gordon's cochair on the Committee was Leone Hankey, an activist lawyer who hadn't even been born when Kazan testified. She indicated, "All the people who were blacklisted died off or are incredibly old. I'm dealing with all these eighty-eight-year-old people whom I have to yell at on the phone to make them hear me. It's poignant that they want to get their message out."

Reporting that "a quiet protest is slowly gathering force in Hollywood against the planned accolade," the Washington Post quoted from another blacklistee, writer Norma Barzman, who, furious about the Award, was soliciting money for an anti-Kazan ad to run in the trade papers: "He's being honored as if he were a hero when in fact he was a heel. It's no joke. He destroyed many, many lives." The Post also had a rebuttal from Kazan's lawyer, Floria Lasky who "said those criticizing Kazan have not accounted for the high-stakes atmosphere of the time. 'It's a big subject,' she said. 'Why one person would decide to do it that way, and somebody else not . . .' she paused. 'They show no respect for another person's point of view' "— as if Kazan's destructive behavior could be sloughed off as a "point of view."

Phoebe Brand was one of the people Kazan had named. Now ninety-one, the actress said, "Almost everyone who named names died shortly after it, they were so guilty. But not Elia Kazan. He felt he did the right thing. But what kind of a person is that? He was an opportunist . . . He justifies himself, which is a mistake. Most others have said they're sorry. I've forgiven many of them, but not him." And John Sanford, whose now-deceased wife Marguerite Roberts was a blacklist victim, said "Kazan is a fink bastard. The son of a bitch deserves nothing more than a kick in the ass."

In contrast, game show host and American Spectator columnist Ben Stein said the thought of the protest "makes me sick. The Hollywood Ten were a disgrace to every decent man or woman in America. Elia Kazan was a hero." For all his pomposity when spouting off trivial facts on Win Ben Stein's Money, he was ignorant on this subject, for Kazan's testimony had nothing at all to do with the Hollywood Ten; the Ten were writers and directors imprisoned after having been fingered during the first round of HUAC's Hollywood investigations in 1947. Stein also said, "I think I'll go there and picket for Elia Kazan. Hollywood and New York are the only places left where Stalinists are heroes."

The Village Voice had a caricature of Kazan on its cover; instead of holding an Oscar, he was gripping a golden rodent, and the accompanying caption was "Hollywood's #1 Rat." Inside, film critic Michael Atkinson profiled Abraham Polonsky, whom he called "easily the most talented and fascinating filmmaker to be blacklisted, and arguably American film's greatest HUAC loss." Polonsky, who was one of the organizers of the Committee Against Silence, had seen his Hollywood career come to a halt after he directed his first movie—the classic socially conscious film noir, Force of Evil. Atkinson asserted that, "It's not going too far today to suggest that Force of Evil is more original, sublime, and lyrical than any Kazan film; equally, what it implies for the career that never subsequently happened is momentous. The '50s, at the very least, would not have been the same decade had Polonsky been working at full cry." Atkinson lamented that "Polonsky is famous now only as the Kazan antithesis, the Hollywood director who lived up to his principles and surrendered his career rather than surrender his friends." About Kazan, the eighty-eight-year-old Polonsky said, "One, I wouldn't want to be buried in the same cemetery with the guy. Two, if I was on a desert island with him, I'd be afraid to fall asleep because he'd probably eat me for breakfast." He did admit, "I don't like Kazan, but I try not to confuse my moral hatreds with my aesthetic hatreds. He made a lot of good pictures, so you could say he deserves an award for his work—I just wouldn't want to give it to him. He was a creep." Polonsky also said, "I'll be watching, hoping someone shoots him. It would no doubt be a thrill in an otherwise dull evening"—a tongue in cheek statement that hysterical, current day right-wing zealots pointed to as proof of the viciousness of commies.

Stuart Klawans of *The Nation* wrote that Kazan's "reputation ultimately rests on five films: *Gentleman's Agreement, A Streetcar Named Desire, Viva Zapata!, On the Waterfront,* and *East of Eden.* That's not a bad record. Then again, Jules Dassin managed to make at least as many memorable pictures—*The Naked City, Night and the City, Rififi, He Who Must Die,* and *Topkapi*—despite being forced out of the United States by the blacklist. I look forward keenly to the news that he, too, has been recognized by the Academy." Dassin's take: "Elia Kazan . . . was a traitor. Some of those he betrayed were his close friends." Film historian Patrick McGilligan pointed out the lie that Kazan was some sort of idealist: "He didn't name everyone in the cell. He named the people he didn't like. He named the people who he felt condescended to him . . . He was a cutthroat guy."

Which Side Are You On?

Hollywood-ites came down on each side. No surprise that Charlton Heston would be all for Kazan; he chortled about this Lifetime Achievement Award,

"Sometimes the good guys win," and said the honor was "richly deserved. Nobody can challenge that he was one of the great directors of his period." That wasn't true, because Kirk Honeycutt of the *Hollywood Reporter* set forth that "few, if any, reputable critics would place Kazan on their list of cinema's greatest artists." He also felt, "a life cannot be separated from the art it creates. What a man thinks and believes and does—his ethos—is what fuels his art."

Director Mark Rydell, while saying he had "only the deepest compassion" for those who had been blacklisted, argued, "It's fifty years ago. The streets are full of Mercedes-Benzes and Toyotas, many driven by writers who were blacklisted. We forgive the Germans and Japanese, do we not? This holier-than-thou attitude that prevents Mr. Kazan from receiving an Award that he deserves for his work is an appalling kind of retribution." Kim Hunter, who won an Oscar for Kazan's *A Streetcar Named Desire* and was blacklisted shortly after, said, "We're through with that friggin' period. Let it go!" Warren Beatty had made his film debut in Kazan's *Splendor in the Grass,* and was now declaring, "Although you and I might feel he made a mistake, neither you nor I were around in that period," and, thus had no right to judge. Ernest Borgnine cooed, "If they want to honor that wonderful man, I say honor him." Tom Arnold felt, "If we didn't honor backstabbers in this town, there would be no Awards ceremony."

Karl Malden, who started the whole mess in the first place said, "As far as I'm concerned, there's no place for politics in any art form. An award like this is about your body of work. And when it comes to a body of work, Elia Kazan deserves to be honored." Malden apparently didn't buy painter Jo Baer's famous statement that "all art is eventually political." The Academy's official argument about the separation of art and politics was highly disingenuous because, for many Honorary Awards, the recipient's off-screen life had been brought into the mix. For instance, three years ago, in honoring Kirk Douglas, Steven Spielberg praised him not simply for his performances but because "he helped to hammer the blacklist to pieces." Douglas's Award was specifically to salute him "as a creative and moral force in the motion picture community." The citation for James Stewart's 1984 Lifetime Achievement said the honor was in part "for his high ideals, both on and off the screen," while a year later, Paul Newman's Award cited "personal integrity." And when Myrna Loy was honored in 1990, it was "in recognition of her extraordinary qualities both on screen and off." (Loy was a politically active progressive Democrat.) The Academy could not in good faith pretend that its Lifetime Honorary Awards were solely for what was on the screen.

On the issue of separating art and politics, Bernard Gordon acknowledged that people with reprehensible politics could sometimes be great artists, "But they are giving Kazan a Lifetime Achievement Award, and the major achievement of his lifetime was to contribute to one of the worst civil liberties violations in the country." Last year's Lifetime Achievement Honorary winner, Stanley Donen, mused, "The man directed some wonderful pictures, and for that he should be applauded. But his activities, as a person, were deplorable. That just comes down to who he is, and whether or not he gets an Oscar doesn't change who he is." Fay Kanin, a former Academy President, said, "I too wonder why the Board of Governors had decided to do this—he has received two Oscars for his own work." Martin Landau said, "He's an old friend of mine. I have a lot of mixed feelings . . . As an artist he deserves to be honored, as a man he doesn't." Oscar-winning actress Lee Grant, who had been blacklisted for many years after refusing to testify before HUAC, told *Daily Variety*'s Army Archerd her opinion of what Kazan had done back in 1952: "What a dumb choice to have made. If I never worked again, I would never have done that."

Archerd, a man known for his temperate nature, would be among those not applauding Kazan. "He has already been honored for his work behind the camera," said Archerd, who then corrected himself. "He has gotten two Oscars. The word 'honor' is inaccurate, because of what he stands for and what he did." The revered columnist explained:

The days now dwindle down to a precious few before the March 21 awarding of the Oscars, and I am regularly interviewed on my guesses for winners. I am also regularly asked my opinion of one winner already announced: the Honorary Academy Award to Elia Kazan. I am not a member of the Academy, and thus not a member of its Board. But I am a member of this showbiz community and feel I must remember the past and speak out at present.

Daily Variety's Front Page, Monday, April 14, 1952, carried the story of Elia Kazan's appearance before the House Un-American Activities Committee . . . . On the back page of *Daily Variety* that same day, Kazan took out a full-page ad. After stating what he claimed were the dangers of Communism, Kazan said, "It left me with the passionate conviction that we must never let the Communists get away with the pretense that they stand for the very things which they kill in their own countries. I am talking about free speech, a free press, the rights of property, the rights of labor, racial equality and about all individual rights." But, after Kazan revealed names, the individual rights of dozens of his peers were soon deprived. Many were forced into poverty, or left this country to work under assumed names for decades. Kazan never has apologized. Will he do so when he is honored by the Academy on March 21? That is something to be seen—and hear. Members of the Board to whom I have spoken claim he is being honored for his "work, not his politics." Another said, "What about all those who decry him but who drive Lexus and Mercedes, haven't they forgiven?" Well I don't know of any cars which have turned in their fellow travelers. Judging from what I hear, there is certain to be an air of disagreement when Elia Kazan is announced as "honored" at the 71st Academy Awards. I, for one, will not be giving him a standing ovation.

Historian Arthur Schlesinger, Jr. jumped into the fray with a *New York Times* op-ed article, in which he showed himself to still be the same Cold Warrior he had been back in the days of the Kennedy Administration, as he condemned the surviving blacklistees for having been "driven into orgies of self-righteous frenzy." He had the gall to write, "If the occasion calls for apologies, let Mr. Kazan's denouncers apologize for the aid and comfort they gave to Stalinism." And Schlesinger fell back upon the tired argument that everyone who feels okay about the blacklist always makes—he drew imaginary, inapposite analogies: "Had Mr. Kazan been a member of the German-American Bund naming underground Nazis, would they have condemned him just as much. Or a former Klansman who informed on his hooded brethren? . . . Mafia thug . . . member of the Nixon White House . . . whistle blower?" Bernard Gordon and Abraham Polonsky wrote back, "Demonizing the left, lumping us all together as unreconstructed Stalinists, is not addressing the issue. This is not about informers in the abstract, as Mr. Schlesinger argues, but informers for the House Committee on Un-American Activities . . . The blacklist was not seriously aimed at Hollywood Communists but at dissenters of every stripe throughout the United States. It succeeded ultimately in silencing all manner of protest on the gravest issues confronting the American people." Whereas Schlesinger quoted screenwriter Dalton Trumbo's famous line, "there were only victims" during the McCarthy era, Gordon and Polonsky gave another Trumbo quote, "Kazan is one of those for whom I feel contempt, because he carried down men much less capable of defending themselves than he." And Trumbo's son, Christopher, said of Kazan's Oscar, "It's a slap in the face to everyone who suffered. They didn't need to do it."

A woman named Carol Travis from Los Angeles wrote to the New York Times and eloquently expressed why a Lifetime Achievement Oscar for this man was considered so contemptible by such a large number of people: "The reason many of us oppose giving this particular award to Mr. Kazan, who already has two Oscars, is that he traded on his power and reputation to deprive others in his own profession of the opportunity to work. His 'lifetime achievement' was built at the cost of theirs. Whether he or his friends were right or wrong about Communism is besides the point."

Perhaps the most unexpected anti-Kazan sentiment came from Rod Steiger who said, "Age and ability in the arts or anything else, in my opinion, does not excuse a crime." Steiger said of Kazan's snitching, "He was our father figure, a man who was supposed to lead us toward honesty and principles in acting. It was a terrible emotional shock . . . It was like my father was found sleeping with my sister." Steiger was vehemently denouncing the director, even though he had appeared in On the Waterfront after Kazan had testified. Moreover, that film was Kazan's—and screenwriter and co-stool pigeon Budd Schulberg's—specious defense of what they had done, an attempt to con audiences into believing that fighting corrupt union bosses was the same as informing on people for their political beliefs. Nevertheless, Steiger told L.A. Weekly, "This man created hell for a lot of people," and on Larry King Live drew an analogy when he said, "I couldn't support Albert Speer no matter how good an architect he was." Steiger appeared on Nightline and said that had he then been aware of Kazan's testimony, he would have walked off On the Waterfront—that he hadn't been known would indicate that he had been appallingly uninformed about current affairs at the time. When Karl Malden heard about Steiger's statement, he said, "Rod is either very stupid or a liar."

On the eve of the Oscars, L.A. Weekly reported that at least two of the thirty-nine Academy Board members now regretted voting in support of Kazan's Award. Cinematographer Haskell Wexler, whose lefty credentials were unimpeachable, told the paper that "My hope had been to heal and that people would understand that in insane times people did things that were reprehensible. But what happened was that people came out of the woodwork to defend the blacklist and things that were indefensible." Veteran screenwriter—and Oscar show writer—Hal Kanter began a speech at the Writers Guild Awards by stating, "My first impulse, always as a human being, is to forgive and let bygones go by. But in the current controversy over an Academy Award, I am ambivalent about honoring Elia Kazan." Army Archerd noted, "That was quite an admission of recanting by Kanter, who was one of those board members who unanimously voted to honor Kazan at this year's Awards." Likewise, director Paul Mazursky told Archerd, "I shouldn't have voted so quickly with the board after Karl Malden's impassioned presentation for Kazan."

"Mr. Kazan has been honored by the Academy for his art and contribution to film," said a spokeswoman for Gilbert Cates. "Our feeling is Mr. Kazan is well enough respected for his art that there will be plenty of people that applaud." But Archerd told the *Los Angeles Times*, "I know the people doing the show are worried," he says. "We could have some real Oscar drama. This is better than any scene Kazan could have directed." Ironically, although the Award was intended to purge Elia Kazan, give him validation and welcome him back into the family of decent citizenry, it had the opposite effect: His actions were being scrutinized as they hadn't been for decades, and whereas his past behavior had lain dormant it was now out in the open for the whole world to see. And if it's true that you can judge a person's character by his friends, well, a pro-Kazan rally was being planned by the lunatic fringe Ayn Rand Institute.

A DreamWorks Nightmare

The day that the nominations were announced, Harvey Weinstein was explaining to the *New York Daily News* what he perceived to be the secret of Miramax's Oscar success: "We're a New York company. We read books. We read scripts. We also happen to love Hollywood movies. We're the outsider Hollywood people like, as opposed to the outsider Hollywood people resent." If this last part was accurate on nominations day, chances are it no longer held true several weeks later.

Miramax had sent screening cassettes to 50,000 Screen Actors Guild members. And wouldn't you know, the three top SAG awards went to Miramax films. Gwyneth Paltrow was named Best Actress, Roberto Benigni Best Actor (on stage, he lifted up, first, the woman carrying out the statuettes and, then, presenter Helen Hunt), and *Shakespeare in Love* won for Best Ensemble cast. (As an indication of the absurd extent to which the adulation for *Life Is Beautiful* had gone, the film was nominated for Best Ensemble, even

though it was essentially a one-man show for its star.) The Supporting Awards were not from Miramax, however, with the prizes going to Robert Duvall for *A Civil Action* and Kathy Bates in *Primary Colors*, meaning that after having been shrugged off as an also-ran in the Oscars, she now had to be considered a serious part of the race.

At the beginning of March, Bernard Weinraub wrote an article in the *New York Times* entitled, "Using The Hard Sell To Grab The Gold." He said that "the Miramax juggernaut . . . was at work, spinning journalists and spending lavishly on trade paper advertisements." Noting that *Shakespeare in Love* "had emerged as *the* rival to *Saving Private Ryan*," Weinraub reported that "this rivalry is unusually intense." He ascertained that "at the moment, *Saving Private Ryan* . . . seems to remain the dominant film of the year and the one to beat for Best Picture." Still, "what resonates at DreamWorks is the sense—and it may be sour grapes—that Miramax is in overdrive with its plethora of publicists and spinners and a seemingly open checkbook." Weinstein insisted that "It's the same kind of Academy campaign we've always run. I don't know how to do it differently." But, Terry Press, the head of marketing at DreamWorks said to Weinraub, "I'm running a competitive *and* respectful campaign." John Hartl of the *Seattle Times* took DreamWorks's release strategy to task. "If it had been released at the end of December, *Saving Private Ryan* might have had a chance to match *Titanic*'s near-record collection," he wrote. "Spielberg's World War II epic, however, was released in July, and it was around just long enough for a backlash to set in." Whereas in the summer she had made a point of saying what a good thing it was for *Saving Private Ryan* to open in July, now Terry Press was complaining that being a more recent release gave *Shakespeare* an advantage, and she yawped, "It is my understanding that the Academy Award for Best Picture is supposed to go to the outstanding achievement in motion pictures—not the most enjoyable in current release or the easiest to watch twice on tape." If she was really so naïve to believe this, then she had no business running an Oscar campaign.

That same week Weinraub's column appeared, an article in *New York* by Nikki Finke spread the word that some industry-ites were complaining about "what many view as Miramax's over-the-line campaign to boost *Shakespeare in Love*'s come-from-behind chances of taking the Best Picture." Finke then reported that things were being said about *Saving Private Ryan* that weren't very nice, that "journalists and critics on both coasts report that they were recipients of negative Miramax spin, including comments from Weinstein himself, who opined to at least one major critic that *Ryan* 'peaks in the first twenty minutes' and 'wouldn't hold up in December.' " When Weinstein got wind of this accusation, he protested, "I would never stoop to that level. I would have to betray my own feelings about *Private Ryan*, which I adored."

There was also widespread bellyaching in the industry about how much Miramax was spending on trade paper ads. Fox Chairman Bill Mechanic joked, "I was told the other day that over 100,000 trees were cut down this year just for Oscar ads, with Miramax responsible for nearly an entire forest." But a Miramax marketing executive said that people were confusing Oscar campaign ads with regular advertising for the movie—although what he didn't say was that the two were pretty much interchangeable. And the publisher of *Variety* said that the spending for *Private Ryan*'s Oscar ads was comparable to that for *Shakespeare*'s.

The *Los Angeles Times* further detailed the hard feelings that were developing between the two film companies. According to reporter Richard Natale, "The massive Miramax ad campaign—in the $15-million range so far, according to sources—in the trades and other publications has caused DreamWorks to fire back with its own stronger-than-anticipated push for its Best Picture nominee *Saving Private Ryan*." One of the poobahs at DreamWorks, Jeffrey Katzenberg told Natale, "There is no question that the aggressiveness of the extraordinary campaign Miramax has run in support of *Shakespeare* has caused us to do more on behalf of *Ryan* than we had initially planned." Miramax threatened legal action against *New York* for the Finke article because, as Weinstein ululated to Natale, "They're trying to take old friends and make it seem like we're enemies. I was strongly bothered by any inference that I would say anything against *Ryan*. . . . I think Steven is our greatest living film-

maker. Why would I want to say anything negative?" Latest estimates were that DreamWorks was now spending twice as much on trade paper ads as it had originally intended. Gerry Byrne, publisher of *Variety* said, "*Private Ryan* had a dominant lead when it was released. Then a bunch of other films came out that were interesting as competitors. Thankfully, they were brought out by distributors who had the money to support their Oscar campaign." He added, "We're not complaining."

Two Miramax executives wrote to the *Los Angeles Times* to complain that the $15-million figure Natale had used was way out of line: "While this sensational number makes for a splashy headline, it is off by a factor of 500 percent. To be clear, our Oscar campaign (including trade ads, publicity, talent, travel, videocassettes and screenings) came in for slightly less than $2 million."

In the *New York Daily News*, Jack Mathews observed that DreamWorks "went to a full-court press, upping its own Oscar budget, and Spielberg himself began doing interviews, reminding folks that a vote for 'Ryan' was a vote for the men who died at Omaha Beach and beyond, and for all the grief-stricken mothers to whom they never returned. Yes, Oscar campaigning is hell."

As part of its aggressive counter-offensive, DreamWorks ran a three-page ad in the *Los Angeles Times* and *New York Times*, with the catch line, "Only one movie inspired the world to remember . . ." thus shifting the focus from *Saving Private Ryan* the movie to *Saving Private Ryan* the "positive real world force." At least all the ads for *Shakespeare in Love* were still treating it as just a movie. The newspaper ads for Miramax's other Oscar hopeful, *Life Is Beautiful,* in contrast, were no longer selling the film, but rather were all about Roberto Benigni, featuring a large photograph of his face, and a pronouncement from Rod Lurie of the local ABC radio affiliate in Los Angeles: "It will be a glorious and popular moment if Roberto Benigni wins Best Actor and it will be the first time in Academy history that an actor in a foreign film wins the top prize." Ads promoting Gwyneth Paltrow in *Shakespeare in Love* were calling attention to "Four Extraordinary Performances By One Actress In The Year's Most Oscar-

Nominated Motion Picture." There was a quartet of Paltrow pictures: she as her character, she in disguise as the young man, as Romeo, and as Juliet. These were obviously just four components of *one* performance, but that's Miramax for you.

Adding to the operatic sense of drama was the bad blood between Disney and Jeffrey Katzenberg. Having been booted out of Disney by studio head Michael Eisner, the DreamWorks cofounder did what he could to make his old company suffer, whether it was making sure DreamWorks' *Deep Impact* and *Antz* were in theaters before Disney's similar-themed *Armageddon* and *A Bug's Life*, or forcing Disney to settle a huge lawsuit with him. With this momentum going, it would be terrible if Katzenberg's sense of vengeance was stymied by DreamWorks losing the Best Picture Oscar to a film by Disney subsidiary, Miramax.

There were also reports of friction between Spielberg and another Miramax figure. The *New York Daily News*'s Rush & Molloy scooped, "Word is that Spielberg doesn't think much of Benigni's *Life Is Beautiful*, because it mixed too much laughter with the tears of the Holocaust. Spielberg said privately that he could barely sit through the movie, 'He wanted to walk out of the theatre,' says one source who has spoken with the *Saving Private Ryan* director. But Spielberg only stayed because his wife, Kate Capshaw, reminded him his exit would be noticed, the source said. 'She said it would send a bad message,' says the source. 'She told him to sit down, which he did.' " Spielberg's official stance on Benigni's film was "I'm happy when anyone makes a movie that says the Holocaust happened." Benigni reported that the Italian press picked up on the reports and ran with them, printing headlines like, "Spielberg: 'I Hate The Movie! The Movie Is Revolting!' "

Let's Do Lunch

The various parties all had to get together for food and photos, though, because it was time for the Nominees Luncheon. *USA Today*'s Claudia Puig was there to bear witness that "The atmosphere was convivial, if a bit strained"; of course, "both Spielberg and Weinstein denied any tension." Spielberg was asked for a

comment about the campaign controversy and would say only, "I have to take the high road when it comes to talking about the competition." Harvey Weinstein was a bit more talkative, blasting the *New York* article and saying of *Private Ryan*, "I think it's a great movie, and I've said it before. It solved a mystery for me about my dad, who was a combat veteran. Anybody trying to spoil my friendship with Steven Spielberg is doing it for their own reasons."

Marilyn Beck and Stacy Jenel Smith were at the Luncheon, and beamed, "What a moment—Gwyneth Paltrow skirting the stage of the grand ballroom of the Beverly Hilton Hotel to get to the table where Cate Blanchett was stationed. The fellow Oscar nominees embraced like long-lost sisters, then Gwyneth crouched next to Cate for more than five minutes, chatting. So much talent, so much blond beauty, so much star power—and both were wearing outfits with dark leather and bulky knit sweaters." The two columnists also reported, "If applause at the Nominees' Luncheon provides any clues—and occasionally it does—Oscar handicappers will find it interesting to note that Ian McKellen drew outstanding response when his name was called. So did Kathy Bates, and so did *Life Is Beautiful* nominee Roberto Benigni."

Benigni had been spending the voting period back in Hollywood and was once again pressing the flesh. Miramax hired the influential publicist Warren Cowan to put together a series of intimate dinners, where Benigni would sup with the likes of Kirk Douglas, Jack Lemmon, and Elizabeth Taylor, the cream of the Old Guard. Benigni was also advised that it would be smart to accept every invitation he received to every party, awards ceremony, or television show.

The previous summer, Ian McKellen had caused a sensation in Los Angeles starring in Ibsen's *An Enemy of the People* at the Ahmanson. During Academy Award voting season, however, he remained in the boondocks of Leeds, England performing Shakespeare, which was not doing his Oscar chances much good at all. When his theatrical commitments were finished, he came to the States. He first spent some time in New York, doing such television programs as *Charlie Rose* and *The Daily Show*, and was guest of honor at a party at the Chelsea gay bar, g. While there, he offered advice for any closeted actors: "Get out and get it over with." McKellen then spent the two weeks leading up to the Oscars in Los Angeles. Bernard Weinraub wrote, "Although obviously buoyed by the nomination, Mr. McKellen also seems puzzled and a bit irritated at the swirl of political-style campaigning for the Award. He is, after all, a serious British stage actor who is unaccustomed to Oscar fever. 'Somehow, I never want to do it again. It takes up an enormous amount of time as you throw yourself into it. And the situation I find myself in is I would very much like to win the Oscar. But I seem to be in a race, a race I didn't enter. It's got a course I'm unfamiliar with. And I'm running along, but I don't know where to run. I'm not complaining about it. It's all a bit complicated for me."

"Complicated" was also the word for the private life of McKellen's costar. A week after she was nominated for an Oscar, Lynn Redgrave filed for divorce from John Clark. The break-up became public a few weeks later, when the *National Enquirer* went to press with details of the unusual circumstances of this fissure. In the article, Clark admitted, "I've been a very naughty boy." Years earlier, he had hired a young woman named Nicolette as his assistant. "One thing led to another and we started an affair," Clark told inquiring minds. The affair resulted in a baby boy but Clark zipped up about it with his wife. "I was afraid it would break her heart," the sentimentalist told the *New York Daily News*'s Rush & Molloy. But, wait, there was more. Because Nicolette was a foreign citizen, Clark and Redgrave's son, Ben—who was in the dark about the real nature of her relationship with his father—agreed, at Clark's urging, to marry her so that she could stay in the United States; this act of kindness led to Ben's real girlfriend leaving him. Clark said, "We were one big happy family—of sorts." He finally fessed up to his wife on Thanksgiving, while she was cooking the turkey. "We had guests. The entire holiday was pretty awful," he admitted. But he also told Rush & Molloy, "I don't regret anything in my life. Everything has a reason. . . . And my kids were so slow giving us grandkids, I had to make our own." E! Online reported that "This story leaves even the *National Enquirer* reporter who broke the news speechless. 'It's . . .

I don't know the words for it,' Patricia Shipp says. But, finally, she does: 'It's very much a soap opera.' "

Cindy Adams wrote, "Lynn Redgrave is my friend since I interviewed her in '67 . . . I love Lynn a whole large lot." Adams mentioned the divorce action and then recounted the *Gods and Monsters* nominee's "bizarre tale": "Husband John fathered a baby with another woman eight years ago. Lynn learned about it just this past Thanksgiving Day. This woman then married their son, Ben, who adopted the baby—not knowing it was his half brother. Ben is no longer wed, the missus having taken up with a married plumber." The columnist rang Lynn, but husband John answered, saying "Lynn's in a hotel. I'm living in this big five acres all by myself." He was grumpy because "She's declared war. She took my Directors Guild ticket away so I couldn't attend Saturday's awards event. She's not talking to me. She froze our bank accounts . . . After managing her all these years, she just quit me to hire the agent of her prime Supporting Actress rival, Kathy Bates." Adams's reaction was a rhetorical, "Is he nuts that he didn't realize how his wife would react when she learned he made a baby with his future daughter-in-law?" Clark's response: "I knew she'd get angry but, in today's world, what's the big deal? We've all got skeletons . . . Yes, I went elsewhere for sex, but always with safe people." Then the wailing commenced: "For thirty-two years, I've lived only for Lynn. Been prepared to die on her behalf. I haven't acted in twelve years or directed anyone but Lynn in twenty years. Where am I supposed to go to earn a living? I've been strictly 'Mr. Redgrave' and only some of this outside activity helped me survive."

Entertainment Weekly's Jim Mullen's "Hot Sheet," stated, "Her husband/manager says he's the father of her daughter-in-law's baby. Who's the matchmaker—Jerry Springer?" Clark was caught by TV cameras being escorted away by security when he tried to crash the SAG awards, after Redgrave had made it clear she didn't want him there. Referring to their annual Cad of the Year award, Marilyn Beck and Stacy Jenel Smith stated, "Every year someone in showbiz stands out for particularly offensive behavior. This year, we've already got a prime candidate in John Clark . . . His appearances on TV this week begging Lynn 'to lighten up' and take him back—or at least take him to the Oscars—are outrageously distasteful."

What Are the Odds?

One week prior to Oscar night, Kenneth Turan began his Oscar-prediction article by declaring, "This has been a strange year—a time that tries Oscar watchers' souls. By this point in the process, a consensus has usually emerged among those whose business or hobby it is to predict the eventual winners. The favorite doesn't always win, but at least there is one. This year, however, the smart money is scratching its collective head."

Whereas Ian McKellen had seemed like a formidable favorite when the nominations were first announced, with each approaching day, the whole Roberto Benigni phenomenon made a victory for the Italian seem more and more possible. David Hunter of the *Hollywood Reporter* still thought Sir Ian would win "because of his elegant spellbinding portrayal of one of Hollywood's own," but, a week before the Awards, *Entertainment Weekly* had the Italian comic as the likely winner. One thing was obvious. If he were to win, it would most certainly *not* be for his performance in *Life Is Beautiful*. Not even Harvey Weinstein would honestly say that Benigni's acting was better than that of his two main rivals, Ian McKellen and Nick Nolte. Rather, an Oscar for Benigni would be for his off-screen "aura." Jack Mathews of the *New York Daily News* said if he could cast the deciding vote, Benigni "would win for Best Person." The *Los Angeles Times* posited that, "If the Elia Kazan controversy is the brooding cloud over this year's ceremony, Benigni is its ray of light—to the point that some in Hollywood are saying that Academy voters could vote for him simply because they want to see what he'll do on stage." Bob Strauss of *Los Angeles Daily News* reluctantly picked Benigni as the likely winner over his own favorite, because "Ian McKellen—whose emotionally intricate work in *Gods and Monsters* towers above the rest— might make some radical gay acceptance speech that, in the year of the Kazan controversy, the Academy just doesn't want to hear."

In his interviews Ian McKellen evidenced a mar-velously dry, and very British, wit, and Nick Nolte— unlike Benigni—was a true eccentric, not a manufactured one. Whereas earlier in the decade he was on the front page of *People* as "The Sexiest Man Alive," now he was known for choosing to make films he found meaningful but which were destined not to be seen by a lot of people. Nolte also had a reputation for making public appearances while wearing pajamas. The *New York Daily News* said, "Once you sit down with him, his antenna goes up and he analyzes your level of gullibility. Then, depending on how he reads you, you may be treated to any number of whoppers: how he was born in a brothel, how he drove around the country with his late father's wooden leg in the trunk of a car (but ended up leaving it in a bar somewhere), how he had his privates cosmetically tucked." When James Coburn was on his show, David Letterman came right out and said of his costar, "Nick Nolte is nuts."

But McKellen's and Nolte's humor was certainly low-keyed and engagingly quirky in comparison to the Italian buffoon. A couple of days before the ceremony, the *Los Angeles Times* looked back and declared, "The awards season in Hollywood hasn't been the same ever since a comic whirlwind from Italy hit town in the form of Roberto Benigni . . . the candle-thin forty-six-year-old star and director of *Life Is Beautiful* bounces, jumps, laughs, cries and claps through press interviews and speeches—a man so full of life that he often leaves those around him speechless." Mark Gill, the West Coast head of Miramax said, "I ran into Penny Marshall who said, 'I heard Roberto Benigni is here. Can I meet him?' That happens over and over and over again. People are desperate to meet him because he has come out of nowhere and all of a sudden he is someone who people want to meet." The week before the Oscars, columnist Mitchell Fink reported, "Here's how big Roberto Benigni has become in Hollywood. He had dinner the other night with Barbra Streisand."

Rush & Molloy reported that two days before the Awards, Steven Spielberg and Roberto Benigni "broke bread in L.A. after months of talk that Spielberg harbored ill feelings for the film." Benigni said, "Spielberg is so nice. He is so full of love for me." He also swore that Spielberg told him, "I really like—love—your movie a lot."

Best Actress had turned into a two-way race between the two Elizabethan actresses, Gwyneth Paltrow and Cate Blanchett, with Paltrow given a slight edge by most handicappers because her vehicle was better liked. Kenneth Turan, however, felt "the favorite has to be Cate Blanchett, easily the best thing (perhaps the only good thing) in *Elizabeth*, a film the Academy liked enough to nominate seven times." Best Supporting Actress was anybody's guess between Lynn Redgrave, Kathy Bates, and Judi Dench, who may have been a slight favorite since Hollywood was now expressing misgivings that she had lost Best Actress to Helen Hunt last year (If Helena Bonham Carter had been nominated in this category this year, she might also have been considered a favorite for the same reason.) E!'s Steve Kmetko believed that Lynn Redgrave was "probably the favorite" and she also had the Golden Globe in her favor. Bates could brag of winning the Screen Actors Guild Award, even if in *Primary Colors* she was just doing her garden variety, boisterous Kathy Bates stuff; Duane Dudek of the *Milwaukee Journal Sentinel* observed, "She was no different here than in *Titanic* or *Misery*, for that matter." Moreover, in *Primary Colors* she came across as such a strong life force that it was impossible to believe her character would contemplate suicide. Redgrave would also undoubtedly receive some sympathy votes because of her marital travails, but the story may have broken too far along in the voting season to aid her too greatly.

Supporting Actor was the most wide-open race of all. Only Geoffrey Rush seemed out of the running, a combination of having won just two years earlier and the lightness of his role. A persuasive case could have been made for any of the other nominees. Ed Harris was picked by *Entertainment Weekly*, *TV Guide* ("for stiffing Harris when he was expected to score for *Apollo 13*"), and Glenn Whipp of the *Los Angeles Daily News*, who said, "Ed Harris has never won, period, which is the ultimate oversight." But Rod Dreher and Jonathan Foreman of the *New York Post* counted him out because they wondered, "What did he have to do in *Truman* besides wear a beret and sound coolly omniscient?" Barry Koltnow of the *Orange County Regis-*

ter predicted Billy Bob Thornton, on the notion that "He was robbed for *Sling Blade* so they'll make it up to him now." Robert Duvall could emerge victorious because he didn't win last year for *The Apostle*; Roger Ebert thought Duvall would be honored because of a "consistently brilliant body of work." Sentimentality over James Coburn was the wild card in this category, but after Lauren Bacall's loss two years ago, and with Peter Fonda, Julie Christie, Burt Reynolds, and Robert Forster all going home empty-handed last year, sentimentality clearly was no longer was what it once was. Moreover sentimental choices tend to go for warm, avuncular performances, such as Sean Connery's in *The Untouchables* a decade earlier, and Coburn's mean old varmint was anything but. Connery was James Bond; it remained to see whether there would be a nostalgic vote for the man who played *Our Man Flint*.

The Final Round

No one was quite sure what the dynamic was in the Best Picture race. Steven Spielberg did win the Directors Guild Awards, a good omen for *Saving Private Ryan*. But *Shakespeare in Love* defeated the war film for the Writers Guild's Best Original Screenplay Award, and the American Society of Cinematographers honored John Toll for *The Thin Red Line*, not *Private Ryan*'s Janusz Kaminski. As Harry Sheehan summed things up prognosticating in the *Orange County Register*, "Most likely: *Saving Private Ryan*. The D-Day landing sequence hits you in the gut, while much of the rest of the movie makes an open appeal to patriotism. That's an Oscar recipe. Long shot: *Shakespeare in Love*. The heavy-handed Oscar campaign Miramax has waged may be starting to backfire, but there's enough enthusiasm for romance within the Academy ranks to make this a contender." The general feeling was that at one point, Miramax's campaign probably had turned the tide for *Shakespeare in Love*, but then somewhere along the line a backlash against that same campaign had kicked in, throwing the lead back to *Saving Private Ryan*. Jay Carr of the *Boston Globe* thought that *Ryan* was still a lock: "For most of us the Oscar race for Best Picture was over last July. *Saving Private Ryan* was the heavy favorite then, and remains the heavy favorite now . . . *Ryan* is the perfect Oscar winner. It's a big film about a big event executed in a big way. It's the kind of film that Hollywood uses to present itself to the world as a class act."

On the Friday before the Awards, three ads appeared in the trade papers on the subject of Elia Kazan. One was from the Committee Against Silence, in the form of a petition condemning the Oscar recipient because "by becoming a star witness for the House Un-American Activities Committee, Kazan validated the blacklisting of thousands, not just Hollywood people, but school teachers, professors, journalists, authors and trade unionists." Interestingly, the ad also castigated the Academy for *its* past history: "Because the Academy was willing to cooperate with the blacklist, Michael Wilson, Dalton Trumbo, and Carl Foreman were denied Oscars until after their deaths. In October 1997, the WGA, SAG, DGA, and AFTRA formally offered their most sincere regrets for their role during the blacklist. The Producers Association joined in. *The Academy has never publicly repudiated its role. Nor has Kazan.*" Finally, the ad asked that those inside the Dorothy Chandler "not stand and applaud Mr. Kazan." Among the persons signing the ad—in addition to blacklist victims, including Phoebe Brand, and their survivors—were Sean Penn, James Cromwell, Carl Reiner, Theodore Bikel, Prof. Irwin Corey, Edward Asner, Charlotte Rae, and Gore Vidal.

Another ad consisted of two parallel columns. The first said, "On February 20, 1999, the Writers Guild of America honored [late blacklisted writer] Paul Jarrico with the Lt. Robert Meltzer Award for Bravery. This is what Paul Jarrico said to the House Un-American Activities Committee: 'I consider the activities of this committee subversive of the American Constitution." The second column consisted of, "On March 21, 1999, the Academy of Motion Picture Arts and Sciences is honoring Elia Kazan with an Honorary Academy Award. This is what Elia Kazan said to the House Un-American Activites Committee: 'Sid Benson, Phoebe Brand, Morris Carnovsky, Ann Howe, Tony Kraber, Lewis Leverett, Paula Miller, Clifford Odets, Art Smith, Robert Reed, Joe Bromberg.' "

Also placing an ad was an outfit going by the name of the "Ad Hoc Committee for Naming Facts,"

whose address coincidentally was c/o the Ayn Rand Institute. This ad was an effrontery to the courage and honor of those who suffered under the blacklist, and was entitled "In Praise of Elia Kazan." Nowhere was Kazan mentioned as an "artist"—even the Committee Against Silence stated "We appreciate and cherish his work"—but from the Ad Hoc ad you wouldn't even know the man made movies, only that he was a snitch who "deserves to be honored, not despite his testimony, but because of it." The ad consisted of nonsense, such as a listing of "Three Big Lies" attributed to those opposing Kazan's Oscar. The first "lie" was that "The Hollywood Communists were noble idealists." (Anyone who did even cursory research into those who were blacklisted would know that—even if, with the hindsight of six decades, they may have been naïve—they absolutely were idealists who were committed to civil rights and the union movement.) The second: "By requiring people to testify about their private beliefs, Congress violated their freedom of speech," and the third was "The Hollywood Communists were unjustly persecuted by the studios that refused to hire them." Even though membership in the Communist Party had not been illegal, the Ad Hoc Committee felt it was a fine thing that party members had been blacklisted because it was "a subversive organization." And then, after espousing its fundamentally un-American positions, these Ad Hoc people were brazen enough to ask those attending the Oscars "to wear an American flag lapel pin as a symbol of support for Mr. Kazan and his opposition to Communism."

A week before the Awards, Marilyn Beck and Stacy Jenel Smith wrote, "We can't recall an Academy Awards laced with so much ill will—out-and-out-hostility—as, sadly, we are seeing this year." The columnists cited the Elia Kazan brouhaha which "has intensified since word got out that both Martin Scorsese and Robert De Niro will present the Award." They also mentioned the accusations that Miramax "has gone way—way—over the top in Oscar campaigning for *Shakespeare in Love.* Even to the point of trying to raise doubts about the worth of *Saving Private Ryan,* something Miramax denies and we never heard." But in addition, the duo reported, "On the other hand . . . there's speculation that it is actually DreamWorks spreading the word that Miramax is putting down *Private Ryan*. We find that hard to believe." Beck and Smith's conclusion: "Whatever the facts, whatever the results, the 71st annual Academy Awards might be remembered most not for the productions and personalities who were honored but for the politics that tore the industry apart."

"In the not-too-distant past, the Academy Awards were mere baubles, glittering prizes bestowed by studio-dependent voters on the members of their club without much rhyme or reason and certainly little controversy," wrote the *Hollywood Reporter*'s Stephen Galloway on Oscar weekend. "This year, something has changed. As the Oscars arrive after weeks of anticipation, they come against a backdrop of controversy unlike anything witnessed in years. While many of these controversies seem like tempests in a teapot, the media attention that they have received has been nothing short of extraordinary and has transferred a once-chummy event into a modern day battlefield." *Entertainment Weekly* referred to "the highly publicized Miramax/DreamWorks war, a conflict so bloody (and expensive) not even Spielberg could film it."

And these observers didn't even bring up Lynn Redgrave and John Clark, or Bobby Geisler, John Roberdeau and Terrence Malick. Malick had made the *Thin Red Line* producers sign an agreement that they wouldn't attend the Academy Awards. They were, however, official Oscar nominees as the coproducers of a Best Picture finalist and, because of that status, were given tickets by the Academy. Malick said if they went, he wouldn't, but Geisler told *Daily Variety*'s Michael Fleming, "John and I feel it is our right to be there, and I feel I deserve to be there and that we were responsible for getting the movie off the ground, and I'm proud to sign my name to it. We are at odds with Terry, but I'd hoped we could create a truce for one night." Mike Medavoy said, "It should be clear that after Phoenix bought the rights from them, they had nothing to do with the picture. And the fact they would abrogate a signed agreement that they wouldn't show up, that becomes the issue."

As a symbol of how standards in Hollywood had fallen to new lows, the Clint Eastwood anti-death penalty mystery, *True Crime,* opened on Oscar week-

end. In full page ads for the movie, Warner Brothers included the statement from one Joanna Langfield from something called "The Movie Minute" enthusing that *True Crime* was "A true potboiler."

A Brand New Lynn

The last official pre–Academy Award event—other than parties—was the Independent Spirit Awards. One thing no one who was there will ever forget was Best Actress winner Ally Sheedy's frightening bid to become the Greer Garson of independent cinema, as she gave a nine minute speech that ranged from incoherent to just plain strange. Much more warmly received was the speech Lynn Redgrave gave after winning Best Supporting Actress. The *Gods and Monsters* actress began by saying, "You don't realize, well you probably do if you've been reading the tabloids, how much this means to me." Alluding to her personal trials, Redgrave continued, "I'm a woman of a certain age and this independence happens at a moment when I'm striking out in a new and independent life. And there are three women who have helped me stand here without crying in front of all of you. And they are my shrink, my lawyer, and my new agent. So, Martha, Emily and Susan Smith, God bless you." Her affirmation of independence brought a rousing reaction from the crowd. Had the speech been made while the Oscar voting was still active, it might have provided the personal connection that would have clinched the Award for Redgrave: instead of being brought down by a tawdry situation, she had risen to a strong new position. And later in the ceremony, Ian McKellen won Best Actor and said, "It's very odd being a foreigner in your country at this time of year. I've enjoyed every minute, but I don't think I want to do it again." *Gods and Monsters* was named Best Independent Picture of the year.

John Hartl of the *Seattle Times* noted, "Once regarded as the prime distributor of independent films in the United States, Miramax was mostly shut out . . . The company did earn one of several facetious prizes: The Shelf, presented in honor of the distributor that had acquired the most films without releasing them." Presenter Illeana Douglas noted that Harvey and Bob

Weinstein were "unavailable" to come to the Independent Spirits and quipped, "They were pressing Gwynie's dress." At Miramax's pre-Oscar bash later that night, Harvey Weinstein could be heard wondering, worriedly, whether he had pushed too hard for *Shakespeare in Love* in his hunt for Oscar glory.

The Big Night

About 500 people were outside the Dorothy Chandler Pavilion protesting Elia Kazan's Oscar. Among the signs they carried were "Honor Courage, Not Kazan," "Best Supporting Snitch," "Blacklisted Directors Coulda Been Contenders" and "Kazan—the Linda Tripp of the '50s"; the demonstrators chanted, "Don't stand, for Kazan." Sixty supporters of squealing were across the street. One of their signs lauded the man who did his best to help stifle free political thought, "Kazan: Defender of Freedom in America"; another declared, "Commies Drool, Capitalists Rule." A delightful individual held a sign stating "I Love Blacklists." Fights broke out between the two groups and the police had to call for reinforcements. Because the anti-Kazan demonstrators were placed along the route for arriving limousines, some fans who hadn't gotten into the bleachers offered the protestors money for their signs, so they could pose as demonstrators and have a better view of the stars as the emerged from their limos.

On account of the Academy's official *Countdown to the Oscars* preshow, the other forecourt programs were forced to sign off a half-hour before the ceremony began. Arriving celebrities did *not* arrive a half hour earlier than usual in order to watch the preshow on monitors inside the Dorothy Chandler Pavilion, however. The result was the programs on E!, KABC, and the WB's KTLA didn't have anywhere near their usual number of interviews, and were instead stuffed with filler material, such as back stories about the nominated films. In fact, Joan Rivers complained that crews were trying to delay the arrivals of stars to keep them away from her and the other shows: "ABC is hogging everything for their preshow ... They're being very cutthroat." This was verified by Keith Olberman in the *Los Angeles Times* who said that the arriving celebs "were funneled down the course an hour later than usual." Rivers sneered that ABC scored a "semi-coup" when it signed Geena Davis to do its show, and she held up a sign to attract the attention of arrivals: "Last shallow question before Geena Davis." Liz Smith wrote, "One man wearing a replica of the *Titanic* on his head had a sign saying, 'I want to be a star.' Another knot of people urged 'More frontal nudity.'"

Awards Ceremony

MARCH 21, 1999, 5:30 P.M.
THE DOROTHY CHANDLER PAVILION

Your Host:
WHOOPI GOLDBERG
TELEVISED OVER ABC

Presenters

Supporting Actor	Kim Basinger
Art Direction	Gwyneth Paltrow
Makeup	Mike Myers
Live Action Short Film	Brendan Fraser
Animated Short Film	Flik and Heimlich
Supporting Actress	Robin Williams
Sound Effects Editing	Chris Rock
Sound	Anjelica Huston
Foreign Film	Sophia Loren
Original Musical or Comedy Score	Andy Garcia and Andie McDowell
Original Dramatic Score	Geena Davis
Scientific and Technical Awards	Anne Heche
Editing	Jim Carrey
Irving G. Thalberg Award	Nicolas Cage
Visual Effects	Liam Neeson
Actor	Helen Hunt
Documentary Awards	Ben Affleck and Matt Damon
Honorary Award to Elia Kazan	Robert De Niro and Martin Scorsese
Costume Design	Whoopi Goldberg
Song	Jennifer Lopez
Cinematography	Uma Thurman
Actress	Jack Nicholson
Writing Awards	Goldie Hawn and Steve Martin
Director	Kevin Costner
Picture	Harrison Ford

Performers of Nominated Songs

"I Don't Want to Miss a Thing"	Aerosmith
"The Prayer"	Andre Bocelli and Céline Dion
"A Soft Place to Fall"	Allison Moorer
"That'll Do"	Peter Gabriel and Randy Newman
"When You Believe"	Mariah Carey and Whitney Houston

Still, KTLA's Laurie Pike was in fine form. The fashion critic said of Jennifer Lopez who was wearing a strapless, jewel-encrusted, black taffeta Badgley Mishka ball gown with an embroidered front, "Usually she dresses so slutty and she's kind of like conservative tonight . . . it's definitely an image change for her. Maybe she's going for a little bit more respectability tonight." Pike also observed that Lynn Redgrave was "looking fabulous. A woman scorned, just like Minnie Driver last year . . . she's totally dressing to impress and maybe find a husband tonight who will treat her better than her last one." Her cohort Sam Rubin also played fashion critic when he said that, in a white tuxedo worn backwards and topped off with a variation on a Borsalino, Céline Dion "looks like a gangster." Laurie Pike thought the word for this outfit by John Galliano for Dior—the hat by Stephen Jones, also for Dior—was "fierce."

The *New York Daily News* reported. "Helen Hunt, last year's winner for Best Actress, showed up at this year's ceremony with such a radically different look from last year's upswept bun hairdo that crowds in the bleachers and even some journalists didn't recognize her. 'Who's that? Who is that?' people murmured as Hunt strolled up the red carpet in a light gray Gucci gown with jeweled trim. Hunt's hair was long, parted in the middle and so straight it looked as if it had been ironed. The actress was also wearing dark eye shadow that gave her a distinctly '60s look." Other observers likened her to *The Mod Squad*'s Peggy Lipton and a raccoon.

Joan Rivers wanted to know why Blythe Danner didn't go down the line with husband and daughter Gwyneth, but walked right into the theater. Bruce Paltrow explained. "My wife's a very independent woman and she just wanted Gwyneth to do this with her father." At which point, Gwyneth jumped in: "He's my date!" She added, "It's just a pleasure to be here with my daddy and my family and it's really lovely." On KABC, Roger Ebert asked Paltrow for her take on the campaign controversy, and she stood up for her guys: "I think it's kind of unfair to say that Miramax spent too much money. I think they just love their films and are being incredibly supportive." "That's the way I feel, too," Ebert assured her. "It's show *business*. You go

out there and fight for your team." *Access Hollywood*'s Nancy O'Dell asked Steven Spielberg if he had brought any good luck charms. Just as the director was saying, "Three kids," wife Kate Capshaw blurted out, "Each other," and Spielberg was forced to admit. "That's a better answer." Tête-à-têting with Lynn Redgrave, Roger Ebert mentioned her acceptance at the Independent Spirit Awards and told her, "Your speech was so inspirational!"

WABC's Laura Spencer asked Meryl Streep, "How did you relax today?" "I'm not relaxed. What makes you think I'm relaxed?" answered Streep. Streep told Nancy O'Dell about her Valentino: "I was in Rome promoting a film and he, you know, sort of made me an offer I couldn't refuse." Cynthia Robins of the *San Francisco Examiner* said she should have turned it down, grimacing because the "sequin-sparkled beige-peach gown may have complemented her complexion but resembled something Hints from Heloise would have recommended to scrub pots." Mariah Carey was thrown for a loss when Joan Rivers told her, "Everybody said you gained weight." Just before cutting to commercials, Rivers said, "Let's go to a break—I have to douche." *Little Voice*'s Brenda Blethyn told Sam Rubin and Leanza Cornett, "I'm relaxed more this time because I think I had more chance of winning last time I was here with *Secrets & Lies*. I don't think I have a chance in hell this year, so I can just relax and enjoy it." By contrast, Kathy Bates noted that on the ballot, "I'm at the top of the list so if anybody was lazy maybe they just thought, we'll just vote for the first one." Roger Ebert informed her, "I'm beginning to hear a lot of groundswell for you." "Me, too," she replied.

Aerosmith was on hand to perform their nominated song, "I Don't Want to Miss a Thing" on the show. Joan Rivers told them, "My daughter Melissa in the middle of her wedding had them play that song. I was not thrilled, guys." Lead singer Steven Tyler had a joke for Rivers, asking "What's the difference between pink and purple?" "What?" replied Joan. "Your grip," said Tyler. Although the band was wearing the same type of flash-and-trash outfits they'd been donning since the Reagan years, Roger Ebert's co-interviewer, Karen Duffy, gushed to them, "You guys look amazing!"

Rivers, though, thought that in her strapless silver Pamela Dennis, Steven Tyler's actress daughter looked much better than her father; "I feel like a princess," said Liv Tyler.

Billy Bob Thornton told Sam Rubin and Leanza Cornett that he didn't prepare an acceptance, but "I actually did write James Coburn's speech." Nick Nolte made fun of all the primping people undergo for the Oscars by telling Laura Spencer, "I sat in the tub, the steambath. Then I had a facial . . . and then I had the scrub and then I had this exfoliation done." He spoke to another reporter about *The Thin Red Line*, saying it's "like one long poem—either you get it or you don't get it." One actor opted for a Western motif, leaving Laurie Pike to wonder, "What is Val Kilmer's Kentucky Fried Chicken look? It's making me hungry for a bucket of chicken." Brendan Fraser carried a piece of paper with the names of all the various designers who contributed to his ensemble. As if by harmonic convergence, Ian McKellen, Ellen DeGeneres and Anne Heche all arrived in front of Roger Ebert at the same time. Heche was chanting McKellen's name as a means of wishing him Best Actor good luck. Ebert noted, "Lots of openly gay people here all at once." "We're all shipped together in the same bus," explained Ellen.

The "Countdown to the Oscars" program was not a good thing. This Gilbert Cates production began with clips of Oscar arrivals from years past and the hepped-up announcer saying, "Tonight, for the very first time, the Academy of Motion Picture Arts and Sciences invites you to a special preview of Oscar excitement! The stars nominated for the gold! Plus the glamour, dazzle and surprises of Oscar fashion! Meet the presenters! Go backstage and enjoy an exclusive glimpse of the lavish Governors Ball!" Things kicked off with Geena Davis walking down the red carpet, saying hello to photographers and fans. Jim Moret, borrowed from CNN for the evening, interviewed arriving stars like Gwyneth Paltrow and Lynn Redgrave, all of whom serenely walked up to the podium where he was positioned—the show lacked the frenetic angling for interviewees and the sheer manic quality of the other programs. Also, Moret did not ask a single person who had designed her or his outfit. There were

also interviews that Davis had pre-taped inside. After a featurette on the making and transporting of Oscar statuettes, Helen Hunt was seen informing Davis that the last episode of *Mad About You* would start filming in the morning, and she was directing it. Davis asked James Coburn, "What do you see yourself doing next? Do you think we perhaps could have a little onscreen chemistry?" Coburn responded, "Well, what do you think?" What Geena thought was, "I'm feeling it now." From time to time, a clock appeared in the corner of the screen, indicating how much time was left before the show started—an attempt to pump a little New Year's Eve excitement into the proceedings.

The clock got to zero and it was time for the main event. Announcer Randy Thomas said, "Ladies and Gentlemen, please welcome our host, Her Majesty, Whoopi Goldberg." Goldberg came out dressed as Queen Elizabeth wearing elaborate frockery and in white face. "Good evening, loyal subjects. I am the African Queen." And the audience responded uproariously. "Some of you may know me as the Virgin Queen, but I can't imagine who." Goldberg announced that "This will be a long show, so we don't want to read about how damned long it was, we know it's long. Tough." And then she added, "I think we've all had our hair done enough times to know that you cannot rush a queen."

Whoopi brought out "Our most Prime Minister, Mr. Bob 'He's Loaded With Dough' Rehme." Goldberg went off to change, and the Academy president began his invocation: "As our globe hurtles towards the millennium and we passengers count the blessings of the Twentieth Century, high among them is the lively art that has enthralled, entertained and educated us, the motion picture." President Rehme continued, that "to celebrate the era now winding down, the Academy asked all 6,000 of its members to select three of their favorite moments from films of the Twentieth Century." Chuck Workman read through the suggestions and put together a montage: "100 Years' Worth of the Academy's Favorite Movie Moments." The compilation was pretty much indistinguishable from all other Chuck Workman Academy Award compilations, although one did wonder whose favorite film moment was Shirley Jones sitting in a chair in *Elmer Gantry*.

For the second time, Randy Thomas introduced the host: "Ladies and Gentlemen, your host for this evening, Academy Award winner Whoopi Goldberg." Goldberg was out of her Elizabethan finery, but was still wiping off make-up, and wondered aloud, "Who knew it was this hard to get a virgin off your face?" Among her other early jokes: "Oscar is seventy-one, honey, so welcome to the early bird special;" "It is the last Oscar show before the millenium, and I get to host it. So I am the last 20th Century Fox"; "The last time I did this, I mentioned all the ribbons people had asked me to wear for all the different causes. Of course the last time I was here the most controversial thing you could put on a dress was a ribbon. But times change." It was the evening's first reference to Bill Clinton's dalliance with intern Monica Lewinsky and to the self-righteous Republican chumps who tried to drive the president from the White House. This led to Goldberg's saying, "I feel I need to get all of this out of my system right now, so here goes," and she started a verse, mentioning some of the touchstones of the Clinton impeachment affair, including "black beret, DNA, interns, rugburns, Henry Hyde, gratified . . . Mr. Trent Lott, out, out damn spot." She wound down with, "Bob Barr, Ken Starr, Harty har har. $50 million down the drain. And for that kind of money, we could have made five good movies, which is what tonight is really all about." And for this sentiment, she heard enormous cheers.

The host said, "I just want to ask, Why is it every time I do this show, I get the year with the controversy? . . . Why'd I get it this time? Y2K? Forget it, Y2Me? . . . I thought the blacklist was me and Hattie McDaniel, shit . . . You know who's having the biggest year of all once again? Shakespeare. Honey, Little Willie is very large, baby . . . Life is so unfair. Ben Stiller does that scene and gets $3 million. George Michael did it, got arrested . . . The Oscar campaigns mounted by DreamWorks and Miramax, honey. Those boys fought World War III over World War II . . . Computers helped make bugs and ants completely lifelike. They couldn't do jack for the House Judiciary Committee . . . I thought *Hilary and Jackie* was about a support group for First Ladies." After the mild laughter this joked elicited, Goldberg said, "You're

missing Billy just about now, aren't you?" Back to the jokes: Gwyneth Paltrow "played a woman who wanted to be an actor so badly, she pretended to be a man, marking the first time in movie history that a woman has had her breasts reduced to get a part." In *Shakespeare in Love,* Geoffrey Rush "played a producer with no money to pay the writer. Here we call that an independent." Finally, "If you stay up here more than thirty seconds, a giant asteroid comes hurtling at you from the balcony. So *Armageddon* is ready to hand out some little bald boys."

Kim Basinger kicked off the Awards. Robert Duvall was the only Supporting Actor nominee not present—speculation was that he was still stewing that he hadn't won last year for *The Apostle*—but it didn't matter because the winner was James Coburn in *Affliction.* "My, my, my," began the seventy-year-old actor. "I've been doing this work for like over half my life, and I finally got one right." He acknowledged, "Some of them you do for money, some of them you do for love. This is a love child." When Bill Conti's orchestra began to give him the musical hook as he expressed his gratitude to a number of people, Coburn shouted, "Wait a minute! Wait a minute! I've gotta say something else here! For my beautiful wife, Paula. She finally got to come to the Academy Awards. This is for you, baby." The smitten actor blew a kiss to his wife of five years.

Whoopi Goldberg then said, "Our next presenter has done Shakespeare. No, I mean in her last movie she *did* Shakespeare . . . I'm cracking myself up. It's okay, y'all will catch up." She then identified the presenter as "Best Actress nominee and sweet kid," Gwyneth Paltrow. Paltrow got to announce that the Oscar for Art Direction was going to her movie. After speaking for a bit, cowinner Martin Childs saw the message on the teleprompter: "Ooh, wrap up . . . The asteroid's coming." This was the first head-to-head between *Shakespeare in Love* and *Saving Private Ryan,* so it was Miramax in the lead 1 to 0. Patrick Stewart introduced the clips from the two sixteenth-century British Best Picture nominees, and then Whoopi returned to joke, "You'll notice that I'm always coming from the wing over here on stage left. It's because of the vast right wing conspiracy."

Mike Myers presented the Makeup Award to *Elizabeth*; *Shakespeare in Love* and *Saving Private Ryan* were the two losing nominees. The best song nominee "When You Believe" from the DreamWorks cartoon *The Prince of Egypt* was performed by a pair of cater-wauling pop divas, Whitney Houston and Mariah Carey; a gospel chorus joined in for the finale.

After a commercial break, Goldberg reappeared on stage, wearing one of the dresses from the Costume Design nominee *Pleasantville* and said, "Good evening. I'm Marilyn Quayle." *Entertainment Weekly* decided this was the night's "Least-Timely Reference," and suggested "Maybe next year Yakof Smirnoff can riff on Pet Rocks." Goldberg said "Judianna Makovsky's cool clothes of the '50s added to the nostalgic look of a make-believe world inspired by those memorable black-and-white television series of long ago. More white than black as I recall, but let's just leave it to Beaver. I didn't say whose." Her off-color comment resulted in a great deal of laughter. The host added, "You know, I may not be doing this show ever again, so let's just go right to the edge and go over, what do you say?"

Even though he had proven his acting prowess in *Gods and Monsters*, Brendan Fraser heard the music from *George of the Jungle* as he came on stage to present the Live Action Short Film Oscar. The winner was *Election Night (Valgaften)* and announcer Randy Thomas told the audience that coproducer Kim Magnusson had been nominated for this award three years in a row. One of the "Trophy Ladies"—which really was the official title for the women who brought the Oscars out on stage—placed a statuette on the floor next to the microphone. Thomas then announced that the next presenters were Flik and Heimlich who had to be identified as characters from *A Bug's Life* since the inhabitants of this Disney/Pixar film hadn't exactly infiltrated the general consciousness. Making it more confusing was that a total of six cartoon characters came out on the floor. Flik, an ant, said, "A small favor of the winners. I realize this is your big night, you know, 'King of the World' and all that [appreciative laughter from the audience] and stepping on the little people is a Hollywood tradition. But, please, when you come up to accept your Award, just watch your

step. Thanks." The winner was *Bunny* and then Whoopi Goldberg asked, "*A Bug's Life*—wasn't that the Linda Tripp story?"

She then said, "Our next presenter is an animated feature all by himself." Other things she said about Robin Williams were "He can't stop playing doctor or with himself" and "He recently starred in <u>What Dreams May Come</u>. I said that . . . that was right, right? They asked me to be very careful about pronunciation." The laughter built as the audience stared to realize what she *might* have said. Williams announced, "In case there is an emergency, we have to follow Academy protocol. Steven Spielberg first, the rest of you, on your own. [Director Louis J. Horvit cut to a smiling Spielberg.] Last week, Jack Valenti went to China to talk about copyright infringement. And he gave an incredible, impassioned speech. And if anyone wants a bootleg copy, I have one right here." He also said, "In terms of the Kazan controversy: 'Let Lainie sing!'" Somebody else had already come up with this joke in a letter to the *Los Angeles Times* but Lainie Kazan herself was at a party in New York. "I was hysterical, and I'm going to write him a little note of thanks," said the songstress. After announcing the names of the contenders for Best Supporting Actress, he made the five women wait as he said, "This is very exciting. I feel like Adam when he said to Eve, 'Back up. I don't know how big this gets.'" Of the five nominees, only Rachel Griffiths laughed. Williams then ruined the suspense by prefacing the name of the winner with, "There is nothing like a dame," meaning, of course, that *Shakespeare in Love*'s Judi Dench had won. Dame Judi said, "I feel for eight minutes on screen I should only get a little bit of him."

After the next commercial interruption, a camera caught Goldie Hawn and Kurt Russell standing in the aisle trying to figure out which seats—now occupied by fillers—were theirs. Goldberg saw them, too, and announced, "Look at Goldie Hawn walkin' around. Hi, Goldie. Hi, Kurt. Sit down, shoot." Then addressing the seat-fillers, "Get up out of their chairs, child. Ain't gonna be anybody looking at me while they're standing there, cute as she is." After Hawn and Russell were comfortably seated, Whoopi said, I've been asked to issue a reminder to the people here in the audience.

Please remember to behave responsibly at the parties after the show. Apparently last year, some producer got so drunk he left with a woman his own age." The camera cut to sixty-one-year-old Warren Beatty and his wife, Annette Bening, forty. She then brought out Sound Effects Editing presenter, "the lethally comic Chris Rock." "Thank you, Oprah. Thank you," he told her. "I say it with love . . . Look at this crowd. It's like the Million White Man March here today." He added, "It's a big controversial night—the Kazan thing. I saw DeNiro backstage. You'd better get Kazan away from DeNiro 'cause you know how he hates rats." There were groans, so Rock said, "Hey, you can't do that, man." One of the winners from *Saving Private Ryan* thanked, "My beautiful trophy wife." Liv Tyler introduced her father's band, and Aerosmith sang the love theme from *Armageddon*; Gilbert Cates tried to make it look "contemporary" by having smoke and flames on stage. Then Angelica Huston presented the Sound Oscar, making it two in a row for *Saving Private Ryan*.

Tom Hanks, with a beard for the movie he was filming, *Cast Away,* arrived on stage to introduce another celebrity, but one who wasn't involved with movies: astronaut and former senator John Glenn. Hanks had fashioned himself into Hollywood's official space program devotee, so he got to do the honors rather than Ed Harris, who had played Glenn in *The Right Stuff* and was sitting in the front row. Glenn had intruded upon Hollywood's big night to introduce a montage of film clips from movies about historical figures. Only Gilbert Cates knew the reason for this compilation, which featured some really bad movies, such as *John Paul Jones* with Robert Stack and the Lewis and Clark *The Far Horizons* (Donna Reed was Sacajawea). Other honorees included Gandhi, Father Flanagan, Oskar Schindler and Glenn Miller. There were also several people playing themselves in their life stories: Muhammad Ali, Jackie Robinson, and Audie Murphy. Of course, the montage ended with Ed Harris as John Glenn.

Goldberg came out dressed in a nominated costume from *Beloved*, and to whom did Louis J. Horvitz cut? Chris Rock. Goldberg said, "I'm a slave to fashion." Then she introduced the Foreign Film presenter, "a legendary international screen beauty . . . Great,

she's gonna look phenomenal. I'm out here looking like Topsy." Before she got around to presenting the Foreign Film Oscar, Sophia Loren introduced clips from *Life Is Beautiful* in its guise as a Best Picture nominee; when she mentioned it was directed by Roberto Benigni, he stood up in the audience. As Loren was opening the envelope and saying "And the Oscar goes to . . ." two loons in the audience yelled "Roberto! Roberto!" Loren made it three as she, too, said "Roberto!"

Showing a distinct lack of class, Benigni then stood up on the top of the chair in front of his, and if he had fallen he could have injured the person sitting there—Billy Bob Thornton—or at least dirtied his tuxedo. He then climbed to the next chair, which, funnily enough, was occupied by Steven Spielberg. Benigni almost lost his balance, and Spielberg had to give him his hand. (When we were growing up, if we even put our feet up on the backs of the seats at the local movie house, the matron would kick us out—we weren't cheered on like Benigni, who clearly was not doing those two chairs at the Dorothy Chandler any good.) He hopped up to the stage, embraced Loren and got a standing ovation. The home audience saw a teary Goldie Hawn. Tim Johnson of the *San Francisco Examiner* wrote, "Note to director: Stop cutting to Goldie Hawn when you want a tear shot." Benigni said to Loren, "I leave here [with] the Oscar, but I want you," even though his wife was sitting in the audience. Now Loren had tears. He then told the audience, "This is too much. I want to thank my parents in Vergaio, a little village in Italy. They gave me the biggest gift, poverty. And I want to thank them for the rest of my life, and would like to dedicate this prize to those . . . who are not here. They gave their lives [cut to Goldie Hawn nodding and looking all solemn] in order we could say that life is beautiful." David Bianculli of the *New York Daily News* said Benigni "made Cuba Gooding Jr. look morose by comparison." But Henry Sheehan of the *Orange County Register* pointed out that "this is just the way the screen comedian acts in his films. That wasn't just Benigni the prize winner up there; it was Benigni the persona."

Andie MacDowell and Andy Garcia presented the Original Music or Comedy Score to *Shakespeare in Love*. Winner Stephen Warbeck thanked, among his inspirations, Bertolt Brecht. Randy Thomas announced, "Direct from her preshow hosting to present the next Award, Oscar winner Geena Davis." Something scary this way came before the Award was given though—the Debbie Allen dance number. According to Davis, Allen had "gathered five of the most talented dancers in the world": Spain's Joaquin Cortez, New Yorkers Savion Glover and Tai Jimenez, the Kirov Academy's Rasta Thomas, and "from *Fosse*, Desmond Richardson." Their task was to "interpret the music of the five nominated Original Dramatic Film Scores."

The number proved that Debbie Allen could stink up the joint with five dancers just as ably as she did with thirty-five. Allen saw fit to interpret *Life Is Beautiful* with a shirtless flamenco dancer, while the other four moved slowly in the background. John Williams's cheap music from *Saving Private Ryan* was accompanied by Savion Glover's tap dancing. *Elizabeth* featured Tai Jimenez doing ballet moves, as the guys behaved like Las Vegas chorus boys. Randy Newman's *Pleasantville* score led to a generic balletic interpretation, and *The Thin Red Line* featured calisthenics and rolling around on the floor. When it was all over, viewers saw Debbie Allen who, as if oblivious to what everyone had witnessed, was flushed with pride. John Hartl of the *Seattle Times* called the choreographer's work, "a tasteless dance sequence," while Liz Smith's column reported, "some people at viewing parties actually hissed the screen!" Tom Shales of the *Washington Post* was amazed that the "bizarre number . . . managed the neat trick of stopping an already dead show cold. Daffy choreographer Debbie Allen was responsible for the hapless, protracted gaffe." And *USA Today*'s Robert Bianco deemed the number "the best Oscar camp since Rob Lowe danced with Snow White." Geena Davis returned to announce that the winner was *Life Is Beautiful*'s Nicola Piovanni, who had worked on some of Fellini's later films. He said, "It's impossible for me at this moment to speak about my emotion in English." Backstage, he told the press he hoped this Oscar would put to rest the rumor that "Nicola Piovanni" was a pseudonym for Ennio Morricone.

John Travolta introduced a tribute to "the most envied, admired, and influential entertainer of our time." This would be Frank Sinatra of whom he was speaking, and the audience would be seeing "a portrait of a proud and charming man"—film clips put together by Martin Scorsese. The next nominated costume worn by Whoopi Goldberg was a Geoffrey Rush outfit from *Elizabeth*. She had a beard to go with it, and thought that perhaps she resembled "George Jefferson in *The Merchant of Venice*. 'Wheezy, pass me that pound of flesh.' " Anne Heche came out to inform the audience what had transpired at the Scientific and Technical Awards' dinner she hosted but, ironically, her body mike was on the blink, and the technical glitch forced her to walk to a standing microphone and start over. She said she enjoyed the speeches at the banquet because, "It was great fun to hear from people who can honestly say that they know what they are doing in this business."

Jim Carrey was up next and he said, "I'm here tonight to present the Academy Award for outstanding achievement in Film Editing. That's all I'm here to do. I have nothing else to worry about. I can just show up and enjoy the parties." *The Truman Show* star then pretended to be crying, composed himself and said, "Winning the Oscar is not the most important thing in the world. It's an honor just to be nominated . . . Oh, God" and again began to weep. "It's my own fault," he admitted. "I screwed it up. About a month ago, I would have thought that voting for myself was going to make the difference, you know. But you really gotta get out there and talk to people. Anyway, who cares." And then in a comically stentorian voice: "I have been beaten by Roberto Benigni! He has jumped into my ocean!" The camera cut to Benigni, jubilating at hearing his name and oblivious to the fact that he had just been ridiculed for being such a media whore. The Film Editing winner was Spielberg veteran Michael Kahn, who read from a piece of paper on which was written "I feel so proud to have played a role in the making of this historical motion picture. I'm so grateful to you, Steven, for giving me the opportunity to excel and grow as a person on this humbling World War II movie." Allison Moorer sang, "A Soft Place to

Fall," the bland country song nominated from *The Horse Whisperer*. " 'A Soft Place to Land,' " mused Goldberg. "I've been called worse."

Norman Jewison's Irving G. Thalberg Memorial Award was being presented by Nicolas Cage, who had costarred in his *Moonstruck*. Cage stated that "his work has received twelve Oscars and forty-one Academy Award nominations. Among his triumphs are landmark films of humanity." Even though this was the Thalberg Award, clips were shown from *In the Heat of the Night* and *The Cincinnati Kid*, two films Jewison hadn't produced. The montage also featured voiceovers from the recipient, including "Films are the literature of this generation. That's why motion pictures are important" and "I love making movies because films are forever." As Jewison made his way onto the stage, the orchestra played "If I Were a Rich Man" from *Fiddler on the Roof* and he did a little dance. "Not bad for a *goy*," he joked. Referring to the clips, he said "They really keep this show going. Forty years of filmmaking and they did it in three minutes." After thanking those who worked on his films, Jewison said, "My one real regret about winning this prize is that, you know, it's not like the Nobel or the Pulitzer. I mean, the Thalberg Award comes with no money attached." Finally, he said, "My parting thought to all those young filmmakers is this. Just find some good stories. Never mind the gross, the top ten, bottom ten, what's the rating, what's the demographic [and an audience composed of people obsessed with such things began cheering]. You know something, the highest grossing picture is not necessarily the best picture [more applause from people who had honored *Titanic* last year]. So just tell stories that move us to laughter and tears and perhaps reveal a little truth about ourselves. And as for myself, I hope to see you again next year." Jewison's *The Hurricane* would be released in December.

Whoopi Goldberg's next double entendre was, "For those of you scoring at home, keep it down, honey, we're doing a show here. But seriously, the score is Shakespeare: 4. World War 2: 2. Insane Italians: 1." Fearing a Pandora's Box, Goldberg ordered Benigni to remain seated: "Don't do it, baby. Don't get up!" Indeed, the *Los Angeles Times* noted that Benigni

"seemed poised to jump onto his feet whenever he heard his name." As Goldberg introduced Liam Neeson, she stroked the microphone stand in a manner that some people found lascivious. Neeson, the star of the upcoming *Star Wars Episode 1: The Phantom Menace*, gave Best Visual Effects to the New Age fantasy, *What Dreams May Come*. One of the winners said, "Love is groovy. Be positive."

The reason Val Kilmer was wearing Western formalwear became clear when he came on stage leading a horse whom he identified as Triggerson, the grandson of Roy Rogers's legendary Trigger. Originally, Kilmer was to have ridden Triggerson on stage, but the horse had been pulling a diva act. Kilmer told the audience, "I grew up next to Roy Rogers's ranch in Chatsworth, California and my daddy eventually bought it. So, of course, I grew up with the innocence and joy of the great matinee movie cowboys." Triggerson, meanwhile, was acting antsy and circling around Kilmer, who joked "Debbie Allen didn't choreograph that part." "Sadly," the actor continued, "both Roy and Gene Autry passed on last year, so I hope you enjoy this affectionate tribute to the Western high ideals that graced the silver screen for nearly a hundred years and sparked our dreams of American adventure." At this point, the horse was knocking into him. "Happy trails, Roy," said Kilmer as he and the Palomino headed off. On the soundtrack was Roy's 1974 recording of "Cowboy Heaven," and a vast array of B Western stars flickered across the screen: Rogers, Autry, Buck Jones, Ken Maynard, Tim Holt, Johnny Mack Brown, Sunset Carson, Rex Allen, and others. One can only imagine what the studio executives sitting in the audience made of this presentation, seeing how they're notoriously ignorant of film history, and most of them were not even familiar with the Westerns of John Ford, Howard Hawks and Budd Boetticher, let alone Lash LaRue's *ouevre*.

Helen Hunt had the duty of opening the envelope and announcing that the Best Actor Oscar was going to Roberto Benigni. Benigni managed to keep off of the seats this time, but he did get another standing ovation. "This is a terrible mistake, because I used up all my English," he said. "My body is in tumult . . . I would like to be Jupiter and kidnap everybody and lie down in the firmament making love to everybody." Showing rare good sense, Bill Conti's orchestra began playing while Benigni was still going on, and he was still at the microphone when the show cut to commercial. A little later, Ian McKellen, Nick Nolte, and Edward Norton met up at the lobby bar and had a good laugh at the absurdity of losing Best Actor to *Roberto Benigni*.

Goldberg next appeared in a 1970s' Glitter Rock outfit—a feather trimmed jumpsuit from *Velvet Goldmine*. Talk about extremes: Sandy Powell, who designed these fabulous threads, was also nominated for *Shakespeare in Love*. Randy Newman and Peter Gabriel performed Newman's nominated song, "That'll Do"; ABC insisted that the Steinway & Sons logo on Newman's piano be painted over since the company wasn't paying a products placement fee. Tom Shales of the *Washington Post* observed, "Who knew until Oscar night that the flop movie *Babe: Pig in the City* contained a beautiful song by Randy Newman?"—one of several reviewers to make this observation. Had voters actually heard the song beforehand, Newman might very well have had his first Oscar.

Ben Affleck and Matt Damon came out to give, not the Screenplay Award they won last year, but the Documentary Oscars. The Documentary Short winner was *The Personals: Improvisations on Romance in the Golden Years*, and Randy Thomas informed us that the film's director Keiko Ibi was "once crowned Miss Japan Grand Prix." The weepy winner said, "Who would have thought that a girl from Japan can make a movie about Jewish senior citizens and actually receive this Award." Damon then said, "There are five films nominated for Documentary Feature, and if it were up to me, every single one of them would win." "Oh, stop it," ad-libbed Affleck. The winning film was about the Holocaust.

At the last commercial break, hordes of audience members escaped to the lobby because they didn't want to be present for the Elia Kazan presentation. Seat-fillers swarmed all over the place. Randy Thomas introduced "Two men who are no strangers to the Academy Awards, Martin Scorsese and Robert De Niro." The *Mr. Showbiz* Web site reported that at the Elton John party, "revelers were poking fun at Robert De Niro's modified-mohawk haircut. Someone yelled, 'They shaved off his sideburns and put it on Scorsese's eyebrows!' " De Niro was sporting this coif for the latest piece of junk he was filming, *The Adventures of Rocky and Bullwinkle*.

The star of Elia Kazan's final film, *The Last Tycoon*, De Niro called the stoolie, "a man whose work is vitally important in the history of American film. He was the master of a new kind of psychological and behavioral truth in acting. The work he did and the actors he used brought a thrilling new reality to the stage and screen." Ironically, De Niro had starred in *Guilty by Suspicion*, a 1991 movie in which he played a blacklisted screenwriter, and Scorsese also had an acting role in the film. Scorsese said, "At a time when the prevailing American voice was bland and glib [one might argue it was because non-bland and glib voices had been silenced by the blacklist], this poetic realist, this angry romantic always spoke fervently to our most basic conflicts." A film montage ensued, and then Kazan appeared onstage with his trophy wife, Frances. Among those director Louis J. Horvitz found standing and clapping were Karl Malden, Warren Beatty, Kathy Bates, Lynn Redgrave, Kurt Russell, Meryl Streep, Billy Bob Thornton and Laura Dern, Helen Hunt, and Debbie Allen. There was a contingent of fence straddlers, people who applauded but remained seated: Steven Spielberg, Jim Carrey, Patrick Stewart. Those the cameras focussed on sitting and not clapping were most prominently Ed Harris and Amy Madigan with wonderfully expressive scowls on their face, and Nick Nolte, arms folded, and his girlfriend Vicki Lewis. Others included Ian McKellen, Brendan Fraser, Holly Hunter and Cate Blanchett's husband, Andrew Upton. Among those sitting and not applauding, but not seen on camera included David Geffen, Sherry Lansing, Bill Condon, and, of course, Army Archerd. Liz Smith reported, "No one booed, most of the audience did not applaud and people were polite." The TV cameras gave a false impression of the crowd reaction, because according to people inside the Dorothy Chandler, no more than a quarter of the people there stood. And the thing to remember is that most of the people who were standing were seat-fillers.

Kazan was waving from the stage and he said, "Thank you very much. I really like to hear that. And I want to thank the Academy for its courage, generosity and I want to tell you that I've been a member of the Academy, on and off, for I don't know how many years. So I'm pleased to say what's best about them— they're damn good to work with." He looked around for Scorsese so he could hug him—Quentin Tarantino was later heard to say that at this moment Scorsese looked "like a cat when Pepe LePew comes around"— and after embracing him and De Niro, Kazan said, "Thank you all very much. I think I can just slip away." And to his wife he asked, "Do you want me to say anything more?" She told him "No," and that was that.

Whoopi's next costume was from *Shakespeare in Love* and she said to the audience, "You think this is easy? I haven't had to take my dress off this many times since my first audition. Steven, you remember how many times I took it off." Cut to a *faux*-appalled Spielberg gesticulating, "No, not me." And, having worn all the nominated costumes, Goldberg got to present the Award, which went to Sandy Powell for *Shakespeare in Love*. Powell began her acceptance with, "I'd like to congratulate Whoopi for having the guts to wear that *Velvet Goldmine* costume." She noted, "Two nominations, one speech. And I want to thank everybody I worked with on both films. There are too many names, it'd be boring." The leading lady from *The Mask of Zorro*, Catherine Zeta-Jones was aboard simply to introduce the performers of the next nominated song, "The Prayer," from a cartoon nobody saw, *Quest for Camèlot*. Zeta-Jones promised "two of the most glorious voices of our time," but it was only Céline Dion and Andrea Bocelli. They were bombastic.

"An actress of depth and beauty," was Randy Thomas's introduction for the Best Song presenter. Jennifer Lopez said it was "time for the respective composers and lyricists to call up the last line from the Oscar-winning song from 1954, 'Three Coins in the Fountain': 'Make it mine, Make it mine, make it mine.' " The reference inadvertently pointed out how ultimately meaningless this category is, for it was a reminder that a disposable pop tune, "Three Coins in the Fountain" had beaten out a song that wasn't as

popular at the time, but went on to become a great standard, "The Man That Got Away." The winner this year was the disposable pop song, "When You Believe." Songwriter Steven Schwartz had stayed in New York.

Annette Bening was in charge of this year's memorial service. In her homily, she said, "Death for makers of motion pictures is not an end for their audience. For as long as there are ways to see, to hear or to feel movies, a filmmaker lives. We pause in our festivities to remember those we cannot forget for the movies they left us before they moved on." Among those commemorated were Robert Young, Alice Faye, Maureen O'Sullivan, E.G. Marshall, Jean Marais, Richard Kiley, Susan Strasberg, Dane Clark, John Derek, Binnie Barnes, Gene Raymond, Esther Rolle, Phil Hartman, and Huntz Hall, whose clip showed him in *Dead End*, and not as his more familiar characterization of Sach from the Bowery Boys. Also included was the first person from last year's Oscar's Family Album to die, Vincent Winter, who had received an Honorary Oscar for "Outstanding Juvenile Performance" in 1954's *The Little Kidnappers*. The loudest applause went to directors Akira Kurosawa and Alan J. Pakula, and the person the montage closed with, Academy Board Member and everybody's pal, Roddy McDowall.

Jack Valenti showed up to give an oration: "When the nation's future is in danger and the dagger's at the nation's belly, ordinary young men and women perform extraordinary acts of heroism." This speech obviously had not been written by Bruce Vilanch. "One man more than any other living American understands these young people who confront fear and death in order to preserve freedom in this free and loving land for generations of Americans yet unborn." Valenti went on like this a little longer; it was all to welcome the homophobic militarist Colin Powell to the stage of the Dorothy Chandler. Powell's appearance was Gilbert Cates's top-secret surprise this year—like pianist David Helfgott in 1996 and Bart the Bear last year. But he received no standing ovation and the natural question was, What the hell is *he* doing here? He and Valenti played soldier and actually saluted each other. On top of Valenti's Civics Class lecture, here was Powell with a history lesson: "Every generation contains the potential for greatness. For the generation that came out of the Depression, that potential was tested on the battlegrounds of World War II. Had those men and women failed that test of their greatness we would live very different lives today. To our and our children's good fortune they did not fail. Instead, they triumphed." The Valenti & Powell show was a lot of idle chatter just to introduce the clips for *The Thin Red Line* and *Saving Private Ryan*, which everyone had already seen on all the pre-Oscar programs anyway.

Following the clips, Whoopi said, "I want to acknowledge someone we lost too recently to include in our film tribute. He wasn't a filmmaker, but he was definitely a member of our film community. Now he clobbered some of us with a great big stick, and sometimes he touched us with a velvet glove. I'm talking about Gene Siskel [applause]. A critic. But even more important, he really loved movies. So, Gene, wherever you are, honey, here's to you." And she gave a thumb's up. Now Siskel was nobody's idea of a serious film critic, but he was a celebrity, so there you go.

Uma Thurman, described by Goldberg as "a vision that any cinematographer is happy to find on the other end of his camera" arrived in a silver Chanel accessorized by cuffs around her upper arms. She announced that this year's wining cinematographer was Janusz Kaminski for *Saving Private Ryan*. The winner received three kisses from his wife, Holly Hunter, and onstage he thanked, "My sugarbear, Holly."

Best Actress presenter Jack Nicholson told the audience, "I'm saying nothing because you've all exhausted every expression you have." The Oscar went to Gwyneth Paltrow in *Shakespeare in Love*, and the winner started welling up with tears as soon as her name was called; she was out-and-out crying as she kissed her parents. Onstage, Paltrow stopped weeping and acknowledged the other nominees, including "my friend Cate Blanchett" [they had recently filmed *The Talented Mr. Ripley*] and "the greatest one who ever was, Meryl Streep," who appeared to be shocked at the encomium. She thanked Harvey Weinstein and Miramax, "my friend Ben Affleck" [the pair had broken up a few months earlier], her 15-percenter, described as "a beautiful man and a wonderful agent, and in his case that is not an oxymoron." Then it was family hour:

I would not have been able to play this role had I not not understood love of a tremendous magnitude [more tears] and for that I thank my family. My mother, Blythe Danner who I [really weeping now] love more than anything, and my brother Jake Paltrow, who is just the dearest person in the whole world. My earthly guardian angel, Mary Wigmore, and especially my father Bruce Paltrow who has surmounted insurmountable obstacles this year. I love you more than anything in the world. And to my grandpa, Buster, who almost made it here tonight, but couldn't quite get here. Grandpa, I want you to know that you created a beautiful family who loves you and love each other more than anything and we thank you for that. I would like to dedicate this to two young men who lost their lives very early, Harrison Kravis and my cousin, Keith Paltrow. We miss you very much. And I thank you so much everybody.

Steven Spielberg came out to eulogize Stanley Kubrick who had died after the memorial film clip was assembled. Spielberg declared, "He wanted to take us places we could never have imagined and so he imagined them for us . . . He dared us to have the courage of his convictions, and when we take that dare, we're transported directly to his world, and we're inside his vision. And in the whole history of movies, there had been nothing like that vision ever. It was a vision of hope and wonder, of grace and of mystery. It was a gift to us and now it's a legacy."

The stars of the soon-to-be-released remake of *The Out-of-Towners*, Goldie Hawn and Steve Martin were the presenters of the Writing Awards. About to announce the Adapted Screenplay winner, Steve Martin said, "And the losers aren't . . ." The winner was Bill Condon for *Gods and Monsters*. Goldie said, "Oh, my God," upon hearing the news. The camera cut away from Condon kissing his boyfriend—Condon later joked to *LGNY* that "they didn't want to turn this into the Tony Awards"—to the thrilled Ian McKellen, Lynn Redgrave, and Brendan Fraser looking around trying to spot the winner. When Condon stopped to embrace them on his way to the stage, McKellen told him, "Go sell the movie." Onstage, the winner mentioned something inaudible to Hawn, who replied, "Too wild." As Condon spoke, the camera showed Brendan Fraser with his arms around Ian McKellen who was in the row ahead of him and Lynn Redgrave nestling on McKellen's shoulder, all enthralled by the man who directed their film. Condon thanked Christopher Bram, saying the film was a "very faithful adaptation" of his novel, *Father of Frankenstein*, and praised, "These actors sitting in front of me, Brendan, Ian and Lynn, three geniuses who made this all work [cheers from the audience]. This is yours." He also acknowledged three people who had died, his parents "Flo and Bill," and Mason Wiley, the coauthor of *Inside Oscar*, who had been a close friend since their college days at Columbia. Condon thanked his boyfriend, "the great Jack Morrissey," concluding, "And, of course, most of all, James Whale. Sixty years ago, Hollywood sort of turned its back on him because he insisted on living the way he wanted. So, Mr. Jimmy, this is for you."

Before announcing the Original Screenplay winner, Hawn revealed why she had said "Oh, my God" and "too wild"—for twelve years she had lived in James Whale's house in Pacific Palisades: "It's so weird, you know." The Original Screenplay Award went to *Shakespeare in Love*. Marc Norman, whose credits included *Cutthroat Island*, said, "We get few enough chances in our lives to put pleasure into the world. I feel very happy and lucky having been connected with *Shakespeare in Love*." Cowinner Tom Stoppard said, "I'm behaving like Roberto Benigni underneath." The camera caught Original Screenplay loser Benigni clapping but looking around for an explanation. Stoppard then instructed the audience, "Don't clap. He'll play the music." He thanked two of the film's producers, Donna Gigliotti and David Parfitt, "good cop and very smart cop to Commissioner Harvey."

"They say the show's running a little long. I like things that run long," began Best Director presenter Kevin Costner. "For the five nominated directors, the hard work is over. It's been over for a long time. The only thing remaining is the anxiety that comes with an impossible night like tonight. You five have been sin-

gled out this evening because . . . you're rotten kids." Terrence Malick was the only nominee not in the building, and instead of his photo, the audience saw an empty director's chair with his name on it. The winning rotten kid was Steven Spielberg for *Saving Private Ryan*. The director received a standing ovation, although home viewers saw Nick Nolte and Vicki Lewis looking at each other with expressions that seemed to say, "He's no Terrence Malick." "Am I allowed to say I really wanted this?" began Spielberg. He thanked "the families who lost sons in World War II," and then said to his father, "Dad, you're the greatest. Thank you for showing me that there is honor in looking back and respecting the past. I love you very much. This is for you." Spielberg was apparently saving his grand pronouncement about the meaning of the Second World War for the Best Picture Award.

The presenter of the final Award, Harrison Ford, pronounced, "And so in the end as it was in the beginning, there are five films nominated for Best Picture." It seemed appropriate that this Award was being announced by Spielberg's Indiana Jones, the only glitch, though, was that the three words he had to read were not "*Saving Private Ryan*" but rather "*Shakespeare in Love*." The *Hollywood Reporter* said the announcement drew "gasps of surprise" in the audience. This upset win meant that Harvey Weinstein finally got to be at an Oscar podium, and after David Parfitt and Donna Gigliotti spoke, he said, "This was a movie about life and art, and art and life combining . . . It's called magic." He also said, "Nobody inspires me more than my brother, Bob, who's my partner and best friend every day." Among the other family members he thanked was "my mom, Miriam—the Miriam of Miramax," and as the music began to play, he got in "who makes Jewish mothers look good." The final count was *Shakespeare in Love*, seven Oscars, *Saving Private Ryan,* five.

Whoopi Goldberg said, "I thought you'd like to know that while you were watching this show another century has gone by." As the credits started rolling, she began dancing to "Hooray for Hollywood."

Aftermath

"Steven Spielberg won't qualify for the Good Sport Award," reported the *New York Daily News*. "Journalists and photographers waited in the press room for the Best Director winner, to no avail. Word came that he was skipping the traditional question and answer session—presumably because he would have been asked how he felt about *Private Ryan* losing the Best Picture Oscar to *Shakespeare in Love*. When questioned about Spielberg's backstage absence, an Oscar official replied: "All I can tell you is we tried—we really tried."

The *Los Angeles Times* deemed it "a glorious night of triumph for Harvey Weinstein," as Miramax won ten Oscars. The *Los Angeles Daily News* opined that Miramax had "cement[ed] its position as Oscar's unofficial tastemaker." Backstage, Weinstein contended, "You know what? I believe in supporting films. People on my movies work so hard ... Isn't it good that somebody goes out and supports you for a change? I think you should get in trouble in this town for *not* supporting your movies." He said his Oscar would go in his four-year-old daughter's bedroom.

Backstage, Roberto Benigni was asked if he ever calms down. He replied, "I let my body do what it wants. ... When you are in love, how can you organize your body?"

Gwyneth Paltrow said the first thing that went through her mind when she heard Jack Nicholson call her name was "Holy shit!" She explained why she had gotten so choked up onstage: "It's hard when you have adrenaline going and your friends and your parents are with you. It's impossible not to be overly emotional or to keep them under control—as is evidenced by my teary acceptance speech." When a reporter told her that the pressroom also got misty-eyed during her speech, she jokingly challenged them: "Come on, you are all a bunch of hardened cynical journalists. Don't try to pull that on me." She was right: the press people were hooting at her acceptance. The next morning, Ray Richmond of *Daily Variety* revealed, "Gwyneth Paltrow is still thanking her butcher and her accountant, but it's such a heartfelt utterance that it deserves

to roll as long as it must." A few weeks after the Awards, actress Imelda Staunton, who played Paltrow's nurse in *Shakespeare in Love*, was performing a nightclub act at New York's Firebird Café. She kidded that onstage Oscar night, Paltrow "seemed to have been starring in *The Crying Game*. Good God, woman. You won an Oscar and you're thin. Cheer up!"

Judi Dench continued on the theme she brought up onstage: "The part was so small. I just didn't think I would be standing here at all. ... I'm delighted to have it, but I'm very taken aback by it." She also said that even though her two Oscar-nominated roles were British Queens, "They are two entirely different people and two entirely different roles. One is just longer than the other." She would later say she didn't understand how she won, and that in her opinion the Oscar should have gone to Lynn Redgrave.

Thalberg winner Norman Jewison also elaborated on points he made during his acceptance speech. "When you get into corporate thinking, I think quality sometimes goes out the window and everybody reaches for the golden ring," he said. "Unless we get back to stories about people, we're going to start losing the audience." He also discussed the other Honorary Award that had overshadowed his, and sided with those protesting Elia Kazan's Oscar: "To betray his friends for his career when he already had a lot of money ... It wasn't like he had to feed his kids." The *Orange County Register*'s Henry Sheehan noted the dramatic difference in the receptions Jewison and Kazan had received, extolling Jewison as "one of Hollywood's genuine nice guys—he's not only polite, he actually wants to do good for each person he meets—Jewison's obvious pleasure was reciprocated by an audience of professionals who were clearly pleased to recognize the filmmaker's combination of craftsmanship and personableness."

The *Los Angeles Daily News* opined, "For Hollywood's old guard, the debut of 'Sunday at the Oscars' was anything but super. Technical glitches and tedious schtick marred the grueling four-hour telecast, the longest in Oscar's seventy-one years. The Academy's controversial decision to bestow an Honorary statuette on Elia Kazan added more gray hues ... Maybe that's why even the Governors Ball, the traditional first stop on the post-Oscar pub crawl, seemed subdued." There was an aquatic look to the Ball, which featured blue-green lighting, matching tablecloths and fabric wall treatments, and Louis XIV furniture, all of which was supposed to add up to the theme of "A Return to the Romance of Period Films." Wolfgang Puck's menu featured herb-crusted white salmon, grilled free-range veal, horseradish mashed potatoes, stir-fried spring vegetables, and chocolates shaped like vintage movie cameras. The *Daily News* noted, "Gil Cates, producer of the interminable telecast, looked like a man who could use a drink—or a nice cup of Earl Grey tea. By half past midnight, only a few die-hards were still getting jiggy with the '70s boogie tunes." Elia Kazan was sitting with Karl Malden and said "I'm glad it's over, but it was a nice evening."

When they were entering the *Vanity Fair* party at Morton's, Ellen DeGeneres was rubbing Anne Heche's stomach and told *Access Hollywood*, "We're recreating our meeting two years ago, so we may be in there a while." Swing legend Artie Shaw was inside Morton's, as were Hollywood legends, Billy Wilder and Kirk Douglas. But garnering the most attention was Monica Lewinsky, who had recently published her memoirs and was in town on a book tour; her date was Jonathan Marshall, a lawyer for the New York film company, Shooting Gallery. When Tom Selleck heard of her presence as he headed into Morton's, he gibed, "Monica has studied her craft and paid her dues in this business and should come and celebrate our industry with us." His fellow Republican, Jane Seymour, heard about the former intern's presence and asked husband James Keach, "Are we gonna leave?" Another television actress, Jenna Elfman said of Lewinsky, "No comment. I'm just over the whole thing. I don't even think I could even stand looking at her face." On the other hand, when *Entertainment Tonight*'s Lisa Canning asked Anthony Hopkins, "Are you gonna get her autograph?" He smiled, and whispered, "Yeah."

"Some of her dinner companions were said to be cool to her at first," reported Rush & Molloy. "But several Republicans like Merv Griffin and Betsy Bloomingdale couldn't resist seeing what she was like. And, one by one, the rest followed. 'Come on,' Ben Affleck said to Matt Damon, 'we're all going to go over

to meet Monica.' Lewinsky's jaw dropped when Affleck introduced himself. After exchanging some banter, Affleck reported, 'She was nice.' 'She thought you were hot,' kidded one of Affleck's pals. 'She called him a "hotty." ' 'She bleeped the President,' said Affleck with a shrug. 'I don't know what she'd want with me? I have to say, though, I admire her—the way she handled herself in the Senate hearings.' " Beverly Hills native Lewinsky chatted for a while with Tony Curtis, who had known her since she used to come over to the house when she was a kid going to school with his son. "Little did we know!" he laughed to the *New York Observer*. The *New York Post*, which referred to her as "the portly pepperpot," reported, "Observers said Lewinsky sat at her table like a queen bee as photographers and reporters jostled each other to speak with her while virtually ignoring Madonna, who sat at a banquette next to her.

Ian McKellen said, "For a man from London to be able to go back and say, 'No, I didn't win the Oscar but I did meet Monica Lewinsky'—that's not bad." McKellen did even better than that. As he told *Entertainment Tonight*'s Bob Goen: "I met Monica Lewinsky and she's gonna be my date for the opening of *Gods and Monsters* in London next Thursday . . . And you thought you were talking to a loser, did you?" Liz Smith's lead in her account of Oscar night was, "I *never* thought my night at the Academy Awards would end up with me meeting Monica Lewinsky at the *Vanity Fair* party and overhearing this exchange—k.d. lang to Monica: 'You know, Monica, I had a sex dream about you!' Monica: 'Wow! That's cool!' " Lewinsky's own take on the evening was "surreal." Sally Kirkland was at Morton's, but she was concerned with something more exciting than Monica Lewinsky: "People are already talking about nominating me for *EdTV* for next year and it isn't even out yet!"

The Elton John party—cosponsored by *In Style* magazine—was held at Pagani across the street from Morton's, so celebrities crossed the street going from one to the other. Bridget Fonda's date was Dwight Yoakam, but when she saw her old boyfriend Eric Stoltz show up at Morton's, she high-tailed it over to Pagani. Those who came here to the John/*In Style* bash to watch the show chowed down on organic carrot and ginger soup, Chilean sea bass with risotto, and warm chocolate tarts. Mitchell Fink of the *New York Daily News* dished that the line for the ladies room was so long "that Janet Jackson's security guard cleared the men's room so Jackson and Lisa Marie Presley could both go in and use the facility." It may have been because of the mingling between the two soirees on Melrose Avenue, but the Elton John party, which in the past had shut down early, went on until two in the morning.

The *Hollywood Reporter* printed a picture of Steven Spielberg at the DreamWorks/Paramount party at Barnaby's on Fairfax Avenue, which was priceless. Here he was with an Oscar in front of him and he was looking as if he had just heard the Germans had won the War. The man who had bore the bad news— Harrison Ford—was at the same table and he, too, looked like Mr. Joyboy. On his way in, Tom Hanks did his best spin for reporters: "I think it's much more interesting for everybody, and a lot more fair, I think, and a lot more judicious when a lot of movies share the grand total of the prizes. I think it's kind of boring when one movie wins them all." When Hanks congratulated Spielberg on that Best Director Oscar, Rush & Molloy transcribed: "Said Spielberg: 'There should be two there.'" The menu here consisted of oysters on the half shell, shiitake mushroom pizza, and chicken pot pie, but the *Los Angeles Times* said that despite "a lavish spread . . . no one seemed particularly hungry. Spielberg was there, looking sober. Jeffrey Katzenberg, who usually talks a blue streak, said little. Paramount chief Jonathan Dolgen looked positively grim." Still, Spielberg's mom, Leah Adler, was in a great mood, and she told *Access Hollywood*, "I'm off the charts. I don't believe it. I mean when I go home and I lie in bed, try to figure it all out, I don't get it. We're just normal people. Look what happened." Roberto Benigni showed up here at one point.

By contrast, there was the Miramax party at the Beverly Hills Hotel's Polo Lounge, which had a huge number of guests. Nick Nolte laughed that "We thought it was supposed to be a private little dinner party but, man, did we make a mistake!" *Entertainment Tonight's* Mark Steines marveled to Blythe Danner and Bruce Paltrow, "She gets up and she says so many wonderful things about you guys." "We pay her well," said Danner. Having heard at the Golden Globes that Gwyneth's grandfather, Buster, had been ailing, everyone was saddened when she said in her acceptance speech that he "almost made it here tonight, but couldn't quite get here," assuming he had lost his battle with stomach cancer. But lo and behold, there he was at the Miramax party. Gwyneth was being literal: he hadn't gotten to the Dorothy Chandler in time for the show because of the traffic. On his way into the party, Mike Myers did his Gwyneth Paltrow imitation for *Entertainment Tonight*: "I got a mama. Boohoohoo!"

Harvey Weinstein was said to be doing his best not to gloat, although the *Hollywood Reporter* noted "there was a certain giddiness in the air, coupled with shock that *Shakespeare in Love* had won." Also observed were Jennifer Lopez and Puff Daddy heading into a bathroom together. After the *Vanity Fair* party, Matt Damon came here, where Ben Affleck's movie was being celebrated, rather than to Barnaby's, where his own movie's loss was being mourned. The *Los Angeles Daily News* observed that, now that he was away from the cameras, Roberto Benigni had turned off his zany persona and was sitting quietly with his family in a booth away from the main party room.

The last guest to leave the last party was Jack Nicholson who departed Dani Janssen's apartment at 5:30 in the morning. This get-together was held in honor of Tom Hanks and Rita Wilson, and Steven Spielberg and Kate Capshaw, Clint Eastwood, Jim Carrey, Harrison Ford, Bridget Fonda, Penny Marshall, and Whoopi Goldberg also attended. In addition to her renowned monkey bread, Janssen's homemade offerings included chicken over rice, sweet-potato casserole, black-eyed peas, and broccoli hollandaise. Rush & Molloy reported, though, that "Shirley MacLaine, Sally Field and Garry Shandling are said to have gotten so worked up talking about Kazan that Shandling finally moved to another room."

The consensus was that the Kazan Award presentation was somewhat anticlimactic—the *Los Angeles Times*, *Daily Variety*, the *Orange County Register*, *USA Today*, the *San Francisco Chronicle* all used that word— perhaps because the Committee Against Silence had from the beginning called for a nondisruptive protest. Screenwriter Walter Bernstein, who had helped organize the demonstration, even admitted, "I was more overwrought over Benigni getting the Best Actor Award because I didn't like the movie." Still, the organizers were delighted with the result. "I think it was wonderful," said Bernard Gordon. "It was much better than I expected. I feel really good." He also said, "It's very encouraging to see so many young people here who understand that civil liberties and civil rights must be protected." Army Archerd wrote, "The joy and exuberance of the winners was matched by the obvious disapproval for the special Oscar to Elia Kazan. Although those who approved were vocally audible, the silence of those who did not far outweighed them. I was seated in the theater in row T, seat 42, where I was able to observe the entire show and, of course, particularly the Award to Kazan. The applause may have sounded loud to the audience at home, but only about 20 percent of the audience stood, and no one at all in my aisle or the one in front of me." Later in the year, Patricia Bosworth wrote an article on Kazan for *Vanity Fair* and asked him if he had enjoyed California. "Hated it," he responded. "Have always hated that place. Liked seeing Karl. Glad I got the Oscar . . . I deserved it." But the bottom line was that it was clear that the majority of people weren't ready to forgive Elia Kazan for his deeds, although he could now go to his grave knowing that he had the seat-fillers on his side.

On *Politically Incorrect* after the Oscars, Rod Steiger was still fuming about Kazan. When host Bill Maher suggested that turning in commies might have been the right thing to do for the good of the country, Steiger said, "Oh, my friend, the Communists had about as much chance of taking over this government as Mickey Rooney, for Christ's sake." David Letterman had a field day with Kazan. The night after the Oscars, he told his audience, "His acceptance speech was, I thought, a little dull. It was a little boring. And then I thought, oh yeah, this guy doesn't have anything to say unless he's testifying in front of Congress." Letterman also ruminated, "What a night. People in the auditorium there, they refused to stand, they refused to applaud. Outside there were protestors, and it was, you know it was very . . . wait a minute, that was the night

I hosted." Which led to "It's interesting. They got Elia Kazan, a very controversial moment last night. They give this guy the Lifetime Achievement Award and he ratted folks out during the McCarthy era, and I'm thinking, 'Well, my God, if the Academy of Motion Picture Arts and Sciences can forgive *this* guy, how about forgiving me?'"

Speaking of louses, as he had threatened to do, Lynn Redgrave's estranged husband had tried to get into the Awards and he said he was sure that if she had taken him as her date she would have won. While Redgrave continued to keep her lips sealed about their breakup, John Clark was a chatterbox. He even invited *Entertainment Weekly* into their house to see what it looked like after Redgrave had moved her things out. He pointed to their wedding picture and said, "Lynn didn't, for some reason, want to take that with her."

Having received tickets to the ceremony, *The Thin Red Line* producers Bobby Geisler and John Roberdeau made plans to attend, even if Terrence Malick and Mike Medavoy didn't want them in the house. But then, after putting on their tuxedos, the pair ultimately decided not to go to the Dorothy Chandler. Geisler told *Entertainment Weekly*, "Ultimately, we went for closure and not another fight. We wanted to do the graceful thing." No one was surprised that their friend-turned-antagonist Terrence Malick hadn't shown up either.

Ray Richmond of *Daily Variety* wrote, "The scenario that many feared inevitable did not materialize Sunday night at the 71st Annual Academy Awards: To the relief of many—and for the first time in recent memory—Céline Dion did not sing "My Heart Will Go On." The *Philadelphia Inquirer*'s Carrie Rickey was perturbed: "An hour into the Oscar telecast Sunday night, with only four of twenty-six statuettes distributed, you could hear remote controls across America click off the tube. An IRS 1040 form would have made livelier TV than the 71st annual Academy Awards, a barrage of tributes to dead cowboys and real-life heroes memorialized on celluloid. In a room containing Gwyneth Paltrow, Whoopi Goldberg and Steven Spielberg, why import Sen. John Glenn and Gen. Colin Powell for glamour?" Fred Shuster of the *Los Angeles Daily News* complained that the telecast, "suffered from uneven comedy material, tepid dance and tribute segments, and the overall feeling of air slowly leaking from an overfilled balloon," while the *Orange County Register*'s Henry Sheehan was particularly displeased with the over-abundance of film montages: "The effect was numbing." David Letterman revealed, "The Academy Awards were so dull, this morning Elia Kazan threatened to name the people responsible." John Hartl of the *Seattle Times* felt, "this was the longest and possibly the dullest Oscar show of the century, clocking in at four hours. That's four and a half hours if you count a pre-Oscar show, hosted by Geena Davis, that rivaled in tackiness the Joan Rivers interviews that also precede the Oscars."

Everybody seemed to tear into *Countdown to the Oscars*. Barry Garron of the *Hollywood Reporter* thought it "was as cheesy and insubstantial as any pre-Oscar show prooduced by E!" Michelle Greppi of the *New York Post* called it "the world's worst Oscar preshow" and took the Academy to task for having it preempt the arrivals on the other shows: "If, indeed, you want seventy or so million viewers to feel good about an event that puts your best and brightest on display, make it easier, not harder, for TV viewers to gawk at the stars (and the fashions provided them at great trouble and expense by designers who actually lost exposure this year) in the most harmless fashion possible." *USA Today* called it "a painfully inane special hosted ineptly by a gushy Geena Davis. It bored us with taped segments when all we wanted to see was the stars' entrances. For this, ABC pushed Joan Rivers off the red carpet?" And the *San Francisco Examiner*'s Tim Johnson said, "Hello, Geena Davis?—come in, this is your career talking. Just yell loudly and we'll pull you out of that hole you've fallen into."

Whoopi Goldberg didn't get off much easier, although there were some TV reviews who applauded her work. The *Orange County Register*'s Kinney Littlefield felt the Oscar telecast "was a warm and winning affair—thanks in large measure to welcoming host Whoopi Goldberg." Robert Bianco of *USA Today* wrote, "Billy Crystal is a smoother host, and he gives the show a higher comfort level. But I also like the sharper, more socially conscious edge Goldberg brings

to the show, though her willingness to work on the edges of good taste sometimes detracts from the event." Matthew Gilbert of the *Boston Globe* felt, "It was the perfect year for Goldberg's wry, smirky sensibility, a year with more than enough Hollywood intrigue and battle for her to play off"; as he watched the show, he was sure she would "win over even the most dour critics with a sharp, frank wit that left no controversy un-goofed upon." He was mistaken. Tom Shales of the *Washington Post* groused, "Goldberg did not distinguish herself as host. She spent a great deal of time laughing at her own jokes, many of which were dirty, a few filthy. Somebody had the not-very-bright idea of parading her out in costumes from each of the five films nominated for costume design. One such outfit was for a slave woman in *Beloved*. Thus what had been merely time-consuming also became tasteless." Rod Dreher of the *New York Post* claimed, "Academy Awards host Whoopi Goldberg drew a coast-to-coast chorus of Bronx cheers yesterday for her vulgarity-spiked performance on Hollywood's High Holy Day. The four-hour show was a ratings disappointment for ABC, and Goldberg's hosting raised inevitable comparisons with David Letterman's 1994 debacle. Goldberg raunched up the normally sedate gala with ribald wisecracks that made many uncomfortable. At one point, she abused a microphone to pantomime stroking Liam Neeson's private parts—a breach of decorum that reportedly caused a shocked ABC executive to send his children from the room."

Entertainment Weekly's Lisa Schwarzbaum felt that "Whoopi bombed last night, she knew it—and yet, crassly, she took it as a sign of her own outrageousness" while the magazine's Ken Tucker told the host, "Third time was the jinx; back into your *Hollywood Squares* box, please." Howard Rosenberg of the *Los Angeles Times* granted that the host had some "nice moments . . . But they were outnumbered by her gratuitously coarse language and one-liners, and cheap political jokes." The *Orange County Register* printed a letter from a very ticked-off Tom Lang of Laguna Niguel who wrote, "I thought Whoopi Goldberg was ridiculous. Her immoral references, her political selling of an impeached president, the put-down of a Republican candidate's wife. The show goes worldwide. Is this how we want the world to think about Americans?" On the East Coast, Joan Nietzschmann of North Bellmore, Long Island, wrote to the *New York Daily News* to complain that, "The Oscars are watched by parents sitting side by side with their children. Do we need to hear such warped comedy? Whoopi looked like a lady, but she didn't sound like one." In the *New York Observer*, Andrew Sarris observed, "A few post-Oscar pundits denounced her for what were perceived as off-the-cuff obscenities threatening the dignity and decorum of the film industry's sacred ritual. Unfortunately, none of her anarchic efforts could stifle the traditional stuffiness that seems to cling to the Oscarcast like moss."

Probably Goldberg's most unexpected admirer was Charlton Heston, who said, "I thought she did very well. I think she's getting better at it, which is not surprising." Heston was full of surprises. The World War II veteran was very happy about the Best Picture upset: "*Private Ryan* was a great film, but *Shakespeare in Love* is the kind of movie you get once every ten years, if you're lucky. I've done a lot of Shakespeare, and I love him."

On the KABC post-Oscar show, Harold Greene said "one of the most poignant moments of the evening was Whoopi Goldberg's tribute to the late Gene Siskel." Roger Ebert responded, "Yes, that was a wonderful moment and it touched my heart. Gene was at the Academy Awards last year . . . And now he's not around any more, but he loved the movies. It was very nice of her to do that." Jonathan Rosenbaum of the *Chicago Reader* winced, however, when he heard Goldberg declare that Siskel "really loved movies." He wrote that film critics in Chicago "were aware that Ebert was a hard-core film buff and Siskel was someone whose interest in film, at least to all appearances, was almost exclusively professional . . . Ebert reviews a good many film books, and to my knowledge Siskel never did; if he ever read any books about film on his own it would surprise me. Inside the profession, Siskel was famous for making so many gaffes about movies in his weekly print reviews . . . If he did love movies independently of his professional duties, he did a superb job of hiding this from his colleagues. The only extended conversa-

tions I ever had with him were on the subjects of Anita Hill (at the time of the Clarence Thomas hearings) and his show."

Despite ABC's high hopes in moving the showing to Sunday, ratings were down 21 percent from the previous year. Some at the network argued that it wasn't fair to compare the two since *Titanic* had led to especially keen interest in the 1997 Oscars, but, then again, these Sunday ratings were a mere 4 percent better than 1996's all-time lowest telecast—the *English Patient* year. In *Entertainment Weekly*, Jim Mullen's "Hot Sheet" stated "Oscar ratings. They were low compared with last year. They should have publicized the tap-dance tribute to *Saving Private Ryan*."

Valli Herman-Cohen of the *Los Angeles Times* began her overview of the night's fashions by clucking facetiously that, "The stars at the 71st Annual Academy Awards ceremonies were derelict in their duty to deliver fashion faux pas—they looked fabulous, disappointing armchair fashion critics and tabloids alike . . . Even gowns that were codesigned by their wearer—usually a guarantee of disaster—emerged with class (notably Liv Tyler's collaboration with Pamela Dennis)." In her own way, Joan Rivers expressed the same thought: "For once the women were pushing class, not ass. I thought it was a fabulous night. Everybody looked just fantastic."

Cynthia Robins wrote in the *San Francisco Examiner* that when "Gwyneth Paltrow stepped onto the red carpet to greet Joan Rivers, there was an audible gasp. Not only was Paltrow, on the arm of her father, Bruce, a bona fide Hollywood princess, she looked the part. Pretty in pink doesn't even describe Paltrow's full-on Ralph Lauren ball gown with its simple princess lines, graceful skirt, deeply veed back and graceful matching organza shawl." Rivers said that Gwyneth Paltrow "looked like a fairy princess. She brought such elegance to the whole evening." Karen Heller of the *Philadelphia Inquirer* raved, "Gwyneth Paltrow is incapable of looking bad," calling her satin gown and matching chiffon stole, "utterly becoming." Orla Healy and Marie Redding of the *New York Daily News*, however, said, "Poor Gwynnie—who looked almost skeletal—spent much of the time struggling to contain herself in the ill-fitting bodice of her Pepto-Bismol-pink princess gown." In some circles, she was criticized for her hair, which was pulled tight into a chignon. David Letterman joked that Bob Vila had applied a coat of polyurethane to her head.

USA Today's Elizabeth Snead picked Cate Blanchett's gown as her favorite, saying the *Elizabeth* star "made the evening's winning style statement. Instead of re-creating old Hollywood elegance, the young Aussie went down the fashion-forward road with avant-garde British designer John Galliano's purple gown with a sheer black embroidered with flowers and a fluttering hummingbird." *W*'s Merle Ginsberg went even further, calling Blanchett's "The most fantastic Oscar dress ever!"

Entertainment Weekly's Degen Pener was especially fond of Catherine Zeta-Jones's Versace: "In a year with so many skinny Grace Kelly wanna-bes, she delivered full-bodied sex-appeal. We think the *Zorro* actress's dark locks perfectly set off the gown's vivacious red." Healy and Redding of the *Daily News* opined that "While Geena Davis may have bombed as pre-show presenter, the former poster-girl for fashion victims should take some comfort in the fact that her knock-out pink frock, at least, looked good"—the satin gown was by Bradley Bayou. The *L.A. Times*'s Herman-Cohen felt that "more mature actresses showed that youth and beauty aren't always synonymous," citing Brenda Blethyn who "looked calm and collected in an etched Escada gown that didn't arrive until nearly show time" and Lynn Redgrave's "pale blue bustle-backed gown" by New York-based Ethiopian designer, Amsale. The *Philadelphia Inquirer*'s Karen Heller said Redgrave was "looking very Kim Novak."

Barbara DeWitt of the *Los Angeles Daily News* wrote, "This was one of the prettiest parades in recent years, but there's always a fashion faux pas or two. And this year it was a pair of vocalists. Mariah Carey looked like a tart in a too-tight '40s halter gown by Lorraine Scott, and Céline Dion (who was fab last year) wore a white Dior tuxedo jacket (backward) and a white hat that some said made her look like a pimp. But somehow she camped it up and it sort of worked." The Associated Press thought that fashion-wise Dion "may be the next Cher." One of Joan Rivers's biggest complaints was Val Kilmer's long, unkempt hair, and she told her daughter, "It's just old-fashioned looking, Melissa. It just looks like one of the guys you would have brought around the house in the early '90s." On the other hand, she said that when Aerosmith's Steve Tyler "went over and goosed Judi Dench, it just made my night."

The Oscars didn't promote a Good-Neighbor policy in South America. "Brazilians who packed bars and nightclubs into the early hours of Monday to watch the Academy Awards vowed their struggling cinema industry would fight back after it failed to win a coveted golden statue," reported Reuters. "In nail-biting scenes reminiscent of the frenzied passion seen during last year's World Cup soccer matches, people fell to their knees to pray in front of giant television screens when the foreign-language film winner was announced . . . *Central Station,* seen by many Brazilians as a chance to wave the flag, fueled a surge of pride in a country rocked by a deep financial crisis and still wounded by a humiliating defeat to France in the World Cup last year." A couple of days after the Oscars, Fernanda Montenegro was back home in Rio and told local reporters she knew neither she nor *Central Station* had much of a chance at winning: "The Oscar really depends on the marketing, which is terrible. Here in Brazil, we talk about cinema as art. In the United States it's different, cinema is only talked about as industry." Regarding Gwyneth Paltrow, she said, "It's easy to understand the reason that she won." That was because Paltrow was "this romantic figure, thin, pure virginal. They don't have much of this type of actress in American cinema. It's an investment." In Montenegro's opinion, *Life Is Beautiful* "didn't deserve to win. I think even Benigni recognized this. As a film it was weak . . . I thought it was just him that won, not the film itself." Still, Montenegro enjoyed the experience. She said, "My generation saw Hollywood as a fantasy. We went to see films as a refuge. You can imagine me as an adolescent gazing at those beautiful actresses without wrinkles, lit with such flattery, and beside them always men who were so handsome. I particularly remember Jennifer Jones in *The Song of Bernadette*. A few weeks ago I met her. Gregory Peck, another dream of my distant past, wrote me a beautiful letter." And on Oscar night itself, "Walking on the red carpet made me feel like a Cinderella."

Paltrow was held in much higher esteem back in the States. *USA Today*'s Dennis Moore decided that while she was "previously known more for what she wears and whom she dates," now "Academy members have found a representative of new Hollywood with whom they're comfortable. She's luminous, well-behaved and, really, one of their own." Wesley Morris of the *San Francisco Examiner* wrote, "Paltrow has single-handedly restored glamour to Hollywood movies. That Paltrow won for being luminous—not for playing a drunk, mentally challenged, disfigured, dysfunctional, dying, socially deficient and/or an odds-defying damsel—is a throwback to classic Hollywood, when a lady could look good for an entire movie and still have the mere infectiousness of her presence be seductive enough to seize Oscar's attention. Her victory was essentially the industry's way of saying 'The children are the future.' "

Bob Strauss of the *Los Angeles Daily News*, who wrote, "Favorite award of the evening: Bill Condon for his brilliantly adapted, psychologically astute *Gods and Monsters* screenplay," tried to find the upside of a victory he was unhappy about: "Roberto Benigni copping the Best Actor award for *Life Is Beautiful* hopefully means that Americans will appreciate foreign films to at least partially the extent that the rest of the world enjoys our movies. (Benigni is the first male actor to win for a non-English language performance.) That, at least, is the optimistic way of spinning the fact that difficult but towering work from *Gods and Monsters*' Ian McKellen and *Affliction*'s Nick Nolte scared the voters off."

Although Goldie Hawn tracked down Roberto Benigni backstage to ooze, "Thank you for your heart" and *Entertainment Weekly*'s Benjamin Svetkey mused, "One man ultimately cornered the market on goodwill," others didn't necessarily agree. *Entertainment Weekly* television critic Ken Tucker said Benigni's "effusiveness turned into schtick pretty fast." Fred Shuster of the *Los Angeles Daily News* wrote, "Italian actor Roberto Benigni's overly ebullient shtick became exhausting," and Denis Ferrara and Diane Judge, filling in for Liz Smith observed: "Roberto Benigni's Oscar

wins for *Life Is Beautiful* were popular, though his buffoonish carrying on is wearing thin. 'Enough already' was the oft-spoken critique in Hollywood." *USA Today*'s Robert Bianco acknowledged that it would "be hard to forget *Life Is Beautiful*'s Roberto Benigni leaping over the seats, screaming out acceptance speeches filled with strange metaphors. But I intend to try." Andrew Sarris wrote, "The man is so completely shameless and uninhibited that he makes Jerry Lewis look like a deadpan stoic. Flatter him, and he hugs you. Insult him, and he kisses your feet. I must concede he had one good line about thanking his parents for giving him poverty so that he could dream, but that is not enough to make up for all his monkeyshines accompanied by the shrewdest broken English since Chico Marx. I believe the Italian word for Mr. Benigni is *basta*." Gary Arnold of the *Washington Times* said, "Having seen his calculated impishness carry *Life Is Beautiful* through the awards season, the time has come to say, 'That'll do, Roberto.' "

A few days after the Awards, Ian McKellen received a telephone call from Harvey Weinstein. The Miramax mogul told him, "You gave the performance of the year. But I saw an opening and I took it."

Two days after the Oscars, the *Los Angeles Times* wrote "After all of Miramax's relentless promotion of *Shakespeare in Love* . . . you might think no one would be surprised when the romantic tale of thespians in love walked away with the Best Picture Oscar. But when Harrison Ford read those three words (and *not* the other three many had been expecting: *Saving Private Ryan*), it hit Hollywood like a frying pan to the forehead. On Monday, as moguls and minions awoke and rubbed the Oscar-party grit out of their eyes, the talk was about how Miramax had pulled it off. Talk that is and a whole lot of sniping." The question being asked, according to the *Times*, was had Miramax "cynically shanghaied the Academy, forever changing the way studios will have to play the game of Oscar pursuit?" The article quoted "a highly placed industry insider" who called Miramax's campaigning "disgusting. The meanness of Washington has splashed over Hollywood. And over what? Some stupid award!" Frank DiGiacomo's take on Harvey Weinstein in the *New York Observer* was, "Yes, he had made a successful landing on a foreign shore. But, oh, those mortars! Oscar or not, he and his little family business were no longer the cute prestige item they had been; in the eyes of Hollywood, Harvey Weinstein had leaped from underdog to Hun."

Bernard Weinraub wrote, "The post-Oscar King of Hollywood lives in New York, behaves like an old-time studio mogul and has plenty of enemies. Especially this morning." Weinraub disclosed that DreamWorks "was nothing less than devastated, even though their World War II epic picked up five Oscars." He also reported that Fox head Bill Mechanic said that Weinstein "was unusual among studio executives because he was consumed above all with winning Oscars. 'More than any other company, Miramax was set up for specialized movies and tend to be movies that the Academy recognizes,' he said. 'They've focused on one thing: the Academy Award process. The rest of us are in the business of making different types of films, some of them meriting Academy attention, some not.'"

Miramax insisted the attacks were sour grapes, and the studio's West Coast president, Mark Gill, said the charges being thrown around were "ludicrous, vicious, uncalled for and wildly inaccurate." He also said, "Ultimately, it isn't about advertising or mudslinging. Ultimately, it's about the movie Academy members liked best." A couple of days after the Awards, Weinstein spoke to the *New York Observer* and maintained, "The newspapers forget that there are 6,000 Academy members. The newspapers report the town from the executive suite, and that can be a very self-serving executive suite. The Academy is made up of filmmakers. People who make movies and know what it takes to make these kinds of films. The executive suite wants to make money. Miramax wants to make movies." Similarly, *Variety*'s Andrew Hindes noted, "Mainstream press reports zeroed in on this year's Oscar campaign, portraying it as a costly trade ad war between Miramax and DreamWorks. But acting and screenwriting awards for little-hyped pictures including Lions Gate's pair of *Affliction* and *Gods and Monsters* show that powerful pictures, however obscure, get the Academy's attention. Industry veterans note that Academy members tend to be an opinion-

ated, independent-minded lot who bring years of experience and a critical eye to the voting process." Saying, "I don't think you can buy the Oscar," Jack Mathews of the *New York Daily News* nevertheless wrote an open letter to Harvey Weinstein stating, "Your campaigns are obnoxious, and they do create the appearance of influence-buying. They're tainting the Oscar process, making Miramax a Cold War villain. and demeaning the films themselves." His conclusion: "What should be remembered as a great night for *Shakespeare* is being remembered as an ugly fight over a gold-plated geegaw."

In the *New York Times*, however, Vincent Canby was having a great deal of fun over the whole contretemps. "There's still nothing quite as exhilarating as the spectacle of some of Hollywood's toughest wheeler-dealers, each of whom has an average income exceeding the G.N.P. of many countries, as they take umbrage at the shabby behavior of an upstart not yet in their club. Such outrage! Such piety! Such wounded feelings!" he wrote. "I refer to the ghastly events that unraveled in slow motion Sunday night at the Academy Awards show when Steven Spielberg's World War II melodrama, *Saving Private Ryan,* the odds-on favorite to control the night, was lyrically humiliated by *Shakespeare in Love.*" Chuckling at the outrage voiced over Miramax's spending, Canby said, "Remember these charges are issuing from Hollywood, a town where the gospel has always been that you have to spend a buck to make a buck. Suddenly everybody's talking as if defending an Augustinian City of God against the forces of that other fellow: not the Devil exactly, but the unfashionable Harvey Weinstein from Brooklyn and Queens, educated at the State University at Buffalo. Even when dressed in designer suits, he gives the impression of having sat up all night in a stalled commuter train. No wonder he lives in New York." Canby concluded that Harvey and Bob Weinstein "are the guys whom their Hollywood colleagues are now bad-rapping for caring only about winning Oscars. Is there anybody even remotely connected to the movie industry that doesn't share that dream?"

When somebody brought up Miramax's profligate spending to Harvey Weinstein backstage on Oscar night, he countered that for all the complaints about his company's campaigning, "I think the most amazing thing we found out from Warren Beatty today was that *Saving Private Ryan* pre-Oscar nomination and post-Oscar nomination spent more money in the trades than we did. Warren spoke to Jeffrey Katzenberg, and they both confirmed that to me. It was fairly amazing to us." And Miramax's West Coast chief, Mark Gill, told Bernard Weinraub, "A lot of people accuse us of spending more than DreamWorks, but actually we spent less. We counted. Basically they bought 165 total pages in the Hollywood trade papers. We bought 118 total pages for *Shakespeare*." Of course, these tallies didn't take into account that Miramax had been using the *Los Angeles Times* and *New York Times* as appendages to the trade papers with ads that were clearly Oscar-oriented. Steven Spielberg pointed out that he himself had remained mum on the subject all along: "I just stayed way beyond that. It was just a bunch of silly publicity."

Rematches were on the way.

1999

The gods seemed to be angry at the Academy.

Fantasy Life

There were certain people out there in the world for whom the arrival of *Star Wars Episode 1: The Phantom Menace* was a religious experience. The first film in the *Star Wars* saga since 1983, and George Lucas's first foray into directing since the original *Star Wars* in 1977, the movie brought about an anxious expectancy similar to that accorded Terrence Malick's *The Thin Red Line* last year, only a different type of person was affected. Some lost souls even camped out ahead of time—literally for weeks—at theaters where the picture would be playing. The publicity machine at 20th Century Fox went into maximum overdrive, and the media happily played along in ballyhooing the film; the hype got to the absurd point where ads for the studio's late winter release *Wing Commander*, more or less indicated that the only reason to go to this Freddie Prinze Jr. vehicle was that before the feature you'd have your first chance to see the trailer for *The Phantom Menace*.

Then in May it opened. J. Hoberman wrote in the *Village Voice, Star Wars Episode I: The Phantom Menace* may be the first movie to peak before its opening. Last year's *Godzilla* was dead on arrival, but *The Phantom Menace*—which (finally!) has its premiere today—has enjoyed a six-month run in the media. Hence, the movie requires scarcely more than six minutes to wear thin. There is nothing in this noisy, overdesigned bore to equal the excitement generated by the mere idea of the trailer. Indeed, days before *The Phantom Menace*'s high-security press junket, fans who penetrated a top-secret distributor's screening were venting their disappointment over the net. By junket time, the backlash was evident." In the estimation of Robert Wilonsky of *New Times Los Angeles*, "This ain't no movie. It's a very long, very tedious infomercial for *Phantom Menace* action figures, on sale now at a Target or Toys 'R' Us near you."

Star Wars Episode I: The Phantom Menace did gross $430 million even though it was hard to find anyone who truly liked it. Ultimately, the film was memorable for two things: as one of the most triumphant examples of flackery in the history of cinema, and for featuring the most reviled film character to be seen in a movie in decades, would-be comic relief Jar Jar Binks. Animosity ran so high that a profusion of Web sites permeated the Internet with names like "Die, Jar Jar Binks, Die!" and "Jar Jar Binks Sucks So Bad I Can't Even Stand It."

Six weeks prior to the premiere of *Star Wars Episode I: The Phantom Menace*, a fantasy film had opened with no particular hype but critical and audience reaction 180 degrees different than that for *Phantom Menace*. The *Philadelphia Inquirer*'s Steven Rea cheered, "A cyberpunk *Alice in Wonderland* in which the rabbit hole is a coaxial cable plugged right into your cerebral cortex . . . *The Matrix* offers the most exhilaratingly inventive action sequences to come down the pike in years," and he lauded the film for "its mix of Lewis Carroll and William Gibson; Japanese anime and Chinese chopsocky, mythological allusions, and machine-made illusion." Kenneth Turan of the *Los Angeles Times* wrote, "*The Matrix* combines traditional science-fiction premises with spanking new visual technology in a way that almost defies description. Like it or not, this is one movie that words don't come close to approximating. Written and directed by the Wachowski brothers, Larry and Andy, *The Matrix* is the unlikely spiritual love child of dark futurist Philip K. Dick and the snap and dazzle of Hong Kong filmmaking, with digital technology serving as the helpful midwife." Extremely positive word-of-mouth and repeat viewings—people wanted to try to figure out how'd they do *that*?—resulted in an unexpected hit, and one that engendered a lot more good will than the George Lucas film. *Entertainment Weekly*'s Dan Fierman wrote, "*The Matrix* out-*Star Wars*-ed *Star Wars*, showing George Lucas what sci-fi *should* look like in '99."

A new kind of buildup was accorded a genre movie opening two months after *The Phantom Menace*. Made at a cost of $60,000, *The Blair Witch Project* became the first film to depend almost exclusively on the internet to get the word out. Its Web site ingeniously intimated that the horrible incidents recounted in the movie had actually happened, and it built up anticipation by setting out all the "facts." Although the general public was unaware of *The Blair Witch Project*'s existence, the Web site itself had developed an intense cult following; between its midnight screening at Sundance and its July release, the film engendered so much discussion on the internet that it was as intensely anticipated by the net community as once upon a time *Phantom Menace* had been. An improvised cinema vérité thriller—three student filmmakers unwittingly record their last couple of days on earth while lost in the woods—*The Blair Witch Project* relied almost exclusively on the power of suggestion: It was sort of a *Friday the 13th* movie in which you never see Jason. Lloyd Rose of the *Washington Post* swore, "*The Blair Witch Project* is the scariest movie I've ever seen. Not the goriest, the grossest, the weirdest, the eeriest, the sickest, the creepiest or the slimiest. Not the most haunting, most disturbing, most horrific, most violent, most beautiful, most dreamlike or most vile. Just flat out the scariest." The *New York Post*'s Jonathan Foreman figured that "For some people *The Blair Witch Project* could do for overnight hiking what *Jaws* did for midnight skinny-dipping." Grossing over $100 million, *The Blair Witch Project* had perhaps the highest gross-to-cost ratio of all time, its triumph even landing it on the cover of *Newsweek*. Harvey Weinstein had seen the film at Sundance but passed on it, acquiring, instead, *Happy, Texas. Premiere*'s "Libby Gelman-Waxner" moaned, "the scariest thing about *Blair Witch* is that I didn't invest in it," while John Hartl of the *Seattle Times* said, "Pity the poor film-festival programmer forced to watch all the inevitable shaky-camera imitations."

Little Boy Boo

One person who was not thrilled about the success of *The Blair Witch Project* was M. Night Shyamalan. An Indian-born filmmaker based in Philadelphia, the twenty-nine-year-old Shyamalan admitted that his heart sank as he witnessed the *Blair Witch* phenomenon: He wanted *his* movie to be the year's sleeper horror film. And certainly, *any* success for *The Sixth Sense* would qualify for sleeper status. Shyamalan had previously made two films—one in which he himself had starred, the other featuring Rosie O'Donnell as a nun—which had resulted in his remaining an un-

known entity. In fact, *USA Today*'s Mike Clark wrote, "The best thing you could say about writer/director M. Night Shyamalan's last film *(Wide Awake)* is that it was shown." The advance word on *The Sixth Sense* was nil; its advertising tag line was "I see dead people" and among smart-alecky filmgoers, the retort was "I see dead movie."

In reality, *The Sixth Sense* turned into a spectacularly successful surprise hit. Shyamalan described his film—a supernatural tale detailing the relationship between a disturbed little boy visited by the spirits of people who had met violent ends and the guilt-ridden child psychiatrist trying to get him out of his funk—as "*Ordinary People* meets *The Exorcist*." Bruce Willis was cast as the shrink and Shyamalan did a Scarlett O'Hara looking for the right moppet to be the centerpiece of the movie. Saying he was "physically and mentally exhausted from the search," the director met Haley Joel Osment: "Haley came in—wearing a little Oxford shirt—and he struck me as a cute, sweet little kid. I just leaned back and Haley started the scene and it was like I had never heard the scene before. It was as though I had never heard the dialogue, all of a sudden every word was perfect. He finished the scene and was crying, and I was crying and all I could say was, 'Who are you? Where did you come from?' Haley started laughing as he wiped the tears away."

A couple of things set *The Sixth Sense* apart from most other movies of its kind. One was that it was, above all, a mood piece, permeated with an intense sense of melancholy. Although it did have its share of shocks, for the most part, the film—like *The Blair Witch Project*—relied on a sense of dread and foreboding. Set in South Philadelphia, it was one of the few movies of recent times to portray matter-of-factly a blue-collar milieu. Finally, and probably most important for its success, *The Sixth Sense* contained one of the great twist endings of all time. Malcolm Johnson of the *Hartford Courant* said, "From its disturbing beginning to its surprising, satisfying ending, *The Sixth Sense* weaves a mysterious spell as it tells a haunting story." The *Chicago Tribune*'s Mark Caro wrote that in the guise of a thriller, *The Sixth Sense* was "an uncommonly serious-minded movie that's brave enough to engage our deepest emotions on issues of death, madness, illusion and forgiveness. That's the biggest thrill of them all."

Eleven-year-old Haley Joel Osment had first garnered attention as Candice Bergen's son, Avery, on *Murphy Brown*, the child whom Vice President Dan Quayle demonized for being born to a fictional single mother; he also played Tom Hanks's kid in *Forrest Gump*. "Though he is hardly a discovery, the eleven-year-old Osment is a revelation in *The Sixth Sense*, an unnerving and astonishing thriller," raved the *Philadelphia Inquirer*'s Carrie Rickey. "While the film about a troubled boy tormented by visions and by schoolmates stars Bruce Willis as a child psychologist, *The Sixth Sense* rests squarely on Osment's hunched little shoulders. He carries the movie, a lyrical and eerie meditation upon loss and hurt and healing, like Atlas swatting away ghosts with his free hand. So transparent is Osment as an actor, and so rare, that the pain on his face stabs you in the heart." Robert W. Butler of the *Kansas City Star* had a similar reaction: "Young Osment gives a heartbreaking performance as the little loner trying bravely to endure horrors that will give him no peace. The kid will have you jumping in fear one moment and sobbing in sympathy the next, achieving breathtaking moments well beyond the capabilities of most adult actors. This is a performance for the time capsule." Osment's summation was, "I'm very honored that I was picked to play Cole. It is an outstanding script and I believe it's going to be a ground-breaker." He also adhered to the Stanislavsky approach. "Good acting is about believing you're the character in the moment," the eleven-year-old expounded. "If you're in that character, nothing is wrong that you do, if you're acting truly as the character." At one point on the set of *The Sixth Sense*, he suddenly threw himself against a wall so that he would look shocked in the next scene: "I needed to be shaken up by something I'd seen, and nothing was really working. It happened sort of instinctively."

Australian actress Toni Collette played Osment's mother and Mick LaSalle commented in the *San Francisco Chronicle*, "Willis and Osment are beautifully supported by Toni Collette as Cole's mother. After years of being known for being heavy, Collette has pulled a Maria Callas and turned svelte. She plays a working-class mom without the usual Hollywood notes of condescension or nobility. She's just a matter-of-fact good mom, and Collette plays her with every nerve frayed, every emotion on the surface of her face."

Stephen Holden of the *New York Times* couldn't stand the movie, though, and slapped it with, "this year's *Touched by an Angel* award for gaggingly mawkish supernatural kitsch." Clearly, he was in the minority, for by the time it had run its course, *The Sixth Sense* had become the second highest grossing film of 1999, behind only *Star Wars: The Phantom Menace*. The *Sacramento Bee* analyzed the success of *The Sixth Sense*: "Ssshhh. Pass it on. People are jumping at the chance to be left in the dark—at least when it comes to this creepy and clever movie . . . Audiences are paying good money to sit in the dark and be stunningly misled until the very end." The article noted that "the secret has become a major component of the movie's buzz," and quoted Robert Thompson, a professor of television, radio, and film at Syracuse University: "There are probably a lot of people a week ago who had no intention of going. Now they've heard something's up with this movie, and they're going to go this weekend." Emphasizing that the way to maximize enjoyment of the film was to know as little about it as possible, the *Bee* advised readers who hadn't yet seen *The Sixth Sense*, "You could always make like little kids do: Cover your ears and sing 'la-la-la-la-la' whenever anyone talks about *The Sixth Sense*, don't read your e-mail or answer the phone, don't turn on the TV or radio and don't read any news publications." Contributing to *The Sixth Sense*'s emerging status as a mega-hit was that people were returning a second time to see what clues had been dropped about the ending that they missed the first time around.

Haley Joel Osment learned what it was like to have been Cuba Gooding Jr., for just as strangers on the street had incessantly demanded that the *Jerry Maguire* actor give them a little bit of "Show me the money!" Haley Joel had to do a rendition of "I see dead people," which was pop culture's second most dominant catchphrase this year—the first being Regis Philbin's "Final answer?" from *Who Wants to Be a Millionaire*. Master Osment would happily oblige. "I never get annoyed about it," he said. "It brings back such good memories."

Stanley Steamy

One of the most anticipated releases of the summer was Stanley Kubrick's posthumous *Eyes Wide Shut*. Although it opened strongly—due to extensive media coverage and the presence of Tom Cruise and Nicole Kidman—word of mouth was on the down side. A minority of critics appreciated the dreamlike, sexually-charged film—in fact, its proponents tended to be intensely passionate about Kubrick's achievement. Mike Clark of *USA Today* said, "It's a precisely modulated and mostly mesmerizing 2 3/4-hour suspense movie, in part because it's one of the most bravely disturbing screen works ever attempted about thoughts withheld by even the most devoted marriage partners and the ramifications of voicing them." He felt that Kubrick, "has managed to make a contemporary New York movie with Cruise and Kidman feel positively Old European. What a distinctive feat this is in a multiplex-driven era when too many comedies, cop pics and space adventures are edited to look and sound exactly the same. All this and enough brooding superstar power, too, which turns the final scene (in a children's toy store, no less) into an emotional corker unlike any other Kubrick directed." Jonathan Rosenbaum of the *Chicago Reader* felt, "This is personal filmmaking as well as dream poetry of the kind most movie commerce has ground underfoot, and if a better studio release comes along this year I'll be flabbergasted."

But most reviewers didn't get the film and treated it with condescension, throwing in just a modicum of respect so they could show that they knew Kubrick was regarded as a great director. *Entertainment Weekly*'s Owen Gleiberman typed, "In *Eyes Wide Shut*, the director's famously over-deliberate, pause-laden style verges, for the first time, on amateurville . . . Stanley Kubrick was a genius, but by the time he died, he'd observed a generation's worth of cultural change from within his self-imposed bunker, and the remove shows. It's his eyes, I'm afraid, that seem to have been wide shut, and his movie that wears a mask." Stephen Hunter of the *Washington Post* said, "it feels creaky, an-

cient, hopelessly out of touch, infatuated with the hot taboos of his youth and unable to connect with that twisty thing contemporary sexuality has become. It's empty of ideas, which is fine, but it's also empty of heat. . . . I still bow before no one in my love for Kubrick's earlier brilliance. But in this one, he lost it, if he had had it in the past decade. . . The sad truth is that *Eyes Wide Shut* must enter that collection of over-inflated zeppelins full of hot air but otherwise rudderless and hopelessly adrift, like *Howard the Duck*, *Ishtar* and *The Flintstones*. It's really nothing more than *American Pie* for the too-smart set."

Eyes Wide Shut did earn 1999's "*Vertigo/The Searchers/Touch of Evil* Award" as the Movie-Most-Destined-To-Be-a-Classic-in-Twenty-Five-Years-While-Reviewers-Who-Dismissed-It-Will-Look-Awfully-Foolish.

Father Knows Best

Eyes Wide Shut was that rarity: a studio summer release intended for adult audiences. More expectedly, once September came around, the studios started rolling out their "mature" fare. DreamWorks didn't have a Steven Spielberg historical epic this year. Instead, it offered up *American Beauty*, a satire about malaise, materialism, the middle class, and midlife crises. The scuttlebutt was that Spielberg read the script on a Saturday and made a bid for it on Monday morning. Indeed, the screenplay was such that you might have thought DreamWorks had bankrolled the film for the specific purpose of propping up Spielberg's thesis that, in comparison to the wonderful World War II generation he lionized in *Saving Private Ryan*, baby boomers were lousy and just plain no good. Making his film debut was British theater director Sam Mendes, who had caused a splash on Broadway by setting a revival of *Cabaret* in a real night club. Kevin Spacey played a husband and father who opts out of responsibility and respectability and Annette Bening was his shrewish wife.

In its Fall Preview, the *New York Daily News* wrote "Stung by the loss of *Saving Private Ryan* to *Shakespeare in Love* for last year's Best Picture Oscar, co-founder Steven Spielberg's DreamWorks is hanging its hopes this year" on *American Beauty*. The article added, "The early word from advance screenings in New York hasn't quite lived up to the buzz launched in a friendly *New York Times* piece in early July, but it's definitely on the radar screen of Oscar watchers." That *Times* article was a Bernard Weinraub "At The Movies" piece that declared, "Forget the summer! The most talked-about film of the moment is *American Beauty*, a drama about a suburban family, set to open in the autumn. Although only a few people have seen the movie, the buzz about it has startled even DreamWorks, which made it and has spent the last few weeks debating the details of how and when to release it." Weinraub also revealed, "Mr. Spielberg has told colleagues it's one of the best films he's seen in years. After Ms. Bening saw the film, the actress was so overcome that she is reported to have burst into tears."

By Sam Mendes's own account, what he filmed over the first three days of production was "crap." Things, he said, were "badly shot, my fault, badly composed, my fault, bad costumes, my fault. And everybody was doing what I was asking. It was all my fault." Horrified by what he was seeing in the dailies, Mendes asked executives at DreamWorks if he could please re-shoot those scenes. He was allowed to start over, and this time he decided he would depend on cinematographer Conrad Hall. Mendes recalled, "I made a very conscious decision early on, if I didn't understand something, to say, without embarrassment, 'I don't understand what you're talking about, please explain it.'" Ultimately, Mendes bragged about the finished product that, "On the one hand, it's a very funny social comedy. But on a subliminal level, it's about change and escape. It goes to some dark places."

Screenwriter Alan Ball was all worked up about the movie having as its theme "how we have preconceived notions about things, but the truth often turns out to be something we never even considered," as if this was something no one had ever considered before. Presumably, this premise was why the film's advertising tag line was "Look closer . . .",—which turned out to be rather ironic, because the more one examined *American Beauty* the more shallow it seemed, the less it had to say. Ball had written for the *Grace Under Fire* sitcom, and later was producer of Cybill Shepherd's series, and the movie possessed the same level of depth

one found in television comedy. This was a satire being marketed as cutting edge and daring, yet it had as its targets such things as the banal conformity of suburban life, loveless marriages, sleazy real estate agents, the military, self-help motivational regimens—subjects that had been done to death by about 1978. At this late date, *American Beauty* actually contained that hoary cliché: the virulent homophobe who is—look closer—really a self-loathing gay man. And Mendes and Ball undoubtedly thought there was something audacious in starting the film with Kevin Spacey masturbating in the shower. Yet they were behind the curve by a year, since Todd Solondz's 1998 film *Happiness* contained overt masturbation, and had an ejaculation shot to boot—and then there was *There's Something about Mary*'s hair gel.

Nonetheless, many reviewers thought *American Beauty* was hot stuff. "Unsettling, unnerving, undefinable, *American Beauty* avoids quick and easy categorization," huzzahed Kenneth Turan of the *Los Angeles Times*. "A quirky and disturbing take on modern American life energized by bravura performances from Kevin Spacey and Annette Bening, *Beauty* is a blood-chilling dark comedy with unexpected moments of both fury and warmth, a strange, brooding and very accomplished film that sets us back on our heels from its opening frames." In the *New York Daily News*, Jami Bernard called *American Beauty* "a tart, funny and tremendously sobering movie about the deepest recesses of personal unhappiness" and a "horrific tour of crossed wires, inchoate longing, dashed illusions, couples grown apart, parents at odds with their children, and resentment that wells from poisoned hearts." To Owen Gleiberman of *Entertainment Weekly*, it was "an exquisitely designed, rather kinky tragicomedy set in a nameless American suburb, and its images have a velvety, saturated richness, as if life had become a candyland of upward mobility." The *Chicago Tribune*'s Michael Wilmington called the film "a stunner: a scathing dark comedy about corruption and doom in the immaculate boudoirs, living rooms and lawns of middle-class suburbia." Rod Dreher of the *New York Post* simply said, "*American Beauty* is a flat-out masterpiece, surely the best movie of the year; indeed, an all-time classic. It is one of the most artistically accomplished, truthful and altogether breathtaking motion pictures I have ever seen. Very few movies are genuinely unforgettable. This is one of them."

The New Republic's Stanley Kauffmann yawned, "All that Ball can tell us is what many American and British and French and Italian films have already expounded. Modern urban-suburban life can be anesthetic; the human spirit often chafes against dehumanizing limits and either explodes or shrivels. Ball has nothing to add." *New York*'s Peter Rainer noted that the "characters are designed to confound our preconceptions and unfold their secret selves. In most cases, though, this two-step agenda comes across as simply one kind of shallowness giving way to another." J. Hoberman of the *Village Voice* called the film a "harsh and hyperbolic, if not particularly funny, satire of suburban angst" and declared, "Bland and nasty, *American Beauty* has the slightly stale feel of a family sitcom conceived under the spell of *Married . . . with Children*." The *Voice*'s Michael Atkinson offered, "Let's have a moment, shall we, to appreciate the irritating, cruel and cartoonish portrait of middle-class families in *American Beauty*, portrayed as they were with all the latitude and respect the Japanese received in *Sands of Iwo Jima*. Certainly this year's Emperor's New Clothes, Sam Mendes's carpet-bomb plays like an outcast child's act of revenge. Wes Bentley's enigmatic dealer aside, there wasn't a character insight that didn't make the cast of *South Park* seem positively three-dimensional."

As for the hot shot young director, Janet Maslin decreed in the *New York Times* that the movie was "directed with terrific visual flair." But Stuart Klawans of *The Nation* felt that Mendes "seems to lack any instinct for linking one shot to another. His camera placement is expressive only when formulaic (he knows when a cut to a long shot will get a laugh), and camera movement is simply beyond him. But by hiring Conrad Hall, he's been able to buy good-looking images."

The ultimate put-down of *American Beauty* came from Alan Vanneman in the film journal, *Bright Lights*: "Okay, *American Beauty* is shallow, pretentious, smug, condescending, and parochial. It radiates the traditional show-biz contempt for the talent-free slobs who inhabit American small towns and suburbia, cut off from high-grade hemp, cutting-edge video equipment, and the other finer things in life. But *American Beauty* does have its good points as well. Specifically, it tells us all the steps we need to take to achieve supreme, continuous, and unending happiness." Some of the steps Vanneman mentioned were "If You Are A Middle-Aged Man: Tell your wife to go fuck herself. Tell your boss to go fuck himself. Negotiate a $50,000-severance package by sexually blackmailing your boss. Have your brains blown out by your next-door neighbor, a repressed homophobic Marine Corps colonel who turns out to be queer (not that there's anything wrong with that)." "If You Are A Teen-Aged Girl: Never crack a book. Hate your parents. Cultivate a 'dark waif' look. Wear 'attitude' lipstick, except in the scenes where the director wants you to look vulnerable." "If You're A Middle-Aged Woman: Forget it, bitch! You're old and ugly and nobody wants you!" On the question of "Why The Critics Love It: They're idiots!—Okay, not all movie critics are idiots. Only those who liked *American Beauty* are idiots."

On the Straight and Narrow

By any reasonable, objective standard, Kevin Spacey was miscast in the lead role. His character, Lester Burnham, is intended to be the quintessential Average Joe who finally gets fed up and loses it, but Spacey brings his snarky, cynical persona to any role he takes, and so, watching *American Beauty* one is left wondering why he hadn't dropped out years ago, and how he and Annette Bening ever ended up together in the first place. Nevertheless, Roger Ebert wrote in the *Chicago Sun-Times* that "Spacey, an actor who embodies intelligence in his eyes and voice, is the right choice for Lester Burnham," and Jay Carr said in the *Boston Globe*, "With his cool, mocking glances and disdainfully curled lip, Kevin Spacey looks like the man who invented sarcasm. . . . Spacey is diamond-brilliant in a role that plays as if custom-made for him."

His leading lady, Annette Bening, was stuck with a caricature rather than a character to play, and Andrew O'Hehir of *Salon* ruminated, "I don't know whether to blame Mendes, the script or Bening, whose formidable acting chops are expended on a feverish, sexually repressed demon whose few tiny moments of possible redemption are undermined by burlesque. This is a woman who, as Lester tells us in his opening voice-over, has matching pruning shears and gardening clogs. In case we haven't figured out that she's the embodiment of American materialism, the script lays it out for us. When Carolyn snaps at Lester for nearly spilling his drink on the couch, he responds, 'This is just stuff. And it's become more important to you than living. And, honey, that's nuts.' ... Perhaps it's not surprising that Carolyn hates both herself and Lester so much. But both parties in a dreadful marriage are always simultaneously the authors and victims of their situation, and absent some understanding of that, *American Beauty* turns Carolyn into a misogynist caricature for no good purpose." Nevertheless, *Variety*'s Todd McCarthy declared, "Bening, perfectly cast as the perfect wife, goes well beyond the expected in such a role and is almost scary at times in the way she defends herself." Kevin Spacey said, "Annette was quite miraculous. In fact, I was a little worried about her; she definitely became possessed."

Despite the critics who saw through *American Beauty*, it did emerge as the best reviewed film of the year—so far. Three more months of prestige items would try to knock it off its preeminent position in the Oscar contest. *Variety* said that "*American Beauty* sounded the opening bell for the race, nabbing what is known as the *L.A. Confidential* slot: It's a mainstream-but-serious pic that the critics have embraced as a signal that summer's over and thoughtful films have arrived." The question with the DreamWorks movie, cautioned *Variety*, was "did the film come out too early?" Helping *American Beauty*'s Oscar odds was that it turned out to be extremely popular—which served to expose the movie for what it was. If it had actually been deep or dark or disturbing, *American Beauty* would not have joined the $100-million club. Hard-hitting, provocative movies don't make $100 million, glib cartoons do.

The *New York Observer* told the sad tale that screenwriter Alan Ball was not completely feasting upon his acclaim, because unlike movie reviewers, those in the world of television weren't according him the proper respect: "His other project, the new ABC sitcom *Oh Grow Up*—about three male roommates living in Brooklyn (one gay, two straight)—is getting slammed." The *Los Angeles Times*'s take was "This is one show that should take its title more seriously." *Entertainment Weekly*'s bottom line on the series: "Suggested alternate title: *Oh Shut Up*." The ratings were anemic, too, and the show was soon canceled.

Ball was openly gay, as were *American Beauty*'s producers Bruce Cohen and Dan Jinks. On the other hand, now that Kevin Spacey was supposedly embodying the middle-class married man, he wanted to make one thing clear. Rumors about his sexuality had been around for years, and a 1996 article in *Esquire* strongly insinuated that he was gay. As *American Beauty* was hitting theaters, Spacey pleaded his case in a *Playboy* interview. He insisted, "Most of the women I know haven't heard about the article. If they have, they know not to believe what they read. Then there are a few women who think the article might be true. It's a challenge for them: They want to be the ones to turn me around. I let them." Michael Musto's reaction in the *Village Voice* was, "Kevin Spacey came out as hetero in *Playboy*, setting the record *straight* and continuing to loudly do so. (He made out with women in public and flirted with one on a talk show.) How depressing! That means that all the people I know who've told me about guys Spacey's dated, done, or come on to are utter, complete liars with a reckless disregard for real life! I must stop hanging out with such disreputable, cowardly worms!"

Deere Heart

An unusually large number of films released toward the end of 1999 were based on real people. Some of these individuals were very well known, others were rescued from anonymity because of their screen portrayals. Perhaps none was more obscure than Alvin Straight, a man who had gained the tiniest modicum of fame for providing the kind of human interest anecdote that often closes television newscasts. Straight was an Iowa septuagenarian who took a trip to see his dying brother, hoping to become reconciled after many years. He made the 240-mile trek to Wisconsin on a John Deere riding mower.

In the *New York Observer*, Andrew Sarris acknowledged that *The Straight Story* "is the kind of movie that no matter how many rapturous reviews it receives, once you find out what it is about, your first reaction almost has to be, you've got to be kidding." Even more unlikely than the subject matter was that this road movie was directed by David Lynch, who in the past celebrated the violently bizarre and the seductively dangerous in such *outré* works as *Blue Velvet* and *Lost Highway*. Lynch said that not too much should be read into the fact that he was making a G-rated movie for Disney, and he insisted, "It's wrong to interpret the film as a barometer of my state of mind. You could draw some strange conclusions from that." While the director admitted, "I guess you'd have to say this is different from the things I've been doing lately," all it meant was that "People react to things and I reacted to this script. It seemed like the right thing to do." He also announced, "Tenderness can be just as abstract as insanity." Richard Farnsworth played Alvin Straight, and said, "The minute I read this script, I identified with this old character, and I fell in love with the story. Alvin is an example in fortitude and a lot of guts."

"*The Straight Story* is nothing short of sublime," said Sarris. "It's clearly one of the three or four best movies of the year. Indeed, in some ways it's too good to be an American movie." He added, "It is suffused with so much unembarrassed but never sappy goodness not only from the principals but from the people along the way as well that it helps make up for all the mean-spiritedness and malignancy that takes up so much screen time these days." An admiring Duane Dudek of the *Milwaukee Journal Sentinel* wrote, "Haunting, gentle and G-rated, *The Straight Story* is as original as anything this esoteric filmmaker has ever produced and quite a bit more profound. It shows Lynch's creative personality, like his protagonist, to be mature, unhurried and still happily subversive."

Wesley Morris of the *San Francisco Examiner* said, "The fragile beauty of Farnsworth's performance is that he makes Alvin appear to be listening to, learning from and entertained by everyone he meets. Farnsworth has eyes as big and chlorine-blue as swimming pools and sometimes the wind makes them leak a little. Other times, he's moved by the kindness of strangers and the quiet, religious magnitude of his own pilgrimage. Farnsworth's mouth is collapsed, pushed in as though he's missing a row of his teeth behind the snowy scraggliness that passes for a beard. . . . What the veteran actor brings is a bemusement—wonder at how fast the world moves around him, at how the years have ravaged him. He may be the only actor I've ever seen whose pensive silences and long drags of contemplative staring have made me want to know what he's thinking about." The *Miami Herald*'s Rene Rodriguez said that Farnsworth "carries the wisdom of an entire life in his eyes. . . . It's a haunting, delicate performance that benefits greatly from Farnsworth's own no-nonsense nature."

The Straight Story was Farnsworth's first feature film in five years and, semi-retired at age seventy-nine, he was spending most of his time these days on his ranch in New Mexico with his forty-one-year-old fiancée. He recalled that when Lynch called him about the movie, "I told him, 'No, I'm slowing down and I've got a bad hip and walk with a cane.' But Lynch replied, 'That's great. Alvin Straight used two canes. You'll be perfect.'" The former stunt man said he and his beloved didn't keep up with current movies. "But I do like to watch the old movies on TV. I get to see so many friends who are long gone—people like Hoot Gibson, Buck Jones, Bob Steele, Tex Ritter, Roy Rogers, Gene Autry."

This Above All

If *The Straight Story* showed middle America at its kindest and most generous of spirit, a second small, fact-based autumn release portrayed the heartland as another world altogether, an intolerant, brutal, and oppressive country. *Boys Don't Cry* told the story of Teena Brandon, a young woman in hardscrabble Nebraska who found fulfillment when she took on a male identity as Brandon Teena, only to be raped and murdered by quintessential rednecks when he was found out. First-time director Kimberly Pierce told CNN that when she first read about Brandon's life after the murder, "It completely blew me away. Here was a girl living in a trailer park, she didn't have much money, she didn't have any role models, and she successfully transformed herself into a fantasy of a boy. That was completely compelling and extraordinary to me—the courage to carry it out and then the cleverness to keep the fantasy alive."

Pierce had cowritten the script as a masters thesis at Columbia and said that when she was preparing the film, "I was looking all over the country, but there was no girl who could play Brandon." She received a videotape containing a screen test in the mail. Eventually, "we popped in the tape, and this beautiful, androgynous person just floated across the screen, cowboy hat on, big sock in his pants, gorgeous boy jaw, boy voice, boy ears, boy eyes, boy forehead. It was stunning." The person on the tape was a twenty-five-year-old actress named Hilary Swank, who was familiar only to people who had seen *The Next Karate Kid*, in which she took over for Ralph Macchio, or watched *Beverly Hills, 90210* in its waning days, or killed time with some negligible TV movies. She would say, "I was lucky *Karate Kid* wasn't a hit and no one noticed me from *90210*. I was afforded this amazing opportunity because they didn't want a famous person." Swank talked about preparing for the role, saying "I had to retrain my brain. I had to take away all my feminine traits. I emulated my father a lot, all the stuff like looking in the mirror and slicking back my hair. It's from watching him a lot growing up."

Swank heard some of the most extraordinary reviews any previously little-known performer had ever received. "Without Hilary Swank's astonishing performance, the film's success would not be possible," marveled Kenneth Turan. "Swank, in a piercing performance, makes us complicit in the agony and glee of Brandon's days and nights, letting us share in the strangeness, the bravado and the yearning desire to connect of this secret life on the edge. It's a bravura piece of work that not only lets us see how the real Brandon convinced so many people she was a man, it just about convinces us of the same thing even though we know the truth from the outset." *Spin*'s Maureen Callahan hosannaed, "Hilary Swank does a remarkable job, and a portrait emerges that renders her not as a martyr, but a naïvely hopeful, unbearably lonely kid." Peter Stack of the *San Francisco Chronicle* rhapsodized that Swank, "is so good it almost hurts to watch her (knowing, of course, the tragedy that awaits). She inhabits the part so fully that it's nearly impossible to remember that she's a woman. . . . She is a he, not just in the way he dresses, but in the way he moves, speaks, gestures, jokes. Every inch of the character exudes a male sensibility so powerfully, and at times so vulnerably, that Swank's performance crosses into a realm of veracity rare in any film acting." Desson Howe of the *Washington Post* wrote, "In Hilary Swank, Pierce has cast the perfect actor—someone who passes convincingly as a man and with whom anyone could fall in love." A few months after *Boys Don't Cry* opened, Winona Ryder took time off from plugging her new movie, *Girl, Interrupted,* on *Charlie Rose* to say about Swank, "I think if she doesn't win the Academy Award, there is no justice. Her performance makes me want to be a better actress."

Mark Caro of the *Chicago Tribune* loved sad-eyed Chlöe Sevigny as the young woman who loses herself to Brandon and stays true to her feelings after she learns her lover is a woman. He said that Sevigny "has a remarkable ability to take a seemingly flat character and quietly make her the movie's heart and soul. Her Lana at first comes across as a bit draggy and off-putting, yet as Brandon woos her, she opens up to reveal depths of sensuality and sympathy." Jan Stuart wrote in the *Advocate*, "As Brandon casts his spell, you can see Sevigny melting down from a hard-bitten B-movie moll to a blushing fool for love," and the *New York Press*'s Armond White opined, "Sevigny is possibly the most unique American actress since Shelley Duvall. With a slightly stoop-shouldered stance, but surprisingly alert, attentive eyes, she's a luscious slug. And her strangeness is disarming." "Chlöe's performance is really what makes us buy Brandon. She is the reason the love affair works, because she makes it so accessible," director Pierce said. "Chlöe has this amazing ability to exteriorize her feelings through her eyes. They're like wells you dive into, like the great silent stars."

A cartoon in *The New Yorker* by Sipress featured

an older man coming out of a theater showing *Boys Don't Cry* and startling his wife by saying, "Marjorie, I've got something to tell you."

Smoke and Mirrors

The television program *60 Minutes* had a reputation as a hard-hitting, truth-seeking, on-the-side-of-the-angels institution, albeit one with an irritating holier-than-thou attitude. But back in 1995, *60 Minutes* did a bad, bad thing, and movie audiences were going to get all the juicy details. For those who enjoy seeing sanctimonious tartuffes squirm when the spotlight is turned on them, correspondent Mike Wallace and executive producer Don Hewitt were providing quite a show.

Directed by Michael Mann, *The Insider* told two interrelated stories. One was about Jeffrey Wigand, a scientist fired by cigarette manufacturer Brown & Williamson, who knows that tobacco industry executives lied to congress in testifying that nicotine was not addictive. The second narrative strand centered on *60 Minutes* producer Lowell Bergman, who urges Wigand to go public with his information on the program, even though anything the whistle blower says would be in violation of a confidentiality agreement he had signed, and might also subject CBS to a mammoth lawsuit for "tortious interference." Giving up his financial security, risking the breakup of his family, and leaving himself open to all manner of judicial and illegal retaliation, Wigand—with his eye on the greater good—taped an interview with Mike Wallace. But then, acquiescing to the demands of corporate CBS, the powers in the news division—with their eyes on windfall profits at a time when a merger with Westinghouse was pending—dispensed with their integrity, leaving Wigand exposed and vulnerable. In the midst of all the tumult, Wigand's personal life becomes a raging shambles.

Shortly before *The Insider*'s premiere, the *New York Post*'s Thelma Adams wrote, "Earlier this year, Wallace and *60 Minutes* creator Hewitt began a campaign to discredit the movie, only to discover that their carping to the press created even more publicity for a serious film that runs 157 minutes and might otherwise be overlooked. Wallace and Hewitt are now keeping mum, declining all interviews about the film. But it may be too late." In Liz Smith's parlance, Wallace had "raised all kinds of hell with the producers," and *Entertainment Weekly*'s Liane Bonin observed that the newsman had "offered his critique of the movie's blend of fact and fiction even before he had seen a frame of celluloid, claiming he had been 'used in a dishonest way' by the filmmakers. Wait, isn't that what scam artists say whenever *60 Minutes* does one of its hidden-camera exposés?" A spokesperson for *60 Minutes* railed that "This movie is purely about putting fannies in seats and has *nothing* to do with the truth."

Ever since Mann had allowed him to see the first draft of the script, Wallace had written a series of angry letters to the director, decrying how he was portrayed as a "soulless and cowardly laggard who lost his moral compass until Lowell set me back on the straight path." Wallace didn't like the way he was shown capitulating—granted, reluctantly—to his bosses rather than fighting for the Wigand interview to air, and he insisted things hadn't happened this way at all. Don Hewitt, who was depicted as an empty suit, had the more general complaint of not liking his dirty laundry to be aired in public. Still, he put on his best public face, maintaining that *60 Minutes* had, in fact, done the right thing. He also said to the *New York Times*, "Like I told Mike, 'It's a movie, O.K.?' I went to see *Gone with the Wind*, but did I really believe there was a guy named Rhett Butler who said, 'Frankly, my dear, I don't give a damn'? No. Movies need heroes and villains, and real life doesn't usually have heroes and villains. Real life has a lot of shades of gray, and movies have black and white even when they're in color." That didn't prevent him from lashing out to the *Washington Post* about what he saw as rampant hypocrisy: *The Insider* was being released by Touchstone, which was owned by Disney. Disney also owned the ABC television network, and Hewitt pointed to Disney's ordering ABC's news magazine *20/20* to deep-six a piece on pedophilia at Disney World.

Michael Mann cowrote the script with Eric Roth, the Oscar-winning screenwriter of *Forrest Gump* and

The Concorde: Airport '79. Al Pacino played Lowell Bergman and Russell Crowe put on forty pounds of flab for verisimilitude in portraying Wigand. In the middle of a publicity interview, Crowe startled a reporter from *Time* by saying, "Time for a cigarette break, mate," adding "I love irony, lovey." Crowe had spent two days with Wigand and said, "He makes it very hard for you to like him. He just doesn't care that much." Crowe was also known for his prickly, the-hell-with-it attitude toward the rest of the world so, despite the two-decade age difference and the lack of physical resemblance, it turned out he was well cast as Wigand after all.

Richard Widmark and Richard Crenna turned down the role of Mike Wallace, each saying he was a friend of the television celebrity and didn't want to be involved with a production that put him in a less-than-flattering light. The part then went to Christopher Plummer, who didn't know Wallace on a personal basis but was certainly familiar with him in his professional capacity. He said he recalled watching Wallace conducting interviews back in the '50s while smoking "endless cigarettes," and "he was riveting. It was a whole new way of attacking guests. He was using the medium correctly, because it is a cruel medium. Edward R. Murrow was laid back and gentlemanly. It was a new way of interviewing and cutting straight to the Achilles." Plummer had himself been interviewed by Wallace in the early 1980s when he was playing Iago on Broadway: "I'd met him in that manner, so I knew what it was like to be in the hot seat." Wallace called him during filming, wanting to have a word with him, but "I didn't return the call," admitted Plummer. "When you're trying to play somebody, for God's sake, you don't want them hanging around under your nose." He also felt the gentleman was protesting too much about *The Insider*. "I don't make him a villain at all," he said. "There's a lot of humor, a lot of fun in my performance." And, averring that "I've seen Wallace be very vulnerable and touching talking about his career and the death of his son," Plummer said he asked Michael Mann to add a scene showing the newsman's tender side—which comes at the end of the picture.

Scary Movie

The critics liked *The Insider* a lot. William Arnold of the *Seattle Post-Intelligencer* called it "a terrific movie—intelligent, magnificently acted, highly compelling as a thriller, and downright scary in its implications for the corporate-run world of the new millennium." *Sight and Sound*'s Mark Kermode was thrilled with what he saw: "That Michael Mann has resisted the temptation to dumb down this material for *The Insider* reaffirms his position as one of the most important and intelligent directors currently working in mainstream cinema. He has created a tense psychological suspenser as complex and uncompromising as it is engaging and enthralling. It is, in short, a masterpiece, a brilliant dissection of recent U.S. politics and the media by a scalpel-sharp screen sensibility." Glenn Lovell of the *San Jose Mercury News* adjudged that, "For the always-interesting Mann ... this real-life cloak-and-dagger thriller represents a major breakthrough. Heretofore known for his visceral action scenes (remember the armored-car robbery in *Heat*?) and ever-prowling camera, Mann for the first time finds just the right balance of style and story." Richard T. Jameson of *Mr. Showbiz* said, "Mann and his great cinematographer, Dante Spinotti, deploy a precariously mobile camera that finds no relief, no stability, wherever it glances. Indeed, *The Insider* constitutes a landmark in the '90s evolution of camera style whereby filmmakers as diverse as Wong Kar-Wai, Olivier Assayas, and *Homicide* lensmeister Jean de Segonzac have searched for a lucid, post-classical vocabulary for describing and distilling modern life."

The *New York Daily News*'s Jack Mathews meditated, "For Wallace and Hewitt, the lesson here is that a movie based on real people and events takes shape much like one of their investigative pieces. Though the format causes details to be lost, and time and events to be condensed, the gist of the story and the salient facts are accurate. Hewitt and Wallace have scores of prouder moments, to be sure, but this is the story of their sorriest failure. It may not be as cut and dried as shown in the film, but in showing them let the big story get away, it's accurate. They've dished it out. Now, with what may be the best movie of the year, it's their turn to take it."

Rolling Stone's Peter Travers raved that Russell Crowe "cuts to the heart of an isolated man who seems to close off his emotions for fear of what might happen if they should spill out. Crowe plays Wigand like a gathering storm. This is acting of the highest level, and fully deserving of award attention." *Time*'s Richard Corliss, who described *The Insider* as "an *All the President's Men* in which Deep Throat takes center stage, an insider prodded to spill the truth," wrote of the film's Wigand, "As played so acutely by Russell Crowe, he is a sullen, stocky, difficult fellow, a Hamlet whose soliloquies have to be read in his nervous blinks and stammers, in the latticework under his tired, wary eyes. They are all the hints we need to detect a soul swamped in ethical dilemmas." *USA Today*'s Mike Clark praised the film's other lead actor: "With Pacino, we get the best of both worlds: a mostly restrained performance that still offers opportunities for the actor's reliable stack-blowing." Stephen Holden of the *New York Times* said, "Christopher Plummer, doing an uncanny impersonation of Mike Wallace, radiates the lethal geniality of a coiled, twitching rattlesnake."

Financial Health Hazard

The internecine struggles at a TV show are hardly of the stuff of interest for the rest of the world, however—as Disney executives learned when the box-office results for *The Insider* started coming in. And just as he had done last year with *Beloved*, Bernard Weinraub was once again conducting a postmortem in the *New York Times* on a high-profile Disney film that had tanked. Weinraub spoke anew to Disney's Joe Roth, who swore, "People say it's the best movie they've seen this year. They say, 'Why don't we make more movies like this?'" Observed Weinraub: "The answer, he implied, was obvious." Weinraub set out the film's problems: "It had scant appeal to younger moviegoers. (Disney executives said the prime audience was over the age of forty.) And the subject matter was dicey and not notably dramatic, marketing executives said. The fact that cigarettes cause cancer is not

new,' said one top studio official. 'The fact is, most people also assume that the media is corrupted by big business.'" Roth said, "It's like walking up a hill with a refrigerator on your back. The fact of the matter is we're really proud we did this movie." But the *New York Observer*, relying on sources at CBS, said that Disney Chairman Michael Eisner had called Don Hewitt: "'He wasn't apologizing to Don, he was venting,'" said a source familiar with the discussion. 'It was him saying, "Jesus, it's been a pain in the ass for me, I'm sorry we ever made the fucking thing." It was his frustration at the lack of money it appears to be making and all the shit they went through and it just wasn't worth it, you know?'"

The Insider's financial travails provided last laugh rights for Mike Wallace, who finally caught up with the film a few weeks after it opened—the eighty-one-year-old multi-millionaire used his senior citizen pass to get in for five bucks instead of $9.50. Not surprisingly, he didn't care for the movie any more than he had liked the first version of the script. He did give Christopher Plummer a backhanded compliment, saying he was "a very fine actor who has all my superficial physical moves down cold." Of *The Insider*'s box-office performance, he declared, "The film is getting what it deserves—a decent burial." The *New York Daily News* noted that Wallace was wearing a trench coat and a baseball cap as he headed into the theater and wondered if he was trying to hide his identity. "I wear a cap on occasion," Wallace insisted. "It was cold."

Buddha in a Ten-Foot Cell

Michael Mann admitted that there was some finagling with time periods in *The Insider* and that several characters were compressed into one. While the film's Lowell Bergman, filled with righteous indignation, quits *60 Minutes* to protest the decision to can the Wigand interview, in actuality, he didn't leave for another three years, when his contract was up. Similarly, in real life, the young woman played by Chlöe Sevigny in *Boys Don't Cry* didn't stay with Brandon Teena after she discovered her boyfriend was a woman. These fabrications didn't cause much of a stir—standard docudrama procedures, people shrugged—

although Don Hewitt certainly made sure people knew about the falsehoods in *The Insider*. Another reality-based movie, however, was practically decimated by negative publicity, as it was relentlessly accused of inventing things out of whole cloth.

At the outset, there seemed little that might be controversial about *The Hurricane*, the story of boxer Rubin "Hurricane" Carter. The fighter had been railroaded on a triple murder charge in 1966 because of racism in the judicial system, and his struggle to clear his name and gain his freedom became a *cause celebre* in the mid-1970s, especially after Bob Dylan cowrote an impassioned song about him—in the lyrics of the song, Carter was likened to "Buddha in a ten-foot cell." Carter was finally freed in 1985. The movie was an ultimately uplifting tale about good people persevering to prevail over a miscarriage of justice, and Universal promoted it as a "triumphant true story." Directed by last year's Thalberg winner Norman Jewison, a man who had long made films evincing a strong social conscience, *The Hurricane* starred Denzel Washington. The actor had himself tried to buy the rights to Carter's life story and, saying "I figured it was the last chance for me to play an athlete other than a chess player," spent a year and a half training as a boxer and getting himself into trim middleweight fighting condition. While Russell Crowe was gaining forty pounds, Washington lost the same amount, and there was Oscar talk about him long before the film was released.

The early reviews measured up. "Denzel Washington delivers a knockout performance that makes him the top contender for the Best Actor Oscar in *The Hurricane*, an expertly crafted, deeply moving film," wrote Lou Lumenick in the *New York Post*, "*The Hurricane* is certainly high-velocity, thoughtful entertainment. Returning to the civil-rights themes of his most memorable films *(In the Heat of the Night, A Soldier's Story)*, veteran director Norman Jewison directs with a passion and precision." Henry Sheehan of the *Orange County Register* said, "A rich and captivating performance from Denzel Washington, a true-life inspirational tale, and solid, occasionally inspired filmmaking all combine to make *The Hurricane* a compelling experience." Kenneth Turan declared, "Denzel Washing-

ton's career has not lacked for exceptional roles; he's been nominated for Oscars and even won one. But nothing really prepares us for what he does in *The Hurricane*. With power, intensity, remarkable range and an ability to disturb that is both unnerving and electric, it is more than Washington's most impressive part, it sums up his career as well, encapsulating the reasons why he's one of the very best actors working in film today." Susan Wloszczyna of *USA Today* proclaimed, "This classic screen bio contains all the elements for a dramatic knockout: a heavyweight star, a master filmmaker and a subject who is an actual folk hero, as celebrated in a Bob Dylan ballad. The combination of Denzel Washington, director Norman Jewison, and middleweight boxer Rubin 'Hurricane' Carter's wrongful triple-murder conviction and subsequent nineteen-year incarceration is an unbeatable one-two-three punch. . . . . Jewison demonstrates that, at age seventy-three, he still has it."

Three days before *The Hurricane* opened, Bernard Weinraub wrote an admiring piece about Norman Jewison: "At an age when many of his contemporaries are no longer working, Jewison is facing the odd prospect of a career resurgence in a business notorious for its obsession with youth. A trim, bespectacled and restlessly enthusiastic man, Jewison said he would probably work in films as long as he could stand. 'I know I'm getting old,' he said with a laugh, seated in his office at a production facility in West Los Angeles. 'But I also know that it's worth it to keep going, worth it to keep fighting and hammering away.' "

But two days later, another *New York Times* reporter, Selwyn Raab, who had covered Carter's case in detail and whose articles were credited as being instrumental in gaining the boxer a second trial, produced a litany of what he said were the film's confabulations. In the movie, justice is brought about primarily by a teenage boy and three strange Canadians. Raab complained that it just wasn't so and that *The Hurricane* "presents a false vision of the legal battles and personal struggles that led to his freedom and creates spurious heroes in fictionalized episodes that attribute his vindication to members of a Canadian commune who unearth long suppressed evidence. While glorifying the Canadians, the film plays down the heroic efforts of the lawyers whose strategy finally won the day for Mr. Carter. And virtually obliterated in the film version is the vital role played by John Artis, Mr. Carter's co-defendant, who was also wrongly convicted and imprisoned for fifteen years." Raab decried the manner in which Carter's less-than-impeccable earlier life was sanitized, and he protested that "A major fabrication is the creation of a racist Javert-type detective who hounds Mr. Carter from the age of eleven until he finally ensnares him in the triple homicide."

One of Carter's lawyers, civil rights activist Lewis M. Steel, also expressed dissatisfaction about *The Hurricane* in both the *The Nation* and the *Los Angeles Times*. In the former he zeroed in on the same fictional racist cop, played by Dan Hedaya, mentioned by Selwyn Raab: "The guts of what occurred was not a single cop after Rubin and John but a police force, a prosecutorial office and a whole list of state court judges who refused to intervene and bring this terrible racial prosecution to an end." And in the *Times*, he complained, "*The Hurricane* crosses the line between reasonable embellishment and pernicious distortion." He felt the movie did Carter a disservice because it "transforms his painful story into a series of false clichés: He was jailed because of one racist cop; he was freed through the efforts of a commune of white people. In reality, Carter was ensnared by an entire criminal justice system." Steel concluded, "Taking the easy way out of a complex story by creating a soap opera instead of engaging in the hard work of crafting a real story cheats the public out of a much more meaningful movie experience." Even before *The Hurricane* was released, Denzel Washington was saying, "This is a film. We have two hours and change, as opposed to the twenty-odd years it took to go through this process. Obviously we leap and jump and combine characters."

Print the Legend

The Hurricane had opened in Los Angeles and New York for Oscar consideration, and when it played other cities a few weeks later, movie critics seemed to be reviewing the accusations almost as much as what was on screen. "News travels fast," wrote Roger Ebert.

"Several people have told me dubiously that they heard the movie was 'fictionalized.' Well, of course it was. Those who seek the truth about a man from the film of his life might as well seek it from his loving grandmother. Most biopics, like most grandmothers, see the good in a man and demonize his enemies. They pass silently over his imprudent romances. In dramatizing his victories, they simplify them. And they provide the best roles to the most interesting characters. If they didn't, we wouldn't pay to see them. *The Hurricane* is not a documentary but a parable." Joe Baltake of the *Sacramento Bee* felt, "In John Ford's *The Man Who Shot Liberty Valance*, a newspaper editor expresses a sentiment that's been threaded throughout all of Ford's movies—and through films by other directors, as well. 'When the legend becomes fact,' he advises, 'print the legend.' This grand old movie tradition is currently being upheld by Norman Jewison in *The Hurricane*, his entertaining, misunderstood biopic about the former middleweight boxing contender Rubin Carter. Movies as an art-entertainment form may be more than a hundred years old, but some people still don't understand them. Sometimes, movies have to lie—to embellish things—to make a point. This is what Jewison does in *The Hurricane* in order to create a truly inspirational film with a social conscience—and this is what has prompted its critics to question its veracity, and to call it 'untrustworthy,' even though Jewison gets the basic facts right."

The harm had been done, though, so Jewison and producer Armyan Bernstein went into damage control; they eventually wrote their own piece in the *Los Angeles Times*, in which they more or less charged Selwyn Raab and Lewis Steele with acting from bruised feelings because the Canadian commune members were highlighted in the movie instead of them. They also similarly addressed the issue with a lengthy article posted on the official *The Hurricane* Web site. Bernstein said that Dan Hedaya's cop was a "composite" chatacter who was doing stand-in duty for the entire "system that convicted Rubin Carter." The trouble that Bernstein and Jewison were facing was illustrated when *New York Daily News* critic Jack Mathews decided, some six weeks after the fact, to remove *The Hurricane* from his Ten Best list. "No, the movie hasn't shrunk. It's still one of the best I saw last year," admitted Mathews, "but there is a point, I believe, when a film that is purportedly based on facts violates the privileges of creative license, and I think *The Hurricane* crosses that line." Mathews shrugged off the fact that "the movie omits important characters, exaggerates Carter's boxing stature, invents villains and writes speeches that were never given" as "minor transgressions." What got to him was "the myth of the Canadian rescue."

The *Tuscon Weekly*'s James DiGiovanna meanwhile was laughing at the film's choice of saviors: "I've always believed that there is a universal force of pure goodness that binds the cosmos together and brings light and justice where there was darkness and injustice. After watching *The Hurricane*, I now have a name for this force: Canadians." Norman Jewison, incidentally, was born in Toronto. Canada was also where Rubin Carter was residing these days. On *The Tonight Show*, Jay Leno mentioned to Denzel Washington, "He lives outside the country now, doesn't he?" Washington's response: "Wouldn't you?"

Imitation of Life

Jim Carrey didn't receive an Oscar nomination for toning it down in *The Truman Show*, but he was back for another try. This time he was teamed with Milos Forman, whose actors had an exemplary track record in receiving Academy recognition. Having survived all the feminist slings and arrows, Forman reunited with Scott Alexander and Larry Karaszewski, the writers of *The People vs. Larry Flynt*, to present another account of a real-life eccentric. *The Man on the Moon* was a biography of Andy Kaufman, the comedian/performance artist who may have had the driest sense of humor ever of anyone who did comedy for a living, or maybe he was simply unable to distinguish between reality and fantasy—no one was ever quite sure. A veteran from *Flynt*, Edward Norton, had been in the running to play Kaufman, as had Kevin Spacey, John Cusack, Hank Azaria, and Sean Penn, but once he saw Carrey's audition, Forman never looked back. And just as Kaufman was (in)famous for refusing to break character when he was doing his contemptuous

Tony Clifton alter ego, so too "Jim Carrey" never came on the set—it was always either Andy Kaufman or Tony Clifton, and they were to be treated as such, even by Milos Forman. Looking back on the production, Forman said, "Andy was a very sweet guy to work with, although he could be very stubborn. When he didn't like something he could be very stubborn. Tony Clifton was a total nightmare to work with. You had to constantly kiss his ass, and flatter him. Beg him to do things."

The film received a mixed response. Just as *The People vs. Larry Flynt* had no visual correlative to its subject's flamboyant lifestyle, *Man on the Moon* "struggles to tell in a conventional, linear manner the story of this most unconventional of entertainers," rebuked Kirk Honeycutt of the *Hollywood Reporter*. And Duane Dudek of the *Milwaukee Journal Sentinel* felt that as opposed to the surrealism that was Andy Kaufman, *Man on the Moon* "is too anxious to be loved and too easy to understand. It's as linear, literal and sentimental as *The Pride of the Yankees*, the film about Lou Gehrig, another public figure whose meteoric rise was followed by an untimely death." But Owen Gleiberman of *Entertainment Weekly* got all worked up about the straightforward film, calling it "a brilliant, maniacally funny, and dizzying experience." *Variety*'s Todd McCarthy shrugged off the entire enterprise, chiding that, "Cinematically, this is undoubtedly Milos Forman's drabbest and least inventive film." McCarthy thought *Man on the Moon* "never comes close to making the case that its subject is worthy of the viewer's interest, that he was anything more than a weird footnote to showbiz history."

Most reviewers felt that Jim Carrey had accomplished something, although there was disagreement as to just what. Steven Rea of the *Philadelphia Inquirer* believed, "If nothing else, the star deserves a prize for delivering the most uncanny impersonation of the year: Kaufman's pop-eyed faux bashfulness, his crazed intensity, his dangerous quirkiness, his repertoire of nutball characters—from the curious Foreign Man (dank you veddy much) to the spurious Tony Clifton—are nailed. You forget that you're watching an actor assay the life, and death, of a man. Instead, you feel like you're watching the man." Marjorie

Baumgarten of the *Austin Chronicle* held that Carrey's "impersonation . . . is as near a DNA cloning as allowed by modern movie technology and the art of imitation. Carrey's performance is a technical marvel, yet it dazzles without edifying," while Rex Reed conceded in the *New York Observer* that, "Watching Jim Carrey go berserk for two hours in a relentlessly punishing impersonation of Kaufman has a certain morbid fascination." Courtney Love, the leading lady of *The People vs. Larry Flynt* who was reunited with Milos Forman in *Man on the Moon*, said of Carrey's work, "This is a sick performance. It's so crazy."

It came to pass that Andy Kaufman's appeal had been highly overestimated by the filmmakers, and *Entertainment Weekly* called Jim Carrey one of the losers of the Christmas holiday movie season: "It turns out his fans love him a lot less than they hate cult comic Andy Kaufman, sending the lengthy bio-pic *Man on the Moon* into an unexpectedly early eclipse." In the end, *Man in the Moon* grossed about half of what Carrey's notorious *The Cable Guy* had taken in.

Head Case

Man on the Moon was a movie about a determinedly odd person. *Being John Malkovich* was a determinedly odd movie. Despite its title, it wasn't a biography—the time hadn't yet come for the John Malkovich life story. And *Being John Malkovich* was more eccentric than a biography of the actor could ever have been. The film's costar, Cameron Diaz, said she couldn't explain the plot "because every time somebody asks me what this movie is about, I go into such a long-winded explanation of it that they inevitably go, 'When can I just see it so that you will shut up?' There are so many layers to it that it takes a lot just to explain." The coproducer, R.E.M.'s Michael Stipe, described the narrative thusly: "An out-of-work puppeteer gets an office job and finds a membranous tunnel that hurls you into the soul of John Malkovich for fifteen minutes, then spits you on the New Jersey turnpike."

Clearly, director Spike Jonze and writer Charlie Kaufman were doing something offbeat here. Jonze— real moniker Adam Spiegel, heir to the Spiegel catalogue fortune and son-in-law of Francis Coppola—had made a name for himself with music videos for Fatboy Slim, Björk, the Beastie Boys, and R.E.M., and commercials for Coke and Nike. Dennis Lim of the *Village Voice* described him as "the most offhandedly avant-garde and whacked-out of the MTV brats." He was also an actor who, concurrently with the release of *Being John Malkovich*, was being seen in David O. Russell's *Three Kings*. Kaufman had written for some television comedies.

David Ansen of *Newsweek* said, "I don't know how a movie this original got made today, but thank God for wonderful aberrations." Among those leading the cheering section was Jack Mathews of the *New York Daily News*: "*Being John Malkovich* is no ordinary comedy. In fact, this film from freshman director Spike Jonze is plain nuts. It's also plain brilliant. It is the most original, off-beat, laugh-out-loud funny comedy I've seen since *A Fish Called Wanda*." In the *Boston Globe*, Jay Carr analyzed, "*Being John Malkovich* is more than just the latest cool, smart, funny movie. It jumps off the screen with the kind of freshness, originality, and light-handed stranglehold on the Zeitgeist that moves movies forward. It bridges for a moment the nervously behind-the-times media establishment and the envelope-pushing energies of the new media-savvy internet and video mavens." He concluded that *Being John Malkovich*, "cheerfully presents the universe as God's own pinball machine." J. Hoberman of the *Village Voice* put it this way: "*Being John Malkovich* is the sort of prize head-scratcher that invites analogy-seekers to cast their nets wide. The most offbeat studio comedy since *Rushmore*, it drafts the brain-twisting conundrums of Jorge Luis Borges, the grotesque humor of Czech animator Jan Svankmajer, and the narrative extravagance of *Céline and Julie Go Boating* in the service of a pop, Warholian riff on celebrity—which is to say, this droll, uncanny, live-action puppet show is actually something new."

While saying that he loved the film, Hoberman acknowledged that *Being John Malkovich* "may not be about anything except itself." Kenneth Turan carped that, "once *Being John Malkovich* determines it has to explain itself, what it comes up with is not only flimsy but barely understandable and harder to credit than what we've experienced with our own eyes." In the *New York Times*, Stephen Holden concluded, "For all its cleverness, the movie doesn't add up to much metaphorically. It's really just a head trip about a head trip," and James Verniere of the *Boston Herald* groused that it was essentially, "a hip variation of those annoyingly contrived body-switching films of the '80s." Rex Reed came up with one of the few out-and-out pans for *Being John Malkovich*, denouncing it as "an exasperatingly precocious one-joke idea that collapses after the first twenty minutes and drags on numbingly, substituting conceit for substance." Thinking back to the good old days of the 1940s, Reed crabbed, "Directed by somebody with the audacity to call himself Spike Jonze, this hyperthyroidal exercise in loopiness only reminds me how much more I prefer the zaniness of the real Spike Jones, with or without his City Slickers, but the people raving about *Being John Malkovich* don't even know what I'm talking about."

The film starred John Cusack as the puppeteer, a de-glamorized Cameron Diaz as his wife, indie stalwart Catherine Keener as the cold-hearted femme fatale they both fall for, and, of course, John Malkovich. The eponymous actor had previously appeared with Cusack in the antithesis of this film, *Con Air,* and he said that when he saw the script for *Being John Malkovich*, "I was very impressed by the writing, but I never imagined anyone being crazy enough to make it. It wasn't like the title was going to bring people out in droves." Malkovich was hailed not simply for being such a good sport in appearing in the movie, but at being so effective in playing a fictionalized version of John Malkovich. Stephen Hunter of the *Washington Post* ruminated, "This may be the first time in history that a man wins an Oscar for playing himself, with the exception of John Wayne in *True Grit*." Roger Ebert said, "Malkovich himself is part of the magic. He is not playing himself here, but a version of his public image—distant, quiet, droll, as if musing about things that happened long ago and were only mildly interesting at the time. It took some courage for him to take this role, but it would have taken more courage to turn it down. It's a plum." Malkovich's assessment of the film: "I just had fun acting like an asshole."

Reviewers analyzed the whys and wherefores of the titular character being John Malkovich. *Slate's* David Edelstein said, "That the vessel is Malkovich might be the movie's most brilliantly unsettling touch, since the actor—although undeniably great—is one of our most distant and weirdly insular. You can understand the masses fantasizing about being Bruce Willis or being Tom Hanks, but being John Malkovich? What's lodged under that thick brow is anybody's guess." Owen Gleiberman *knew* the reason for the casting: "Why Malkovich? Because he's nearly invisible in his own celebrity. He needs his own occupiers as much as they need him." In actuality, screenwriter Charlie Kaufman said that Malkovich was always his first choice to play the host-consciousness mainly because the word "Malkovich" sounded funny when it was repeated so often.

Identity Crisis

The advertising tag line for *Being John Malkovich* was "At last, a movie for anyone who wanted to be someone . . . else." It would have been equally applicable for *The Talented Mr. Ripley*, which used as a come-on in its trailer, "I always thought it would be better to be a fake somebody than a real nobody." Based on a Patricia Highsmith novel filmed by Rene Clement as *Purple Noon* in 1960, *The Talented Mr. Ripley* was Anthony Minghella's follow-up to *The English Patient*. Once again he was adapting a complex book, but if the hero of *The English Patient* was morally ambiguous, the title character in his new film was an out-and-out sociopath—although one whose heart had its reasons.

Taking place in the late 1950s, the film told of a poor young man with severe self-image problems who falls in with the privileged and beautiful living *la dolce vita* in Italy. The movie was character study, suspense film, travelogue, and dissection of the nefariousness of class distinctions. Minghella acknowledged that he had been attracted to the book because of its protagonist's outsider status. His own parents were Italian immigrants who sold homemade ice cream on the Isle of Wight and he said, "This sense of a man with his nose pressed up against the window, the sense that there's a better life being led by other people—to me, these feelings are familiar and pungent."

The Talented Mr. Ripley was populated by some of the cinema's current best and brightest. Matt Damon had the title role—he was signed just before *Good Will Hunting* made him a star. Last year's Best Actress winner, Gwyneth Paltrow, was also on hand, as was a woman she had defeated at the Oscars, Cate Blanchett. The least well known of the principals was Jude Law, who had received nice notices for both his acting and his looks in such films as *Gattaca* and *Midnight in the Garden of Good and Evil* but who had yet to be in a movie that connected with the general public. In *Mr. Ripley*, he had the "Golden Boy" role that Central Casting would have instinctively assigned to Matt Damon. Minghella said of Law, "I had followed Jude's work and I think he's just going to explode into movies. I thought, 'This is the part that can really show to a big audience what he's capable of.' I think he's an enormously magnetic old-style film star. He has everything going for him, he's the luckiest guy on the planet as far as I'm concerned. He's very, very talented. He's incredibly charismatic. That was a case of my knowing exactly who I wanted in that role and just going after him. I'm very terrier-like when I decide who I want." Looking at this cast, a beginning-of-the-year preview issue of *Entertainment Weekly* declared, "Lord knows '99 will not produce a movie as easy on the eyes as *The Talented Mr. Ripley*."

Movieline had high praise for Damon's essaying the dark title role, calling it "a commendably ambitious gamble . . . the material defies any conventional notion of a good career move." Damon said, "Ripley is a very complicated, interesting character. His sexuality is a lot more complicated than one might think. It's 1958. He doesn't have any outlets to discuss what and who he is. He just wants love returned to him. So he gives it and puts it out to everybody and fantasizes about love. He's somebody who's deeply uncomfortable with his own body—he does not like himself. He feels worthless." The actor also stated, "I loved the character of Ripley. He's *so* different from me. He subordinates himself to the people he's with." But a *Time* interviewer noted a similarity: "Both Ripley and Damon work their way through conversations like poachers in Yellowstone. They sense they're being watched, so they constantly observe themselves."

The film opened on Christmas Day. Joe Baltake of the *Sacramento Bee* was delighted with the gift, applauding that "The sheer, insouciant nastiness of Anthony Minghella's terrific *The Talented Mr. Ripley* offers us the guilty seasonal pleasure of wallowing in evil in its most luxuriant form. This film runs counter to all the pervasive holiday joyousness by perversely hitting us with a little, well, bad cheer." Bob Strauss of the *Los Angeles Daily News* wrote, "*The Talented Mr. Ripley* is as luxurious a psycho-thriller as anyone could wish for. Sumptuous, sensual, stately and twisted, it's a class act all the way—especially in its insistence on viewing abundant beauty with an uneasy eye. Filmed in just about every corner of Italy you'd ever want to see, the movie is a sunny noir exercise in the tradition of Hitchcock's continental romps—but very, very different from the master's work in its particular sense of dread." The *San Francisco Examiner*'s Wesley Morris was also an admirer: "Minghella takes Highsmith's already-gloomy novel through an allegorical looking glass in which a persona is a work of art, and a single self will never do. It's that rare movie with a sense of timeliness that is eternal, and a protagonist whose soul-crushed angst, even at its most fatal, speaks to the little boy/girl lost in everyone."

"Mr. Damon's performance works on multiple levels," extolled Philip Wuntch of the *Dallas Morning News*. "In the initial scenes, you'll want to coddle him for his unyielding niceness, but a tiny hint of something sinister keeps you from embracing the character. Mr. Damon's greatest triumph is in locating Tom's self-loathing. It lurks beneath the surface in all scenes and sometimes explodes in homicidal rage." This was Gwyneth Paltrow's first screen appearance since *Shakespeare in Love* and John Hartl said in the *Seattle Times*, "Paltrow, playing an essentially helpless character, has never been so moving," while *Variety*'s Todd McCarthy felt that "The wondrous Blanchett exactly captures a particular sort of flighty American aristocrat." *Entertainment Weekly*'s Lisa Schwarzbaum raved, "Law, in a star-making performance, is the sexually magnetic center of every scene he's in," a sentiment echoed by Janet Maslin, who said, "This is a star-making role for the preternaturally talented English actor Jude Law. Beyond being devastatingly good-looking, Mr. Law gives Dickie the manic, teasing powers of manipulation that make him ardently courted by every man or woman he knows. During the first half of the film, Dickie is pure eros and adrenaline, a combination not many actors could handle with this much aplomb."

Not everyone was so taken with the film. The *Chicago Reader*'s Jonathan Rosenbaum groaned, "Familiarity is the watchword of this overblown opus, which neglects holes in the plot to play up its postmodern theme of identity as pastiche." And Amy Taubin sneered in the *Village Voice,* "Minghella, a would-be art film director who never takes his eye off the box office . . . turns *The Talented Mr. Ripley* into a splashy tourist trap of a movie. The effect is rather like reading *The National Enquirer* in a café overlooking the Adriatic."

In the Mainstream

The Talented Mr. Ripley was a coproduction of Paramount and Miramax—the former owned domestic rights, the latter, international—but Miramax was going solo on another Christmas release. *The Cider House Rules* was based on John Irving's 1985 best seller—in Miramax's advertising parlance it was "John Irving's Classic American Novel"—a sprawling tale of a young man's coming of age in Maine in the early '40s, against a backdrop of orphans, illegal abortions and a distant world war. Irving suggested the reason screen rights to his novels were inevitably snapped up despite their bulk and unwieldy plots was that, "I write nineteenth-century stories; they're supposed to affect you emotionally. I'm not interested in writing about people I feel superior to. I'm interested in writing about heroes. I think that's what's interesting to film. If it's not moving, it's nothing." By his own admission, he wasn't much of a moviegoer, rarely heading out to the theater, mostly because, "It drives me crazy when people talk." Irving began writing a screen adaptation of *The Cider House Rules* shortly after the book was published, and working on his first script gave him a break from the solitude of writing novels: "I'm not complaining," he insisted. "I've liked being alone since I was a kid . . . and I like my 'day job' bet-

ter than writing screenplays. But when your working life is circumscribed by a four- or five-year cycle—which is what a novel represents to me—and in that working life you share what you're doing with no one, other than reading an occasional chapter to your wife, there's something very beckoning about the idea that you could have a successful collaboration. I just loved the friendship of it." He must have been thinking of a long-term collaboration, because the first draft he completed would have made for a nine-hour movie.

Irving had director approval on the project and was collaborating with Phillip Borsos, until the Canadian filmmaker died of cancer at age forty-one. Others who were attached at various points were Wayne Wang, Michael Winterbottom, and Ang Lee, but ultimately it was Lasse Hallström who was signed. Although he had made a handful of films in America, Hallström was still best-known for his 1985 Swedish film, *My Life as a Dog;* one reason he was considered ideal for *The Cider House Rules* was because of his proven skill at directing children, and there sure were a lot of orphans in this picture. Asked about his expertise with kids, the fifty-three-year-old Hallström said, "I don't know if I have a special method with children. I feel like I stopped growing at age twelve and, in a weird way, I can relate to that twelve-year-old experience." He also related to Irving's writing: "I love his combinations, his sense of humor, and his absurdities. The bizarre and the comedic and the dramatic; that mix is really familiar to me from *My Life as a Dog* to *Gilbert Grape.*"

Tobey Maguire played the lead role of Homer Wells, the surrogate son of the orphanage's director, Michael Caine. Maguire, with his memorably reticent manner (*Variety*'s David Rooney referred to his "fragile, strangely moving voice") had emerged, thanks to *The Ice Storm* and *Pleasantville,* as the movies' current preeminent personification of sensitive youth, and the film provided Michael Caine with a rare foray at playing an American character as he exchanged his Cockney accent for the voice of a Mainer.

In the *New York Times*, Stephen Holden called *The Cider House Rules,* "a gentle, beautifully acted fable about a young man's journey into the world, his loss of innocence and his acquiring of values that reflect the lessons learned on his journey," while Jean Oppenheimer of *New Times Los Angeles* said, "No other film this year captures the complex, bittersweet nature of life so movingly." Richard T. Jameson of *Mr. Showbiz* praised the director, asserting that "Lasse Hallström, a past master at cockeyed coming-of-age chronicles, has a near-genius for unpatronizing tolerance, and for seeing beauty in the world and nature and seasons without turning them into postcards."

The word "Dickensian" seemed to pop up in most reviews of the film although Joe Baltake also mentioned Grace Metalious, the author of *Peyton Place*. Bob Graham of the *San Francisco Chronicle* hit upon the film's appeal when he said that *The Cider House Rules* possess "that Dickensian spirit wherein simple acts of kindness can bring an audience close to tears." Terry Lawson of the *Detroit Free Press* noted, "Those who consider the novel Irving's finest still may take exception to the alterations, which include paring away much of the book's final third and eliminating a key complication. As a consequence, the debate over the ethics of abortion has been effectively diluted, leaving a pro-choice position unchallenged. What remains is updated Dickens, a compassionate story of one orphan's education at the hands of a world that didn't want him—but needs him nevertheless." Lawson also honed in on what detractors of *The Cider House Rules* would claim was wrong with the picture: "Irving's book was far more morally complex than the film, and much, much funnier. Though Hallström's best films, *My Life as a Dog* and *What's Eating Gilbert Grape*, share Irving's love of the absurdly defining act, this film errs on the side of sentimentality and sweetness." But then again, Michael O'Sullivan of the *Washington Post* found the film to be "a sensitive but not overly sentimental adaptation."

No Wire Hangers!

Shortly before the film premiered, a *New York Daily News* article by Sean Mitchell delved into a paradox about *The Cider House Rules*: "How is it that a movie that makes a subtle and historic argument for a woman's right to an abortion also seems to be about the old-fashioned importance of family?" Answering his own question, Mitchell said, "While *The Cider House Rules* is making the case (some would say) for a woman's right to choose and a doctor's right to help her, it then does something else unexpected and at least as powerful. It makes us appreciate the values of the nuclear family—by its absence." He added that, "In a season when the most highly praised movie of the year, *American Beauty*, trashed the family as a grotesque joke, the family values, so to speak, of *The Cider House Rules* can seem more than a little unfashionable."

Referring to his movie's abortion stance, Hallström had said he hoped the film wouldn't be "overshadowed by the controversy and bring out the right-wing lunatics," but Bob Strauss of the *Los Angeles Daily News* didn't see anything to worry about because "*Cider House* is nothing if not the most conservative abortion-rights movie ever made." Lisa Schwarzbaum, said, "The story slips tough and even incendiary subject matter into an old-fashioned coming-of-age yarn—there are few topics more fiery than abortion, and *Cider House* comes out unwafflingly pro-choice—but Hallström's signature style is to allow moments of moral drama to rise and fall without fanfare, while sustaining a gentle pace suitable to stories of vulnerable childhood." Stephen Hunter did complain in the *Washington Post*, "the movie is pure pro-choice agit-prop, as it tracks Homer's conversion to the cause of choice and posits the heroism of the abortionist. Pro-lifers will hate it on that point alone, and they should be forewarned." But, on the contrary, Amy Taubin of the *Village Voice* found *The Cider House Rules* to be "as paternalistic, puffed-up, and dull as a congressional debate about abortion rights," griping also that it was "being passed off as a film in support of a woman's right to choose, but its implicit position is that abortion is wrong except in cases of rape or incest. Worse still, it makes men the arbiters of what happens to a woman's body and the abortion debate a defining factor of manhood. The mind boggles at the plethora of patriarchal assumptions."

Jan Stuart of *Newsday* said, "*The Cider House Rules* may well be remembered as the career coming-of-age of Tobey Maguire, a handsome young actor of such laconic grace and serenity that it is easy to under-

INSIDE OSCAR 2: 1999 271

estimate the power of his work here . . . Charisma is a mysterious gift, and Maguire is proof positive that understatement can be its best ally." Kevin Thomas of the *Los Angeles Times* called Michael Caine's "a career-crowning portrayal," elaborating that the actor, "in his understated yet towering portrayal, reveals in Dr. Larch the vulnerability that lurks within—and, indeed, informs—individuals of formidable resolve and strength of character." Glenn Kenny of *Premiere* found that, "The performances are almost all stunning . . . Caine, trying on an accent not his own for the first time in memory, projects an aura of saintliness without even half trying, it seems."

It's Not Easy Seeing Green

Another movie adapted from a best-seller by a New England–based writer opened the same day as *The Cider House Rules*, but *The Green Mile* had more in common with some other current releases. This, the fiftieth film based on the writings of Stephen King, was even nuttier than *Being John Malkovich* and as off-the-wall as Andy Kaufman—the frightening thing, though, was that *The Green Mile* was playing it straight. Set in a Louisiana prison in the 1930s, *The Green Mile* was the second film directed by Frank Darabont, the first being *The Shawshank Redemption*—*Variety*'s Todd McCarthy laughed that Darabont was "positioning himself as the unassailable specialist in adapting Stephen King period prison novels for the screen." Even though *The Shawshank Redemption* had been generally well received—especially by television reviewers—the thin-skinned Darabont said he went for five years between projects because, "You spend a year-and-a-half making something, it's enormously demanding, and then some bonehead on TV spends sixty seconds passing judgment."

The pre-release buzz somehow had *The Green Mile* as the film to beat for Best Picture. Set in Louisiana in 1935, it was about a humongous but childlike black fellow wrongfully convicted of murder and waiting to be executed. He's not merely a death row inmate, though, he's a painfully obvious Christ figure—his name's John Coffey, which conveniently provides him with the right initials—who has the mi-

raculous power of curing what ails you, although with the unfortunate side-effects of disrupting electrical service and discharging swarms of bugs from his mouth.

Tom Hanks was the head guard, and if in *Saving Private Ryan* he was supposedly doing his bit for realism, with *The Green Mile* he was back in a world that had as little basis in reality as *Forrest Gump*. The silver-tongued Frank Darabont told *Premiere*, "I have a deep, abiding fear of turning out something crappy," and then he went and made *The Green Mile*. One sat in the theater dumbfounded because Darabont seemed to have a kind of genius for piling absurdity upon absurdity to such a point that it got to seem utterly postmodern. *Newsweek*'s David Ansen very nicely summed up the terribleness of it all: "Darabont's movie, trawling for Oscars, arrives amid a flurry of expectation and hype. What's up there on screen, however, is a lumbering, self-important melodrama that defies credibility at every turn. Who are these people? What planet are we on? Not only is Hanks's blissfully married character the nicest, most sensitive prison guard in the history of the Southern penal system, his three death row colleagues are nearly as caring and genteel. Running a close third is the warden, whose loving wife is dying of cancer (can you guess where that plot strand is heading?). In keeping with the movie's Old Hollywood view of reality, the villains are painted in strokes broad enough for any two-year-old to hate them."

There were numerous other exquisitely awful ingredients, as well. Not only, as Ansen mentioned, are the prison guards decorous and unfailingly civil, the death row inmates likewise—with one exception—are grand hail-fellow-well-met types, and the Depression-era prison itself is the most immaculate and pleasant institution imaginable. A lot of fuss is made about a mouse in the cell-block—as if a backwoods penitentiary in 1935 wouldn't have been crawling with rodents. Moreover, this little mouse was so precious that he could have had the title role in *Stuart Little*. Making it all even more dear was that one of the death row inmates gives him the name "Mr. Jingles." *The American Spectator*'s James Bowman was aghast: "The giveaway of the film's fatal sentimentalism is that damned mouse. Cute in itself, it is captured and trained to do cute tricks with a wooden spool by an almost equally cute inmate, Eduard 'Dell' Delacroix (Michael Jeter)." The film aimed to move its audience to joyous tears of relief when John Coffey brings Mr. Jingles back to life after the one non-saintly guard—named "Percy," no less; nobody called Percy in a movie can be a good egg—stomps on the mouse because he's a wicked man.

Director-writer Darabont blithely ignored the fact that in 1935 Louisiana a black man found with the bodies of two little white girls who had been raped and murdered would have faced Deep South-style justice and never would have lived to see prison. And as a treat before he gets to offer his life up for his fellow man in the electric chair, J.C. is shown his first movie—*Top Hat* with Fred Astaire and Ginger Rogers. Now, back in the '30s, the Rogers and Astaire films were the height of sophistication; their appeal was to swank audiences, and they were box-office poison in rural areas. There was no way that an illiterate, dirt poor man from bayou country would have sat still through Fred and Ginger's witty rapport and ballroom dancing, or have been enthralled by the comic stylings of Edward Everett Horton and Eric Blore. A Buck Jones or Ken Maynard cowboy movie, perhaps; an Irving Berlin musical, no way. But "Cheek to Cheek" does get the big lug thinking profound thoughts when he hears the song's metaphorical "Heaven, I'm heaven . . ." which he pronounces as "Heaben." Darabont also threw in some end-of-millennium New Age stuff, and the whole thing took up over three hours of one's life. Screenwriter Larry Gelbert quipped, "I haven't seen *The Green Mile* yet, so don't give away the middle."

Father, Forgive Them

As enacted by an ex-bodyguard Michael Clark Duncan, the John Coffey character was equal parts Noble Savage and Stepin Fetchit. Edward Guthmann of the *San Francisco Chronicle* observed, "There's not a trace of cynicism in *The Green Mile* . . . Instead, there's a naiveté that turns offensive: Why, for example, is a strong and powerful black man considered palatable only when he's got the brain of a three-year-old? *Forrest Gump* had the same problem with the mush-

headed Bubba character. In this case, John Coffey speaks in deze-and-dem clichés ('I needs to see you, boss'), sweats profusely when he works his miracles and has the humble, innocuous manner of a plantation field hand in a moldy melodrama." The *Philadelphia Inquirer*'s Carrie Rickey believed the film "trades in bigotry by presenting a black man as a 'fraidy cat." "With a grating combination of naiveté and arrogance," wrote Ann Hornaday of the *Baltimore Sun*, "*The Green Mile* consistently overplays its melodramatic material, including a portrait of a black man that is as breathtakingly offensive as it is earnest."

In the *San Francisco Examiner*, Wesley Morris noted that two of the film's messages are: "Some Negroes aren't evil, child-killin' vermin, they're supernatural specimens of divine benevolence; the mouse is God's most artful breed of rodent." He also said, "Coffey's kindness in a cruel white world is meant to be inspirational or transcendent. But what more does Darabont tell us about him? He seems to have wandered off the highway to heaven with his body by Gold's, heart by Hallmark and manner of speaking by way of Harriet Beecher Stowe. And for what, to cure some ailing white folks and to help a dead mouse?" When Darabont heard that critics saying that his treatment of the J. C. character was racist, he cried to Marilyn Beck and Stacy Jenel Smith, "To me, part of what the movie is about is that we're all creatures of God under the skin. It's anti-racist." Which just emphasized how clueless he was.

Warner Brothers was selling this piquant brew as serious Oscar stuff, and sure enough there were reviewers who obliged. David Sheehan of KCBS-TV would have to live with the knowledge that he was on record calling *The Green Mile* "Unquestionably, the best picture of the year." (Then again, he was also quoted as saying that, given 1,000—or more precisely 105—years worth of possibilities, *Bicentennial Man* was "the most beautiful film of the millennium.") Mark S. Allen of UPN-TV said—at least according to the ads (most of the quotes in the advertisements were from obscure individuals familiar only because of being quoted in advertisements): "Undoubtedly, one of the last great films of the century." Roger Ebert must have mixed up his review of *The Green Mile* with what he had come up with for *The Cider House Rules* because, according to him, *The Green Mile*, "tells a story with beginning, middle, end, vivid characters, humor, outrage and emotional release. Dickensian."

Gary Thompson of the *Philadelphia Daily News* was distracted by a particular element of the movie: "One thing confirmed by *The Green Mile* is that if Tom Hanks' head gets any bigger, the rest of his movies are going to have to be filmed in IMAX. That's not a brace around his neck. That IS his neck. Hanks has the jolly jowls of a successful man, and he is certainly that—one of the world's biggest box-office draws, and a man with an unerring instinct for movies that touch audiences." Hanks's instinct was intact—despite its ludicrousness, *The Green Mile* was one of the year's top grossing pictures. Darabont got something out of the movie besides large ticket sales: as a souvenir, he took "Old Sparky," the film's electric chair, back with him to his house in Los Feliz.

Down in the Valley

Every bit as long (three hours, eight minutes), pathetic and silly as *The Green Mile* was *Magnolia*, Paul Thomas Anderson's highly ballyhooed and much-anticipated-in-some-circles follow-up to *Boogie Nights*. *Magnolia* did, however, come with a hip patina that Frank Darabont could only have dreamed of as he sat at home on his electric chair. A series of superficial and highly contrived character studies about cheerless people in the San Fernando Valley, the movie was all fol-del-rol. It did have some cool special effects with frogs, though.

Anderson seemed to make a point of creating an arrogant persona for public consumption, doing things like spouting off to the *New York Times*, "Most people don't share my moral sense which is I'll masturbate, but I have to clean it up very quickly afterwards." He also said, "I consider *Magnolia* a kind of beautiful accident. It gets me. I put my heart—every embarrassing thing that I wanted to say—in *Magnolia*." One wouldn't necessarily have minded the arrogance if the guy actually had something to say, but he revealed himself to be a classic *poseur* and *Magnolia* was an extravagantly pointless film. John Anderson of *Newsday*

wrote, "In a lot of ways, *Magnolia* is a perfect movie to close out the '90s, because it extrapolates from all the vices of '90s mainstream cinema: vacuous visual agility, big-name actors in search of a point and a black hole where its soul should be." Desson Howe of the *Washington Post* observed, "Over the course of three hours, these characters—all residents of the San Fernando Valley and few of them happy—never stop flipping their lids, venting their spleens and blowing head gaskets. Did California run out of Prozac or something? . . . Anderson instructs his performers to go long on the hot-button emotions. Most scenes—or so it seems—begin and conclude with anger, bitterness, yelling or shouting. Anderson considers himself an actor's director, but he's something far less romantic: a star-struck enabler." Howe's conclusion: "When you strip away the surface intensity of this movie, nothing remains but Anderson's desire to make a movie. Shouldn't there be something more?"

Of the large cast—many of them repeaters from *Boogie Nights*—Tom Cruise garnered the most attention, not because he was particularly good (although the *Wall Street Journal*'s Joe Morgenstern called his "a fearless, absolutely flawless performance"), but because he was Tom Cruise taking a smallish role in an ensemble piece, turning off his usual facile charm and sitting around in his underwear. He portrayed a ridiculously misogynistic and crude character who, like most of the people in *Magnolia*, had only the vaguest connection to life as we know it. The *Village Voice*'s J. Hoberman said, "Tom Cruise plays a sexual self-help guru as an outrageous parody of the pumped-up roles he played in *Cocktail* and *Top Gun*. (A later scene in which he emotes is mercifully short.)" There were many jokes at the actor's expense because he kept repeating the line, "Respect the cock!" The *Observer* of London said, "Everyone who has seen *Magnolia* has been impressed—make that stunned—by just how nasty Tom Cruise is willing to act. 'Respect the cock' could well be this spring's surprise catchphrase. Hence much muttering about how brave he was to risk his shiny image. But you are only as brave as you can afford to be: this week it emerged that he had made a massive $70 million as star and producer of 1996's *Mission: Impossible* . . . With *Mission: Impossible 2* coming up this year, its clear that Cruise can play any creep or pervert that takes his fancy." Still, *The Daily Show*'s Frank DeCaro was impressed by Cruise's "amazingly accurate portrayal of a heterosexual in *Magnolia*."

Because every character in the movie was more or less miserable, *Magnolia* presented itself as hard-hitting and realistic, and some people fell for it. *Rolling Stone*'s Peter Travers raved, "startling, innova-tive, hugely funny and powerfully, courageously mov-ing . . . *Magnolia* is a near miracle." Calling *Magnolia* "Part poem, part jungle blossom, all brilliance," F.X. Feeney of *L.A. Weekly* said that Anderson was "at-tempting, whatever the outcome, to embrace reality with the same encyclopedic, comedic vigor that James Joyce did in *Ulysses*. Anderson maps the Valley, his Dublin, with the same fond but pitiless eye."

Armond White of the *New York Press* advised, "If you're one of the suckers thinking about seeing *Mag-nolia*, here're some necessary caveats. Question the general middling critical opinion that director-writer Paul Thomas Anderson is a 'great talent.' By what standards? It's incredible that Anderson, by imitating Robert Altman's 1993 *Short Cuts* so blatantly, and lengthily, has received such high praise. *Magnolia*'s L.A.-sprawl plot, its apocalyptic interlude, parallel do-mestic dysfunctions—even some of the same Altman actors—only show Anderson's shamelessness. This isn't great talent; at best it's *merely* talent: the imitative skill of the second rate. Such theft wins tenure for third-rate professors and now wins kudos for third-rate di-rectors." White added, "1999 proved how craven critics are toward rich, powerful Cruise. Never an ade-quate actor, he gets praise just for trying."

On the "Dumbass and the Fag" Web site, "Jarett" summarized his feelings about *Magnolia*: "The people you always hated and never wanted to know. The movie you never wanted to see. The director you al-ways hoped would turn up hanging from a light fix-ture in a Las Vegas hotel room." Kevin Smith, the director of *Dogma* and *Chasing Amy*, posted his feel-ings about *Magnolia* on his Web site: "They sent me an Academy screener DVD of [*Magnolia*] this week. I'll never watch it again, but I will keep it. I'll keep it right on my desk, as a constant reminder that a bloated sense of self-importance is the most unattrac-tive quality in a person or their work." The filmmaker also referred to *Magnolia* as "cinematic root canal." The movie opened big, but putrid word-of-mouth killed it, as audiences stayed away in droves. *60 Min-utes* producer Don Hewitt said, "I went to a screening of *Magnolia*. It was so bad I liked *The Insider* better."

A Bunch of Film Critics Sitting Around Voting

Despite all the movies that had been released since September, the National Board of Review began the year's Awards process by naming *American Beauty* Best Picture. Best Director, however, went to Anthony Minghella, even though the Board had been shown an unfinished version of *The Talented Mr. Ripley*, and the Best Screenplay Award was given to John Irving for *The Cider House Rules*. Russell Crowe won Best Actor for *The Insider*, while the Best Actress prize winner was British stage actress Janet McTeer for playing a flighty Southern mom in the road movie, *Tumbleweeds*. Ubiquitous character actor Philip Seymour Hoffman was chosen Best Supporting Actor for playing an earnest male nurse in *Magnolia* and an overbearing specimen of the upper class in *The Talented Mr. Ripley*. Julianne Moore was cited as Supporting Actress for four movies: *Cookie's Fortune*, *An Ideal Husband*, *A Map of the World* and *Magnolia*; her most acclaimed performance was in Neil Jordan's rendering of the Graham Greene classic, *The End of the Affair*, but it couldn't be included in this list because she was the lead in the film. In lieu of being named Best Actress, *Boys Don't Cry*'s Hilary Swank was acknowledged for having given a "Breakthrough Performance," which certainly sounded like a Come-Back-When-You're-Older consolation prize.

The Los Angeles Film Critics Association voted second this year. Russell Crowe was the sole National Board winner to repeat, and *The Insider* also won Best Picture, Cinematography, and Supporting Actor for Christopher Plummer's enactment of Mike Wallace. Michael Mann did not win Best Director, though, that distinction going to Sam Mendes for *American Beauty*. The Best Screenplay winner was *Being John Malkovich*.

Both female acting awards went to *Boys Don't Cry*: Hilary Swank and Chlöe Sevigny.

Unlike the other two groups, the New York Film Critics Circle awarded Best Picture and Best Director to the same film: Mike Leigh's unfocused Gilbert & Sullivan tale, *Topsy-Turvy*. The Best Actor victor was Richard Farnsworth in *The Straight Story* and Hilary Swank had her second Best Actress Award. Both Supporting winners were in *Being John Malkovich*: Catherine Keener and John Malkovich. The Screenplay Award went to the social satire, *Election*.

Finally, the National Society of Film Critics' Best Picture voting ended in a tie between *Being John Malkovich* and *Topsy-Turvy*; Mike Leigh won Best Director for the latter, and Russell Crowe had another prize to add to his collection, as did Supporting winners Christopher Plummer and Chlöe Sevigny. The Best Actress winner was a new face on the awards circuit, Reese Witherspoon as the high school go-getter of your worst nightmare in *Election*. Charlie Kaufman received the Screenplay award for *Being John Malkovich*.

Primary Season

Surveying things, Harvey Weinstein could see that the only awards his company had taken were one National Board of Review citation for each of *The Cider House Rules* and *The Talented Mr. Ripley*, plus half of Philip Seymour Hoffman's prize from the Board—and since *Ripley* was a coproduction, Seymour's award equaled a quarter of a credit for Miramax. The front page headline on the century's last edition of *Variety* was devoted to Weinstein: "PUSHED TO THE MIRAMAX? The Talented Mr. Weinstein survives a bumpy '99" The article, by the paper's editor, Peter Bart, stated that profits had dropped to $80 million, $45 million less than the previous year. It also indicated that his biggest gaffe was a "misbegotten" release of an English-dubbed version of *Life Is Beautiful*, at a time when everyone just wanted Roberto Benigni to go away. As for Oscars, Bart felt that, "Miramax may not have a *Shakespeare in Love* or an *English Patient* this year, but several of its movies should win a slew of nominations in different categories." *Entertainment Weekly* described the company's year thusly: "If Miramax were a character out of Greek mythology, it would be Icarus, the guy who flew high enough to feel the warm rays of the sun—and then got burned and came whirling back to earth."

Tom Sherak, the domestic chairman of 20th Century Fox, expressed the common attitude when he told CNN, "This year there's a lot of films, but there's really nothing that you can say, '*That*'s it!' And I think that's gonna be kind of fun as the Academy votes." Publicist and Oscar strategist Tony Angellotti, who was working on behalf of Miramax, had a similar opinion. "It's a strange year," he said to *USA Today*. "Everything is still in the running. Certain films that have not been acknowledged in any shape or form, yet still have a chance, and little pictures that have gotten some recognition are now candidates." Kenneth Turan also sized up the situation and wrote, "Everyone loves a favorite at Oscar time, even if it's only as a highly visible target it would be fun to unseat. But this year not only is there no *Saving Private Ryan* on the horizon, there's no *Shakespeare in Love* either, and the Oscar races across the board look as wide open as possible."

Because no one or two films were dominating critical or popular favor and because support for *American Beauty* was palpably soft, DreamWorks was already waging an aggressive campaign for the film by December, advertising much more vigorously than Miramax was doing for either of its two most likely entries, *The Talented Mr. Ripley* and *The Cider House Rules*. The *American Beauty* ads—many of which took up two pages—contained chunks of dialogue transcribed from the screenplay. The ploy was intended to bring back memories of the movie—without making people actually sit through it again. DreamWorks had to hope that voters would decide that such lines as "You're the one to talk, you bloodless, money-grubbing freak" were so scintillating that the film deserved to take its place alongside such genuinely witty Best Picture winners as *All About Eve*, *The Apartment* and *Shakespeare in Love*. Adding a new element to campaigning was Universal. While in the past, Miramax's general ads in the *Los Angeles Times* and the *New York Times* were to some degree directed to Oscar voters,

Universal took it one step further this year: it announced in these general circulation papers the schedule of Academy screenings for its Oscar hopefuls, *The Hurricane*, *Man on the Moon* and *Snow Falling on Cedars*.

Entertainment Weekly noted that "Harvey Weinstein has been uncharacteristically quiet this year," but with the arrival of the new year, Miramax kicked its campaigning up a notch as it started to play catch up with DreamWorks. The cover of the first edition of *Variety* of the new millenium featured a full-page ad for Meryl Streep in *Music of the Heart*, the little-seen Wes Craven movie based on the 1995 Documentary nominee, *Fiddlefest*. The issue also featured a two-page ad for *The Cider House Rules* and full pages for *Mr. Ripley*'s Matt Damon, Jude Law, Gwyneth Paltrow, Cate Blanchett, and Philip Seymour Hoffman (Paramount was handling Academy screenings of the film), and the Jane Austen adaptation, *Mansfield Park*, as well as half-pages for Kate Winslet in Jane Campion's latest, *Holy Smoke* and Kirk Douglas in *Diamonds*. The latter was a critically dismissed, warm family comedy in which the veteran actor played an ex-boxer who helps his grandson get laid in a bordello; it, however, contained Douglas's first performance since his stroke, and Miramax was hoping for an auld lang syne nomination. Other than *American Beauty* and the Miramax collection, the trade papers were dominated by ads from the "independents." U.S.A. Films—which had been formed by the merger of October and Gramercy—for *Being John Malkovich*, *Topsy-Turvy* and Ang Lee's unsuccessful Civil War drama, *Ride with the Devil*; Sony Classics for some movies targeted to specialized audiences: David Mamet's adaptation of the Terrence Rattigan play, *The Winslow Boy*, Agnieszka Holland's *The Third Miracle*, Chan Kaige's *The Emperor and the Assassin* and Woody Allen's *Sweet and Lowdown*; and Fine Line for three movies that had not permeated the public consciousness, *Tumbleweeds*, *Simpatico* and *The Legend of 1900*. "We've never had so many Oscar ads," enthused *Variety*'s Peter Bart. In addition to *American Beauty*, the studio releases getting the biggest push were Universal's *The Hurricane* and Disney's *The Insider*. And as technology marched on, there was a new campaign component this year:

DreamWorks with *American Beauty* and New Line with *Magnolia* were giving Academy members the option of receiving a screener DVD rather than the traditional videocassette.

Foreign Press Reports

After the New York Film Critics awards, the Golden Globe nominations were announced; it was *The Talented Mr. Ripley*, not *The Cider House Rules*, that was representing Miramax in the Best Picture contest. *American Beauty*, however, led with six nominations. With five nods, *Ripley* tied *The Insider* for the second-place position; *The Cider House Rules* only had two nominations, one for Michael Caine as Supporting Actor, the other for John Irving's screenplay. The most notable sidebar from this year's nominations, though, was a revelation about Globe favorite, Sharon Stone. The actress received a somewhat unexpected nomination for Best Actress (Musical or Comedy) as the title role in Albert Brooks's *The Muse*, and it turned out she had generously purchased gold watches from Coach for all eighty-two members of the Hollywood Foreign Press, so that they could keep track of time while mulling over their ballots. The president of the Foreign Press, Helmut Voss, ordered his members to return the gifts, which were estimated to have cost in the $350 range. Voss told *Daily Variety*, "This watch was way, way, way beyond the edge of the envelope as far as promotional considerations, like T-shirts. We were touched by her generosity, but this is definitely a no-no for a group like ours that wants to protect the integrity of its award." No one seemed to want to accept credit for this act of kindness, as Stone's publicist said it was U.S.A. Films that paid for the watches, something the company denied. "Hardly a day goes by without one of these stupid crises arising," sighed President Voss.

When the Globes were handed out in mid-January, *American Beauty* emerged victorious in the top three categories: Best Picture (Drama), Best Director, and Best Screenplay. It didn't make it in the acting categories, though, as Best Actress (Drama) went to Hilary Swank in *Boys Don't Cry*, Best Actor (Drama) to Denzel Washington in *The Hurricane*. Washington brought Rubin Carter up to the stage with him and said, "This man right here is love. He's all love." On the Musical or Comedy side, *Toy Story 2* beat *Being John Malkovich* for Best Picture, Janet McTeer in *Tumbleweeds* won Best Actress—over Sharon Stone—and Jim Carrey received his second Globe in two years for *Man on the Moon*. Backstage, he echoed what many other people felt about his category placement, telling the show's producer, Dick Clark, "I thought I did a drama." The Supporting winners were Tom Cruise in *Magnolia* and Angelina Jolie, who played a fearlessly uninhibited mental patient in what had been designed to be a Winona Ryder showcase, *Girl, Interrupted*; wags referred to the film as "*One Flew Over the Cuckoo's Nest* meets *The Facts of Life*." Jolie, who had previously won two Globes for her television work, brought her brother, James, on stage with her because "I always wanted him to see . . . the view from up here. It's kind of amazing." On her way into the ceremony, while talking to a reporter, she had pulled James over and said, "I get so nervous without my brother." He kissed her on the head and said, "I love her so much. I love her more than anything in the world."

Three of the films which had been up for Best Picture (Drama) nominees received nothing from the Foreign Press: *The End of the Affair*, *The Insider* and *The Talented Mr. Ripley*. While Miramax came out of the Globes empty-handed, Fine Line took home a pair of Globes: Janet McTeer's and one for Ennio Morricone for the score of *The Legend of 1900*. The following day, DreamWorks announced it would be re-opening *American Beauty* at 750 theaters in order to have it back in the spotlight during Oscar voting season. Bernard Weinraub of the *New York Times* spoke to Terry Press, head of marketing at DreamWorks, who "said the notion of being seen as a front-runner appalled her and the company." Having witnessed *Saving Private Ryan* go down in defeat last year, she insisted, "We presume nothing now. We're grateful to have won the Golden Globes. But I'm not going to repeat the sins of last year. We've been there. We've been front-runners before. This is our second time around with this. It didn't work out last year, and we're not counting on anything this year." Press acknowledged that playing a game of tit for tat last year, DreamWorks

may have overdone the advertisements for *Private Ryan*, but that would not happen again. "We'll have a presence, but a restrained and tasteful presence."

Spurned by the Hollywood Foreign Press, Miramax now really went into high gear. The spin coming from screenings was that Academy members absolutely adored *The Cider House Rules*. And while some of that was, of course, Miramax hyperbole, it was undeniable that *Cider House* was ideal Academy fodder—a warm, sentimental movie with an unreproachably liberal slant presented in a "conservative" style. Meanwhile, *The Talented Mr. Ripley*, with its murders and homosexual overtones, was turning out to be a bit much for some Academy voters. So advertisements for *Cider House* began running at full throttle. John Hartl of the *Seattle Times* wrote that the movie "is being pitched as if it were a Hallmark Hall of Fame production. In a series of full-page ads that have been appearing daily in *Variety* and other papers, it's been touted as 'an American classic about family,' or 'an American classic about compassion,' or 'an American classic about choices.' The ads include a series of darling, Kodak-ready pictures of Michael Caine with his orphanage and/or Charlize Theron playing piggyback with Tobey Maguire. No mention is made of the fact that the film deals with incest, abortion, infidelity, murder and ether addiction." *USA Today* did a head count and when the nominating process was over, the count was forty-six ads asking for consideration for *The Cider House Rules*, thirty-six for *American Beauty*. No other movie came close.

Raging Bull

The *Hollywood Reporter*'s Martin Grove said that because of his Golden Globe victory, Denzel Washington was now "the guy to beat" in the Best Actor Oscar race. The weekend of the Globe ceremony was when *The Hurricane* opened wide and it finished number one at the box office. Unfortunately for everyone connected with *The Hurricane*, it was all going to go downhill from here. The accusations that had been leveled about the film's accuracy began to gain momentum. *Entertainment Weekly* ran a piece which not only repeated and expanded upon the accusations made by Selwyn Raab and Lewis Steel regarding false-hoods within the film, but also detailed the tortuous history of bringing Hurricane Carter's story to the screen. The implication was that the filmmakers used a number of contributions from writers without credit or adequate compensation. Moreover, the accusations about the dubiousness of the film's narrative opened the way for a new group of disgruntled people to make some noise. A former newspaper reporter from Pater-son, New Jersey—where the murders occurred—began a Web site dedicated to the proposition that Ru-bin Carter was indeed guilty as sin. Family members of the three victims and of the detectives and police offi-cers who worked to haul Carter in on the murder charges also joined in, and the ad hoc group called it-self "Graphic Witness." At least they were upfront, be-cause the Web site contained the statement: "This is not intended to be a balanced presentation, just an ac-curate counterweight to the Hollywood Justice Sys-tem." In addition to insisting upon Carter's guilt, the group claimed that the detective on whom the Dan Hedaya character was primarily based, far from the racist thug portrayed in the movie was actually "a big, sensitive teddy bear of a man."

Universal finally took out trade paper ads in late January defending its movie, but, a week before the nominations were announced, *Los Angeles Times* re-porter Patrick Goldstein surveyed the wreckage and summarized that the studio had been "embroiled in an ugly media battle over the movie's veracity, which many in Hollywood believe has badly tarnished its Os-car aura." He added, "some in Hollywood are wonder-ing why the studio didn't react more quickly to the attacks. It also calls into question whether Universal was fully aware of the factual discrepancies surround-ing the film and the likelihood that the film's truthful-ness would be questioned." Goldstein explained that "Oscar experts say that studios, like political cam-paigns, must react immediately to negative attacks. But Universal and [production company] Beacon dawdled, waiting three weeks before sending a letter to the *New York Times* responding to Raab's broadside." Screenwriter and industry observer William Goldman told Charlie Rose he didn't understand why the truth squad was hounding *The Hurricane* when "*Boys Don't Cry*, which no one hammered, was not quote-unquote accurate. *The Insider* was really not quote-unquote ac-curate . . . For some reason, whether it's because the *New York Times* wrote a rotten article and the *New York Times* is very powerful, everybody's picked up on *The Hurricane* and slammed it for not being accurate and all these other movies got away with it." Similarly, Lou Lumenick of the *New York Post* was incensed that "*The Hurricane* fell victim to a vicious campaign that held it to a much higher factual standard than such past Oscar winners as *Out of Africa*." "Sometimes I wish we'd made a movie about Julius Caesar," sighed Universal's publicity chief Terry Curtin. "At least none of his Roman legions are around to complain about whether every little detail of his life is accurate or not."

What's Up, Documentarians?

In its seemingly never-ending quest to bring credibility to the Documentary Feature Awards, the Academy this year had a preliminary list of semifinal-ists decided upon by nearly eighty Academy members who actually made documentary films. Thus, the cate-gory would—like the other Awards—be first voted upon by specialists in the field, rather than Academy members from any old branch who just happened to have time on their hands. These documentarians would each watch a number of the eligible films—this year, there were fifty-five such movies—and whittle them down to a dozen, and then any Academy mem-ber who saw all twelve semifinalists would be wel-comed to vote to determine the five finalists. Perhaps the most significant aspect about the dozen semifinal-ists was that the closest to a Holocaust film among them was Errol Morris's *Mr. Death: The Rise and Fall of Fred A. Leuchter Jr.*, about an oddball who designed electric chairs and was a Holocaust-denier. The fact that the never-nominated Morris had made it this far in the proceedings was fairly remarkable in itself, though he was a member of the Documentary Branch's executive committee.

There's a Change in the Weather, There's a Change in the Sea

The best reviewed Oscar show of the past decade had been the one that Gilbert Cates had *not* produced, 1995's Quincy Jones telecast. So for Oscar fans, it was joyous news when Cates said he wouldn't be available this year. Replacing him was the husband-and-wife team of Richard and Lili Fini Zanuck—she would be the first woman ever to produce the ceremony. In making the announcement, Academy President Bob Rehme said, "I'm on Cloud Nine. We're very excited to have the Zanucks produce the Oscars." He did acknowledge Gilbert Cates's "yeoman work," but said, "With this new producing team in place, I look forward to a whole new perspective." Richard Zanuck initially wouldn't get into details about what they might be bringing to the show, other than saying that their production would be "new and different."

As they began to put plans into place, the Zanucks admitted they were waiting to hear if Billy Crystal would agree to return after last year's hiatus. In the meantime, they announced that actor Peter Coyote would serve as an on-camera announcer, who, it was hoped, would help expedite the proceedings. "Peter will be the voice of the show," Richard Zanuck said. "The last time that Billy Crystal hosted, he had to walk out onto the stage more than twenty times. The host comes out onstage too much. Now people will walk onstage with the voice of Peter Coyote." *Daily Variety* also recounted that, "Asked about dance numbers, both rolled their eyes and grimaced and said they aren't big fans of such segments. Finally they admitted that they've ruled out a dance number for the show—which drew applause from the media reps." *Daily Variety* later reported, "Richard and Lili Fini Zanuck were sitting in a restaurant in Sun Valley, Idaho, when some people at a nearby table sent over a bottle of wine. The reason? 'They wanted to thank us for cutting the dance numbers,' Richard explains. 'They were from Oklahoma. We didn't know them at all.' " He elaborated, "We just didn't think the dance numbers fit in. It's a celebration of films and film music." The Zanucks also said there would be fewer film

montage segments than in a Gilbert Cates show, Lili explaining, "One of the things Dick and I decided when we accepted this assignment is to remember all the things in the telecast that occur during which we got up to go get food." The couple, who had never worked in television before, said their number one priority would be to bring the show in at three hours, and Fini Zanuck joked to reporters that because she's a woman "the sets will all be pink." Her husband, the son of 20th Century Fox mogul Darryl F. Zanuck, said, "I bring a history," since he'd been attending Oscar ceremonies for half a century. "This awards ceremony is practically in my DNA."

In mid-December, the producers got their Christmas wish: "This is something that we really wanted," jubilated Fini Zanuck. "Our audience is going to be thrilled. The No. 1 question that Richard and I get from people is, 'Do you have Billy Crystal?' Now we do. . . . I assume every year the first call from the Oscars office is to Billy Crystal," she said. "When Dick and I decided to do this, we wanted to put a new spin on every aspect but one. My husband went on a huge campaign to get a commitment from Billy. He said to Dick, 'You know, there's a cab driver in Chicago who knows you're trying to get me to do the Oscars again. Everybody knows this.' "

The next goal the Zanucks set for themselves was increasing the hipness level of music. That, of course, meant getting rid of hack film composer, Bill Conti, and his "lite-music" orchestrations. Instead, the producers signed as co-musical directors, Burt Bacharach, who had been embraced by Gen X in recent years as a quintessence of cool, and record producer Don Was, who was currently working on albums with Iggy Pop and Ziggy Marley, so he was clearly no Bill Conti. Was revealed, "There will be a lot of rhythm and every star entrance will have a groove under it. This will be the first show in Oscar history to feature a DJ and turntable in the orchestra." Everything bode well.

The Zanucks had received Oscars ten years earlier as the producers of Best Picture winner *Driving Miss Daisy*, and Richard had also been given the Thalberg Award in tandem with his former partner, David Brown. He said, "We know what it's like to have that once-in-a-lifetime thrill. By the same token, as this year's producers we know we have to be cognizant of the fact that there will be 800 million people watching around the world. We don't want to bore them in any way. It's not in our nature to have a quick trigger finger, but I hate lists. There's something insincere about that. If you can't remember who you want to thank when you get up there, maybe they shouldn't be thanked."

As for Honorary Oscars, the Board of Governors announced that the Irving G. Thalberg Memorial Award was going to Warren Beatty, a man who had been in the news recently because he had been mulling over a run for the White House. One would be hard put to argue that Beatty was undeserving of recognition by the Academy, but Beatty had been an actor, director, writer, and producer; to give him an Oscar only for the latter made very little sense. According to the *Hollywood Reporter*, "The Academy said Wednesday that its Board of Governors chose Beatty because he is the only person to receive multiple Oscar nominations as an actor, writer, director and producer." Which was all good and fine, but that has nothing to do with the Thalberg Award, and a general Lifetime Achievement Award would have been much more appropriate.

There was hope in some circles that the Academy would try to make amends for its offensive anointing of Elia Kazan by giving a Lifetime Achievement to someone who had been blacklisted—director Jules Dassin's name came up most often. Instead, it was going to be one of those Awards that seemed more obligation than celebration. Polish filmmaker Andrzej Wajda was to be honored, although it was doubtful that greater than a handful of people currently working in Hollywood had seen any of his films. His reputation was primarily for having been a voice of freedom and creative expression in a totalitarian state rather than for the quality of his movies themselves, the best known of which was *Man of Marble*. Cynics wondered if giving an Award to a filmmaker who had had run-ins with a Communist regime was the Academy's sly way of declaring that Kazan had done the right thing in snitching. Wajda was also on record as saying that Kazan was one of his idols. Head writer Bruce Vilanch was happy though, laughing that as opposed to last year, "The Board of Governors gave us a

break: They didn't give an Award to anybody half of the world hates."

The Nominations

The four movies most widely touted as Best Picture nominees made the cut. *American Beauty* had the most nominations, but its total of eight was the lowest for a leader since *Rain Man* in 1988. Right behind were *The Cider House Rules* and *The Insider* with seven and *The Sixth Sense* with six. There had been no agreement among Oscar prognosticators as to what the fifth Best Picture would be, as some early favorites became weighed down with baggage: *Being John Malkovich*, because it was a little too "hip" by the Academy's standards; *The Talented Mr. Ripley*, because it seemed to be a little disturbing (even though it did very well at the box office); *The Hurricane*, because of all the controversy; *Magnolia*, because people loathed it; and *The End of the Affair*, because it never caught on beyond sophisticated urban audiences. But the film that made it in was not at all expected. Although it had been considered a likely contender before it opened, once it had been released, *The Green Mile* simply didn't seem to possess the stature of an Academy Award nominee. But there it was in the final five, with a total of four nominations. Granted Frank Darabont had received a Directors Guild nomination, but most members of the DGA are from television, many working as stage managers, and they are usually pinpointed whenever a nomination like this shows up among the Guild's finalists. Indeed, as was usually the case, the Academy's Directors Branch showed itself to be more sophisticated than the general membership, as it gave a Best Director nomination to Spike Jonze for *Being John Malkovich* rather than to Frank Darabont. Similarly, in 1994, the Directors Branch denied Darabont a nomination even though *The Shawshank Redemption* was up for Best Picture; that year, his spot had gone to Krzysztof Kieslowski for *Red*. No argument there, either.

The biggest surprises—both in terms of exclusion and inclusion—came in the Best Actor race. Jim Carrey was not nominated for *Man on the Moon*. Although the movie wasn't a hit and although there was disagreement over whether Carrey had created a full character or had simply done an accurate but skin-deep impersonation, most analysts thought that a nomination would be coming to Carrey, if for no other reason than that he didn't receive one last year for *The Truman Show*. His non-nomination sat fine with the *Los Angeles Daily News*'s Bob Strauss, who mused, " Yes, the voters do appear biased against the approval-seeking funnyman, but not because he's a comedian; he just hasn't played a convincingly human character yet." Army Archerd reported, "A lot of Andy Kaufman material had been planned for Billy Crystal by the Oscar show's head writer Bruce Vilanch and Billy's writing team of (ten) writers," but now that had to be scratched. Compounding the surprise was that in Carrey's stead was Sean Penn in *Sweet and Lowdown*, Woody Allen's little-seen, little-discussed film about a badly behaved Django Reinhardt-esque guitar player. If Carrey wasn't going to make it, *The Cider House Rules*'s Tobey Maguire or *The Talented Mr. Ripley*'s Matt Damon had seemed more likely. The other four nominees had all been anticipated: Russell Crowe in *The Insider*, Richard Farnsworth in *The Straight Story*, Kevin Spacey in *American Beauty*, and Denzel Washington in *The Hurricane*—this was the sole nomination for the Hurricane Carter movie. (Noting the seven-to-one difference in nominations for two less-than-entirely-accurate fact-based movies, Kenneth Turan maintained that *The Insider* was "much more proactive in how it handled its own truth-or-fiction controversy" than *The Hurricane*.) Henry Sheehan of the *Orange County Register* said, "It's a testament to the funnyman's publicity machine that his presence or absence from this or that awards list is always touted as a major event . . . Also, take a look at the five best-acting nominees; does any single one of them deserve not to be there? No. So if Carrey had been nominated, we'd just have someone else crying foul."

The five women who had been deemed the most likely Best Actress nominees all made it in: Annette Bening in *American Beauty*, Janet McTeer in *Tumbleweeds*, Julianne Moore in *The End of the Affair*, Meryl Streep in *Music of the Heart* (for this one, the overachiever learned how to play the violin in four months), and Hilary Swank in *Boys Don't Cry*. Simi-

larly, the Supporting Actor finalists had all been expected: Michael Caine in *The Cider House Rules*, Tom Cruise in *Magnolia*, Michael Clarke Duncan in *The Green Mile* (despite the queasiness some people felt about his role), Jude Law in *The Talented Mr. Ripley*, and Haley Joel Osment in *The Sixth Sense*. The Supporting Actress balloting produced one surprise: Samantha Morton, for playing a deaf-mute lovesick laundress in *Sweet and Lowdown*, rather than the widely expected Golden Globe and Screen Actors Guild nominee, Cameron Diaz from *Being John Malkovich*. Woody Allen revealed his secret of working with Morton. "I wanted her to think of Harpo Marx when she approached playing Hattie," Allen said. "It turned out she'd never even heard of the Marx Brothers. That's the gap between us. But she made it her business to see a lot of Marx Brothers films, and when she got back, she could do Harpo perfectly." Diaz's fellow Malkovich actress, Catherine Keener, did receive a nomination, as did Toni Collette in *The Sixth Sense*, Angelina Jolie in *Girl, Interrupted*, and Chlöe Sevigny in *Boys Don't Cry*. At age forty, Keener was the grand old lady of this group—all of her fellow nominees were in their twenties.

When critics and Oscar watchers discussed which non-nominees they wished had made the cut, the name most often mentioned was National Society of Film Critics winner, Reese Witherspoon of *Election*. "I am still smitten with a tremendously underrated performance by actress Reese Witherspoon in the tremendously underrated movie *Election*," said Mike Downey of the *Los Angeles Times*. "Awards are forever going to actors and actresses for playing characters with physical and mental disabilities. I'd be glad to see Witherspoon get one, just for playing a major pain in the butt." *Newsday*'s John Anderson said of one of the women who were nominated for Best Actress: "Meryl Streep for *Music of the Heart* proved that she apparently really *could* get nominated by reading the phone book." Richard Natale of the *Los Angeles Times* wrote, "Miramax head Harvey Weinstein had reportedly promised Streep a nomination if she agreed to do the film (after first choice Madonna abruptly left the project over "creative differences") and he's clearly a man who delivers." Kathie Lee Gifford commented of

Streep, "She never gives anything other than a stellar performance." This was the actress's twelfth nomination, tying her with Katharine Hepburn for the most acting nominations ever.

Disney's two Best Picture nominees, *The Insider* and *The Sixth Sense* were the studio's first finalists in the category since *Beauty and the Beast* in 1991. And its seventeen nominations were the most of any studio, the first time ever that Disney had this distinction. Studio executive Richard Cook admitted, "This is uncharted territory for us. We don't do Academy Best Pictures, so this is a real thrill." Ironically, Joe Roth, the studio chairman who had been behind Disney's 1999 releases was no longer at the studio, having left in January to start his own company. Oscar pundits suggested that perhaps it was time to stop giving too much credence to the Hollywood Foreign Press: Three of this year's Best Picture Oscar nominees had not been Golden Globe finalists.

Right after last year's ceremony, an ABC executive had said that he was hoping that *Star Wars Episode 1: The Phantom Menace* would dominate the nominations, on the assumption that ratings would then be huge. Of course, now, nobody cared about the movie any more, and it garnered just three technical nominations; *The Matrix*, a movie people actually did care about, did it one better. *The Blair Witch Project* was shut out, not that a different scenario was expected; Hollywood considered the *Blair Witch* team a bunch of amateurs who got lucky, and, besides, there was no Oscar for best Web site.

That four of the five Best Picture nominees were bunched so closely together in number of nominations attested to how at this point there was no out-and-out frontrunner. The *Los Angeles Times* posited that it was "one of the tightest Oscar races in years," and Rick Lyman wrote in the *New York Times*, "Share the wealth seemed to be the theme of the day. . . No single film dominated the nominations, and there were no clear favorites in any of the leading categories, meaning that this year's Oscars will be the most hard-fought and unpredictable in recent years." *Daily Variety*'s Timothy M. Gray said that this year, "The term 'wide-open race' is an understatement." Despite its Golden Globe victory, Jack Mathews of the *New York Daily*

News said that *American Beauty* was merely now "one of four pictures with about an even chance . . . Actually, if you're a believer in the kind of momentum shift that saw *Shakespeare in Love* overtake *Saving Private Ryan* last year, you might give an edge to *The Cider House Rules* or *The Sixth Sense*." *Daily Variety*'s Dana Harris asked, "Rematch, anyone?" Noting that Dream-Works and Miramax were at the center of the Best Picture race, she reminisced that a year ago, "a victorious Harvey Weinstein could be seen gripping his Best Picture statuette while a dour DreamWorks team flanked Steven Spielberg and his Oscar for Best Director. Second-guessing about overconfidence on the part of DreamWorks began within nanoseconds of the best pic announcement. Now it's déjà vu all over again. DreamWorks has the critical and popular favorite with *American Beauty* while Miramax is squarely positioned in the feel-good category with *The Cider House Rules*."

"For Miramax, it was a day to celebrate. For other studios, the good news was tempered with a mixture of fear and loathing," wrote Glenn Whipp of the *Los Angeles Daily News*. "Tuesday's Oscar nominations produced several story lines—the large number of first-time nominees, the absence of favorites both perennial (Tom Hanks) and otherwise (Jim Carrey) and the Academy's propensity to reward mainstream films over more inventive fare. For industry insiders, however, one topic dominated above all others: Miramax had somehow done it again. Get ready to be bombarded (again) with television and newspaper ads for a movie that many people have been more than happy to ignore for the past three months." Even though the overall feeling was that none of the nominees had a concrete lead over the others, DreamWorks's marketing head Terry Press still told *USA Today*, "I'm not ashamed that our film is the front-runner. But do I presume that we will stay the front-runner? No. The race is wide open." And, immediately laying claim to the high ground, she insisted, "It's distasteful to me to turn the Academy Awards into a marketing derby." Although to anyone who had been paying attention, *Cider House*'s showing came as no surprise, executives at rival studios immediately began venting. "To get seven nominations for that film is unbelievable," said one unnamed executive from another studio. "But that's Miramax. That's the way they play. They'll spend whatever it takes." Someone else kvetched to the *Daily News*, "Miramax isn't in the movie business. They're in the Oscar business." One studio honcho, though, was magnanimous enough to acknowledge, "Their campaigns aren't any different from other studios—only more successful."

Even though Andrzej Wajda would be receiving an Honorary Oscar, the Foreign Film committee didn't see fit to nominate his latest movie, *Pan Tadeusz*, Poland's entry this year. The second round of voting in the Documentary Feature category was pretty much the same as in the old days: Errol Morris again came away waiting for his first nomination. But for once, the year's most popular documentary did end up among the final five: *Buena Vista Social Club*, Wim Wenders's exuberant account of a group of aged Cuban musicians having a career renaissance. *Newsweek*'s David Ansen cautioned fans of the film, though: "The rule of thumb is: if there's a movie about the Holocaust, it will win. There isn't one this year, but there is a film about the Palestinian terrorist attack on the Israeli athletes at the Munich Olympics called *One Day in September*. Look for it to edge out the front-runner, *Buena Vista Social Club*." Kevin Macdonald, the director of *One Day in September*, told the *London Times* that his movie would certainly be helped out by "the Jewish aspect."

Annette Bening was wide awake watching the announcements in bed with Warren Beatty, and then she immediately went into full campaign mode, talking to *Good Morning, America* over the phone and saying that her baby—who was due right around Oscar night—was kicking. She also was on the horn with *Access Hollywood*'s Pat O'Brien joking that "I will be wearing a tent" on Oscar night, but when she tried to chat with E!'s Steve Kmetko, technical difficulties prevented the home audience from hearing what was on her mind. Even though Bening hadn't won any critics' awards or the Golden Globe, Claudia Cohen was on *Live with Regis and Kathie Lee* decreeing, "She has got to be the favorite at this point. She's Hollywood royalty. She's having a baby practically on the day of the Academy Awards. And she showed she's a really good sport and a team player, respectful of Hollywood institutions—she

was on the air by telephone this morning on *Good Morning, America*."

Hilary Swank was on the set of her new movie, *The Gift*, in the boondocks of Georgia with no television set in sight. Husband Chad Lowe called her from L.A. and held the phone to the TV so they could listen to the nominations together. She said that hearing the news with her "best friend," in this fashion made the nomination even more special. Janet McTeer told the *Los Angeles Times*, "I think the whole thing is quite funny, to be honest. You make a film for a coffin of spit and twelve-and-a-half dollars, and here we are at the Oscars. You never know, do you?"

Richard Farnsworth, who at seventy-nine, became the oldest Best Actor nominee ever, said, "I got up at four this morning and couldn't sleep and threw some hay to the stock and came on in," he said. "When we got the message, it just tickled me to death." He said he was going to celebrate with a martini and a burrito. Kevin Spacey was in Las Vegas making his new movie, *Pay It Forward*, but he was up bright and early to speak to the media. After he talked to the *Today* show, host Matt Lauer stated, "Good things sometimes happen to good people and Kevin Spacey is good people." Spacey told *Entertainment Tonight* he was upset because he hadn't been able to reach his mother—her line was constantly busy.

Spacey's costar in *Pay It Forward*, eleven-year-old Haley Joel Osment, was also making the television rounds from Vegas. He said of his competition, "I haven't been allowed to see them. A lot of them are R-rated. I hope to see them in years to come. I'm not old enough now." He certainly sounded like an old showbiz pro, though, when he told *E! News Daily*, "It's really not a competition, and there is no winner, there is no loser. It's a huge honor to be nominated and I'm just happy to be on that list." And also when he said on *Good Morning, America*, "I was just thrilled, but especially for Night Shyamalan and Toni Collette. It was really, really, really great for both of them to get the nominations they really deserved. I'm so happy for everyone on *The Sixth Sense*." As for his own nomination, "It was just incredible. I never would have thought that it was going to happen this early." After Haley Joel signed off, *Good Morning, America* host

Charles Gibson said, "That's neat." Jay Leno joked that now when Osment looked around him he'd be saying, "I see jealous people."

The Green Mile's Michael Clarke Duncan had allowed *Access Hollywood* into his New York hotel room to capture his response to getting—or not getting—a nomination. When he heard his name, he was instantly screaming and jumping and then he wrestled some other guy in the room. Next, Duncan was on his knees making the sign of the cross, but the show respectfully cut away from him before he actually began praying. An hour-and-a-half later Duncan was on *The Rosie O'Donnell Show* saying that he had wanted to call his mother immediately to share the news but he couldn't remember her phone number. The reason he blanked out was "I was so amped. I was so geeked up from being an Academy Award nominee." Duncan's director, Frank Darabont, showed up on *Showbiz Today* talking about not being a Director nominee despite *The Green Mile*'s Best Picture nomination. Darabont name-dropped: "It puts me in very good company. I was just on the phone this morning with Steven Spielberg who called to congratulate me, who's a friend. And I said, 'Steven, how many times has this happened to you?' He said, 'twice.' I said, 'Ha! I finally matched one of your records.' "

American Beauty screenwriter Alan Ball and his two producers, Dan Jinks and Bruce Cohen were on *The Morning Show*, live from Jinks's house. When Bryant Gumbel asked him where he'd go from here professionally, Ball responded, "I just hit the jackpot with this movie . . . so I think I'm going to have to leave the business and go to Montana." The two producers laughed, as if he had said something witty. Their director Sam Mendes told *Access Hollywood*, "I'm thrilled and delighted and honored, as well, which you can't say for most awards, but this occasion is the big one, so I'm really, really delighted."

Toni Collette said, "My younger brother was like, 'You rock!' and for him to say that, I mean, he must be pretty impressed." Chlöe Sevigny had just arrived in Germany where her newest film, *American Psycho,* was being shown at the Berlin Film Festival. She was awakened with news of her nomination by her friend, Best

Actress nominee Julianne Moore, who was in the hotel room next to hers. Sevigny laughed that over the course of the day, she received so many flowers that her room looked like a funeral parlor. When Sevigny was back in the States, she appeared on *The Tonight Show*, and offered an endearing contrast to her cutting-edge film appearances by showing up with ashes on her forehead—it was the first day of Lent.

There's Always Something

The Zanucks were putting more plans into place. They now realized that their original goal of a three-hour show was probably a pipe dream, but they were shooting for a maximum of three-and-a-half, and insisted it couldn't be allowed to go for four hours, as last year's telecast had. The producers also promised to improve the Academy's half-hour preshow, hiring Joe Gallen, who had created the *MTV Movie Awards*, to produce it. *TV Guide* pointed out that publicity for last year's countdown program "had promised peeks at stars schmoozing in the lobby and much backstage craziness—none of which happened." Producer Gallen said, "I don't want to sound like the boy who cried wolf, but we *will* deliver what was hoped for last year. And then some." The presence of an official Oscar preview show meant that once again the other preshows would be abbreviated. "I take it as a compliment," said Joan Rivers. "They can't do what we do. We're just a little bitty show that everyone enjoys stopping by. . . . We have a good time, they have a good time. Go and be well."

Although it seemed that any sane person would cheer the demise of the dance numbers in general, and the nonparticipation of Debbie Allen in particular, Army Archerd reported, "It was bound to happen: at Sunday's Professional Dancers Society 14th annual Gypsy Awards, honoring Fred Astaire, Buddy Ebsen and Marge Champion at the BevHilton, a loud chorus of 'boo's' protested the elimination of dance numbers from the Oscar show this year. (Protest was brought up by chair Joni Berry and advisory board chair Bob Sidney). The theme was picked up by presenters Dick Van Dyke, Donald O'Connor, Carol Channing and

Betty Garrett." Actually, the producers did hire a choreographer, Kenny Ortega. In his words, "The Zanucks want a choreographer to keep the show flowing. That involves everything that moves—from the performers and sets to the sweep of a camera angle." And although the producers had ditched big production numbers, the show would not be entirely bereft of musical performances. In addition to the five Best Song nominees, there would be what the Zanucks hoped would prove a showstopper—performances of past Oscar-winning and nominated songs performed by Garth Brooks, Ray Charles, Isaac Hayes, Whitney Houston, Queen Latifah, and Dionne Warwick.

Even though they didn't have to worry about choreographic embarrassments, the producers still faced a musical problem: what to do with one of the Best Song nominees, "Blame Canada." The song, from the cartoon feature *South Park: Bigger, Longer & Uncut*, contained lyrics that clearly weren't going to pass muster with ABC's Department of Standards and Practices. The tongue-in-cheek number about scapegoating and abrogating responsibility contained the words "fuck" and "fart" and a reference to "that bitch, Anne Murray." Lili Zanuck told songwriters Trey Parker and Marc Shaiman that they needed to come up with a "creative solution." Parker insisted that "we won't tolerate changing the lyrics. That's the wrong way to go—the song got nominated for what it is." His solution was, "I want to say 'bleep' instead. I'm trying to convince ABC to bleep the words and not change them. I'm not going to write new words."

Shaiman said to CNN, "We're not being unreasonable. We understand there's the F-word, and you're not going to say that on network TV, the big F-word. But there's the other F-word they don't want to say: that's 'fart.' And they're like, 'We can't say that on the air,' and I was really surprised. We're like, 'Fart'? What's wrong with 'fart'?" He observed, "It would be ironic to have to change the words in a song in a movie about censorship." Shaiman also said that Canadian songbird Anne Murray was "cool" with the reference to her, although she did turn down the offer to perform the song at the Oscars.

Grudge Match

It hadn't taken long after the nominations were announced for the DreamWorks and Miramax troops to take battle positions. Ads for *American Beauty* and *The Cider House Rules* were omnipresent. On CNN, *Premiere*'s Deputy Editor Howard Karren observed, "This year, it's definitely personal." He believed that if a Miramax come-from-behind victory "happened again, I think there would be a lot of bitterness" on the part of DreamWorks. But *American Beauty* coproducer Dan Jinks said, "I think it's an injustice to the other films to reduce it all to *American Beauty* and *Cider House*," insisting that all five nominees "are terrific movies. And I feel everyone is rooting for everyone." *Cider House*'s producer, Richard Gladstein agreed. "There's not the least bit of tension among the filmmakers," he said. "All this banter over who's going to win, that doesn't exist in my world." Miramax publicity maven Cynthia Schwartz said, "Contrary to popular belief, our goal in life is not winning Oscars; it's to reach as wide an audience as possible."

Sean Mitchell of the *New York Daily News* heard all this nice touchy-feely talk and said, "Maybe so, but if it were all so collegial, why have DreamWorks, Miramax and other studios spent bankbreaking sums promoting their nominees through prime-time commercials and trade ads . . . ? Front cover ads for *American Beauty* have wrapped *Daily Variety* regularly in the last few weeks, reflecting what everyone assumes is the studio's granite determination not to allow a repeat of last year." The *Washington Post*, meanwhile, was watching TV, and couldn't help notice Miramax's commercials, saying, "The studio's syrupy television spots, part of a national campaign that Miramax says has cost it as much as $15 million, have been emphasizing not only the film's 'life-affirming, resonant' qualities, as one Miramax executive puts it, but also its status as 'an American classic.'" DreamWorks's marketing head Terry Press was in full self-righteous mode, saying "I never hid the darkness or the unsavory elements of *American Beauty* in my advertising campaign—and that's a real difference between us and *Cider House*. That's one thing I really draw the line at."

Lasse Hallström got booked for an excellent gig. He was invited by Academy Award winner Rabbi Marvin Hier to screen *The Cider House Rules* at the Simon Wiesenthal Center's Museum of Tolerance, followed by a question and answer segment. Hallström would be representing a pro-choice stance a day after an appearance by George W. Bush, the simpleton Texas governor running for the Republican Presidential nomination. Bush was there on behalf of the "pro-life" side—even though he had never seen anything so forlorn as an electric chair not in use.

Jack Valenti in the Garbage, Cobwebs on Michael Caine

Never mind that *The Hurricane* was only in the running for the Best Actor Oscar, "Graphic Witness," the anti–Rubin Carter crowd back in Paterson, New Jersey didn't pull back. Washington was Universal's only nomination in any of the major categories (it had a mere total of five, the others spread among four films in the Cinematography, Original Score, Sound, and Makeup categories) so the studio continued to advertise heavily for the actor. In response, "The Families of Rubin 'Hurricane' Carter's Victims" tried to place an ad in *Daily Variety* and the *Hollywood Reporter* that was addressed to members of the Academy. It declared that there was "substantial, credible" evidence that Carter had committed the three murders—but don't just take their word for it, "twenty-four jurors—including two African-Americans—were convinced." The ad then asked Academy members "Please do not support an Oscar for this false and terribly hurtful film." The two trade papers refused to run the ad. Graphic Witness even attacked Jack Valenti, because the Motion Picture Association head had defended the movie in an open letter, praising it because it "illuminates the rightness of American justice." The New Jersey-ites disagreed, saying "The movie illuminates nothing. Instead it casts a dark shadow over the truth and does harm to the good people who worked hard to send Rubin Carter to prison. . . . Hollywood is trashing our country, and

Mr. Valenti is saluting the garbage." Poor Denzel Washington. It was March, the Oscars were fast approaching, and he found himself still defending *The Hurricane*. He was on *Charlie Rose* stating that in preproduction, "I was sort of lobbying for 'Let's show his violent side a little more and not make him so sweet.' " As for those real-life heroes disgruntled over their exclusion from the film, Washington said, "There are a lot of people who played a role. There are a lot of writers. There are a lot of lawyers, there are a lot of people who played a role. But you've got to pick. Or maybe they should have done a crawl at the end and given all the people credit."

The backlash may have been having effect, because at the Screen Actors Guild Awards, Washington lost to *American Beauty*'s Kevin Spacey, who was victorious for the first time this awards season. Or it may have simply been that SAG members were enamored of *American Beauty*, since Annette Bening was named Best Actress and the film won for Best Ensemble, beating, among others, the cast of *The Cider House Rules*. This was also Bening's initial award, and for the first time it seemed as if maybe Hilary Swank wasn't necessarily going to have an easy go of it at the Oscars. Angelina Jolie won Best Supporting Actress for *Girl, Interrupted*, while the one saving grace for Miramax at the SAGs was Michael Caine's being named Best Supporting Actor. Shortly before the Oscars, Caine was on *The Tonight Show* and was talking about the conflicting results of the multitudinous awards leading up to the Academy Awards. "It's such a miasma of awards," he said to Jay Leno. "It's a sort of puzzle that goes across your face like cobwebs." Turning to the audience, Caine said, "You've never heard awards described like that before, have you?"

You'll Be in My Heartburn

Reporting on the Nominees Luncheon, the *Los Angeles Times* said that, "From Tom Cruise congratulating the creators of *South Park* to Hilary Swank excited to meet Meryl Streep, Monday appeared to be a day of generosity in Hollywood." Kevin Spacey told the press that as far as he was concerned, the Oscars were "an unnatural pitting of actors against one another, and I'm honored to be a part of one of the more extraordinary years for actors, inventive filmmakers and for studios taking risks." The *Times* observed that "First-time nominees like Swank and Russell Crowe seemed almost giddy and somber, respectively, with the attention the nominations afforded them."

Barry Koltnow of the *Orange County Register* was observing the get-together and he wrote that Russell Crowe "is a real-life, no-nonsense tough guy. He walks into a room ready for a fight, and nothing gets past him. He will deliver a devastating verbal jab without hesitation and without regard for its implications. He seems to exude extreme confidence and fearlessness. He is truly a man's man, whom one would assume would dismiss the Oscars as frivolous and a waste of time. That's what I expected him to say. I certainly didn't expect him, the macho cop from *L.A. Confidential*, to turn into a sentimental slob. 'I don't have any funny lines and I don't have a cynical opinion of it,' the actor said, in almost a reverential tone. 'An Oscar nomination to me is a very important thing. It's a great privilege. I know lots of people who have had stellar and very long careers who have never had the benefit of being acknowledged by their peers in that manner. I'm really appreciative of it and very thankful.' "

Among the highlights at the repast was Michael Clarke Duncan's running into the room just as the "class photo" was about to be snapped and yelling "Sorry, I'm late." Duncan explained that he had lost his keys in the limo coming home from partying after the Screen Actors Guild Awards the previous night and spent the morning waiting for a locksmith. "What an entrance," said President Rehme, while Academy Governor Marvin Levy, who was at the podium at the time, quipped "This may be the first time we've ever had a homeless person at the Nominees Luncheon."

The other most memorable moment came from "Blame Canada" cowriter, Trey Parker, who provided a welcome contrast to the afternoon's sense of camaraderie. Meeting the press, Parker began, in the words of the *Hollywood Reporter*, "firing off profane taunts at fellow Best Song nominee Phil Collins." Collins, who, once Peter Gabriel left the band, had epitomized the worst of corporate rock as a drummer with Genesis (Wesley Morris of the *San Francisco Examiner* called

him "the cheesiest drummer on earth"), was now an offensively insipid balladeer and songwriter. He was nominated for the year's most vapid Song nominee, "You'll Be in My Heart" from a Disney cartoon, *Tarzan*. Fielding questions from the press, Parker informed those assembled, "Incidentally, people don't realize this, but Phil Collins's song was originally called 'You'll Be in My Fucking Heart.' " He also said that his one hope about the Best Song contest was that Collins not win, elaborating that under that awful scenario, "Everything I've achieved in life, the small things I've achieved, will come down to 'You lost to Phil Collins.' " Parker's cowriter Marc Shaiman said that, yes, it was true that with less than two weeks before the Awards, no one had yet agreed to perform "Blame Canada" on the show; he said his personal choice was KTLA-TV entertainment reporter and Oscar forecourt interviewer, Sam Rubin.

Insider Trading

What to do about the lyrics for "Blame Canada" would be the least of the Academy's worries—the *South Park* dilemma was just one of an unprecedented number of problems affecting this year's Awards. The *Wall Street Journal* decided it would be fun to take a poll of Academy voters so it could let everyone know prior to Oscar night who the winners were going to be. A month before the Awards, reporters began calling Academy members at home, managing to pry some information out of them. The *Journal's* news hounds found that older, not-so-active Academy members were particularly forthcoming with information and that many not only didn't want the reporters to hang up, but were willing to discourse upon a wide range of topics. As soon as the Academy hierarchy got wind of things, it swung into action. President Bob Rehme wrote a letter to the membership, warning that "someone claiming to be a journalist has been attempting to poll a wide cross-section of Academy members. . . . For what it's worth, the publication she claims to represent is disavowing any knowledge of this project." Suggesting that, "I think you'll agree that it's more fun for everybody if our voting results aren't announced until Oscar night," the Academy president said, "This seemed like a good time to remind all members that our policy is not to chat with the press about how we intend to fill out our ballots."

Despite Rehme's gentle admonition, some members continued to respond to reporters, so two weeks later the president sent out another missive, stating, "Although its west coast office originally disclaimed (perhaps legitimately) any knowledge of the project, the *Wall Street Journal* in fact recently made the most concerted attempt in history to predetermine the outcome of our awards." The president did declare happily that "most of us recognized the threat to the Academy Awards process and quite properly declined to provide data for the poll." But, "on the other hand, if just a few hundred of us were inveigled into participating, the *Journal* stands a good chance of scooping us before Oscar Night. That would be unfortunate in the extreme, of course, but I'm confident that this year's assault on our privacy will at least sensitize all members to the reality of the danger, and guarantee that any entity attempting to conduct a similar poll in the future will encounter nothing but stony silence." Meanwhile, Academy Executive Director Bruce Davis was proud of the cunning shown by some members who had been contacted because they "said they deliberately gave misleading information." Davis conceded that "As long as you don't do anything deceptive, it's probably legal . . . [but] it's not in our interest to cooperate, and we're sure most of the members did not." According to the *New York Post*, the state of Oscar campaigning had gotten to the point where industry-ites had been saying that either Miramax or DreamWorks must have been in some way connected with this telephone poll, although no one could pinpoint to what purpose.

The Paper Chase

Next problem: Two weeks before they were due, Army Archerd reported, "A search for missing Academy Awards ballot papers has gone into high gear as Academy of Motion Picture Arts & Sciences executives concluded that 4,000 Oscar ballots—or four-fifths of the voting total—hadn't been received by voters, five days after they were delivered to the post office. Academy public relations director John Pavlik said the U.S. Postal Service had not yet found the ballots even though the Academy had 'lit a fire' under them." That something was awry had first come to the Academy's attention a few days earlier when guests at the Scientific and Technical Awards dinner inquired why they hadn't received their ballots. The ballots that had been sent out earlier to out-of-state and international members reached their destinations, it was the 4,000 ballots going to local destinations—ten bags' worth of mail sent off from the Beverly Hills post office—that were MIA. Archerd reported, "Pavlik said he understands how this could happen—because he once worked at the post office."

After giving the postal service another day to do right by it, the Academy sent out 4,200 replacement ballots. Archerd said, "The Post Office told me the new ballots will positively be delivered today to Acad members. Acad and PricewaterhouseCoopers staffs were busy until late Tuesday night stuffing (and supervising) the replacement ballots in new, yellow envelopes. An enclosed letter warns members not to use the original envelope, should they receive it in the mail. 'If the Academy gets back (ballots in) white envelopes, they will be destroyed,' warned Acad PR director John Pavlik." Archerd also detailed how the snafu had occurred in the first place: "The Postal Service's Terri Bouffiou claimed the Academy brought in the ballots in gray sacks, 'traditionally for bulk mail, so we processed it as such and the sacks were sent to the L.A. Processing Center.' " The post office graciously told the Academy that it would bear the cost of mailing the replacement ballots, and the Academy ended up extending the voting deadline by two days, giving PricewaterhouseCoopers only three days to tally the votes. The extension provided a nice little windfall for the trade papers because it meant two more days' worth of campaign ads.

Willie and the Gold Boys

The Academy's travails weren't over, though. On March 10, just over two weeks before the ceremony, fifty-five Oscar statuettes were stolen from a Roadway Express loading dock in the city of Bell, California, as they were making their way to Los Angeles. (By coincidence, Bell was also where the missing ballots had turned up in a corner of a bulk mail facility.) The trucking company immediately put up a $50,000 reward for the safe return of this precious cargo. Back in Chicago, R. S. Owens & Company was working on an intense overtime schedule to create thirty-five replacements, as the Academy did have twenty extra Oscars hanging around. At a news conference, Executive Director Bruce Davis said the new statuettes would be flown in rather than trucked, but wouldn't say when, explaining, "We're going to be a little coy about that just in case there's an Oscar gang out there." Davis was keeping his sense of humor and he said, referring to the *Wall Street Journal*, the lost ballots, and the stolen Oscars, "Three weeks ago we were kind of tiptoeing around saying, 'Things are going awfully smooth. Something's going to happen.' It's been a strange year." When a reporter suggested that the robbery was a hoax intended to bring attention to the Awards, Davis insisted, "It is not a publicity stunt. There isn't much of a dearth of Academy publicity this time of year."

On the Sunday prior to the Awards, fifty-two of the fifty-five Oscars were discovered next to some trash bins behind the Food-4-Less grocery store on Western Avenue in L.A.'s Koreatown section. The man coming across the booty was sixty-one-year-old Willie Fulgear, who declared, "I've got more Oscars than any of the movie stars." Fulgear, who was in the salvaging and recycling game, said that he climbed into a dumpster and saw a shiny gold object—an Oscar. Digging deeper into the bin and checking out the immediate surrounding area, he found fifty-one more statuettes, most of which were in their original packaging, wrapped in plastic and padded with Styrofoam in boxes. The Associated Press set the scene of the crime: "The bins were in a parking lot with a tall wrought iron fence topped with razor wire. The L-shaped lot served a coin-operated laundry, smog-check station and grocery store. It wasn't clear when the trash bins were last emptied." Fulgear hadn't been aware that the Oscars had been hijacked, but his son called the police to let them know his dad had them.

Two employees at the Roadway Express dock in Bell were charged with the theft and would have to miss the Oscar telecast because they'd be in jail in lieu of posting $100,000 bail. "They did it for profit. They thought they could make money," explained police Detective Marc Zavalla. Fulgear said, "I had no idea how many I had. I just knew that if I didn't get them, somebody else would," and revealed he'd use the reward money to help his son put a down-payment on a house. The hero not only copped the fifty grand, he was also given two tickets to the ceremony by a grateful Academy, as well as transportation and a tuxedo. As *Daily Variety* put it, "That's Hollywood for you: One minute you're rummaging around in a garbage bin, and the next minute you're invited to the Oscars." But Fulgear balked when he heard the Academy was only springing for a town car, so *Access Hollywood* provided him with a stretch limo. His escort for the Oscars would be his proud son, Allen, who said, "My dad has always been a silent hero, the one that nobody ever talks about. I think the good guy finally wins here." Fulgear said he was especially hoping to meet Denzel Washington and Billy Crystal, and during the news conference at which he was given his reward, declared, "If anybody says honesty doesn't pay, send them to me. Honesty just paid me $50,000." At first, Fulgear wouldn't hear of it when police Commander David Kalish called him a hero. "I didn't save anybody's life," Fulgear said, thought for a second, and amended his statement, "But wait, yes I did—Oscar's."

Down the Stretch

As Oscar night approached, it seemed that *American Beauty* had opened up a commanding lead. The SAG awards were just one of several omens indicating that the idea of a *Cider House* upset wasn't catching on. Like *Saving Private Ryan*, this year's DreamWorks entry had won the Directors Guild and Producers Guild Awards. Unlike *Saving Private Ryan*, *American Beauty* also received the Writers Guild Award for Original Screenplay. At the same time, the Writers Guild Adapted Screenplay Award went not to Miramax's *The Cider House Rules* but, in an upset, Paramount's little-seen springtime release, *Election*.

Kenneth Turan analyzed that, "For a while, it looked promising for the adaptation of the John Irving

novel, which surprised many people with its seven nominations. But though *Cider House* has closed the gap
considerably and turned a rout into a horse race, it's not
as universally admired a film as *Shakespeare* was, and
DreamWorks has fought back effectively for its candidate. And while last year's winner built momentum
right through the final day, *Cider House* feels like it's already peaked." Peter Keough of the *Boston Phoenix* analyzed, "The Miramax machine tried its best, and indeed
that may be the problem: after a decade of domination
by the pushy pseudo-independent studio, perhaps
Hollywood has decided to start off the new millennium
fresh." Citing the Guild awards won by *American
Beauty*, David Ansen wrote in *Newsweek*, "The Oscar
race itself was supposed to be the nail-biter, the closest
race in years. The big shocker could be *American
Beauty*'s total dominance on Oscar night." He also said,
"How *The Cider House Rules* went from being a movie
no one was talking about to the only film given a chance
to upset the *Beauty* apple cart says a lot about the
Academy Award process. The Oscars, sadly, have become as much about campaigning as the national elec-
tions. The two perceived front-runners, *Beauty* and
Cider happen to be the two that have spent the most
money. Everyone in town concedes that Miramax is the
master of spin. This year it has succeeded in taking a
pro-choice, incest-tinged movie and positioning it via
soft-focus TV ads as the family-values movie of the season. Like George W. convincing folks that he's a 're-
former with results,' *Cider House* . . . is a crowd pleaser
in spite of the fact that it's almost impossible to say what
the movie is about." Ansen also got in one last dig at his
least favorite nominee: "As for that gas-bag populist *The
Green Mile*, it seems as out of place in this runoff as William Jennings Bryan."

DreamWorks's Terry Press said the *Cider House*
print ads had backfired: "I don't think anybody in the
end believed all those pictures of just orphans." The
ultimate reason that *The Cider House Rules* seemed not
to be pulling a *Shakespeare in Love*, though, was that
DreamWorks was playing hardball. Jeffrey Katzenberg
said, "Harvey skunked us last year." Still, he described
Weinstein as a "buddy," and said that just as in the
Democratic primary campaign where, "Bill Bradley
made Al Gore a better candidate," Miramax had

pushed DreamWorks to a higher level of campaigning.
This meant taking a page from Miramax's strategy
book and bringing in outside p.r. consultants—one of
whom was the formidable Dale Olsen—to come up
with a specialized strategy. They convinced Dream-
Works to produce a "Making of . . ." documentary
about *American Beauty* to run on local cable—something Miramax had been doing for years. Displays focusing on *American Beauty* were put up in bookstore
windows so that thoughts of the movie might dance in
the heads of more literary-minded voters, as well as
those who might just be passing a bookstore in the
mall on their way to get a frozen yogurt at TCBY.

One of the consultants, Bruce Feldman, went
with screenwriter Alan Ball to an Anthony Hopkins
tribute at the Santa Barbara Film Festival. The *Los Angeles Times* talked to Feldman about the event. " 'Alan
was invited to be on a panel. I took him up the night
before to go to the tribute, got him seated in the front
with all the board members, then took him to a private
dinner [for Hopkins] at Citronella, where for two
hours it was, "This is Alan Ball from *American
Beauty*," ' Feldman said, estimating that thirty to forty
academy voters reside in Santa Barbara, and that several of those were at the tribute. 'Look, if you show up
at a dinner, it doesn't make anybody vote for the guy.
But it's human nature to be influenced by personal
contact. We figured five, ten or twenty-five votes could
make a difference. Who's to say that it wouldn't?' "
The stunt that had Miramax crying foul, though, was
that on the same day that Academy voters were expected to receive their ballots, DreamWorks had faxed
many of them invitations to a large-scale fundraising
party that President Clinton and Vice President Gore
would be attending, thus subliminally tying Democratic politics to supporting *American Beauty*. Let us
not forget that DreamWorks's head of marketing,
Terry Press, had earlier said about the studio's campaign strategy, "We'll have a presence, but a restrained
and tasteful presence." And also, "It's distasteful to me
to turn the Academy Awards into a marketing derby."

People were amazed at the level of campaigning
Annette Bening was doing in her very enceinte condition. Her newest film, the Mike Nichols–Gary Shandling vehicle, *What Planet Are You From?* was released

during the voting season, so Bening had an excuse to be on talk shows without coming across as too crassly Oscar-hungry. Peter Travers said, "Annette Bening is playing that pregnant thing so much all during this point and I think they're loving her being pregnant and being married to Warren Beatty. So she will win." The combination of Kevin Spacey's SAG award and the continuing assault on *The Hurricane* had also turned the tide to at least a point where Denzel Washington, who had once seemed a prohibitive favorite was now in a toss-up situation with the *American Beauty* actor. *American Beauty* also added a sympathy element into the mix—it was revealed that Steven Spielberg had undergone an operation to remove a kidney.

The Washington Post relayed one person's thoughts: " 'I have never thought that our real competition was *Cider House Rules*,' says one DreamWorks executive, somewhat disingenuously. 'I think the very fact that Harvey got the movie multi-nominated is amazing. But the real competition as far as I am concerned has always been *The Sixth Sense*.' " When Miramax West Coast head, Mark Gill, heard this, he snorted, "That makes her the only person in Hollywood who thinks that. Wishful thinking doesn't make it so."

Disney, in fact, was getting not so much failing marks on its campaigns for its two Best Picture nominees, as a grade of "Absent." *The Sixth Sense* had been given very little financial support for its Oscar run because an Academy Award would not bring in any kind of windfall to the studio; the film had already racked up a fortune and it didn't have much more life left in theaters—it would be released on video and DVD two days after the Awards. Former studio chairman Joe Roth admitted, "Of course it's a disappointment" that Disney was negligent in promoting *The Insider* for the Oscars, but between Michael Eisner's dislike of the film, Roth's departure and the film's underachieving box-office performance, the campaign for *The Insider* was at best perfunctory. For conspiracy enthusiasts, a rumor was making the rounds that Harvey Weinstein convinced Eisner not to spend money on the two Disney films, because doing so would hurt a movie from Miramax, which, after all, was a Disney subsidiary. *The Washington Post* said, "Disney seems to have con-ceded the whole Academy Awards contest in advance; the studio isn't even planning a post-Oscars party, telling a reporter that it already had a party for the Golden Globes."

Capitalist Tools

Two days before the ceremony, the *Wall Street Journal* revealed the results of its poll. The paper stated that the bottom line reason for the survey was, "in an election year, with everyone being bombarded by polls anyway, we figured: Why not?" The *Journal* covered itself for possible mistakes by stating that of the 5,607 members of the Academy "precisely 356 of them agreed to reveal at least one of their choices. That's over 6 percent—a respectable sampling, but by no means a scientific one." The results of the poll were: *American Beauty* for Best Picture, in front of *The Cider House Rules* by fifty-two votes, or sixteen percent. Best Actor was the closest race, with Denzel Washington twenty-two votes ahead of Kevin Spacey, while Hilary Swank won almost two to one over Annette Bening. In the Supporting categories, Michael Caine led Haley Joel Osment, and Angelina Jolie had a comfortable lead over Chlöe Sevigny. Sam Mendes was well ahead of Lasse Hallström. Amy Stevens, entertainment editor of the *Weekend Journal*, insisted that the paper was not trying to destroy the Academy Awards as we know them. "This was journalism, a series of interviews and an evaluation of what they told us," she said. "We did not steal the Oscars or the nominations."

Bob Rehme told CNN, "I'm very distressed by what the *Wall Street Journal* did . . . It's like going to a big sports event and having them tell you the score before it starts." At a press conference addressing the *Journal*'s article, the Academy's Bruce Davis said that while trying to predict the winner was a time-honored and integral part of the whole Oscar process, actively working to ascertain the winners was going too far. "We clearly don't like this. They are trying to take the fun out of this." Getting metaphorical, he also said, "There's always a kind of geek in real life that we're all familiar with who goes to the movie early and then comes running up and says, You've got to see this movie. The kid says 'I see dead people.' I think right now the *Wall Street Journal* is beginning to sense that they have done a geeky thing in the journalism world."

When the *Journal*'s Stevens heard that her paper had been likened to a "geek," she shrugged, "I imagine we've been called worse." The Associated Press quoted Joe Saltzman, a journalism professor at the University of Southern California: "The Academy should maybe open its eyes and realize the Oscars aren't that important to everyone in the world. It's just the bloody Oscars, for heaven's sake." Another editor at the *Journal*, Joanne Lipman, argued that the poll made the Awards "so much more fun because it shed so much light on the process and the thinking that goes into the people's choices." Indeed, perhaps more damaging to the Academy's reputation than the listing of predicted winners—which were essentially the same as those of most Oscar prognosticators—were the quotes from some people who had spoken to the paper, for they revealed what kind of deliberations went into filling out an Oscar ballot. Old-time comedian Buddy Hackett was giving his Supporting Actor vote to Michael Caine and said he wouldn't vote for Haley Joel Osment because, "In another five years, he'll have pimples, and no one will want to talk to him." Seventy-five-year-old character actor Norman Alden—who was particularly memorable in 1977's *I Never Promised You a Rose Garden* (a sort of Jimmy Carter-era version of *Girl, Interrupted*)—said he would never vote for *American Beauty* because, "I don't care about bad marriages and fooling around and all these crazy things."

A Peek into the Future

The *USA Today* Oscar predictions article began with, "Missing ballots. Purloined statues. Sneaky journalists prying into information out of unsuspecting Academy members. So many mysteries have unfolded in the weeks leading to Sunday's ceremony, it's almost anticlimactic to try to solve what usually is the biggest question of the night: Who will take home the Oscar?" Almost all Oscar watchers agreed that *American Beauty* would win Best Picture, although not everyone was happy about it. Wesley Morris of the *San Francisco Examiner* said that he himself would vote for *American Beauty*, "Only if I'd never been to the suburbs and had

never read a John Updike or Philip Roth novel." Then he made his prediction: "Will win: *American Beauty*. ('John or Philip who?')." Mark Steyn of the *Spectator* of London pointed out that *American Beauty* is "a compendium of clichés from a thousand other films. It's narrated by a corpse—like William Holden in *Sunset Boulevard*. The guy salivates over a nymphet—like James Mason in *Lolita*. There's a bit of *sex, lies, & videotape*, a soupçon of *Reflections in a Golden Eye*. At this year's ceremony, *American Beauty* could be the first Oscar winner that's indistinguishable from the montage salute to Hollywood greats."

Jack Mathews felt Hilary Swank would win because he imagined "other actors (who represent more than half of the Academy) saying to themselves, 'My God, I could not do that.' " But, he acknowledged, "you cannot ignore Annette Bening's popularity, and the sentimental prospect of her having her fourth baby and receiving her first Oscar at the same time." *USA Today*'s Mike Clark said, "Six weeks ago, I would have said Swank. But *Boys Don't Cry* is even less of an 'Academy' movie than *American Beauty* is and just enough voters might like the symmetry of seeing Bening get an Oscar the same night as husband Warren Beatty gets the Irving G. Thalberg Award. I pick Bening—without confidence."

In the Best Actor contest, predictions were evenly divided between Denzel Washington and Kevin Spacey. John Hartl of the *Seattle Times* thought, it would be Washington, "By the slimmest of margins." Kenneth Turan ruminated, "What a difference a few weeks make. The night before nominations were announced, Denzel Washington's performance in *The Hurricane* seemed a sure thing not only for a nomination but for the actual Award as well. Washington got his nod; but surprisingly it was the only one his unlucky film, trapped in a tempest-in-a-teapot controversy over its accuracy, received. Without broad-based support in several branches, it's difficult to win a major award. While Washington was losing momentum, *American Beauty*'s impressive Kevin Spacey was gaining support. Spacey won the Screen Actors Guild Award, and while Washington could still take the Oscar, that is looking less and less likely." *Entertainment Weekly* felt that "With Washington's buzz fading fast,

Spacey looks to repeat—but watch out for Crowe." *USA Today*'s Susan Wloszczyna still felt, "No one would feel bad if either Farnsworth or Spacey walked away with the little man. But how can the Academy ignore the chance to honor a deserving black lead actor for the first time since Sidney Poitier's barrier-breaking win for 1963's *Lilies of the Field*? Washington will come out the champ." Barry Koltnow of the *Orange County Register* believed that one thing Washington did have going for him was that "he should have gotten the Oscar for *Malcolm X*."

Glenn Whipp of the *Los Angeles Daily News* spoke for the majority when he said, "Angelina Jolie has a flamboyant role and an outsized personality that voters seem drawn to. (Just ask the Hollywood Foreign Press Association, which has given her three Golden Globes.) Factor in Jolie's lineage (she's Jon Voight's daughter) and her SAG win and you have a pretty convincing case in her favor." Mike Clark was one of the few not to predict Jolie; his Supporting Actress choice was Toni Collette. He reasoned, "I think people are weary of Jolie's squirrelly off-screen personality." Clark's colleague at *USA Today*, Susan Wloszczyna said, "All will be *très* Jolie—unless voters are frightened off by tales of her real-life wild behavior." (The actress was always happily forthcoming with the press about her encounters with sado-masochism and bisexuality.)

Most up in the air was the Supporting Actor contest. As Henry Sheehan of the *Orange County Register* analyzed the situation, "Tom Hanks may get more respect and Jack Nicholson more affection, but when it comes to sheer pizzazz, Tom Cruise is the biggest star in Hollywood. And while Cruise has generated hundreds of millions at the box office, won critical plaudits and respect from his peers, he doesn't have a nice little statuette to put on the mantle. And like every other big star, he really, really wants one. His portrayal of a nasty infomercial huckster in *Magnolia*, while hardly his best work, is a classic bit of Oscar bait and should make Cruise a favorite. But wait—who is that? Why, it's good old Michael Caine sporting a New England accent and a misty smile in underdog *The Cider House Rules*. And who is that hiding behind him but little Haley Joel Osment from *The Sixth Sense*, just the sort to warm the cockles of the elder Academy voters'

hearts. That dynamic makes this one of the most fraught moments of the evening."

James Verniere of the *Boston Herald* thought the eleven-year-old would prevail, "for his spine-tingling performance in *The Sixth Sense*, which is fine with me since without this kid, there would have been no movie." *Entertainment Weekly* agreed, saying, "the winner is . . . scarcely tall enough to see over the podium. (No that's not a Tom Cruise joke.)" David Sterritt of the *Christian Science Monitor* thought it would be Tom Cruise's night because his performance was "the kind of acting that the Academy really likes: It's really over the top. There's nothing subtle about it." The *Village Voice*'s Michael Musto also predicted Cruise "for a heavy-handed turn in a rotten movie's most nonsensical role . . . he's a favorite for 'guts,' premature lifetime achievement, and his own pudendum expansion. (All right, who wants to tell the kid from *The Sixth Sense* that it's all over? Boys do cry.)" Peter Keough wrote in the *Boston Phoenix*, "SAG winner Michael Caine as the ether-addicted abortionist in *The Cider House Rules* will allow the Academy to cast its timid pro-choice vote. Michael Clarke Duncan's black idiot saint in *The Green Mile* would be a candidate for a racial consolation prize except that the role makes Hattie MacDaniel's Mammy from *Gone with the Wind* look visionary." Appearing on CNN's *He Said/She Said*, Lisa Schwarzbaum said, "Jude Law would win everything from me . . . He rocks my world!"

Last Words

Michael Clarke Duncan told Marilyn Beck and Stacy Jenel Smith he was sure *The Green Mile* "will go down as a cinematic masterpiece no matter what awards it does or doesn't win." *American Beauty*'s Dan Jinks was asked if he and coproducer Bruce Cohen would pull a Cameron if they won and declare themselves "Kings of the World!" "Oh, that would so never come out of our mouths," he said. Someone pointed out to Michael Caine that he might have to witness a little boy crying if Haley Joel Osment didn't win. Laughed Caine, "I'll cry if *I* don't win."

Hilary Swank talked about the perks that come along with being an Oscar nominee. "Let me tell you, the things that are left on my doorstep as little gifts," she said. "My closet is the most beautiful girl's dream— you have no idea. Sweaters. Shoes. Purses. It's amazing. And I love clothes. I love shoes." Toni Collette said, "It's very strange to think that people I know have been involved with the Oscars and it's even stranger that I'm involved." She said that for her, the Oscars had always entailed being with her family in Sydney for a "lazy evening around the television speculating about American culture." When Jay Leno asked Angelina Jolie about the prospect of being interviewed by Joan Rivers on Oscar Night, Jolie admitted, "I don't like to talk to her . . . I figure if she ever says anything about my brother, yeah, I'm gonna have it out with her."

Meanwhile, Harvey Weinstein phoned Jeffrey Katzenberg a week before the ceremony to concede. Katzenberg revealed, "He said he called to say, 'Congratulations. You saw the playbook and outplayed us.'" The Miramax chief also wanted to know, "What's your Oscar movie for next year?"

One of Miramax's stars from last year, Roberto Benigni would be returning to Hollywood for the Awards. Ruthe Stein of the *San Francisco Chronicle* wrote, "many in Hollywood hope the effervescent Italian will stick a sock in it while presenting the Best Actress Oscar and not upstage the winner. His impossibly fractured English got to be too much for a lot of people last year, sparking a rumor that when there's no mike in sight, Benigni speaks the Queen's English."

"Blame Canada"'s Marc Shaiman finally came up with someone to perform the song. He suggested Robin Williams, who happily accepted. "We thought he could pull it off and he would get it, and not cheese it up too much," explained cowriter Trey Parker. "It was either that or go the other route and have, like, Jewel do it acoustically."

On the Friday before the Oscars, Army Archerd revealed, "The Top Five Rejected Billy Crystal Entrances at the Oscars Sunday":

5. Billy comes out on a lawnmower with Richard Farnsworth, who drops Billy off and drives himself to his seat at the Shrine.

4. Billy comes out in an electric (execution) chair. The *Sports Illustrated* swimsuit models enter to wet his sponge.

3. Tony Clifton stumbles out and reveals himself to be John Malkovich, who is Being Billy Crystal.

2. Billy enters from the back of the house and climbs over seats to get to the stage, babbling effusively in Italian all the while.

And No. 1: A giant garbage bin comes out and cracks open, spilling out Billy, fifty-five Oscars, Debbie Allen and a dance number. . . . So now, head writer Bruce Vilanch goes back to his drawing board.

The Big Night

The LAPD put the kibosh on one of the enduring traditions leading up to Oscar Night. Several days prior to the Awards, cops gave about thirty fans who were camped out around the corner from the Shrine less than an hour to pack up; the officers said that students from a nearby school needed the sidewalk for access to their buses. In the words of bleacher fan Lola Lopp from Riverside County, "We were scrambling like cockroaches when the light goes on." At the front of the line of the time, like clockwork, had been Sandi Stratton and Babe Churchill. In three decades, "we've never been kicked out before," Sandi said, and the two of then had to pack up their inflatable couch, folding chairs, tent, and food supplies and head off to a motel. The *Orange County Register* told its readers that "Sandi's gall bladder surgery went fine, and her daughter will be married next month," and noted that "The women have been interviewed by television crews from Thailand to Toronto. A French woman who saw them on TV back home was so intrigued she flew across the ocean this year and is camping out behind them." Another bleacher regular, Marge DiNovi, who had become friends with the sisters over the years said, "I have a porcelain doll who doesn't have skin as beautiful as Annette Bening."

The Academy proved itself to be a good egg by issuing tickets to ensure that the people who had been forced to disperse would be the first ones admitted when access to the bleachers was finally allowed. A spokesperson for the Academy rued the police action, saying that it was something the officers decided to do on their own. A dueling mouthpiece for the LAPD said the officers were merely enforcing the law because neighborhood folks had complained about their sidewalks being blocked. He spoke with disdain about the Academy: "They're trying to say we're the heavies in this. No way. They are just so weird. They don't want any bad publicity . . . like no one is going to watch the Oscars because they moved people."

Bad publicity did come about anyway, because for the second year, the Academy was hogging the final half-hour before the ceremony—crush time in terms of arriving celebrities—for its own preshow. Forced to

---

Awards Ceremony

MARCH 26, 2000, 5:30 P.M.
THE SHRINE AUDITORIUM, LOS ANGELES

Your Host:
BILLY CRYSTAL
TELEVISED OVER ABC

Presenters

Costume Design	Drew Barrymore, Cameron Diaz and Lucy Liu
Sound	Heather Graham and Mike Myers
Makeup	Erykah Badu and Tobey Maguire
Supporting Actress	James Coburn
Live Action Short Films	Cate Blanchett and Jude Law
Animated Short Film	Jessie, Buzz Lightyear and Woody
Song	Cher
Documentary Short Subject	Wes Bentley, Thora Birch and Mena Suvari
Documentary Feature	Ethan Hawke and Uma Thurman
Supporting Actor	Judi Dench
Honorary Award to Andrzej Wajda	Jane Fonda
Sound Effects Editing	Chow Yun-Fat
Scientific and Technical Awards	Salma Hayek
Visual Effects	Arnold Schwarzenegger
Foreign Film	Antonio Banderas and Penelope Cruz
Original Score	Keanu Reeves and Charlize Theron
Art Direction	Russell Crowe and Julianne Moore
Editing	Tommy Lee Jones and Ashley Judd
Irving G. Thalberg Award	Jack Nicholson
Cinematography	Brad Pitt
Adapted Screenplay	Kevin Spacey
Original Screenplay	Mel Gibson
Actress	Roberto Benigni
Actor	Gwyneth Paltrow
Director	Steven Spielberg
Picture	Clint Eastwood

Performers of Nominated Songs

"*Blame Canada*"	Robin Williams
"*Music of My Heart*"	Gloria Estefan and 'N Sync
"*Save Me*"	Aimee Mann
"*When She Loved Me*"	Sarah McLachlan and Randy Newman
"*You'll Be in My Heart*"	Phil Collins

begin early, the other programs had to rely on filler material during the first hour of their broadcasts. Joan Rivers kicked things off on E! with a taped segment in which she dumped out the contents of her pocketbook while looking for i.d. so she could get her press credentials. Among the items in her bag were a box of Tampax ("I don't need these anymore"), two rubber chickens, and a vibrator ("for my neck"). Once she was live from the red carpet—with a picture of "Chucky" from the *Child's Play* movies around her neck as her supposed press identification picture—Rivers announced, "In exactly one hour and fifty-nine minutes from now, in every gay bar all over America, you're gonna hear the same words: 'Shhh! Stop it, bitch. It's starting.'" She also said, "Dr. Laura, of course, is here to support *The Straight Story*," a reference to the gay-hating radio talk show host who was trying to make it on television despite an unappealing personality and the opposition of good people everywhere. "Monica Lewinsky is here pushing her new toy line, the 'Monica Gives Good Mr. Potato Head' toys," but, "O. J. Simpson is not going to be here tonight. He's out looking for the real thieves of the Oscars." Libby Callaway of the *New York Post* critiqued that "Joan's Oscar night look was as impeccable as her pre-show red carpet commentary was vulgar. The night's most feared woman was dressed by her friend Vera Wang in a gorgeous pale lilac off-the-shoulder tulle gown studded with milky crystals."

Rick Lyman of the *New York Times* observed that "a bright red banner was strung across the front of the Shrine Auditorium as though announcing some kind of Stalinist reunion." *Access Hollywood* printed up signs with one word directions and questions: "Wave," "Spin," "Jewels?" and "Designers?" The reason, explained a segment producer, was "Last year we got hoarse screaming out the questions. This year we'll just hold up these." Unfortunately, because they had the *Access Hollywood* logo on it, the signs were not allowed. Companies paid good money to the Academy to have their corporate names prominently displayed around the forecourt and the kind of signage *Access Hollywood* was trying to display "would cost you a couple million," explained somebody from the Academy. Fifteen minutes had passed without a single star showing up,

so Joan Rivers lamented about the forecourt situation: "There's nobody here but a lot of dopey people looking for other people." She then apologized for being "in such a rotten mood. If I seem snippy and snappy tonight, it's just that I haven't had sex in six months. I lost the vacuum cleaner attachments."

The first celebrity to arrive was Garcelle Beauvais, from *The Jamie Foxx Show*, followed by 1970s icon Karen Black. Rivers greeted Black by saying "I haven't seen you in a while. We go back forever together. You look terrific." Cindy Adams of the *New York Post* maintained that Black's "bosom puffed out like an omelet and must've been corseted from her ankles up." Comedian D. L. Hughley was covering the forecourt proceedings for the *Los Angeles Times* and said, "I saw Joan Rivers and Joan Rivers's daughter. I don't know her name but I know her job is being Joan Rivers's daughter. They were commenting on the dresses. I saw a couple of actresses (who shall remain nameless) spot Joan and then walk the other way, with a look of terror on their faces."

On KTLA, the home base for the WB network's broadcast, fashion critic Laurie Pike was disappointed in the first nominee who showed up. "I was dying to see what Chlöe Sevigny was going to wear," she said, "and she's shown up in a fairly simple black dress. I mean with a *huge* amount of diamonds around her neck. She came with her boyfriend, Harmony Korine, and his hair's all messy but otherwise he's just in a tux. So it's kind of interesting that she came out and actually said, 'I'm not into Badgley Mischka, I'm not into the beaded dresses, I'm not into Pamela Dennis.' So I thought she'd wear something really, like European and progressive, and she's got on kind of a simple black dress." The belted, halter V-necked dress was by Yves St. Laurent and the thing that Pike didn't realize is that even though Sevigny was a mainstay of independent films, she was also from Darien, Connecticut, and simple good taste goes hand-in-hand with Fairfield County. Sevigny told Joan Rivers, "I just really want to go home and be with my friends in New York." A little later Sevigny's *Boys Don't Cry* director Kimberly Pierce arrived and revealed to KTLA's on-site hosts Sam Rubin and Mindy Burbano that Chlöe had originally wanted to play Brandon in *Boys Don't*

Cry, but Pierce had come right out and told her, "You can't pass for a boy." Pierce also elaborated to Joan Rivers how difficult it was to cast Hilary Swank's role, because "I looked at every butch lesbian and transsexual and they were great, but they couldn't pull off the role." Cindy Adams reported, "Kimberly Pierce, bare midriff. Her bellybutton's an innie."

Lucy Liu, one of the title roles in the upcoming *Charlie's Angels*, admitted to Rivers, "I was afraid to come over here actually." Liu was wearing a one-shoulder bright red Versace and she had nothing to fear from Joan, who commented after she left, "She is one great looking piece of rear end." In the *New York Observer*, Simon Doonan wrote, "Who's that with the green Christo-wrapped factory chimney on her head? It's Erykah Badu, and her Miriam Makeba–St. Patrick's Day creation is rocking the house. It's an Afrocentric couture fantasia constructed from patches of leprechaun-green leather held together with raffia crochet and it has the refreshing whiff of amateurism." Badu, the singer who had a featured role in *The Cider House Rules*, said of her Charlene Shepherd outfit, "it's divinely me." The "chimney" referred to by Doonan was one of Badu's signature high turbans, and woe to him who got stuck sitting behind her trying to see anything on stage. (It was Tommy Lee Jones who'd be in the unlucky seat, but Badu later revealed, "He didn't say anything. He was just chilling.") Laurie Pike, calling Badu a "style icon," joked that "usually her turbans are one foot. The Academy Awards: two feet."

Richard Farnsworth told Cindy Adams, "If I win, I'll put the Oscar on the mantel. I'll have to move a steerhead but it's okay, I don't mind." Haley Joel Osment, who began his day by going to Mass, was in a custom-made Hugo Boss, and told *Good Morning, America*'s Lara Spencer, "I've never had so much fun in my life." KTLA's Mindy Burbano asked the youngster, "Now you going to be doing *A.I.*, the Stanley Kubrick, is that right?" "Stanley . . . ?" responded a confused Haley. Sam Rubin clarified: "The Steven Spielberg movie." "Probably just rumors, right now," said the actor. "Haley's in negotiations," joked Rubin. After the boy had moved on, Rubin told the audience, "Let me tell you what Kevin Spacey told me. He said, that is not an eleven-year-old boy. That is a forty-five-year-old man pretending to be an eleven-year-old boy."

Michael Clarke Duncan wanted to make sure Joan Rivers knew that his watchband had a diamond-encrusted sculpture of "Mr. Jingles-the-Mouse" on it: "Look at there. Are we rockin' tonight or what, baby? . . . Anybody messes with you, they've got to mess with me." When his *Green Mile* director Frank Darabont arrived at the WB spot, Sam Rubin revealed that he and Darabont were roommates in college "and look what happened to me, and look what happened to him." *Access Hollywood* wondered how Darabont would feel if he won the Oscar but was given one that had been in the dumpster. "Hell, I'd climb into the dumpster after it if I had to." Asked about the *Wall Street Journal* article, President Rehme said, "I canceled my subscription. They should go back to Wall Street and leave Hollywood alone." When Laurie Pike saw Gloria Stuart in Carolina Herrera, she cheered "Total fogey chic rules!" Sarah McLachlan, who would be singing Randy Newman's nominated, "When She Loved Me," from *Toy Story 2*, was wearing a pink India-print sarong. Pike's take was that she's "usually kind of dowdy with that kind of Lillith Fair thing she has going on. I think she looks amazing."

Joan Rivers said, "Gwyneth, you look fabulous!" She was speaking to Matt Stone, the *South Park* cocreator who was wearing an homage to Paltrow's pink number from last year. One of *South Park: Bigger, Longer and Uncut*'s nominated songwriters Trey Parker was also in drag, dolled up in a green knockoff of Jennifer Lopez's notorious, wide-open Versace Grammy outfit. The other "Blame Canada" writer, Marc Shaiman was in a grotesque powder blue suit accessorized with a blue fedora and blue fur stole. Fashion critics couldn't decide if he was reworking Céline Dion's backwards tux from last year or whether he was going for a Sean "Puffy" Combs look to accompany Parker's Lopez. Rivers asked Parker, "Are your parents watching, I hope?" He replied, "My mom and dad are watching I think." "My mom was watching 'til right about now," said Stone. He also told CNN's Jim Moret, "It's just such a magical evening, and everyone looks so spectacular, we just wanted to be a part of it all." "It's a night of magic," agreed Parker. When

Variety asked him how he keeps it all in place, Parker replied, "I was just blessed with a beautiful body and it hangs perfectly. I don't use tape." According to the *Los Angeles Times*, "Some security personnel were reluctant to let the pair in, saying they would have to go home to change. But ultimately they were allowed in with their offbeat attire." Right behind this ebullient trio was everybody's least favorite Best Song nominee, Phil Collins—ironic given what Parker had said about him at the Luncheon. Collins told Rivers, "I had an interview with your daughter at the Grammys . . . she's a good girl." He had originally agreed to have a KTLA camera in his limousine with him as he drove to the show. But as correspondent Mark Kriski explained things, "This is Hollywood's biggest night, and you know when you're trying to arrange something, our people have to talk to Phil Collins's people, and then he's got people who talk to their people, and people talk to people with people and all of a sudden we ended up with twenty people in the car. So Phil decided, 'You know what, I'm gonna take another limo.' "

Mindy Burbano got a gander at Hilary Swank in her rust-colored, Rudolph Duke ball gown and commented that the *Boys Don't Cry* star was "looking all of the woman that she is." Burbano also noted that Kevin Spacey was "with an American Beauty right on his arm"—his date—"isn't she a beauty!" and complimented Richard Farnsworth on his "very nice cane." D. L. Hughley wrote, "Kevin Spacey came by. He's an extremely talented actor, but he is one scary dude. I think if he moved in next door, I'd put my house up for sale."

'N Sync was performing on the program, and by common consent the Boy Band caused the most feverish response from the bleacher fans. J. C. Chasez said of the group's being part of the Oscars, "It's overwhelming. It really is. I mean, this is the biggest event on television, uh, in the world." He added, "I'm looking forward to meeting Harrison Ford and maybe even hang out with somebody like Brad Pitt or somebody like that." Joey Fatone was happy because, "I just met Ashley Judd. That was nice. That was nice." And Lance Bass said, "I'd just like to see Julia Roberts but I don't think she's gonna be coming tonight." From a completely different musical vantage point than

'N Sync, Supporting Actress contender Samantha Morton was wearing a Sex Pistols' "God Save the Queen" T-shirt with her Paul Smith pantsuit.

Cindy Adams reported that "a fan in the stands yelled at me: 'You wore that same dress last year.' Shouted her companion: 'No. It was two years ago.' " Rivers asked Lasse Hallström what he thought about the twenty or so pro-life, anti-*Cider House Rules* protestors across the street. "We missed them all," he acknowledged. Joan assured him, "I wanted to open up the limo door and say just go to hell."

At 5 o'clock, ABC and the Academy took over with *Countdown to the Oscars 2000*. The program began with film clips from earlier Oscar shows, featuring shots of Danny Thomas, Lucille Ball and Desi Arnaz, Joan Crawford and Alfred Steele, Burt Reynolds and Dinah Shore, Rock Hudson and a beard, Eddie Fisher with Debbie Reynolds, Eddie Fisher with Elizabeth Taylor. The clips also juxtaposed different through-the-years images of Sharon Stone, Sophia Loren, Meryl Streep, and Jack Nicholson. The musical accompaniment to all this included Madonna's "Vogue" and Frank Sinatra's version of "The Way You Look Tonight." Meredith Vieira from the talk show *The View*, was the program's primary host, and she introduced herself by saying, "For the next twenty-seven or so minutes, watch me grovel shamelessly in front of the greatest stars in Hollywood." Chris Connelly from MTV was also on hand, and he had the first interview: Tom Cruise and Nicole Kidman in what would be their last Oscar appearance as husband-and-wife. The actress was looking bored in a shiny gold gown until Connelly gushed, "We have a first round knockout in the fashion department. Nicole, what a fantastic dress. How'd you choose it?" "A friend of mine who's a wonderful designer designed it for me," said Kidman. "He just happens to be one of the best designers in the world, so I just got lucky." The designer wasn't so fortunate, since Kidman never identified him by name. (It was John Galliano for Dior.) Cruise piped in with, "She's gorgeous." During the course of the show, trivia about the interviewees flashed on the bottom of the screen, such as "While filming *Moulin Rouge*, Nicole fractured her ribs . . . she's fine now."

The third interviewer on the program was model

Tyra Banks. Anyone who ever had voiced a single complaint about Joan Rivers or Sam Rubin should be forced to watch a nonstop loop of Banks's interviews as penance. When Cameron Diaz told her she was wearing Versace, Banks's reply was "Versace? This is amazing!" without ever following through on why that was particularly amazing. Meanwhile, the trivia on the bottom informed us that "Cameron's father Emilio Diaz had a small role in *There's Something About Mary*." When Banks was jawing with Ashley Judd, the trivia ticker let it be known that "Ashley's mom is Naomi Judd and her sister is Wynona Judd. They are *The Judds*." Tyra Banks's segue after learning that Ashley's gown was by Valentino, was "There were a lot of serious, really high impactful movies this year. Which one had the most impact on you?" *(The Insider.)*

Meredith Vieira described Kevin Spacey's date as "his lovely lady," and when he went on about the popular success of *American Beauty* being more important to him than winning an Oscar, Vieira rejoined, "You little liar." She also told Denzel Washington, "I love a nominee who says publicly, 'I want to win.'" "Oh, is that what I said?" replied Washington. For some reason, Chris Connelly said that this year's was "one of the most wide-open Best Actress races maybe of all time." Tyra Banks called Keanu Reeves "Mr. Fine. Mr. Sexy." (Did you know that Keanu was once the manager of a pasta shop in Toronto?) And she told Angelina Jolie, "Now, Miss Thing, you are amazing in this movie."

With show time approaching, Meredith Vieira headed toward the Shrine. On her way in, she passed some people with cigarettes and commented, "Oh my goodness. There are people from *The Insider* and they're smoking. Did they learn nothing from that movie?" Vieira was usually a sophisticated and charming television presence, but one winced as she entered the theater and gave a running commentary: "I am not in Kansas anymore. Oh, wow. See, you have to understand that as a little kid, I used to dream that I would be here one day and I'm here." While still in the back of the auditorium, she said "And I don't recognize anybody. I think these are the muckety-mucks here. Where are the stars?" She said hi to Charlize Theron from *The Cider House Rules* and, getting to the front

row, stopped to ask Tom Cruise about seating arrangements, told Clint Eastwood "I think you're in my seat," and then sat in his lap. With about thirty seconds to go, we were with Tyra Banks in the wings. To three women she passed, she said, "Look at the Trophy Girls! Say 'hi,' Trophy Girls!" and then she was high-fiving President Bob Rehme. Well, the preshow at least was as stilted as last year's . . .

The telecast began with a welcome from Peter Coyote, who was performing his announcing chores from a station just off stage right. Then, in his opening speech, Bob Rehme said, "Well, it's certainly been an interesting year, or at least an interesting last few weeks in which the focus in Hollywood shifted from who in the world's going to win the least predictable year in memory to what in the world are we going to present them with?" The president then introduced the night's first set of film clips by saying that a quarter of the movies that will be judged for next year's Oscars had already been seen, and "It's not too early to ask, what might we see in 2001." The initial scene was the monkey throwing a bone up in the air in the beginning of *2001: A Space Odyssey*. When the bone came down, it hit Billy Crystal—in the film—on the head, knocking him out. As a result, he started seeing bits and pieces from classic movies, and hearing such lines as Bette Davis's "Fasten your seatbelts . . ." wicked witch Margaret Hamilton's "I'll get you my pretty," Marlon Brando's "Stella!" and James Stewart's "Merry Christmas" from *It's a Wonderful Life*. Finally, Crystal found himself with Charlie Chaplin in the scene from *The Gold Rush* where Chaplin is cooking his shoe. In a subtitle, Crystal said, "I see dead people," and Chaplin told him, "I loved *Analyze This*," the host's comedy from a year earlier. *Taxi Driver*'s Travis Bickle, of course, wanted to know, "You talking to me?" and Crystal replied, "Al Pacino, I'd know you anywhere." Crystal was in drag as *The Graduate*'s Mrs. Robinson ("Baby, I'm in Anne Bancroft's clothes and digging it") and was seen "squealing like a pig" in *Deliverance*. As a Roman slave, Crystal said, "I am so not Spartacus," and pointed out Kirk Douglas; he was in what looked like the shower from the Bates Motel but which turned out to be Kevin Spacey's *American Beauty* shower; and he had the passenger seat when James Dean was playing chicken in *Rebel Without a Cause*. Ultimately, he landed in a New York City streetscape as one of the gangs from *West Side Story* showed up, singing, "The Jets ain't gonna get their chance tonight. They're telling us that we can't dance tonight." Cut to Crystal on a fire escape singing, "Tonight, tonight. There'll be no dancing tonight. And yet this show will run too long . . . Make this endless show end tonight!"

The filmed segment over, Crystal was carried out on stage by a cop and said, "I just wanted to make sure I got here. That's why I had the LAPD *plant* me here"—a little topical, local police corruption humor. Crystal editorialized, "All right, edgy. That's a speeding ticket for me." Truth to tell it was not nearly as good an opening as any of the discarded ones Army Archerd had written about. The host continued, "Welcome to the Oscars, or as ABC likes to call it, 'Regis's Night Off.'" Regis Philbin and wife Joy heard this *Who Wants to be a Millionaire* reference while watching the show from the *Vanity Fair* party at Morton's. Leading into his Best Picture medley, Crystal referred to *The Green Mile* as "The feel good death row movie of the year." To the tune of the theme from *Green Acres*, he sang "White lights, last rights. Sponge dry? You fry . . . Don't get me wrong. But it was a little bit long. Three hours, tell me why."

Before getting to the other nominees, Crystal stopped for a few jokes. Seeing Richard Farnsworth, he mentioned "*The Straight Story,* which is the story of Dr. Laura Schlesinger. Couldn't be here tonight— couldn't get anyone in town to do her hair and makeup." He said that Hilary Swank was "nominated in the new category, Best Performance by an Actress with a Supporting Part." Seeing the hero of the stolen Oscars story, Willie Fulgear, Crystal remarked, "Willie got $50,000 for finding the fifty-two Oscars. It's not a lot of money when you realize that Miramax and DreamWorks are spending millions of dollars just to get one." He noted that Haley Joel Osment was "eleven years old. I've had movies in development longer than that."

Returning to the medley, Crystal sang Barbra Streisand's anthem from *Funny Girl* for *The Sixth Sense.* "People. People who see dead people, are the spookiest people in the world. You're eleven, having chats with folks in heaven . . . you see things that aren't there, like Bruce Willis with hair." The lyrics about *The Insider* were sung to the "Minute Waltz." "I know everybody there thinks I'm a loony. They have got their nerve, they hired Andy Rooney . . . Watch this little whacko bring down big tobacco." There was a shot of a glum-looking Russell Crowe. *The Cider House Rules* song was all about Michael Caine and the music was "Mame": "He never met a script that he didn't like. Caine. . . . How many movies can one actor make? Caine. You'll make one in the next station break." This was a curiously dated reference because it was back in the '80s that the actor was a not-always-discriminating workaholic, his pace these days had slowed down considerably. Crystal got the audience to join in on the "Caine" refrain, and the actor later said, "I thought it was wonderful . . . I thought, this is the cream of Hollywood here singing my name. I thought, it's okay if I don't win. It's okay." Finally, *American Beauty* got "The Lady is a Tramp": "He just turned forty, but he digs a teen. Loves to shower, never gets clean."

Crystal addressed Jack Nicholson in the first row, and Nicholson chatted back. The host said, "Feel free to talk to me anytime, Big Daddy," and then predicted "It's a four-hour show." Crystal also noted, "Jack has three Oscars . . . which is no big deal, since so does some guy in Bell."

The first presenters were the stars of the upcoming *Charlie's Angels* movie: Drew Barrymore, Cameron Diaz, and Lucy Liu. A gushy Diaz said to the other two, "Don't we have the best job in the whole world, you girls? We're actresses. We get to go to work every day. We get to put on costumes. Tonight we get to put on gowns." The three of them then started sharing information about their outfits and Robert Dominguez of the *New York Daily News* described them as "giggling like schoolgirls at a pajama party." The winner of the Oscar for Best Costume Design was *Topsy-Turvy*; prior to this Gilbert and Sullivan film, a Mike Leigh movie winning Costume Design was about the last thing anyone could have imagined. One sign that this wasn't a Gilbert Cates show was that as winner Lindy Hemming came to the stage, the Burt Bacharach/Don Was ensemble was providing a techno-beat to accompany her—a far cry from Bill Conti gooeyness. "I'd like to thank all of you for giving our little film such a brilliant start," said the winner, and she then walked back into the audience rather than going backstage to meet the press, and none of the Angels stopped her. Another innovation by the Zanucks was that when Barrymore, Diaz, and Liu went offstage, the camera followed them into the wings as they walked past Peter Coyote, thus giving the home audience the feel of being right in the thick of operations.

A commercial break followed, including an ad for Charles Schwab, the discount broker, in which Sally Field parodied her "You like me" Oscar speech. And when the show returned, a saxophone in the orchestra was blaring jazz riffs. "Welcome back to the Academy Awards," said Billy Crystal, "where the races are tight and security isn't." He noted that "There's somebody walking around Bell, California, right now with three Oscars. Police describe him as armed and pretentious. They're still investigating but . . . I, for one, think that the answer lies in the world of Faye Resnick"—a nostalgic reference to the O. J. Simpson case. And the host also assured everyone that "If Roberto Benigni gets out of hand, I've got the stun gun." There was a cut to Benigni laughing too hard and clapping.

Introducing Haley Joel Osment, Crystal said, "He had the best idea of all. He said to me, backstage, he said, 'Uncle Bill, since now we have fifty-two extra statues, why don't you just make it like Little League where everyone gets a trophy?' " Crystal then referred to the lad as "a brilliant actor." Osment said, "I'm very excited to be here, and to look out on this beautiful and elegant crowd of people, and realize, you're all alive." He was here to introduce "Children in the Movies," a Gilbert Cates-esque montage of film clips, though at least, unlike in a Cates show, this one did have some relevance since there was a kid nominated for an Oscar. The participants ranged from Jackie Coogan in the 1920s to "Fuzzy the Orphan" (Erik Per Sullivan) from *The Cider House Rules*.

Mike Myers and his leading lady from *Austin Powers: The Spy Who Shagged Me*, Heather Graham, gave the Sound Award to *The Matrix*, and then Tobey Maguire and Erykah Badu announced that the Makeup Award was going not to *Austin Powers*, but

Topsy-Turvy. This was a surprising result because the Makeup in the film was essentially stage makeup—beards and mutton chops, and not the elaborate prosthetics that usually win in this category. It may have been simply that the Mike Leigh movie was a more reputable endeavor than the other nominees, which were comedies of varying degrees of rudeness and schmaltz (*Austin Powers*, *Bicentennial Man* and *Life*). Unlike previous shows where the presenters went to one podium or another on either stage left or right, this year the presentations were made in dead center, and recipients could make use of a set of stairs that led right up from the middle aisle. With a pulsating musical beat, and clublike lighting effects on the stage itself, it really was a whole new show.

Winona Ryder, who on past Oscar nights was noted for her flapper fashions, had moved ahead in time: her antique dress was a Pauline Trigère from the '40s. The *San Francisco Examiner*'s Cynthia Robins described the frock as "a stark vintage ball gown with spaghetti straps and a white-and-black satin evening wrap that emphasized her elegant carriage and pale beauty (her only gems were large diamond studs in her ears.)" Ryder introduced the clip from *The Cider House Rules* and, of course, the script had her referring to John Irving's novel as a "Dickensian fable." Ryder's boyfriend, Matt Damon, was watching the show at Ben Affleck's house, but he and Winona would rendezvous later at the *Vanity Fair* party. When Billy Crystal reappeared, he joked, "They searched Erykah Badu's hat and found one of the missing Oscars."

Best Supporting Actress presenter James Coburn sounded like he was having whatever the *Charlie's Angels* had had, when he giddily went on as to how "It's wonderful to work in a town with so many creative, talented, gorgeous, *sexy* women and I have that enviable job of getting close to one of them and presenting her with an Oscar." Another Zanuck novelty was having a bank of video monitors built into the top of the stage where, first, clips of the nominated performers were shown and then the nominees were seen for reaction shots. The winner was Angelina Jolie for *Girl, Interrupted*, and she immediately hugged her brother, who was sitting next to her. (He later said, "we locked heads," while she explained, "I was hiding in his shoulder.") Jolie's first comment on stage was, "God, I'm surprised nobody's ever fainted up here. I'm in shock, and I am so in love with my brother right now," a declaration that evoked laughter from the crowd. "He just held me and said he loved me, and I know he's so happy for me. Thank you for that." She also addressed the star and executive producer of *Girl, Interrupted*: "Winona, you're amazing," and praised "my mom, who's the most brave, beautiful woman I've ever known, and my dad, you're a great actor but you're a better father." Then Jon Voight's daughter was back to her brother, "And Jamie, I'd have nothing without you [there was a cut to him crying]. You are the strongest, most amazing man I've ever known, and I love you." And because the Zanucks had cameras backstage, the audience got to witness upcoming presenters Jude Law and Cate Blanchett hugging Jolie.

Billy Crystal said, "I would like to assure the American public that despite what the *Wall Street Journal* said, the results of our Awards are the best kept secret in America, with the possible exception of what George W. Bush did in the '70s." Morgan Freeman arrived to introduce another set of film clips, this one of rather dubious relevance: 200 Million Years of History as portrayed in the movies, which meant going from old cavemen movies to the fetus from *2001: A Space Odyssey*, with antiquity, the Bible, the Middle Ages, various wars, Isadora Duncan, *Sullivan's Travels*, and the Beatles thrown in. Chuck Workman was inconsistent in putting the montage together because while most of the clips were from movies that looked back on history, there were others from films that were dealing with contemporary events and qualify as historical only because the films themselves are now old (such as *Casablanca*, *Open City*, and *The Human Comedy*). *South Park* producer Matt Stone was livid about this segment, describing it as, "Hollywood representing itself with these movies as historical fact—when it's Hollywood movies that are the reason why American kids are so dumb in history. I was so offended. They show *The Birth of a Nation* or John Wayne movies and it's like Hollywood patting itself on the back for something it didn't deserve. It would have been different if they'd done it with the attitude of 'Look how dumb we were!' "

Cate Blanchett and Jude Law were the presenters of the Live Action Short Film Award. Law commented that the category, "contains the most interesting title of any film this year." Twice he could be heard saying "not that one," as Blanchett read the nominations for *Bror, Min Bror (Teis and Nico)* and *Kleingeld (Small Change)*, but said, "That's the one!" when she got to *My Mother Dreams the Satan's Disciples in New York*. That one was also the winner, and as the recipients made their way to the stage, Peter Coyote said that it was director Barbara Schock's "American Film Institute thesis film." Hannah Brown raved in the *New York Post* that Blanchett and Law were the evening's "Most Elegant Presenters," and that they "had the kind of understated, old-fashioned glamour and poise that makes kids dream about becoming actors."

The next bit of business was Billy Crystal and Michael Clarke Duncan carrying out two *Toy Story* dolls and the Rock 'Em, Sock 'Em Robots. Crystal said to Duncan, "I'm a big fan of yours. I saw *The Green Mile* three times. Which one were you?" He also made the enigmatic remark, "Standing next to me, we look like a semicolon." When Duncan touched the dolls, the stage lights flashed on and off and gave off sparks, just like in his movie. As they walked off, Duncan could be heard saying to Crystal, "What was that about?" Buzz Lightyear and Woody bantered a bit before making the presentation for Animated Short Film, so there was a cut to Mr. Potato Head in the audience, saying, through the voice of Don Rickles, "Hey, will you get on with it? Will you two dummies hurry it up. I wanna see the interpretive dance." His date, Mrs. Potato Head, yelled, "Stop it! You're embarrassing me in front of Don Rickles." Turned out, Woody and Buzz didn't have the envelope with them, so another character from the movie, Jessie, came out riding the horse, Bullseye, and announced that the winner was a cartoon version of Hemingway's *The Old Man and the Sea* from Russia. Announcer Coyote disbursed the information that director Alexander Petrov's "animation technique for this film involved painting each frame on glass plates with his fingers."

Citing the flashing lights on stage, Billy Crystal said, "I wanna thank *Soul Train* for lending us their floor." The Zanucks had decided to have all five songs performed within one segment. Randy Newman and Sarah McLachlan, along with a cellist, started with Newman's beautiful ballad, "When She Loved Me," from *Toy Story 2*. To keep things moving without interrupting the flow, the next group of musicians was already on stage adjacent to Newman and McLachlan, but they had been blocked by a panel, which now opened to reveal them. Aimee Mann, accompanied by three other guitarists, a keyboardist, and drummer, sang "Save Me" from *Magnolia*, which had been a hit on college and progressive radio stations. When Laurie Pike had glimpsed Mann entering the Shrine, she commented, "I thought Aimee Mann looked kind of cute. You know, a little casual for the Academy Awards but, you know, she's a singer. That's okay." Mann shared Trey Parker's opinion of Phil Collins, and had said she would boo if he won. He was up next, mewling in the same space where Newman and McLachlan had performed. The banality of his "You'll Be in My Heart" was emphasized by its being performed after the first two—altogether superior—nominees. On the same level as Collins's number, though, was the Diane Warren song, "Music of My Heart," performed listlessly by Gloria Estefan and 'N Sync. 'N Sync's Lance Bass admitted, "We were totally out of our element 'cause our fans weren't there like we're used to in the balcony." And finally, there was the troublesome "Blame Canada." Robin Williams appeared with masking tape over his mouth; ripping it off he gave one of *South Park*'s catch phrases, "Oh my God, they killed Kenny!" Williams was joined by a group of about two dozen people of various ages and sizes all dressed in bright cartoon colors. "Fart" and "that bitch Anne Murray" made it into the performance, but when it came time for "go fuck yourself" Williams turned his head away and didn't sing anything, but the rest of the ensemble gasped. This boisterous number did include dancing, including Williams and some Northwest Mountain Policewomen making like the Rockettes.

Cher tripped on the fishnet train of her outfit as she came out to present the Best Song Oscar. "Damn this dress," she said at the microphone. She then pulled up the offending garment and started finagling with it, telling the audience, "Don't pay any attention

to anything that's going on below my knees, okay?" Cynthia Robins laughed in the *San Francisco Examiner* that "After all those years of wearing dresses that required a degree in structural engineering to construct, it's amazing that her most conventional costume yet almost killed her." Cher said, "Alright, you probably noticed already that I am dressed like a grown-up. I wish to apologize to the Academy and I promise that I will never do it again." The crowd applauded her vow. The black velvet gown was, as usual, a Bob Mackie, it just wasn't the completely over-the-top fun frock generally associated with Bob Mackie. Still, Michael Musto wrote, "only Cher would think electrified seaweed hair and a jeweled cross hanging over her crotch are tasteful, which is why we love her to death." Actually, rather than Cher, it was Academy voters who should have been apologizing because the winner was, in the words of E! Online's Erik Pedersen, "that dweeb Phil Collins" for "You'll Be in My Heart." He and Randy Newman—now a thirteen-time nonrecipient—were together backstage, and Collins hugged him and got all choked up. Unfortunately, the two highly vocal anti-Collins nominees, Trey Parker and Aimee Mann were nowhere in sight. Somebody with no taste stood up in the audience—it was his wife. Onstage, Collins said, "Now my life can go on. It's been hell, I'll tell you." In the *Los Angeles Daily News*, David Kronke seethed that " 'Blame Canada' lost to whatever lame bit of kiddy self-empowerment Phil Collins slapped together."

The presenters of the Documentary Short Subject were the three young things from *American Beauty*, Wes Bentley, Thora Birch, and Mena Suvari. Valli Herman-Cohen of the *Los Angeles Times* harumphed that Suvari had "stepped out of her *American Beauty* high school character to look like a well-preserved matron. The silver Escada dress worked, but the high Jacqueline Susann hair didn't." The winner was *King Gimp*, about an artist with cerebral palsy. Dan Keplinger, the subject of the film was in the audience with the winning producers, Susan Hannah Hadary and William A. Whiteford, and was so excited by the victory that he tumbled out of his wheelchair. Hadary and Whiteford had to maneuver him back into his chair before they could come to the stage. ABC's cameras remained focused on the scene and John Carman of the *San Francisco Chronicle* wrote that Keplinger, "provided one of those jaw-dropping Oscar moments out in the audience when he fell from his wheelchair, flailed his arms and kicked his legs in joy. Atta guy; that's saying it." The *New York Post* was a little more respectful, calling this, "the heart-wrenching surprise of Oscar night . . . instead of focusing on a triumphant smile, the camera caught Dan, twenty-seven, jumping off his wheelchair, flailing his arms in the air like a windmill, and writhing around on the floor of the Shrine Auditorium. The Academy and audiences watched—at first in shock. Then it dawned on them that this crazy man rolling around on the floor was screaming with joy. 'Well, we didn't expect it,' said *King Gimp* producer William Whiteford. Keplinger can't celebrate conventionally because he has cerebral palsy. 'Dan's jump for joy is a little bit different,' says his mother, Linda Ritter. 'He has to get down on the ground.' "

The Documentary Feature Award was given by the evening's only husband-and-wife presenters, Uma Thurman and Ethan Hawke. Known for his grungy dressing down, the tuxedo-clad Hawke was holding his own with his famously glamorous wife, who was dressed in a classic red silk Alberta Ferretti. He was described by Peter Coyote as a "noted actor and novelist," having written an eloquently heartfelt story of young love, *The Hottest State*. Sure enough, as David Ansen and other cynics had predicted, the winner was not the joyous *Buena Vista Social Club*, but *One Day in September*. Producer Arthur Cohn also won the award as the night's most pompous speaker as he intoned, "In contrast to all the films you are honoring tonight, this film was only completed in October. Consequently, the film *One Day in September* hasn't been released anywhere in the world. And, as a result, with this Oscar you members of the Academy have given a terrific sign to members of all the world of the filmmakers that the Academy in its judgment is not basing itself at all and is not influenced by box-office success, but is harping and insisting only on the outstanding quality of a film which can be remembered for a long time." Besides getting in a graceless dig at *Buena Vista*, Cohn told a blatant lie, because the film

was released for one week—otherwise it wouldn't have qualified for the Award. Wim Wenders, the director of *Buena Vista Social Club*, told *The Nation* that Cohn's acceptance "left me speechless. Congratulating the Academy for being able to distinguish between commercial success and artistic value was a slap in the face of all the other nominees. You just don't do that to your competitors when you get up there to receive an Oscar. Some of the other nominees sitting just behind us were just as appalled."

When Billy Crystal next appeared, he was carrying one of those huge bags of oranges migrant workers sell along highways in Southern California. "Such good news," he explained. "We found the other two Oscars." Sure enough there was a pair of statuettes in the bag along with the fruit. "Somebody bought these coming off the Santa Monica Freeway on an off-ramp. $3.99—this is a bargain."

Judi Dench announced that the winner of the hotly-contested Best Supporting Actor race was Michael Caine in *The Cider House Rules*. Michael Clarke Duncan was the first one on his feet in what soon became a standing ovation. Tom Cruise embraced the winner as he made his way to the stage. The *New York Post*'s Hannah Brown meowed that the "never-nominated Nicole Kidman . . . looked relieved when husband Tom Cruise lost." Caine said, "I was looking, watching all the others and thinking back when I saw the performances. And I was thinking of how the Academy changed 'The winner is . . .' to 'And the Oscar goes to . . .' and if ever there was a category where the Oscar goes to someone without there being a 'winner,' it's this one because I do not feel [I'm] a 'winner.' " Amidst the applause there was a shot of Haley Joel Osment clapping and smiling. Caine then began to speak of each other nominee individually. "You have Michael Clarke Duncan, who I'd never heard of quite frankly [meaning Caine was lucky enough to have missed *Armageddon*] who is astonishing." Duncan stood up. "You have Jude, who's gonna be a big star no matter what happens. You have Tom who, if you had won this, your price would have gone down so fast. Have you any idea what supporting actors get paid? [Caine was chuckling as he said this and the audience applauded.] And we only get one motor home, a small one. And Haley Osment,—what an astonish . . . Haley, when I saw you, I thought, well, that's me out of it. So really I'm basically up here, guys, to represent you as what I hope you will all be: a survivor." Caine still needed to make some personal thanks, so he addressed the show's producer, "Dick, I wasn't here . . . the last time I won so give me a bit extra time, okay?" The Zanucks allowed the actor to say what he wanted to say. In the *Los Angeles Times*, Kenneth Turan called the winner, "a model of graceful generosity . . . Caine is well-liked in the industry because he is the kind of person everyone saw." And on the subject of "graceful generosity," it was also becoming quite apparent that the Zanucks were not nearly as quick with the rude get-off-the-stage-music as Gilbert Cates.

The next thing Billy Crystal had to say was, "Ladies and gentlemen, let's welcome home Jane Fonda." This was the two-time Best Actress winner's first time at the Oscars since 1992, having spent most of the decade otherwise engaged in her role as Mrs. Ted Turner. She was presenting the Honorary Award to Andrzej Wajda and said of the recipient, "often at odds with government censors, his films not only chronicled the politics of Eastern Europe, they paved the way for change." The film clips were no day at the beach: grim scenes of people being shot, folks crying, refugees making their way through a war-torn street, freedom fighters stalking the sewers, Danton about to face the guillotine, people herded on a train to a concentration camp, a corpse being carried on a slab. To make things a little more upbeat, there were also a few scenes of people dancing and a shot of Lech Walesa. The montage ended with a quotation superimposed upon the screen: "My task as a director is not just to provide a nice evening's entertainment. . . . The most important thing is to make people think."

In contrast to the mood of the montage, Wajda was a spry, cheerful-looking gentleman of seventy-four. His acceptance speech was in his native language, but it was subtitled, and he explained, "Ladies and Gentlemen, I will speak in Polish because I want to say what I think and feel, and I have always thought and felt in Polish." He went on to say, "I thank the American friends of Poland and my compatriots for helping my country rejoin the family of democratic nations,

rejoin the Western civilizations, its institutions and security structures. My fervent hope is that the only flames people will encounter will be the great passions of the heart—love, gratitude, and solidarity." After he and Fonda headed offstage, the camera cut to Peter Coyote while he made the next introduction: "From *Anna and the King*, make way for his majesty, Chow Yun-Fat." As the presenter started to walk out, the camera caught Wajda kissing Fonda on the hand. *Us Weekly* was delighted with Fonda's appearance, saying she "looked like she hadn't lost a step in the ten years since her last movie role."

Chow was handing out the Sound Effects Editing Award, and rather than film clips, only sound bites from the nominees were presented: cheers, whoops, and punches from *Fight Club*; an explosion and things breaking in *The Matrix*; and laser guns being shot off from *Star Wars Episode I: The Phantom Menace*. The winner was *The Matrix* and recipient Dane A. Davis, who looked like he could have been Richard Dreyfuss's brother, said, "So this is where the rabbit hole goes." Next, a rather stiff Salma Hayek talked about the Science and Technical Awards dinner that she had hosted. Billy Crystal commented, "You know, just think. Andrzej Wajda, Chow Yun-Fat, and Salma Hayek. John Rocker must be going nuts," a reference to the cracker Atlanta Braves reliever. Arnold Schwarzenegger, whom Crystal described as "Austria's biggest export since the von Trapp family," announced that the Visual Effects Awards was also going to *The Matrix*. There were four recipients, but only one spoke. And he did so for so long that even the Zanucks' patience was tried and he was the first one this evening to get the musical hook.

Diane Keaton introed the *American Beauty* clip by saying, "Sometimes it's hard for us to remember how beautiful ordinary things are. But watching *American Beauty* makes it impossible for even the most cynical of us not to fall in love with the beauty of a garage door opening, or a kitchen window late at night, or a white plastic bag dancing in the wind." Sylvia Rubin of the *San Francisco Chronicle* wrote that Keaton "once again marched to her own drummer in blue granny glasses, a black velvet gown with long black gloves, covering every inch of skin, accented by an enormous brooch of red satin roses."

Then the host returned with a new bit. He said, "A lot of people want to know what the stars are thinking during the show." As the camera zeroed in on individuals in the audience, "because I've sort of a sixth sense for what they're thinking," Billy Crystal shared what was on their minds. Among them were Arnold Schwarzenegger ("I can't believe there's no party at Planet Hollywood. I can't believe there's no Planet Hollywood."); Annette Bening ("Ooh, I hope the baby doesn't look like David Crosby."); Denzel Washington ("I hope they don't try to pin that missing Oscar thing on Hurricane Carter." Washington didn't laugh.); Meryl Streep, who covered her mouth when she saw herself on the monitor ("The designated hitter rule is ruining baseball." Streep appeared not to understand the joke.); Dame Judi Dench ("Oh, this thong is killing me."); Michael Clarke Duncan ("I see white people." The audience cheered for this one.); Russell Crowe ("I could use a cigarette right around now." The actor nodded in agreement.); statuette saver Willie Fulgear ("This is cool, but what I really want to do is direct."); and finally Jack Nicholson ("You know what, I'm still the coolest guy in the room.").

Crystal then announced "something really special for you. This is a wonderful treat, ladies and gentlemen." It was Burt Bacharach leading a series of songs that either won or were nominated for Oscars. The only problem was that the first song, performed by Garth Brooks, was "Everybody's Talking," which wasn't nominated for Best Song; in fact, it wasn't even eligible for an Oscar because Fred Neil hadn't written it for *Midnight Cowboy*. Next was Faith Hill singing "Over the Rainbow," which was surprising because the country singer hadn't been scheduled to appear on the show. On the other hand, the expected Whitney Houston was nowhere to be found. Others on stage were Ray Charles, Queen Latifah, and Isaac Hayes. The latter performed "Theme from *Shaft*" in a production number not unlike the one in which he had performed the Oscar-winner back at the 1971 show, as go-go girls in 1970s' retro—including a woman with a blonde Afro wig—did their stuff; there was so much smoke on stage that one could hardly see Hayes. While each singer performed, clips from the movie in which his or her song was featured played out on monitors

around the stage. The climax of the segment had Dionne Warwick singing Burt Bacharach's and Hal David's "Alfie," and the audience got to see plenty of clips of Michael Caine as he looked in 1966. The participants received a standing ovation.

Billy Crystal said, "I couldn't see Isaac Hayes. How do you lose Isaac Hayes? First the ballots. Then the statues. Then Isaac Hayes." Presumably because Crystal was talking about an African American, director Louis J. Horvitz cut to Denzel Washington who wasn't laughing. Kenneth Turan would declare, "If there was anyone in the Shrine who did not look happy to be there it was Denzel Washington."

A veteran of Pedro Almodovar movies, Antonio Banderas, and a star of the director's *All About My Mother*, Penelope Cruz, got to announce that the Foreign Film winner was *All About My Mother*. Or as Cruz announced the winner, "Pedro!" This time director Horvitz cut to Gloria Estefan for a reaction shot. Speaking in *very* broken English, Almodovar paid homage to his compatriots: "You know, I come from a country, from a culture very different from this. And you know, in that country it is six o'clock in the morning. So let me dedicate this to the Spanish people that are watching TV now, and they sacrifice their Monday just to look you and me with this." He spoke of his family's dedication: "You know, I also want to thank my sisters Maria Jesus and Antonia for the amount of candles that they lit to their favorite saints during the last months. You know, culture different. Thanks to the Virgin of Guadalupe, the Virgin of La Cabeza, La Milagrosa, the Sacred Heart of Mary, San Judas Tadeo, and El Jesus de Mendinacelli. I told you that we live in a different country, a different culture." And he had some advice for Miramax: "Harvey Weinstein. Well, listen, so for yes to Harvey. One idea. What? Consider my sisters' Oscar campaign. You know they, they, yes, lighting a lot of candles to these saints, presided by a photograph of my mother with Penelope and me. Next to a twig of laurel, which brings good luck." Almodovar kept speaking, despite the musical cue from the orchestra, and Banderas eventually kiddingly pulled him away from the microphone. When the Foreign Film winner was finally finished, Billy Crystal said, "He makes Benigni look like an English teacher," and because Almodovar was chubby and had a frightful head of big black hair reminiscent of that of half of a 1960s comedy team, Crystal added, "I do miss Steve Rossi, though."

Keanu Reeves and Charlize Theron announced the Original Dramatic Score Oscar winner was John Corigliano for the Canadian film, *The Red Violin*. The winner, who had only scored two previous movies, said, "I'm from another world, of classical music, and when I write my symphonies and concertos, it's a very lonely profession. And one thing I've learned about film writing is how communal it is."

Edward Norton had the honor of introducing the "In Memoriam" section which, this year, ran the gamut from the lyrically austere French director, Robert Bresson, to "Ernest," Jim Varney. Also included were stars from the 1920s: Buddy Rogers; the '30s: Sylvia Sidney; the '40s: Hedy Lamar and Victor Mature; the '50s: Ruth Roman and Rory Calhoun; the '60s: Dirk Bogarde; and the '70s: Oliver Reed and George C. Scott. Also, character actors Henry Jones (in character as *The Bad Seed*'s LeRoy), James Bond's "Q," Desmond Llewelyn, Lila Kedrova, Ian Bannen, and Madeline Kahn, who received the biggest round of applause; two wonderful character actresses eligible for inclusion were not in the mix: Peggy Cass and Hillary Brooke. Also seen were *Godfather* writer, Mario Puzo; writer-director, Garson Kanin; blacklisted Oscar-winning writer, Frank Tarloff; Hollywood-Ten-victim-turned-stool-pigeon, director Edward Dmytryk; and producer Allan Carr, who will forever be associated with Snow White and Rob Lowe at the Oscars, but who should also be acknowledged as the one who made the switch from "And the winner is . . ." to "And the Oscar goes to . . ." But the most moving of all the faces shown in the segment was blacklisted director Abraham Polonsky, the noble man who a year earlier was one of the leaders of the Elia Kazan Oscar protest.

As the saying goes, from the sublime to the ridiculous as the clip from *The Green Mile* unreeled; introducing it, Samuel L. Jackson called the film "a ripping yarn of good and evil." Film Editing presenter Ashley Judd said, "With all due respect to Jack, I'd like to say he doesn't totally have the corner on the coolest guy in the room," and pointed to her copresenter and costar from *Double Jeopardy*, Tommy Lee Jones. He intoned, "It's important to remember the editors because without the work of these talented artists, this year's movies might have been really long," and received appreciative laughter. *The Matrix* received its fourth Oscar and then Billy Crystal assured everyone, "They just found Isaac Hayes in a dumpster in Bell, California."

Jack Nicholson began the presentation of the Irving G. Thalberg Award to Warren Beatty by saying, "Because of the dignity of the occasion, Miss Bening's condition and the age of the recipient, there will be no sex jokes, and I'm very sorry about that." Noting Beatty's hands-on approach to things, Nicholson also kidded that his friend had "seen to it that all of the seat-fillers are board-certified obstetricians." Along with the usual movie clips, there were filmed testimonials from people who had worked with Beatty, including his wife, who enthused, "He works so hard!" Faye Dunaway, who said, "He's always pushing the boundary . . . He has enormous courage. He has guts," and Gary Shandling who testified that, "He makes me feel like I have nothing." Before handing Beatty the bust of Irving Thalberg, Nicholson called him, with "all due respects to the late, great Sam Spiegel, the handsomest recipient of this Award ever." *The Washington Post*'s Tom Shales complained that "Jack Nicholson introduced Beatty with sly old-boy jokes just as the two had done when the Golden Globes bestowed a Lifetime Achievement Award on Nicholson a couple of years ago; this is getting to be a vaudeville act."

Talking about people who taught him and were kind to him when he first arrived in Hollywood, Beatty mentioned producer Sam Goldwyn, who "was in his eighties, God bless him, and he treated me like a grown-up. Now, it's very interesting. I think that most of the people teaching me now all seem to be in *their* early twenties, and I do whatever I can, I think, to keep them, I try to get them to stop treating me like a grown-up, but I thank them." He had more gratitude: "I thank my profession for giving me freedom and access—the freedom to live a much fuller life apart from the movies and the access to get out and know the world and then come back and go back to making movies." Beatty added, "Please forgive me for not making more of them, I'll try to do better. Thank you so much for encouraging my voice in public affairs. Please forgive me if I've used it stridently or, in fact, not often enough, I'll try to do better." Next, it was "To my fellow actors, I would like to say thank you—thank you for making me look good. I'm first, last, and always an actor. My pride in that is unbounded. Please forgive me for being a producer. I'll try to do better."

He then addressed "those of you who may have heard rumor here or there of my life in Hollywood as a single man [laughter from the audience], the poet wrote, 'Only solitary men know the true joy of friendship. Others have their family, but to a solitary man, his friends are everything.' So I want to thank you," Beatty continued, "my friends for leading me through those days and finally, in fact, leading me to Annette. Please forgive me for making her unavailable to your movies four times. That's four times. I would like to say that I'll try to do better, but you and I know that I won't. So let's just say that I'll try to do less." He went on about how corny it was that he was being honored, his wife was up for an Oscar, and she was on the verge of giving birth, all at the same time, eventually saying that the baby "could join us any minute in the second row if I don't wrap this up." But before he did, he spoke to his three kids at home about how "the things that don't have to change for us are our reliability of friendship, the sanctity of our family and the dignity of our work." David Hinckley of the *New York Daily News* called the speech—which lasted for five minutes and forty seconds—"disjointed," while the *Los Angeles Times* deemed it, "long-winded but touching and sometimes humorous." Ken Tucker of *Entertainment Weekly* sighed, "Suddenly—shockingly—Beatty looked only a few years younger than Richard Farnsworth, and his rambling remarks were only slightly more coherent than those of the widely feared Roberto Benigni."

Brad Pitt announced that the winner of Best Cinematography was *American Beauty*'s Conrad Hall, his second Oscar after having won for *Butch Cassidy and the Sundance Kid* thirty years earlier. Hall said that after reading Alan Ball's script, "I didn't know how we were going to get a movie that anybody liked because there were sure unusual characters, until Sam pointed

out to me, 'Don't you ever have any unusual thoughts yourself, Conrad, about 16-year-old girls that accompany your daughter home?' "

Kevin Spacey noted that originally Annette Bening was supposed to be presenting the Adapted Screenplay Oscar with him but, because of her condition, "I could not ask her to climb stairs, unless, of course, she wins the Oscar and she'll crawl up here on all fours on her own." The winner, as expected, was John Irving for *The Cider House Rules.* He said, "You must be trying to get me to reconsider my day job," and concluded his thanks by acknowledging "everyone at Planned Parenthood and the National Abortion Rights League." The cheers and thunderous applause he received for this sentiment proved once again that people don't mind political statements at the Oscars as long as they agree with the sentiment being expressed.

Original Screenplay presenter Mel Gibson read, "Consider the writer. Locked away in a lonely room, waiting for Lady Muse to alight gracefully and turn the stark blank empty void of a page into the stuff of masterpiece . . . Jeez, who writes this stuff?" The Oscar went to the guy who wrote *American Beauty*. Loser Paul Thomas Anderson thought he was being funny by making a face into the camera when he heard the result, but he only looked like a loser, and *Entertainment Weekly* said, "Good thing pouting squeeze Fiona Apple was there to tell him what misunderstood geniuses they are." After some standard-issue thank yous, winner Alan Ball gave gratitude to "that plastic bag in front of the World Trade Center so many years ago for being whatever it is that inspires us to do what we do." In the wings, viewers got to see Kevin Spacey hug Ball, and then John Irving hugging him, too. Before the next set of commercials, Peter Coyote warned, "He's back. Academy Award winner Roberto Benigni presents the Best Actress Oscar."

After the break, Billy Crystal appeared at the podium with a huge butterfly net and said, "Okay, the good news is it's Roberto Benigni. The bad news is he's had nine espressos." Benigni ran around on the stage and then said, "I wish I possessed a tail I could wag," and went on about how nice it would be to be a dog but "since my acceptance speech last year they asked me to stay the hell off the furniture." *Entertainment*

Weekly advised Benigni, "Dude, they're no longer laughing *with* you, they're laughing at you." And *Premiere*'s "Libby Gelman-Waxner" mused, "When Roberto Benigni appeared, and everyone remembered that last year he actually won Best Actor, couldn't you feel the entire planet trying to look away, and blame someone else?"

The Best Actress winner was Hilary Swank in *Boys Don't Cry*. The recipient began by noting, "We have come a long way." She also called her film a "labor of love" because "God knows, nobody got paid"—she had been paid $75 a day scale for what she did for love. The camera saw her husband Chad Lowe weeping, which, of course, led everyone to joke, "Boys *Do* Cry"; the Swank-Lowe household now had an Oscar to go along with his Emmy. Addressing her mother, Swank said, "It looks like living out of our car was worth it." She concluded by thanking "Brandon Teena for being such an inspiration to us all. His legacy lives on through our movie to remind us to always be ourselves, to follow our hearts, to not conform. I pray for the day when we not only accept our differences but we actually celebrate our diversity." Cintra Wilson of *Salon* wrote that Swank, "came out of nowhere and outclassed everyone with her poise and talent." Waiting offstage to present, last year's winner Gwyneth Paltrow embraced Swank.

When Paltrow was onstage she told everyone, "you probably all remember how wimpy I was" when she made her acceptance speech. Sean Penn was the only one of the twenty acting nominees not to be in the Shrine, but the winner was Kevin Spacey in *American Beauty*. Spacey began by saying, "This is the highlight of my day," a quote from his onanism shower scene. He dedicated the Award to "the man who inspired my performance. A man who has been my friend and my mentor and, since my father died, a little bit like my father, who's performance in *The Apartment* stands as one of the finest we've ever had. Jack Lemmon, wherever you are, thank you, thank you, thank you." Like Lemmon, Spacey now had a Best Actor Oscar after having first won a Supporting Award. Army Archerd would report that "Jack Lemmon admits he was overwhelmed by Kevin Spacey's dedication of his Oscar to him. Jack heard this dedica-

tion as he watched the Oscars at the home of Veronique and Gregory Peck." Spacey then gave thanks, "To my friends for pointing out my worst qualities. I know you do it because you love me. And that's why I loved playing Lester. Because we got to see all of his worst qualities and we still grew to love him." He addressed his date, "Diane, thank you for teaching me about caring about the right things, and I love you." Finally, "And, Mother, I don't care what they say about bringing you to awards shows. I will always bring you to awards shows because I'm proud of you and I love you." It wasn't clear who "they" were.

Steven Spielberg kept it in the studio when he announced that the Best Director Oscar was going to *American Beauty*'s Sam Mendes. After people connected with *American Beauty* and family and friends had been taken care of, Mendes cited a director associated with Jack Lemmon: "I'd like to say thank you to a personal hero of mine, who is a really big influence on this movie. I want to say thank you to Billy Wilder, and I want to say to him, if my career after this point amounts to one-tenth of what yours has been I will be a very happy man." Finally, Clint Eastwood announced that the Best Picture winner was *American Beauty*, its fifth win out of eight nominations. Coproducer Bruce Cohen said nothing of interest, but Dan Jinks did at least come up with thanks to "all of my parents."

Billy Crystal closed the four-hour, ten-minute show by saying, "It's been a great night, and I've been told that this is the shortest Oscar show of this century."

Aftermath

Hilary Swank was fairly distraught because she had forgotten to thank her husband, who was now backstage with her. As soon as she met the press, she said, "First of all, I have to say something that I didn't say when I was up there. As you can all imagine, it's very surreal up there. I have got to thank my husband, Chad Lowe [applause from the reporters] and I'm doing it right here because without him I could never have made it through this experience. So, thank you, honey. You're my everything." She said it hit her that she had forgotten Chad as she was walking offstage and "I was, like, trying to get back, but the music was on." Swank said that when Roberto Benigni opened the envelope and called her name, Chad told her, "Breathe and be free. Congratulations." She admitted that "I do feel like a princess. It's been quite an amazing journey." And she talked about Brandon Teena and *Boys Don't Cry*. "I can't honestly stand here and say I know what it feels like to be a boy, but . . . I know how it feels to be a human being with dreams and desires." She was hopeful about the movie's impact, saying, "I think this movie opens the door to letting people know what goes on in society and putting an end to intolerance."

Lowe was having a lot of fun with his wife's gaffe, and he told *Access Hollywood*, "I get to now choose what movie we go to for the next year." She explained, "He was the one person I didn't write down on my little list because who forgets their husband, their most important person in their life?" Chad added, "And now she takes out the garbage. I'm gonna use this for a *long* time."

"I was actually experiencing an aneurysm," was Kevin Spacey's description of being onstage. He elaborated on his comment about his friends who point out his "worst qualities": "What I meant by that was that real friends are not just the ones that congratulate you and tell you that you're great and tell you you do terrific work . . . Real friends are the ones that keep you on your toes, keep you real, keep you trying to focus on the things that are important in your life . . . I was thanking those friends of mine, and they know who they are, who smack me in the head every time when I get a little ahead of myself." His director, Sam Mendes, said, "I would've done this movie for free, and I practically did so."

Explaining what had led him to praise his fellow nominees, Michael Caine said, "When you see them on that enormous screen, one after another, and obviously the best parts of all our performances are picked, it's quite astonishing. And this air that I had was that everyone was just as good as me here, and we all were just as good as each other . . . that was when I decided . . . this can't go by without mentioning their performances." He later told *Good Morning, America*'s Charles Gibson, "I walked up to the stage and my back was to the people and I'm very in charge of myself. You know, I'm an actor, I've been a stage actor, so it doesn't worry me. And I turned and they were all standing and cheering and clapping. And it completely blew me away. It's one of the first times in a public sort of thing like that, that I've ever really been that overwhelmed."

When Angelina Jolie was asked who had inspired her for *Girl, Interrupted*, she responded, "My inspiration is everybody. I like everybody. I don't judge anybody. I find everybody attractive and interesting and kind of great. So I get all these different roles and I can slide into one side of something I've seen in the world that I think is great. I'm fascinated by people, and I like to see them get up and yell and shout and be happy and say what they want and what they mean, and so that was my inspiration." She also said, "My dad said he was proud of me and that I was a good actress. For him to think I'm a good actress is kind of a big deal for me." And even though Jon Voight was an Academy Award winner, Jolie said, "I've never really held an Oscar before. My dad's mother had his in a goldfish bowl or something, high up on the mantel. I don't remember much about it. You just kind of grow up thinking it's the strange thing in Grandma's house." Speaking of family, "My parents came over to the hotel when I was getting ready. . . . My dad gave me something that said 'We love you and we're proud of you' from my whole family. . . . My mom was in the car with me the other day and I said, 'Mom, you need a new car,' and she said, 'But you went on all your auditions in this car. You lost a hundred jobs in this car.' "

When Jolie was asked, "Can you explain the nature of your closeness to your brother?" she said, "Oh, God, well, I don't know if it's divorced families or what it is, but he and I were each other's everything, always, and we've been best friends. He's been always my strongest support . . . He's the sweetest human being I know. He's a good person, and he's just given me so much love and taken care of me, and, you know, it makes life great."

"I've been to an awful lot of these," said Warren Beatty. "And I look at this as an expression of a community. I don't look at it as a competitive horse race. I've lost thirteen of these. I've won one. I enjoy coming down here. I'm very caught up in the community; I'm very proud of the profession." Still pontificating, he said, "The influence of movies on body politic throughout the world is not getting less. I think it's a big responsibility for all of us. I think that we have to take special care not to be driven solely by making money." When Beatty was asked what he would say to his soon-to-be-born child about this night, he replied, "I'll show her the videotape." This was considered a scoop because it was the first indication that Beatty and Bening knew the sex of their baby. But Beatty caught himself and said, "It looks like there's a chance" that it was a girl.

When Pedro Aldomovar won at the Golden Gobes, he said it was "like an orgasm." Winning the Oscar, however, was "a multiple orgasm."

The *Hollywood Reporter* observed that, entering the Governors Ball, "guests flowed into a room with hundreds of catering staff decked out in starched white uniforms standing at military attention." The Shrine's Exposition Hall was festooned with white parachuting, onto which multicolored images of clouds and flames were projected. People stayed longer than usual, perhaps because, with the show having run so long, everyone was particularly hungry. The party favor was a flashing red ring that looked like something that would be sold at a boy band concert.

"It was tough knowing where to look at *Vanity Fair*'s Sunday night Oscar party at Morton's," averred the *New York Post*'s "Page 6," but it did case out "the four nearly identical blondes towering over smiling Hugh Hefner," as well as Uma Thurman and Ethan Hawke "getting advice about private schools for their two-year-old." Liz Smith was at Morton's, too, and she reported that "The 'Old Guard' was on hand positioning themselves to see all incoming missiles—I do mean Betsy Bloomingdale, Denise Hale, Connie Wald, Lynn Wyatt, Angie Dickinson—and these ladies add a touch of class wherever they go." Rush & Molloy of the *New York Daily News* said, "Good thing they had a big tent at the *Vanity Fair* party after the Oscars. Some of Tinseltown's ex-lovers seemed to need some space between them. Brad Pitt and Gwyneth Paltrow kept a safe dis-

tance. Pitt and current girlfriend Jennifer Aniston tucked themselves into one corner, while Paltrow stuck close by Ben Affleck, whose lip-locking removed any doubt they were back together. Minnie Driver and beau Josh Brolin also situated themselves at a remove from her ex, Matt Damon, who had his arm around Winona Ryder." Damon told *Us Weekly*, "I'm so happy right now. I'm really at a great place in my life." Cameron Diaz and boyfriend Jared Leto were also seen constantly engaged in mouth-to-mouth. Cher and Courtney Love both said they were especially happy that Hilary Swank was victorious, and Jude Law professed that Michael Caine's tribute "was a huge compliment, more than winning it, probably, for me." Tom Cruise said, "That's the greatest thrill about the whole experience, feeling how much actors respect each other. Michael captured that."

Frank DiGiacomo of the *New York Observer* was less than thrilled with what *Vanity Fair* had brought forth this year, saying, "the Morton's bash felt anything but clubby; the guest list, nine single-spaced pages long, seemed to lack only the name of Spike Jonze." And whereas not long ago this party had been *the* party, now, observed DiGiacomo, it "was the place to go before you went to your own little party somewhere else." His analysis of the scene was, "it takes a sense of community for people to dance; an atmosphere where confidence overrides self-consciousness. Last year, the *Vanity Fair* Oscar party was a virtual boogie fest, with Madonna and Ricky Martin and a whole lot of less-famous people shaking their liposuctioned hips to a hot Cuban band. This year, however, the dance floor was barren for stretches at a time, save for a few excursions by George Hamilton and Danielle Steele and Jay and Mavis Leno. It didn't help that the singer for the big band-style group that was performing was doing an excellent job channeling Chet Baker, an artist who's best listened to when pain is the order of the day." DiGiacomo also wrote that Angelina Jolie and her brother James's "cuddling appeared to surpass sibling affection. One partygoer told *The Observer* that even father Jon Voight, who was at the party, seemed to be a little unnerved by their closeness." Jolie met up at Morton's not only with her father, but also her godmother, Jacqueline Bissett. The *Hollywood Reporter* said, "The party ended surprisingly early when the band broke at 2:30 A.M."

The DreamWorks bash for *American Beauty* was at Spago Beverly Hills, and in contrast to last year's glum celebration for the multi-Oscar winning *Saving Private Ryan*, this year the joint was jumpin'. The Associated Press described Spago as the place where "hundreds of fans pushed against metal barricades for a glimpse of the famous and the sort of familiar. It's the place Kevin Spacey hoisted his best actor Oscar over his head, while Steven Spielberg ran down the red carpet shouting 'Great! Great! Great!' " On his way in, Sam Mendes boasted, "I'm gonna be hung over for a week!" Annette Bening, who did go to the Governors Ball, thought better of attending this one. A buffet consisted of beef stew, salmon, stir-fry chicken, and breakfast entries, and the restaurant was overrun with both bouquets of roses and rose petals. Haley Joel Osment was eating French toast and said that Michael Caine;s comments had meant a lot to him; he described Caine's speech as "really cool. He had a really nice speech." Judi Dench dropped by to offer congratulations to Sam Mendes, a friend from the London stage. Citing the wins by Mendes and Michael Caine, Dame Judi said, "I was surprised at how generous everybody was to the British. I was very shocked by that because we're not like that. That kind of generosity is wonderful to us." The AP quoted someone standing outside Spago: "I wonder what's going on in there," said twenty-seven-year-old Judy Feldman of Los Angeles. The place had pretty much emptied out by 1 A.M., as most people headed over to Mortons, and those who were still here at 2 A.M. were asked by the management to leave.

Even though *The Cider House Rules* had won but two Awards, *USA Today*'s Claudia Puig said "the atmosphere was still upbeat" at the Miramax party at the Beverly Hills Hotel's Polo Lounge. In fact, in typical Miramax fashion, the soiree kept going until 4 o'clock. David Kronke of the *Los Angeles Daily News* also bore witness that, "Miramax's runners-up ball 2000 was nothing near the depressing dirge last year's Dream-Works party was." But a contrarian *Entertainment Weekly* said, "Without Best Picture bragging rights, the studio's bash was so muted that Patrick Swayze was the

life of the party." At one point, Harvey Weinstein said, "I understand the resentment. I consciously decided to let the other company spend more money than us." Ashley Judd, Ann-Margret, Roberto Benigni, Jane Fonda, Ethan Hawke and Uma Thurman, and Limp Bizkit's Fred Durst were present, as was Walter Cronkite, even though when he was asked if he thought *The Cider House Rules* should have won, he replied, "Not really."

Anthony Minghella, the Man of the Hour at the Miramax party three years earlier, was empty-handed tonight and made just a brief appearance. Stephen Schaefer of the *Boston Herald* asked him if it was easier to go to the Oscars without having the pressure of being the front-runner. He laughed and said, "No! It's easier to *win*." Sounding like his kindly *Cider House Rules* character, Michael Caine had said that he was worried how not getting the Oscar might affect Haley Joel Osment, and that was the main impetus for his acceptance speech: "Losing something at his age can hurt you, so I thought I'd take the edge off that." Claudia Puig reported that "Quentin Tarantino, Harvey Keitel, Malcolm McDowell and Don Rickles were engaged in raucous conversation." The biggest surprise about this party was that three of the most prominent members of the Miramax "family"—Gwyneth Paltrow, Matt Damon, and Ben Affleck—were no-shows; *Entertainment Weekly* printed a poignant picture of a place card reading "Affleck/Damon/Paltrow—Reserved" sitting desolate on an unused table. Trey Parker had changed from his Jennifer Lopez outfit into a tuxedo, although he set it off with thong sandals. He had nothing but praise for Robin Williams's rendition of "Blame Canada," admitting that when cowriter Marc Shaiman suggested him, "I said, 'If it's the '80s Robin Williams, I'm happy, but if it's the *Patch Adams* one, forget it.' " Parker hadn't changed his opinion of Phil Collins, though. He told *Entertainment Weekly*, "I was just so fucking angry losing to Phil Collins. Fuck him. It sucks. It sucks. I could have lost to Aimee Mann and been like, 'Okay, that's cool, she's cool.' My grandkids are going to be like, 'Fuck you, Grandpa. You lost to Phil Collins.' " And the *Los Angeles Daily News* transcribed another of Parker's musings as, "Parker replied:

"(Really filthy expletive) Phil Collins up the (anatomical region) five times."

The two complaints at the Elton John/*In Style* party were that it took up to a half-hour to get in and then, once inside, the live music was too loud. The bash was in the same building across the street from Mortons that had hosted last year's party, except that then it was Pagani; now the restaurant had closed, but the kitchen fixtures were intact and 160 people ate dinner here. Olivia Newton-John, Lesley Ann Warren, Chow Yun-Fat, Jennifer Tilly, Billie Jean King, Martina Navratilova, Jeffrey Katzenberg, Gloria Estefan, Laurence Fishburne, Farrah Fawcett, Dyan Cannon, Toni Collette, Lucy Liu, Michael Stipe, Haley Joel Osment, Soleil Moon Frye, James Woods, Marie Osmond, Joan and Melissa Rivers, and some of the Backstreet Boys were all here at one point or another.

The Night of 100 Stars benefit party for Martin Scorsese's Film Preservation Foundation held its annual event at the downstairs ballroom of the Beverly Hills Hotel. The chicken dinner was enjoyed by a generally mature crowd, including Mickey Rooney, Cliff Robertson, Jack Klugman, Red Buttons, Judd Nelson, and Sally Kirkland. Jayne Meadows, here with Steve Allen, gushed, "I love Billy Crystal, next to my husband, more than anyone in the world. He's a total genius." Tony Curtis took time out from partying to complain to Rush & Molloy about Jane Fonda's presence on the show. "She gets picked out only because of her notoriety," he groused. "I'm not dumping on Jane. But there are a lot of great actors in the hills of Hollywood who'd love a few minutes of that sunlight. That's all right. We shall overcome."

Every so often, a newcomer steps up hoping to gain a place in the hierarchy of Oscar parties. This year the challenger was the Hollywood Stock Exchange, an internet site on which people could buy and trade movie stars—on *Politically Incorrect*, Adam Carolla described it as "Rotisserie Baseball for the gays." The *Hollywood Reporter* depicted the soiree at the House of Blues as "Digerati meets glitterati. As many new media millionaires were there as old media movie stars." The music was cool—Moby and Earth, Wind and Fire—and the guests included Tom Arnold, Kelsey Gram-

mer, Edward Furlong, Jerry O'Connell, Mario Van Peebles, and what the *Los Angeles Daily News* said was "about half the classes from *Roswell* and *Popular*." Working as a reporter for an online site, Gary Coleman was there with a statuesque blonde investment banker, who reportedly bid $4,000 to win a date with him, while the *Hollywood Reporter* caught sight of a 1970s teen idol, saying, "a visibly upset Leif Garrett got into it with an overzealous security man who kept a line of guests outside the overcrowded concert venue."

Examining *American Beauty*'s Oscar success, the *Los Angeles Times* said, "clearly this year, something—either a general desire to leave no stone unturned or a more pointed analysis of Miramax's grass-roots marketing—led DreamWorks to partake in Hollywood's sincerest form of flattery: imitation. Just one year after Miramax was widely accused of hijacking the Oscar race, its executives were struck by how familiar certain aspects of the DreamWorks campaign looked to them." The paper also wrote, "According to one rival studio, the number of ad pages DreamWorks bought in the three trade papers—*Daily Variety*, *Weekly Variety* and the *Hollywood Reporter*—was twice that of any other studio. And that ratio was borne out in an independent tally by the *Times* of the advertising for Best Picture contenders in *Daily Variety* during the four weeks after the nominations were announced. DreamWorks spent more than $774,000 to promote *American Beauty* during that period, as compared to about $350,000 Miramax spent to promote *Cider House*." Athough Bob Strauss of the *Los Angeles Daily News* was pleased that *American Beauty* had won, he acknowledged that its victory, "wasn't just earned. It was also bought. While rival studio Miramax got most of the criticism for spending too much money on its Oscar campaign for the sappy *Cider House Rules*, there is no denying that DreamWorks spent all that it could and more to keep *Beauty* a constant presence on local airwaves and periodical covers. And since fellow big spender Miramax's film was the only other Best Picture nominee to win awards this year, it's sadly evident that money drives these races now at least as much as merit." *Daily Variety* said, "Miramax walked away with a terrific consolation prize: Since *Cider House*'s nomination, the gross for the Lasse Hallström-directed drama has more than doubled to $48 million. 'They knew it was a nomination, not a win,' said a rival studio marketing exec. 'They got what they wanted out of it.' " Harvey Weinstein's take on not triumphing this year: "We're fucking mortal."

Daily Variety reported, "Disney-owned Miramax has come to be known as a kudos machine, spending generously every year to spin straw into Oscar gold. Not so, however, for its corporate parent. After snagging an industry-leading seventeen noms—including a rare two for best pic—Disney all but disappeared Sunday night." Its only victory came with Phil Collins, and who'd want bragging rights for *that*? The paper also said, "Geoffrey Ammer, the studio's co-prexy of marketing, conceded Disney didn't spend as aggressively as some of its rivals. He estimated that Disney spent one-fourth the amount that DreamWorks and Miramax did on trade ads. But, he stressed, that was also the case prior to the noms, and the studio got good results." Disney remained the only major Hollywood studio not to have won a Best Picture Oscar. Ever.

Kenneth Turan declared "it was exhilarating to see four below-the-line Oscars (more than any film except *American Beauty*) go to the cutting-edge visual pyrotechnics of *The Matrix*. In years past, it would have been a given that the appeal of this technically brilliant film skewed too young to make much of an impression on the Academy, but clearly that is no longer the case." But Henry Sheehan of the *Orange County Register* seemed to wish it still was the case. He wrote, "As the evening went on its rather monotonous way, with more and more favorites winning, you might have longed for the old, antagonistic years of the 1970s. Then, the cultural clash between succeeding Academy generations would routinely cause fireworks, with presenters criticizing remarks by winners, the old guard disdaining the new, the oncoming newcomers chafing under Hollywood traditions."

Evan Henderson of the *Los Angeles Daily News* said, "Ultimately, the *Wall Street Journal* blew it. Its crystal ball was about as clear as the movie-savvy guy running the Oscar pool at Maytag. OK, maybe it was a little clearer. The six predictions in the Oscars top categories, based on a pre-Oscar survey of 6 percent of Academy members, yielded five winners. The Journal, in its Friday edition, picked *American Beauty* as the Best Picture winner. Not too difficult since just about every film critic in the country also got it right . . . But is four out of five (80 percent) a measure of accuracy or simply of a bunch of educated guesses?" Hilary Swank said that knowing that the *Journal* had predicted her hadn't made things any easier, and that she was still "very surprised" by her win. "There are something like 5,000 voters, and you know all 5,000 of them didn't call and say, 'This is who I voted for,' " she explained. The few voters who were quoted in the article received a letter of admonishment from the Academy because, said Executive Director Bruce Davis, "This will sensitize even the most naive members of the need to keep their choices to themselves." The *Journal* did not do a similar investigation for the 2000 Awards.

"The ABC telecast was the best in recent memory," raved Monica Collins of the *Boston Herald*. "The show was clean, snappy, high-gloss and very well-produced by Richard and Lili Fini Zanuck. The Zanucks said they would cut the needless fat from the show and build back the muscle of movies. They succeeded brilliantly . . . the Oscar show touched all the right places and hit all the high notes." She was also thrilled that "Billy Crystal didn't have to save the show this time," because "everything seemed to come together. The presenters were well-paired, their chatter lacked the usual embarrassing excess. The acceptance speeches seemed particularly gracious. It was as if everyone got with the program. The set was a marvel—shiny and interesting, with computer-esque touches and neon. The stage became an exciting showcase, instead of an irrelevant excuse for the podium. It was an Oscar show with heart, with a mind, with impeccable production choreography. . . . This year's Oscar show left me and my friend wondering why we've suffered through all those awful Oscars through the years."

Wesley Morris wrote in the *San Francisco Examiner* that "aided by Crystal's unsparing and punctual spontaneity, the show was downright hip, more so than it's been in decades. The decaying conductors, Bill Conti and Marvin Hamlisch, were put back on ice and replaced with the verve of Burt Bacharach, and there was an air of techno-chic that was enhanced by the four Oscars *The Matrix* took home." Paul Brownfield of the *Los Angeles Times* was delighted that, "the 72nd annual Academy Awards telecast was hipper than in years past, sleeker in look and edgier in tone. . . Finally, you thought, as if the Oscars had set up a customer-service center and listened to complaints." Somewhat less enthused was the *San Francisco Chronicle*'s James Carman, who called the show, "a solid, tidy Oscarcast that never quite managed the big surprises, sloppy excesses and emotional highs we hope to see."

It was also as if the verve and ingenuity of the new producers had rubbed off on Billy Crystal. Kenneth Turan cheered that the host and his writers were "the event's most reliable source of pleasure. With some jokes just for local consumption (like finding the missing Oscars in a bag of oranges bought on a freeway off-ramp) and a strong sense of film history (his opening 'I am so not Spartacus' montage of clips, all co-starring himself, was the evening's best), Crystal seems to be embracing his destiny as the nonpareil Oscar host for our time." Robert Bianco of *USA Today* thought that Crystal's opening montage segment "may be his cleverest clip trick ever," and the *Milwaukee Journal Sentinel*'s Joanne Weintraub declared that, "This wasn't the first time computer imaging inserted Crystal into a series of vintage film clips, but last night's montage was the best and most elaborate yet." *Daily Variety*'s Paul F. Duke said, "Oscar host Billy Crystal got so much mileage out of the snafus and nuttiness besetting the Academy in recent weeks that you almost had to wonder—was it all an inside job for comedy's sake?"

Marie Borek of Wytheville, Virginia, wrote to *USA Today* with a bee in her bonnet. "I am appalled that there is no time censorship anymore. It used to be that we knew that the hours between 7 P.M. and 9 P.M. were 'safe-viewing' times for children," she repined. "After the first five minutes of the opening monologue by Billy Crystal, I realized we would not be sharing the Oscar show with our children any more. My two daughters, ages three and ten, saw repeated pictures of *The Exorcist* during those so-called 'safe-viewing' hours. How are we supposed to shield our children from such images when they are thrust upon us without warning? I should add that my ten-year-old is extremely upset, since she had been looking forward to the Awards all week." Another complaint was lodged by Tony Chuisano of Brooklyn, who wrote to the *New York Daily News*, "The same hypocrites who denounced Elia Kazan's Award because he names Communists came out this year to honor Hanoi Jane, who aided the commies. What jerks."

The *Los Angeles Times* talked to Peter Coyote, noting that "Some wondered why the actor, who has appeared in films such as *E.T.*, *Jagged Edge* and the current hit *Erin Brockovich*," was positioned as a mere announcer. 'I'm really flattered,' said a tired but exhilarated Coyote, still jubilant a day after his stint. 'I would do it again in a hot minute. Most of the time when the Oscars come around, I'm in a motel working, or I would be hosting a "sore losers" Oscar party. So it was really nice to be asked to the dance. And the Zanucks actually booked me before they booked Billy Crystal to host.' Coyote, who has become a frequent voice-over presence on commercials, added he was uncertain whether he would be shown during the show. 'I told them, "I used to have a career as an actor, so it would be nice to be seen." They told me not to worry. And they meant it. It just can't hurt to have your mug in front of a billion people, and to be associated with the Oscars.'"

Despite the determination of Richard and Lili Fini Zanuck to speed up the show, the telecast set a new record, although that was at least partially because of how nice they were in according winners ample time to give their thanks. John Carman of the *San Francisco Chronicle* chortled, "Funniest thing is that the danceless, patterless Oscars, after all the promises and hand-wringing about the show's notoriously ungainly length, clocked in at four hours and ten minutes, the longest ever. Maybe they ought to turn the thing inside out and do the entire show as an interpretive dance." *USA Today*'s Robert Bianco said of the countdown show, "For the second time, ABC produced its own pre-show—and for the second time, ABC would have been better off had it just trained a camera on the red carpet and left the hosts at home."

Taking an overview of the night's fashions, Sylvia Rubin of the *San Francisco Chronicle* said, "There were no major embarrassments, no serious fashion victims— only elegant, old-fashioned glamour—dangling diamonds, bare shoulders, plenty of cleavage and upswept hair. Gone was the Technicolor red lipstick that had always signaled a night on the town, gone in favor of pale, shiny lips in sheer shades of bronze, blush and pink. Red dresses were also noticeably absent, after a big buildup during the last couple of weeks, showing up only on Uma Thurman, Angela Bassett and Lucy Liu." The *New York Post*'s Libby Callaway said simply, "taste was the night's biggest trend," while *People* declared that we "were witnessing a new era in Oscar fashion, one in which subdued elegance not only plays a part but prevails." *In Style*'s Hal Rubenstein quipped that, "When Cher shows up looking ready to curtsey, you can't help wondering, is this the Oscars or an inaugural ball—a Republican one?"

Elizabeth Snead of *USA Today* said, "This year, the Academy Awards were brought to you in living color. At Sunday night's hipper, slicker Oscar ceremony, Hollywood's hottest stars chose headline-grabbing gowns in bright, over-the-rainbow hues." Valli Herman-Cohen said, "Oscar's big fashion trends? Colorful clothes, big diamond jewelry, matching accessories, jeweled minaudieres and twirled, upswept hair. But vividly colored evening wear, like Keith Richards, doesn't age well. Ten years from now when we look back at Oscar 2000, we may recoil at Uma Thurman's pleated rose sheath by Alberta Ferretti, or the bright lavender Valentino gown on Ashley Judd (who wore lavender glitter eye shadow) or the terra cotta Vera Wang slip dress on Charlize Theron. But for now, the colors and the dresses worked perfectly because the dresses were so flattering." Orla Healy of the *New York Daily News* pointed out that not everyone went for color and that "many fashion plates like Lara Flynn Boyle, Cate Blanchett and Angelina Jolie played it terribly safe in basic black." Joan Rivers felt this year's trend was "We see less breasts and a lot more butt"—

her way of saying that plunging necklines had been replaced by bare backs.

Almost everyone agreed that Hilary Swank truly looked like the Belle of the Ball. She had decided on her strapless Randolph Duke gown only at the last moment, weighing it back and forth against an effort by Christian Dior's John Galliano. Sylvia Rubin said, "She looked every bit the movie star, even though most of the audience had never heard of her before *Boys Don't Cry* was released." Charlize Theron also received widespread kudos for her Vera Wang, which evoked the 1930s, or at least Sharon Stone evoking the 1930s. Wang had found antique art deco clips and they formed the starting point for the outfit; the clips were sewn onto the straps of the eventual dress. When Stephen Lynch of the *Orange County Register* asked her if the outfit "was a return to classic Hollywood," Theron "made a 'well, duh' expression. 'It's glamorous, I like that,' she said, then sashayed away quickly." And Chlöe Sevigny also received high marks. In *USA Today*, Elizabeth Snead said she "looked like a young, vampy Marlene Dietrich," while Hal Rubenstein thought that Sevigny "showed how youth can look sophisticated without raiding Mommy's closet."

Cynthia Robins of the *San Francisco Examiner* declared that "Fashion faux pas were few and far between, although the most glaring was Gwyneth Paltrow, experiencing a bad hair day and gowned in a flapperish, silver Chloe that did nothing for her complexion." E! Online's Ted Casablanca also castigated her, saying, "Gwyneth Paltrow made even less of an impression with her dress at Morton's than she did at the Oscars. The sorry frock was noticed as much as Monica Lewinsky's notorious presence was last year. 'What was she thinking?' was the dress-diss heard round the (two) party rooms."

As for other miscues, Jill Radsken of the *Boston Herald* adjudged: "Worst sequel: Meryl Streep's beaded brocade jacket. The legendary actress seems to be getting more repetitive than Sylvester Stallone. Streep has worn the same tired jacket at too many award shows and events. She'd be wise to hang it up." Joan Rivers also complained about Streep's fashion couture choices, and couldn't figure out why "she dresses like a matron." Orla Healy said, "Overlooking the gag pulled by those wacky *South Park* dudes, fashion victim No. 1 was Julianne Moore in a beyond-frumpy, black Chanel number that hit her in all the wrong places. Go figure." And Cynthia Robins was distressed that Moore "wore sheer Chanel couture and still looked like somebody's maiden aunt." But proving that fashion critics are no more in accord than film reviewers, Sylvia Rubin wrote, "The best black dress was worn by the elegant Julianne Moore, in a Chanel couture gown with a sheer midriff and softly pleated skirt."

But there was unanimity that Angelina Jolie had made the night's worst impression. Valli Herman-Cohen observed that when she "appeared in her black Versace gown, onlookers outside the Shrine Auditorium variously murmured, 'Morticia,' 'Elvira' or 'Who is she?' Her dyed-black, hip-length hair and skull ring may have been Oscar's latest glimpse of Goth." (Her hair was dyed black for the movie she was shooting, *Original Sin,* and she also had hair extensions.) Declaring, "I See Dead People," Hannah Brown of the *New York Post* said that Jolie "seemed to be going for a necrophiliac-chic look with her chalk-white skin, jet-black, waist-length hair extensions and long, loose black sleeves," while next to her picture, *Entertainment Weekly* simply wrote, "Eek!" The dress was designed by Donatella Versace, and Joan Rivers said it was "Donatella's dress for Trick or Treat," and wondered, "What in God's name was that all about?"

Just before the 2000 Awards, Matt Stone and Trey Parker looked back on Oscar Night 1999, and shared with the *Los Angeles Times.* Stone complained about the whole setup of the Oscars, that "It's so self-congratulatory. It's supposed to be for the people who have excelled in the industry, not just for the whole industry. And it's disgusting to be there. It really was." Parker explained, "That's why we had to wear dresses. If we had been there in tuxes, and like, 'Here we are, we're a part of this whole thing.' ... We wanted to go, because, you know, how many times do you get nominated for an Academy Award? But I cannot wear a [expletive] tux and walk into that thing that I just think is the most disgusting part of our country. How

can you do that? Still, probably out of everything I've done, maybe the movie's No. 1, but [dressing in drag] is the thing I'm most proud of, No. 2."

Gossippers wanted to know what was up with Whitney Houston. An obliging *New York Post* dished, "Pop diva Whitney Houston claims she backed out of performing at the Oscars because of a sore throat—but sources say the singer was yanked after she flubbed her songs in rehearsal. Legendary songwriter Burt Bacharach—one of the Academy Awards' musical directors—got so frustrated with Houston at a rehearsal, he told her to hit the road, sources say. 'Just leave. It's not going to work out,' Bacharach told Houston, according to a source who was at the rehearsal. ... When she showed up for rehearsal on Thursday, she gave Bacharach no more than fifteen minutes and was 'totally out of it,' a source said. Her performance at the Friday rehearsal was no better. She came in on cue for one number, but missed her cue for the second and sang the wrong song, the source said." The *Los Angeles Times* reported, "Several sources said Houston was 'fired' by orchestra leader Burt Bacharach during a rehearsal Friday, where she reportedly was unprepared and unresponsive to direction." Houston's publicist issued a statement saying, "Whitney Houston arrived in Los Angeles with a sore throat. After participating in rehearsals for the 72nd Academy Awards show both Thursday and Friday nights, she was unsure that she would be better by Sunday. She therefore regretfully withdrew from the performance." A spokesperson for the Academy came out on the singer's side, saying, "The poor girl was sick. She couldn't sing to the best of her ability. She wasn't fired; it may have been a mutual decision but she was certainly part of the process." Houston's cousin, Dionne Warwick, who had participated in the musical segment, affirmed, "Her throat was gone. And, doctor's orders not to open her mouth to do anything but hum." But *Us Weekly* quoted an "Oscar insider" as saying, "There was a little drama. It's just really sad." Houston's publicist later went to *USA Today* to proclaim that the singer was not using drugs. Saying that "the most talked-about celebrity at [the Oscars] was the one who didn't show up," *Newsweek* reported that

"According to people who were there, the thirty-six-year-old singer seemed to be in her own world, humming tunes (not the ones being practiced) and playing an invisible keyboard as she walked around in circles." Because the singer had recently missed a celebration at the Rock and Roll Hall of Fame and didn't show up as scheduled at the American Movie Awards in January, Ted Casablanca ruminated, "My, that gal is really getting to be the Elizabeth Taylor of the music biz. One very public physical malady after another. How many more spectacles can she create?"

Snickering was widespread about the closeness Angelina Jolie felt for her brother. E! Online's Erik Pedersen, for example, said, "What man—or woman, for that matter—wouldn't like to be, even for just a moment, Angelina Jolie's unusually beloved brother?" while *Entertainment Weekly* said the siblings "just generally gave everyone the heebie jeebies." And on the post-Oscar edition of *Politically Incorrect*, Bill Maher asked, "What's going on with Angelina Jolie and her brother? Something's not right there." James Voight told *Us Weekly*, "I've heard what people are saying, and it's a very weird thing. We love each other. If that's unusual these days, that's sad." He also said that he and his sister hadn't slept together since he was seven and she was five, when "we fell asleep in our mom's bed while watching television." A week after the Oscars, Rush & Molloy wrote that "Hilary Swank stood up for Oscar-winner Angelina Jolie at Sunday's Gay & Lesbian Alliance Against Defamation Media Awards. Swank looked decidedly unamused when comic Julie Gold did an impression of Jolie—staggering out on stage in a black wig—and hinted that the actress and her brother James may be a little too loving toward each other. Swank, who cross-dressed so memorably in *Boys Don't Cry*, reminded gay-rights supporters that Jolie had been admirably frank about her bisexuality. Swank also hailed Jolie for living as she pleases." Six weeks later Jolie was pleased to marry Billy Bob Thornton.

Kevin Spacey learned how the spotlight becomes much more focused when one goes from well-respected character actor to full-fledged movie star. Within weeks of winning the Best Actor Oscar he was a cover story for the supermarket tabloid, the *Star*, which shouted "KEVIN SPACEY ROMPS WITH MALE MODEL! Amazing photos of Oscar winner's secret double life." And as an extra little tweak the words, "Oh, Boy!" were added. In the paper's centerfold were photos, taken a week before the Oscars, of the actor and "a good-looking, well-toned hunk half his age." The pictures showed the two men on top of some rocks in a public park near Topanga, and had such captions as "The young man and Spacey get comfortable on the rocky precipice," and "The pair tussle and then a tired Spacey rests his head in his buddy's lap." (The same issue of the *Star* contained exclusive photos of Jodie Foster changing her kid's diaper in a Hollywood park.)

There were sad conclusions regarding two of this year's memorable Oscar participants. In October, six-and-a-half months after the Awards, Best Actor nominee Richard Farnsworth committed suicide. His fiancée Jewely Van Valin said "I was just in the other room and I heard the shot. He was in incredible pain today. He was going downhill." Farnsworth had been diagnosed with terminal cancer several years earlier, and Van Valin disclosed that he had endured a great deal of pain while making *The Straight Story*. "He was very ill in that movie," she said, "but phenomenally he made it through. He didn't want the world to know he was sick." More recently, his health had taken a steep decline, leaving him partially paralyzed and in intense chronic pain.

And the story of the missing Oscars did not have a happy ending after all. In June, Willie Fulgear called the police to report that he had returned from vacation to find that thieves had stolen the safe in which he had put his $50,000 for safekeeping. "I didn't get a chance to even enjoy my money," he lamented. "They took the safe. They took some of my movies, my VCR and they just messed everything up."

2000

Photo finish.

The Nutty Professor

At the 1999 Oscars, held on March 26, 2000, Academy President Bob Rehme pointed out that a quarter of the contenders for the 2000 Awards had already been released. Among those films, many critics had actually found two that they considered award-worthy. Originally intended to be a 1999 year-end release for Academy Award consideration, *Wonder Boys* got bogged down in postproduction and had to wait until February to make its debut—while five other movies were fighting it out at the Oscars. Andrew Sarris wrote in the *New York Observer* that "*Wonder Boys* is certainly superior to any of the Oscar nominees for Best Picture of 1999. Indeed, it is the kind of wittily literate satire of bookish academe that I am used to seeing only in rare British and French movies." He deemed it, "the most civilized and compassionate entertainment we are likely to see this year."

Steve Kloves adapted the comic novel by well-regarded aging *wunderkind* Michael Chabon, but although Kloves was also a director—having made two films, *The Fabulous Baker Boys* and *Flesh and Bone*—Michael Douglas convinced him to turn things over to *L.A. Confidential*'s Curtis Hanson. Sure it would be a sacrifice on Kloves's part, but Douglas was making a sacrifice, too—he was only taking $5 million for the film.

Wonder Boys had the feel of a '70s movie, in that it evidenced nothing approaching a "high concept" and rather meandered in a pleasing sort of way. The film also hearkened back to an earlier era because, as Amy Taubin of the *Village Voice* appreciated, it "has a good attitude. Tolerance for eccentricity—not to mention for recreational drugs, adultery, and homosexuality—has been all too rare in movies of late." It told of a weekend in the life of one Grady Tripp, a pothead creative writing professor who can't bring himself to finish a follow-up to his long-ago-acclaimed first novel—that would constitute a sign of growing up. Among those interacting with him over these couple of days are his pregnant girlfriend—who is also the wife of the English department chairman—his gay agent and, in particular, his most gifted student,

an inveterate liar who is discovering both his muse and his sexuality. Director Hanson said, "*Wonder Boys* is a coming-of-age story—but a coming-of-age story about a guy who's fifty. Grady's still finding his way and struggling to figure things out. All the characters are disparate and yet similar in certain ways. They're all mucking around trying to figure out how to lead their lives, just like we all are—only they're funnier."

New York's Peter Rainer declared, "I don't think I've ever seen another American comedy that mixed rue and slapstick and sentiment in quite this way." Kenneth Turan of the *Los Angeles Times* said, "this smart, literate film is especially noticeable for its generosity of spirit, for the sympathetic compassion and warmth it displays toward people who don't always receive it, on screen or off." "Few things are harder to pull off than picaresque comedy," opined *Newsweek*'s David Ansen. "One false move and you're drowning in whimsy. One contrivance too many and the whole thing can seem forced and arbitrary. . . . With a sleight of hand so casual we don't see how the trick is accomplished, Hanson and his cast convince us these people are real, our intimate acquaintances. No one is playing the farce for laughs—and as a result, the laughs come tumbling out on their own. Who knew that Hanson had such an uncanny comic touch? Typecast for many years as a director of thrillers (*Bad Influence, The Hand That Rocks the Cradle*), Hanson finally made the A-list with his terrific neo-noir *L.A. Confidential*, which confirmed his status as a top-notch genre director. *Wonder Boys* convinces me he can do anything."

Douglas was the least reined-in he'd been on screen for a long, long time, and he resultingly received his best reviews in years. The *Wall Street Journal*'s Joe Morgenstern, who said, "the most surprising thing about *Wonder Boys* is how glad it makes you feel, even though it's mostly concerned with antic or romantic misery," decreed, "Michael Douglas has never played such a raffishly eccentric role, and he has never been so appealing." John Hartl of the *Seattle Times* said that *Wonder Boys* featured, "Michael Douglas delivering what may be the most relaxed and inventive performance of his career," and the *Sacramento Bee*'s Joe Baltake called his "a blazing comic performance." The rest of the cast included Tobey Maguire, Frances Mc-Dormand and Robert Downey Jr., and Andy Klein of *New Times Los Angeles* felt, "The combination of this gentle comedy and Curtis Hanson's previous film, *L.A. Confidential,* mark him as a truly great director of ensemble performance. Everyone in the film is doing the best work of their careers."

Peter Rainer laughed that "Douglas has a shaggy, scraggly look, as if he'd spent way too many nights fully dressed in a sleeping bag. Who would believe Douglas could look like a blood brother to Michael J. Pollard?" While Michael Douglas may have not been his usual impeccably groomed self in the movie, he still was not the spitting image of the novel's Grady, who is described as fat and homely. Nevertheless, author Michael Chabon had no qualms about the casting. "I was pleased when it became Michael Douglas because he would get the movie made, but the more I thought about it the more I realized he had this kind of character in him," Chabon said. "I thought back to *The China Syndrome,* where he played kind of a longhair, and to *The Streets of San Francisco,* where even though he was playing a cop he was loose and rangy, and you thought there might be a joint in the breast pocket of his tweed jacket."

If Curtis Hanson thought he had had problems with the marketing of *L.A. Confidential,* he had a rude awakening awaiting him. Ads for *Wonder Boys* featured a close-up of Douglas resembling, in one critic's opinion, Elmer Fudd; to another he looked "like a jowly leprechaun with a three-day growth of beard." The *San Francisco Examiner's* Wesley Morris began his review of the movie by reviewing the ad, and it was no rave: "The poster for *Wonder Boys* is a dare to expect the worst. An uncomfortable close-up of a self-satisfied-looking Michael Douglas peering out over his glasses, wearing what could be a bathrobe or a tweed overcoat with a red scarf. He could be called Pumblewitch, Magchook or any variety of names Charles Dickens liked to mix and match. He could be Doctor Who. All we can feel for him is embarrassment." The ads were not the only thing working against the movie. Despite the presence of Tobey Maguire as a young man undergoing the rite of self-discovery, the film seemed bereft of youth appeal—*L.A. Weekly*'s Manohla

Dargis noted that "A young friend calls *Wonder Boys* a middle-aged-man movie, and it's easy to see her point. The soundtrack features songs by Neil Young, Leonard Cohen and Bob Dylan, midlife droners all, and the story turns on a fifty-year-old's crises of faith." Not many people went to see *Wonder Boys* and it was sad to watch the movie—despite all the raves—die a quick death.

Don't Drink the Water

A second film opened to sterling reviews in the midst of the 1999 Oscar season. And this one made a lot of money. *Erin Brockovich* was a true story about a divorced single mother who investigates the source of cancer-causing toxins in drinking water and who, despite a lack of training, is the spark behind a huge lawsuit against California's monolithic power company, PG & E. The film was directed by Steven Soderbergh, who had made his mark with *sex, lies, & videotape,* and had worked steadily in the decade since that 1989 debut—*Erin Brockovich* was his eighth picture in ten years—primarily within the parameters of independent filmmaking. (He also won the admiration of film lovers everywhere when he referred to Don Simpson and Jerry Bruckheimer, Hollywood's dominant purveyors of swill during the 1980s and early 1990s, as "slime, barely passing for human.")

Soderbergh laughed that, "I haven't made a movie that's returned its money since *sex, lies, & videotape.* But there must be enough people who think, 'This is the one where people show up.'" *Erin Brockovich* was the one. Of course, that wasn't unexpected because *Erin Brockovich* starred Julia Roberts, who, having gotten the urge to appear dowdy on-screen out of her system with *Mary Reilly* and *Michael Collins,* was on a roll that was even more impressive than Tom Hanks's. Anyone who could get people to see something as dire as *Runaway Bride* was by definition a true megastar.

According to studio publicity, producer Carla Shamberg was visiting her chiropractor when he told her about a plucky friend who had brought environmental polluters to their knees. "I couldn't believe what my doctor told me," Shamberg said, so she went home and recounted the story to her husband, a part-ner in the production company Jersey Films, and things took off from there. The sassy, down-to-earth title character was something of a floozily-dressed, foul-mouthed throwback to the spunky Depression-era screen heroines that a Joan Blondell or Barbara Stanwyck played. Julia Roberts had been cast before Soderbergh became attached to the movie, but he was delighted with the actress he had been handed. "Un-like some movie stars, who you see playing somebody 'real' and it looks like they're totally slumming," the director said, "I thought she absolutely could play a real person." He also felt that Roberts would be com-fortable playing a woman with a blue collar back-ground because, "I knew that she grew up in a sort of lower-middle-class small town in Georgia. She just knew what that was like."

When the actress was going through her somber period in the mid-90s, it seemed she was intent on proving to the world she was a "serious actress." Ironi-cally, in *Erin Brockovich* she showed off her talents as a thespian in a movie about a weighty subject, while, at the same time, her patented charm remained front and center. As Amy Taubin said in the *Village Voice,* "What's pretty original about the picture is that it fo-cuses an investigative drama based on a true story around a comic performance. Without Roberts's com-bination of exuberance and irony, *Erin Brockovich* would have been a replay of the earnest *A Civil Action,* in which John Travolta brings suit against a big corpo-ration that's been dumping toxic waste in a town's wa-ter supply. *Erin Brockovich* has an almost identical plot, but it's closer in tone, and even politics, to *Thelma & Louise.* Outlaw humor is its survival tool."

The *Boston Globe*'s Jay Carr felt that, "From start to finish, Roberts's warmth and energy pour off the screen in this film, which is boldly contoured enough to accommodate her outsize persona. Tapping bril-liantly into her high-strung maverick side, Roberts really makes this film stand up and march, or, rather, totter fearlessly ahead on eight-inch heels. Never has she filled a role with so much fire and conviction." Philip Wuntch of the *Dallas Morning News* also ex-tolled her performance: "During her first decade of stardom, Ms. Roberts repeatedly displayed a sharp de-

livery of one-liners, and *Erin Brockovich* contains her most pungent repartee yet. The difference here is that she allows us to see the sadness beneath the sarcasm. It's a dynamic performance, one that retains its mo-mentum throughout the movie. If Sally Field's Norma Rae seemed too much a blue-collar saint, Ms. Roberts's Erin would snicker at such a sanctimonious label and continue behaving like the most human of beings." Roger Ebert was one of the few dissenters, as he groused, "her performance upstages the story; this is always Roberts, not Brockovich, and unwise wardrobe decisions position her character somewhere between a caricature and a distraction. I know all about the real Erin Brockovich because I saw her on *Oprah,* where she cried at just the right moment in a filmed recap of her life."

With a flawless American accent, Albert Finney played the often-exasperated lawyer who takes Erin under his wing. Glenn Kenny of *Premiere* enthused, "Albert Finney is pure genius, sly, crusty, put-upon and genuinely lovable." But it wasn't just the performances that made the critics happy. *Variety*'s Todd McCarthy raved, "An exhilarating tale about a woman discover-ing her full potential and running with it, *Erin Brocko-vich* is everything that 'inspirational' true-life stories should be and rarely are." He observed that "At the moment, Soderbergh is working in a manner closer to that of the top directors of the old studio era than any-one has in years; turning out pictures at a rate faster than one per year, he's impressively adjusting his style according to the demands of his eclectic material, col-laborating with a wonderfully unpredictable assort-ment of actors and building a fascinating career in the process. He sacrifices nothing here on what promises to be his most commercial film to date, which in turn should lead to more opportunities on even bigger proj-ects." And Ella Taylor of *L.A. Weekly* wrote, "Soder-bergh never confuses serious with solemn, the kind of highmindedness that may have sunk *The Insider* at the box office. *Erin Brockovich* is a sexy, hugely enjoyable romp, hedged with lyrical grace notes and intimate de-tail. The film's moods rise and fall in fluid rhythms."

Others, however, were pining for the more eso-teric Soderbergh. After stating that Soderbergh "has, in the years since *sex, lies, & videotape,* matured into a

cinematic stylist of striking erudition and originality,"
A. O. Scott—one of two people hired to replace Janet
Maslin, who had switched to reviewing books at the
New York Times—lamented that "This time out he re-
strains some of his bolder impulses: there are none of
the sudden flashbacks that kept *Out of Sight* so brilliantly off balance, and certainly no brazen jump cuts,
as in *The Limey* last year." Robert Wilonsky of *New
Times Los Angeles* carped that "It's the first Steven
Soderbergh film to smack of work for hire. It's a let-
down after *Out of Sight* and *The Limey*, an overlong
and earnest whimper after two rollicking blasts. Replace Julia Roberts with costar Marg Helgenberger,
and you've got what amounts to made-for-Lifetime
uplift: Out-of-work, twice-divorced single mother
takes on the Man and knocks him on his ass to the
tune of $333 million. Think *A Civil Action* with
cleavage."

Some critics may have moped that he was being
conventional, but Soderbergh insisted, "I love the fact
that it is about the least hip thing you can imagine.
There's absolutely nothing in this movie for a film student to enjoy. I love to think of the Columbia film
students looking at it going, 'What happened to you?' "
But coproducer Stacey Sher maintained that it wasn't
all that different from his other films: "Steven loves
stories where what the world sees and what the character sees are two different things." And, referring to his
rather complex (or convoluted, depending on your
take) previous film, Soderbergh said, "I read *Erin
Brockovich* in the middle of round three of deconstructing *The Limey*, and I thought, Oh God, this is
exactly what I want to do. You know, none of that shit.
I just felt tired of it. To make an aggressively linear
movie was really appealing."

The last Universal release that was based on a real
person's encounters with the judicial system, *The Hurricane,* had been pummeled by negative publicity
regarding factual omissions, exaggerations, and fabrications. Determined to avoid a repeat of that scenario,
the studio hired a firm that—as the *Los Angeles Times*
described it—"specializes in crisis management public relations." The p.r. people, the filmmakers and
lawyers for Universal sat down with the real Erin
Brockovich and, said the studio's head of publicity,

Terry Curtin, "We asked every question imaginable.
Did we change any names? If so, why? What facts were
changed? Whose life rights did we buy? Who had a
gripe against Erin? We essentially ran two press campaigns at the same time. One was offensive—selling
our movie—and one was defensive—protecting our
movie."

Julia Roberts was not only enjoying the best reviews of her career, she was also a woman in love. Appearing on *Oprah*, the actress was so buoyant when
talking about her boyfriend, Benjamin Bratt, that the
host observed, "Obviously, just thinking about him
gives you goosebumps." Said Roberts, "We're just ec-
statically happy . . . We're drunk with joy twenty-four
hours of the day. We're sickening."

The Erin up There

One of the most memorable aspects of *Erin
Brockovich* was what *Entertainment Weekly*'s Steve Daly
called "Julia Roberts's jaw-dropping bustline." He then
asked, "Given her usually modest silhouette, how'd
they *do* that?" Costume designer Jeffrey Kurland
replied, "That's all Julia up there." The most that Kurland would reveal was that "precisely engineered" gar-
ments (i.e., push-up bras) were involved and that
"three-inch heels helped a lot to push Julia's bust
forward." Benjamin Bratt joked, "It takes a village to
raise that cleavage." Sheryl Connelly of the *New York
Daily News* said she "decided to do a home test. Of
the heels, that is. Sorry to report, but the only discernible difference the heels made was suddenly—no
surprise—I was taller. The movie magic was definitely
in that bra."

Army Archerd attended *Erin Brockovich*'s Hollywood premiere and reported, "Julia Roberts told me
it's her favorite film. And the real Brockovich told me
she was thrilled with Julia's portrayal—and she certainly should be. Julia is masterful, dramatic, comedic,
sexy (and revealing). The real Brockovich parlayed
Roberts' baring movie wardrobe by arriving at the Village preem in a gown (from Nicole's on the Sunset
Strip) barebacked, bare-sided and more. It caused as
much eyebrow-lifting (and eye-lowering) as Jennifer
Lopez's at the Grammys." Benjamin Bratt praised

Roberts's performance to *Access Hollywood*: "She was all legs, breasts and balls and they're made of brass!"

At the end of *Erin Brockovich*, the title character is thrilled beyond measure because she is given $2 million. Covering the premiere, *Variety* reported, "One recurring comment at the tented after-party was the need to suspend disbelief when the Julia Roberts character gets excited over a $2 million check. 'Like she would leave the house for $2 million,' was one industry-ite's comment."

Seems Like Old Times

Looking at the upcoming summer movies, the entertainment media's burning question was which of the two Fourth of July weekend releases would come out on top: Mel Gibson as an American Revolutionary War soldier in *The Patriot*, from the team that made *Independence Day* (and also *Godzilla*), or *The Perfect Storm*, the adaptation of the best-selling book about an actual maritime tragedy, starring George Clooney. And would it be one of these films or *Mission: Impossible-2*, with Tom Cruise and directed by John Woo, or perhaps even a sleeper hit, that would win the title of the summer's number one movie? Last year, *The Mummy* showed that a film opening pre-pre-Memorial Day, could make a financial splash by being the first summer release out of the gate, even though the calendar said it was still the middle of spring. This year, DreamWorks's *Gladiator* grabbed that position. Lewis Beale of the *New York Daily News* said, "If *Gladiator* seems as anachronistic as lava lamps and vinyl 45s, there's a reason. It's been nearly four decades since anyone has made a big-budget film about the Roman Empire and audiences haven't exactly been clamoring for this kind of fare."

The story that DreamWorks circulated was that producer Douglas Wick and studio executive Walter Parkes showed up at director Ridley Scott's office with a reproduction of a poor-man's-neoclassical painting from the nineteenth century, "Pollice Verso"—which means "Thumbs Down" in Italian—by Jean-Leon Gerome. In the picture, an emperor is about to give the signal to a gladiator to off his defeated opponent. Scott said he took one look at the picture and, "That

image spoke to me of the Roman Empire in all its glory and wickedness. I knew right then and there I was hooked." *Gladiator*'s title role went to Russell Crowe, after Mel Gibson told Scott he was too old to be wearing a toga. The good thing for Crowe was that he'd be showcased in a big budget popcorn movie, the downside was that he had to lose the extra poundage he had put on for *The Insider*. It wasn't easy: "After five weeks of working out I'd only dropped five pounds. For some people dropping thirty-eight pounds is nothing, but my cholesterol was ridiculously high and I had trouble getting out of cars, I was so fat." Having Russell Crowe in the lead did not make for an easy shoot. One DreamWorks executive admitted, "Russell was not well behaved. He tried to rewrite the entire script on the spot." When not on the set, he more than once brawled with the local citizenry, and the caretaker of the house in which Crowe was living in Morocco was so appalled by his behavior that he insisted, "He must leave! He is violating every tenet of the Koran!"

Gladiator opens with a battle sequence that was an homage to—or, given that this was Ridley Scott, a rip-off from—Anthony Mann's *The Fall of the Roman Empire*; *Gladiator* included many of the same historical characters as that 1964 epic, an expensive flop that was the last example of the ancient spectacle genre until now. As it went on, however, *Gladiator* crossed over to *Spartacus* territory (with *Amistad*'s Djimon Hounsou in the Woody Strode role), but whereas Kirk Douglas was fighting for oppressed peoples in the Kubrick film, Russell Crowe's (fictional) character, Maximus, was out for personal revenge. The psychological underpinning of the film was that this Maximus was the favorite of—and a surrogate son to—Emperor Marcus Aurelius (Richard Harris), much to the consternation of his actual son, Commodus (Joaquin Phoenix). Commodus has Maximus's kin killed and is also responsible for our hero's downward mobility as he goes from general to slave. Over the course of the movie, Maximus shakes off his chains and becomes a hotshot gladiator, and when all is said and done, the film had all the cheesy trappings of a movie about a sports star.

David Franzoni, who wrote the original screenplay—which was then rewritten by two other credited scripters—was given to making pompous statements, such as "I want to hold a mirror to our society. That's why I insisted Maximus be a pagan, that honor and morality is [sic] not defined by religion, but by the human spirit. Every more or less successful epic piece was about 'Rome is evil because they're not Christians or Jews.' That was a statement of the 1950s and mine is that it has nothing to do with it, that morality lives inside a man or a woman." He also maintained that audiences were again ready for "great stories of people standing up and dying for what is right. We've gone through the MTV version of reality, where there is no right or wrong—every man for his own dot-com—and I think people are looking back at the great moral tales."

Elvis Mitchell, the other successor to Janet Maslin at the *New York Times*, called *Gladiator* "grandiose and silly" and mused that the film "suggests what would happen if someone made a movie of the imminent extreme-football league and shot it as if it were a Chanel commercial." The *Hollywood Reporter*'s Kirk Honeycutt felt, "The movie is impressive in scope, but like the gladiator games themselves, designed for mindless spectacle to please the multitudes." Marc Savlov of the *Austin Chronicle* said, the "story seems cribbed from previous, better tales (notably John Milius' *Conan the Barbarian*, John Boorman's *Excalibur*, and Stanley Kubrick's *Spartacus*). . . . It's a loud, obnoxious, and pleasant-enough entertainment, but hardly the soaring tale of one man's struggle that it was so clearly envisioned to be. Better luck next time, Rid."

A large part of the appeal of earlier spectacles was their sumptuous production values and gargantuan sets. Most of the exteriors in *Gladiator*, by contrast, were created through Computer Generated Imaging (CGI), and the film looked terrible. For instance, less than a third of the Colosseum in the movie was an actual physical set, and most of the extras all too clearly were not real people either, just globs of pixels. Sounding defensive, the producers attributed this corner-cutting to "time constraints and area limitations." Godfrey Cheshire of the *New York Press* sighed that, "When Mankiewicz staged Liz Taylor's grand entrance to Rome in *Cleopatra*, you knew that all those costly extras and gargantuan sets were real. In *Gladiator*, where so many of both are conjured by CGI, that sub-liminal sense of tangible reality evaporates. Somewhere between De Chirico and Disney, the film's Forum and Colosseum are foreshortened, overstuffed, overstylized, sternly insubstantial; it's hard to be impressed with impossible vistas that are so clearly cartoonish. (The concentration of special effects may partly account for the film's unappealingly dark and flat look.)" Still, he conceded, "In summer-movie terms, sure it's better than *Twister*." the *Village Voice*'s J. Hoberman said, "The digital animation is far more evident here than in *The Phantom Menace*—the fights often seem lifted from a Mack Sennett two-reeler, undercranked for comic effect." He also found the film to contain, "turgid narrative and mediocre dialogue."

That's not to say some reviewers didn't like *Gladiator*. On *Today*, Gene Shalit called it, "A slam-bang, sword-clang, wallop of adventures in epic dimensions," and Desson Howe of the *Washington Post* said, "if you enjoy visceral (and I mean visceral) action, crowd-whooping heroics and stirring acts of resistance against tyranny, if the aphorism 'hack or be hacked' rings true, then *Gladiator* is one extended guilty pleasure." Jami Bernard of the *New York Daily News* found the movie to be "a sweaty, stylish hunkfest," and said "the camera only has eyes for Crowe. The glowering! The seething! The hooded gaze! The quiet suffering! (Watch him carve away a tattoo he no longer has use for. No anesthetic! No disinfectant!)"

Where's the Beef?

Lisa Schwarzbaum of *Entertainment Weekly* also had a thing for the leading man. Saying that "this is the rare Ridley Scott production in which individual characters have relatively secure separate identities," she then got all feverish: "*Gladiator*, though, is Crowe's to win or lose—Caesar's thumb up or thumb down, as it were. And he wins, colossally. The New Zealand-born, Australian-raised actor's performances have each been so completely different from one another, his transformation so complete and self-abnegating as to erase the notion of a fundamental Russell Crowe. Previously, this disarming lack of a portable, consistent, publicity-friendly acting personality has gotten in the way of his becoming a marquee star. Not any more.

The puffy, ashen whistle-blower Crowe played in *The Insider* (for which he jolly well deserved the Oscar) has vanished, replaced by a brawny army general used to working the land. This Maximus, with his lovely, meaty 1950s body mass like that of a William Holden or Robert Mitchum, has a farmer's vanity-free self-confidence; he needs to hold and smell a handful of the earth before each battle. Heartily masculine, commanding yet capable of temperance, and with a warily, wearily understanding gaze, Crowe makes Maximus' desire to go home when his job is done the greatest aspiration a man can have."

But Susan Wloszczyna felt short-changed. The *USA Today* critic wrote, "A lop here. A lop there. 'Off with their heads' could practically be *Gladiator*'s slogan. There haven't been so many decapitations on screen since the horrid B-picture *8 Heads in a Duffel Bag*. But what director Ridley Scott should have been shouting instead during his bash-'em, slash-'em effort to revive the long-dormant sword-and-sandal epic is 'Off with their shirts.' What's the use of hiring a fabulous specimen like Russell Crowe, getting him all sweaty and bruised as victorious general-turned-arena warrior Maximus, then covering him up most of the time in a powder-blue shift or an ornate chest protector? Scott gave us *Thelma & Louise* and christened Sigourney Weaver the first truly feminist action hero in *Alien*. More than most male filmmakers, he should know what women want from a Roman circus. And it isn't tiger attacks, torso slicing or a lethal game of dodge the chariot. A healthy slab of beefcake will do it."

The Nation's Stuart Klawans, who referred to Maximus as "a disagreeably virtuous general," wrote that "Crowe is a wonderful actor, as you can see from *The Insider* and *L.A. Confidential*, yet no one in charge of this film thought to allow him an emotion, other than a single-minded desire for revenge and an equally dull rectitude. Crowe gamely wears whatever costume he is given; he tromps along with his arms held out from his sides, like a tough soldier whose muscles ache. And that's about all he can do under the circumstances, other than work his basso into ever more alarming registers."

Twenty-four-year-old Joaquin Phoenix beat out Jude Law for the role of the film's villain, and Ridley Scott said, "When we offered him the part, I think the most surprised person was Joaquin himself. He is not the physically imposing type one might have envisioned in the role, but he conveys the complexities of this corrupt ruler in a very courageous way. He exposes the vulnerability that is juxtaposed with the ruthlessness of Commodus." Mick LaSalle of the *San Francisco Chronicle* said, "a fair amount of [the film's] success must be ascribed to Joaquin Phoenix, who makes Commodus a frightening and contemptible character. Commodus is not the typical Roman decadent. Phoenix plays him more as an amoral, insecure young man driven to near madness by total power and the inherent loneliness that attends it." *Entertainment Weekly*'s Chris Nashawaty said, "Russell Crowe may have been the one to get audiences all hot and bothered with his command to 'unleash hell!' But back in Rome, brooding away in the chilly palace shadows, a more nuanced star-making performance was in the works, replete with its own catchphrase: 'It vexes me. I'm terribly vexed.' . . . Phoenix was the anti-Crowe: the wounded foil, who says more with a whispery malevolent snarl than a throat-shredding bark." Phoenix said of Commodus, "I thought he was complex. You don't expect to find a character dealing with issues like parental neglect and paranoia in a movie like this." While Russell Crowe had to lose weight for *Gladiator*, Phoenix needed to flab out in order to portray Commodus, which the vegan actor accomplished by devouring peanuts.

But the actor garnering the most attention was Oliver Reed, who played a sardonic slave trader. *Time*'s Richard Corliss said, "The boozy, exuberant Reed gave a superbly knowing performance." The hard-living actor died of a heart attack two days before his scenes were finished and his role was taken over by computer graphics, which grafted a 3-D image of his head and face on a body double. Mark Morris of the *Observer* of London said, "As Reed wears North African clothing for much of the film, the void is much better disguised than it might have been, but still easy to spot. Proof again that the much maligned Ed Wood—who got his wife's chiropractor to complete Bela Lugosi's role in *Plan 9 from Outer Space*—was simply ahead of his time."

I Just Killed to Say I Love You

Terry Press and her marketing people at Dream-Works had to conjure up a way to attract women to a movie that felt like an evening spent at a Worldwide Wrestling Federation event. They came up with a commercial emphasizing the film's romantic moments—even though there were scarcely enough for a sixty-second spot—and booked it to run on such female-oriented programs as *Oprah*. But, reported the *Wall Street Journal*, "the studio yanked the ads when it got reports men were seeing them." Press said, "We did not want to confuse men and have them think the movie was softer than it really was." Besides, women were going anyway—a well-toned Russell Crowe proved to be a draw. After the movie opened strongly, and word-of-mouth made it clear that men knew what it was all about, DreamWorks again began running the sappy ads. Press said, "There's a very emotional and heartfelt message for women in the movie"—which was that the hero was so in love with his murdered wife that his passion for her fuels an obsessive revenge that borders on the psychotic, and what woman wouldn't want that kind of devotion in her man? In other words, despite his ferociously violent nature, Maximus is really just an old pussycat. But, said Press, "Meanwhile the guy kills a lot of people so men don't care. It's the best of both worlds."

Gladiator did well, taking in $35 million its opening weekend—although that was $8-and-a-half million less than what *The Mummy* had done when it opened on the first weekend of May last year. For the Fourth of July weekend, *The Perfect Storm* far outdrew *The Patriot*, which was scorned by reviewers (Jack Mathews of the *New York Daily News* said *The Patriot* "anticipated the burning question: What does it look like when a man's head is taken off by a cannonball—and answered it twice!"), with Mel Gibson receiving particularly harsh treatment, Kirk Honeycutt of the *Hollywood Reporter* said, "Gibson gives a mechanically precise but soulless performance in which he seems more concerned with how he looks than what his character is thinking or feeling." But poor dim Joel Siegel of *Good Morning, America* popped up and said,

Gibson "always a remarkable actor (his Hamlet is a personal favorite), has never been better." The notices for *The Perfect Storm* was pretty bad, as well. *Variety*'s Todd McCarthy called it, "a picture that leaves one thinking less about the fates of the characters than about how the actors had to spend most of their working days soaking wet." The ads for the film did carry a quote attributed to Jess Cagle of *Time*, calling this Wolfgang Petersen effort, "A milestone in filmmaking. Nearly perfect. A wonder to behold. A rocking testament to the places moviemaking can take us. Petersen's film is traveling the highest plane of the state-of-the-art." And the *Chicago Tribune*'s Michael Wilmington would actually put it on his Ten Best list. The summer's box-office champ, though, was *Mission: Impossible-2*, which was no better nor particularly less bad than any of the other loud movies cluttering theaters during the dog days. Terry Lawson of the *Detroit Free Press* said, "*M:I-2* is just another summer stock item, like sunscreen and barbecue coals. It's something you buy unthinkingly, or at least so the filmmakers hope."

All About Me

Last September, DreamWorks had great success employing a platform release for *American Beauty*. This fall, the studio had two movies to which it was giving similar, slow rollouts, in the hope that word of mouth would build them into must-see hits as they expanded to more theaters. *Almost Famous*, writer-director Cameron Crowe's first film since *Jerry Maguire* four years ago, was inspired by Crowe's own experiences as a writer for *Rolling Stone* while he was still a teenager. In its fall preview issue, the *Village Voice* warned readers this was Crowe's "self-mythologizing coming-of-age navel-gaze." The director said he was fretting about reaction to the film because, "It's a little different if somebody says about *Jerry Maguire*, 'Oh, I'm not really into sports. I didn't care for it.' That's different than, 'I'm not really into your life. It bored me.'"

The film was the most highly publicized of the early autumn releases. Set in the early '70s, it was filled with bell-bottoms, tie-dye, and Yes, Black Sabbath, and Rod Stewart on the soundtrack. Reviewers liked it a lot. Roger Ebert of the *Chicago Sun-Times* wrote, "Oh, what a lovely film. I was almost hugging myself while I watched it. *Almost Famous* is funny and touching in so many different ways." While Ebert was contemplating putting his arms around himself, the reviewer for the town's other daily, Michael Wilmington of the *Chicago Tribune*, was dabbing his eyes because the film "actually brought me tears of happiness." *Variety's* Todd McCarthy called it "a sweetly amiable memoir of one boy's coming of age with rock 'n' roll that's more gentle and modestly insightful than it is exhilarating or revelatory." Robert Hilburn, the rock critic for the *Los Angeles Times*, said *Almost Famous* was "a movie about loss of innocence in the early '70s that is so sweet it ought to have a happy-face logo attached to every frame." And from *Rolling Stone* itself, Peter Travers wrote, "It's pure pleasure. Just don't expect the dark side *(Gimme Shelter, Sid and Nancy)*. Not since *A Hard Day's Night* has a movie caught the thrumming exuberance of going where the music takes you." But Edward Guthmann of the *San Francisco Chronicle* felt the film was "a sweet but curiously unfulfilling story about journalism, music and one kid's loss of innocence."

A quick perusal of the favorable reviews for the film showed that most of those who praised *Almost Famous* were baby boomers, people who were up and about in 1973, and for whom this material was wistfully affecting. A Gen X critic, Ed Gonzalez of *Slant Magazine*, said, however, "*Almost Famous,* a nostalgia factory of popular music, is such a starstruck film that it is easy to see why it makes people like Roger Ebert want to hug themselves. This is less a movie than it is a vehicle for baby boomer reminiscence." He added, "Is there something I'm missing here? I like good classic rock as much as I like all good music but watching a bunch of Jesus-types singing along to expendable Elton John anthems isn't my kind of feel-good experience. This can't be a purely generational thing. Maybe it's the fact that the film's light tones will automatically prevent the infusion of much darker facets. A film of this nature is prone to some sort of cathartic drug or alcohol moment but when it comes it feels like an after school special." And a rock critic older than the baby

boomers, Richard Meltzer, called *Almost Famous*, "insufferable dogmeat, coming from the same neverneverland as a bad episode of *Happy Days*"; it was all "sentimental slop: the sort of film if it wasn't nominally a rock film you'd bring in violins."

Goldie Hawn's twenty-one-year-old daughter, Kate Hudson, played a groupie named Penny Lane, and Cameron Crowe described the actress as a cross between her mother and Claudette Colbert. Crowe cast Frances McDormand as the character based on his own mother, and when his real mom showed up on the set to enact her small role, he ordered her to stay away from the actress. "I said, 'I don't want you influencing her; I want her to have her own interpretation.' And then I had to leave the set for a few minutes, and when I came back my mom and Frances were having lunch together!"

DreamWorks had poured $60 million into *Almost Famous*, and it was too bad for them that moviegoers couldn't have cared less how Cameron Crowe spent his formative years. The studio's biggest miscalculation was not realizing that a movie about the "classic rock" era would have a very small natural constituency. A lot of people who grew up on this music had developed more refined taste, so even they had no interest in the world of a fictional band that sounded sort of like Lynard Skynard. So the gossip mill started dishing that the bigwigs at DreamWorks were now seething at Crowe, and executives from other studios gloated— off the record, of course—that Spielberg-Katzenberg-Geffen had shown exceedingly poor judgment in giving the director so much money to get all warm and fuzzy about himself.

A month after the film opened, the *Los Angeles Times* stated, "*Almost Famous* is a head scratcher. Seeing Cameron Crowe's entertaining ode to his days as a 1970s teen rock journalist, you'd think: Hit. And a profitable one because, with no stars, it certainly couldn't have cost much. Neither is turning out to be true . . . Crowe is understandably pained. So much so that the man who granted tons of interviews before his movie's release refuses to come to the phone now to discuss it." The article went on to say, "Relations between the writer-director-producer and DreamWorks SKG, which financed and released the movie, sources say, are strained. Crowe is questioning whether the studio, run by Steven Spielberg, Jeffrey Katzenberg and David Geffen, could have done, and spent, more to sell his movie. Meanwhile, DreamWorks, which has been enormously supportive of Crowe and paid the overhead of his production company for three years before his deal expired this summer, is said to be deeply disappointed with the filmmaker. The movie as much as $15 million over budget and a month over schedule . . . Sources close to Crowe said that even before the movie opened, the DreamWorks partners were making snide remarks about how perturbed they were that their company had spent $60 million on 'an art film,' 'his little personal movie.' " Of course, one might ask what had induced them to give Crowe a $7-million salary in the first place. And to the chagrin of DreamWorks, Crowe had not only indulged himself by telling his story, but also by reshooting and reshooting scenes far beyond the norm.

A week after the *Los Angeles Times* article appeared, Rick Lyman of the *New York Times* reported that Crowe and DreamWorks executives were "reeling, they say, from a growing chorus of articles and rumors in Hollywood taking them to task for the film's high budget and for its lack of top-name actors, and from suggestions that the experience has somehow ruptured relations between the director and the studio. . . 'I am just so grateful that they made the movie and they made it right,' Mr. Crowe said. 'They handled this movie with great personal care, from the very start until today.' " Jeffrey Katzenberg's official word was "We are hurt and despondent that it has not done more at the box—that's our shared disappointment." Speaking in tones that strained to sound rose-colored, Katzenberg added, "It was such a good experience for everyone involved in making this movie. At least let us have that as something we can share for having traversed this journey together."

Conspiracy Theory

Bad feelings were engulfing DreamWorks' other fall release. *The Contender* was a political thriller, the second movie written and directed by former radio talk show host and ex-movie critic, Rod Lurie. The *Los Angeles Times* had described him as a "vituperative reviewer," although he likened his critiquing style to "your next-door-neighbor after a couple of beers." He may also have found that by having purposefully tried to seem "outrageous" in his reviews, he had caused some problems for himself in his filmmaking endeavors. When the *Times* profiled him shortly before *The Contender* opened, the paper received a letter from a reader, Ramin Zahed of West Hollywood, who said, "I still remember fuming when I read critic-turned-screenwriter Rod Lurie's xenophobic review of *Mississippi Masala* in *Los Angeles* magazine a few years back. The story in [the *Times*] confirmed my views that the guy is also racist, homophobic, mean-spirited and a real opportunist . . . Sorry, but I'd rather be forced to watch the new *Digimon* movie than sit through a film made by a weasel."

The Contender told of the fuss that arises when a right-wing congressman exposes the party-hearty past of a female vice presidential candidate. Lurie said, "It's titillating to ask what would happen if a woman had to deal with the same obnoxious questioning that Clinton had to go through. Would the country be as ready to forgive her as quickly? The answer, I think, is no." He felt, "Our Puritanism would consume us. All female leaders of the last century—Indira Gandhi, Golda Meir, Margaret Thatcher, Janet Reno—none of them have been overtly sexual beings. We tend to view our female leaders as mother figures, and the last person you want to view in a sexual way is your mom."

Gary Oldman played the conservative politician behind the intrigue. The British actor and his manager, Frank Urbanski, who served as the film's executive producer, were also the ones causing headaches for DreamWorks. The two of them vented to *Premiere*, raising a stink because they said the finished project had become a pro-liberal, anticonservative tract, which was not what they had signed on to do. Their objections—which were duly noted and reported on by the national press—arose after the independently-made movie was picked up for distribution by DreamWorks and reedited. This was the first completed film the studio had bought and Lurie said that Steven Spielberg told him, "Thank you for letting us have your wonderful movie." The three heads of

DreamWorks, Spielberg, David Geffen, and Jeffrey Katzenberg were all prominent backers of Al Gore in the presidential race, whereas Frank Urbanski was supporting the *Forrest Gump*-like thing that was the vice president's opponent. You wouldn't have guessed it from the pugnacious style he had used for reviewing films, but Lurie—the son of political cartoonist Ranan Lurie—claimed he had been a dyed-in-the-wool liberal his entire life. Poppycock, said Urbanski, who insisted, "Rod Lurie has transformed from being an ultra-right-wing conservative in one year to saying that he has always been a liberal Democrat, because his benefactors are Katzenberg, Spielberg, and Geffen." Getting personal, he added "I think Rod lost his courage along the way," and, absurdly, called the released cut of *The Contender*, "almost a Goebbels-like piece of propaganda."

Meanwhile, Gary Oldman was keeping tabs to verify that his puss would be given enough prominence in the ads for the movie, and making sure he was conspicuous in the trailer. Marketing chief Terry Press moaned, "Everyone is trying to keep Gary Oldman happy, which does not seem possible."

Despite all the foofaraw, *The Contender* opened as planned—to mixed reviews. Roger Ebert applauded, "This is one of those rare movies where you leave the theater having been surprised and entertained, and then start arguing. *The Contender* takes sides and is bold about it. Most movies are like puppies that want everyone to pet them." Rene Rodriguez of the *Miami Herald* said, "What *The Contender* lacks in sophistication and subtlety, it more than makes up for with sheer verve and chutzpah," while Glenn Lovell of the *San Jose Mercury News* felt, "What it lacks in credibility, it more than makes up for in energy and scandalous wit." But Robert Wilonsky of *New Times Los Angeles* raged that "There's no getting around it: *The Contender* is the most offensive movie of the year. It pretends to be high-minded even while it slings mud and semen at the audience in its attempt to make its bludgeoning point." William Arnold of the *Seattle Post-Intelligence* complained, "It's timely, intriguing and often salaciously entertaining to be sure, but also rather annoyingly shallow, filled with one-note characters, and not half as daring as it seems to think it is . . .

The characters all talk as if they're in a bad Quentin Tarantino movie, the subplots are unbelievably melodramatic, and the cop-out ending makes the heroine look more stupid than noble." *The Contender* also contained a line that belongs in camp dialogue heaven: "The one thing that the American people cannot stomach is a vice president with a mouth full of cock."

The film did give meaty parts to two great actors: Joan Allen as the eponymous character—the first time she had the lead role in a movie—and Jeff Bridges as the president. Lurie had met Allen when he presented her with the Los Angeles Film Critics Supporting Actress Award for *Pleasantville* and told her, "I'm gonna write a script for you. Something you can't say no to." When Allen was making the television rounds publicizing the movie, Regis Philbin observed, "This is your breakthrough film as a starring leading lady," and his cohost, Jason Alexander (this was the interim period between Kathie Lee Gifford and Kelly Ripa), added, "And long overdue." Kenneth Turan wrote that "Allen, without doubt as fine an actress as is working today, makes the difficult role of a woman who cannot reveal her increasingly intense feelings in public look natural, seamless and completely convincing." Bob Strauss of the *Los Angeles Daily News* felt that the commander-in-chief was "played by Bridges with delectably shrewd drollery." Then there was Gary Oldman. *Salon*'s Charles Taylor said, "chain-smoking while outfitted in a curly fright wig and horn-rimmed glasses, he looks like the Three Stooges' Larry Fine reincarnated as an evil bookkeeper. Oldman gives a performance of such total phoniness that it will be a miracle if he doesn't win an Academy Award for it."

Despite all the publicity, *The Contender* was a nonstarter at the box office. And its plot machinations paled in comparison to the real life skullduggery that occurred a few weeks later when the presidential election took place, with Florida Secretary of State Katherine Harris working overtime to turn America into Topsy-Turvy Land so that the guy who lost could move into the White House anyway. Two days after the voting—but still weeks before five thugs on the Supreme Court acted as willing accomplices to the Bush/Harris *coup d'etat*—the *Los Angeles Times* asked a numbers of writers and directors how they'd like the election scenario to play out. The *Times* reported that Rod Lurie "envisions a fairy-tale ending in which a winsome young child finds a forgotten Florida ballot box, brings it to his despondent Democratic parents who leap in their SUV and rush to the Attorney General's office. 'They'd run into all sorts of obstacles, get pulled over for speeding by a cop wearing a Bush button, and then, at the last minute, arrive just in time,' he says, lowering his voice dramatically. 'They open the box which has only a few ballots and then, *Survivor*-like, they count them out, and Gore wins by a single vote.' The movie's final scene would feature the young child standing outside the Oval Office. 'The door opens and the child is greeted by Al Gore, played by a thin Tom Hanks. The music comes up,' Lurie says, 'there's a happy ending, and America is good again.' "

Feets, Do Your Stuff

According to Rod Lurie, Steven Spielberg told him he considered *The Contender* to be "an intellectual *Rocky*." Another fall release could more accurately claim the triumph-of-the-underdog mantle and, being British, it had the aura of *The Full Monty*, as well. Taking place in Northern England against the backdrop of the 1984 miners' strike during Margaret Thatcher's assault on working men and women, *Billy Elliot* told of an eleven-year-old boy who finds fulfillment by taking up ballet. What set it apart from most movies of its kind was that the characters and their environment had a genuinely hard edge to them.

Billy Elliot was the first film for stage director Stephen Daldry and was written by playwright Lee Hall, who, Daldry noted, shared his own "old leftie" convictions; Daldry described the movie as equal parts Ken Loach social drama and MGM musical. Two thousand boys tried out for the lead role, and the part went to twelve-year-old Jamie Bell, who, like his character, had studied ballet. He acknowledged that he had heard "hassle from the lads at school," explaining that his friends "called me a 'poof' and asked me where my tutu was. Them saying that made it more of a challenge for me. I wanted to prove to them that it wasn't just for girls, it was for boys, too." Daldry said that

Bell "was too good at first. We had to work on making him worse." The kid wasn't even all that keen on the project originally because, "I thought movies were kind of a waste of time. That they were, you know, cheap theater." Once he made the film, though, Bell decided that "Being in movies is pretty cool." The star and his forty-year-old director had a terrific rapport. "I've never met anyone like him," said Jamie. "Sometimes he pretends he's my age; sometimes I pretend I'm his age. He's a really good person to talk to."

A sensation at Cannes, the movie came to America as the first release from Universal's "arthouse division," Universal Focus, which had visions of *Billy Elliot* as an Oscar contender. *USA Today*'s Susan Wloszczyna said, "If Dickens had written *Flashdance* after seeing *The Full Monty*, it probably would have come out something like this infectious, feel-good bundle of ambition in the face of adversity. In the deft hands of Stephen Daldry . . . *Billy* tiptoes awfully close but never completely gives in to obvious sentiment. It feels old but also quite fresh, with a whirling dervish of a newcomer, Jamie Bell, in the title role, an energetic narrative and a cheeky wit undercut with flashes of violence." Mark Caro of the *Chicago Tribune* said that "like *The Full Monty*, the new movie finds its humor not in cheap gags but in the way sympathetic, complex people react to harsh circumstances in a working-class English town." He concluded, "Such crowd-pleasing tales are deceptively tough to make; most filmmakers wind up pushing predictable buttons to elicit predictable audience reactions. *Billy Elliot* earns its sentiment by vividly reconstructing the conflicts of a specific time and place while showing the artistic birth of someone raised in that environment. It's enough to inspire you to go home and jump on your bed."

David Elliott of the *San Diego Union-Tribune* felt that the "astonishing" Bell was "like a younger, scrawnier version of Tom Courtenay's working-class dreamer in *Billy Liar*" and Terry Lawson said in the *Detroit Free Press*, "It may be that the most fierce performance of the year comes from Jamie Bell. . . . Bell is at once gangly and poised, primitive and self-possessed, smart and smart-alecky, and you can't wait to see which way he'll turn from one second to the next. His dance numbers are effectively integrated into the story, but when he takes off, so does the film. Bell's unleashing of Billy's rage to the Jam's 'Town Called Malice' may be the most exhilarating 3 minutes you'll spend in a theater this year, and *Billy Elliot* has an immensely entertaining 108 more to go with it." Steven Rea of the *Philadelphia Inquirer* said simply, "You'd have to have a heart of stone, or Mrs. Thatcher's, to not be moved."

In the film, Billy comes under the tutelage of a no-nonsense dance instructor, portrayed by Julie Walters, who was best known in America for her Oscar-nominated performance in 1983's *Educating Rita*. Jan Stuart wrote in *The Advocate*, "As played with flinty ennui by Julie Walters, she's Glenda the Good Witch by way of Miss Hannigan." In the *New York Times*, A. O. Scott said that the character, "clinging to the frayed edge of middle-class respectability, harbors a lifetime of compromise and frustration behind her businesslike demeanor, and Ms. Walters gets it across without a wasted word."

When Jamie Bell was in America, he was asked by the *New York Daily News* what the movie was about. "*Billy Elliot* is about a boy and a miner's strike," he responded. Seeing a look of disappointment on the interviewer's face, he sheepishly explained, "They told me to keep my answers short." He appeared on the *Late Show with David Letterman*, and when later asked about the host, Jamie said, "He was good. He was on a lead. Probably because he didn't know me. I'm only fourteen, so he probably didn't know how to, um, talk to me or anything. He was okay. He had Sarah Jessica [Parker] on as well, and he was having quite an open chat with her. He was quite naughty there. But when I came on he calmed down. Thank God." One thing that struck Bell about the United States was, "You have weird MTV . . . Whenever I turn it on, it's not playing music."

Three Strikes

In his review of *Billy Elliot*, *Rolling Stone*'s Peter Travers said, "Watch your back, Haley Joel Osment: Bell explodes onscreen in a performance that cuts to the heart without sham tear-jerking." And what about *last* year's boy wonder? He was also in theaters this fall,

in *Pay It Forward*. Because it involved Oscar winners Kevin Spacey and Helen Hunt, as well as Osment, there had been pre-release Oscar talk surrounding the film. All it took to put an end to that was for people to see it: *Pay It Forward*—a meeting of the minds between *Deep Impact* director Mimi Leder and *Look Who's Talking Now* writer Leslie Dixon—was probably the worst-reviewed studio release of the year. Jonathan Rosenbaum of the *Chicago Reader* spoke for critics everywhere when he said, "This programmatic Christian parable is pretty unbearable—glib, often myopic, and reeking with sentimentality and self-pity." A maudlin message movie, it put forth the proposition that this would be a wonderful world if only everyone would perform three acts of unsolicited kindness. One wag said, "I took the lesson of *Pay It Forward* to heart. I told three people not to see it."

Up on the Roof

Ever since it played at Cannes in May, people had been enthusing about the new Ang Lee movie. The director showed yet again that you could never predict what he'd be attempting next. Having gone from contemporary Taiwan to 1820s' England to 1970s' Connecticut to Kansas during the Civil War, now, with *Crouching Tiger, Hidden Dragon*, Lee had set down in early nineteenth-century China. Stephen Garrett of *Time Out New York* was at Cannes and called the movie—which was shown out of competition and, therefore, not eligible for awards—"the unqualified hit of the fest." Garrett said, "With gravity-defying rooftops, sinewy swordplay and enough acrobatic kicks to make Jet Li proud, the high-velocity fable was proof that the melodrama maestro of *The Ice Storm* has reinvented himself as the international scene's hottest action director."

Scarlet Cheng of the *Far East Economic Review* noted, "With his newest movie, *Crouching Tiger, Hidden Dragon*, Lee is tapping back into the culture he was raised in, and working for the first time in the land of his ancestors." The director told her that making a martial-arts film was "the fulfillment of my childhood fantasies." The movie was of the classical Chinese genre known as *wu xia*, which means "martial chivalry," and is the mythic form that is considered in large degree to define the Chinese national identity, holding the same import as samurai tales do for Japan and Westerns do for America. As such, it has been found in Chinese operas and fiction for hundreds of years, although *Crouching Tiger, Hidden Dragon* was specifically based on a pulp novel from the 1930s that Lee had read as a child. Leading lady Michelle Yeoh, a veteran action-film star, said, "When Ang spoke to me about *Crouching Tiger*, it was obvious that this was a dream he had been harboring since he was a kid. It would be a dream for any Asian filmmaker because the material is so ingrained in our being."

Lee contemplated, "The more movies I make, the more I realize they're my form of therapy. Maybe I'm in a midlife crisis, I don't know. But I felt it was very important to get back to my roots." (Although he was born in Taiwan, his parents hailed from mainland China.) He also admitted, "There's a part of me that says unless you make a martial-arts film, you're not a real filmmaker. It's pure cinema energy—it's raw, it's cool, it's fun. It's why you want to be a filmmaker." But then again, when he approached the traditions of *wu xia*, "I found I could no longer do a pure action movie, I found I had to bring the drama along with it. I cannot move too far away from the characters, even when I stage an action scene." Elizabeth Weitzman of the *New York Daily News* picked up on this dual aspect when she observed, "Lee, intent on putting the 'art' in martial arts, has combined seemingly incompatible elements to create both a heart-stopping action extravaganza and a love story for the ages. The result is a film for those thrilled either by head-spinning, *Matrix*-style fight choreography or lush period epics." Lee also said his intent was to downplay the genre's "macho" aspects and create a movie more female-oriented: "I wanted to take a journey through these women's emotions. I felt it was important to bring back old-fashioned storytelling, and the best way to do it was through the emotional lives of the women in my film." James Schamus, Lee's frequent collaborator who cowrote and coproduced *Crouching Tiger*, said that in Asian action movies, "there is the tradition of female warriors kicking butt. Why this film resonates is that it does something new: It depicts female heroes as people

and as women. Unlike previous incarnations of sexually charged, castrating leather-and-lace butt-kicking chicks, these are women with emotions." And Lee added, "They fight like women, they're not simulating men.".

Crouching Tiger, Hidden Dragon married the action sequences to a pair of love stories, one involving world-weary, middle-aged warriors, the other emphasizing the full-blooded passion of youth. Thus, Lee wasn't being entirely facetious when he referred to the film as "*Sense and Sensibility* with martial arts." The forty-six-year-old filmmaker also felt, "On the surface, the younger couple is more romantic. They're the tiger. But that doesn't last. The older couple have more repressed feelings, a more tacit understanding. That's the hidden dragon, and to me, that's much more romantic. They represent the Confucian model. Their spirit and morality are more important than their swordsmanship. That's my heart of hearts, too."

West Meets East

In America, Hong Kong action films had a small, but intense, following which, interestingly, consisted of highbrow critics who rhapsodized over the metaphysical implications of the other-worldly agility and the pure motion of the action sequences found in the best of the genre, and urban audiences, whose reaction to some of the mind-boggling stunts was along the lines of "That's some crazy shit!" For most American audiences and reviewers alike, however, *Crouching Tiger, Hidden Dragon* was their first contact with the genre—even though it wasn't a pure-breed—and the fact that it represented something entirely new to them at least partially explains the unfettered enthusiasm the film received in most circles.

Jonathan Foreman of the *New York Post* raved, "You have never seen a movie like *Crouching Tiger, Hidden Dragon* because there has never been a movie like it. If you liked *The Matrix*, you will love *Crouching Tiger, Hidden Dragon*, and if you liked *The Ice Storm* you'll love the martial arts epic, too." He also believed that, "At least one of its breathtaking action sequences—a spectacular swordfight in the upper branches of a bamboo forest—will be a milestone in film history." Susan Stark of the *Detroit News* said that the film "will have you blinking to make sure your eyes are telling you the truth," because "Hollywood action pictures have made us rather blasé about characters leaping from rooftop to rooftop. Yet, *Crouching Tiger* refreshes the conventional, loony hyperbole in the most disarming way. These people aren't leaping at all, you come to realize. They're flying. And before the film is done, it will have them doing balletic battle from the top of swaying trees—in broad daylight. There's really no adequate way to communicate the surge of amazement and delight this film inspires. Leave it at this: It's just one of those wonders of imagination and craft that confirm your wildest dreams about the magic of movies."

Dave Kehr of *Citysearch* granted that "*Crouching Tiger* is a fine introduction to the genre for newcomers, though specialists might find it thin in comparison to the real thing." But even some sophisticated critics who were well versed in the genre were happy about Lee's movie. *Newsweek*'s David Ansen, for instance, felt, "At once elegant and sublimely silly, contemplative and gung-ho, balletic and bubble-gum, a rousing action film and an epic love story, *Crouching Tiger, Hidden Dragon* is one bursting-at-the-seams holiday gift, beautifully wrapped by the ever-surprising Ang Lee." He explained that, "It's an artful pastiche of many Hong Kong movies before it, from King Hu's 1971 historical martial-arts epic *A Touch of Zen* to the wild, gender-bending acrobatics of the Tsui Hark production *Swordsman II* (1991), next to which this looks positively sedate. *Crouching Tiger* doesn't so much break new ground as reconfigure the genre with the pomp and ceremony of Western production values and the psychological nuance that only the director of *Sense and Sensibility* and *The Ice Storm* can add to the brew. Lee grounds the high-kicking mayhem in poetic gravity, which gives it a flavor all its own, as plangent and lovely as the cello strains of Tan Dun's memorable score." The *Chicago Reader*'s Jonathan Rosenbaum, too, knew it was a hybrid, intended to be a tribute to the work of earlier Chinese maestros, but still he said, "This is the first Ang Lee film I've seen that I've liked without qualification. More important, it's the most exuberant action movie in ages, putting most re-

cent Hollywood blockbusters to shame," and he felt that the film, "succeeds in putting the same spirited spin on martial arts that *Singin' in the Rain* did on early Hollywood."

Andy Klein of *New Times Los Angeles* said, "It is ironic that *Crouching Tiger, Hidden Dragon*—which, in a poor field of competitors, is shaping up as one of the year's best films—may well be least enthusiastically received among diehard fans of its genre. What appears striking and new to most audiences is likely to be less riveting to those who have loved this form of cinema for years . . . and who may feel peevish that it's taken a relative interloper from the art houses to bring its glories to broader attention. 'We've been trying to turn you on to this stuff for *years!*' they might justifiably cry. 'And you wouldn't listen! And now you're giving all the credit to Ang Lee, who is largely recycling standard elements of the genre!'" Klein nonetheless had amiable feelings toward the film and suggested, "In truth, if longtime fans try to look objectively at *Crouching Tiger, Hidden Dragon*, they will see a first-rate entry in the field, worthy of comparison to its forebears. And they should welcome anything that brings attention to their beloved genre. Meanwhile, the rest of you should go see *Crouching Tiger, Hidden Dragon*. And, assuming you like what you see, should go out and rent *The Bride with White Hair* already."

But, writing in *Movieline*, Michael Atkinson, a long-standing admirer of the real thing, had little patience for *Crouching Tiger, Hidden Dragon* and those who loved it: "Hong Kong films are generally cheap and slapdash; Lee, working from a classic pre-WWII novel, has offered up a calm, gorgeous fable using every luxury, digital or otherwise, at his disposal. The movie has a Merchant-Ivory gloss to it that would've killed the fun of any of its authentic predecessors." And as for those movie reviewers out there whose raves sounded to him like the mindless gurgling of babies, Atkinson wrote, "Heralded as the film that will save 2000 from being the worst year for movies since 1929, Ang Lee's *Crouching Tiger, Hidden Dragon* is nothing less than a confectionery indulgence: it's a sugar high, fast, simple, polished and energetic. What it isn't is original or revolutionary or any of the other bogus adjectives piled upon it by critics who, almost by definition, have no business being critics." Atkinson said that "The best of these films have been seen in theaters and available on video for years . . . So, any reviewer stunned out of his shoes by *Crouching Tiger* is as valuable a critical voice as a sportswriter who's never heard of Willie Mays." Atkinson didn't specify any of the clueless reviewers who so irked him, but there was *Good Morning, America*'s addled Joel Siegel spouting off that "The way Bergman took us into his subconscious, Lee takes us into his dreams. It was filmed in Mandarin, but after the first few moments you won't notice the subtitles." He also said, "*Crouching Tiger, Hidden Dragon* isn't just one of the best movies of the year; it's one of the best movies, period. If someone were to ask me to list the hundred greatest movies of all time, *Crouching Tiger* would be on that list."

Chow Yun-Fat was a last-minute replacement for Jet Li, who decided to take a Hollywood offer instead. According to the director, Chow "had never touched a sword in his life." The film was so grueling that Chow grimaced as he recollected, "I had to see the chiropractor every day. My wife had to give me massages." Even more difficult than the duels for the actor—who had appeared in a couple of Hollywood films, including last year's unasked-for remake of *Anna and the King of Siam*—was the dialogue: he spoke Cantonese, not Mandarin. He admitted, "The first day I had to do twenty-eight takes just because of the language. That's never happened before in my life." Lee insisted that his actors speak in the Mandarin language of the original book because "Otherwise, it would be like watching John Wayne speak Chinese in a Western." Michelle Yeoh damaged her knee and had to spend a month in the United States for rehabilitation, but it was not like the production was any easier for the director. "We shot around the clock with two teams," Lee recalled. "I didn't take one break in eight months, not even for half a day. I was miserable—I just didn't have the extra energy to be happy. Near the end, I could hardly breathe. I thought I was about to have a stroke." Despite his quiet demeanor, Lee was quickly seen as a stern force on the set. But leading lady Yeoh said she based her fearless and fierce combatant character on Lee's wife. "I'm more physical and she's more verbal. But she can definitely kick Ang's ass."

High Art

Another altogether different type of epic was also on movie screens at the end of December and, coming nine months after *Erin Brockovich*, it was also the second Steven Soderbergh release of 2000. *Traffic* was a tripartite look at different aspects of drug commerce and usage, and was based on *Traffik*, a five-hour British miniseries about the trajection of illegal substances from Pakistan through Europe to Great Britain. Soderbergh said he had been interested in doing a film that somehow dealt with drugs but wasn't quite sure what to focus on. A friend, producer Laura Bickford, had obtained rights to the miniseries and, because he himself had seen *Traffik* and "thought it had a shape I could work with," Soderbergh signed on to the project. He and Bickford contacted a writer they were both impressed by named Stephen Gaghan. When they told him they wanted to do a movie about drugs, he said, "Funny you should mention that . . ." because he was already committed to writing a drug trafficking project for producers Ed Zwick and Marshall Herskovitz. After the particulars had been sorted out, the various parties all joined forces. The movie transposed the proceedings to North America and focused on a Mexican drug cartel, local law enforcement efforts in Southern California, and a personal story stemming from the federal government's so-called "War on Drugs," with all three stories converging at the end of the two-and-a-half-hour film. Soderbergh described the different strands as constituting "a sort of 'Upstairs, Downstairs' glimpse of what's going on, from how policy gets made to how the stuff gets from Mexico to a street corner in Cincinnati."

Soderbergh tried to sell the project by pitching it as "*Nashville* meets *The French Connection*"—"but I don't know that that was helping," he said. *Traffic* was turned down by all of the major Hollywood studios, but finally indie upstart USA Films agreed to bankroll the project. Soderbergh shot the film himself, but when he tried to have his credit read, "Directed and Photographed by" he was told "no can do" by the Writers Guild. The reason was that the Guild had an agreement with producers stating that no other credit can come in between those for the director and the writer. Not wanting to have two separate credits, Soderbergh used a pseudonym, based on his father's first two names and, thus, the film's cinematography was officially by one "Peter Andrews." There was no love lost between Soderbergh and the Writers Guild, as he had resigned from the union several years earlier after a credits dispute. "They told me that you can't quit the Guild, but I sent them a letter of resignation, and as far as I'm concerned, I'm out for good."

"It fulfills the promise Soderbergh showed with *sex, lies & videotape* in 1989," adjudged Duane Dudek in the *Milwaukee Journal Sentinel*. "His more recent films, *Out of Sight*, *The Limey* and *Erin Brockovich*, were all exceptionally good, but *Traffic* is groundbreaking. It is a lucid and ferocious examination of a tail-chasing and finger-pointing drug war driven by political self-interest, personal self-indulgence and self-denial in both cases. . . . Its argument that the personal is political is made potent by a precariously balanced assortment of characters whose motives may be unique but whose behaviors are interdependent. The scathing subject matter is reinforced by a style whose alternately bleached and bruised, Pavlovian visual cues summon a distinct, equally detached, sense of place and circumstances." Edward Guthmann of the *San Francisco Chronicle* believed that "With *Traffic*, his most ambitious and complex film to date, Soderbergh again proves himself one of our most inventive filmmakers. Soderbergh doesn't play it safe: With each project he erects a new set of dramatic and logistic challenges; instead of being intimidated by those challenges, he's galvanized by them, inspired to greater and more exciting work." A. O. Scott mused about Soderbergh in the *New York Times*: "A director who began his career with a deft chamber piece has now at last attempted a symphony. Is it a populist art film or an especially arty popular movie? Is Mr. Soderbergh an independent who has infiltrated Hollywood, or was he always a mainstream director in maverick's clothing? Such questions are based on rather wobbly distinctions, the kind Mr. Soderbergh, early on, seemed likely to uphold. Now, at the top of his game, he may help to abolish them, which would be good news indeed."

Joe Baltake of the *Sacramento Bee*, however, felt

that "*Traffic* is essentially a glorified public-service message that not only warns about the insidiousness of the drug culture and the dangers of drugs themselves, but also analyzes this country's War on Drugs campaign with a harsh, critical eye . . . The result is a movie with an intensely contemporary, up-to-date feeling that is as immediate as tonight's newscast. *Traffic* is the kind of movie that will probably age rather quickly, but right now it resonates in the present tense." Kenneth Turan had a number of reservations: "In its eagerness to make its points in an emotional way, it falls back too readily on the excesses of melodrama. Sometimes we feel we're watching an updated version of *Marijuana: The Weed with Roots in Hell*, or, to go back even further, a dramatization of the titillating horrors faced by young women in the dread clutches of the white slave trade." Furthermore, he felt that, "As a big-budget film in a controversial area, *Traffic* seems especially eager to be seen balanced, to be fair—for instance, to the hard-working and sincere anti-drug agents putting their lives at risk. So though it takes important steps in that direction, the film pulls back from what seems to be its own logical conclusion: No matter how much money we throw at the drug problem ($45 billion per annum at last count) and how heroically they're implemented by those at the front lines, current policies simply do not work." Turan's conclusion was, "Given what this film shows, a clearer stand on decriminalization or even treatment in place of prison seems in order. Without one, watching *Traffic*, artfully made though it is, feels a little like seeing a version of *The Insider* that thought it politic to waffle on whether cigarettes were a danger to your health."

Time's Richard Schickel said that such plot twists as a federal "drug czar" discovering his daughter is a junkie and a drug dealer being killed before he can turn state's evidence were "the clichés of a hundred crime movies, and bringing them all together in one place does not, finally, constitute an act of originality, no matter how interesting the details sometimes are, no matter how expertly they are presented. It may be that the magnitude of the problem is bound to strike dumb anyone who addresses it. It may also be that a mainstream movie doesn't dare consider more than offhandedly the radical alternatives to an official policy. We win tactical victories of the kind this film chronicles. But we are losing the 'war' because its strategies are undiscussible." *Newsweek* essayist Jonathan Alter didn't mind that *Traffic* came across as rather muddled in its proscriptions about what to do regarding drugs in America, saying that "One of the beauties of the film is that it somehow manages to satisfy both drug-enforcement officials by showing them as heroes and drug-policy critics by exposing the futility of sealing the border. The horrors of addiction and interdiction get equal time. By staying descriptive rather than didactic, Soderbergh reenergizes the drug-policy debate without actually entering it. That's up to the rest of us." The director did have his own opinion, even if it wasn't clearly elucidated in the movie: "You talk to any cop, they'll tell you, education and treatment pays off like gangbusters. The supply? We're never gonna stop that."

The film was packed with big name actors including Michael Douglas as Our Man in Washington (a late replacement for Harrison Ford), Dennis Quaid as a drug kingpin, Catherine Zeta-Jones as his wife, Amy Irving, Julia Roberts's boyfriend, Benjamin Bratt, and, in cameos, James Brolin, Peter Reigert, and *Erin Brockovich*'s Albert Finney. A number of U.S. Senators appeared in a Washington cocktail party sequence; producer Laura Bickford said, "We invited a bunch of senators to participate. Being liberal Hollywood types, the ones we called first were the Barbara Boxers." Several Republicans also took part, though, including a chief critic of Hollywood movies, Utah's obnoxious Orrin Hatch, and Iowa's Charles Grassley, whose pinched-face and mealy-mouth manner would have had him perfectly cast as a dyspeptic small-town banker in a Depression-era movie. (The *Los Angeles Times* reported that Hatch agreed to participate "after being assured that the movie would neither glorify drug use nor contain what he considers gratuitous violence." His spokesperson told the paper, "The first question we had is 'What is the movie rated?' We said, 'We really have to know: Is there anything that's going to make it embarrassing for a U.S. senator, particularly a Mormon U.S. senator, to participate in this movie?'") Offsetting the appearance of these unsavory individuals were some of the best character actors working in movies, particularly Don Cheadle and Luis Guzmán as drug agents, and Miguel Ferrer as a middle-level deal provider. The reviewers, however, focused on one person in particular. Jami Bernard said in the *New York Daily News*, "This actor's paradise is packed with outstanding performances. But first among equals is Benicio Del Toro, a consistently surprising young man (he was the one nobody could make out in *The Usual Suspects*). Del Toro plays Javier Rodriguez, a Mexican border cop trying to balance nine-to-five corruption with a job well done in a place where you can't tell the good guys from the bad. Del Toro's part is almost entirely in Spanish, and almost entirely cerebral. You see him chewing over the latest turn of events, trying to make a plan. He can do a poker face with an unusual amount of animation, which makes him incredibly magnetic." Desson Howe of the *Washington Post* said, "Benicio Del Toro, as his name suggests, is a majestic bull. An acting bull, that is, who overwhelms anyone with the sheer naiveté to enter his ring. Stomps them and eviscerates them, his eyelids drooping like half-drawn blinds. . . . He isn't just one of the many performers in *Traffic*, Steven Soderbergh's sinfully watchable ensemble movie about the drug trafficking scene. He owns it."

The *New York Times* treated some drug law enforcement veterans, academics, and recovering drug addicts to a screening of *Traffic* in order to get their reactions to the film. One nineteen-year-old man who was an ex-user said that the film's young druggie, played by Erika Christensen, was way too pretty. "She looked healthy throughout the movie," he complained. "Real heroin addicts don't look healthy. They start losing weight, their teeth start getting messed up, their skin gets scaly." A sociologist from the John Jay College of Criminal Justice in New York, Travis Wendel, was hopeful the movie would help refocus attention on narcotics, noting that illegal drugs were no longer at the forefront of governmental debate and were scarcely discussed in the recent presidential campaign. "Drug policies were in the headlines," he said "but they were all about prescription drugs for the elderly."

Crash Diet

America's favorite Average Joe, Tom Hanks, was kicking around in movie theaters this Christmas season. He was back with Robert Zemeckis, a reunion that chilled everyone who hated *Forrest Gump*, which, like *Dances with Wolves*, was one of those acclaimed movies it was becoming increasingly difficult to find someone who'd admit to liking. What brought them together was *Cast Away*, all about a hot shot FedEx employee whose plane crashes, meaning that Hanks got to be all virtuosic while solo on a desert island. Hanks had come up with the idea all by himself—never mind Daniel Dafoe—telling Jay Leno that the concept had been planted in his head while he was watching a documentary on Amelia Earhardt.

The actor also got to do De Niro-ize—because being stuck on an island will take off the weight. *Cast Away* was filmed in two parts. The production shut down for a year while Hanks took off fifty pounds; director Zemeckis took advantage of the time off to make a disposable piece of junk, the ghost story, *What Lies Beneath*. Hanks—who coproduced the film—pontificated that, "*Cast Away* offers high adventure. But at the same time, it presents a simple Zen-like understanding of what things in the world are truly important"—like Oscars, because one didn't need to be too cynical to believe that the primary raison d'être for the movie was to get Hanks Academy Award number three. The actor told E!'s Steve Kmetko that the project "did become this long, kind of like, personal quest of how to do this in a way that was going to be contrary to standard cinematic narrative, that we do things that were kind of bold and kind of scary" as if he were collaborating with Wong Kar-Wai, not the guy who made *Death Becomes Her* and *Contact*.

Mick LaSalle of the *San Francisco Chronicle* had a grand time at *Cast Away*, calling it "a laugh-out-loud delight, easily the funniest picture since *South Park*. It will bring joy to audiences, though not in the way it was intended—as an uplifting tale of the human spirit. Instead it will bring joy in a way certainly not intended, as one of the most gloriously and unwittingly silly films ever devised by a major American filmmaker. Still, joy is joy, so even if Tom Hanks and director Robert Zemeckis had no idea they were making a comedy, we shouldn't hold that against them." Doug Kim of the *Seattle Times* said the film's "message seems to be about the value of time, and Hanks' mastery of it/slavery to it, but that's not a whole lot more profound than the message we get in those ten-second beer commercials where the guy on the beach throws the ringing cell phone in the water."

Any number of reviewers did go for *Cast Away*. There was, for instance, Jeff Vice of the *Deseret News* who said, "The very idea of being deprived of everyday luxuries is so horrifying to most of us that the film's premise might seem a bit ridiculous. But the fine cast, which includes Helen Hunt (who's very good in what seems like her twelfth role this month), makes it very believable. . . . It also includes a wry, fitting ending that might best be described as Capra-esque (as in Frank Capra, the maker of such films as *It's a Wonderful Life*)." Rex Reed wrote in the *New York Observer*, "It is very much a film about survival, of both physical ardor and the dignity of the human spirit. I'm almost embarrassed to admit it, but I spent half the time in *Cast Away* covering my eyes and the other half in tears."

Hanks received the kind of reviews that this type of prefabricated tour-de-force is calculated to procure. Andrew Sarris said, "this movie offers Mr. Hanks ample opportunity to tear every scene to tatters, and this should impress the Oscar voters." *The New Yorker*'s David Denby, as usual, was saying nothing but saying it with much pomposity: "Tom Hanks's physical transformation is one of the most moving things in recent films—a progression toward death and, at the same time, toward life."

Although Helen Hunt was officially Hanks's costar, appearing in the film's "civilization" bookends, he spent much of the film talking to a piece of product placement, a volleyball named Wilson. *Mad*'s parody of *Cast Away* had Hanks saying to the ball: "Finally, a companion! I've painted a face on a volleyball! For the next ninety minutes you're going to be my new best friend! We will chat, we will bond! I'm going to spend the movie talking to an inanimate costar! I haven't experienced this since Meg Ryan!" Writer Salman

Rushdie said that when he was in the theater he was distracted by "a five-year-old girl insistently asking her parents during *Cast Away*, 'Mommy, when is the volleyball going to talk?'" In the movie, Hanks returns home to find that Hunt has married someone else, but not to worry, because as Bruce Newman of the *San Jose Mercury News* saw it, the film "can't seem to wait to pair Hanks off again, this time with somebody even sexier than Helen Hunt, the love of his life until five minutes earlier. So what's the big lesson here? That if you take your lumps like a man, you wind up with somebody who maybe *hasn't* been in every movie released since Labor Day?" In the *Mad* version, the happy ending has Hanks hanging out in a sporting goods store fondling volleyballs.

Sweet and Sour

And where was Harvey Weinstein? Back in January Weinstein, uncharacteristically, didn't buy a single movie at Sundance and, for most of the year, he was a less noticeable presence than normal. He expended a great deal of his time and energy on Al Gore's presidential campaign and Hillary Clinton's successful run for the U.S. Senate, and was out of sight for a while because of a hospital stay. Miramax's most acclaimed 2000 release was Michael Almereyda's stylized, modern-day adaptation of *Hamlet*, with Ethan Hawke earning terrific reviews in the title role, supported by an eclectic, highly praised supporting cast that included Sam Shepard as the Ghost, Julia Stiles as Ophelia and Bill Murray as Polonius. Elvis Mitchell of the *New York Times* called *Hamlet* the best film of the year, saying it was "voluptuous and exhilarating." But, as *Slate*'s David Edelstein pointed out, Weinstein and company "tested *Hamlet* on the multiplex crowd, were horrified by the numbers, and buried the movie without a second thought." The film was not widely seen, and had to wait to go to video to develop a burgeoning cult following.

Miramax had three Christmas releases. One was the high-budget (by Miramax standards) *All the Pretty Horses*. Even though it was based on the Cormac McCarthy best-seller, was directed by Billy Bob Thornton and starred Matt Damon, what little pre-release atten-tion the movie garnered was negative, largely because its premiere was constantly being postponed and rescheduled. Army Archerd revealed, "Miramax's prais-ery has been mounting a campaign to undo any preconceived mal de mouth. F'rinstance, they had Thornton, Weinstein and the film's star Matt Damon conference-call Liz Smith to erase the evil droppings of fellow fourth-estaters. She printed the trio's denials of problems and praise of one another. But, with due appreciation of Liz's power, it didn't seem to be enough for Miramax because they then called yours truly to ask if I'd talk to Damon." The *Daily Variety* columnist said "Of course I would be happy to talk to Damon, any time," and the actor spun that "This is a very special picture. Hopefully it will be for everyone. It is truly profound and I am prouder of this than anything I have ever done. I wish I could make it over and over again." Damon called Billy Bob Thornton, "a miracle worker; I learned so much from him." Despite the damage control, *All the Pretty Horses* proved to be a nonevent during the holiday season.

There was also *Malena*, a sappy Italian film that Miramax unsuccessfully tried to manipulate into a crossover hit as it had done with *Life Is Beautiful* two years ago.

That left the Weinsteins with *Chocolat*. The film was dappled with reminders of past Miramax successes. It was directed by Lasse Hallström who had given the studio a presence at last year's Oscars with *The Cider House Rules*, and it starred Juliette Binoche from Miramax's first Best Picture winner, *The English Patient*, and Judi Dench from its second, *Shakespeare in Love*. An allegorical tale set in France, *Chocolat* had the not-too-convincing premise of the Catholic Church launching an attack on the title commodity—though the candy was really a surrogate for all of life's sensuous pleasures—and it was rather a precious little thing upon which to base a studio's Oscar hopes. Director Hallström said "To me, *Chocolat* is a very funny fable about temptation and the importance of not denying oneself the good things in life. It's about the constant conflict between tradition and change. And at its very center it is about intolerance and the consequences of not letting other people live out their own lives and beliefs." And so, as his last film was a sweet-natured broadside against right-to-lifers, this one was a gentle denunciation of the misnamed "family values" crowd. Producer David Brown said, "It's not the average conventional one-two-three kick movie story. It's unusual but at the same time it has this immense likability." *Politically Incorrect*'s Bill Maher loved *Chocolat*, and said the village in which it takes place was "a very Republican town; They do not want anyone to have fun . . . He's like Mayor Newt Gingrich and she's Bill Clinton."

An optimistic sign for the movie was that on-site reports had pegged the production as an extremely happy experience. David Gritten of London's *Observer* said that he had learned to approach Juliette Binoche in the middle of a movie set "with trepidation; she is not known for being upbeat. I have observed her tense and moody on two previous films. Yet there she was Juliette Binoche, tramping across a field, her beautiful dark eyes darting slyly about her, her trademark vestigial smile dancing on her lips in perpetual celebration of some private joke." And she was saying, "This is a light piece, a happy piece. It's about chocolate, you know, how bad can that be?" Meanwhile, Judi Dench was telling the *New York Times* that she had met Lasse Hallström at the last Miramax pre-Oscar party "and he had a wonderful sense of humor. I knew it would be glorious working with him and it was. A sense of humor is so important to me, it's the key that unlocks everything." She also admitted, "I am notorious for not reading the script, and I really don't. I just get a kind of funny feeling that tells me when to do a role. Did you ever see *The Glenn Miller Story*? Do you remember how his wife, June Allyson, always said that she got this funny prickly feeling up the back of her neck when she heard a piece of music that was special? It's just like that. I'm entirely instinctive, as far as that goes."

Some reviewers seemed to enjoy themselves watching *Chocolat* as much as the cast did making it. Others did not. Kevin Thomas of the *Los Angeles Times* was perhaps the film's most pronounced cheerleader, as he gushed, "*Chocolat* is a work of artistry and craftsmanship at the highest level, sophisticated in its conception and execution, yet possessed of wide appeal. It's that rarity, a movie that opens at Christmas that re-flects the true (as opposed to commercial) spirit of the season." The *Chicago Tribune*'s Michael Wilmington was also crazy for *Chocolat*, calling it "a romance that is really romantic and a comedy that is really funny. It floods the screen with genuine magic. A feast of fine actors and every one of them is a joy to watch." Lou Lumenick of the *New York Post* described *Chocolat* as "a bittersweet confection that few holiday filmgoers will be able to resist, thanks to melt-in-your-mouth performances by Juliette Binoche, Alfred Molina and Judi Dench. . . . it's not exactly cutting-edge filmmaking, but rather the soothing cinematic equivalent of a warm cup of decadently rich cocoa." *Time*'s Richard Schickel, though, complained that the movie, "may suggest to those who find themselves unsusceptible to its fabulistic charms how easy it has become to travesty the manner of what used to be thought of as 'art' movies. This one has something of their air—an attractive, slightly exotic setting, characters who appear to have some substance and some curious quirks. But everything is spun toward sugary sentimentality. And relentless predictability." David Sterritt of the *Christian Science Monitor* said, "the unsubtle story is full of simplistic divisions between right and wrong, and the filmmaking is pretty but predictable. As the title inadvertently hints, the picture's aftertaste is more sugary than satisfying."

Elvis Mitchell wrote that the characters played by Juliette Binoche and Johnny Depp—the chocolate purveyor, Vianne, and Roux, the "river rat," with whom she falls in love—"are in touch with the natural parts of themselves—D. H. Lawrence-inspired figures for people who don't want the messy sexuality that Lawrence also calls for. With her bright eyes and generous spirits, Vianne is so good-natured she takes the seediness out of bohemia. *Chocolat* might be a little more fun if she were somewhat aware that she is creating a village of sugar abusers. Instead, she mystically fulfills the needs of everyone with whom she comes into contact because, in the end, the people who inhabit *Chocolat* all have voids in their lives. They're people who need people, and thanks to Vianne, they're the luckiest people in the world."

As part of their mutual admiration society, Bill Clinton invited Harvey Weinstein—along with Lasse

Hallström—to the White House and had him bring along *Chocolat*. Army Archerd reported, "Looking around the simple projection room, Harvey told the Clintons, 'Wait'll you see my projection room.' And the Clintons will probably see a lot more of it as Bill C. soon takes offices in the city and their house in Chappaqua. The president and Hallström had a long schmooze after the screening—about the movie whose theme of tolerance the Clintons loved. The president also talked of other moviemakers—including Ingmar Bergman. And also talks of soon being neighbors—the Hallströms live in Bedford."

In the Sewer

In mid-November, a front page story in *Variety* stated, "If you thought voting in Palm Beach was a challenge, imagine trying to cast a ballot in the 2000 Oscar race. With just six weeks left until the end of the year, there is still no front-runner. There's not even a middle-runner. . . .The vacuum is so noticeable that even Wolfgang Puck, the celebrity chef who works many Oscar parties was seen approaching Acad prexy Robert Rehme asking, 'Where are all the Oscar pictures?' " Three weeks later, the trade paper's piece on the National Board of Review stated that this year's was "an awards field generally considered the most wide open in years."

USA Today's Mike Clark looked back from the vantage point of late December and mourned, "Despite a late spate of cinematic salvations (many tucked away in faraway art houses), the movie year is widely considered dreadful, with some calling it Hollywood's worst since sound. Now that is one rash statement, but I was hearing complaints everywhere—at my son's baseball games, at my high school reunion, and from people who love movies enough to own sixty-one-inch TV screens, satellite dishes and large DVD collections. The lament went like this: I'm a mortgage-paying grown-up to whom the bank will lend money, yet I pick up the paper, and there's nothing I want to see." He noted, "Look up any movie year on the internet, and you'll see that the early '60s were soft for Hollywood and the mid-'80s softer—but nothing like this." Jack Mathews of the *New York Daily News* said, "If you

look at 2000 as a report card, Hollywood flunked. It had a dismal winter and spring, almost went 0 for the summer, had a weak fall followed by a holiday line-up that barely contained a single legitimate Oscar contender." A. O. Scott wrote in the *New York Times* that there was plenty of reason for cinematic pessimism: "Nobody wants to see serious movies; fewer and fewer foreign films make it into American theatres. The big studios are content to make hundreds of millions of dollars on overhyped, mediocre pictures—*M:I-2*, *Gladiator*, *The Grinch*—that people see more out of habit than enthusiasm." James Schamus, the co-producer and cowriter of *Crouching Tiger, Hidden Dragon* told *Newsweek*, "I think this was a bad year for crappy movies. The crappy movies really were *so* crappy that they kind of made a bigger splash in the sewage system of the world."

But Steve Erickson wrote in *Chronicle of a Passion*, "It's become received wisdom that 2000 was a horrible year for film, a judgment that leaves me baffled. If one views mainstream American cinema as the center of the universe (and far too many critics do), only then does it make sense." And his contention was borne out by the *Village Voice*'s film critics poll in which Clair Denis's dreamy, erotically charged reimagining of *Billy Budd*, *Beau Travail*, was named the number one movie of the year, with the rest of the top ten including the Taiwanese *Yi Yi*, Edward Yang's wise and humane family drama; the devastating adaptation of Edith Wharton's *The House of Mirth* by Britain's Terence Davies; Iranian giant Abbas Kiarostami's meditation on life's ebbs and flows, *The Wind Will Carry Us;* and Bruno Dumont's *L'Humanité* from France, a mesmerizing rendering of a world filled with regret, despair and longing. (Erickson noted that *L'Humanité* was so good that *Entertainment Weekly*'s Owen Gleiberman "stayed true to form by putting it on his Bottom Five list."). Most of these films, obviously, weren't going to curry much enthusiasm from the people who made up the Academy's membership, though the warmly humanistic *Yi Yi*, did have real Academy-type virtues and Edward Yang might have been a dark horse possibility for a Best Director nomination. Unfortunately, even though *Yi Yi* had a successful run in Los Angeles, it was not included on the Academy's reminder list of eligible pictures and, thus, would not be in the competition. Apparently, the film's distributor, Winstar, didn't do the paperwork required to get it on the list; still, the company could be proud of having emerged as 2000's most exciting independent film company. Back in the mainstream, Terry Press, head of marketing at DreamWorks, didn't want to hear anything from the nabobs of negativism: "It wouldn't be Christmas without Oscar complaining. 'Ho, ho, ho. This year is the worst ever.'"

The Season for Giving

Even though it had received mixed reviews, Philip Kaufman's *Quills*, in which the Marquis de Sade becomes a heavy-handed symbol of free speech, was the National Board of Review's selection as the Best Picture of the year. (Gerald Peary of the *Boston Phoenix* described the film's de Sade thusly: "Geoffrey Rush as a lovably dirty old man who leers but never gets to debauch. Someone like your toothless uncle Billy, who makes sexist remarks and tries to pinch the girls at the Thanksgiving table, but slap his wandering hand and the old geezer is pretty harmless. Nope, there's no raping of nuns or thirteen-year-old virgins for this Marquis, just lots of overwritten claptrap monologues and a philosophy of life that's less about destroying church, state, and hymens than about defending First Amendment rights.") Julia Roberts won Best Actress for *Erin Brockovich*, and while this acting award went to the most popular woman in the movies, Best Actor went to a man who was almost completely unknown in this country. A major star in Spain, Javier Bardem played Reinaldo Arenas, a persecuted gay Cuban writer, in *Before Night Falls*, the second film made by artist Julian Schnabel. (*Newsday*'s Jan Stuart said, "Bardem performs one of those triumphs of total immersion that make us marvel at the occasional heroism of screen actors.") The Supporting Actress winner was also obscure: Lupe Ontiveros, who made for a wry mother-figure in *Chuck and Buck*, a dark independent film about a modern day Peter Pan's obsession with a childhood friend. Joaquin Phoenix received Best Supporting Actor, not just for *Gladiator*, but also for the little-seen Miramax crime drama, *The Yards*, and *Quills*, in which

he played a compassionate young priest who develops an active libido. The Board anointed Steven Soderbergh Best Director for both *Erin Brockovich* and *Traffic*.

Soderbergh was likewise cited as Best Director for his two 2000 releases by the New York Film Critics Circle, which also named *Traffic* Best Picture. The group selected Tom Hanks as Best Actor in *Cast Away*, a somewhat surprising result because members of the organization often seem to be making a show of trying to come off as hip, and Hanks bordered on the retro. Best Actress was Laura Linney in *You Can Count on Me*, playwright Kenneth Lonergan's directorial debut about a woman and her ne'er-do-well brother; the film was inexplicably popular among critics despite its monumental banality, and never mind that it was so uncinematic it resembled something you might have seen on *American Playhouse* around 1981. The film also received the Best Screenplay Award. Go figure. The New Yorkers' named Marcia Gay Harden Best Supporting Actress for playing painter Lee Krasner, Jackson Pollock's wife, in *Pollock*, Ed Harris's ten-years-in-the-making labor-of-love. Benicio Del Toro had been runner-up to Hanks for Best Actor, so the Critics turned around and gave him the Supporting Actor Award. *Time*'s Richard Corliss wrote of Del Toro, "He has the sleepy sensuality of the young Robert Mitchum—a narcoleptic dreamboat quality that suggests a sleek predator roused from slumber by a poke through his cage. So when Benicio Del Toro got a call around noon Los Angeles time to be told that he'd won the New York Film Critics Circle's Best Supporting Actor prize for his performance as a Mexican narc in *Traffic*, the thirty-three-year-old emitted something like a growl. The new lion of Hollywood is a late sleeper and, he says, 'I'm not a happy camper when I get woken up.'" Some card thought he or she was being funny by voting for Wilson, the volleyball from *Cast Away*, just as in 1978 some card thought he or she was being funny by voting for Rex Reed who was seen walking into the Daily Planet building in *Superman*.

The runner-up for Best Picture in the New Yorkers' voting was *Crouching Tiger, Hidden Dragon*, meaning that this group of people believed it was the second best movie released in 2000, and that only *Traffic* was better. (Ang Lee was also second to Steven Soderbergh for Best Director.) But then, illogically, *Crouching Tiger* lost Best Foreign Film to *Yi Yi*. *The House of Mirth* came in third in the Picture and Director races, and its star, Gillian Anderson, was second for Best Actress. J. Hoberman of the *Village Voice* said, "I . . . think that *The House of Mirth* was ineptly handled and am convinced that had the movie been promoted with one-quarter the energy that Miramax puts into flogging its Oscar bait, Gillian Anderson would have won the New York Film Critics' Circle Award for Best Actress. A number of critics never got to screenings; nor, so far as I know, were any screeners sent out." Sony Classics was the inept distributor, but then again the company may have been preoccupied with promoting *Crouching Tiger, Hidden Dragon* and *Pollock*.

Crouching Tiger, Hidden Dragon received the Los Angeles Film Critics Association's Award for Best Picture, but Steven Soderbergh's double-barrel was too much for Ang Lee in the Director contest. Michael Douglas was named Best Actor for *Wonder Boys* and Julia Roberts took Best Actress honors. The L.A. Supporting prizes went to two people who lived in New York: Frances McDormand for both *Wonder Boys* and *Almost Famous*, and Willem Dafoe for *Shadow of the Vampire*, in which he played *Nosferatu* actor Max Schreck, who in the movie's premise actually was a vampire. As with the New York critics, *You Can Count on Me* won Best Screenplay and *Yi Yi* was named Best Foreign Film. Later, when Julia Roberts accepted her award at the Los Angeles Critics' ceremony, she joked, "I'm kind of freaking out because critics, in general, I don't eat with." And, according to the *Los Angeles Times*, she joked that, "The chicken here sure beats the [expletive] out of the fish at the National Board of Review!"

Yi Yi did best of all with the National Society of Film Critics—it won Best Picture. But even here, no one could dislodge Steven Soderbergh; he was now four for four. The acting winners were Javier Bardem, Laura Linney, Benicio Del Toro and one person not previously heard from in this year's awards: Elaine May, who played seriously dumb in *Small Town Crooks*, Woody Allen's reworking of both an old Lloyd

Bacon comedy, *Larceny, Inc.*, and the Bowery Boys movie, *Blonde Dynamite*. *You Can Count on Me* was the Screenplay winner.

The Marquis de Cates

It was too good to last—after just one year's sabbatical Gilbert Cates was coming back to produce the Oscar ceremony. Richard and Lili Fini Zanuck had made clear that they intended their producing duties to be a one-shot only deal, but hopes that another new face would be brought in to continue with the revitalization of the show were in vain. This would be Cates's tenth time, and he said, "Ten is a nice round number. I'm thrilled to be back and delighted that Bob has asked me once more. Hopefully, this year's show will be fun for all. I love to try to surprise viewers." President Rehme sounded a bit skeptical, as he said, "Hopefully the show will be somewhat entertaining."

Billy Crystal had already stated that he would be unavailable for hosting duties, as he was in the middle of filming a movie, *America's Sweethearts*. A few days after Cates was designated as producer, he announced that Steve Martin would be emceeing this year. "He is everything," said Cates. "He's a movie star, he's funny, he's classy, he's literate—he'll be a wonderful host." Although Martin had made many memorable quips during his eight Oscar appearances, there was some thought that his humor might prove to be too dry to sustain an entire show, that he would be too cerebral a presence. Cates, though, zeroed in on the host's appeal when he said, "Steve has an elegance about him that harkens back to the days of Johnny Carson. He can do comedy, but he's also very graceful, very funny and very intelligent." As work got underway on the show, veteran Oscar writer Bruce Vilanch said that "Steve is trying to be very smart. He doesn't want to try to impose too much of himself on the show. I think that he saw Dave and decided that he doesn't want to do too much of his own schtick." The host himself said, "Carson was great. Billy's been great. I'm hoping to be mediocre."

The *Los Angeles Times* had invited readers to send in their suggestions as to who should host, and Martin, along with Jim Carrey—whom Billy Crystal had suggested—was mentioned the most often. Other suggestions from readers included Jon Stewart, Eddie Izzard, the return of Johnny Carson (or else Kevin Spacey doing his Johnny Carson imitation), Martin Short, Chris Rock, Paula Poundstone and Regis Philbin. Gary Clifford of Limerick, Ireland was a lonely voice requesting, "Letterman again, please. It's only the dumb masses who didn't get him last time! Dave was the only host in the last ten years not to make the Oscar night resemble a funeral procession! Please, no more blandness." And Glendale's Neal Bakke wanted something completely different: "Let's get some elegant women at the reins. Here are some suggestions: Julie Andrews (Oscar winner), Shirley MacLaine (Oscar winner), Barbra Streisand (double Oscar winner), Angela Lansbury (triple Oscar nominee). One thing that these woman can bring to the Oscars is elegance." Waxing nostalgic in his letter to the *Times*, Neal said, "I remember watching the Oscars when I was little, and it was such a thrill. Part of the excitement of the evening was watching until the very last Award so you could see what Elizabeth Taylor was wearing and how she looked. There is no glamour and elegance to the Oscars anymore."

One prayed that Cates had at least taken notes while seeing the improvements Richard and Lili Fini Zanuck had brought to the ceremony last year. But not only did he announce that he was hauling out musical director Bill Conti again, he seemed to possess sadistic tendencies, because he uttered the five worst words any Oscar viewer could hear: "Debbie Allen is coming back." It was a toss-up as to what was more surprising: that Cates had so little respect for the audience that he would again hire this woman, or that, with her *Saving Private Ryan* tap-dancing number right up there with Snow White in Oscar infamy, Allen wouldn't have had the grace, and good sense, to just say no.

Taking stock of everything that went wrong last year—the stolen Oscars, the missing ballots, the *Wall Street Journal* poll—the Academy's executive director, Bruce Davis, was guardedly optimistic about the upcoming Awards. "The likelihood of having such a confluence of extreme improbabilities occur again is tiny," he said. Bob Rehme pointed out that the Academy

Awards "happened the same way for years and years and nothing ever happened. Then all of a sudden a couple of things happened the same year. It was simply a strange, weird coincidence." But just in case . . . The Academy put into effect a contingency plan of having a slew of Oscars locked away in its vault as backup statuettes. The newly minted statuettes, meanwhile, would be flown in from Chicago, rather than making the trip halfway across the country in the back of a truck. In addition, postal workers would make a personal pick-up of this year's ballots at the Academy's headquarters to ensure they didn't get waylaid. And the Academy didn't have to worry about an interloper from the New York financial world spilling the beans this time out. Jonathan Dahl, editor of the *Wall Street Journal*'s "Weekend Journal," said that the Oscar poll was a "once-in-a-lifetime idea," and was not going to become an annual rite of spring. He maintained that, "We thought it was a great idea, it got great response and we are very glad we did it. It did a service to our readers, not only how the results might be, but just in how the Academy operated and the thinking behind how people voted."

Terry Press's Busy Season

A new Oscar promotional gimmick took hold this year. Academy members were sent scripts for over two dozen Oscar hopefuls. Studio publicity departments didn't expect voters actually to read the screenplays, it was more that they were playing mind games. The thinking was that if a voter saw that it had gone to the bother and expense of sending the thing out, the studio must believe the movie was really good. Also, the major companies gave members the option of receiving films on DVD rather than video, with just a few of the small, independent companies sitting on the more recent technology.

When it came to advertising for nominations, DreamWorks was putting Miramax to shame. The studio's marketer, Terry Press, bragged to the *Hollywood Reporter*, "I think we have a lot of eggs in the basket this year, and our Oscar hopes are spread among a variety of our pictures." With its two fall releases, *Almost Famous* and *The Contender*, having failed at the box office, however, the studio worked on convincing Academy members that its big hit of 2000 was actually a serious movie, one which was deserving of Oscar recognition. And so ads for *Gladiator* proliferated. Many of them took up two pages and were in black and white or sepia-toned, an attempt to give the movie a tony feel. The studio wasn't forgetting *Almost Famous*, though. The film was showing up on Ten Best lists and was nominated for many of the guilds' awards, so apparently it was better liked than its money-losing ways would have indicated. Moreover, DreamWorks could look back to last year when *The Insider* was a Best Picture finalist despite flat box-office returns. DreamWorks was going with the same ploy for the Cameron Crowe movie it had used last year for *American Beauty*—chunks of dialogue littered the page. Tellingly, the studio did not do so with *Gladiator*: it would have been self-defeating to bring to the attention of Academy voters such ludicrous lines as Marcus Aurelius's "There was a dream that was Rome. You could only whisper it. Anything more than a whisper and it would vanish, it was so fragile"; Maximus's "If you find yourself alone, riding through green fields with the sun on your face, do not be troubled, for you are in Elysium, and are already dead"; and Proximo's: "Those giraffes you sold me, they won't mate. They just walk around, eating, and not mating. You sold me . . . queer giraffes. I want my money back." Instead, the focus of the ads was entirely on Russell Crowe.

Variety noted that because of "the anything-goes nature" of this year's races, "a movie like *Gladiator*—which many consider essentially a well-crafted summer action movie with the Oscar-friendly trappings of large scale and period setting—boasts the kind of awards profile it might not wield in any other year. With the film out of theatrical circulation, DreamWorks pumped new life into its campaign with a lavish DVD launch at the Academy theater in Los Angeles, including appearances by director Ridley Scott and star Russell Crowe. It was as if the film had premiered all over again." This December screening was followed by a panel discussion, and Scott showed examples of how the film used Computer Graphic Imaging; much of the film's behind-the-camera talent

was also in attendance to mingle with guests, many of whom were Academy voters. The studio did run some ads for *The Contender*, and Gary Oldman was still making Terry Press's life miserable by insisting that, star that he was, he be positioned in the Best Actor category, not Supporting.

Selling the Product

Miramax was by no means standing on the sidelines, although the *Hollywood Reporter* said that the studio "is looking to many industry insiders like it will lag behind in this year's Oscar race with its Christmas releases . . . However, as one critic points out, 'Never underestimate Miramax.' In response to whether or not Miramax has lost its Oscar edge, a spokesperson for the company asserts that Miramax will, indeed, be heavily campaigning for performers in all three of its Christmas releases." This spokesperson boasted to the *Reporter*, "We always pull it out in the home stretch."

A more objective voice, Mike Clark of *USA Today*, had grim news for Harvey Weinstein's hopes of being at the Shrine Auditorium via *Chocolat*: "Given its title and its almost fablelike story, *Chocolat* leads one to expect the cinematic equivalent of an éclair or some other lightweight sweet. But what we get recalls that classic *New Yorker* cartoon in which a husband bites into one of his wife's just-baked delicacies and asks, 'What did you use for mortar?' Adapted from Joanne Harris's 1999 novel, the movie is directed with so little whimsy by Lasse Hallström that the standard Miramax hype machine might overheat to the point of catching fire if it tries revving up the kind of dubious huzzahs it did for Hallström's *The Cider House Rules* a year ago. At least with that film, reasonable minds could differ."

Also highly prominent this Oscar season was Universal, which was going all out for *Erin Brockovich* and *Billy Elliot* (and doing its bit for Ron Howard's *Dr. Seuss's How the Grinch Stole Christmas*; it also had partnered with DreamWorks on *Gladiator*). The *Los Angeles Times*'s Richard Natale said of *Brockovich*, "Earlier in the year it was assumed the film might be too lightweight for the top prize and would do best in categories such as Best Actress (Julia Roberts) and

Supporting Actor (Albert Finney). But with few viable candidates for the Best Picture slot at this point, Universal is mounting a full-scale campaign as well as an exclusive re-release of the film in theaters." But Universal's Terry Curtin told *USA Today* that the studio had thought of *Erin Brockovich* as an Oscar contender back in March when it opened, and averred, "We always looked at it as a key Academy picture. It's so frustrating to read that it is only in the running because other movies have fallen short." In fact, the year's first ad of this Oscar season was for *Brockovich*, placed by Universal back in mid-November. And it didn't run in a Hollywood trade paper but, rather, to give the campaign a classier launch, in the *New York Times Magazine*. Disney was pushing the high school football/racial drama, *Remember the Titans*, the Coen Brothers' *O Brother, Where Art Thou?* and *Unbreakable*, M. Night Shyamalan's follow up to *The Sixth Sense*. Fox Searchlight was doing its bit for *Quills*, even as audiences were turning away from it, and Warner Brothers was promoting *Pay It Forward* as if it had been an acclaimed box-office hit.

Paramount did a *mea culpa* and reissued *Wonder Boys* in November—with a brand new advertising campaign. But it was not a wide re-release, and the film didn't garner any more attention than it had the first time around. Universal also put *Erin Brockovich* back into a few theaters; the main reason was not to increase revenues for an already very successful film, but to give the studio an excuse to run high-profile, Oscar-oriented advertising in the *Los Angeles Times* and *New York Times*.

All My Children

Erin Brockovich was half of a problem for Steven Soderbergh. With both of his films considered strong possibilities for Best Picture Oscar nominations, the question was would his admirers be splitting votes so that his two movies canceled out each other? He refused even to hint that he might prefer one just a smidgen more. *Brockovich*'s coproducer Stacey Sher said, "I'm such a fan of Steven's that I just root for them both . . . And Steven will not take a position of one film versus the other. People keep saying, 'Steven,

you are going to have to jettison a film if you want to win.' And he says, 'Would you jettison a child?' " But *USA Today* reported that at USA Films, the company that made *Traffic*, "The hope is that *Brockovich* will be viewed as a Roberts vehicle, and *Traffic* will be seen as the artistic achievement."

Sony Classics saw the grosses for *Crouching Tiger, Hidden Dragon* steadily build as the movie evidenced an appeal across the board, from art house cineastes to action fans and then, as it opened in more theaters, to just plain multiplex folks. The company's copresident, Michael Barker, said "The film appeals to every demographic, and as we proceed around the country it proves that occasionally a picture comes along that says subtitles are a nonissue." In early January, David Davis, a senior vice president and media analyst at Houlihan, Lokey, Howard and Zukin, told *Daily Variety* that he saw the movie grossing $35 million, while Sony Classics was predicting anywhere from $30 to $50 million.

Under the Hollywood Foreign Press's rules, *Crouching Tiger* was only eligible for Foreign Film Golden Globe, not for Best Picture. It was eligible in all other categories, though, and, in addition to Foreign Film, was nominated for Best Director and Original Score. The big news from the nominations was that Steven Soderbergh received nominations for both *Erin Brockovich* and *Traffic*, the first time in the Globes' fifty-seven-year history that such a double nomination had occurred in the Directing category.

When the Globes was handed out, Soderbergh was no longer the pacesetter. Although his film couldn't win Best Picture, Ang Lee did take the Best Director Globe, and—indicative of the esteem in which he and *Crouching Tiger* were held in Hollywood—received a standing ovation. After losing in all four of the categories for which it had been nominated earlier in the evening, *Gladiator* was resuscitated at the last minute and won Best Picture (Drama). Cameron Crowe had a good night. Although he lost the Screenplay Award to *Traffic*'s Stephen Gaghan, *Almost Famous* did win Best Picture (Musical or Comedy), defeating *Chocolat*, and Kate Hudson received the Supporting Actress prize. *Traffic* also received a Globe for Benicio Del Toro as Best Supporting Actor. The two biggest stars in Hollywood won the Drama awards: *Cast Away*'s Tom Hanks, who now had to be considered the favorite for the Oscar, and Julia Roberts in *Erin Brockovich* (she thanked her family, saying "It can't be easy to be related to me, trust me"). *Chocolat*'s Juliette Binoche lost Best Actress (Musical or Comedy) to Renee Zellweger in *Nurse Betty*, and Jim Carrey failed to make it three in a row at the Globes. His performance in *Dr. Seuss' How the Grinch Stole Christmas* lost to George Clooney's in *O Brother, Where Art Thou?* The ceremony also featured the incongruous sight of Bob Dylan in the midst of the members of the Hollywood Foreign Press Association; "Things Have Changed," his song from *Wonder Boys* was a Globe winner and, like Ang Lee, he was given a standing ovation. The highlight of the night came later, though. Patrick Goldstein wrote in the *Los Angeles Times*, "There was so much enmity between Miramax and Sony Pictures Classics that when Miramax czar Harvey Weinstein ran into Sony's co-chief Tom Bernard at a post-Golden Globes party, a brawl nearly broke out."

Crystal Ball of Confusion

Daily Variety's take on the Golden Globe results was "Many Oscar pundits look to the Globes as a clue to Academy Award voting but, in a year with no critical consensus, members of the Hollywood Foreign Press Association may have confused things even more." The fact that *Gladiator* won Best Picture, however, certainly gave it visibility—if not necessarily credibility—with Oscar voters. The same could be said for the Broadcast Film Critics Association, which also decided that *Gladiator* was the best of all the movies released during the calendar year of 2000. No one was going to base his or her Oscar ballot on what a bunch of people who review movies on TV or radio thought, but again, this prize did provide DreamWorks with additional text to put in its *Gladiator* campaign ads.

Steven Soderbergh replicated his Golden Globe achievement with the Directors Guild by being nominated for both *Erin Brockovich* and *Traffic*. Ang Lee and Cameron Crowe were also nominated, as was, goofily enough, Ridley Scott—more and more, all the money DreamWorks was spending to convince that

Gladiator was an important achievement was harvesting results.

The objective truth was that while there were likely contenders for Best Picture, not a single film was absolutely assured of being a finalist for the Award—all of the most plausible Best Picture contenders had factors working against them. One would have to have assumed that, deep down, voters knew *Gladiator* was no more than an entertaining enough time-killer. *Crouching Tiger, Hidden Dragon* was in Mandarin and it didn't play to the tear ducts like the last foreign language film to be nominated for Best Picture, *Life Is Beautiful*. Audiences in the States hadn't flocked to *Billy Elliot* in nearly the numbers that the pre-release buzz had suggested, so it was looking as if the proper Oscar antecedent for the film might not be *The Full Monty* but *Waking Ned Devine*. The film, however, was playing well at Academy screenings, and would be helped by the fact that, traditionally, Academy members tended to vote emotionally rather than intellectually; Universal publicist Eddie Egan told *USA Today*, "People are turning to it in waves." *Almost Famous* had all those guild nominations, but although its status as a box-office dog wasn't a fatal condition, it certainly wasn't an asset. *Wonder Boys* received better reviews than *Almost Famous* but it was even more of a box-office failure. *Erin Brockovich* may have had Steven Soderbergh's name on it, but to a lot of people it did seem a lot like a TV movie. Then again, the appeal of movies about a spirited underdog bucking the system (which trace their ancestry to such Best Picture nominees from sixty years earlier as *Mr. Deeds Goes to Town* and *Mr. Smith Goes to Washington*) could not be discounted, and the fact that *Erin Brockovich* has such a strong, feisty heroine meant the film would likely strike a particular cord with female Academy members. The other Soderbergh release, *Traffic* was perceived in some circles as being too dark for the Academy, but as it opened in additional theaters, it showed more signs of becoming a popular success, a development that might be enough to put it over. Then there was *Chocolat*. Granted the film was nobody's idea of a serious Oscar contender, but at this point in time, it was unwise to bet against Miramax pulling out small miracles.

Julia Roberts was as sure a sure thing for a Best

Actress nomination as one could possibly be. New York Film Critics winner Laura Linney was also likely for *You Can Count on Me*, and the fact that her little movie played better on a screener video than the big screen would help her chances. Ellen Burstyn was garnering the most attention she had received in years: *Requiem for a Dream* presented her with a particularly flamboyant role because she both faced the dire consequences of popping pills *and* got to speak with a heavy Brooklyn accent. Burstyn was also the comeback story of 2000. In addition to all the attention she was garnering for *Requiem for a Dream*, she was also receiving glowing reviews for *The Yards*, starred in a new—albeit inconsequential—television series, and was widely seen in multiplexes when *The Exorcist* was very successfully re-released with additional footage. *Entertainment Weekly* even included her as one of the "Twelve Top Entertainers of the Year." *Requiem* was rated NC-17, however, which was not the label that you wanted when Oscar voters were sizing you up.

Beyond these three women, however, things were much less clear. The well-liked Joan Allen would also be helped by the fact that she was playing an appealingly strong, gutsy woman. Many critics adored Gillian Anderson in *The House of Mirth*—she won the *Village Voice*'s critics poll for the most outstanding performance of the year from any actor or actress—but the movie wasn't moving beyond its art house bookings, despite the actress's following from *The X-Files*. Michelle Yeoh's work in *Crouching Tiger, Hidden Dragon* also received some ecstatic notices, but the issue was how receptive would Academy voters be for a Hong Kong action star giving a performance in a language other than English? Renee Zellweger had momentarily seen her standing rise when she won the Golden Globe for *Nurse Betty*, but that unloved autumn release was pretty much forgotten. *Chocolat*'s Juliette Binoche had her personal charm and old-style movie star elegance working for her, not to mention the Miramax campaign organization.

Finally, there was Kewpie doll-faced Icelandic singer Björk in Lars Von Trier's *Dancer in the Dark*. She had won the Best Actress prize at Cannes for playing a Czech immigrant who is going blind and kills the man who's absconding with the money for the opera-

tion that will prevent her son from also losing his sight. The film was a determinedly downbeat musical that provoked as extreme reactions as any movie this year, and its leading lady was proved equally divisive. To *Time*'s Richard Corliss, she was a "clueless amateur" and in a piece titled "Björk is a Bjerk," he reported that her director had "declared that Björk was no actress, as if those who'd seen the film needed reminding." Edward Guthmann of the *San Francisco Chronicle*, though, called hers a "landmark performance that's impossible to forget," and *Newsweek*'s David Ansen said, "Björk gives what may be the most wrenching performance ever given by someone who has no interest in being an actor." On various film-oriented Web sites, the former lead singer of the Sugarcubes was spoken about reverently by her followers—dubbed Björkheads—who were as impassioned and singular in their devotion as the Streisand-obsessed and the Christian Bale cultists were in theirs. What did it all mean in terms of Academy recognition for Björk? Well, her character ends up singing and dancing her way to death row, and older Academy members probably didn't want their musical numbers any darker than Cyd Charisse and Fred Astaire's "Girl Hunt Ballet" in *The Band Wagon*.

With the critics' awards all over the place, predicting the Best Actor nominees was no easy chore. The showboating that *Cast Away* provided New York winner Tom Hanks pegged him as a definite nominee, and it also helped that *Cast Away* was a very big moneymaker. (Because people disliked the non-castaway scenes so much, the film wasn't talked up much for a Best Picture nomination—David Ansen said, "once he returns to the world, the movie takes one wrong turn after another.") Despite the sorry box-office performance of *Wonder Boys*, Michael Douglas was also rated a definite nominee, because he was an industry insider and, after all, he gave a superb performance; his work in *Traffic* wasn't going to get him a Supporting nomination, but being on screen in a current, acclaimed movie served to remind voters of his existence. As for Javier Bardem, the Best Actor winner from the National Board of Review and the National Society of Film Critics, although the Spanish actor had appeared in some two dozen films in his homeland (the titles of which included *Between Your Legs* and *The Tit and the Moon*), he remained an unknown presence in Hollywood. And playing a gay Cuban poet wasn't exactly the type of career move to raise one's visibility. It seemed that if he wanted to be nominated, he might have to pull a Roberto Benigni and play the fool on American talk shows and at Hollywood parties, which was not a likely scenario for the articulate actor.

The word on Ed Harris had always been that he was a highly respected "actor's actor," and the title role in *Pollock* offered him plenty of bravura moments. The problem was that the film played only one-week Oscar-qualifying engagements in Los Angeles and New York and was not in theaters during the nominating period, meaning no one at all was talking about it. Geoffrey Rush's turn as the Marquis de Sade in *Quills* could catch the fancy of Academy voters, particularly if they were in the mood for some scenery chewing, but not many people had taken this sanctification of the Marquis de Sade to their hearts. Sean Connery had early on been considered a strong possibility as a reclusive writer who nurtures a gifted-but-troubled youth in *Finding Forrester*, but, like *Quills*, his vehicle left little impression on the world; while Connery was a beloved icon, to many people, this Gus Van Sant film seemed merely to be a redux of Van Sant's *Good Will Hunting*.

The Screen Actors Guild nominations made things even murkier when *Traffic*'s Benicio Del Toro was nominated in the *lead* performance category. Also nominated for the SAG Best Actor Award was *Billy Elliot*'s Jamie Bell. Kid actors always got shunted off into the Supporting category at the Oscars, but there was no way that Bell, who was in nearly every scene in *Billy Elliot*, could be placed as a Supporting ringer—to make the Academy short list, he'd have to buck history, since no child had been nominated for a lead Oscar since Jackie Cooper in 1931. Director Stephen Daldry said he had talked to Jamie and "The thing I keep telling him and myself is to put the awards in context. As the old adage says, treat success and failure as the impostors that they are."

An Errol Flynn for a New Millennium

Then there was Russell Crowe and his stolid performance in *Gladiator*. People were beginning to rewrite history, suddenly deciding that he had been robbed last year when he didn't win for *The Insider*, even though at the time it was Denzel Washington who had been perceived as the aggrieved party. What Crowe truly had going for him though, was that during 2000 he had at last crossed over into the realm of big time movie star, both on-screen and off. In the movies, enacting a traditional heroic role, he finally showed the world some old-style charisma and sex appeal. And whereas in real life he previously had been considered a somewhat eccentric and curmudgeonly character, now he had a public persona as a dashing throwback to Errol Flynn and the young Warren Beatty. The reason: when he was filming *Proof of Life*, his first post-*Gladiator* movie, he and costar Meg Ryan had an affair while she and her husband of nine years, Dennis Quaid, were calling it quits. Adding to Crowe's new renown as an alluring rogue: by the time the movie came out, he and Ryan were no longer an item—the word was that when she started talking up having a baby, he was out of there. Without missing a beat, he was then linked to other women in gossip columns and the tabloids. Of course, some in the media tried to demonize Crowe as a womanizer and home-wrecker, but in any case, he was now a household name as a man with a seductively dangerous quality. Around the time *Proof of Life* was opening late in the year, Michael Musto reported in the *Village Voice*, "My sources tell me that Russell Crowe was just at Tower Video, enthusing to a salesgirl about the Aussie band Dead Can Dance. He became so worked up that he ran across the street to Tower Records, bought the group's latest release, and then ran back to give it to her, proving that he's not a skanky bitch after all. Just then, Meg Ryan came racing in with a hatchet and chopped the girl's head off in a jealous rage. All right, I made that last part up." Jamie Bell was asked what he was taking away from the experience of making the Hollywood publicity rounds during awards season, and replied, "Russell Crowe is teaching me how to pick up girls!"

The Ryan-Quaid dissolution was just one of several marital bust-ups that had Hollywood reeling. Like Ryan and Quaid, Alec Baldwin and Kim Basinger were perceived to have a Gable and Lombard kind of union, but in January, 1997's Best Supporting Actress began divorce proceedings. There was also Tom Cruise and Nicole Kidman. After nearly a decade of ostentatiously going on about how in love with "Nic" he was, Cruise filed for divorce in February. And to think they had just renewed their vows in December.

Shortly before the nominations, Miramax's West Coast head, Mark Gill, pretty much admitted that whatever Oscar dreams the studio had once held for *All the Pretty Horses* had dissipated: "Look, you hope everything is going to end up in the wonderful zone," Gill says. "Sometime the critics and the audiences don't see it. We're still proud of the movie." But he insisted that most prognostications to the contrary, *Chocolat* would be heard from on nominations morning: "We always thought in its own subtle way that *Chocolat* had a tremendous message about tolerance and inclusion. There is also the sweet, charming element to it." To the consternation of some critics, the film also was the beneficiary of strong word-of-mouth. "It's one of those rare movies where people are recommending it like crazy," he says.

In addition to a blitzkrieg of ads, the studio looked to the world of public service to aid and abet in selling *Chocolat*. "Miramax even held a special screening for the Reverend Jesse Jackson, figuring *Chocolat*'s message of tolerance would appeal to him," reported *BusinessWeek*'s Thane Peterson. "Tolerance for whom, you have to wonder—candymakers?" The Reverend Jackson loved the movie, saying that in detailing the oppression faced by Juliette Binoche's character, *Chocolat* allegorized "the classic struggle of our time." He felt that the film paralleled the recent presidential election where black voters in Florida were systematically disenfranchised: "The movie is as dramatic as November 7, and it is as though it was written about our times instead of for our times. It's about the great theme of our time, intolerance. You can just see the religious right narrowly defining the rights of others."

Although *Chocolat* is set in France in 1959, Jackson saw an historical parallel to America in the 1960s, asserting that "The movie is really about us going to Birmingham to get the right to vote. People said: 'You're not from here, you don't belong here. Go away.' " Reverend Jackson's conclusion was, "Everyone should see this movie." The studio also showed the film to the Anti-Defamation League, which awarded it a citation for its "commitment to tolerance." Mark Gill, the studio's West Coast head, was particularly pleased, saying "The ADL endorsement was useful to us because our competitors were out there saying that our movie was only a trifle."

Steven Soderbergh hadn't changed his stance: "I'll just let it all shake out," he said. "There's nothing I can do about splitting my own vote if that happens. I'm just proud of both movies." Patrick Goldstein of the *Los Angeles Times* even took note that "At the New York and Los Angeles Film Critics awards, he sat with *Traffic*'s USA Films contingent; at the Broadcast Film Critics Awards and National Board of Review dinner, he sat with *Brockovich*'s Universal team. When he won best director at the Broadcast Film luncheon, he began his speech by saying, 'I'm going to go chronologically.' (*Erin* came first.)" Goldstein also wrote an open letter to the director, advising, "If you campaign, you become just another Oscar slut, since you're basically disowning one of your own films. Obviously it sends a me-myself-I message to the film's actors, crew, studio, etc. Right now you're putting your movies ahead of yourself, which buys valuable goodwill."

Tom Hanks had some final pre-nomination thoughts about the Academy Awards. "The Oscar race has become like flu season," he ruminated. "Asking me if I'm going to get nominated is like saying, 'Hey, Tom, do you think you're gonna get the flu this year?' It makes me ask myself, 'Do I want to get the flu?' On one hand, yeah, I could enjoy a few days of the lavish attention, which is similar to being nominated for an Oscar. But like the flu, there's nothing you can do about it, man! You can't avoid it. You can't covet it. You just have to let it wash over you."

The Nominations

Damned if spending that campaign lucre hadn't paid off—*Gladiator* received the most nominations, twelve. But perhaps even more impressive was that—subtitles notwithstanding—*Crouching Tiger, Hidden Dragon* followed with ten, thus becoming, by far, the most-nominated foreign language film ever. With these two action movies leading the pack, *Daily Variety* adjudged that Academy members "were in a fightin' mood as two combat films paced the race." Most impressive of all, though, was that Steven Soderbergh did receive nominations for both *Erin Brockovich* and *Traffic*, and that both films were nominated for Best Picture, garnering five nominations apiece. Soderbergh was the first person to be nominated for Best Director twice in the same year since 1938, when Michael Curtiz had been up for *Angels with Dirty Faces* and *Four Daughters*. (He lost to Frank Capra for *You Can't Take It with You.*) And, in another case of campaigning paying off, sure enough *Chocolat* ended up among the chosen five, although Lasse Hallström was not a nominee for Best Director, the fifth spot going to *Billy Elliot*'s Stephen Daldry.

This year's biggest surprise was the failure of Michael Douglas to be nominated for Best Actor in *Wonder Boys*. (*Time*'s Jess Cagle suggested, "Next time he should show some cleavage, which seems to be working for Julia Roberts and Russell Crowe.") Jamie Bell was also an also-ran. The Actors branch chose two men from small, not widely released movies, Javier Bardem in *Before Night Falls* and Ed Harris in *Pollock*; Harris especially was a bit of a surprise, not because of the quality of his work but because he hadn't received any critics awards and hadn't been up for a Golden Globe or SAG award. Also nominated were Russell Crowe in *Gladiator*, Tom Hanks in *Cast Away* and Geoffrey Rush in *Quills*. On the distaff side, Julia Roberts in *Erin Brockovich* was joined by Joan Allen in *The Contender*, Juliette Binoche in *Chocolat*, Ellen Burstyn in *Requiem for a Dream,* and Laura Linney in *You Can Count on Me*. The Björkheads would have to content themselves with their girl being nominated for one of the songs from *Dancer in the Dark*, "I've Seen It

All." Of course she would be competing against an icon of much longer standing than she: Bob Dylan, nominated for "Things Have Changed" from *Wonder Boys*. Björk was born in November 1965, a time when *Highway 61 Revisited* was a new release.

There were no real surprises in the Supporting categories. Benicio Del Toro was nominated here, not as a lead, and he faced the same four men who had made up his competition at the Golden Globes: Jeff Bridges (not Gary Oldman) in *The Contender*, Willem Dafoe in *Shadow of the Vampire*, Albert Finney in *Erin Brockovich* and Joaquin Phoenix in *Gladiator*. In the Supporting Actress race, *Pollock*'s Marcia Gay Harden was the only nominee who hadn't been up for the Golden Globe, as she replaced Globe nominee Catherine-Zeta Jones from *Traffic*, although Zhang Ziyi, the young warrior of *Crouching Tiger, Hidden Dragon* had seemed as equally likely a nominee as Harden and Jones. (With Zeta-Jones and her husband both left out, there were jokes about Hollywood being jealous of the newlyweds/new parents; Bob Strauss of the *Los Angeles Daily News* said, "While complaints about overlooking Michael Douglas's thoughtful turn in *Wonder Boys* are certainly justified, Oscars are about knee-jerk impressions as much as they are about artistic merit, so let's face it: This guy has had a good enough year already.") The four other Supporting Actress contenders were Judi Dench in *Chocolat*, Kate Hudson in *Almost Famous*, Frances McDormand in *Almost Famous,* and Julie Walters in *Billy Elliot*. The chauvinistic headline of the *Dallas Morning News*'s Oscar story complained, "Marcia Gay Harden Only Texan in Batch."

This year's oddball nomination was *O Brother, Where Art Thou?* being cited in the *Adapted* Screenplay Award. The Depression-era comedy contained a title card stating, "Based upon the *Odyssey* by Homer," but Joel and Ethan Coen claimed they had never read the work. Joel did say that they did have a look at the Classic Comics Illustrated version and that they had some vague recollections of Kirk Douglas in *Ulysses*. At one point, the brothers were going to add the credit, "Portions also based on *Moby Dick*," which would have really confused things.

Bob Strauss felt that this year's nominations

"represent the Oscar voters' split tendency to think progressively while clinging to retrograde tastes. Most laudable is the recognition that film is indeed an international art form. The unprecedented ten nominations for the Mandarin-language *Crouching Tiger, Hidden Dragon* was accompanied by a Best Picture nomination for *Traffic*, a third of which is spoken in Spanish, and a supporting actor nod for that section's main player, Benicio Del Toro." On the other hand, Strauss was less than thrilled that the voters gave the most nominations to *Gladiator*, which "is at core a *Death Wish*-grade revenge story done big and pretentious."

Steven Rea of the *Philadelphia Inquirer* lamented that "*Crouching Tiger* failed to land any acting nods, a pity since Chow, Michelle Yeoh and newcomer Zhang Ziyi give this technical marvel real human dimension." The *Boston Herald*'s Stephen Schaefer decreed, "Harvey Weinstein, the pugnacious, irrepressible head of Miramax Pictures, has to rate as the year's biggest Oscar winner. With *Chocolat* named one of the five Best Picture nominees in yesterday's Academy Award nominations, Weinstein trumped his arch rivals at DreamWorks who were hoping to put *Almost Famous* in that *Chocolat* spot." But Jack Mathews of the *New York Daily News* felt it wasn't Miramax's campaigning skills that had sunk that DreamWorks film: "The failure of Cameron Crowe's *Almost Famous* to make the Best Picture and Director ballots may well be a reaction to Crowe's vulgar whining about the way the film was handled by DreamWorks. Knowing how hard it is to get a personal movie made, especially one costing $60 million, industry people tend to think, 'Ah, shaddup!' " Crowe said that despite not getting those two big categories, "It's cool. It's good. And I was completely thrilled that our actresses got noticed. That was amazing. You dream of getting Oscar nominations for your actors and actresses because then everybody wants to work with you." Harvey Weinstein insisted, "*Chocolat* is just one of those movies that touch people emotionally. People love it; we've had very few films that have played this well with audiences." And showing that he didn't live and breathe only Miramax, he cited one disappointment. It wasn't Lasse Hallström's omission, but rather Michael Douglas's. "He was fantastic in *Wonder Boys* and great in *Traffic*," said Weinstein. "He had a really good year."

A lot of critics seemed to take *Chocolat*'s Best Picture nomination as a personal affront. John Hartl of the *Seattle Times* wrote, "Can Academy Award nominations be bought? The question was raised last year when Miramax spent a fortune to earn several nominations for Lasse Hallström's *The Cider House Rules*. Yesterday was déjà vu all over again." Henry Sheehan of the *Orange County Register* fulminated that "Certainly relentless propaganda seems the only explanation for the nominations for *Chocolat*, a fluffy, innocuous and somewhat fake trifle at best. The movie became the subject of what is by now an annual Oscar campaign by its distributor, Miramax, which used the same huge promotional muscle it has in the past on films such as *Il Postino (The Postman)* and *The Cider House Rules*." He continued, "The two big victims of the Academy's blinders this year were *Wonder Boys* and, especially, *The House of Mirth*. *Boys* did get three nominations, including Best Editing (the film's editor was the legendary Dede Allen), Best Song and Best Adapted Screenplay, which helps. But the movie's droll sophistication puts it head and shoulders above other nominees; the exclusion seems peculiarly willful. *Mirth* is worse because the movie is not only outstanding, but features a career-altering performance by Gillian Anderson. Of course, in her characterization of Lily Bart, a player in New York society circa 1905, Anderson deliberately avoided cheap displays of emotion. She pursued a more honest and true line in portraying a woman whose mind is at war with her heart, though in agreement that that war should go undetected by all around her. Instead, *Requiem for a Dream*'s Ellen Burstyn, playing a hysterical woman addicted to diet drugs, shot with a fish-eye lens and wearing a fright wig for much of the time, gets the nod. Oh, well. No use getting your dander up over something as fleeting as the Oscars. After all, the rack of Oscar winners at your local video store is generally the dustiest in the place. Cary Grant and Alfred Hitchcock must be laughing even now." *Entertainment Weekly*'s Lisa Schwarzbaum wrote, "I'll leave the analysis of why a fable about the magical power of candy bars got as far as it did in the Oscar race to colleagues calmer than I am about the phony message of 'tolerance' promoted by its backers." She added, "Wouldn't it have been fabulous if Gillian Anderson, so radiant in *The House of Mirth*, had gotten the Best Actress spot gobbled by Juliette Binoche?"

Time's Richard Corliss said, "Haven't seen *Chocolat* yet? Then here's a synopsis: It's the story of a smug, sleepy town invaded by a charismatic outsider who feeds the villagers sweets and makes them do crazy things. The town is Los Angeles; the outsider is Miramax boss Harvey Weinstein; and what could be nuttier than voting *Chocolat* a nomination for the year's best film. *Chocolat* is at best a trifle, and at most a tribute to a man who can feed the Academy anything and have them say 'mmmm, good.' If commercial movies are the art of the sell, and they are, then Weinstein is *The Music Man*'s Professor Harold Hill, and Hollywood is River City." Gary Thompson of the *Philadelphia Daily News* drew a more contemporary analogy, saying, "Surely there's a place for Katherine 'The Fixer' Harris at Miramax." He said of the Florida secretary of state, "Her reputed ability to engineer a favorable result for a pet candidate would be a valuable skill at the Disney unit, which somehow soft-monied, ballot-stuffed and poll-taxed its way to five Oscar nominations yesterday for *Chocolat*." He also suggested that, "Perhaps notoriously elderly Academy voters were confused by the Miramax-designed butterfly ballot, with pre-punched holes next to *Chocolat*, and titanium manhole covers over the designated slots for *Almost Famous*, *Cast Away*, *Billy Elliot*, *Wonder Boys*, *You Can Count on Me*, *Before Night Falls*, *Shadow of the Vampire*, *Thirteen Days*, *High Fidelity* or any one of perhaps fifty movies that would look less ridiculous with a Best Picture nomination next to their names."

Juliette Binoche was on *CBS This Morning* and Bryant Gumbel told her the other nominees in her category. Hearing Julia Roberts's name, she said, "I know who's gonna win . . . She deserves it . . . I'll clap for her many beautiful years of beautiful work." According to the *New York Times*, "Joan Allen had just taken a shower with her pet parrot and was watching the Oscar nominations in her Manhattan apartment while blow-drying

the bird. ('You're not supposed to let them get a chill.')" Later she was in the midst of doing an interview with *Access Hollywood* when her seven-year-old daughter called to say that her play date had been canceled because her friend was sick and she needed someone to pick her up from school. Ellen Burstyn, the 1974 Best Actress winner, laughed that, "It's been awhile. My Oscar is getting kind of tarnished. I looked at it a couple of years ago and thought I really needed a new one." Barry Koltnow talked to Laura Linney and joked with her that five years earlier she had been in "arguably one of the worst movies of the past twenty years." "I get knocked around a lot for *Congo*," she admitted, " but I always defend that movie. I knew nothing about making films when I did *Congo*, which made it the perfect movie to learn about filmmaking. I had a lot of time to observe and ask questions because the movie required no acting whatsoever."

Geoffrey Rush issued a statement from an airplane: "Having left the Berlin Film Festival on Monday and arriving in Melbourne on Wednesday, not only have I missed Tuesday's announcement, but I missed an entire day to celebrate." Ed Harris told the *Los Angeles Daily News*'s Glenn Whipp, "I wasn't really expecting too much but I had a sneaking suspicion they might respect the work. I don't live and breathe and die by these things, you know what I'm saying, but I can tell you I'm not unhappy." Javier Bardem's reaction was, "This is more food for my ego, which is always hungry. There are two things that can happen when an actor is nominated for such a prestigious honor. The first is a danger to be avoided, and that is that you can start thinking that you are something special, that you are an important person. The second is a blessing, and that is simply to be proud of what you have done and what your movie has done." He promised, "In the coming weeks, I will try very hard to put all my energy into the second, and not the first. After all, it is important to remember that I am only one tomato in a very big salad." Bardem continued the food motif with another reporter, saying "The only Oscars I am accustomed to are Oscar Meyer sausages," and he also talked to Army Archerd about his compatriots: "They are treating me like the king of Spain—

which is weird, because I don't believe in the monarchy!"

Marcia Gay Harden was in a Denver hotel and had just gotten out of the shower when the phone rang. "I wasn't expecting a call," she recounted. "It was my lawyer. He said, 'Oh my God, you did it, girl!' So I had all this energy and all this joy and no place to put it." Just then a waitress arrived with breakfast and, said the actress, "I attacked her and said, 'I just got nominated for an Oscar!' and she saw me crying and said, 'Well, come over here and give me a hug.' " *Shadow of the Vampire*'s Willem Dafoe said, "A lot of people in the Academy, let's face it, they're actors. They know the lay of the land. And there's a part of them that enjoys balancing those bigger movies like *Gladiator* with smaller movies, like ours." He also compared the atmosphere surrounding this nomination to that of when he was nominated for *Platoon* in 1986. "It was so different years ago. You didn't campaign," he recollected. "But I think Miramax changed all of that. They developed this nomination process complete with lobbying and marketing." He also reminisced that "back then, I just got a call from my son's baby-sitter in the morning, telling me that they had been announced. I had no awareness of it. And I don't think that the press anticipated them so far in advance. It was better."

Michael Shamberg said he and his fellow *Erin Brockovich* producers were looking at things from an historical perspective: "We calculate there have been about 420 nominations for best picture out of about 20,000 Hollywood pictures," he said. "That's amazing to be a part of that group." Marshall Herskovitz, one of the producers of the other Stephen Soderbergh film said, "I happen to love *Erin Brockovich*, but I love *Traffic* more." *Gladiator*'s coproducer Douglas Wick said, "The movie audience usually has a short memory and I honestly felt that coming out in May was a liability for us. Then the DVD sales started before Christmas and we got an extraordinary response. Suddenly, we weren't old news anymore. People started talking about us again." *Chocolat* producer David Brown was in London when he heard of his film's strong showing and said, "I'm on my way to the airport, flying to New York—and I doubt if I'll need a plane." He had figured things could have gone either way: "We knew we had a

wonderful movie, but we also know how this business works," he said. "We all watched the announcement this morning and you've never seen such nervous people. You never assume anything in Hollywood. Believe me, if we had gotten nothing this morning, and I mean no nominations, it wouldn't have surprised me." Army Archerd said, "I laughed when Harvey Weinstein told me, 'I'm humbled,' as response to congrats on *Chocolat*'s five Oscar nominations. But seriously, folks, Harvey *was* humbled, he explained. 'I am gratified after what happened last year: two months in the hospital, one month recuperating—and then the presidential and senatorial (Demo.) campaigns.' About the film, he reminds, 'We delivered it late and started up at the last minute.' As for his feelings about his confection's Oscar chances, 'It's a wide-open race.' "

Ang Lee, who had spent the night and early morning hours working on an internet movie for BMW, said "I am very excited and confused." He said he was especially surprised by one of the movie's nominations. "Nobody ever mentioned the song, so I didn't think it would be nominated." The other exciting news for Lee was that over the previous weekend *Crouching Tiger, Hidden Dragon* had overtaken *Life Is Beautiful* to become America's highest grossing foreign language film ever. Steven Soderbergh was in Las Vegas filming *Ocean's Eleven* and issued a statement: "I can't even put into words what I'm feeling. I think if I didn't have the distraction of shooting a film I would have to be sedated. I'm so happy for everyone associated with both films and so honored to be recognized with this wonderful group of nominees. I wish I weren't being so statesman-like about this, but I'm really having trouble wrapping my mind around it." It was a best-of-times-worst-of-times situation for Ridley Scott, and his official statement said, "Sadly I lost my mum this week, but she is obviously looking after me." Stephen Daldry was filming *The Hours* and somebody asked him if he spoke with one of his cast members about his nomination. "Tell Meryl?" he asked, laughingly. "She's got twelve of them, she wouldn't be impressed."

In the *New York Daily News*, Jack Mathews said, "What the year 2000 failed to produce in the way of great movies, it's making up for with a great Oscar race." Citing Steven Soderbergh's double nomination for Best Director and his having two films in the Best Picture race, Mathews declared, "the Academy's largess on behalf of Soderbergh may well have sealed his fate as a non-winner. His fans among the 5,700 Academy voters are likely to be split between his two films, clearing the way for a *Gladiator/Crouching Tiger* duel." Soderbergh's dilemma was widely discussed, as he continued to refrain from stating a preference. One of his *Traffic* stars, Michael Douglas, was quoted as saying, "Steven is going to have to make a choice which film to campaign for." At the Directors Guild Awards, where Soderbergh lost to Ang Lee, emcee Carl Reiner advised him that in the future if he wanted to have two films released in a year and still be honored, "Make one great and one not so great."

A week after the nominations, Julia Roberts appeared on the *Late Show with David Letterman*. Her attitude about Academy Award night was, "One must be hopeful but expect to remain seated." She referred to the Oscar as "the golden man," and then told Letterman, "You know what, I say that and I realize I don't have to win because I have my own golden man at home." It was almost a year after her appearance on *Oprah* and she was still just as mushy about Benjamin Bratt.

It's an Honor

The Academy was handing out three Honorary Awards this year. The Thalberg was going to Dino De Laurentiis, the veteran Italian producer who already had a pair of Oscars for Federico Fellini's *La Strada* and *Nights of Cabiria*, from back in the days when the statuette for Best Foreign Film went to the producer rather than the director. The mogul's output ranged from the highs of Roberto Rossellini's *Europa '51*, John Milius's *Conan the Barbarian*, David Lynch's *Blue Velvet*, and Michael Mann's *Manhunter* (the first and by far the best of the Hannibal Lecter movies) to the lows of *Death Wish*, *Orca*, and *Mandingo* and his latest release, the Ridley Scott-directed, *Hannibal*. There were also a lot of bloated spectacles along the way, such as *The Bible*, *Waterloo*, and *The Bounty*. Bob Rehme declared, "De Laurentiis' body of work speaks for itself. His love of, passion for, and dedication to making

motion pictures has suffused through his career. He has always had the courage to make the films that he believes in." De Laurentiis's reaction was "It is a big honor and a big surprise for me. I work with passion and integrity, and now I have to do better." The eighty-one-year-old honoree also laughed and said, "This is what happens when you become older."

An Honorary Award was going to British cinematographer Jack Cardiff, who had won an Oscar in 1947 for *Black Narcissus* and received two other cinematography nominations. He had also been nominated for Best Director for *Sons and Lovers* in 1960. Known as one of the great masters of color photography, Cardiff had, coincidentally, shot three films for Dino De Laurentiis: *War and Peace*, *Cat's Eye*, and *Conan the Destroyer*.

Jack Cardiff would be the first cinematographer to receive a Lifetime Achievement Oscar. Ernest Lehman was going to be the first recipient who was primarily a screenwriter (as opposed to writer-director). The curious thing about this Award was that although Lehman—who was credited with fifteen films—was involved in a number of movies considered classics, they were primarily works in which either the script was not the primary component of the movie's reputation (*North by Northwest*, *West Side Story*, *The Sound of Music*) or else films with strong scripts written with collaborators who were more prominent (*Sabrina*'s Billy Wilder, *The Sweet Smell of Success*'s Clifford Odets). He also had made his fair share of potboilers, such as *Executive Suite*, *From the Terrace*, and *The Prize*. The official word from President Rehme on Lehman was, "He is not only a prolific screenwriter but an accomplished novelist, journalist and motion picture producer whose films rank as genuine classics." Lehman was eighty-five, Cardiff eighty-six, meaning that Dino De Laurentiis was the spring chicken in the group.

Crime Blotter

A rather uneventful Oscar season received a shot of adrenaline. As E! Online's Marcus Errico put it, "Mysterious kidnappers scheming to abduct one of the hottest celebs in the world and hold him ransom for millions. Sounds like the plot of a cheesy movie, right? The scary thing is, it's true." The hot celebrity was Russell Crowe, and a British tabloid had feverishly reported that "mystery gangsters" were planning to abscond with the *Gladiator* star and cause him bodily pain. The FBI confirmed that there had been threats, that it was treating them very seriously and that it had briefed the actor and his security people. *Entertainment Tonight* disclosed that Scotland Yard had been intently keeping an eye on Crowe when he was in London for the *Proof of Life* premiere. Crowe had been told of the investigation just prior to the Golden Globes, and the actor had been escorted to the ceremony by a beefed-up security contingent that night. "That explains the army of security guards that flanked Crowe at the Golden Globes," mused *Entertainment Weekly*. "And we thought he just wasn't a people person." The magazine also said that Crowe continued to be "under protective surveillance." Gossip maven Ted Casablanca's reaction was "The only question I have is: What idiot would want to take him? And don't think for a second that his people aren't going to use this as an excuse for his sour demeanor."

Lunch Hour

At the Academy's Nominees Luncheon at the Beverly Hilton, Crowe made light of the kidnapping threat when speaking to the press, emphasizing that anybody who took him would be stuck in a *Ransom of Red Chief* situation. He said he could picture the culprits after having been saddled with him for a few days: "They'd be on the phone going, 'Look, we've passed the hat around. We got a couple hundred dollars. Can you take him off our hands?'" Changing subjects to speak about the nominations, Crowe made the cryptic comment, "I think it's wonderful for Joaquin. He can't hide anymore. We all know he's fantastic. And that's just bad luck for him."

Tom Hanks said that even though this was his fifth go-around, all the Oscar attention still "feels like a wedding day—win or lose, I know both sides." Laura Linney was asked how she thought she'd be feeling on Oscar day. "Probably I will be in the same state that I've been in for the last month," she said, "which is

sort of this wonderful heightened sense of hilarity. I've just been having a ball." A reporter asked Ellen Burstyn how this nomination compared to her previous nods, "Well, I've had a long rest," the *Requiem for a Dream* star said. "This is my sixth nomination. But there was twenty years between nominations, so it feels like springtime after a long winter." She also admitted that she "totally" wanted to win. Kate Hudson talked about growing up with an Oscar in the house. She said that her mother's statuette was on the mantle and "wasn't locked in a cabinet, it was just standing out there. We always thought someone was going to steal it. And one time we had a huge party. My parents were out of town. It was horrible. We ended up having, like, 500 people at our house. And at the end of the night, my brother and I were upstairs and he goes, 'Oh, my God. The Oscar!' And we go running down the stairs and, thank God, it was there." Joan Allen talked about her daughter's view of the Academy Awards: "She is beginning to understand it a little bit now. But when I was nominated for *Nixon*, she was really little. She was only a couple of years old. And I said, 'I've been nominated for an Oscar.' And she said, 'Oscar's a grouch!' "

While last year's producers, Richard and Lili Fini Zanuck, were lenient with the time constraints on speeches, Gilbert Cates emphasized to the nominees at the luncheon the importance of keeping acceptances down to forty-five seconds. He showed film clips of such winners as Alfred Hitchcock, Sammy Cahn and Jimmy van Heusen, and William Holden giving the briefest of thanks, but he didn't mention that Holden complained backstage about having been told to button his lip because a commercial was coming up. Cates had exciting news, though. If there was a whole gaggle of people you wanted to mention and could not do it in forty-five seconds, you could give an Academy representative a list of the names, and it would be posted on the Academy's official Web site for the whole world to see. Reuters reported that the offer "was greeted with a long silence from a crowd of more than a hundred nominees, including the likes of Russell Crowe, Tom Hanks and Joan Allen, and then laughter." Cates had another, even more exciting, proposition, as well. Whoever gave the evening's shortest acceptance speech would win a spanking brand new state-of-the-art high definition television set, with a retail market value of $2,500!

Clear As Mud

As Oscar night approached, things had not become any clearer. Best Picture had settled into a three-way race between *Crouching Tiger, Hidden Dragon*, *Gladiator*, and *Traffic*. When Ang Lee received his standing ovation at the Golden Globes, it was an indication that *Crouching Tiger, Hidden Dragon* was probably the town's favorite movie. But then, in quick succession, *Gladiator* received the "Eddie" from the American Cinema Editors as the Best Edited Feature Film (Drama); the Cinema Audio Society Award for Outstanding Achievement in Sound Mixing; and the Art Directors Guild Award for Excellence in Production Design, Feature Film—Period or Fantasy. This last was especially noteworthy given that so many of *Gladiator*'s sets were not sets per se, but CGI work. One might have thought that members of this Guild would be a little concerned that the more this computer-generated stuff was encouraged, the more precarious their job security would become. The bottom line was that it had become clear movie craftspeople loved *Gladiator*.

Momentum was, for the time being, with *Gladiator*. But Ang Lee won the Directors Guild Award and *Crouching Tiger* was then perceived to have snatched back the lead; this marked the first time that the DGA prize went to the director of a foreign language movie. Then, because it was that kind of year, *Traffic* went and won the Screen Actors Guild Award for Best Ensemble Cast. USA Films was employing the "Important Statement" strategy with *Traffic*. Ads quoted from editorials and op-ed pieces to indicate that—unlike the competition—*Traffic* had crossed over from merely being a movie into becoming a part of the current social fabric. From reading the ads you'd find out, for instance, that Senator John McCain saw *Traffic* with his sixteen-year-old daughter "and it had a very powerful effect. It caused me to rethink our policies and priorities." And that columnist Arianna Huffington was "not neutral about which film wins Best Picture this year. Shouldn't we reward a movie that is not

only great enough to move us, but great enough to move our world?"

For what it was worth, *Gladiator* was the big winner across the pond at the British Academy Awards and it also took top honors at the Producers Guild Awards. Edward Guthmann of the *San Francisco Chronicle* wrote, "*Gladiator* probably has the best shot because it's such a clear affirmation of Hollywood craft. It wouldn't be a disgraceful choice, as the 1995 Oscar to *Braveheart* was, but it wouldn't show much imagination or largesse on the Academy's part, either. It's also possible that Oscar voters are finally ready to honor a foreign-language film with the top prize. It helps that Ang Lee, director of *Crouching Tiger*, is a U.S. resident and director of such English-language films as *Sense and Sensibility* . . . It's a tough call, but *Gladiator*, clearly a company product in a company town, probably has the strongest chance." Gene Seymour of *Newsday* wrote, "*Gladiator*, an ancient Roman ripsnorter mixing old-fashioned sword-and-sandals bloodshed with up-to-the-minute digital staging, has both revived a once-dominant Hollywood genre and opened new possibilities for technicians and storytellers alike. Add to this mix its approximately $187-million box-office take—third for all movies released last year—and it's easy to see where that love came from." *The Seattle Times*'s John Hartl wrote of *Crouching Tiger*: "The momentum for the most popular foreign-language movie in U.S. history has not flagged since Ang Lee's Taiwan-based adventure-romance made its sensational debut last spring at the Cannes Film Festival." Because "It's such a beloved movie," Hartl felt Ang Lee's film would triumph.

Sony Classics' Michael Barker figured that *Crouching Tiger* had an extra something in its corner: "Every year *Entertainment Weekly* has a special pre-Oscar issue. That Oscar issue has portended good things for the cover picture. *American Beauty* was last year. The year before was *Shakespeare in Love*. We basically asked our publicist Reid Rosefelt to do everything he could to see if there was a possibility of them selecting *Crouching Tiger* as the cover art—and they did. These are all things that you plan way ahead of time. You're never sure if you're going to get them, but if those things happen then it becomes in the mind of an Academy member, 'Well, we should take this film pretty seriously.' We're lucky they did." In the Director's race, the smart money seemed to be on Ang Lee, given the combination of his DGA award and the Steven Soderbergh double-nomination conundrum. *Gladiator* was conceded to have been more of a producer's and technician's accomplishment than a director's. Ridley Scott had been receiving additional media attention because his new movie, *Hannibal,* was in theaters, although that served to remind people what a hack he was.

Carrie Rickey of the *Philadelphia Inquirer* said, "In this most contentious Oscar year, the wizards agree on one thing alone: that come Sunday, Julia Roberts will bag the Academy Award." Barring an upset of Lauren Bacall proportions (and Juliette Binoche was present in this race), the entire world expected her to win. "Julia Roberts is the reigning female star of this particular moment and there is a great desire to reward her," said *Time*'s Richard Schickel. "Hers is a big brassy performance, a hugely attractive performance." Liz Smith quoted Groucho Marx from when *A Star Is Born*'s Judy Garland lost to Grace Kelly in *The Country Girl* ("It's the biggest robbery since Brinks!") and said, "That's how I'll feel if Julia Roberts is denied the Oscar for her sensational work in *Erin Brockovich*. This should be Julia's golden moment, with Academy voters recognizing not just this performance, but also the body of her work, which has been a joyous growth process ... Julia is a real star, more grounded than many of her self-important predecessors. Her gifts are still blooming." David Ansen felt, "Let's put it this way, if Julia Roberts acts surprised when they call her name, she should get a second Oscar for best performance at an awards ceremony. Early on there were a few folks who thought Ellen Burstyn could pull off an upset, but whatever sentimental support she has was cancelled out by the audience-punishing *Requiem for a Dream,* not the kind of movie the Academy cozies up to."

Best Actor was still up in the air. Geoffrey Rush was out of the running, and the front-runners were generally considered to be Tom Hanks and Russell Crowe. Intriguingly, the Best Actor winner at the SAG Awards was neither of these men, but Supporting Ac-

tor Oscar nominee, Benicio Del Toro of *Traffic*. USA Films' president, Russell Schwartz, said that the company submitted Del Toro in the lead category for the Screen Actors Guild as "an experiment. We felt we had nothing to lose if he didn't win, and it would call more attention to his work if he did. It was a long shot. Amazingly, it paid off."

Looking at the two perceived Best Actor frontrunners, Richard Corliss wrote in *Time*, "Crowe has movie-star swagger (though *Gladiator* is his only hit) to go with his movie-actor talent. But can his gifts overcome his nonpareil rep as a hard case? Let the tabloids count his ways: steals Meg Ryan from her husband; dumps Ryan when she says she wants to have a baby with him; spends the evening with Courtney Love; puts a move on eighteen-year-old Leelee Sobieski. He also pisses off most of the people who have worked with him and written about him. The Aussies have a word for Crowe: lout. Hanks—genial, hardworking, good ol' Joe Oscar—is the anti-Crowe. He carried *Cast Away* alone on his sunburnt shoulders. And he would win ... if he didn't always win. This guy must be running out of mantelpiece. Maybe Oscar will take a year's vacation from Tom, and take a walk with the Wild Man of Oz." But the *Hollywood Reporter*'s Martin Grove said, "Hanks is very well-liked in Hollywood and clearly a member of the Club. Hanks' performance is what most critics seem to have responded to best in *Cast Away*. Crowe seems less well-liked and something of a Hollywood outsider whose image in the media and sometimes controversial love life may detract from his popularity with Academy voters. The recent news about the horrible plot to kidnap and possibly maim Crowe probably broke too late in the month to make him seem more sympathetic to the voters. I'm betting on Hanks."

James Verniere of the *Boston Herald* wrote, "The most recent buzz suggests that Crowe's homewrecker reputation may tip the scale to happily married good guy Tom Hanks." At the same time, however, there were small cracks in Tom Hanks's status as Mr. Beloved in Hollywood, with traits that had previously been seen as genuine Nice Guy qualities now being perceived by some people as pompousness and holier-than-thou smarminess. Hanks had gotten involved in so many noncontroversial causes—the World War II monument, anything at all portraying astronauts as salt-of-the-earth heroes—that he was coming across like the head of the local Kiwanis Club. There was also evidence of the unseemly high regard in which Tom Hanks held Tom Hanks: When Ruby Dee and husband Ossie Davis were being honored with a lifetime achievement honor at the SAG Awards, he had taken it upon himself to escort Dee to the stage. Hanks's serving as a walker was an act of startling presumptuousness, especially since Dee was in no need of assistance, and her husband was right there and, if anyone should have been arm-in-arm with the actress, it was he. The fact that he lost the Best Actor SAG Award to *Traffic*'s Benicio Del Toro could be taken as an indication that affection for Hanks might not be what it used to be.

While most attention centered upon Crowe and Hanks—they were the only Best Actor nominees from major studios—Ed Harris was not out of it. Roger Ebert picked the *Pollock* actor to win, saying he "has been working in Hollywood for twenty years, in a whole lot of pictures, and has been nominated twice before and is not only popular but respected, and who did what every actor dreams of doing: Found the perfect role for himself, developed the picture, and personally directed it. *Pollock* is the kind of film many Academy members *will* have seen, because it's about the most famous of modern American artists and because even the clips on TV make it clear it's not another potted biopic." Javier Bardem might have seemed like an unlikely victor, but he did have a campaign volunteer *par excellence*: Jack Nicholson was so taken with the actor's work in *Before Night Falls*—as well as being a friend of artist-turned-director, Julian Schnabel—that he hosted a private screening of the movie, and told the audience, "This is a great and beautifully made film, and I hope you feel the same way about it as I do." He urged everyone to get out there to vote for Bardem. Truth to tell, it didn't seem that Nicholson would be any more successful than when he was urging people to get out and vote for George McGovern in 1972.

Supporting Actor appeared to have narrowed down between the hot young actor and the respected veteran, Benicio Del Toro and Albert Finney; while Del Toro was taking the leading honor at SAG, Finney was named in the Supporting category. *USA Today*'s Susan Wloszczyna said, "The *Traffic* cop was just too arresting to be ignored, and Benicio Del Toro will be honored," and David Ansen concurred, saying that Del Toro "seems to be Hollywood's man of the moment." Albert Finney, who had never gone to the Oscars, was not helping his cause by hemming and hawing over whether he would show up this year. (Richard Corliss suggested that *The Contender*'s Jeff Bridges "makes good acting look too easy, and won't get Oscar's attention til he plays King Lear in La Jolla or gets arrested on Sunset Boulevard.") Best Supporting Actress was generally thought to be a more-or-less open five-way race, although SAG winner Judi Dench's and Golden Globe victor Kate Hudson's names came up a little more frequently than those of the other three women. Calling this a "race of devilish complexity," Kenneth Turan decided, "It sometimes helps to imagine who the voters would most like to see up on the stage, and the tears flowing between Hudson and her mother, Goldie Hawn, in the audience might be too much to resist." *Entertainment Weekly* also cited "the recent trend toward rewarding ingénue actresses" in picking Hudson.

And the campaigning continued. With memories of the *Saving Private Ryan* loss still on her mind, DreamWorks's Terry Press said, "I do not think anyone goes into the Oscars expecting a sweep. That would be moronic." So the studio put *Gladiator* into Los Angeles's AMC Century 14 Theatre for a special one week engagement, buttressed by two-page ads in the *Los Angeles Times*. And each day, somebody connected with the film would be on hand to chew the fat with the audience, including coproducer Douglas Wick, composer Hans Zimmer, and Russell Crowe. Ridley Scott was shooting a movie in Morocco, but even he made an appearance via a live satellite feed. Ted Casablanca said that Russell Crowe was "really plugging for it. He's workin' this town. You can tell he really wants it." Meanwhile, to help marshal support for *Crouching Tiger, Hidden Dragon*, Sony Classics had projectionists travel out to twenty film locations so that casts and crews who were working out of town would have a chance to catch the film. The company was docked some tickets to the ceremony because it sent both videos *and* DVDs to Academy members instead of one or the other. An Academy spokesperson noted that this was a clear violation of the Oscar campaign rules, but Sony Classics' copresident Tom Bernard pleaded extenuating circumstances, saying that the company had originally sent out the videos before the DVDs were ready and then gave the DVD only to members who had specifically requested it. Besides, said a Sony spokesperson, "everyone else" was doing it too, a claim pooh-poohed by the Academy. DreamWorks was similarly penalized, having used images of the Oscar statuette in *Gladiator* ads in a manner displeasing to the Academy.

Adding to feelings of strangeness and uncertainty regarding this year's Awards, just prior to the Oscars, to be filed under "Who Would Have Thunk It?" *Crouching Tiger, Hidden Dragon* and *Traffic*—a subtitled film in Mandarin and highly topical "problem" film no studio wanted to touch—both hit the $100-million box-office mark. It was only two months earlier that Sony was thrilled with estimates that *Crouching Tiger* might earn as much as $35 million.

A Statesman Reflects

On the day before the Oscars, the *Los Angeles Times* carried a piece by Harvey Weinstein in which he talked about what the Oscars have meant to him throughout his life. After starting, "When I was a kid, the two seminal television events in my family were the World Series and the Academy Awards," he wrote

"Despite the movie being embraced by audiences, the odds are probably twenty to one against our film, *Chocolat*, winning Best Picture, so this year I feel more like a statesman. I'm relaxing and enjoying the opportunity to pat people on the back and root for some of my friends and favorite filmmakers. For instance, I couldn't be more excited for Julia Roberts. When I was having trouble promoting the movie *Il Postino*, Julia came to my rescue. She was a huge fan of Pablo Neruda's poetry and recorded his work for a soundtrack and a TV show promoting the film. For no fee. She has done this anonymously for many other companies and causes. Russell Crowe pretends to be a bad boy, but he's got a good heart underneath. Javier Bardem gave a memorable performance in *Before Night Falls*. Geoffrey Rush and Ed Harris are the Spencer Tracys of our generation. And what more can you say about Tom Hanks—he's extraordinary." But Weinstein didn't neglect to put in a plug for his own movie and to remind readers that the Academy had smiled upon it: "When *USA Today* was challenging me on the Best Picture nomination for *Chocolat*, I challenged them to pick a movie theater anywhere in this country to gauge audience response to the film. I flew down and met them at a randomly selected theater in Washington, D.C. The audience, a high-end, intelligent group that crossed all racial and economic lines, loved the movie. Even the *USA Today* writer was impressed by this random audience's affection for the film. What pundits don't realize is that Academy members are people." Gossip columnists Rush & Molloy reported that Weinstein said that he suggested to Juliette Binoche that she vote for her competitor, Julia Roberts.

The Big Night

I n contrast to last year, everything leading up to the ceremony had gone completely smoothly. That is until three days prior to the Awards, when scaffolding that was being erected outside the Shrine Auditorium collapsed, injuring five workers, one seriously. According to *Daily Variety*, "People at the scene said a slight breeze caused the accident." *Good Morning, America* reporter Lara Spencer was on-site when the mishap occurred and said, "I heard a crack, crack, then workers screaming 'Whoa! Whoa! Whoa!' It's almost like it fell in slow motion." "Things were going smoothly and it looked like it was going to be flawless this year. Now it's not," commented John Pavlick, the Academy's communications director. By Oscar day, however, everything was ship-shape.

The *San Francisco Chronicle*'s Ruthe Stein had talked to people who had been waiting in line to get bleacher accommodations and reported, "First in line are a group of thirty-two who call themselves the Oscar Chatter. Some have occupied bleacher seats for two decades and tell stories of ogling Audrey Hepburn and Federico Fellini. Eighteen-year-old Allison Henkel of Orinda is the group's newest member. She's hoping to score a seat near the front and catch the eye of Oscar nominee Ed Harris, who went to Tenafly High School in New Jersey with her mother. Henkel made a poster with a blowup of Harris's yearbook photo inscribed to her mom, 'Take good care of yourself—you're a beautiful girl!'" Stein also noted, "Most people have a motel room nearby where they can get an occasional good night's sleep, shower and use the facilities. When nature calls in the middle of the night, the twenty-four-hour restaurants in the area have been accommodating. 'I go into Denny's at two in the morning in my orange duck slippers. They just look at me and think I'm nuts,' said Tina Hernandez, forty-seven, leader of the Oscar Chatter. She's grateful that they have not had to contend with rain, as in past years. 'We don't say the "r" word around here.'"

Bob Tourtellotte of Reuters talked to one person in the bleachers, Tommy Korioth of Austin, Texas "who has been cruising the nation's highways in his car seeing the country and just got the itch to head to

Awards Ceremony

MARCH 25, 2001, 5:30 P.M.
THE SHRINE AUDITORIUM, LOS ANGELES

Your Host:
STEVE MARTIN
TELEVISED OVER ABC

Presenters

Art Direction	Catherine Zeta-Jones
Supporting Actress	Nicolas Cage
Editing	Russell Crowe
Short Films	Ben Stiller
Costume Design	Penelope Cruz
Supporting Actor	Angelina Jolie
Sound	Mike Myers
Sound Editing	Mike Myers
Cinematography	Julia Roberts
Makeup	Kate Hudson
Honorary Award to Jack Cardiff	Dustin Hoffman
Documentary Awards	Samuel L. Jackson
Visual Effects	Chow Yun-Fat and Michelle Yeoh
Scientific and Technical Awards	Renee Zellweger
Original Score	Goldie Hawn
Irving G. Thalberg Award	Anthony Hopkins
Foreign Film	Juliette Binoche and Jack Valenti
Song	Jennifer Lopez
Actor	Hilary Swank
Honorary Award to Ernest Lehman	Julie Andrews
Actress	Kevin Spacey
Adapted Screenplay	Arthur C. Clarke (in Sri Lanka)
Original Screenplay	Tom Hanks
Director	Tom Cruise
Picture	Michael Douglas

Performers of Nominated Songs

"A Fool in Love"	Susanna Hoffs and Randy Newman
"I've Seen It All"	Björk
"A Love Before Time"	Coco Lee
"My Funny Friend and Me"	Sting
"Things Have Changed"	Bob Dylan (in Sydney)

Tinseltown and see some stars." Korioth said, "I don't really like the movies. I'm a professional stalker, and I thought, well, there are so many stars out there on the carpet that if I came here, I wouldn't have to stalk again until next year." He wanted to make sure the reporter knew he was joking, though—an FBI Agent working the Russell Crowe case might have been nearby. It goes without saying that Sandi Stratton and Babe Churchill were on hand. E!'s David Adelson was working the stands this year and had never met the sisters, who were holding court with their bleacher friends. After taking a look at their well-appointed tent, he said to Babe, "You guys are certifiably crazy, has anybody ever told you that?" "All the time" was her honest answer. The people from Krispy Kreme were at the Shrine on Oscar day, handing out doughnuts to the fans, although sticky confections may not have been the best thing to be handling on a warm day like this one. Among the T-shirts being worn in the stands, alongside those advocating favorite nominees, were two directed at "President" George W. Bush: "Bush Is America's Emperor Commodus" and "Dude, Where's My Democracy?"

Joan Rivers had been hit with a barrage of criticism in the days leading up to the Oscars, as television critics accused her of all sorts of offenses, most specifically, dissembling misinformation and general ineptitude. So she began her preshow telecast by looking into the camera and intoning very seriously, "Before we start the festivities today, and it will be, I hope, a very festive two hours here on the red carpet, I would just like to say something, okay? Just hold it for a second. In the last few weeks I have received a lot of criticism for mispronouncing names, not knowing people perhaps that I should know. Well, you're all going to have to forgive me out there in TV Land because I'm an old lady now, and I can't read the TelePrompTer the way I used to, and if you're having a problem out there with that then . . . " At this point, she pretended to be struggling to make out what was on the prompter, and said, "Eat shoot."

Then she became her usual self. Rivers, who was wearing Vera Wang and a pair of $6-million earrings from Harry Winston, made a prediction: "Michael Jackson will see *Billy Elliot* forty-seven times, and we're

not talking about the movie." She also indicated that she had hated *Chocolat* and asked, "Will someone out there please e-mail me and tell me how can you run a candy store without ever once ringing up a purchase?" She then deprecated the "really ugly Shrine Auditorium . . . soon to be a Home Depot." Other *bon mots* included, "Marcia Gay Harden—if you're from New York, you know that's Latin for 'excited sissy' " and, regarding Harvey Weinstein, "His ass has been kissed so often it's now referred to as the Blarney Stone." Finally, Rivers said, "People are farting. Brian Dennehy just cut one . . . Three cameramen collapsed."

While Joan Rivers had her elaborate introduction, on KTLA-TV and the WB network, Sam Rubin said simply, "They've been doing it for seventy-three years, but it seems to get bigger and genuinely more exciting each and every year." He and cohost Mindy Burbano handed out containers of Altoids to everyone who stopped by. Meanwhile, Joan Rivers asked Coco Lee, the singer who would be performing "A Love Before Time" from *Crouching Tiger, Hidden Dragon*, "What were you brought up to speak? Mandarin? What do you think in?" Responded Lee, "Actually English, 'cause I grew up in San Francisco." Willem Dafoe told Rivers, "We've never talked." "No, we've never spoken," concurred Rivers, "but I think you're an amazing actor." The actor continued that, "Everybody was saying, 'I hope you talk to Joan Rivers.' " Rivers told him she hoped he won. Dafoe was there with his eighteen-year-old son, St. Ann's graduate, Jack, and the pair wore matching Prada tuxes and neckties. Fashion critic Laurie Pike, in the KTLA studios, commented that neckties with tuxes constituted "a sort of 'Like I Really Hope I Win But If I Don't I'm Gonna Pretend I'm Just Casual' look." Laura Linney told the *Los Angeles Times* that her vintage red Valentino cost "far more" than what she was paid for *You Can Count on Me*. "But I would have made that movie for free," declared the Best Actress nominee.

When Chow Yun-Fat stopped by, Rivers mistook his wife for his costar, Michelle Yeoh, and said "How lovely to see you. I feel like I know you. Congratulations." Chow stepped away to talk to someone else while Rivers continued with her, asking, "Are you going to stay and do more American features now, do you think? . . .What's happening so far, have they been sending you scripts?" Perhaps thinking it was an American custom to treat a married couple as a single unity, Mrs. Chow said, "Yes, so far. The agent's working on it." Rivers then asked her, "When you were doing your own stunts, were you scared?" Fortunately, at this point, Chow broke off his other conversation and came to his wife's rescue. Laurie Pike said "Chow Yun-Fat's wife looked incredible. She was working that androgynous look with the white shirt and the black jacket . . .with her little '20s ringed hairdo." The *Los Angeles Daily News* felt the elegantly dressed couple— he was in classic tie and dinner jacket—was "looking very 1930s Shanghai." As they moved on, Joan Rivers mused, "It's wonderful to see so many Asians here."

Joaquin Phoenix, who brought his mother as his date, was asked by Sam Rubin, "As you walk through all this, you think . . .?" "I don't," he responded, "I don't. I guess I'm on auto-pilot and I just hope for the best." After they shook hands and Phoenix moved on, Rubin commented, "First sweaty palm of the evening." Phoenix admitted to reporters that he just rolled out of bed, climbed into his Armani and didn't have time to devote a lot of time to his appearance, which accounted for his hair being disheveled and his shirt-tail sticking out. Laurie Pike said, "He's cute, let me tell you. You can give him my number. But dude needs to get a hairdresser." Heather Wood of the *Los Angeles Daily News* observed, "Phoenix walked down the red carpet chewing gum and clutching a bottle of water . . . he seemed to have a lock on the most-unkempt award. Perhaps a bit nervous by all the commotion, he lit up a cigarette on the red carpet and even offered friend Winona Ryder a puff. She was happy to accept." Phoenix was feeling exuberant though, and ran over to high-five fans in the bleachers. *Entertainment Tonight* also caught him "planting a kiss on a very surprised Jamie Bell."

Sam Rubin asked Jamie, "How nutty is all this?" "It's crazy," he responded. "I can't believe how excited you get. I don't think there's something like this we English get too excited about. I think the only thing we get excited about is probably having a good final in football." After a commercial break, Rubin told the audience what it had just missed: "What a terrific

moment—Marcia Gay Harden exchanging a squeeze with Benicio Del Toro." Harden said, "That was fun. If the Oscars are always like this, I'll come back." When she got to Joan Rivers, the Supporting Actress nominee pointed to her father, a colonel in the Navy, and said, "This one, he wanted to design the dress. We wouldn't allow him." The actress was in a burgundy Randolph Duke gown and Rivers asked her how she had decided upon it. "I think it's so beautiful and it's so dramatic," Harden responded. "And I think the Oscars may only come along once in a lifetime, and I just wanted to feel and look like a movie star." She laughed, but Rivers assured her, "You do." Of the next arrival, Rivers said, "And now someone that it would not be a show without . . . Now you're gonna watch me grovel. How fabulous to see you!" The person she was addressing was Mindy Herman, CEO of E!. As the executive twirled around to show off her dress, Rivers literally "kissed her ass."

Julia Roberts and Benjamin Bratt drove up not in a limousine but an Expedition SUV. As soon as Roberts, who was in a vintage Valentino, made it through security and onto the red carpet, she was hugged by Hilary Swank. This year's front-runner whispered to last year's winner, "I'm freaking out." *Entertainment Tonight*'s Mark Steines asked Roberts if she would keep her speech to forty-five seconds, but Bratt answered for her, "That ain't gonna happen, baby." Thirty-two-year-old bleacher fan, Spencer Greenwood, had been shouting out Roberts's name, and he beamed to *USA Today*, "I am pretty sure she looked our way. I think she was flirting with me." After Tom Hanks went through the metal detector, he took his wife's hand, only to discover it wasn't Rita Wilson he was holding. "You're not my wife," he told the woman. "No, but I'm available," she said.

Sam Rubin asked Steven Soderbergh, "What kind of year has this been for you?" "Disappointing," was the double-nominee's dry response. Mindy Burbano wondered why so many top actors seemed to want to work with him. Soderbergh said, "Well, I *like* actors, which puts me ahead of a lot of people, believe it or not." Julia Stiles enthused, "I saw Puff Daddy in the elevator of my hotel and I was really excited about that!" Javier Bardem pronounced the scene on the red carpet "a nightmare . . . everybody's screaming here." He also complained to Cindy Adams that "When I was nominated, my friends in Madrid were so excited. They said, 'There must be a party for you.' But I was the one who had to make it. Also the one who had to pay for it." Kate Hudson told the KTLA duo that she had a great time getting dressed with her mom, and that Goldie Hawn had told her, "Tomorrow's another day and you're going to be looking for another job." At one point, Yo-Yo Ma, with his cello strapped to his back, stopped in front of the KTLA space to take a box of Altoids. Mindy Burbano saw him and got all excited: "Now here's an accessory we have not seen before, carrying a guitar on his back. . . . I take it you're performing this evening?" "Yes, absolutely," said Ma, "I'm performing with Itzhak Perlman." Even with that clue, the pair didn't seem to know who he was, but Rubin had him turn around so the audience could see the Pokemon sticker on his cello case.

Surveying the crush of people entering the forecourt, Laurie Pike caught sight of an unusually dressed woman, and exclaimed, "Santa Claus!" Indeed, the woman was wearing the traditional red outfit with (fake) white fur trim. Sam Rubin joined in with, "Merry Christmas! Happy Hanukkah!" And Pike added, "I love Christmas, too, but it's March. I don't know what her story is. Please find out for me. I need to know why she wore that." It turned out she was Costume Design nominee, Rita Ryack, who was attired this way in tribute to her movie, *Dr. Seuss' How the Grinch Stole Christmas*. Talking to Sigourney Weaver about the just-released film *Heartbreakers*, Joan Rivers said, "The success of the new movie is so amazing . . . And they're saying you're the best since Norma Shearer with a Russian accent." She then wanted Jennifer Lopez to tell her who she was now dating in the post–Puff Daddy era. "Cris. He's around here somewhere." "Is it serious?" pressed Joan. "It's nice . . . I'm having a good time." Lopez and Cris Judd would marry in September. James Coburn told Rubin and Burbano, "I can't stay away because my old lady got a taste of it a couple years ago." Draped in beads, Juliette Binoche didn't want to turn around to show off her dress to the E! audience, protesting that "I'm not a model." "You look wonderful. You always look

so chic," cajoled Rivers. "Do it for France." So, for her country, Binoche spun. Laurie Pike's overall feeling was that everyone was so well dressed that, "even the people in the stands look fantastic this year." *Los Angeles Times* fashion reporter Valli Herman-Cohen took stock of what she had witnessed on the red carpet and said, "Amid all of the commotion, it's easy to forget that this almost gross display of wealth (most of it borrowed or granted gratis) takes place near USC, in a working-class neighborhood."

The Academy was trying again with a preshow. From "backstage at the Shrine," cohost Jim Moret said, "For the first time our cameras are behind the scenes." But except for the fact that you could see Best Song nominee Sting standing off to the side, Moret might have been in any nondescript hallway in any building anywhere. Another host, Julie Moran—whose day job was with *Entertainment Tonight*—talked to Michael Douglas and Catherine Zeta-Jones and learned that their son Dylan was now seven months old and was at home with the nanny. It became evident that, once again, the Academy's official show was completely orchestrated and was once again going to lack any kind of spontaneity, as the interviewers waited for their guests to calmly step up in an orderly fashion. Missing was the frenetic jockeying for position that marked the unofficial programs.

The third host, Chris Connelly from MTV, introduced the recently married Kate Hudson as "the only woman who's had a year in love and in the Hollywood wars as good as Michael and Catherine." He didn't draw anything interesting out of her. Apropos of nothing, Jim Moret said to Morgan Freeman, "I understand that you are a song and dance man." "Well," replied the actor, "I used to do a little soft shoe and a little hoofing." Freeman was entirely in black and wore a spider pendant designed by his daughter, Deena—it was a plug for his upcoming movie, *Along Came a Spider*.

The next interchange involved Julie Moran inquiring of Sigourney Weaver, "Is it a much different red carpet when you're not nominated and you can kind of relax?" Responded Weaver, "Oh, yes. I think it's much more nerve-wracking being nominated." "As always, you look statuesque and beautiful," said

Moran. While Rita Wilson was straightening it, Tom Hanks told Moran, "Julie, this bow-tie is gonna be driving me nuts all night. It's always going off to the side." "You look fabulous," complimented Moran. *Newsday*'s John Anderson said, "Tom Hanks, wearing a tiny fuzz of moustache, looked like Mr. Spacely on *The Jetsons.*"

Things slid into the nauseatingly obsequious, when Chris Connelly said to his next interviewee, "If I could be cast away on a desert island, I would choose you, Jennifer Lopez." Wearing a pale green Chanel, the singer-actress was much more covered up than usual, but almost immediately it was clear that, because of the diaphanous quality of the dress's sheer top, she was being more revealing than in even her notorious Versace outfit from the 2000 Grammys. Connelly kept going: "You are once again the goddess of the red carpet. How did you choose this fabulous dress tonight?" "I always choose at the last moment, which is bad," said Lopez. "No, it's good," insisted Connelly. "It makes you more improvisational."

The program broke away from this scintillating conversation to give the first results of an online poll from the Awards' official site, in which the public voted for their favorite "great Oscar moments." Number four was "John Wayne's Last Oscar Appearance." Nine percent of the participants voted for this not-particularly-eventful moment. Next was the Billy Crystal/David Letterman filmed *English Patient* parody from 1996, with 10 percent of the vote. And in second place, with 14 percent, was "Oscar's Family Album" from 1997. The announcer said the participants included "eighty-eight-year-old Louise Brooks," thus confusing Luise Rainer with the deceased star of *Pandora's Box*; what was confounding about the mistake was that the narration had been taped, so this wasn't a spontaneous error. Time for new fact checkers at the Oscars.

People's Steven Cojocaru was on the program to discuss fashion. When he had appeared with Joan Rivers on *E!'s Academy Award Fashion Review* in the past, he had been completely bitchy. Here, Cojocaru apparently had been told to be all sweetness and light, because he couldn't say enough about how lovely the ladies were looking tonight. Winona Ryder was "funky yet formal at the same time. I like the shredding at the bottom of her dress. Looking absolutely beautiful." And Catherine Zeta-Jones was "pure Oscar perfection. I'm having a fashion heart attack."

Julie Moran asked Julia Roberts, "What did you guys do this morning?" "We had breakfast with our family and a bunch of our friends," answered the Best Actress favorite. Turning to Benjamin Bratt, Moran informed him, "I know what you love about this lady is her spontaneity," and asked, "Has she prepared a speech tonight or is she gonna fly solo?" "She never does. Why would she start tonight?" he responded. "Which I find kind of amazing, given the things that come out of her mouth sometimes."

After Jim Moret took viewers on a brief visit to the Shrine's Exhibition Hall where the Governors Ball would be held, Steven Cojocaru was back to do some additional cooing over the fashions. Hilary Swank was "Phenomenal. Very Marilyn Monroe. Happy Birthday, Mr. President." Moran asked him, "What would you say is the fashion trend tonight?" "Skin. Nature's fashion," replied Cojocaru. "And for the men?" "For the men, a traditional mix, with some envelope-pushers." Next, Björk was talking to Jim Moret about her foray into acting: "I prefer the music, but it was great to try it once." It was a little difficult to pay attention to what she was saying, because one was distracted by her unique dress. The singer was wearing a full body stocking that was covered with a swan whose neck wrapped around hers, the head and beak resting upon her breast. Taking note of her outfit, Moret commented, "This is a very unusual creation." "Yes, my friend made it."

It was almost showtime, so we learned that the number one most memorable Oscar moment, according to the Internet poll, was David Niven and the Streaker from 1973, although, even as it topped all other Academy Awards incidents, it had garnered only 17 percent of the vote. The streaker gave Chris Connelly the opportunity to say, "I guess like Steven was saying, skin was in even then, I suppose." Julie Moran saw her opportunity and seized it: "Skin is always in." To which Connelly answered, "You know, Jim. I think a lot of people wish Russell Crowe had worn *that* outfit, huh?" Moret closed with, "Well, you think about Russell Crowe. I'll think about Jennifer Lopez."

Because it was March 25, *2001,* the broadcast began with Deodato's version of "Thus Spake Zarathustra" on the soundtrack, as announcer Gina Tottle gave the lowdown on some of the celebrities seen arriving in the opening montage of clips: "We've watched her grow from teen actress to full-fledged Hollywood star, Winona Ryder"; "She will always be the Pretty Woman, Oscar nominee, Julia Roberts"; "No one wants to sit next to him at the banquet, Sir Anthony Hopkins." Then the Shrine was filled with the sounds of Oscar ceremonies past, including Bob Hope saying, "Welcome to the Academy Awards. Or as it's known at my house, Passover," Gary Cooper announcing that James Cagney was the Best Actor winner in 1942, and Cooper again presenting to Bing Crosby in 1944. Among other sights and sounds included were Elizabeth Taylor winning for *Butterfield 8*, Barbra Streisand saying, "Hello, Gorgeous," Jack Lemmon acknowledging, "I think it's one hell of an honor," Sally Field's "You like me!," Billy Crystal as Hannibal Lechter and, finally, two unseemly Oscar participants: Roberto Benigni climbing on chairs and James Cameron declaring himself "King of the World."

From King of the World, the show went out of this world with a remote from the International Space Station Alpha—another *2001: A Space Odyssey* allusion. Astronaut Susan Helms said that she and her colleagues up there "are all big movie fans. When we want a little time to relax 235 miles above the earth, we watch movies. And we like to keep track of those who have been nominated for Hollywood's highest honor. So tonight we're gonna stay up a little bit late to root for our favorites and to learn who the big winners are." Helms continued, "There's another guy hanging around here . . ." The camera pulled back to reveal a cardboard cutout of Steve Martin. "And I think there's only one way to get rid of him . . ." "Steve Martin" was then ejected from the space station, but there was no corresponding effect on the stage, such as him coming through a screen or dropping from the ceiling. Instead, Martin just walked out. And in a continuity error, he had on a bow tie in the space station picture, but here on earth he was wearing a necktie. This segment—which had been pretaped so as not to upset the astronauts' sleep schedule—was Gilbert Cates's idea, not Steve Martin's.

It was already manifest that we were back to a Gilbert Cates show, because in contrast to the cool music heard last year, Bill Conti was playing the same schlocky arrangements as always, things that sounded as if they might have been written for a Mitzi Gaynor TV special from 1966. Looking at a giant Oscar on stage, Martin began by saying, "You know, we live in a great country. If this statue were in Afghanistan, it would have been destroyed by now"—a reference to the ancient Buddha statue being demolished by that country's ruling Taliban. He also said, "Right now, all over the world, there are 800 million people watching us right now, and every one of them is thinking the exact same thing—that we're all gay."

Looking into the audience, he said, "Miss Ellen Burstyn. Ellen Burstyn has . . ." Martin was interrupted by clapping and he said, "Please, hold your applause until it's for me." Returning to the actress, he continued, "Ellen Burstyn did something that not many actresses would do for a role in a movie. She made herself look thirty pounds heavier and twenty years older. And Russell Crowe *still* hit on her." Amidst the laughter there was a cut to Russell Crowe *not* laughing, which made the rest of the audience laugh even harder—this would be a recurring theme on the program. Sitting next to Crowe, Joaquin Phoenix rubbed his fingers together in a "shame, shame" gesture to Martin. One can only imagine what Crowe's reaction would have been to a Martin joke that didn't make the final cut: "I've heard Russell Crowe's been in a lot of things this year."

The host then mentioned, "Kate Hudson. Twenty-one years old. I love welcoming the young stars to show business because it reminds me of my own death . . . Look how beautiful Julia Roberts looks. Julia, I miss our phone calls. But it seems like ever since you got caller i.d., you're never home . . . Let's see how we're doing on time [he looked at his watch]. Oh, we've got five hours." Again peering into the audience, Martin said, "There's Javier Bardem, who gave such a brilliant performance in a movie about a homosexual poet persecuted by hostile military forces, a movie the rapper Eminem called the feel-good movie of the year. And there's Charlton Heston [the actor raised up his arm in acknowledgment]. Now be careful what you say to him because he thinks he was in *Gladiator*." Heston laughed heartily, but then the camera caught Russell Crowe not laughing, a situation which, again, made everyone else chortle even more.

Referring to Tom Hanks and his wife, Martin noted, "Tom and Rita have one of the most enduring marriages in show business. And it is not easy to keep a marriage together in Hollywood because, well, we sleep with so many different people . . . There's Ang Lee, director of *Crouching Tiger, Hidden Dragon*. Now, at first I didn't realize that was a movie because to me *Crouching Tiger, Hidden Dragon* sounds like something Siegfried and Roy do on vacation." The host mentioned that "Ticket prices went to $10 in New York. And I understand why . . . Julia." Viewers saw Julia Roberts react in mock horror by covering her mouth with her hands. Martin continued, "But I'm concerned because the audience still has valid complaints, and we have to listen to them. One, they feel that the trailer gives away too much of the movie [applause]. Like, I saw the trailer for *Dude, Where's My Car?* and it *ruined* it for me. Now, maybe that's not fair because I had read the book." Addressing another problem, he said, "But maybe critics are right, maybe Hollywood movies are too violent. Now, I took a nine-year-old kid to see *Gladiator* and he cried through the entire film. Now maybe it was because he didn't know who I was . . . You know what I just realized: That hosting the Oscars is like making love to a beautiful woman—it's something I only get to do when Billy Crystal's out of town." Finally he mentioned the eighty-one-year-old Thalberg recipient, Dino De Laurentiis "or as Anna Nicole Smith would call him, 'fresh meat.'"

The stage set was dominated by panels with checkered designs. They resembled the tiling in a bus station bathroom built in the 1960s, or an example of a rendering of the "look-of-the-future" as it may have been presented at the 1964 New York World's Fair. The first presenter was Catherine Zeta-Jones, the first category was Art Direction and the first winner of the night was *Crouching Tiger, Hidden Dragon*. Unfortunately for recipient Tim Yip, he took a breath in between his thanks and, as the *Hollywood Reporter*'s Barry Garron observed, "might have inadvertently won the trapdoor prize by inserting a pause in his acceptance

speech too tempting for Bill Conti's orchestra to pass up." The band played and Yip was gone. Tom Hanks and Rita Wilson were sitting just in front of Julia Roberts and Wilson later said, "the conductor started the music right away, so he didn't get to finish his speech, so she was already looking at him saying, 'Oh-oh, he's got the stick out.'"

Michael Caine was far away filming a movie, so his Supporting Actress duties were handled by Nicolas Cage. The 1995 Best Actor winner led into the presentation by saying, "The words 'dame,' 'Tony-nominated,' 'critically acclaimed,' 'Oscar-winner' and 'national treasure' have all been used to describe tonight's nominees for Outstanding Performance by an Actress in a Supporting Role. But I say, they're simply the best." It made for an amusing parlor game to try to determine which designation went with which nominee. The winner was the "Tony-nominated" one, Marcia Gay Harden in *Pollock*. After hugging and kissing director/costar Ed Harris, the winner handed her purse to her husband, Thaddaeus Scheel. On stage, she said, "Members of the Academy, thank you for taking the time to even view the tape and consider our film. Ed Harris, thank you for inviting me to share your passion. You are a brave director and an even braver actor and I love you. Dad, who's here tonight, thank you for teaching me how to soldier through tough situations, and Mom, for teaching me how to do it gracefully."

After a commercial break, Steve Martin said, "You know, they used to say when they opened the envelope, 'And the winner is . . .' and if you notice, they've changed it to 'And the Oscar goes to. . . .' Because God forbid anyone should think of this as a competition. It might make the trade ads seem crass." He then introduced "a man I like to call a close personal friend, but he asked me not to." It was Russell Crowe, who said, "G'day, folks. How ya doin'?" And then he said that the winner of the Oscar for Film Editing was *Traffic*.

Of the next presenter, Martin gushed, "You loved him in *There's Something About Mary*. You loved him in *Meet the Parents*. And you were fine with him in *Mystery Men*." Before announcing the winner of the Live Action Short Film Award, Ben Stiller said, "You know, there's an old saying in Hollywood: It's not the length of your film, it's how you use it." The Oscar went to *Quiero Ser (I Want to Be . . .)*. Producer Florian Gallenberger declared, "I want to thank Mexico where we shot the film for being such a strange and hard to understand country with so much magic." Before announcing the winner of the Animated Short Film Award, Stiller said, "You know, there's another old saying in Hollywood: Don't try to be funny while introducing the nominees for Best Animated Short Film." Presumably because there hadn't been a major cartoon feature released in 2000, this award wasn't being presented in its traditional fashion—by animated characters. The Oscar went to *Father and Daughter* and winner Michael Dudok de Wit offered brief thanks. Introducing the first nominated song, "My Funny Friend and Me," Halle Berry said that *The Emperor's New Groove*—a nonmajor Disney cartoon feature—was "a family film that is truly for the whole family." Even though it was cowritten and performed by Sting, the song was lethargic and lacking in melody.

Penelope Cruz announced that the Costume Design winner was *Gladiator*, which was somewhat surprising because *Crouching Tiger*'s frocks were both more unusual and aesthetically pleasing. For *Gladiator*, winner Janty Yates essentially took the same basic sword-and-sandal costumes one saw way back in *The Sign of the Cross* and *Quo Vadis* and made them look silly by adding froufrou accessories. Joaquin Phoenix had influenced some of Yates's designs, because the animal-friendly actor insisted that he "would wear only fake-leather outfits." Steve Martin then said, "By the way, Penelope Cruz has starred in such movies as *Live Flesh*, *Woman on Top* and has just finished a new movie called *Blow* [the audience laughed]. And now, here to erase that imagery from your mind is the president of the Academy, Bob Rehme." Rehme, who was that rarity, a charismatic Academy president, received appreciative applause as he noted he was finishing his fifth and final year as head of the organization, a position which has been "an honor and, frankly, a great thrill." He concluded his last official speech by saying, "For seventy-three years, the Academy has endeavored to advance the arts and sciences of motion pictures and to recognize outstanding achievements in filmmaking by conferring our golden Oscar. Filmmakers are extraordinary artists, based all around the world

and supply that world with its most glorious and powerful art form. Let's use that power with a high and humane sense of purpose, And, uh, for some of you who've fallen a little short of that mark, you'll be given another chance between now and the end of my term—I'll be considering some presidential pardons." This last comment, which evoked laughter from the crowd, was a joking reference to Bill Clinton, who was still getting into hot water with rabid right-wingers even though he was no longer in office.

Next, the voice of announcer Gina Tottle was heard saying, "Last year's Oscar winner for her role in *Girl, Interrupted* returns to deliver one this year," a sentence that didn't parse properly because it sounded as if Angelina Jolie was handing out an Oscar winner. Jolie's look was a complete opposite from her much criticized appearance when she was on the receiving end. *Los Angeles Times* fashion critic Valli Herman-Cohen said, "Last year's Morticia Addams shocker, Angelina Jolie, flouted convention again, but with a classy white Dolce & Gabbana pantsuit." Lisa Marsh of the *New York Post* gave Jolie "the most improved award," saying "last year's fashion-loser-Supporting Actress winner looked to have figured out how to let her beauty shine through in a simple white satin tuxedo." Jolie was also minus 1999's dyed black hair and extensions. When she was on the red carpet, *Access Hollywood*'s Pat O'Brien said to her, "This is a major fashion statement, wearing a pants suit to the Oscars." "Oh-oh," she replied. "I'm gonna get in trouble again for something."

Albert Finney hadn't made it to Los Angeles after all and just as Jolie was to announce the winner, Joaquin Phoenix leaned over and kissed his mom. When he heard that the winner was *Traffic*'s Benicio Del Toro, Phoenix gave a spontaneous thumbs up. Del Toro dedicated his Oscar to the people of Nogales, Arizona, and Nogales, Mexico. The actor later told *Us Weekly*, "I'm a pretty quiet guy. My first thought when they announced the Award was 'Oh, God, now I have to go up there and talk.' "

Steve Martin introduced Mike Myers by referring to his aborted *Sprockets* project, saying he "this year refused to do a movie because he felt the script wasn't any good. What Hollywood is *he* in?" Myers said,

"Now, ladies and gentlemen, the awards we've all been waiting for, Sound and Sound Editing. Now I know what you're asking yourself. Will the winner this year be Chet Flippi or Tom [Myers then made a nonsense sound] or perhaps even Chad [more gibberish]. We don't know, but what I do know is that what's in this envelope is gonna send shock waves through the industry!" Sound went to *Gladiator*, Sound Editing to *U-571*. Jon Johnson, winner of the latter award, thanked among others, Dino and Martha De Laurentiis, his film's producers, "who make it exciting and an honor to be in this business." He also offered "my whole crew, my deepest thanks, and I'd like to mention a few of them that I've tortured the longest." Johnson concluded by thanking "my partner, chief antagonist, fiercest promoter, most loyal friend—my wife Jill. I love you forever and after. Kids, don't stay up tonight, we'll be out real late." This year Gilbert Cates was dispatching his camera crews to wherever the winners had been sitting so that the reactions of the people they were with could be captured, even if it was just a technical category—Mrs. Johnson was smiling broadly.

Julia Stiles described the next song, "A Love Before Time" from *Crouching Tiger, Hidden Dragon*, as "combining the flavor and texture of Eastern music with the orchestral color and sensitive lyrics of Western culture." But the ballad—with lyrics by James Schamus—was as insipid as anything Diane Warren might have come up with. Coco Lee was unenviably stuck with the song. This was also to be the night's one major appearance of Debbie Allen's choreography and, surprisingly enough, it was not at all aggressively awful. She had three dancers approximate the fights seen in the movie, and when they flew through the air, their cables were much less invisible than those in the film. Nevertheless, *Entertainment Weekly*'s Ken Tucker declared, "Even when the Oscars jettison the traditional garish dance number, an overproduced stink bomb still manages to clear living rooms across America."

Steve Martin returned to announce, "This next actress is so beautiful and so talented. She is one of the great movie stars of this generation, and there's nothing bad you can say about her . . . However. I did hear this. Last week she got all liquored up, stole a lawn boy, and tried to mow her pool. And yet, if you ask her about it, she'll deny it. Here she is, America's Sweetheart, Julia Roberts." The *Erin Brockovich* star said, "If it weren't for great cinematographers, we'd all be in radio," and then announced that the Oscar for Cinematography was going to Peter Pau for *Crouching Tiger, Hidden Dragon*. He read a litany of forty-four names at a furious pace—the better to outrun Bill Conti's orchestra—and concluded by allowing that "It's a great honor to me, to the people of Hong Kong, and Chinese people all over the world." KABC-TV's Jerry Penacoli said that Pau "sounded like a Chinese version of the Energizer Bunny" and *Entertainment Weekly* noted, "The audience laughs as . . . Peter Pau thanks a long list of Chinese people. Foreign names are funny!" The audience saw an example of Pau's work after Morgan Freeman introduced a montage from the movie. Martin then said, "I saw the movie *Crouching Tiger, Hidden Dragon* and I was surprised because I didn't see any tigers or dragons. And then I realized why: they're crouching and hiding."

Bill Conti's orchestra played a Vegas-style version of "Mrs. Robinson" to greet Dustin Hoffman who, for no discernible reason, had been selected to present the Honorary Oscar to Jack Cardiff; Hoffman hadn't any connection to the cinematographer, and, meanwhile, Charlton Heston, who had appeared in Cardiff's *Crossed Swords*, was right there in the audience. Anyway, Hoffman said, "For those of us here tonight that are seventy years or younger, Jack Cardiff was shooting film before we were born . . . For three generations, Jack brought something extraordinary into our lives, an indelible vision of cinematic splendor." The film clip salute lifted interviews from a documentary about the cinematographer, *Painting with Light*, including testimonials from Martin Scorsese, who said, "Every time I saw Cardiff's name, I knew I was in for something very, very special . . . It's a painting he's made. Paintings that move, extraordinarily. He's using the lens like brush strokes"; and Kathleen Byron, who had starred in *Black Narcissus*, said, "He gave me half of my performance with the lighting." When Cardiff came on stage, Hoffman stepped aside and put the statuette down on the floor, and the recipient asked, "Where's the Oscar?" "It's here," said Hoffman. "Well, for God's sake," said Cardiff, as the presenter hurried to hand him the award. "Can't take him anywhere." Cardiff clutched the statuette to his chest as he said, "This has to be a dream. I often dream I'm working on a movie, but this one tonight is a biggie. I mean, God, all these film extras. And black tie, too, that's extra. God, we'll be over budget. It's a nightmare. And this wonderful Oscar, it's not real, it's special effects. It's amazing, isn't it? Alright, I'm not dreaming, but it's mighty close . . . Thank you all for being on the set."

Gina Tottle said, "The Oscars will return in a California minute," and when they did, Steve Martin said, "I'm a little upset with our next presenter, Samuel L. Jackson, who beat me out for the role of Shaft. He had a whole black take on the role that evidently I didn't have." Jackson was presenting the Documentary Awards. The Short Subject went to first-time director Tracy Seretean for *Big Mama*, who said "beginner's luck," and dedicated the Oscar to her film's subject, Viola Dees, who had died in December: "I'm sure she would want . . . to share this award with the grandmothers like her who are struggling to raise a generation of children whose own parents abandoned them." In predicting the winner of the Feature Documentary Award, *Entertainment Weekly* had indicated that one of the nominees, *Into the Arms of Strangers: Stories of the Kindertransport* was "about a mission to save children from the Holocaust. Need we say more?" No.

Randy Newman was accompanied by Susanna Hoffs to sing his song from *Meet the Parents*, "A Fool in Love"; the Bangles singer was married to Jay Roach, who had directed *Meet the Parents*. The number had a tango influence, and the lyrics were a nice throwback to the witty cynicism of Newman's recordings from the '70s. He and Hoffs were joined by a chorus of women dressed in white wearing white boas and two men in white tuxedos. This group swayed and gestured with their hands, but it is not known if these movements were the work of Debbie Allen.

"The FBI has just announced a suspect in the plot to kidnap Russell Crowe," said Steve Martin. "And all I can say is, Tom Hanks, you should be ashamed of yourself." Kenneth Turan wrote, "The camera went to Hanks for a reaction shot, and the actor not only sor-

rowfully hung his head like Opie caught in a misdeed, but had the presence of mind to mumble 'Sorry' as well. It was a classic moment, worth an entire night full of obligatory thank-yous, and more." Chow Yun-Fat and Michelle Yeoh announced that the Visual Effects Award was going to what was by far the least impressive of the three nominees. Roger Ebert would declare, "One of the most inexplicable Oscars all evening was for Visual Effects for *Gladiator* because they were noticeably bad." The only one of the four recipients to speak thanked Ridley Scott "for his genius" and gave thanks to "my mom in heaven and my dad and family in Detroit."

Renee Zellweger was on hand to report on the Scientific and Technical Awards ceremony, which she described as "an impressive gathering of Hollywood's version of the Silicon Valley." A clip was shown of Irwin Young, the recipient of the Gordon Sawyer Award, saying "I have always felt that there is no better relationship between the scientist and the artist, more so because science and art are the same."

Goldie Hawn misread the TelePrompTer and, giggling, said, "Damn. Oh, you know, you think that when you grow up you get to learn to at least read." She was there to introduce cellist Yo-Yo Ma and violinist Itzhak Perlman who were playing selections from the five Original Score nominees; Debbie Allen had stayed away from them. Hawn then announced that the Original Score winner was *Crouching Tiger, Hidden Dragon*'s Tan Dun. Taking a piece of paper out of his pocket, he provoked laughter when he said, "I prepared something exactly forty-five seconds." He read, "My music is to dream without boundaries. Tonight, with you, I see boundaries being crossed. As a classical music composer, I'm thrilled to be honored here. *Crouching Tiger, Hidden Dragon* breeds East and West, romance and action, high and low culture." He finished with, "This is for two tigers in my family"—his wife and son—"both born in the Year of the Tiger." His speech actually came in at three seconds short of forty-five.

Anthony Hopkins noted that "the legendary" Irving Thalberg's career lasted only eighteen years. "The career of the legend we honor here tonight with the Thalberg Memorial Award has lasted sixty years so far . . . His legend lives as film's most influential independent producer. An energetic, creative fountain of film, his passion for the entire movie-making process has made him one of the most fascinating—and fascinated—producers of all time." After the film clips, Dino De Laurentiis said to the audience, "Thank you very much for this big hug." He added that "My gratitude goes to six beautiful women. They love me, they keep me young." They were his wife and five daughters, and the camera revealed that a couple of them were quite young, prompting *Entertainment Weekly* to gibe that the recipient's "cheering section looked like recess at an Italian preschool." De Laurentiis continued by saying in heavily accented English, "Let me dedicate this happy hour to the Italian film industry, with the hope that they come back alive with new talent and fresh ideas. In my life, I'm proud especially about one thing: To give the opportunity to so many young directors for the first time. And I want to say something to the big studios—don't be afraid about young talent. New minds, young minds, are the future of tomorrow's films. And remember Irving Thalberg himself was only twenty-three years old when he ran MGM." De Laurentiis concluded by thanking "everybody who goes to buy tickets—especially for my movies."

Winona Ryder came onstage and announced, "This is an incredible view. Boy." Gleaning some people connected with *Before Night Falls* in the audience, Ryder said, "Javier, Julien, John, thank you for your movie [putting her hands over her heart]. Thank you so much." Then, "I am so incredibly excited to be here to introduce our next performer because I'm a huge fan and have been for a long time." The performer was "the phenomenal Björk." The singer's rendition of the haunting "I've Seen It All" was a great Oscar moment, a chillingly direct and unadorned performance, the likes of which have seldom been seen on the Awards. After, commenting on Björk's frock, Steve Martin said, "I was going to wear *my* swan, but to me they are so last year."

John Travolta, who had come close to killing his career this year with *Battlefield Earth*, handled the "In Memoriam" introduction. He said, "Goodbye to the names we knew, the faces we loved, for all of us are

better that you visited us for a while." Those remembered included Oscar-winning writers Edward Anhalt, Ring Lardner Jr. (a member of the Hollywood Ten), and Julius J. Epstein (a *Casablanca* cowriter); director Stanley Kramer, the unforgettable B-movie actress Marie Windsor, Hollywood's most famous "little person," Billy Barty, Douglas Fairbanks Jr., Beah Richards, gladiator star Steve Reeves, dancer Harold Nichols, actor and furniture maker George Montgomery, Jean-Pierre Aumont, Claire Trevor, Loretta Young, three heavyweight thespians: John Gielgud, Jason Robards Jr., and Alec Guinness, the one and only Dale Evans, Richard Farnsworth—who a year earlier was seated in the Shrine as a Best Actor nominee—and Walter Matthau, who received a huge response from the audience. Robert Bianco of *USA Today* complained, "It's lovely to do a film-clip salute to the movie people who passed away, but when will they teach the crowd that it's incredibly tasteless to clap for some people and not others? It's a memorial, not *Queen for a Day*."

Jack Valenti took the stage, which meant it was time for the Foreign Film Award. His copresenter, Juliette Binoche, was stuck with telling us that "The camera speaks to the world in every tongue. A baby's smile, an old man's tears, and a stolen kiss are universal. They need no translation." Valenti added, "The five nominees for Best Foreign Language Film truly illuminate the diversity and ever-increasing popularity of foreign films today." The winner was, of course, *Crouching Tiger, Hidden Dragon*. Ang Lee read a list of names.

The telecast's director Louis J. Horvitz apparently had gotten a load of what Jennifer Lopez was wearing when she appeared on the preshow because he now handled her appearance the same way Ed Sullivan had dealt with Elvis Preseley's pelvis-gyrating in 1956: he had the cameraman shoot her from the neck up. Still it took a few seconds to get the camera into position so the television audience could take note that the lights inside the Shrine made the sheer quality of her dress's top even more translucent. Tara Solomon of the *Miami Herald* said, "Her Chanel gown was beautiful; it's just a shame the auditorium was so cold." Lopez was also wearing false eyelashes made of mink. She introduced Bob Dylan, who performed "Things Have

Changed" by satellite from Sydney where he was on tour. Although there were occasional wide shots of his four band members, most of the performance was seen with the singer-songwriter in extreme close-up. He was sporting a pencil-thin moustache, and people seemed to find him a little scary. *Entertainment Weekly* opined that that he looked like a cross between Vincent Price and Cesar Romero as the Joker on *Batman*, and Jay Leno said, "At first I thought it was Willem Dafoe in the Vampire makeup . . . He looked like Floyd the Barber on *The Andy Griffith Show*." David Letterman joked, "This is how dumb I am. Toward the end there they bring down the big screen and you see Bob Dylan, and I thought it was the beginning of the dead actor montage."

Director Horvitz would sometimes cut to members of the audience during the performance, so viewers got to see Goldie Hawn bopping in her seat and Catherine Zeta-Jones moving her head. And also, *Erin Brockovich* coproducer Danny DeVito munching on a carrot. Then Lopez returned to announce that, as expected, Dylan had won the Oscar. Beginning, "Oh, God, this is amazing," Dylan thanked Curtis Hanson and his longtime label, Columbia Records, and then said, "I want to thank the members of the Academy who were bold enough to give me this Award for this song, a song that doesn't pussyfoot around or turn a blind eye to human nature. God bless you all with peace, tranquility, and good will." Richard Corliss said, "Dylan, who turns sixty in May, looked like a desiccated Snidely Whiplash, slim mustache and all. But it was worth it to hear the geezer hipster enunciate that grand cliché, 'I want to thank the members of the Academy,' and then congratulate them 'for being so bold' in giving an Oscar to a song whose lyrics most of them could not decipher."

Steve Martin went running into the audience with a bowl and stopped at Danny DeVito's seat, saying, "Here's some dip." Back onstage, he said, "It was great seeing Bob Dylan live from Australia, which had an eighteen hour time difference—which to Bob is normal." Martin then mentioned, "A homosexual poet. A drunken artist. A man who has a relationship with a volleyball. A sexual deviate. A guy who likes to wear gladiator outfits. But enough about me." Hilary

Swank arrived to present Best Actor, but first said, "Last year, much was made about someone that I forgot to thank. But Chad knows how grateful I am for him, so I would like to take this quick moment to thank someone else I forgot. Dad, thank you for all your support." Her sentiment received applause, and then Swank got to the business at hand, announcing that this year's Best Actor winner was Russell Crowe in *Gladiator*. Crowe looked stunned and some guy in the row behind him grabbed him and was holding onto him, then bumped heads with him. Joaquin Phoenix hugged and kissed Crowe, and onstage the Best Actor kissed Hilary Swank on both cheeks. He dedicated the Oscar to his grandfather who was a cameraman in World War II, and an uncle who died last year, calling them "two men who still continue to inspire me." He thanked "my mum and dad, who I just don't thank enough, I suppose," praised a number of other individuals and said, "But really, folks, you know I owe this to one bloke, and his name is Ridley Scott."

Crowe concluded by saying, "You know, when you grow up in the suburbs of Sydney, or Auckland, or Newcastle, like Ridley or Jamie Bell, or the suburbs of anywhere, you know a dream like this seems kind of vaguely ludicrous and completely unobtainable [at this point, there was a shot of Jamie Bell listening intently]. But this moment is directly connected to those childhood imaginings. And for anybody who's on the downside of advantage and relying purely on courage: It's possible." Of course, one doesn't necessarily connote growing up in the suburbs with being on "the downside of advantage," but it was a nice sentiment nevertheless.

There was still an Honorary Oscar to take care of, and the strands of "The Sound of Music" signaled the arrival of Julie Andrews. She was there to give the Award to the writer of the non-nominated screenplay of *The Sound of Music*. After a filmed retrospective of his career, Ernest Lehman came out as "Tonight" from *West Side Story* played. He could be heard asking Andrews—with whom he was arm-in-arm—"When do I speak?" Looking to make sure the TelePrompTer was ready, Julie said, "Go." What was on the prompter was, "Thank you, you big beautiful audience. As for my fair lady [at this point, he halted and stared into the audience, providing for six nervous seconds of dead air time], your words were the sound of music to my ears. To the Board of Governors of our blessed Academy, you cannot imagine how happy you've made me. I accept this rarest of honors on behalf of all screenwriters everywhere, but especially those in the Writers Guild of America." It turned out Lehman had a chip on his shoulder: "We have suffered anonymity far too often. I appeal to all movie critics and feature writers to please always bear in mind that a film production begins and ends with a screenplay." This sentiment received cheers in the Shrine. Lehman's comments were also the evening's only passing reminder of a threatened strike by the Writers Guild, which had the entire town in a tizzy. (The strike never did occur.)

When Kevin Spacey walked onstage to present the Best Actress Award, Bill Conti had the boys in the band play "Don't Rain on My Parade" from *Funny Girl*, perhaps because it was heard in *American Beauty*, or maybe Spacey was just partial to show tunes. Before getting to the business at hand he told an anecdote: "I got off the plane yesterday and realized that I had left my tuxedo in Nova Scotia. And I would like to thank Dame Judi Dench for traveling across the country with my tuxedo so that I could be dressed this evening. (He and Dench were filming *The Shipping News* for director Lasse Hallström.) She is, without a doubt, the classiest delivery service I have ever had."

The Best Actress winner was Julia Roberts in *Erin Brockovich*. With a long train on her gown, she had trouble maneuvering the steps to the stage in her high heels, so Benjamin Bratt gave her his arm. Later, at the Governors Ball, he explained, "It was an emergency save," because he noticed that "there was a water bottle stuck under the gown, gathered up in the cloth of the dress." Onstage she put her arms around Kevin Spacey and began her speech by saying, "I'm so happy," and then laughed hysterically. Gaining her composure, Roberts said, "I have a television, so I'm going to spend some time here to tell you some things. And, [addressing Bill Conti] sir, you're doing a great job. But you're so quick with that stick, so why don't you sit because I may never be here again" [the audience clapped]. After paying tribute to the other nomi-

nees, she mused, "I can't believe this," and then looking at her Oscar, "This is quite pretty . . . I want to acknowledge so many people that made *Erin Brockovich Erin Brockovich*, but let me make my dress pretty" [she straightened her gown]. After thanking Albert Finney and some other individuals who worked on the movie, Roberts pleaded, "Turn that clock off, it's making me nervous." She told Steven Soderbergh, who was sitting with his *Traffic* compatriots tonight, "You made me want to be the best actor that I suppose I never knew I could be, or aspire to and I made every attempt—Stick Man, I see you—so I thank you for really making me feel so . . ." and then she again laughed exuberantly. " I love it up here!" she exclaimed as she held up her arms in triumph and received the audience's cheers. She thanked her family, and Benjamin Bratt, and Elaine Goldsmith-Thomas "who's been my agent since God was a boy." She concluded by declaring, "I love the world! I'm so happy! Thank you!" Army Archerd said, "The Shrine shook with joy along with Julia Roberts, who finally topped Sally Field's 'You like me, you really like me!' with her joy-filled 'I love the world!' Three hours into the show, she gave it new life." The *Hollywood Reporter*'s Barry Garron called Roberts's speech, "the night's most spontaneous, witty and genuine outpouring of gratitude," and *USA Today*'s Susan Wloszczyna said it was the "best excuse for breaking the forty-five-second speech rule."

The show wasn't going to let go of the *2001* motif just yet, and Tom Hanks appeared in order to introduce the Adapted Screenplay presenter. That was Sir Arthur C. Clarke, who had written the story upon which Kubrick's *2001: Space Odyssey* was based and who had shared a 1968 Original Screenplay nomination with the director for the film. He wasn't in the Shrine, though; he was at home in Sri Lanka, but because of the marvels of modern satellite technology his image was there in Los Angeles. The eighty-three-year-old writer, who was wearing a Nehru jacket that was much more 1968 than 2001, said, "Somewhere in my files is the best Academy Awards speech never delivered." He had taped five different openings of the envelope, each time reading a different winner, and the PriceWaterhouseCoopers representative told director Louis J. Horvitz to run the one in which Clarke said the words, "And the Oscar goes to Stephen Gaghan for *Traffic*." The winner began by saying, "If I made up a story where someone like me would find himself in a place like this, no one would believe it." Gaghan, who was open about his own past involvement with drugs, also said, "Four years ago, a lot of people reached out their hands to me and helped me out. This is for you guys."

Tom Hanks stuck around to present the Original Screenplay Award. Receiving it was Cameron Crowe for *Almost Famous*. Russell Crowe—no relation—stood up and shook hands with the winner as he made his way to the stage. Once there he said, "The movie was a love letter to music and to my family, so I dedicate this to all musicians who inspire us and to my family." He also name-dropped by finishing with, "It wouldn't be complete without saying hello to the master himself, Mr. Billy Wilder. So here's to you, Audrey and Billy."

Announcer Gina Tottle short-changed Tom Cruise by calling him a "two-time Academy Award nominee." The orchestra played the theme from *Mission: Impossible* to greet the actor, who wore not a tux but a suit, hadn't bothered putting on a tie, and hadn't seen fit to button his top button. John Carman of the *San Francisco Chronicle* wrote, "Tom Cruise might have bothered to dress up, just a little. Nicole got all the neckties?" And Jonathan Foreman of the *New York Post* condemned his "disrespectful refusal to change out of his street clothes." Rather robotically, Cruise read, "Their visions varied in scope and size but in each instance they demonstrated the magic and power of movies." He was speaking of the Best Director nominees and, opening the envelope, he disclosed that Steven Soderbergh hadn't canceled himself out after all. Soderbergh had won for *Traffic*. All the *Traffic* contingent mobbed him, and in another section Julia Roberts stood up. "Suddenly, going to work tomorrow doesn't seem like such a good idea," the winner said at the microphone. "My daughter Sarah's asleep in London. She's missing this, unfortunately. There are a lot of people to thank. Rather than thank some of them publicly, I think I'm gonna thank all of them privately. What I wanna say is, I want to thank anyone who spends part of their day creating. I don't care if it's a book, a film, a painting, a dance, a piece of theater,

[rising applause], a piece of music. Anybody, anybody who spends part of their day sharing their experience with us. I think this world would be unlivable without art and I thank you. That includes the Academy, that includes my fellow nominees here tonight. Thank you for inspiring me. Thank you for this."

Earlier, presenter Tom Cruise hadn't walked down the red carpet but entered the Shrine in the back, and hadn't sat in the audience. Now that he had done what he had to do, he took off for the *Vanity Fair* party—and even there he went through the back door. His publicist fielded questions about his casual attire, and she insisted, "It wasn't anything last minute. It's not like he went to the Salvation Army. It was the choice he made."

As Kenneth Turan noted, "All night long *Gladiator* and *Crouching Tiger, Hidden Dragon* had traded victories and putative knockout punches, with *Dragon* winning three out of four head-to-head contests. The two films were tied at four wins apiece with but two categories left to go when suddenly it seemed that a third picture might sneak in and take it all." Since *Traffic* had won Best Director and Best Adapted Screenplay, it seemed entirely fitting that one of its actors, Michael Douglas, came onstage to complete the anointing with the Best Picture Award. The problem was that the title in the envelope was not *Traffic* but *Gladiator*, which became the first film since *All the King's Men* in 1949 to take Best Picture without winning Best Director or a Writing Award. (Even *The Greatest Show on Earth* won for Best Motion Picture Story.) Douglas hid his disappointment very well. Co-producer Douglas Wick's eloquent oration was: "It takes a lot of people to make a coliseum. But it only takes one or two to mess it up. To all the wizards who brought to life the sights, sounds, and citizens of a faraway world, we should take a chisel to this statue and give you your fair share. But instead, I hope you will accept our thanks for not messing it up."

Steve Martin had the last word: "Well, I know what you're thinking. Just as you really start to get into it, it's over." After two years at clocking in at over four hours, this year's show seemed positively brief at three hours and twenty-three minutes.

Aftermath

Last year Hilary Swank was self-flagellating about forgetting to thank Chad Lowe onstage, this year Julia Roberts was furious with herself for not mentioning Erin Brockovich. "During my out-of-body experience earlier tonight, I didn't acknowledge her, shamefully, shamefully," Roberts said backstage. "And really, she is the center of the universe which was our movie. And I've said so many things about her and so many things to her that she knows the esteem in which I hold her, which is quite, quite high. But I was remiss in not acknowledging her tonight. So, with great humility, I acknowledge her profusely." The Best Actress winner admitted, "I'm thrilled to bits. You know, I don't know how people act cool and calm, because this is so huge." Roberts also predicted that, "I won't have a proper thought for, I'd say, six to ten days, which is unfortunate because I start a movie in three. But it's with Steven Soderbergh, so I think he'll understand. I don't think he'll be making sense for a good four to five days." When she was asked about her determination not to let "Stick Man" Bill Conti put an end to her speech, Roberts laughed, "Everybody tries to shut me up. It didn't work with my parents, it doesn't work now."

If Roberts was her vivacious self, Russell Crowe, too, lived up to his reputation. He told the members of the fourth estate assembled backstage, "I'm only into short answers, so ask me questions that I can answer 'yes' or 'no' to, and we'll all get along really well." Asked what he felt when he heard Hilary Swank call his name, he said, "Absolutely nothing." He elaborated, "There was no connection with the world. I didn't have any legs. I was just sitting there thinking that this was one of those remarkably bad-taste kind of gags that your brain plays on you." Crowe said that a few months ago he had assumed Michael Douglas would win the Best Actor Award for *Wonder Boys* and "I thought it was very strange that he was not nominated." He described making *Gladiator* as "a really enjoyable experience. Little skirts and stuff aside, I quite enjoyed the costumes and everything." He explained about the medal he had pinned to his chest: "This is my grandfather's MBE, which stands for Member of the British Empire. He was awarded this by the Queen of England for his work as a war photographer in the Second World War." Before leaving, Crowe declared, "For the opportunities at destiny's forge, God bless America, God save the Queen, God defend New Zealand, and thank Christ for Australia."

"I would be a liar to say that as an actress who came up in New York City in the theater, waiting tables, that I never dreamt of this," said Marcia Gay Harden. "I swore if I ever won an Oscar that I would say thank you to all the waiters and waitresses who used to cover my shift for me so I could run downtown on the subway and audition." Her regret was that, "with forty-five seconds, you just can't give it to the waiters." Of Ed Harris, the Supporting Actress winner said, "I never felt Ed was a first-time director. He never seemed awkward in the process. As a veteran actor and director, the combination of that meant that Ed could help me access things in a faster way. Ed would direct me live as the camera was rolling, and so in that process, he was able to help me unzip things and access things that usually take a lot of time to get to. It was thrilling because he's tough, and he's raw, and he would ask me to go to that place with him." Finally, before moving on, the Supporting Actress winner emphasized, "For me, it's not a career victory; it's a fruition of a dream come true," she said. "I'm a New York theater actress, and now I'm here—with Oscar!"

Benicio Del Toro explained why in his brief acceptance he had paid tribute to the citizenry of Nogales, Mexico, and Nogales, Arizona: "When you go on location, you go into people's neighborhoods all over the country, all over the world," he said. "As an actor, the location is so important—the people were so humble, so beautiful that it really made it easy for me to get into it. I think it helped all the actors, and I think it helped the film. So that's what I meant." Asked if he considered himself a sex symbol, he quipped, "You tell me, how do I look?"

Steven Soderbergh said, "I think I looked pretty surprised, didn't I? I mean, all of you must know that I really didn't anticipate this—I didn't see it coming. I was having a great time. I got to see a lot of my friends get up there and was very happy already. But this is going to take a while to process." He also expressed his belief that whether a movie was from the studios or was an independent was irrelevant: "I've always followed the same methodology from my first film up until the one I am shooting right now," he said. "Coming up the independent route, I didn't imagine this situation. But frankly, from the beginning I have said that I don't delineate between studio films and independent films; I delineate between good movies and bad movies. And we would all like to see good movies. I don't care who's writing the check." As for the movie he won for, "Certainly, none of us anticipated what would happen to *Traffic* because it was a difficult movie to set up, and one that we were told time and time again had no commercial potential."

Gladiator coproducer Branko Lustig—who also won a Best Picture Oscar in 1993—claimed that even when his movie lost the Screenplay and Director Awards, "I had the same feeling like *Schindler's List.* We will get it."

The winner of the TV for giving the shortest acceptance speech was Michael Dudok de Wit, the recipient of the Animated Short Subject Oscar. He had gotten off the stage after only 17.8 seconds. But even he, a lowly cartoonist, said he had "many television sets" and this one would be going to a worthy charity: Hollygrove, a home for troubled youth in Los Angeles. For the record, his entire speech was: "I would like to thank my two producers, Claire Jennings from London and Willem Thijssen from Amsterdam, and both for their dedication and very hard work. And I would like to thank especially my wife Arielle for her support. Thank you, Academy members. This is fantastic."

At the Governors Ball, Benjamin Bratt said of his beloved, "Even now she seems to be in a slight state of shock." Tom Hanks was at the Ball and said that when Steve Martin accused him of being behind the Crowe kidnapping, "I did not know what was going on! Steve did great. It was a very elegant show." Sting mentioned Bob Dylan and said, "I'm glad he won. I have all his records. I learned to write songs at his feet." Steven Soderbergh accepted congratulations for just an hour and then he was off to LAX because he had arranged for a 6 A.M. shoot on the Las Vegas *Ocean's Eleven* set. But because the show itself was over relatively early,

most people stayed at this first function longer than usual, and danced to music provided by a Cuban band. Wolfgang Puck's menu consisted of yellow Finnish potato with crème fraîche and osetra caviar, chino chopped salad, trio-salad and roasted "veal Oscar" with sweet main lobster, asparagus and sauce choron; dessert was Bavarian chocolate mousse on which stood a little chocolate-filled Oscar. The Best Actress winner left the party through the employee exit, and Wolfgang Puck said, "The highlight of my night was not only the great food, but Julia Roberts came in the kitchen."

One very noticeable difference this year was the absence of studio-sponsored Oscar night parties. The *Los Angeles Times* observed that "For almost a decade, the Miramax post-Oscar party, held first at the Mondrian Hotel and later at the Beverly Hills Hotel, was a key late-night destination for the young and hip. Yet the studio, which has been criticized in the media for its lavish spending on the Oscar campaign for *Chocolat,* is curtailing this annual rite. The reason, says Marcy Granata, president of Miramax publicity, is simply a bow to the realities of Oscar-night protocol. Partygoers, she notes, often don't reach their own studio parties until after *de rigueur* stops at the Governors Ball and the *Vanity Fair* event. 'All the parties seem to be getting more and more truncated. You have very little time to rush from one to the next,' says Granata." Executives at rival studios laughed that the real reason was that Miramax had realized it wasn't going to have much to celebrate, and as things turned out, it didn't—for the first time since 1987, the studio hadn't copped a single Oscar, and *Chocolat* was the sole Best Picture nominee not to be awarded at least one Oscar.

Vanity Fair editor Graydon Carter fretted that because there were fewer soirees this year, he was overwhelmed with requests for invitations: "It's much more frantic. I wish there were other parties. Maybe we should just merge this with the Governors Ball. It would make life a lot easier." Monica Lewinsky made a return appearance to Morton's and the *New York Observer*'s Frank DiGiacomo reported, "There were whispers that during the dinner portion of the evening, there had been some tense moments at the table where handbag designer Monica Lewinsky had been seated with DreamWorks SKG partner Jeffrey Katzenberg and actor Kevin Spacey, who were both big supporters of Mr. Clinton. When I asked Ms. Lewinsky about it at the party, she denied that anything of the sort had happened. DreamWorks head of marketing Terry Press said, without an ounce of equivocation in her voice, 'There was no tense moment.' But a source at *Vanity Fair* acknowledged that there was some strain and said that, at one point, Mr. Carter had to go over to sit down with Ms. Lewinsky. Referring to Mr. Katzenberg and Ms. Lewinsky, the source said: 'Graydon thought it would be a perfect match, because they were both so close to Clinton.' " Liz Smith raved about this party, "The actual Academy Awards themselves are but a whisper on this blasting phantasmagoria of stars, all crushed together, defying the fire laws, intimately rubbing Armani shirtfronts and silicone enhancements against one another."

Dinner here consisted of crab cakes, New York steak, and mushroom risotto and private reserve Francis Ford Coppola wine, the tables decorated with tulips flown in from the Netherlands. As with the Governors Ball, post-Oscar dance music at Morton's was Cuban in flavor. Cindy Adams noticed artist-turned-film-director Julian Schnabel "admiring his own painting on the wall." He informed her, "I am not someone who does things. Like paint pictures or direct films. I am an artist who creates." And James Woods confided to Adams that, "My girlfriend Hillary and I have almost the same color heads because I'm using her hair products." Frank DiGiacomo reported that "in the center of Morton's, Anthony Hopkins and James Woods, two of the most convincing screen psychos in town, were laughing and joking like a couple of fratboys. I asked the two men if the movie business was more or less fun than it was ten years ago. 'It's fun for him,' Mr. Woods replied. 'He just got paid $45 million. I get paid in fucking food stamps.' " DiGiacomo also saw Angelina Jolie talking to PBS documentarian Ken Burns who she said was giving her "some pointers" about how to "look smart" when Billy Bob Thornton discussed baseball. Jolie had told *Access Hollywood* that the best part of this evening was "talking to my husband on the phone on the way over

here." What did she tell him? "That I miss him and I wish I was in bed with him."

Liz Smith said that single man Tom Cruise "was jovial and friendly to all who approached, but he did have PR maven Pat Kingsley nearby, nervous, in case she needed to step in." Smith counted among the party's most memorable sights, "the alluring spectacle of Pamela Anderson and Elizabeth Hurley, just a couple of single chicks on the town together, leaning bountifully over Warren Beatty and Annette Bening's table, sharing a compact, touching up their famous lips, keeping heads close while strong men watched and wept." Sean "Puffy" Combs, who a week-and-a-half earlier had been acquitted of gun possession and bribery, told the party girls, "You two have to come to New York. We could have so much fun." Hurley told him, "I saw you on *Charlie Rose* and you were quite brilliant." Warren Beatty was overheard saying, "Everyone talks about the length of it. I wouldn't care if the Academy Awards ran nine hours. We've lost sight of its meaning. To me it's not primarily a television show. It's our industry." Matt Damon and ex-girlfriend Winona Ryder chatted briefly and then mingled separately. Liz Smith sighted "Courtney Love, as bombastic and bodacious as ever, in her transparent, bosom-baring gown, circling the room with Chloë Sevigny. 'We're just trolling for boys,' Love said." Seeing a picture of Love's outfit, Joan Rivers said, "God bless this old slut." Outside Morton's, Love said to CNN, "Relationships break up. Relationships are formed. It's like Fellini in there."

When Julia Roberts and Benjamin Bratt were making their way into the *Vanity Fair* party, *Access Hollywood*'s Shaun Robinson informed the Best Actress winner that her acceptance speech had taken three minutes and forty-seven seconds. Roberts's response: "Oh, I'm sorry." The Best Actress winner also told *Entertainment Tonight*'s Jann Carl that Bill Conti "was so brutal with that stick." Roberts predicted to *Today*'s Jill Rappaport, "It's gonna take months for my cheeks to recover from smiling so hard." On *Good Morning, America*, Diane Sawyer said she heard that "the biggest surprise of the entire Oscar event" was that Julia Roberts, covered by Benjamin Bratt, used the men's room at Morton's, and on *Entertainment*

Tonight, Mary Hart said that her presence in that male domain was "eliciting cheers from the guys." Roberts explained, "I've never needed anything so much in my life." Winner Marcia Gay Harden was the last one to leave Morton's, closing the joint at 3 A.M. Harden said that when she and her family had ended their partying, "we got back in the limousine and were chased by paparazzi for miles and miles. Fortunately we had our bodyguard [because of her borrowed Harry Winston diamonds] and he was able to get away from them. I don't know what they thought they were going to get. Maybe they thought it was Russell Crowe's car."

Lara Spencer of *Good Morning, America* reported that at the *Vanity Fair* party, "Once you're in, it's so crowded that a lot of people said, 'Forget it. You know what, forget it. We're going over to *In Style.*' So *In Style* had a really great year." Elton John was hosting this AIDS fund-raiser at Moomba and guests included a quartet from *Traffic*: Michael Douglas, Catherine Zeta-Jones, Topher Grace, and Erika Christensen; also Sting, Tim Allen, Whitney Houston, Kim Cattrall, k.d. lang, Kevin Spacey, Melissa Etheridge, Gabriel Byrne, LeAnn Rimes, and Bridget Fonda and boyfriend Dwight Yoakam. The prize in the Oscar pool, a diamond-encrusted Chopard watch, was won by director John Waters who had predicted every category correctly. Eventually, the dance floor got so crowded that one had to wait in line to get to it. For the first time ever at his Oscar night party, John got up and sang for the guests, performing a duet with Nelly Furtado. Most people headed back over to Morton's at 11:30 after the duo had finished singing. As Tom Hanks was leaving, KABC-TV's Carlos Granda asked him what he thought when the Best Actor winner was announced. "I always thought it was going to be a toss-up," said the *Cast Away* star. "I always thought Russell stood as good a chance as I and I was happy for him."

Daily Variety said, "Further west at the Beverly Hills Hotel, Norby Walters hosted the 10th annual Night of 100 Stars gala, which benefits the Film Foundation and was hoping to raise $140,000 for the restoration and preservation of films made before 1952. This is an older crowd (many of the attending stars probably saw career peaks around 1952) and Wal-

ters said the dinner 'brings Old Hollywood and Young Hollywood together in a fashion they normally wouldn't meet. Old Hollywood thinks the way they did it was right. And Young Hollywood, sort of, doesn't care less.'" Lara Spencer described this affair slightly differently, saying, "those not on the *Vanity Fair* guest list are welcomed at the Night of 100 Stars . . . it attracts a different crowd—stars we all know and love and haven't seen for a while." The assortment of guests included Sally Kirkland, Robert Stack, Sid Caesar, Thora Birch, Lee Iacocca, David Hasselhoff, Sean Young, Vivica A. Fox, Gary Busey, Pat Boone (in a mustard yellow tuxedo), and Brian Dennehy, who said to Lara Spencer, "They certainly didn't invite *me* to the *Vanity Fair* party."

DreamWorks had planned a private little get-together at Dominick's in Beverly Hills, but after *Gladiator* won Best Picture, the studio decided to make it an open house and told celebrities and members of the press to come on down. It was a quickie though: Ridley Scott, Steven Spielberg, Jeffrey Katzenberg, and David Geffen stopped by briefly and left. By the time Joaquin Phoenix arrived after hanging out at Morton's, the place was empty. Russell Crowe made a pit stop and then headed to the Bel-Air Hotel, where he was hosting his own private party. While he was at Dominick's, Ridley Scott told CNN, "Russell is so cocksure usually and he really wasn't tonight. He was actually stunned that he got it I thought, and that was very sweet."

Sony Classics, which had released *Crouching Tiger, Hidden Dragon*, did have an Oscar-night bash. The company's copresident, Tom Bernard said, "The funny thing about it is that we've never had a party. Everybody said you have to have a party, so we decided to have a party because it was something we were supposed to do. Then we find out that nobody's having parties! Yet there are so many people involved in this movie coming from around the world—from Taiwan, Hong Kong, New York—we felt this would be some kind of event to help them celebrate." The party was held at Crustacean in Beverly Hills. Chow Yun-Fat and Michelle Yeoh mingled with the large assemblage of fans who were gathered outside the restaurant. A reporter asked Chow if he was surprised at how many people—mostly Chinese Americans—had shown up to catch a glimpse of the *Crouching Tiger* stars. "Oh, I paid for them," he kidded. Yeoh's attitude was, "Such a wonderful feeling. We have four Oscars. Whoever would have thought?"

Los Angeles magazine sponsored a party at Spago, which was significant because it would be the last Oscar party ever for Wolfgang Puck's Sunset Strip fixture. KABC reporter Garth Kemp was there before things were in full swing and said, "Already we've seen some people here, everybody from Tom Arnold to . . . we saw Gladys Knight here earlier as well. We've got Buzz Aldrin, the astronaut that was down here, a lot of celebrities. Jay Leno was here as well." Later in the week, the celebrated restaurant, home of Swifty Lazar's parties in the 1980s and early 1990s, closed its doors for good after nineteen years. Chef-owner Puck had opened another Spago in Beverly Hills and the old place had fallen out of favor, suffering the same fate that decades earlier had befallen the Brown Derby—it had been commandeered by tourists.

The front page of *Women's Wear Daily* featured a full-length picture of Julia Roberts and said, "It was a fabulous blast from the past . . . an evening that could have come right out of the heyday of the silver screen capital." The *San Francisco Chronicle*'s Cynthia Robins declared, "True Hollywood glamour stalked the red carpet at the Oscars last night. Not the cheap imitation kind that has marred what is truly the glossiest evening of the year, but old-fashioned, '50s sleekness—the red lip, the carefully arched brow, the entrance dress and the gems to match. For those women who really 'got it,' i.e., who realized that breast-baring decolletage and a plethora of sequins do not star power make, it was an evening to glisten, not to flash." Heather Wood of the *Los Angeles Daily News* felt that, "Young stars and starlets may be taking over Hollywood, but during Sunday's Academy Awards, old Hollywood glamour ruled on the red carpet. And this year's list of leading ladies led the way sporting dresses in an array of colors and chic styles."

It was nearly unanimous that Julia Roberts not only gave the night's best acceptance speech—people were disarmed by her high spirits and palpable joy—but that she had also made the most impressive fashion statement. Her Valentino was from the designer's Fall 1982 *haut couture* collection and the black gown was offset by white silk piping. Cynthia Robins said, "Julia Roberts was nothing short of spectacular . . . with her long, dark hair so piled and full that it rivaled Baby Jane Holzer's for loft and volume." The Best Actress winner did admit that as the evening wore on the gown was beginning to feel a little snug. She laughed that Hilary Swank, "every time she passed me, would say, 'Breathe, just breathe.' Not so easy in this dress, but I'm doing the best I can!" Observers were also delighted that she and Benjamin Bratt were color-coordinated—he wore a white shirt and tie with his black one-button Armani tuxedo—although Roberts claimed they hadn't planned it that way. On *Access Hollywood*, Steven Cojocaru said, "Remember this, folks. The couple that coordinates together stays together, and these two are in it for the long haul." The couple also had a coordinated accessory: they were wearing rings, which fueled speculation that marriage was imminent.

Among other highly praised women was Renee Zellweger, who wore a lemon yellow Jean Dessés from the late '50s. "It's old and it fit and I loved it," she told reporters; various fashion experts compared her to Rita Hayworth and Veronica Lake. Joan Allen also received high marks in her Michael Kors, and Heather Wood of the *Los Angeles Daily News* wrote, "*The Contender* actress arrived early during the pre-show parade of celebrities, giving photographers and journalists ample time to soak in her unaging beauty. Allen wore a crystal-encrusted tangerine gown that hugged her body like a glove, revealing every lovely feature. Sporting a new, trendy haircut, Allen looked as young and vivacious as some of the night's youngest stars . . . Allen, whose hair was in a bob, said it took 'about five hours' to achieve her simple yet elegant look." *Entertainment Weekly* declared, "Sleek, sexy, and thoroughly modern, this gown demonstrated that even a serious actress can look as stunning as any starlet." Allen said, "It was a color that I had been told by friends looked good on me, and when I went to see Michael, he had designed one dress in this color. I said, 'That's the one!' "

The *Philadelphia Inquirer*'s Jennifer Weiner said,

"Marcia Gay Harden accepted her Oscar in 1940s elegance, wearing a strapless sheath of cranberry with a matching wrap by Randolph Duke." Harden told *People*, "My father said to me, 'Honey, I want you to wear a strapless dress. You've got what it takes to hold them up!'" She also said that in choosing her simple-yet-dramatic red gown, she had looked to Hollywood's past. "I once played Ava Gardner, and she inspired me," said the Supporting Actress winner. Randolph Duke explained to Larry King that Harden's "got light skin, she's got dark hair. It started with Daddy wanting her to wear champagne . . . Champagne washed Marcia out. She needs a deep strong color because when you walk on the red carpet it's gotta be, Wow!, because you want to set the carpet on fire." The *Mogambo* star's name was also brought up by Hal Rubenstein who asked, "Is Catherine Zeta-Jones channeling Ava Gardner?" The *New York Daily News*'s Alev Aktar said of Zeta-Jones, "The Welsh bombshell was a knockout in a black beaded Versace corset dress that showed off her aerobicized curves." Anne Bratskeir of *Newsday* wrote, "Underscoring that black is back, Catherine Zeta-Jones—having shed her pregnancy weight—flaunted the figure in a body-skimming black Versace number, a sequined bustier with structured satin skirt."

On *Live with Regis and Kelly*, Kelly Ripa mentioned Jennifer Lopez's dress and said, "This time she went for a ball gown, but she still managed to be naked in a ball gown . . . but I think all the men were very, very happy." Indeed, Lopez's gown was widely discussed—and praised—by a group that usually doesn't pay much attention to fashion: straight men. *Good Morning, America*'s Charles Gibson said, a little coyly, "There was one dress I couldn't help noticing . . . She looked great." Jonathan Foreman wrote in the *New York Post*, "Jennifer Lopez proved, by being more naked on the Oscar stage than anyone since that streaker who dashed past David Niven back in 1973, that the Hollywood tradition of outrageous sexiness didn't die with Marilyn Monroe." Jay Leno said of Lopez, "She finally figured out a way to get people to quit looking at her butt."

But Hal Rubenstein of *In Style* was exasperated by director Louis J. Horvitz's apparent fear of breasts. He

complained that for the television audience, "Basically, this girl had no dress, she just had a neckline . . . My feeling is, has anybody been at a beach lately?" Alev Aktar of the *New York Daily News* said Lopez's "shockingly transparent top gave new meaning to the word titillating."

Ellen Burstyn received raves for her cream-colored Catherine Bacon gown and especially for her sapphire white-and-gold "Sun King" diamond necklace from Christian Dior. The actress had said, "I wanted to attract as much sun as I could. I wanted to bring in the light and send it out." *Newsday*'s Anne Bratskeir felt "Halle Berry stunned in a sequined lavender cowl-necked gown from Badgley Mishka." Joan Rivers said one of the actress's breasts was called Badgley, the other went by Mishka.

The same two names kept coming up when critics were citing their least favorite outfits. For some reason, people seemed seriously offended by the fun Björk was having with her swan outfit. In 1994, everyone was delighted by Lizzy Gardiner's American Express dress, and one might have assumed that Björk's offbeat outfit would receive a similarly pleased reaction. But Jay Carr of the *Boston Globe* said, "Björk's wraparound swan frock . . . made her look like a refugee from the more dog-eared precincts of provincial ballet." Heidi Oringer of the ABC News Radio Network squawked that the frock was a "disaster" and a "crazy-looking number." Steven Cojocaru declared the outfit to be "probably one of the dumbest things I've ever seen" and Kelly Ripa announced, "She's always known for her hideous attire." *Women's Wear Daily* wrote, "Björk—surprise, surprise—provided, if not the Cher factor, then at least the requisite kook factor. When the Icelandic singer-actress was asked the age-old question, 'What are you wearing?' she laid an egg. Literally. Björk lifted up the tulle script of her swan dress and dropped a toy egg on the red carpet." The egg doubled as a purse, which should have indicated that the Best Song nominee was just enjoying herself. Comic actress Tracey Ullman, appearing on *Today* for a morning-after Oscar post-mortem, said, "At least she wasn't styled by somebody. She just decided to look like a lunatic on her own." Jay Leno said "that thing was so bad even heterosexuals are making fun of it," and,

"The camera caught Danny DeVito eating a carrot . . . then they saw Björk's dress eating a box of popcorn." Joan Rivers said, "later I saw her in the ladies room spreading papers on the floor . . . this girl should be put into an asylum." Melissa Etheridge, though, said, "Loved the dress, and I love Björk" and in the *New York Observer*, Simon Doonan gave Björk a "total, overall *j'adore*!" The outfit had been designed by Marjan Pejoski, who hailed from Macedonia, and Björk said, "It's just a dress."

The other woman treated mercilessly was Juliette Binoche who had a flapper-cum-dominatrix look going in a form-fitting black corset dress designed by her pal and compatriot, Jean-Paul Gaultier. She was also wearing a beret and studded boots and was festooned with pearl necklaces from Chanel, accessories suggested by Gaultier, although she arranged them herself. John Anderson wrote in *Newsday* that Binoche "looked as if fans had pelted her with strands of pearls as she strode along the red carpet," while Hal Rubinstein's comment was, "Doo-wacka-doo." Binoche told the press that her look was inspired by the character Lulu who Louise Brooks played in G. W. Pabst's *Pandora's Box*, but Tracey Ullman wanted to know, "Why did Juliette Binoche look like Jack Lemmon in *Some Like It Hot*?" On second thought, said Ullman, "She looked like she'd been in a fight at a garden party." Escada's Brian Rennie was Joan River's guest on *E!'s Academy Award Fashion Review* and said Binoche looked "like a French school boy's wet dream."

Also receiving mostly thumbs down was Kate Hudson. "I wanted to look youthful and sexy and beautiful," she said, but most observers concluded that Stella McCartney didn't help her attain these goals. Her gray dress had a fringed and beaded shoulder cape attached, and it was those fringes in particular that set people off. Hal Rubenstein said, "We'll blame it on youth—the one thing Kate Hudson's Annie Oakley look forgot to celebrate," while Joan Rivers felt "the top looked like something Chuck Connors wore on *The Rifleman*." In the *Miami Herald*, Tara Solomon wondered, "Since when did Stella McCartney start doing couture lamp shades?" *Entertainment Weekly* didn't like Hudson's hair, either, asking, "weren't curly perms over, like, ten years ago?" while *Us Weekly*'s

Susan Kaufman felt the actress's hair was "kind of like a poodle."

Simon Doonan remarked on hairdos in the *New York Observer*, saying "Asian style . . . penetrated the ranks of the white girls who all had some kind of Dewi Sukarno–Imelda Marcos upswept hairdo. Catherine Zeta-Jones and Laura Linney had identical coffee-cake bouffants, and Julia Roberts toted an oversized Styrofoam bun. Matronly as these coiffures are, they are age-appropriate and lend an aura of timeless stature where none might exist." Joan Rivers observed that Charlton Heston was wearing "the best toupee he's ever had," although Jay Leno felt that "Björk's dead swan . . . kind of matched the dead muskrat on Charlton Heston's head."

The majority of men acted as if it were the mid-'90s again as they said fie! on traditional tuxes. Neckties dominated, but there were also string ties and the no-tie look reappeared, making those who opted for traditional formal wear—such as Sting—look particularly elegant in comparison. The *New York Post*'s Lisa Marsh called the singer's "perfectly tailored Gucci three-button . . . a timeless classic without a single thread out of place." In the *San Francisco Chronicle*, Cynthia Robins suggested, "Russell Crowe should run his stylist through with that sword from *Gladiator*. He was High Fop with fouffed-up hair, a preacher coat, a string tie and an inexplicable medal hanging from his coat pocket. Get that boy a pair of jeans, a cigarette and a ticket back to his farm in Australia. He could use a break." Crowe had joked to *Entertainment Tonight* about his duds, "This is what happens when me and Giorgio Armani have a couple bottles of red wine." Watching the red carpet arrivals, Jennifer Weiner wrote in the *Philadelphia Inquirer*, "David Carradine looked positively weird in a two-tone beige-and-white tuxedo with matching white hair, causing men all over America to say, as one, 'Hey, I could've done better than that.' "

On *Politically Incorrect* the next night, host Bill Maher complained that so many fashion critics were gay men. "I'm a little tired of hearing gay men telling me what's sexy about women. How would *they* know?" he groused. "They don't know what's sexy about a woman." One of the guests was Richard Roeper, the man whom Roger Ebert had personally selected as his post-Siskel television partner, even though Roeper had no background in film. If Siskel and Ebert could fairly have been called Tweedledum and Tweedledee, then now it was Tweedledee and the Village Idiot. Roeper piped up to disagree with Maher, declaring that gay men "know what's sexy about women's clothes—they wear them."

From the nation's press, there was good news for both Steve Martin and Gilbert Cates. Eric Mink of the *New York Daily News* called the Oscar telecast "one of the freshest, smartest and most bracing in recent memory. And, at three hours, twenty-three minutes, one of the most concise. Nothing reflected this combination of intelligence, confidence and the edgy wit of a knowing insider better than first-time host Steve Martin . . . Martin alternated between poking fun at himself and biting the Hollywood hand feeding him. And biting hard." The *Los Angeles Daily News* noted, "You might not have been able to tell it from perpetually dour Russell Crowe's face, but host Steve Martin was consistently funny throughout the evening, rather than peaking early and running out of steam, which has been a problem in recent years." Similarly, Ken Tucker opined in *Entertainment Weekly*, "As host, Martin was typically dapper and comfortably low-key, pacing himself throughout the evening. (People invariably praise Billy Crystal's hysterical opening-song parodies and forget that for the rest of the show he's often just a manic yuk machine.)"

Carrie Rickey wrote in the *Philadelphia Inquirer* that "The urbane Martin, whose delivery was drier than the Mojave and reminiscent of the glory days of Johnny Carson, ribbed all the nominees. . . . The emcee was like the perfect waiter, always appearing when the show needed comic service. Between his blitzkrieg humor and the elimination of production numbers, the evening moved if not as fast as an action movie, not at its usual slo-mo pace." And *USA Today*'s Susan Wloszczyna cheered that Martin was "very classy and with just the right air of mocking self-importance. I forgot just how funny he is as a standup comic. He made something as crass as an awards ceremony seem grownup and tasteful. I thought I would miss those

song parodies and Billy's manic presence but I didn't at all. I hope he does it again and again."

Entertainment Tonight's Leonard Maltin deemed Martin "the perfect mix of class and class clown." Robert Bianco of *USA Today* raved, "Steve Martin didn't have to be wild and crazy to be hilarious, or to make Oscar night his own. Hosting Sunday's blessedly quick Academy Awards, Martin was a droll delight—as amusing as Oscar star Billy Crystal, but in an entirely different way. Where Crystal was all hard work and good humor, the more deadpan and deceptively proper Martin let his nastier jokes sneak up on you, almost mimicking the image of the perfect host." He did say, "Otherwise, aside from Roberts' charming acceptance speech, it was not a particularly exciting or emotional night, but it sure did move. Producer Gil Cates, back for his tenth show after skipping last year, presented a streamlined Oscar show, without any extraneous movie-history film salutes or production numbers. Anyone who can get the Oscars in at under three and a half hours can even be forgiven for a remarkably ugly set that often made presenters look like they were standing inside a sewer pipe."

Andrew Sarris focused on one aspect of the show: "The single switch from the age-old practice of sending up a pair of presenters for almost every award to this year's steady stream of solo presenters was little short of a stroke of genius. Still, there was a big morning-after complaint: that the show lacked 'spontaneity.' It was as if the inane exchanges at the podium over the past decades were Wildean models of repartee. Too many movie journalists have forgotten, or perhaps never read, F. Scott Fitzgerald's devastating description of William Powell and Norma Shearer fumbling through cocktail parties without their scriptwriters to provide them with the appropriate dialogue. No, the last thing the Oscar telecast needs is the 'spontaneity' of the big stars, not unless what the movie journalists are really looking for are opportunities to laugh derisively at the gaffes, slips and bloopers coming from the lips of overdressed celebrities."

Army Archerd felt the show "was certainly one of the best in years" and said of Steve Martin, "Judging by this Shrine aud last night, he can come back any time he wants." Many of the show's participants were raving about the host. To Mike Myers, he was "brilliantly hilarious," while Ben Stiller called him, "the best, totally. He really took his personality and used it." From the music side of things, Sting said Martin was "the best in a long time, funny and inside." Tom Hanks told *Us Weekly*, "Steve did a service to mankind, hosting this thing. He always left us wanting more, and it was a really quick, fabulous show." One of the show's writers, Rita Cash, noted in *Entertainment Weekly* that in the green room she had observed "several stars remark how much they love Steve Martin ... words like 'smart,' 'witty,' 'genuine' are used. The consensus: Billy Crystal no longer owns the Oscars."

You can't please everyone, though, as *Hollywood Reporter*'s Barry Garron meowed that "Here was veteran producer Gil Cates presiding over one of the few Academy Award presentations that ended on time and still managed to be too long." He added, "If nothing else, tonight's show proved that, despite the many Awards most viewers have no interest in, the show can be done in three and a half hours."

Of course ABC and the Academy had also taken up thirty minutes of airtime prior to the Awards ceremony. Robert Bianco complained, "Once again, ABC demanded exclusive rights to the pre-show—and once again, ABC produced an excruciating half-hour. We don't need 'how do you feel' interviews, and we don't want to see the inside of an empty ballroom. We just want to see who's there and what they're wearing. How hard can that be?"

The show did have its lowest ratings in five years—one would have to assume people did not tune in because they heard Debbie Allen was coming back.

The day after the Awards, a member of the Academy's Board of Governors from the Sound branch wrote to President Bob Rehme to complain about the way Mike Myers had made fun of his field of endeavor. Rehme wrote a letter of apology to members of the branch, because the Academy had a rule written down saying that presenters on the show were forbidden from cracking jokes at the expense of any of the Award categories.

Taking stock of the voting results, the *Hollywood Reporter*'s Kirk Honeycutt said, "Yes, *Gladiator,* an epic tale of ancient Rome and its blood-sport warriors, won the Best Picture statuette. But in its collective wisdom, the Academy of Motion Picture Arts and Sciences voters divvied up thirteen Oscars so neatly among these films as to create a virtual three-way tie." Rene Rodriguez of the *Miami Herald* wrote, "no single movie dominated the ceremony, which more than lived up to its billing as a night of surprises. It even ended on time." Kenneth Turan contemplated, "Finally, eerily, it was a cliffhanger not unlike the one that decided that other election back in November, with the winner in doubt until the final envelope was opened."

Bob Strauss complained in the *Los Angeles Daily News* that, "the event concluded on the most conservative, conventional note that it possibly could have. Best Picture winner *Gladiator* was the biggest production, the biggest box-office hit and, by a long shot, the most violently mind-numbing nominee of the five. The Academy could have chosen to honor a film bold enough to attack a gnarly social issue in all of its hopeless complexity or broken a nearly three-quarter-century tradition by recognizing that cinema speaks in an international language. But, as they often do, the voting members went for the obvious, spectacular choice. Not hook, line and *Titanic,* though, and for that the group deserves some praise." Strauss also mused that one tradition, "we should be elated to see bite the dust, however, is Miramax Films' relentless efforts to promote mediocre work to Oscar glory. The Academy reacted strongly to being bamboozled into nominating the soft-centered *Chocolat* for Best Picture, resulting in a Miramax shutout ... Maybe now the company will consider going back to its true glory of making films like *The Crying Game*, *The Piano* and *Pulp Fiction*—which aesthetically timid Oscar may not have liked all that much, but was forced to show respect for. Now, if only the voting members had been a little more resistant to the equally emphatic, Oscar-pimping ways of DreamWorks, the studio that pushed so hard for *Gladiator* and Best Original Screenplay winner *Almost Famous.*"

The *Hollywood Reporter*'s Martin Grove suggested

that "DreamWorks' *Gladiator* screenings may also have played a part in the film's Best Picture win and in Russell Crowe's Best Actor victory. The film was considered the Best Picture front-runner given that with twelve nominations it had more than any other film this year and that it had won the Golden Globe for Best Picture/Drama. Nonetheless, the steadily increasing momentum for *Traffic* and for *Tiger* as the Oscar race progressed turned this into a real nail-biter. DreamWorks could just as easily have lost for Best Picture, so anything and everything it did on the marketing front to support *Gladiator* must be regarded as having been important. The Century City showings, in particular, appear to have been very worthwhile. For many films, the goal is to get Academy members to look at them, even if it's on tape or DVD at home. For *Gladiator*, it was important to get the voters to take a second look—but, hopefully, on a big screen with proper projection and good sound because of the epic nature of the film."

In the *Los Angeles Times*, Patrick Goldstein lamented that, "The Oscars have fallen prisoner to the same forces that dominate the movie business the rest of the year—the reliance on multimillion-dollar marketing campaigns. Miramax took great umbrage when I dismissed its Best Picture nomination for *Chocolat* as a triumph of marketing. But I would argue that DreamWorks' transformation of *Gladiator* from a summer popcorn movie to Best Picture winner was also a victory of advertising over artistry. When *Entertainment Weekly*, whose motto should be 'All Oscars All the Time,' does its annual ranking of the best Oscar winners of all time, *Gladiator* will no doubt be near the bottom." On the *Late Show with David Letterman* Top Ten list the night after the Oscars, the topic was "Top Ten Things You Should Never Say in an Academy Award Acceptance Speech." While number four was "I'd like to tell you all about the exciting 2001 line of Amway products," number one was "Is it me, or did *Gladiator* blow?"

Roger Ebert was on KABC-TV's *An Evening at the Academy Awards* immediately after the show and said that voting *Gladiator* Best Picture "was kind of a case of temporary insanity on the part of the Academy and in years to come this will be cited as an example of

years in which the voters just got carried away with some thing or the other." Steven Spielberg told *Access Hollywood*'s Pat O'Brien, "You have to understand that every picture that was nominated this year could have easily and honorably walked off with the Best Picture Award. Nobody would have blinked. They would have said, 'Yeah, that film deserves it.' So I think we were very lucky this year." The DreamWorks triumvirate of Spielberg, Jeffrey Katzenberg, and David Geffen made a joint appearance on *Today* after the ceremony and Spielberg expressed the same sentiment as he admitted, "everything's about luck." Both Katzenberg and Geffen said that a year from now at the Oscars they'd all be talking about Spielberg's *A.I.*

Shortly after the Oscars, Pauline Kael, interviewed by the *New York Times*, weighted in on *Gladiator*. "I was shocked at how bad *Gladiator* was technically," she said. "It has the worst editing, and it's absurd casting that actor—what's his name—as a gladiator; you look at him flexing his muscles and you want to laugh. He's like one of the Three Stooges."

Having rooted for Tom Hanks, Lou Lumenick of the *New York Post* was dismayed about the result of the Best Actor race, partially blaming 20th Century Fox's "truly pathetic campaign" for *Cast Away* and adding, "But what really riles me is the nagging suspicion that the much-publicized Russell Crowe kidnap plot may have put him over the top. I am in no way suggesting that the FBI was in cahoots with DreamWorks to boost Crowe's Oscar chances, or that Crowe's life wasn't actually in danger. But decades in the news game tell me such plots are a lot more common than people suspect—and more often than not they never become public knowledge. That the Crowe plot broke into print just as most Academy members were casting their votes makes me very, very skeptical." Martin Grove also felt that the kidnapping story may have worked to the actor's advantage: "Academy members who hadn't yet sent in their ballots when those stories broke in early March may have changed their opinion of Crowe in view of that disturbing news. To many of those who thought Crowe seemed unfriendly and aloof at the Globes, he now appeared much more sympathetic considering the kidnapping plot. That sort of threat would unnerve anyone and could easily explain his behavior. Now the beefy security guards who were always surrounding Crowe were seen as being necessary rather than a celebrity affectation. Voters who waited to mail in their ballots had an awareness of Crowe's situation that earlier voters didn't have. Their more sympathetic view of Crowe may have contributed to his victory."

Liz Smith couldn't stand Russell Crowe, and wrote, "I see that the Oscar winner is still determined to be a sour puss. He was eerily out of sorts in his Oscar seat with his corkscrew curls of hair and his turn-of-the-century frock-coat costume. But he redeemed himself with smart remarks from the podium. Still, the grim visage, the impatient demeanor and the gum-chewing are all very off-putting. And, what kind of guy can't take a joke when Steve Martin has him hitting on Ellen Burstyn." Andrew Sarris, on the other hand, appreciated "Russell Crowe's catatonic expression" because it "merely showed on the outside what many people were feeling on the inside under their mandatory good-sport smiles." David Letterman said, "Russell Crowe won for Best Actor for *Gladiator*. He celebrated by breaking up another Hollywood marriage."

Chocolat producer David Brown may not have carried home an Oscar on Academy Award night, but later in the year he received a different type of honor. The New York Landmarks Conservancy designated the eighty-five-year-old Manhattanite a "Living Landmark."

Any number of news accounts of the 2000 Oscars referred to the ceremony as a "coronation" of Julia Roberts. For those who believe a happily-ever-after tale concludes with a marriage knot, the post-Oscar coda was bound to disappoint. In June, Roberts and Benjamin Bratt announced that they were no longer together. There were rumors surrounding Roberts's *Ocean's Eleven* costar George Clooney, but the good-

natured actor shrugged them off, kidding, "I didn't have time. I was too busy breaking up Tom and Nicole." With all sorts of speculation circling around in the tabloids, Roberts went on *Late Show with David Letterman*, officially to publicize her new movie, *America's Sweethearts,* but it was anticipated that the topic of her break-up with Bratt would be discussed.

She first talked about the Academy Awards with Letterman, and laughed when he reminded her that on her last, pre-Oscar appearance on his show, she had said that "doing good work is its own reward." Roberts said she still believed that but "an Oscar is a nice little kick." The Best Actress winner also expressed dismay about having forgotten to thank Erin Brockovich in her speech, lamenting that accepting an Oscar "doesn't bring out the Einstein moment that you hoped that it would. And one can hope to either be really smart or incredibly Audrey Hepburn about it all and just very tall with a long neck. And I was just slumped over and yakkin' like I was at a hayride."

Then it was time to get personal. The actress was momentarily taken aback when bandleader Paul Shaffer bluntly asked, "So, Julia, you getting laid these days?" "Bad, bad Paul!," she scolded. "That is so wrong . . . I didn't come out of a cake . . . I'm shocked." Letterman also chided Shaffer, then eventually said to Roberts, "But what about it?" Roberts said that her relationship with Bratt had "come to a kind and tenderhearted end and my only regret is that it seems that in some odd form, though, the media, not surprising, can't acccept that it's tenderhearted and kind. It has to make it messy and ugly." She added, "Here's the thing. I love Benjamin. He's a good man, he's a fine man. He is, to the exultation of the female single population, not my man anymore, sad, but true . . . We're just two kids trying to find our way in the world."

Nominations

T his appendix lists every Academy Award nomination for films eligible in the years from 1995 through 2000. **Winners are indicated by a * next to their names or titles.**

1995

Picture
Apollo 13, Imagine Entertainment, Universal. Produced by Brian Grazer.

Babe, Kennedy Miller, Universal. Produced by George Miller, Doug Mitchell, and Bill Miller.

* *Braveheart*, Icon/Ladd Co, Paramount. Produced by Mel Gibson, Alan Ladd, Jr., and Bruce Davey.

The Postman (Il Postino), C. G. Group Tiger-Pentafilm/Esterno Mediterraneo/Blue Dahlia, Miramax. Produced by Mario and Vittorio Cecchi Gori, and Gaetano Daniele.

Sense and Sensibility, Mirage, Columbia. Produced by Lindsay Doran.

Actor
* Nicolas Cage in *Leaving Las Vegas* (United Artists/Lumiere Pictures, MGM/UA).

Richard Dreyfuss in *Mr. Holland's Opus* (Interscope Communications/Polygram Filmed Entertainment, Buena Vista).

Anthony Hopkins in *Nixon* (Illusion Entertainment Group/Cinergi, Buena Vista).

Sean Penn in *Dead Man Walking* (Working Title/Havoc, Gramercy).

Massimo Troisi in *The Postman (Il Postino)* (C. G. Group Tiger-Pentafilm/Esterno Mediterraneo/Blue Dahlia, Miramax).

Actress
* Susan Sarandon in *Dead Man Walking* (Working Title/Havoc, Gramercy).

Elisabeth Shue in *Leaving Las Vegas* (United Artists/Lumiere Pictures, MGM/UA).

Sharon Stone in *Casino* (De Fina/Cappa, Universal).

Meryl Streep in *The Bridges of Madison County* (Amblin/Malpaso, Warner Bros.).

Emma Thompson in *Sense and Sensibility* (Mirage, Columbia).

Supporting Actor
James Cromwell in *Babe* (Kennedy Miller, Universal).

Ed Harris in *Apollo 13* (Imagine Entertainment, Universal).

Brad Pitt in *12 Monkeys* (Atlas Entertainment, Universal).

Tim Roth in *Rob Roy* (Talisman, MGM/UA).

* Kevin Spacey in *The Usual Suspects* (Blue Parrot, Bad Hat Harry, Gramercy).

Supporting Actress
Joan Allen in *Nixon* (Illusion Entertainment Group/Cinergi, Buena Vista).

Kathleen Quinlan in *Apollo 13* (Imagine Entertainment, Universal).

* Mira Sorvino in *Mighty Aphrodite* (Doumanian/Sweetland, Miramax).

Mare Winningham in *Georgia* (City 2000, Miramax).

Kate Winslet in *Sense and Sensibility* (Mirage, Columbia).

Director
Chris Noonan for *Babe* (Kennedy Miller, Universal).

* Mel Gibson for *Braveheart* (Icon/Ladd Co, Paramount).

Tim Robbins for *Dead Man Walking* (Working Title/Havoc, Gramercy).

Mike Figgis for *Leaving Las Vegas* (United Artists/Lumiere Pictures, MGM/UA).

Michael Radford for *The Postman (Il Postino)* (C. G. Group Tiger-Pentafilm/Esterno Mediterraneo/Blue Dahlia, Miramax).

Writing
(SCREENPLAY WRITTEN DIRECTLY FOR THE SCREEN)

Braveheart, Icon/Ladd Co, Paramount. Randall Wallace.

Mighty Aphrodite, Doumanian/Sweetland, Miramax. Woody Allen.

Nixon, Illusion Entertainment Group/Cinergi, Buena Vista. Stephen J. Rivele, Christopher Wilkinson, and Oliver Stone.

Toy Story, Pixar, Buena Vista. Joss Whedon, Andrew Stanton, Joel Cohen, and Alec Sokolow. Story by John Lasseter, Peter Docter, Andrew Stanton, and Joe Ranft.

* *The Usual Suspects*, Blue Parrot, Bad Hat Harry, Gramercy. Christopher McQuarrie.

(SCREENPLAY BASED ON MATERIAL PREVIOUSLY PRODUCED OR PUBLISHED)

Apollo 13, Imagine Entertainment, Universal. William Broyles Jr. and Al Reinert.

Babe, Kennedy Miller, Universal. George Miller and Chris Noonan.

Leaving Las Vegas, United Artists/Lumiere Pictures, MGM/UA. Mike Figgis.

The Postman (Il Postino), C. G. Group Tiger-Pentafilm/Esterno Mediterraneo/Blue Dahlia, Miramax. Anna Pavignano, Michael Radford, Furio Scarpelli, Giacomo Scarpelli, and Massimo Troisi.

* *Sense and Sensibility*, Mirage, Columbia. Emma Thompson.

Cinematography
Batman Forever, Burton, Warner Bros. Stephen Goldblatt.

* *Braveheart*, Icon/Ladd Co, Paramount. John Toll.

A Little Princess, Johnson/Baltimore Pictures, Warner Bros. Emmanuel Lubezki.

Sense and Sensibility, Mirage, Columbia. Michael Coulter.

Shanghai Triad, Shanghai Film Studios(China)/Alpha, UGC Images, La Sept Cinema (France), Sony Pictures Classics. Lu Yue.

Art Direction—Set Decoration

Apollo 13, Imagine Entertainment, Universal. Michael Corenblith; Merideth Boswell.

Babe, Kennedy/Miller, Universal. Roger Ford; Kerrie Brown.

A Little Princess, Johnson/Baltimore Pictures, Warner Bros. Bo Welch; Cheryl Carasik.

* *Restoration*, Segue Prods.-Avenue Pictures, Miramax. Eugenio Zanett.

Richard III, British Screen, Bayly/Pare, First Look, MGM/UA. Tony Burrough.

Sound

* *Apollo 13*, Imagine Entertainment, Universal. Rick Dior, Steve Pederson, Scott Millan, and David MacMillan.

Batman Forever, Burton, Warner Bros. Donald Mitchell, Frank Montano, Michael Herbick, and Petur Hliddal.

Braveheart, Icon/Ladd Co, Paramount. Andy Nelson, Scott Millan, Anna Behlmer, and Brian Simmons.

Crimson Tide, Simpson/Bruckheimer, Buena Vista. Kevin O'Connell, Rick Kline, Gregory Watkins, and William Kaplan.

Waterworld, Gordon Co., Davis Entertainment Co., Licht/Mueller Film Corp., Universal, Steve Maslow, Gregg Landaker, and Keith Wester.

Music
(ORIGINAL SONG)

* "Colors of the Wind" (*Pocahontas*, Disney, Buena Vista); Music by Alan Menken. Lyrics by Stephen Schwartz.

"Dead Man Walking" (*Dead Man Walking*, Working Title/Havoc, Gramercy); Music and lyrics by Bruce Springsteen.

"Have You Ever Really Loved a Woman" (*Don Juan DeMarco*, American Zoetrope, New Line); Music and lyrics by Michael Kamen, Bryan Adams, and Robert John Lange.

"Moonlight" (*Sabrina*, Mirage/Rudin/Sandollar, Paramount in association with Constellation Films); Music by John Williams. Lyrics by Alan and Marilyn Bergman.

"You've Got a Friend" (*Toy Story*, Pixar, Buena Vista); Music and lyrics by Randy Newman.

(ORIGINAL MUSICAL OR COMEDY SCORE)

The American President, Wildwood Enterprises, Columbia. Marc Shaiman.

* *Pocahontas*, Disney, Buena Vista. Alan Menken, music; Stephen Schwartz, lyrics; Alan Menken score.

Sabrina, Mirage/Rudin/Sandollar, Paramount in association with Constellation Films. John Williams.

Toy Story, Pixar, Buena Vista. Randy Newman.

Unstrung Heroes, Roth/Arnold, Buena Vista. Thomas Newman.

(ORIGINAL DRAMATIC SCORE)

Apollo 13, Imagine Entertainment, Universal. James Horner.

Braveheart, Icon/Ladd Co, Paramount. James Horner.

Nixon, Illusion Entertainment Group/Cinergi, Buena Vista. John Williams.

* *The Postman (Il Postino)*, C. G. Group Tiger-Pentafilm/Esterno Mediterraneo/Blue Dahlia, Miramax. Luis Bacalov.

Sense and Sensibility, Mirage, Columbia. Patrick Doyle.

Film Editing

* *Apollo 13*, Imagine Entertainment, Universal. Mike Hill and Dan Hanley.

Babe, Kennedy Miller, Universal. Marcus D'Arcy and Jay Friedkin.

Braveheart, Icon/Ladd Co, Paramount. Steven Rosenblum.

Crimson Tide, Simpson/Bruckheimer, Buena Vista. Chris Lebenzon.

Se7en, Kopelson, New Line. Richard Francis-Bruce.

Costume Design

Braveheart, Icon/Ladd Co, Paramount. Charles Knode.

* *Restoration*, Segue Prods.-Avenue Pictures, Miramax. James Acheson.

Richard III, British Screen, Bayly/Pare, First Look, MGM/UA. Shuna Harwood.

Sense and Sensibility, Mirage, Columbia. Jenny Beavan and John Bright.

12 Monkeys, Atlas Entertainment, Universal. Julie Weiss.

Makeup

* *Braveheart*, Icon/Ladd Co, Paramount. Peter Frampton, Paul Pattison, and Lois Burwell.

My Family, Mi Familia, American Zoetrope, Thomas-Newcomm, New Line. Ken Diaz and Mark Sanchez.

Roommates, Interscope Communications, Polygram Filmed Entertainment, Nomura Babcock & Brown, Buena Vista. Greg Cannom, Bob Laden, and Colleen Callaghan.

Visual Effects

Apollo 13, Imagine Entertainment, Universal. Robert Legato, Michael Kanfer, Leslie Ekker, and Matt Sweeney

* *Babe*, Kennedy Miller, Universal. Scott Anderson, Charles Gibson, Neal Scanlan, and John Cox.

Sound Effects Editing

Batman Forever, Burton, Warner Bros. John Leveque and Bruce Stambler.

* *Braveheart*, Icon/Ladd Co, Paramount. Lon Bender and Per Hallberg.

Crimson Tide, Simpson/Bruckheimer, Buena Vista. George Watters II.

Short Films

(ANIMATED)

The Chicken from Outerspace, Stretch Films Inc., Hanna-Barbera Cartoons Inc., Cartoon Network. John R. Dilworth, producer.

* *A Close Shave*, Aardman Animations. Nick Park, producer.

The End, Alias/Wavefront. Chris Landreth and Robin Bargar, producers.

Gagarin, Second Frog Animation Group. Alexij Kharitidi, producer.

Runaway Brain, Walt Disney Pictures. Chris Bailey, producer.

(LIVE ACTION)

Brooms, Yes/No. Luke Cresswell and Steve McNicholas, producers.

Duke of Groove, Chanticleer Films. Griffin Dunne and Thom Colwell, producers.

* *Lieberman in Love*, Chanticleer Films. Christine Lahti and Jana Sue Memel, producers.

Little Surprises, Chanticleer Films. Jeff Goldblum and Tikki Goldberg, producers.

Tuesday Morning Ride, Chanticleer Films. Dianne Houston and Joy Ryan, producers.

Documentary

(SHORT SUBJECTS)

Jim Dine: A Self-Portrait on the Walls, Outside in July Inc. Nancy Dine and Richard Stilwell, producers.

The Living Sea, MacGillivray Freeman. Greg MacGillivray and Alec Lorimore, producers.

Never Give Up: The 20th Century Odyssey of Herbert Zipper, American Film Foundation. Terry Sanders and Freida Lee Mock, producers.

* *One Survivor Remembers*, Home Box Office and the United States Holocaust Memorial Museum. Kary Antholis, producer.

The Shadow of Hate, Guggenheim Prods. Inc. for the Southern Poverty Law Center. Charles Guggenheim, producer.

(FEATURES)

* *Anne Frank Remembered*, Jon Blair Film Co. Ltd. Jon Blair, producer.

The Battle Over 'Citizen Kane,' Lennon Documentary Group. for "The American Experience." Thomas Lennon and Michael Epstein, producers.

Fiddlefest—Roberta Guaspari-Tzavara and Her East Harlem Violin Program, Four Oaks Foundation. Allan Miller and Walter Scheuer, producers.

Hank Aaron: Chasing the Dream, TBS. Mike Tollin, producer.

Troublesome Creek: A Midwestern, West City Films Inc. Jeanne Jordan and Steven Ascher, producers.

Foreign Language Film

All Things Fair (Sweden).

* *Antonia's Line* (The Netherlands).

Dust of Life (Algeria).

O Quatrilho (Brazil).

The Star Maker (Italy).

Irving G. Thalberg Memorial Award

Not given this year.

Jean Hersholt Humanitarian Award

Not given this year.

Gordon E. Sawyer Award

Donald C. Rogers.

Honorary Awards

Kirk Douglas, for fifty years as a creative and moral force in the motion picture community.

Chuck Jones, for the creation of classic cartoons and cartoon characters whose animated lives have brought joy to our real ones for more than a half century.

Special Achievement Award

John Lasseter, for the development and inspired application of techniques that have made possible the first feature-length computer-animated film.

Scientific or Technical

ACADEMY AWARD OF MERIT (STATUETTE)

None.

SCIENTIFIC AND ENGINEERING AWARD (PLAQUE)

Arnold & Richter Cine Technik for the development of the Arriflex 535 Series of Cameras for motion picture cinematography.

Martin S. Mueller for the design and development of the MSM 9801 IMAX 65mm/15 perf production motion picture camera.

Iain Neil for the optical design, Rick Gelbard for the mechanical design, Eric Dubberke for the engineering, and Panavision International, L.P. for the development of the Primo 3:1 Zoom Lens.

Ronald C. Goodman, Attila Szalay, Steven Sass, and Spacecam Systems, Inc. for the design of the SpaceCam gyroscopically stabilized Camera System.

Digital Theater Systems for the design and development of the DTS Digital Sound System for motion picture exhibition.

Dolby Laboratories for the design and development of the SR-D Digital Sound System for motion picture exhibition.

Sony Corporation for the design and development of the SDDS Digital Sound System for motion picture exhibition.

Howard Flemming and Ronald Uhlig for their pioneering work leading to motion picture digital sound.

Colin Mossman, Joe Wary, Hans Leisinger, Gerald Painter, and Deluxe Laboratories for the design and development of the Deluxe Quad Format Digital Sound Printing Head.

David Gilmartin, Johannes Borggrebe, Jean-Pierre Gagnon, Frank Ricotta, and Technicolor, Inc. for the design and development of the Technicolor Contact Printer Sound Head.

Alvy Ray Smith Ed Catmull, Thomas Porter, and Tom Duff for their pioneering inventions in Digital Image Compositing.

TECHNICAL ACHIEVEMENT AWARD (CERTIFICATE)

Al Jensen, Chuck Headley, Jean Messner, and Hazem Nabuls of CEI Technology for the production of a self-contained, flicker-free, Color Video-Assist Camera.

Peter Denz of Prazisions-Entwicklung Denz for the development of a flicker-free Color Video-Assist Camera.

Institut National Polytechnique de Toulouse for the concept, Kodak Pathe CTP Cine for the prototype, and Eclair Laboratories and Martineau Industries for the development and further implementation of the Toulouse Electrolytic Silver Recovery Cell.

Pascal Chedeville for the design of the L.C. Concept Digital Sound System for motion picture exhibition.

James Deas of the Warner Bros. Studio Facility for the design and subsequent development of an Automated Patchbay and Metering System for motion picture sound transfer and dubbing operations.

Clay Davis and John Carter of Todd-AO for their pioneering efforts in creating an Automated Patchbay System for motion picture sound transfer and dubbing operations.

BHP, Incorporated for their pioneering efforts developing Digital Sound Printing Heads for motion pictures.

Gary Demos, David Ruhoff, Dan Cameron, and Michelle Feraud for their pioneering efforts in the creation of the Digital Productions Digital Film Compositing System.

Douglas Smythe, Lincoln Hu, Douglas S. Kay Industrial Light & Magic for their pioneering efforts in the creation of the ILM Digital Film Compositing System.

Computer Film Company for their pioneering efforts in the creation of the CFC Digital Film Compositing System.

David Pringle and Yan Zhong Fang for the design and development of "Lightning Strikes," a flexible, high-performance electronic lightning effect system.

Joe Finnegan (a.k.a. Joe Yrigoyen) for his pioneering work in developing the Air Ram for motion picture stunt effects.

Points of Interest

1. The family way: Best Actress Susan Sarandon is the companion of Best Director nominee Tim Robbins.
2. Renaissance people: Emma Thompson nominated for Best Actress and Best Adapted Screenplay, Massimo Troisi nominated for Best Actor and Best Adapted Screenplay.
3. Female firsts: Emma Thompson is the first woman nominated for acting and writing awards in the same year. *Antonia's Line* is the first Foreign Film winner directed by a woman (Marleen Gorris). Anna Behlmer is the first woman nominated for Best Sound.

Rule Change

1. The more the merrier: Original score award is divided into two categories.

Eligible Films That Failed to Be Nominated for Best Picture

Dead Man Walking; Leaving Las Vegas; Nixon; Rob Roy; The Bridges of Madison County; Se7en; Heat; The Usual Suspects; Kids; Get Shorty; To Die For; Richard III; The Glass Shield; Smoke; 12 Monkeys; The Secret of Roan Inish; Nadja; A Little Princess; Toy Story; Muriel's Wedding; Funny Bones; Clueless; Safe; Exotica; The Incredibly True Adventures of Two Girls in Love; Before Sunrise.

Submitted Films Rejected by the Foreign Language Film Award Committee

Flower of My Secret (Spain), directed by Pedro Almodovar; *Ulysses' Gaze* (Greece), directed by Theo Angelopoulos; *Underground* (Yugoslavia), directed by Emir Kusturica; *The White Balloon* (Iran), directed by Jafar Panahi.

Eligible Songs That Failed to Be Nominated

"Exhale (Shoop, Shoop)" (Babyface)—*Waiting to Exhale*; "Hold Me, Thrill Me, Kiss Me, Kill Me" (U2)—*Batman Forever*.

1996

Picture
* *The English Patient*, Tiger Moth, Miramax. Produced by Saul Zaentz.
  Fargo, Working Title, Gramercy. Produced by Ethan Coen.
  Jerry Maguire, TriStar. Produced by James L. Brooks, Laurence Mark, Richard Sakai, and Cameron Crowe.
  Secrets & Lies, Ciby 2000 and Thin Man, October. Produced by Simon Channing-Williams.
  Shine, Momentum, Fine Line. Produced by Jane Scott.

Actor
  Tom Cruise in *Jerry Maguire* (TriStar).
  Ralph Fiennes in *The English Patient* (Tiger Moth, Miramax).
  Woody Harrelson in *The People vs. Larry Flynt* (Ixtan, Columbia).
* Geoffrey Rush in *Shine* (Momentum, Fine Line).
  Billy Bob Thornton in *Sling Blade* (Shooting Gallery, Miramax).

Actress

Brenda Blethyn in *Secrets & Lies* (Ciby 2000 and Thin Man, October).

Diane Keaton in *Marvin's Room* (Rudin/Tribeca, Miramax).

* Frances McDormand in *Fargo* (Working Title, Gramercy).

Kristin Scott Thomas in *The English Patient* (Tiger Moth, Miramax).

Emily Watson in *Breaking the Waves* (Zentropa Entertainment/La Sept Cinema, October).

Supporting Actor

* Cuba Gooding Jr. in *Jerry Maguire* (TriStar).

William H. Macy in *Fargo* (Working Title, Gramercy).

Armin Mueller-Stahl in *Shine* (Momentum, Fine Line).

Edward Norton in *Primal Fear* (Lucchesi, Paramount/Rysher Entertainment).

James Woods in *Ghosts of Mississippi* (Castle Rock Entertainment, Sony).

Supporting Actress

Joan Allen in *The Crucible* (20th Century Fox).

Lauren Bacall in *The Mirror Has Two Faces* (Milchan/Barwood, TriStar).

* Juliette Binoche in *The English Patient* (Tiger Moth, Miramax).

Barbara Hershey in *The Portrait of a Lady* (Propaganda, Gramercy).

Marianne Jean-Baptiste in *Secrets & Lies* (Ciby 2000 and Thin Man, October).

Director

* Anthony Minghella for *The English Patient* (Tiger Moth, Miramax).

Joel Coen for *Fargo* (Working Title, Gramercy).

Milos Forman for *The People vs. Larry Flynt* (Ixtan, Columbia).

Mike Leigh for *Secrets & Lies* (CiBy 2000 and Thin Man, October).

Scott Hicks for *Shine* (Momentum, Fine Line).

Writing

(SCREENPLAY WRITTEN DIRECTLY FOR THE SCREEN)

* *Fargo*, Working Title, Gramercy. Ethan Coen and Joel Coen.

Jerry Maguire, TriStar. Cameron Crowe.

Lone Star, Castle Rock Entertainment, Sony Pictures Classics. John Sayles.

Secrets & Lies, CiBy 2000 and Thin Man, October. Mike Leigh.

Shine, Momentum, Fine Line. Screenplay by Jan Sardi. Story by Scott Hicks.

(SCREENPLAY BASED ON MATERIAL PREVIOUSLY PRODUCED OR PUBLISHED)

The Crucible, 20th Century Fox. Arthur Miller.

The English Patient, Tiger Moth, Miramax. Anthony Minghella.

Hamlet, Castle Rock Entertainment, Sony. Kenneth Branagh.

* *Sling Blade*, Shooting Gallery, Miramax. Billy Bob Thornton.

Trainspotting, Channel 4/Figment Film, Miramax. John Hodge.

Cinematography

* *The English Patient*, Tiger Moth, Miramax. John Seale.

Evita, Vajna/Cinergi/Stigwood/Dirty Hands, Buena Vista. Darius Khondji.

Fargo, Working Title, Gramercy. Roger Deakins.

Fly Away Home, Sandollar, Sony. Caleb Deschanel.

Michael Collins, Geffen/Woolley, Warner Bros. Chris Menges.

Art Direction—Set Decoration

The Bird Cage, United Artists, MGM/UA. Bo Welch; Cheryl Carasik.

* *The English Patient*, Tiger Moth, Miramax. Stuart Craig; Stephanie McMillan.

Evita, Vajna/Cinergi/Stigwood/Dirty Hands, Buena Vista. Brian Morris; Phillippe Turiure.

Hamlet, Castle Rock Entertainment, Sony. Tim Harvey.

William Shakespeare's Romeo & Juliet, Bazmark, 20th Century Fox. Catherine Martin; Brigitte Broch.

Sound

* *The English Patient*, Tiger Moth, Miramax. Walter Murch, Mark Berger, David Parker, and Chris Newman.

Evita, Vajna/Cinergi/Stigwood/Dirty Hands, Buena Vista. Andy Nelson, Anna Behlmer, and Ken Weston.

Independence Day, Centropolis Entertainment, 20th Century Fox. Chris Carpenter, Bill W. Benton, Bob Beemer, and Jeff Wexler.

The Rock, Simpson/Bruckheimer, Buena Vista. Kevin O'Connell, Greg P. Russell, and Keith A. Wester.

Twister, Amblin, Warner Bros./Universal. Steve Maslow, Gregg Landaker, Kevin O'Connell, and Geoffrey Patterson.

Music

(ORIGINAL SONG)

"Because You Loved Me" (*Up Close and Personal*, Touchstone/Cinergi/Avnet/Kerner, Buena Vista); Music and lyrics by Diane Warren.

"For the First Time" (*One Fine Day*, Fox 2000/Via Rosa, 20th Century Fox); Music and lyrics by James Newton Howard, Jud J. Friedman, and Allan Dennis Rich.

"I Finally Found Someone" (*The Mirror Has Two Faces*, Milchan/Barwood, TriStar); Music and lyrics by Barbra Streisand, Marvin Hamlisch, Bryan Adams, and Robert "Mutt" Lange.

"That Thing You Do!" (*That Thing You Do!*, Clinica Estetico/Clavius Base, 20th Century Fox); Music and lyrics by Adam Schlesinger.

* "You Must Love Me" (*Evita*, Vajna/Cinergi/Stigwood/Dirty Hands, Buena Vista); Music by Andrew Lloyd Webber. Lyrics by Tim Rice.

(ORIGINAL MUSICAL OR COMEDY SCORE)

* *Emma*, Matchmaker/Haft Entertainment, Miramax. Rachel Portman.

The First Wives Club, Rudin, Paramount. Marc Shaiman.

The Hunchback of Notre Dame, Disney, Buena Vista. Alan Menken, music and orchestral score; Stephen Schwartz, lyrics.
James and the Giant Peach, Disney/Allied Filmmakers, Buena Vista. Randy Newman.
The Preacher's Wife, Touchstone/Goldwyn/Parkway Prods./Mandy Lane Ent., Buena Vista. Hans Zimmer.

(ORIGINAL DRAMATIC SCORE)
* *The English Patient*, Tiger Moth, Miramax. Gabriel Yared.
Hamlet, Castle Rock Entertainment, Sony. Patrick Doyle.
Michael Collins, Geffen/Woolley, Warner Bros. Elliot Goldenthal.
Shine, Momentum, Fine Line. David Hirschfelder.
Sleepers, Polygram Filmed Ent./Propaganda-Baltimore, Warner Bros. John Williams.

Film Editing
* *The English Patient*, Tiger Moth, Miramax. Walter Murch.
Evita, Vajna/Cinergi/Stigwood/Dirty Hands, Buena Vista. Gerry Hambling.
Fargo, Working Title, Gramercy. Roderick Jaynes (aka Joel and Ethan Coen).
Jerry Maguire, TriStar. Joe Hutshing.
Shine, Momentum, Fine Line. Pip Karmel.

Costume Design
Angels & Insects, Playhouse Int'l, Goldwyn. Paul Brown.
Emma, Matchmaker/Haft Entertainment, Miramax. Ruth Myers.
* *The English Patient*, Tiger Moth, Miramax. Ann Roth.
Hamlet, Castle Rock Entertainment, Sony. Alex Byrne.
The Portrait of a Lady, Propaganda, Gramercy. Janet Patterson.

Makeup
Ghosts of Mississippi, Castle Rock Entertainment, Sony. Matthew W. Mungle and Deborah La Mia Denaver.
* *The Nutty Professor*, Imagine Entertainment, Universal. Rick Baker and David Leroy Anderson.
Star Trek: First Contact, Berman, Paramount. Michael Westmore, Scott Wheeler, and Jake Garber.

Visual Effects
Dragonheart, De Laurentiis, Universal. Scott Squires, Phil Tippett, James Straus, and Kit West.
* *Independence Day*, Centropolis Entertainment, 20th Century Fox. Volker Engel, Douglas Smith, Clay Pinney, and Joseph Viskocil.
Twister, Amblin, Warner Bros./Universal. Stefen Fangmeier, John Frazier, Habib Zargarpour, and Henry La Bounta.

Sound Effects Editing
Daylight, Davis Entertainment/Singer, Universal. Richard L. Anderson and David A. Whittaker.
Eraser, Kopelson, Warner Bros. Alan Robert Murray and Bub Asman.
* *The Ghost and the Darkness*, Douglas/Reuther, Paramount. Bruce Stambler.

Short Films
(ANIMATED)
Canhead, Hittle. Timothy Hittle and Chris Peterson, producers.
La Salla, National Film Board of Canada. Richard Condie, producer.
* *Quest*, Thomas Stellmach Animation. Tyron Montgomery and Thomas Stellmach, producers.
Wat's Pig, Aardman Animations Ltd. Peter Lord, producer.

(LIVE ACTION)
De Tripas, Corazon, IMCINE/DPC/Universidad de Guadalajara. Antonio Urrutia, producer.
* *Dear Diary*, DreamWorks SKG. David Frankel and Barry Jossen, producers.
Ernst & Lyset, M & M. Kim Magnusson and Anders Thomas Jensen, producers.
Esposados, Zodiac Films/Juan Carlos Fresnadillo P.C. Juan Carlos Fresnadillo, producer.
Wordless, Film Trust Italia. Bernadette Carranza and Antonello De Leo, producers.

Documentary
(SHORT SUBJECTS)
* *Breathing Lessons: The Life and Work of Mark O'Brien*, Inscrutable Films/Pacific News Service production; Jessica Yu, producer.
Cosmic Voyage, Cosmic Voyage Inc., IMAX. Jeffrey Marvin and Bayley Silleck, producers.
An Essay on Matisse, Great Projects Film Co. Inc. Perry Wolff, producer.
Special Effects, Nova/WGBH Boston, IMAX. Susanne Simpson and Ben Burtt, producers.
The Wild Bunch: An Album Montage, Tyrus Entertainment. Paul Seydor and Nick Redman, producers.

(FEATURES)
The Line King: The Al Hirschfeld Story, Times History. Susan W. Dryfoos, producer.
Mandela, Island Pictures, Clinica Estetico Ltd. Jo Menell and Angus Gibson, producers.
Suzanne Farrell: Elusive Muse, Seahorse Films Inc. Anne Belle and Deborah Dickson, producers.
Tell the Truth and Run: George Seldes and the American Press, Never Tire. Rick Goldsmith, producer.
* *When We Were Kings*, Gramercy, DASFilms Ltd. Leon Gast and David Sonenberg, producers.

Foreign Language Film
A Chef in Love (Georgia).
* *Kolya* (Czech Republic).
The Other Side of Sunday (Norway).
Prisoner of the Mountains (Russia).
Ridicule (France).

Irving G. Thalberg Memorial Award
Saul Zaentz.

Jean Hersholt Humanitarian Award
Not given this year.

Gordon E. Sawyer Award
Not given this year.

Honorary Award
Michael Kidd, in recognition of his services to the art of the dance in the art of the screen.

Scientific or Technical

ACADEMY AWARD OF MERIT (STATUETTE)
Imax Corporation for the method of filming and exhibiting high-fidelity, large-format, wide-angle motion pictures.

SCIENTIFIC AND ENGINEERING AWARD (PLAQUE)
John Schlag, Brian Knep, Zoran Kacic-Alesic, and Thomas Williams for the development of the ViewPaint 3D Paint System for film production work.

William Reeves for the original concept and the development of particle systems used to create computer-generated visual effects in motion pictures.

Jim Hourihan for the primary design and development of the interactive language-based control of particle systems as embodied in the Dynamation software package.

Jonathan Erland and Kay Beving Erland for the development of the Digital Series Traveling Matte Backing System used for composite photography in motion pictures.

TECHNICAL ACHIEVEMENT AWARD (CERTIFICATE)
Richard A. Prey and William N. Masten for the design and development of the Nite Sun II lighting crane and camera platform.

Nestor Burtnyk and Marceli Wein of the National Research Council of Canada for their pioneering work in the development of software techniques for Computer Assisted Key Framing for Character Animation.

Grant Loucks for the concept and specifications of the Mark V Directors Viewfinder.

Perry Kivolowitz for the primary design and Dr. Garth A. Dickie for the development of the algorithms for the shape-driven warping and morphing subsystem of the Elastic Reality Special Effects System.

Ken Perlin for the development of Perlin Noise, a technique used to produce natural appearing textures on computer generated surfaces for motion picture visual effects.

Brian Knep, Craig Hayes, Rick Sayre, and Thomas Williams for the creation and development of the Direct Input Device.

James Kajiya and Timothy Kay for their pioneering work in producing computer generated fur and hair in motion pictures.

Jeffrey Yost, Christian Rouet, David Benson, and Florian Kainz for the development of a system to create and control computer generated fur and hair in motion pictures.

Award of Commendation (Special Plaque)
Joe Lombardi for celebration of fifty years in the motion picture industry.

John A. Bonner Medal of Commendation
Volker Bahnemann and Burton (Bud) Stone for outstanding service and dedication in upholding the high standards of the Academy of Motion Picture Arts and Sciences.

Points of Interest

1. Nothing to it: Marianne Jean-Baptiste, Edward Norton, and Emily Watson nominated for their film debuts. Scott Hicks nominated for his nondocumentary debut.
2. The family way: Best Actress Frances McDormand married to Original Screenplay co-winner and Director/Film Editing nominee Joel Coen. Joel Coen shares Original Screenplay Oscar with brother Ethan Coen.
3. Thanks, honey: Frances McDormand first person to be directed in an Oscar-winning role by a spouse.
4. Pseudo nominee: Roderick Jaynes, nominated for Film Editing for *Fargo* is actually a pseudonym for Joel and Ethan Coen.
5. Renaissance men: Original Screenplay co-winner Joel Coen also nominated for Best Director and Film Editing. Original Screenplay co-winner Ethan Coen also nominated as producer of Best Picture nominee, *Fargo* and for Film Editing. Adapted Screenplay winner Billy Bob Thornton also nominated for Best Actor.
6. I am woman, hear me score: Emma Portman becomes first woman to win an Oscar for composing a musical score.
7. Television is better than ever: Live Action Short Film winner, *Dear Diary*, was an unsold television pilot.

Rule Change

1. Medal of Commendation now the "John A. Bonner Medal of Commendation."

Eligible Films That Failed to Be Nominated for Best Picture

Lone Star; Sling Blade; Mother; The People vs. Larry Flynt; Trainspotting; Welcome to the Dollhouse; Grace of My Heart; Big Night; Neon Bible; The Portrait of a Lady; Emma; Evita; Breaking the Waves; Looking for Richard; Everyone Says I Love You; The Crucible; Hamlet; Beautiful Thing; A Midwinter's Tale; Michael Collins; Citizen Ruth; Once Upon a Time . . . When We Were Colored; William Shakespeare's Romeo & Juliet; Scream; Land and Freedom; The Funeral; Bottle Rocket; Dead Man.

Submitted Films Rejected by the Foreign Language Film Award Committee

Drifting Clouds (Finland), directed by Aki Kaurismaki.

Eligible Songs That Failed to Be Nominated

"God Give Me Strength" (Burt Bacharach and Elvis Costello)—*Grace of My Heart*; "I Believe I Can Fly" (R. Kelley)—*Space Jam*.

1997

Picture
As Good As It Gets, Gracie, TriStar. Produced by James L. Brooks, Bridget Johnson, and Kristi Zea.
The Full Monty, Redwave, Fox Searchlight. Produced by Uberto Pasolini.
Good Will Hunting, Be Gentlemen, Miramax. Produced by Lawrence Bender.
L.A. Confidential, Regency Enterprises, Warner Bros. Produced by Arnon Milchan, Curtis Hanson, and Michael Nathanson.
* *Titanic*, Lightstorm Entertainment, 20th Century Fox and Paramount. Produced by James Cameron and Jon Landau.

Actor
Matt Damon in *Good Will Hunting* (Be Gentlemen, Miramax).
Robert Duvall in *The Apostle* (Butcher's Run, October).
Peter Fonda in *Ulee's Gold* (Nunez-Gowan/Clinica Estetico, Orion).
Dustin Hoffman in *Wag the Dog* (New Line Cinema).
* Jack Nicholson in *As Good As It Gets* (Gracie, TriStar).

Actress
Helena Bonham Carter in *The Wings of the Dove* (Renaissance, Miramax).
Julie Christie in *Afterglow* (Moonstone Entertainment, Sony Pictures Classics).
Judi Dench in *Mrs. Brown* (Ecosse, Miramax).
* Helen Hunt in *As Good As It Gets* (Gracie, TriStar).
Kate Winslet in *Titanic* (Lightstorm Entertainment, 20th Century Fox and Paramount).

Supporting Actor
Robert Forster in *Jackie Brown* (Mighty, Mighty Afrodite, Miramax).
Anthony Hopkins in *Amistad* (DreamWorks).
Greg Kinnear in *As Good As It Gets* (Gracie, TriStar).
Burt Reynolds in *Boogie Nights* (New Line Cinema).

* Robin Williams in *Good Will Hunting* (Be Gentlemen, Miramax).

Supporting Actress
* Kim Basinger in *L.A. Confidential* (Regency Enterprises, Warner Bros.).
Joan Cusack in *In & Out* (Rudin, Paramount in association with Spelling Films).
Minnie Driver in *Good Will Hunting* (Be Gentlemen, Miramax).
Julianne Moore in *Boogie Nights* (New Line Cinema).
Gloria Stuart in *Titanic* (Lightstorm Entertainment, 20th Century Fox and Paramount).

Director
Peter Cattaneo for *The Full Monty* (Redwave, Fox Searchlight).
Gus Van Sant for *Good Will Hunting* (Be Gentlemen, Miramax).
Curtis Hanson for *L.A. Confidential* (Regency Enterprises, Warner Bros.).
Atom Egoyan for *The Sweet Hereafter* (Ego Film Arts, First Line Features).
* James Cameron for *Titanic* (Lightstorm Entertainment, 20th Century Fox and Paramount).

Writing
(SCREENPLAY WRITTEN DIRECTLY FOR THE SCREEN)
As Good As It Gets, Gracie, TriStar. Mark Andrus and James L. Brooks, screenplay; Mark Andrus, story.
Boogie Nights, New Line Cinema. Paul Thomas Anderson.
Deconstructing Harry, Doumanian, Fine Line Features.
The Full Monty, Redwave, Fox Searchlight. Simon Beaufoy.
* *Good Will Hunting*, Be Gentlemen, Miramax. Ben Affleck and Matt Damon.

(SCREENPLAY BASED ON MATERIAL PREVIOUSLY PRODUCED OR PUBLISHED)
Donnie Brasco, Mandalay Entertainment, TriStar. Paul Attanasio.
* *L.A. Confidential*, Regency Enterprises, Warner Bros. Brian Helgeland and Curtis Hanson.
The Sweet Hereafter, Ego Film Arts, First Line Features. Atom Egoyan.
Wag the Dog, New Line Cinema. Hilary Henkin and David Mamet.
The Wings of the Dove, Renaissance, Miramax. Hossein Amini.

Cinematography
Amistad, DreamWorks. Janusz Kaminski.
Kundun, Touchstone, Buena Vista. Roger Deakins.
L.A. Confidential, Regency Enterprises, Warner Bros. Dante Spinotti.
* *Titanic*, Lightstorm Entertainment, 20th Century Fox and Paramount. Russell Carpenter.
The Wings of the Dove, Renaissance, Miramax. Eduardo Serra.

Art Direction—Set Decoration
Gattaca, Jersey, Columbia. Jan Roelfs; Nancy Nye.

Kundun, Touchstone, Buena Vista. Dante Ferretti; Francesca Lo Schiavo.

L.A. Confidential, Regency Enterprises, Warner Bros. Jeannine Oppewall; Jay R. Hart.

Men in Black, Amblin Entertainment, Columbia. Bo Welch; Cheryl Carasik.

* *Titanic*, Lightstorm Entertainment, 20th Century Fox and Paramount. Peter Lamont; Michael Ford.

Sound

Air Force One, Beacon Picture/Columbia, Columbia. Paul Massey, Rick Kline, D. M. Hemphill, and Keith A. Wester.

Con Air, Touchstone, Buena Vista. Kevin O'Connell, Greg P. Russell, and Arthur Rochester.

Contact, Warner Bros. Randy Thom, Tom Johnson, Dennis Sands, and William B. Kaplan.

L.A. Confidential, Regency Enterprises, Warner Bros. Andy Nelson, Anna Behlmer, and Kirk Francis.

* *Titanic*, Lightstorm Entertainment, 20th Century Fox and Paramount. Gary Rydstrom, Tom Johnson, Gary Summers, and Mark Ulano.

Music
(ORIGINAL SONG)

"Go the Distance" (*Hercules*, Disney, Buena Vista); Music by Alan Menken. Lyrics by David Zippel.

"How Do I Live" (*Con Air*, Touchstone, Buena Vista.); Music and lyrics by Diane Warren.

"Journey to the Past" (*Anastasia*, 20th Century Fox); Music by Stephen Flaherty. Lyrics by Lynn Ahrens.

"Miss Misery" (*Good Will Hunting*, Be Gentlemen, Miramax.); Music and lyrics by Elliott Smith.

* "My Heart Will Go On" (*Titanic*, Lightstorm Entertainment, 20th Century Fox and Paramount); Music by James Horner. Lyrics by Will Jennings.

(ORIGINAL MUSICAL OR COMEDY SCORE)

Anastasia, 20th Century Fox. Stephen Flaherty, music; Lynn Ahrens, lyrics; David Newman, orchestral score.

As Good As It Gets, Gracie, TriStar. Hans Zimmer.

* *The Full Monty*, Redwave, Fox Searchlight. Anne Dudley.

Men in Black, Amblin Entertainment, Columbia. Danny Elfman.

My Best Friend's Wedding, Zucker/Predawn, TriStar. James Newton Howard.

(ORIGINAL DRAMATIC SCORE)

Amistad, DreamWorks. John Williams.

Good Will Hunting, Be Gentlemen, Miramax. Danny Elfman.

Kundun, Touchstone, Buena Vista. Philip Glass.

L.A. Confidential, Regency Enterprises, Warner Bros. Jerry Goldsmith.

* *Titanic*, Lightstorm Entertainment, 20th Century Fox and Paramount. James Horner.

Film Editing

Air Force One, Beacon Picture/Columbia, Columbia. Richard Francis-Bruce.

As Good As It Gets, Gracie, TriStar. Richard Marks.

Good Will Hunting, Be Gentlemen, Miramax. Pietro Scalia.

L.A. Confidential; Regency Enterprises, Warner Bros. Peter Honess.

* *Titanic*, Lightstorm Entertainment, 20th Century Fox and Paramount. Conrad Buff, James Cameron, and Richard A. Harris.

Costume Design

Amistad, DreamWorks. Ruth E. Carter.

Kundun, Touchstone, Buena Vista. Dante Ferretti.

Oscar and Lucinda, Dalton, Fox Searchlight. Janet Patterson.

* *Titanic*, Lightstorm Entertainment, 20th Century Fox and Paramount. Deborah L. Scott.

The Wings of the Dove, Renaissance, Miramax. Sandy Powell.

Makeup

* *Men in Black*, Amblin Entertainment, Columbia. Rick Baker and David LeRoy Anderson.

Mrs. Brown, Ecosse, Miramax. Lisa Westcott, Veronica Brebner, and Beverley Binda.

Titanic, Lightstorm Entertainment, 20th Century Fox and Paramount. Tina Earnshaw, Greg Cannom, and Simon Thompson.

Visual Effects

The Lost World: Jurassic Park, Universal/Amblin Entertainment. Dennis Muren, Stan Winston, Randal M. Dutra, and Michael Lantieri.

Starship Troopers, TriStar/Touchstone, TriStar. Phil Tippett, Scott E. Anderson, Alec Gillis, and John Richardson.

* *Titanic*, Lightstorm Entertainment, 20th Century Fox and Paramount. Robert Legato, Mark Lasoff, Thomas L. Fisher, and Michael Kanfer.

Sound Effects Editing

Face/Off, Douglas/Reuther, WCG, Permut, Paramount and Touchstone. Mark P. Stoeckinger and Per Hallberg.

The Fifth Element, Gaumont, Columbia. Mark Mangini.

* *Titanic*, Lightstorm Entertainment, 20th Century Fox and Paramount. Tom Bellfort and Christopher Boyes.

Short Films
(ANIMATED)

Famous Fred, TVC London, Channel 4 and S4C. Joanna Quinn, producer.

* *Geri's Game*, Pixar Animation Studios. Jan Pinkava, producer.

La Vieille Dame et Les Pigeons (The Old Lady and the Pigeons), Pascal Blais/Les Armateurs/Odec Kid Cartoons. Sylvain Chomet, producer.

The Mermaid, Film Company "DAGO"/"SHAR" School-Studio/Studio. "PANORAMA," Yaroslavl production. Alexander Petrov, producer.

Redux Riding Hood, Walt Disney Television Animation. Steve Moore, producer.

(LIVE ACTION)

Dance Lexie Dance, Raw Nerve, Northern Lights. Pearse Moore and Tim Loane, producers.

It's Good to Talk, Feasible Films. Roger Goldby and Barney Reisz, producers.

Sweethearts?, MetronomeProductions/Victoria Film. Birger Larsen and Thomas Lydholm, producers.

* *Visas and Virtue*, Cedar Grove. Chris Tashima and Chris Donahue, producers.

Wolfgang, M&M, Dansk Novellefilm. Kim Magnusson and Anders Thomas Jensen, producers.

Documentary

(SHORT SUBJECTS)

Alaska: Spirit of the Wild, Graphic Films Corp. George Casey and Paul Novros, producers.

Amazon, Ogden Entertainment. Keith Merrill and Jonathan Stern, producers.

Daughter of the Bride, Terri Randall Film and Video. Terri Randall, producer.

Still Kicking: The Fabulous Palm Springs Follies, Little Apple Film. Mel Damski and Andrea Blaugrund, producers.

* *A Story of Healing*, Dewey-Obenchain Films. Donna Dewey and Carol Pasternak, producers.

(FEATURES)

Ayn Rand: A Sense of Life, A G Media Corp. Ltd., Strand Releasing. Michael Paxton, producer.

Colors Straight Up, Echo Pictures. Michèle Ohayon and Julia Schacter, producers.

4 Little Girls, HBO Documentary Film/40 Acres and a Mule Filmworks. Spike Lee and Sam Pollard, producers.

* *The Long Way Home*, Moriah Films production at the Simon Wiesenthal Center, Seventh Art. Rabbi Marvin Hier and Richard Trank, producers.

Waco: The Rules of Engagement, SomFord Entertainment/Fifth Estate. William Gazecki, producer.

Foreign Language Film

Beyond Silence (Germany).

* *Character* (The Netherlands).

Four Days in September (Brazil).

Secrets of the Heart (Spain).

The Thief (Russia).

Irving G. Thalberg Memorial Award

Not given this year.

Jean Hersholt Humanitarian Award

Not given this year.

Gordon E. Sawyer Award

Don Iwerks.

Honorary Award

Stanley Donen, in appreciation of a body of work marked by grace, elegance, wit and visual innovation.

Scientific or Technical

ACADEMY AWARD OF MERIT (STATUETTE)

Gunnar P. Michelson for the engineering and development of an improved, electronic, high-speed, precision light valve for use in motion picture printing machines.

SCIENTIFIC AND ENGINEERING AWARD (PLAQUE)

Eben Ostby, Bill Reeves, Sam Leffler, and Tom Duff for the development of the Marionette Three-Dimensional Computer Animation System.

Richard Shoup, Alvy Ray Smith, and Thomas Porter for their pioneering efforts in the development of digital paint systems used in motion picture production.

Kirk Handley, Ray Meluch, Scott Robinson, Wilson Allen, and John Neary for the design, development, and implementation of the Dolby CP500 Digital Cinema Processor.

Craig Reynolds for his pioneering contributions to the development of three-dimensional computer animation for motion picture production.

John Gibson, Rob Krieger, Milan Novacek, Glen Ozymok, and Dave Springer for the development of the geometric modeling component of the Alias PowerAnimator system.

Dominique Boisvert, Rejean Gagne, Daniel Langlois, and Richard Laperriere for the development of the "Actor" animation component of the Softimage computer animation system.

Bill Kovacs for his creative leadership and Roy Hall for his principal engineering efforts that led to the Wavefront Advanced Visualizer computer graphics system.

Joel Johnson of the O'Connor Laboratories for the unique design improvement in fluid-head counter-balancing techniques as used in their Model 2575.

Al Jensen, Chuck Headley, Jean Messner, and Hazem Nabulsi of CEI Technology for the production of a self-contained, flicker-free, Color Video-Assist Camera.

TECHNICAL ACHIEVEMENT AWARD (CERTIFICATE)

Clark F. Crites for the design and development of the ELF 1-C Endless Loop Film Transport and storage system.

Dan Leimeter and Bob Weitz for the development and implementation of a Portable Adjustment Tool for T-Style Slit Lens Assemblies.

Greg Hermanovic, Kim Davidson, Mark Elendt, and Paul Breslin for the development of the procedural modeling and animation components of the Prisms software package.

Jim Keating, Michael Wahrman, and Richard Hollander for their contributions that led to the Wavefront Advanced Visualizer computer graphics system.

James M. Reilly, Douglas W. Nishimura, and Monique C. Fisher of the Rochester Institute of Technology for the creation of A-D Strips, a diagnostic tool for the detection of the presence of vinegar syndrome in processed acetate-based motion picture film.

Philip C. Cory for the design and development of the Special Effects Spark Generator.

Jim Frazier, for the concept, and Iain Neil and Rick Gelbard for the design and development of the Panavision/Frazier Lens System for motion picture photography.

James F. Foley, Charles Converse, and F. Edward Gardner of UCISCO; and to Bob Stoker and Matt Sweeney for the development and realization of the Liquid Synthetic Air system.

Richard Chuang, Glenn Entis, and Carl Rosendahl for the concept and architecture of the Pacific Data Images (PDI) Animation System.

James A. Cashin, Roger Hibbard, and Larry Jacobson for the design, development and implementation of a projection system analyzer.

John A. Bonner Medal of Commendation
Pete Clark.

Points of Interest

1. Never too late: At age eighty-seven, Gloria Stuart becomes the oldest acting nominee ever.
2. Tie-tanic: *Titanic* ties *All About Eve*'s record of fourteen nominations, and *Ben-Hur*'s record of eleven Oscars.
3. Seeing double: For the first time ever, two people are nominated for playing the same character in the same movie—Kate Winslet and Gloria Stuart in *Titanic*.

Eligible Films That Failed to Be Nominated for Best Picture

The Ice Storm; Ponette; The Sweet Hereafter; Eve's Bayou; Gabbeh; Happy Together; Waiting for Guffman; Donnie Brasco; Fast, Cheap & Out of Control; Ulee's Gold; Jackie Brown; Crash; In the Company of Men; The Wings of the Dove; Men in Black; The Apostle; All Over Me; Grosse Pointe Blank; Boogie Nights; The Quiet Room; Lost Highway; Kundun; Gattaca.

Submitted Films Rejected by the Foreign Language Film Award Committee

Deep Crimson (Mexico), directed by Arturo Ripstein; *Destiny* (Egypt), directed by Youssef Chahine; *For Ever Mozart* (Switzerland), directed by Jean-Luc Godard; *Gabbeh* (Iran), directed by Mohsen Makhmalbaf; *Journey to the Beginning of the World* (Portugal), directed by Manoel De Oliveira; *Ma Vie en Rose* (Belgium), directed by Alain Berliner; *Princess Mononoke* (Japan), directed by Hayao Miyazaki.

1998

Picture
Elizabeth, Working Title, Gramercy. Produced by Alison Owen, Eric Fellner, and Tim Bevan.
Life Is Beautiful, Melampo Cinematografica s.r.l., Miramax. Produced by Elda Ferri and Gianluigi Braschi.
Saving Private Ryan, DreamWorks. Produced by Steven Spielberg, Ian Bryce, Mark Gordon, and Gary Levinsohn.
* *Shakespeare in Love*, Miramax, Universal, Bedford Falls Co, Miramax. Produced by David Parfitt, Donna Gigliotti, Harvey Weinstein, Edward Zwick, and Marc Norman.
The Thin Red Line, Fox 2000 Pictures in association with Phoenix Pictures, 20th Century Fox. Produced by Robert Michael Geisler, John Roberdeau, and Grant Hill.

Actor
* Roberto Benigni in *Life Is Beautiful* (Melampo Cinematografica s.r.l., Miramax).
Tom Hanks, in *Saving Private Ryan* (DreamWorks).
Ian McKellen in *Gods and Monsters* (Regent Entertainment, Lions Gate).
Nick Nolte in *Affliction* (Tormenta, Lions Gate).
Edward Norton in *American History X* (Turman-Morrissey Co. New Line).

Actress
Cate Blanchett in *Elizabeth* (Working Title, Gramercy).
Fernanda Montenegro in *Central Station* (Sony Pictures Classics).
* Gwyneth Paltrow in *Shakespeare in Love* (Miramax, Universal, Bedford Falls Co, Miramax).
Meryl Streep in *One True Thing* (Universal).
Emily Watson in *Hilary and Jackie* (Oxford Film Co., October).

Supporting Actor
* James Coburn in *Affliction* (Tormenta, Lions Gate).
Robert Duvall in *A Civil Action* (Touchstone/Paramount, Buena Vista).
Ed Harris in *The Truman Show* (Rudin, Paramount).
Geoffrey Rush in *Shakespeare in Love* (Miramax, Universal, Bedford Falls Co, Miramax).
Billy Bob Thornton in *A Simple Plan* (Mutual Film Co. in association with Savoy Pictures, Paramount).

Supporting Actress
Kathy Bates in *Primary Colors* (Universal/Mutual Film Co., Universal).
Brenda Blethyn in *Little Voice* (Scala, Miramax).
* Judi Dench in *Shakespeare in Love* (Miramax, Universal, Bedford Falls Co, Miramax).
Rachel Griffiths in *Hilary and Jackie* (Oxford Film Co., October).
Lynn Redgrave in *Gods and Monsters* (Regent Entertainment, Lions Gate).

Director

Roberto Benigni for *Life Is Beautiful* (Melampo Cinematografica s.r.l., Miramax).

* Steven Spielberg for *Saving Private Ryan* (DreamWorks).

John Madden for *Shakespeare in Love* (Miramax, Universal, Bedford Falls Co, Miramax).

Terrence Malick for *The Thin Red Line* (Fox 2000 Pictures in association with Phoenix Pictures, 20th Century Fox.).

Peter Weir for *The Truman Show* (Rudin, Paramount).

Writing

(SCREENPLAY WRITTEN DIRECTLY FOR THE SCREEN)

Bulworth, 20th Century Fox. Warren Beatty & Jeremy Pikser, screenplay; Warren Beatty, story.

Life Is Beautiful, Melampo Cinematografica s.r.l., Miramax. Vincenzo Cerami and Roberto Benigni.

Saving Private Ryan, DreamWorks. Robert Rodat.

* *Shakespeare in Love*, Miramax, Universal, Bedford Falls Co, Miramax. Marc Norman and Tom Stoppard.

The Truman Show, Rudin, Paramount. Andrew Niccol.

(SCREENPLAY BASED ON MATERIAL PREVIOUSLY PRODUCED OR PUBLISHED)

* *Gods and Monsters*, Regent Entertainment, Lions Gate. Bill Condon.

Out of Sight, Jersey, Universal. Scott Frank.

Primary Colors, Universal/Mutual Film Co., Universal. Elaine May.

A Simple Plan, Mutual Film Co. in association with Savoy Pictures, Paramount. Scott B. Smith.

The Thin Red Line, Fox 2000 Pictures in association with Phoenix Pictures, 20th Century Fox. Terrence Malick.

Cinematography

A Civil Action, Touchstone/Paramount, Buena Vista. Conrad L. Hall.

Elizabeth, Working Title, Gramercy. Remi Adefarasin.

* *Saving Private Ryan*, DreamWorks. Janusz Kaminski.

Shakespeare in Love, Miramax, Universal, Bedford Falls Co, Miramax. Richard Greatrex.

The Thin Red Line, Fox 2000 Pictures in association with Phoenix Pictures, 20th Century Fox. John Toll.

Art Direction—Set Decoration

Elizabeth, Working Title, Gramercy. John Myhre; Peter Howitt.

Pleasantville, Larger Than Life, New Line. Jeannine Oppewall; Jay Hart.

Saving Private Ryan, DreamWorks. Tom Sanders; Lisa Dean Kavanaugh.

* *Shakespeare in Love*, Miramax, Universal, Bedford Falls Co, Miramax. Martin Childs; Jill Quertier.

What Dreams May Come, Interscope Communications in association with Metafilmics, Polygram. Eugenio Zanett; Cindy Carr.

Sound

Armageddon, Touchstone, Buena Vista. Kevin O'Connell, Greg P. Russell, and Keith A. Wester.

The Mask of Zorro, Amblin Entertainment, TriStar. Kevin O'Connell, Greg P. Russell, and Pud Cusack.

* *Saving Private Ryan*, DreamWorks. Gary Rydstrom, Gary Summers, Andy Nelson, and Ronald Judkins.

Shakespeare in Love, Miramax, Universal, Bedford Falls Co, Miramax. Robin O'Donoghue, Dominic Lester, and Peter Glossop.

The Thin Red Line, Fox 2000 Pictures in association with Phoenix Pictures, 20th Century Fox. Andy Nelson, Anna Behlmer, and Paul Brincat.

Music

(ORIGINAL SONG)

"I Don't Want to Miss a Thing" (*Armageddon*, Touchstone, Buena Vista); Music and lyrics by Diane Warren.

"The Prayer" (*Quest for Camelot*, Warner Bros.); Music by Carole Bayer Sager and David Foster. Lyrics by Carole Bayer Sager, David Foster, Tony Renis, and Alberto Testa.

"A Soft Place to Fall" (*The Horse Whisperer*, Touchstone, Buena Vista); Music and lyrics by Allison Moorer and Gwil Owen.

"That'll Do" (*Babe: Pig in the City*, Kennedy Miller Media Pty. Ltd., Universal); Music and lyrics by Randy Newman.

* "When You Believe" (*The Prince of Egypt*, DreamWorks SKG, DreamWorks); Music and lyrics by Stephen Schwartz.

(ORIGINAL MUSICAL OR COMEDY SCORE)

A Bug's Life, Walt Disney Pictures/Pixar Animation Studios, Buena Vista. Randy Newman.

Mulan, Walt Disney Pictures, Buena Vista. Matthew Wilder, music; David Zippel, lyrics; Jerry Goldsmith, orchestral score.

Patch Adams, Universal. Marc Shaiman.

The Prince of Egypt, DreamWorks SKG, DreamWorks. Stephen Schwartz, music and lyrics; Hans Zimmer, orchestral score.

* *Shakespeare in Love*, Miramax, Universal, Bedford Falls Co, Miramax. Stephen Warbeck.

(ORIGINAL DRAMATIC SCORE)

Elizabeth, Working Title, Gramercy. David Hirschfelder.

* *Life Is Beautiful*, Melampo Cinematografica s.r.l., Miramax. Nicola Piovani.

Pleasantville, Larger Than Life, New Line. Randy Newman.

Saving Private Ryan, DreamWorks. John Williams.

The Thin Red Line, Fox 2000 Pictures in association with Phoenix Pictures, 20th Century Fox. Hans Zimmer.

Film Editing

Life Is Beautiful, Melampo Cinematografica s.r.l., Miramax. Simona Paggi.

Out of Sight, Jersey, Universal. Anne V. Coates.

* *Saving Private Ryan*, DreamWorks. Michael Kahn.

Shakespeare in Love, Miramax, Universal, Bedford Falls Co, Miramax. David Gamble.

The Thin Red Line, Fox 2000 Pictures in association with Phoenix Pictures, 20th Century Fox. Billy Weber, Leslie Jones and Saar Klein.

Costume Design
Beloved, Touchstone Pictures, Buena Vista. Colleen Atwood.
Elizabeth, Working Title, Gramercy. Alexandra Byrne.
Pleasantville, Larger Than Life, New Line. Judianna Makovsky.
* *Shakespeare in Love*, Miramax, Universal, Bedford Falls Co, Miramax. Sandy Powell.
Velvet Goldmine, Zenith/Killer Films, Miramax. Sandy Powell.

Makeup
* *Elizabeth*, Working Title, Gramercy. Jenny Shircore.
Saving Private Ryan, DreamWorks. Lois Burwell, Conor O'Sullivan, and Daniel C. Striepeke.
Shakespeare in Love, Miramax, Universal, Bedford Falls Co, Miramax. Lisa Westcott and Veronica Brebner.

Visual Effects
Armageddon, Touchstone, Buena Vista. Richard R. Hoover, Pat McClung, and John Frazier.
Mighty Joe Young, Walt Disney Pictures, Buena Vista. Rick Baker, Hoyt Yeatman, Allen Hall, and Jim Mitchell.
* *What Dreams May Come*, Interscope Communications in association with Metafilmics, Polygram. Joel Hynek, Nicholas Brooks, Stuart Robertson, and Kevin Mack.

Sound Effects Editing
Armageddon, Touchstone, Buena Vista. George Watters II.
The Mask of Zorro, Amblin Entertainment, TriStar. David McMoyler.
* *Saving Private Ryan*, DreamWorks. Gary Rydstrom and Richard Hymns.

Short Films
(ANIMATED)
* *Bunny*, Blue Sky Studios. Chris Wedge, producer.
The Canterbury Tales, S4C/BBC Wales/HBO Prod. Christopher Grace and Jonathan Myerson, producers.
Jolly Roger, Astley Baker/Silver Bird production for Channel Four. Mark Baker, producer.
More, Bad Clams Prods./Swell Prods./Flemington Pictures. Mark Osborne and Steve Kalafer, producers.
When Life Departs, A. Film. Karsten Klerich and Sefan Fjeldmark, producers.

(LIVE ACTION)
Culture, False Alarm Pictures. Will Speck & Josh Gordon, producers.
* *Election Night (Valgaften)*, M&M. Kim Magnusson and Anders Thomas Jensen, producers.
Holiday Romance, Jovy Junior Enterprises. Alexander Jovy, producer.

La Carte Postale (The Postcard), K2 S.A. Vivian Goffette, producer.
Victor, Bergvall Bilder/Hemikrania. Simon Sandquist and Joel Bergvall.

Documentary
(SHORT SUBJECTS)
* *The Personals: Improvisations on Romance in the Golden Years*, Keiko Ibi Film. Keiko Ibi, producer.
A Place in the Land, Guggenheim. Charles Guggenheim, producer.
Sunrise over Tiananmen Square, National Film Board of Canada. Shui-Bo Wang and Donald McWilliams, producers.

(FEATURES)
Dancemaker, Four Oaks Foundation. Matthew Diamond and Jerry Kupfer, producers.
The Farm: Angola, U.S.A., Gabriel Films. Jonathan Stack and Liz Garbus, producers.
* *The Last Days*, Survivors of the Shoah Visual History Foundation, October. James Moll and Ken Lipper, producers.
Lenny Bruce: Swear to Tell the Truth, Whyaduck Prods. Robert B. Weide, producer.
Regret to Inform, Sun Foundation. Barbara Sonneborn and Janet Cole, producers.

Foreign Language Film
Central Station (Brazil).
Children of Heaven (Iran).
The Grandfather (Spain).
* *Life Is Beautiful* (Italy).
Tango (Argentina).

Irving G. Thalberg Memorial Award
Norman Jewison.

Jean Hersholt Humanitarian Award
Not given this year.

Gordon E. Sawyer Award
Not given this year.

Honorary Award
Elia Kazan, in appreciation of a long, distinguished and unparalleled career during which he has influenced the very nature of filmmaking through his creation of cinematic masterpieces.

Scientific or Technical
ACADEMY AWARD OF MERIT (STATUETTE)
Avid Technology, Inc. for the concept, system design and engineering of the Avid Film Composer for motion picture editing.

SCIENTIFIC AND ENGINEERING AWARD (PLAQUE)
Arnold & Richter Cine Technik and the Carl Zeiss Company for the concept and optical design of the Carl Zeiss/Arriflex Variable Prime Lenses.

ARRI USA, Inc. for the concept, and Walter Trauninger of Arnold & Richter Cine Technik and the Arnold & Richter Cine Technik engineering staff for the engineering (Arnold & Richter Cine Technik/Trauniger) of the ARRI 435 Camera System.

Roy B. Ference, Steven R. Schmidt, Richard J. Federico, Rocky Yarid, and Michael McCrackan, for the design and development of the Kodak Lightning Laser Recorder.

Stephen J. Kay of K-Tec Corporation for the design and development of the Shock Block.

Derek C. Lightbody of OpTex for the design and development of Aurasoft luminaires.

James A. Moorer for his pioneering work in the design of digital signal processing and its application to audio editing for film.

Colin Mossman, George John Rowland, and Hans Leisinger for the concept and design of the Deluxe High Speed Spray Film Cleaner.

Iain Neil for the optical design, Takuo Miyagishima for the mechanical design, and Panavision, Incorporated for the concept and development of the Primo Series of spherical prime lenses for 35mm cinematography.

Robert Predovich, John Scott, Mohamed Ken T. Husain, and Cameron Shearer for the design and implementation of the Soundmaster Integrated Operations Nucleus operating environment.

Mark Roberts, Ronan Carroll, Assaff Rawner, Paul Bartlett, and Simon Wakley for the creation of the Milo Motion-Control Crane.

Dr. Thomas G. Stockham and Robert B. Ingebretsen for their pioneering work in the areas of waveform editing, crossfades, and cut-and-paste techniques for digital audio editing.

Michael Sorensen and Richard Alexander of Sorensen Designs International, and Don Trumbull for advancing the state-of-the-art of real-time motion-control, as exemplified in the Gazelle and Zebra camera dolly systems.

Gary Tregaskis for the primary design and Dominique Boisvert, Phillippe Panzini, and Andre LeBlanc for the development and implementation of the Flame and Inferno software.

Ronald E. Uhlig, Thomas F. Powers, and Fred M. Fuss of the Eastman Kodak Company for the design and development of KeyKode latent-image barcode key numbers.

TECHNICAL ACHIEVEMENT AWARD (CERTIFICATE)

Thaddeus Beier, for the design and implementation of ras_track, a system for 2D tracking, stabilization and 3D camera and object tracking.

Dr. Mitchell J. Bogdanowycz of the Eastman Kodak Company and Jim Meyer and Stan Miller of Rosco Laboratories, Inc. for the design of the CalColor Calibrated Color Effects Filters.

Garrett Brown and Jerry Holway for the creation of the Skyman flying platform for Steadicam operators.

Mike Denecke for refining and further developing electronic time-code slates.

Edmund M. Di Giulio and James Bartell of Cinema Products for the design of the KeyKode Sync Reader.

David DiFrancesco, Bala S. Manian, and Thomas Noggle for their pioneering efforts in the development of laser film recording technology.

Nick Foster for his software development in the field of water simulation systems.

Dr. Carl F. Holtz, David F. Kopperl, Dr. A. Tulsi Ram, and Richard C. Sehlin of the Eastman Kodak Company for the research and development of the concept of molecular sieves applied to improve the archival properties of processed photographic film.

Manfred N. Klemme and Donald E. Wetzel for the design and development of the K-Tek Microphone Boom Pole and accessories for on-set motion picture sound recording.

Ivan Kruglak for his commitment to the development of a wireless transmission system for video-assisted images for the motion picture industry.

Ivan Kruglak for his pioneering concept and the development of the Coherent Time Code Slate.

Mike Bolles, Udo Pampel, Mike MacKenzie, and Joseph Fulmer of Industrial Light & Magic for their pioneering work in motion-controlled, silent camera dollies.

Takuo Miyagishima and Albert K. Saiki of Panavision, Inc. for the design and development of the Eyepiece Leveler.

Cary Phillips for the design and development of the "Caricature" Animation System at Industrial Light & Magic.

Dr. Douglas R. Roble for his contribution to tracking technology and for the design and implementation of the TRACK system for camera position calculation and scene reconstruction.

James Rodnunsky, Bob Webber, and James Webber of Cablecam Systems, and Trou Bayliss for the design and engineering of Cablecam.

Remy Smith for the software and electronic design and development and James K. Branch and Nasir J. Zaidi for the design and development of the Spectra Professional IV-A digital exposure meter.

Barry Walton, Bill Schultz, Chris Barker, and David Cornelius of Sony Pictures Imageworks for the creation of an advanced motion-controlled, silent camera dolly.

Bruce Wilton and Carlos Icinkoff of Mechanical Concepts for their modular system of motion-control rotators and movers for use in motion control.

Ed Zwaneveld and Frederick Gasoi of the National Film Board of Canada and Mihal Lazaridis and Dale Brubacher-Cressman of Research in Motion for refining and further developing electronic time-code slates.

John A. Bonner Medal of Commendation

David W. Gray for his past and ongoing dedication to the advancement of motion picture sound technology.

Points of Interest

1. The family way: Cinematography nominee John Toll is married to Makeup nominee Lois Burwell.
2. Renaissance man: Best Actor Roberto Benigni also nominated for Director and Original Screenplay.
3. Two-timer: Foreign Film winner, *Life Is Beautiful*, also nominated for Best Picture.

Eligible Films That Failed to Be Nominated for Best Picture

Gods and Monsters; *Rushmore*; *The Opposite of Sex*; *Pleasantville*; *The Truman Show*; *Central Station*; *A Simple Plan*; *The Butcher Boy*; *Happiness*; *Affliction*; *Waking Ned Devine*; *High Art*; *Hilary and Jackie*; *The General*; *The Big Lebowski*; *Bulworth*; *Your Friends and Neighbors*; *Life of Jesus*; *Live Flesh*; *Out of Sight*; *Chinese Box*; *A Soldier's Daughter Never Cries*; *Mrs. Dalloway*.

Submitted Films Rejected by the Foreign Language Film Award Committee

The Celebration (Denmark), directed by Thomas Vinterberg; *The Dreamlife of Angels* (France), directed by Erick Zonca; *Eternity and a Day* (Greece), directed by Theo Angelopoulos; *Flowers of Shanghai* (Taiwan) directed by Hou Hsiao-Hsien; *Inquietude* (Portugal), directed by Manoel De Oliveira; *Rosie* (Belgium), directed by Patrice Toye; *Run Lola Run* (Germany), directed by Tom Tykwer.

1999

Picture
* *American Beauty*, Jinks/Cohen Company, DreamWorks. Produced by Bruce Cohen and Dan Jinks.
  The Cider House Rules, FilmColony, Miramax. Produced by Richard N. Gladstein.
  The Green Mile, Castle Rock, Warner Bros. Produced by David Valdes and Frank Darabont.
  The Insider, Touchstone, Buena Vista. Produced by Michael Mann and Pieter Jan Brugge.
  The Sixth Sense, Hollywood/Spyglass Entertainment, Buena Vista. Produced by Frank Marshall, Kathleen Kennedy, and Barry Mendel.

Actor
  Russell Crowe in *The Insider* (Buena Vista).
  Richard Farnsworth in *The Straight Story* (Buena Vista).
  Sean Penn in *Sweet and Lowdown* (Sony Pictures Classics).
* Kevin Spacey in *American Beauty* (DreamWorks).

Denzel Washington in *The Hurricane* (Universal).

Actress
  Annette Bening in *American Beauty* (DreamWorks).
  Janet McTeer in *Tumbleweeds* (Fine Line).
  Julianne Moore in *The End of the Affair* (Columbia).
  Meryl Streep in *Music of the Heart* (Miramax).
* Hilary Swank in *Boys Don't Cry* (Fox Searchlight).

Supporting Actor
* Michael Caine in *The Cider House Rules* (Miramax).
  Tom Cruise in *Magnolia* (New Line).
  Michael Clarke Duncan in *The Green Mile* (Warner Bros.).
  Jude Law in *The Talented Mr. Ripley* (Paramount & Miramax).
  Haley Joel Osment in *The Sixth Sense* (Buena Vista).

Supporting Actress
  Toni Collette in *The Sixth Sense* (Buena Vista).
* Angelina Jolie in *Girl, Interrupted* (Columbia).
  Catherine Keener in *Being John Malkovich* (USA Films).
  Samantha Morton in *Sweet and Lowdown* (Sony Pictures Classics).
  Chloë Sevigny in *Boys Don't Cry* (Fox Searchlight).

Director
* Sam Mendes for *American Beauty* (DreamWorks).
  Spike Jonze for *Being John Malkovich* (USA Films).
  Lasse Hallström for *The Cider House Rules* (Miramax).
  Michael Mann for *The Insider* (Buena Vista).
  M. Night Shyamalan for *The Sixth Sense* (Buena Vista).

Writing
(SCREENPLAY WRITTEN DIRECTLY FOR THE SCREEN)
* *American Beauty*, DreamWorks. Alan Ball.
  Being John Malkovich, USA Films. Charlie Kaufman.
  Magnolia, New Line. Paul Thomas Anderson.
  The Sixth Sense, Buena Vista. M. Night Shyamalan.
  Topsy-Turvy, USA Films. Mike Leigh.

(SCREENPLAY BASED ON MATERIAL PREVIOUSLY PRODUCED OR PUBLISHED)
* *The Cider House Rules*, Miramax. John Irving.
  Election, Paramount. Alexander Payne and Jim Taylor.
  The Green Mile, Warner Bros. Frank Darabont.
  The Insider, Buena Vista. Eric Roth and Michael Mann
  The Talented Mr. Ripley, Paramount and Miramax. Anthony Minghella.

Cinematography
* *American Beauty*, DreamWorks. Conrad L. Hall.
  The End of the Affair, Columbia. Roger Pratt.
  The Insider, Buena Vista. Dante Spinotti.
  Sleepy Hollow, Paramount and Mandalay. Emmanuel Lubezki.
  Snow Falling on Cedars, Universal. Robert Richardson.

Art Direction—Set Decoration
Anna and the King, 20th Century Fox. Luciana Arrighi; Ian Whittaker.
The Cider House Rules, Miramax. David Gropman; Beth Rubino.
* *Sleepy Hollow*, Paramount and Mandalay. Rick Heinrichs; Peter Young.
The Talented Mr. Ripley, Paramount & Miramax. Roy Walker; Bruno Cesari.
Topsy-Turvy, USA Films. Eve Stewart; John Bush.

Sound
The Green Mile, Warner Bros. Robert J. Litt, Elliot Tyson, Michael Herbick, and Willie D. Burton.
The Insider, Buena Vista. Andy Nelson, Doug Hemphill, and Lee Orloff.
* *The Matrix*, Warner Bros. John Reitz, Gregg Rudloff, David Campbell, and David Lee.
The Mummy, Universal. Leslie Shatz, Chris Carpenter, Rick Kline, and Chris Munro.
Star Wars Episode 1: The Phantom Menace, 20th Century Fox. Gary Rydstrom, Tom Johnson, Shawn Murphy, and John Midgley.

Music
(ORIGINAL SONG)
"Blame Canada" (*South Park: Bigger, Longer & Uncut*, Paramount and Warner Bros.); Music and lyrics by Trey Parker and Marc Shaiman.
"Music of My Heart" (*Music of the Heart*, Miramax); Music and lyrics by Diane Warren.
"Save Me" (*Magnolia*, New Line); Music and lyrics by Aimee Mann.
"When She Loved Me" (*Toy Story 2*, Buena Vista) Music and lyrics by Randy Newman.
* "You'll Be in My Heart" (*Tarzan*, Buena Vista). Music and lyrics by Phil Collins.

(ORIGINAL SCORE)
American Beauty, DreamWorks. Thomas Newman.
Angela's Ashes, Paramount and Universal Pictures International. John Williams.
The Cider House Rules, Miramax. Rachel Portman.
* *The Red Violin*, Lions Gate. John Corigliano.
The Talented Mr. Rupley, Paramount & Miramax. Gabriel Yared.

Film Editing
American Beauty, DreamWorks. Tariq Anwar and Christopher Greenbury.
The Cider House Rules, Miramax. Lisa Zeno Churgin.
The Insider, Buena Vista. William Goldenberg, Paul Rubell, and David Rosenbloom.
* *The Matrix*, Warner Bros. Zach Staenberg.
The Sixth Sense, Buena Vista. Andrew Mondshein.

Costume Design
Anna and the King, 20th Century Fox. Jenny Beavan.
Sleepy Hollow, Paramount and Mandalay. Colleen Atwood.
The Talented Mr. Ripley, Paramount & Miramax. Ann Roth and Gary Jones.
Titus, Fox Searchlight. Milena Canonero.
* *Topsy-Turvy*, USA Films. Lindy Hemming.

Makeup
Austin Powers: The Spy Who Shagged Me, New Line. Michèle Burke and Mike Smithson.
Bicentennial Man, Buena Vista. Greg Cannom.
Life, Universal. Rick Baker.
* *Topsy-Turvy*, USA Films. Christine Blundell and Trefor Proud.

Visual Effects
* *The Matrix*, Warner Bros. John Gaeta, Janek Sirrs, Steve Courtley, and Jon Thum.
Star Wars Episode I: The Phantom Menace, 20th Century Fox. John Knoll, Dennis Muren, Scott Squires, and Rob Coleman.
Stuart Little, Columbia. John Dykstra, Jerome Chen, Henry F. Anderson III, and Eric Allard.

Sound Effects Editing
Fight Club, 20th Century Fox. Ren Klyce and Richard Hymns.
* *The Matrix*, Warner Bros. Dane A. Davis.
Star Wars Episode 1: The Phantom Menace, 20th Century Fox. Ben Burtt and Tom Bellfort.

Short Films
(ANIMATED)
Humdrum, Aardman Animations Limited. Peter Peake, producer.
My Grandmother Ironed the King's Shirts, National Film Board of Canada & Studio Magica a.s. Production. Torill Kove, producer.
* *The Old Man and the Sea*, Productions Pascal Blais/Imagica Corp./Dentsu Tech./NHK Enterprise 21/Panorama Studio of Yaroslavl. Alexander Petrov, producer.
3 Misses, CinéTé Film. Paul Driessen, producer.
When the Day Breaks, National Film Board of Canada. Wendy Tilby and Amanda Forbis, producers.

(LIVE ACTION)
Bror, Min Bror (Teis and Nico), Nimbus Film & Dansk Novellefilm. Henrik Ruben Genz and Michael W. Horsten, producers.
Killing Joe, Joy Films and Chelsea Pictures. Mehdi Norowzian and Steve Wax, producers.
Kleingeld (Small Change), Die Hochschule für Film und Fernsehen "Konrad Wolf" Potsdam-Babelsberg. Marc-Andreas Bochert and Gabriele Lins, producers.
Major and Minor Miracles, Dramatiska Institutet. Marcus Olsson, producer.
* *My Mother Dreams the Satan's Disciples in New York*, American Film Institute/Kickstart. Barbara Schock and Tammy Tiehel, producers.

Documentary
(SHORT SUBJECTS)

Eyewitness, Marbert Art Foundation. Bert Van Bork, producer.

* *King Gimp*, Whiteford-Hadary/University of Maryland/Tapestry International. Susan Hannah Hadary and William A. Whiteford, producers.

The Wildest Show in the South: The Angola Prison Rodeo. Gabriel Films. Simeon Soffer and Jonathan Stack, producers.

(FEATURES)

Buena Vista Social Club, Road Movies, Artisan. Wim Wenders and Ulrich Felsberg, producers.

Genghis Blues, Wadi Rum, Roxie Releasing. Roko Belic and Adrian Belic, producers.

On the Ropes, Highway Films, WinStar Cinema. Nanette Burstein and Brett Morgen, producers.

* *One Day in September*, Cohn. Arthur Cohn and Kevin Macdonald, producers.

Speaking in Strings, CounterPoint, Seventh Art. Paola di Florio and Lilibet Foster, producers.

Foreign Language Film
* *All about My Mother* (Spain).
Caravan (Nepal).
East-West (France).
Solomon and Gaenor (United Kingdom).
Under the Sun (Sweden).

Irving G. Thalberg Memorial Award
Warren Beatty.

Jean Hersholt Humanitarian Award
Not given this year.

Gordon E. Sawyer Award
Roderick T. Ryan.

Honorary Award
Andrzej Wajda, one of the most respected filmmakers of our time, a man whose films have given audiences around the world an artist's view of history, democracy, and freedom, and who in so doing has himself become a symbol of courage and hope for millions of people in postwar Europe.

Scientific or Technical
ACADEMY AWARD OF MERIT (STATUETTE)
None.

SCIENTIFIC AND ENGINEERING AWARD (PLAQUE)

Nick Phillips for the design and development of the three-axis Libra III remote control camera head.

Fritz Gabriel Bauer for the concept, design, and engineering of the Moviecam Superlight 35mm Motion Picture Camera.

Iain Neil, Rick Gelbard, and Panavision, Inc. for the optical design, mechanical design, and for the development of the Millennium Camera System viewfinder.

Huw Gwilym, Karl Lynch, and Mark Crabtree for the design and development of the AMS/Neve-Logic Digital Film Console for motion picture sound mixing.

James Moultrie, Mike Salter, and Mark Craig Gerchman for the mechanical design and optical design of the Cooke S4 Range of Fixed Focal Length Lenses for 35mm motion picture photography.

Marlowe A. Pichel for development of the process for manufacturing Electro-Formed Metal Reflectors which, when combined with the DC Short Arc Xenon Lamp, became the worldwide standard for motion picture projection systems.

L. Ron Schmidt for the concept, design, and engineering of the Linear Loop Film Projectors. These radically new motion picture film projectors provide superior print handling, image steadiness, screen illumination, and enhanced viewer experience by means of an extremely simple air-driven mechanical transport system.

Nat Tiffen of Tiffen Manufacturing Corporation for the production of high-quality, durable, laminated color filters for motion picture photography.

TECHNICAL ACHIEVEMENT AWARD (CERTIFICATE)

Vivienne Dyer and Chris Woolf for the design and development of the Rycote Microphone Windshield Modular System.

Leslie Drever for the design and development of the Light Wave microphone windscreens and isolation mounts from Light Wave Systems.

Richard C. Sehlin, Dr. Mitchell J. Bogdanowicz, and Mary L. Schmoeger of the Eastman Kodak Company for the concept, design, and development of the Eastman Lamphouse Modification Filters.

Hoyt H. Yeatman Jr. of Dream Quest Images and John C. Brewer of the Eastman Kodak Company for the identification and diagnosis leading to the elimination of the "red fringe" artifact in traveling matte composite photography.

John A. Bonner Medal of Commendation
Edmund M. Di Giulio and Takuo Miyagishima.

Points of Interest

1. The family way: Supporting Actress Angelina Jolie and 1978 Best Actor Jon Voight become only father-daughter acting winners. Thalberg winner Warren Beatty is married to Actress nominee Annette Bening. Best Song nominee Aimee Mann is Best Actor nominee Sean Penn's sister-in-law.

2. Nothing to it: Sam Mendes wins Best Director for his first movie, Spike Jonze nominated for his.

Rule Changes

1. Musical chairs: The Original Musical or Comedy Score category is deep-sixed. It is replaced by Original Song Score, but there are only two 1999 releases eligible for the Award (*South Park: Bigger, Longer and Uncut* and *Tarzan*), so the Award is not given.
2. Clear the stage: No more than three producers will be eligible for a film's Best Picture statuettes. They "shall be those three who have performed the major portion of the producing functions."

Eligible Films That Failed to Be Nominated for Best Picture

Eyes Wide Shut; The End of the Affair; The Straight Story; The Talented Mr. Ripley; Boys Don't Cry; Election; The Winslow Boy; Being John Malkovich; The Matrix; The Blair Witch Project; True Crime; Man on the Moon; Fight Club; The Hurricane; The Limey; Mansfield Park; Mr. Death: The Rise and Fall of Fred A. Leuchter, Jr.; Titus; Rosetta; After Life; Holy Smoke; eXistenZ ; My Name Is Joe; The City (La Ciudad); Topsy-Turvy; Xiu Xiu: The Sent Down Girl; The Muse; The War Zone; Magnolia; Limbo; Three Kings; Cookie's Fortune; Notting Hill; 10 Things I Hate about You; Joe the King.

Submitted Films Rejected by the Foreign Language Film Award Committee

The Color of Paradise (Iran), directed by Majid Majidi; *Earth* (India) directed by Deepa Mehta; *Mifune* (Denmark), directed by Søren Kragh-Jacobsen; *Ordinary Heroes* (Hong Kong), directed by Ann Hui; *Pan Tadeusz* (Poland), directed by Andrzej Wajda;. *Rosetta* (Belgium), directed by Luc and Jean-Pierre Dardenne; *Three Seasons* (Vietnam), directed by Tony Bui.

2000

Picture
Chocolat, Brown, Miramax. Produced by David Brown, Kit Golden, and Leslie Holleran.
Crouching Tiger, Hidden Dragon, Zoom Hunt International, Sony Pictures Classics. Produced by Bill Kong, Hsu Li Kong, and Ang Lee.
Erin Brockovich, Jersey Films, Universal and Columbia. Produced by Danny DeVito, Michael Shamberg, and Stacey Sher.
* *Gladiator,* Wick in association with Scott Free, DreamWorks and Universal. Produced by Douglas Wick, David Franzoni, and Branko Lustig.

Traffic, Bedford Falls/Laura Bickford, USA Films. Produced by Edward Zwick, Marshall Herskovitz, and Laura Bickford.

Actor
Javier Bardem in *Before Night Falls* (Fine Line).
* Russell Crowe in *Gladiator* (DreamWorks and Universal).
Tom Hanks in *Cast Away* ((20th Century Fox and DreamWorks).
Ed Harris in *Pollock* (Sony Pictures Classics).
Geoffrey Rush in *Quills* (Fox Searchlight).

Actress
Joan Allen in *The Contender* (DreamWorks and Cinerenta/Cinecontender).
Juliette Binoche in *Chocolat* (Miramax).
Ellen Burstyn in *Requiem for a Dream* (Artisan).
Laura Linney in *You Can Count on Me* (Paramount Classics/Shooting Gallery/Hart Sharp Entertainment in association with Cappa Productions).
* Julia Roberts in *Erin Brockovich* (Universal).

Supporting Actor
Jeff Bridges in *The Contender* (DreamWorks and Cinerenta/Cinecontender).
Willem Dafoe in *Shadow of the Vampire* (Lions Gate).
* Benicio Del Toro in *Traffic* (USA Films).
Albert Finney in *Erin Brockovich* (Universal and Columbia).
Joaquin Phoenix in *Gladiator* (DreamWorks and Universal).

Supporting Actress
Judi Dench in *Chocolat* (Miramax).
* Marcia Gay Harden in *Pollock* (Sony Pictures Classics).
Kate Hudson in *Almost Famous* (DreamWorks and Columbia).
Frances McDormand in *Almost Famous* (DreamWorks and Columbia).
Julie Walters in *Billy Elliot* (Universal Focus).

Director
Stephen Daldry for *Billy Elliot* (Universal Focus).
Ang Lee for *Crouching Tiger, Hidden Dragon* (Sony Pictures Classics).
Ridley Scott for *Gladiator* (DreamWorks and Universal).
Steven Soderbergh for *Erin Brockovich* (Universal and Columbia).
* Steven Soderbergh for *Traffic* (USA Films).

Writing
(SCREENPLAY WRITTEN DIRECTLY FOR THE SCREEN)
* *Almost Famous*, DreamWorks. Cameron Crowe.
Billy Elliot, Universal Focus. Lee Hall.
Erin Brockovich, Universal. Susannah Grant.
Gladiator, DreamWorks. Screenplay by David Franzoni, John Logan, and William Nicholson; story by David Franzoni.
You Can Count on Me, Paramount Classics/Shooting Gallery/Hart Sharp Entertainment in association with Cappa Productions. Kenneth Lonergan.

(SCREENPLAY BASED ON MATERIAL PREVIOUSLY PRODUCED OR PUBLISHED)

Chocolat, Miramax. Robert Nelson Jacobs.

Crouching Tiger, Hidden Dragon, Sony Pictures Classics. Wang Hui Ling, James Schamus, and Tsai Kuo Jung.

O Brother, Where Art Thou?, Touchstone. Ethan Coen and Joel Coen.

* *Traffic*, USA Films. Stephen Gaghan.

Wonder Boys, Paramount. Steve Kloves.

Cinematography

* *Crouching Tiger, Hidden Dragon*, Sony Pictures Classics. Peter Pau.

Gladiator, DreamWorks and Universal. John Mathieson.

Malèna, Miramax. Lajos Koltai.

O Brother, Where Art Thou?, Touchstone, Buena Vista. Roger Deakins.

The Patriot, Columbia. Caleb Deschanel.

Art Direction—Set Decoration

* *Crouching Tiger, Hidden Dragon*, Sony Pictures Classics. Tim Yip.

Dr. Seuss' How the Grinch Stole Christmas, Universal. Michael Corenblith; Meredith Boswell.

Gladiator, DreamWorks and Universal. Arthur Max; Crispian Sallis.

Quills, Fox Searchlight. Michael Childs; Jill Quertier.

Vatel, Miramax. Jean Rabasse; François Benoit-Fresco.

Sound

Cast Away, 20th Century Fox and DreamWorks. Randy Thom, Tom Johnson, Dennis Sands, and William B. Kaplan.

* *Gladiator*, DreamWorks and Universal. Scott Millan, Bob Beemer, and Ken Weston.

The Patriot, Columbia. Kevin O'Connell, Greg P. Russell, and Lee Orloff.

The Perfect Storm, Warner Bros. John Reitz, Gregg Rudloff, David Campbell, and Keith A. Wester.

U-571, Universal and Studio Canal. Steve Maslow, Gregg Landaker, Rick Kline, and Ivan Sharrock.

Music

(ORIGINAL SONG)

"A Fool in Love" (*Meet the Parents*, Universal and DreamWorks). Music and lyrics by Randy Newman.

"I've Seen It All" (*Dancer in the Dark*, Fine Line). Music by Björk. Lyrics by Lars von Trier and Sjon Sigurdsson.

"A Love before Time" (*Crouching Tiger, Hidden Dragon*, Sony Pictures Classics). Music by Jorge Calandrelli and Tan Dun. Lyrics by James Schamus.

"My Funny Friend and Me" (*The Emperor's New Groove*, Buena Vista). Music by Sting and David Hartley. Lyrics by Sting.

* "Things Have Changed" (*Wonder Boys*, Paramount and Mutual Film Company). Music and lyrics by Bob Dylan.

(ORIGINAL SCORE)

* *Crouching Tiger, Hidden Dragon*, Sony Pictures Classics. Tan Dun.

Chocolat, Miramax. Rachel Portman.

Gladiator, DreamWorks and Universal. Hans Zimmer.

Malèna, Miramax. Ennio Morricone.

The Patriot, Columbia. John Williams.

Film Editing

Almost Famous, DreamWorks and Columbia. Joe Hutshing and Saar Klein.

Crouching Tiger, Hidden Dragon, Sony Pictures Classics. Tim Squyres.

Gladiator, DreamWorks and Universal. Pietro Scalia.

* *Traffic*, USA Films. Stephen Mirrione.

Wonder Boys, Paramount and Mutual Film Company. Dede Allen.

Costume Design

Crouching Tiger, Hidden Dragon, Sony Pictures Classics. Tim Yip.

Dr. Seuss' How the Grinch Stole Christmas, Universal. Rita Ryack.

* *Gladiator*, DreamWorks. Janty Yates.

102 Dalmations, Disney. Anthony Powell.

Quills, Fox Searchlight. Jacqueline West.

Makeup

The Cell, New Line. Michèle Burke and Edouard Henriques.

* *Dr. Seuss' How the Grinch Stole Christmas*, Universal. Rick Baker and Gail Ryan.

Shadow of the Vampire, Lions Gate. Ann Buchanan and Amber Sibley.

Visual Effects

* *Gladiator*, DreamWorks. John Nelson, Neil Corbould, Tim Burke, and Rob Harvey.

Hollow Man, Columbia. Scott E. Anderson, Craig Hayes, Scott Stokdyk, and Stan Parks.

The Perfect Storm, Warner Bros. Stefen Fangmeier, Habib Zargarpour, John Frazier, and Walt Conti.

Sound Editing

* *U-571*, Universal. Jon Johnson.

Space Cowboys, Warner Bros. Alan Robert Murray and Bub Asman.

Short Films

(ANIMATED)

* *Father and Daughter*, CinéTé Filmproductie bv/Cloudrunner Ltd. Michael Dudok de Wit, producer.

The Periwig-Maker, Ideal Standard Film. Steffen Schäffler and Annette Schäffler, producers.

Rejected, Bitter Films. Don Hertzfeldt, producer.

(LIVE ACTION)

By Courier, Two Tequila. Peter Riegert and Ericka Frederick, producers.

One Day Crossing, Open Eyes. Joan Stein and Christina Lazaridi, producers.

* *Quiero Ser (I want to be . . .)*, Marc-Andreas Bochert and Gabriele Lins. Florian Gallenberger, producer.

Seraglio, Seraglio. Gail Lerner and Colin Campbell, producers.

A Soccer Story (Una Historia de Futebol), UM Filmes. Paulo Machline, producers.

Documentary
(SHORT SUBJECTS)

* *Big Mama*, Birthmark. Tracy Seretean, producer.

Curtain Call, NJN/White Whale. Chuck Braverman and Steve Kalafer, producers.

Dolphins, MacGillivray Freeman Films. Greg MacGillivray and Alec Lorimore, producers.

The Man on Lincoln's Nose, Adama Films. Daniel Raim, producer.

On Tiptoe: Gentle Steps to Freedom, On Tip Toe. Eric Simonson and Leelai Demoz, producers.

(FEATURES)

* *Into the Arms of Strangers: Stories of the Kindertransport*, Sabine Films, Warner Bros. Mark Jonathan Harris and Deborah Oppenheimer, producers.

Legacy, Nomadic Pictures. Tod S. Lending, producer.

Long Night's Journey into Day, Iris Films, Seventh Art. Frances Reid and Deborah Hoffmann, producers.

Scottsboro: An American Tragedy, Social Media. Barak Goodman and Daniel Anker, producers.

Sound and Fury, Aronson Film Associates and Public Policy Productions, Artistic License. Josh Aronson and Roger Weisberg, producers.

Foreign Language Film

Amores Perros (Mexico).

* *Crouching Tiger, Hidden Dragon* (Taiwan).

Divided We Fall (Czech Republic).

Everybody Famous (Belgium).

The Taste of Others (France).

Irving G. Thalberg Memorial Award
Dino De Laurentiis.

Jean Hersholt Humanitarian Award
Not given this year.

Gordon E. Sawyer Award
Irwin W. Young.

Honorary Awards
Jack Cardiff, one of the greatest visual artists ever to work in film.
Ernest Lehman, in appreciation of a body of varied and enduring work.

Scientific or Technical
ACADEMY AWARD OF MERIT (STATUETTE)

Rob Cook, Loren Carpenter, and Ed Catmull for their significant advancement to the field of motion picture rendering as exemplified in Pixar's *Renderman*.

SCIENTIFIC AND ENGINEERING AWARD (PLAQUE)

AKAI Digital for the design and development of the DD8 Plus digital audio dubber specifically designed for the motion picture industry.

Fairlight for the design and development of the DaD digital audio dubber specifically designed for the motion picture industry.

Advanced Digital Systems Group (ADSG) for the design and development of the Sony DADR 5000 digital audio dubber specifically designed for the motion picture industry.

Timeline, Incorporated for the design and development of the MMR8 digital audio dubber specifically designed for the motion picture industry.

Joe Wary, Gerald Painter, and Colin F. Mossman for the design and development of the Deluxe Laboratories Multi Roller Film Transport System.

Alvah J. Miller and Paul Johnson of Lynx Robotics for the electronic and software design of the Lynx C-50 Camera Motor System.

Al Mayer, Sr. and Al Mayer, Jr. for the mechanical design, Iain Neil for the optical design, and Brian Dang for the electronic design of the Panavision Millenium XL Camera System.

TECHNICAL ACHIEVEMENT AWARD (CERTIFICATE)

Vic Armstrong for the refinement and application to the film industry of the Fan Descender for accurately and safely arresting the descent of stunt persons in high freefalls.

Bill Tondreau of Kuper Systems, Alvah J. Miller and Paul Johnson of Lynx Robotics, and David Stump of Visual Effects Rental Services for the conception, design, and development of data capture systems that enable superior accuracy, efficiency, and economy in the creation of composite imagery.

Leonard Pincus, Ashot Nalbandyan, George Johnson, and Tom Kong for the design and development of the Softsun low pressure xenon long-arc light sources, their power supplies and fixtures.

Glenn Berggren for the research, Horst Linge for the design and development, and Wolfgang Reineke for the optical design of the Isco-Optic lenses for motion picture projection.

Udo Schauss, Hildegard Ebbesmeirt, and Karl Lenhardt for the optical design, and Ralf Linn and Norbert Brinker for the optical and mechanical design of the Schneider Super Cinelux lenses for motion picture projection.

Philip Greenstreet of Rosco Laboratories for the concept and development of the Roscolight Day/Night Backdrop.

Venkat Krishnamurthy for the creation of the Paraform Software for 3D Digital Form Development.

George Borshukov, Kim Libreri, and Dan Piponi for the development of a system for image-based rendering allowing choreo-

graphed camera movements through computer graphic recon-
structed sets.

John Pytlak for the development of the Laboratory Aim Density
(LAD) system.

John A. Bonner Medal of Commendation

Paul Kenworthy Jr. for his pioneering efforts and innovations in the
design of equipment for shooting feature films using optical
relays.

Award of Commendation (Plaque)

Ioan Allen for the concept, Mark Harrah for the design, and
Robin Bransbury for the implementation of the TASA Trailer
Loudness Standard. In 1997, cinema sound engineers, exhibitors, and the major studios formed the Trailer Audio Standards Association to develop a trailer volume standard.

Points of Interest

1. Nothing to it: Stephen Daldry nominated for Best Director for
his first movie.
2. The family way: Joaquin Phoenix and his late brother, 1988
Supporting Actor nominee River, are the first brothers to have
been nominated for acting awards.
3. Universal language: With ten nominations, *Crouching Tiger,
Hidden Dragon* is the most honored foreign-language film in
Oscar history.
4. Two-timers: Steven Soderbergh nominated twice as Best Director, the first double nominee in this category since Michael
Curtiz in 1938. Foreign Film winner *Crouching Tiger, Hidden
Dragon* also nominated for Best Picture.

5. Interrupted melody: Best Original Song Score is not given due
to lack of eligible entries.

Rule Change

1. The name game: Sound Effects Editing Award becomes Sound
Editing.

Eligible Films That Failed to Be Nominated for Best Picture

*Hamlet; Wonder Boys; Billy Elliot; The House of Mirth; The Color of
Paradise; A Time for Drunken Horses; High Fidelity; American
Psycho; Ratcatcher; Chuck & Buck; Before Night Falls; Dancer in
the Dark; Nurse Betty; O Brother, Where Art Thou?; Best in Show;
Requiem for a Dream; Girl on the Bridge; Not One Less; Space
Cowboys; Quills; The Ninth Gate; Unbreakable; The Virgin Sui-
cides; Almost Famous; Charlie's Angels; State and Main; Pollock;
Ghost Dog: The Way of the Samurai.*

Submitted Films Rejected by the Foreign Language Film Award Committee

Chunhyang (Korea), directed by Im Kwon-Taek; *In the Mood for
Love* (Hong Kong), directed by Wong Kar-Wai; *A Time for
Drunken Horses* (Iran), directed by Bahman Ghobadi; *Vertical
Ray of the Sun* (Vietnam), directed by Tran Anh Hung.

Index

Zakim, Stu, 91
Zane, Billy, 143, 145, 164
Zanett, Eugenio, 388, 399
Zanuck, Darryl F., 90, 279
Zanuck, Lili Fini, 279, 285,
301–3, 305, 314–15,
343–44, 356
Zanuck, Richard, 279, 285,

301–3, 305, 314–15,
343–44, 356
Zargarpour, Habib, 392, 406
Zavalla, Marc, 289
Zea, Kristi, 393
Zeffirelli, Franco, 75
Zellweger, Renee, 73,
347–48, 361, 370, 379

Zemeckis, Robert, 39, 53,
338
Zeta-Jones, Catherine, 237,
246, 337, 351, 361,
364–65, 367, 372, 378,
380–81
Zimmer, Hans, 31, 359,
391, 394, 399, 405

Zinnemann, Fred, 115
Zippel, David, 394, 399
Ziyi, Zhang, 351–52
Zonca, Erick, 401
Zwanevelt, Ed, 401
Zwick, Edward, 200, 335,
396, 404

Don't forget the classic original. . . .

INSIDE OSCAR

by

MASON WILEY and DAMIEN BONA

The Unofficial History of the Academy Awards®
1927–1994

Published by Ballantine Books
Available at your local bookstore.